Randy Manning

DEMOCRACY UNDER PRESSURE

An Introduction to the American Political System

MILTON C. CUMMINGS, JR.
The Johns Hopkins University

DAVID WISE

Democracy

HARCOURT BRACE JOVANOVICH, INC.

New York   Chicago   San Francisco   Atlanta

Under Pressure

An Introduction
to the American Political System

DEMOCRACY UNDER PRESSURE
An Introduction to the American Political System

Milton C. Cummings, Jr. and David Wise

Cover: *Itata*, a lithograph
by the American artist Frank Stella. © Gemini G.E.L. 1968.

© 1971 by Harcourt Brace Jovanovich, Inc.

ISBN: 0-15-517336-7

Library of Congress Catalog Card Number: 77-149616

Printed in the United States of America

Illustrations by J & R Technical Services, Inc.

ACKNOWLEDGMENTS AND COPYRIGHTS

Textual Material

The American Political Science Association. For excerpt from Robert A. Dahl, *The American Political Science Review,* December, 1967. Reprinted by permission of the publisher and the author.

Atheneum Publishers, Inc. For excerpts from *The Making of the President 1968* by Theodore H. White, published by Atheneum. Copyright © 1969 by Theodore H. White. Reprinted by permission of the author and publisher.

The Bodley Head. For excerpt from *The City* by John V. Lindsay.

Columbia Broadcasting System. For excerpt from the transcript of the television news special, "LBJ: Why I Chose Not to Run," December 27, 1969.

The Christian Science Monitor. For excerpt quoted by permission from the article, "Auto repairs sputter, miss" in The Christian Science Monitor. © 1970 The Christian Science Publishing Society. All rights reserved.

Doubleday & Company, Inc. For excerpt from *Sexual Politics* by Kate Millett, copyright 1969, 1970 by Kate Millett. Reprinted by permission of Doubleday & Company, Inc., and by permission of Rupert Hart-Davis, Ltd. Also for excerpt from Arthur Bernon Tourtellot, *The Presidents on the Presidency* (Doubleday, 1964).

E. P. Dutton & Co., Inc. For excerpts from the book *Plunkitt of Tammany Hall* by William Riordon. Introduction by Arthur Mann. Introduction Copyright, ©, 1963 by Arthur Mann. Dutton Paperback edition. Published by E. P. Dutton & Co., Inc. and reprinted with their permission. Also for excerpt from the book *Justice: The Crisis of Law, Order and Freedom in America* by Richard Harris. Copyright, ©, 1970 by Richard Harris. Published by E. P. Dutton & Co., Inc. and reprinted with their permission and by permission of the author.

Esquire Magazine. For excerpt from article by James Farmer in Esquire Magazine, May 1969. Reprinted by permission of Esquire Magazine © 1969 by Esquire, Inc.

Acknowledgments and copyrights for textual material and for illustrations continue on p. 691.

Preface

Democracy Under Pressure: An Introduction to the American Political System is an attempt to provide a new approach to a textbook on American politics and government.

As the title indicates, the authors frankly recognize that the American political system is under pressure today, that it is being vigorously questioned and tested by many students and other groups in our society. In such a time, we believe it useful to provide a book that focuses, not only on the very considerable achievements of the American system of government, but on its shortcomings as well, on the reality as well as the rhetoric of American democracy. We have tried to do this in a textbook specifically designed for teachers and students in the 1970's.

In writing the book, we set three goals. First, we believe that a textbook should be exciting and stimulating to read. So we have attempted to provide a text that is as clear and readable as possible without sacrificing scholarship or content. That goal, in part, was the basis of our collaboration—that of a political scientist, and a political writer based in Washington. The book is relatively brief but is intended to cover the essentials of American politics and government.

Second, although we present American governmental and political institutions in their historical context, we have sought to relate politics and government to contemporary issues. We have examined many of the problems of American democracy that concern students and other Americans today—issues such as the environment, minority rights, Vietnam, Black Power, the military-industrial complex, poverty, consumer protection, electoral reform, student dissent, and the urban crisis. We have, for example, devoted a chapter to a discussion of the problems of groups struggling for equal rights in the American political system—blacks, Indians, Mexican Americans, Puerto Ricans, and women.

Third, we have attempted to focus on gaps, where they exist, between American myths and American realities, between the political system's promise and its performance. Few students today are disillusioned with the principles of American democracy; but they do ask that the political system practice those principles.

In examining the structure and processes of American politics and government, we have tried to ask: How is the political system supposed to work? How does it actually work? What might be done to make it work better? Each chapter is organized around a series of basic questions about the workings of the political system. The book does not, in every case, provide ready "answers" to these questions, but it raises them for the student's consideration and, if desired, for classroom discussion. At a time when the values and processes of the political system are being challenged, we believe it appropriate and necessary to raise fundamental questions sharply and clearly.

At the same time, the book emphasizes the individual responsibility of each citizen for the quality of American society and American government. It provides specific examples of participation in the political process by students and other citizens. It examines both the rights and responsibilities of citizens in a democracy.

The authors deeply appreciate the assistance of the many people who helped them to produce this book. We are especially grateful to our painstaking and resourceful research assistant, Norma J. Elliott, and to Thomas A. Horne, whose research contribution was also invaluable. Additional research assistance was provided by Diane O. DeLand, Beatrice Diebold, and Jack Fischer, and by Esther Safran and Jean Vandervoort of the Congressional Quarterly research staff. We are also indebted to Connie de Launay, who uncomplainingly typed the manuscript, and to Exa Murray, who typed the bibliographies. Legare H. B. Obear, Chief of the Loan Division of the Library of Congress, generously extended the library's loan privileges to the authors.

We also wish to express our gratitude to the many persons who read parts of the manuscript in advance or assisted in other ways. That list is too long to include in its entirety, but it must begin with Frederick L. Holborn, of the School of Advanced International Studies, The Johns Hopkins University, whose interest in the project dates from its start and whose counsel was helpful at many points along the way; John M. Elliott, of Kenyon College, whose comments on Part Two were particularly useful;

Herbert E. Alexander, of the Citizens' Research Foundation; Dom Bonafede, Andrew J. Glass, and William Lilley III, of the *National Journal*; Jack Rosenthal, Fred P. Graham, Benny L. Kass, Joseph Laitin, Charles G. Bennett, Frank W. Schiff, and John D. Tierney; Congressmen Fred B. Rooney and Morris K. Udall, who provided helpful comments on Chapter 12; Raymond L. Wise, Matthew A. Crenson, Philip Brenner, and Curtis J. Newby.

We also wish to acknowledge the assistance of the many scholars who were kind enough to review portions of the manuscript during its development. These include: James David Barber, Yale University; Allen K. Campbell, Syracuse University; Fred Gantt, Jr., North Texas State University; Barbara Hinckley, Cornell University; William S. Holley, El Camino College; Stanley Kelley, Jr., Princeton University; Robert E. Lane, Yale University; Theodore J. Lowi, University of Chicago; Kenneth Prewitt, University of Chicago; Michael D. Reagan, University of California, Riverside; Donald L. Robinson, Smith College; John P. Roche, Brandeis University; Henry S. Ruth, Director of the Criminal Justice Coordinating Council of New York City; Burton M. Sapin, George Washington University; Richard M. Scammon, Governmental Affairs Institute, Washington, D.C.; William S. Wagner, Foothill College. We are especially indebted to Dr. Rafael L. Cortada, Dean of Urban Resources and Development at the Medgar Evers College of the City University of New York, for his valuable comments on Chapter 5. The comments of all of these reviewers were consistently helpful; at the same time, responsibility for the final result, including any errors or shortcomings, is ours.

Finally, we wish to express our thanks to William A. Pullin, Vice-President of Harcourt Brace Jovanovich, who first proposed this project to the authors and gave it his continued support; and to Everett M. Sims, Director, and Thomas A. Williamson, Executive Editor, of the College Department, both of whom provided valuable editorial guidance and assistance at every stage of the book's development. We owe a special debt of gratitude to Virginia Joyner, our talented, untiring, and unflappable manuscript editor, whose editorial skills added immeasurably to the clarity and precision of the book. The editing benefited greatly as well from the gifted and perceptive copyediting of Linda Reiman. Alice Sanchez, Production Manager, efficiently saw the book through the various stages of production. As Chief Art Editor, Vivian Fenster brought great enthusiasm, care, and patience to the selection of the many photographs in the book and the preparation of the graphs, charts, and other illustrations. Designer Harry Rinehart applied his creative talent to integrate the whole, type and graphics, into a result that captures in visual form the spirit and purpose of our examination of *Democracy Under Pressure*.

Milton C. Cummings, Jr.
David Wise

Contents

2

The Constitutional Framework, 41

3

The Federal System, 77

4

Civil Liberties and Citizenship, 107

5

The Struggle for Equal Rights, 145

PART TWO *Politics U.S.A.*

6

Public Opinion and Interest Groups, 189

7

Political Parties, 227

8

Political Campaigns and Candidates, 271

Voting Behavior and Elections, 315

12

The Congress, 451

13

Justice, 497

PART FOUR *Government in Operation*

14

Foreign Policy and National Security, 547

PART FIVE **The American Community**

16

State and Local Government, 639

DEMOCRACY UNDER PRESSURE
An Introduction to the American Political System

PART ONE

The American Democracy

1

Government

and People

On a clear day in April in the spring of 1968, a gray pall of smoke hung over the White House in Washington. The smoke came from burning buildings ten blocks away. The fires had been set by enraged black citizens following the tragic assassination of Dr. Martin Luther King, Jr., by a white man. A minister who preached nonviolence, Dr. King had been both the leader and the symbol of the civil rights movement in America for more than a decade. Now he was gone.

With the center of the city in flames, Washington was seized by panic. Downtown stores closed, office workers poured into the streets and tried to flee the city, creating a massive traffic jam. Telephones went dead as equipment failed under the heavy volume of calls. The President signed a proclamation authorizing federal troops to move into the capital to restore order.

Some idea of the atmosphere can be gained from this description of the first soldiers entering the city:

It was an incredible sight for Captain Leroy Rhode, commander of the 3d Infantry's D Company, as he led 150 men over Memorial Bridge, across the Potomac River, into Washington. Immediately ahead was the Lincoln Memorial. To the right was the Washington Monument. In the distance was the Capitol, obscured by billows of smoke coming from fires in the center of the city. . . . By 5 p.m., the men in D Company were mounting machine guns on tripods, on the white marble steps of the Capitol, and setting up a command center, under the frescoed dome in the rotunda. . . . A few minutes later, another company of the 3d Infantry surrounded the White House.[1]

For twelve days, Washington was occupied by a total of 13,600 federal troops, more than had been sent to the capital at any time since the Civil War. For seven consecutive nights, authorities declared a curfew in the District of Columbia. Residents of the capital of the United States, as well as tourists who had come to watch the annual Cherry Blossom festival, were confined to their homes and hotel rooms. Even United States senators, representatives, and Cabinet officials were technically barred from the streets by the curfew rules, although they were able to move about with police escort.

When it was all over, twelve persons were dead, 1,000 fires had been set, more than 7,600 men, women, and children had been arrested, and the cost, if such events can be measured in dollars, was $27 million in property damage and other expenses. In cities across America, this pattern of violence, vandalism, arson, and looting was repeated.

Later that same month, students at Columbia University seized several buildings and staged a lengthy strike, demanding basic changes in the structure and policies of the university and setting a pattern for student demonstrations on many other campuses. The strike ended after six weeks, but not before police clubbed and bloodied the Columbia students.

To many people, it appeared that violence, never far below the surface of American society, had emerged as a dominant force. Throughout that spring, the divisions and tensions continued to build.

Senator Eugene J. McCarthy, a liberal Democrat from Minnesota, announced in late 1967 that he would seek his party's nomination for President. He entered the March New Hampshire presidential primary in a challenge to the Democratic incumbent, President Lyndon B. Johnson; McCarthy opposed the increasingly unpopular war in Vietnam that John-

---

[1] Ben W. Gilbert and the staff of the *Washington Post*, *Ten Blocks from the White House, Anatomy of the Washington Riots of 1968* (New York: Praeger, 1968), pp. 88–89. Most of the details of the Washington riots are based on this contemporary account, compiled by newspaper reporters at the scene.

Columbia student enjoying chair and cigar of the university's President during student strike, spring 1968.

son had escalated. Flocking to McCarthy's banner, busloads of college students converged on New Hampshire and turned his campaign into a peace crusade.

Senator Robert F. Kennedy of New York also entered the race for the Democratic nomination. He drew extraordinary crowds. He called for a restoration of "decency" in America and he won the support of blacks, migrant Mexican farm workers, Indians, and the poor. At the same time, he showed considerable strength among other traditional Democratic party ethnic voting groups. His words had a special appeal to young people. Then, like his older brother, President John F. Kennedy, and like Martin Luther King, he, too, was struck down. During a victory celebration in a Los Angeles hotel, only moments after he had won the important California primary, an assassin put a bullet in his brain. He died the next day.

There were more horrors to come. At the Democratic National Convention in Chicago, police brutally beat young antiwar protesters, as Americans across the nation watched their television screens in disbelief. Yet many Americans apparently agreed with the argument of Chicago Mayor Richard Daley that the police had been provoked by the demonstrators. According to a Gallup Poll conducted immediately after the street demonstrations, 56 percent of Americans interviewed approved of the actions of the police in Chicago.[2] Another view, stated in a later staff study of the

[2] Gallup Poll, September 17, 1968. The question asked of 1,507 persons was, "Do you approve or disapprove of the way the Chicago police dealt with the young people who were registering their protest against the Vietnam war at the time of the Chicago convention?" The nationwide findings were:

	Approve	Disapprove	No Opinion
National	56%	31%	13%
Humphrey backers	44	41	15
Nixon backers	63	25	12
Wallace backers	71	20	9

National Commission on the Causes and Prevention of Violence, adjudged the events at Chicago "a police riot." [3] The report included such episodes as these:

> A volunteer medic from Northwestern University's medical school described the scene: "When someone would fall, three or four cops would start beating him. One kid was beaten so badly he couldn't get up. He was bleeding profusely from the head. . . ." The witness saw another medic, wearing a white coat, struck by an officer. When he yelled, "I'm a medic," the officer said, "Excuse me," and hit him again. . . .

> About 25 persons had broken north from the barricade, down the slope from the Garibaldi statue, toward the South Pond. Task Force police at the northern end of the line charged after them. . . . A young man and his girlfriend were both grabbed by officers. He screamed, "We're going, we're going," but they threw him into the pond. The officers grabbed the girl, knocked her to the ground, dragged her along the embankment and hit her with their batons on her head, arms, back and legs. The boy tried to scramble up the embankment to her, but police shoved him back in the water at least twice. [4]

Against this background of violence, the Democratic nominating convention at Chicago chose Vice-President Hubert H. Humphrey to oppose

THE POLICE AND PROTEST: CHICAGO, 1968

The tape of the Police Department radio log discloses the following conversation at 1:29 a.m. on Tuesday morning:

Police Operator: "1814, get a wagon over at 1436. We've got an injured hippie."
Voice: "1436 North Wells?"
Operator: "North Wells."

In quick sequence, there are the following remarks from five other police cars:
"That's no emergency."
"Let him take a bus."
"Kick the f....."
"Knock his teeth out."
"Throw him in a wastepaper basket."

—From *Rights in Conflict*, The Walker Report to the National Commission on the Causes and Prevention of Violence.

[3] Daniel Walker, *Rights in Conflict*, report of the Chicago Study Team to the National Commission on the Causes and Prevention of Violence (New York: Bantam Books, 1968), p. 5. President Johnson named the commission on June 5, after the shooting of Senator Kennedy, "to look into the causes, the occurrence and the control of physical violence across this nation."
[4] *Ibid.*, pp. 147, 176–77.

We felt horror and grief and rage. We wanted to shake President Johnson and tell him to stop! stop! And the more we spoke out and marched and felt horror, the more the killing grew. . . . We watched our cities crumbling and dying. We saw people of black and brown and red being denied their humanity. . . . An election approached and we once again had hope. . . . At Chicago we grew up and felt our youth withering. Whom to turn to? Most of the people in the nation approved of the beating we received. . . . The "defense" budgets for the major countries of this earth are staggering, criminal.

"The System"—does it work? To some extent, yes. But not enough, not quickly enough. What are we supposed to do with our lives? . . . There comes a time when pure frustration builds and breaks out and is ugly. You throw a bottle and it feels good. . . . You say America is better than other places in the world. It is better than most, but brother, it's nothing to be proud of, and it's getting worse each day.

—Linda Eldridge, student at Monterey Peninsula College, California, quoted in *Time*, May 11, 1970.

Richard M. Nixon, who had been nominated by the Republicans at Miami Beach. (President Johnson, faced by dissent and mounting political opposition, had earlier announced that he would not seek reelection.) George Wallace, former governor of Alabama, ran for President as the nominee of the American Independent party. His campaign had a particular appeal in the South and among many blue-collar workers, in the South and elsewhere, who were fearful of the black man and responsive to the issue of "law and order."

Many voters, particularly liberals in both parties, were discontent, feeling that the American political system had not produced the best candidates to go before the voters. According to one CBS preelection poll, 43 percent of the American electorate would have preferred a choice among candidates different from that offered in 1968.[5] Nixon won the election by a narrow popular margin. He became the first President since Zachary Taylor in 1849 to begin his first term with both the House and Senate controlled by the opposition party.

The violence, the assassinations, the riots, the alienation of youth, blacks, and other disaffected groups, the fear, the divisions, and the frustration of the American people dominated the political landscape. It even seemed to some in 1968 as though America was breaking apart. What had gone wrong? Was the American political system in danger of disintegrating? Were its institutions outmoded and irrelevant to the times? Or was the system still workable and merely being subjected to unusual strains? These questions remain urgent today.

[5] Walter Dean Burnham, "Election 1968: The Abortive Landslide," *Trans-action*, Vol. 6, No. 2 (December 1968), p. 21.

THE RECIPROCAL NATURE OF DEMOCRATIC POWER

In July 1945, a small group of scientists stood atop a hill near Alamogordo, New Mexico, and watched the first atomic bomb explode in the desert. At that instant, the traditional power of government to alter the lives of men took on a terrifying new dimension. Since the onset of the nuclear age and the development of intercontinental ballistic missiles, man has lived less than thirty minutes away from possible self-destruction. That is all the time it would take for ICBMs to reach their targets, destroying whole cities and perhaps entire nations.

Today, the President of the United States is often described as a man with his finger "on the nuclear button." The existence of such chilling terminology, and of atomic weapons, reflects the increasingly complex, technological, computerized society in which Americans live. As America has changed through the development of science, technology, and industrialization, government has changed along with it. Government has expanded and grown more complex; it is called upon to perform more and more managerial tasks. Government today touches the lives of individuals as never before.

The Impact of Government on People

Obviously, government can affect the life of a student by drafting him into the armed forces and sending him overseas to fight in a war in which he may be killed. Less obvious, perhaps, are the ways in which government pervades most aspects of daily life, sometimes down to minute details. For example, the Federal Government regulates the amount of windshield that the wipers on a car must cover and even the *speed* of the windshield wipers. (At the fast setting, wipers must go "at least 45 cycles per minute.") [6]

A family sits down to a breakfast of orange juice, bacon and eggs, toast, and coffee. Half a dozen agencies of the Federal Government may have dealt with the food before it arrived at the breakfast table: the orange juice, if the frozen kind, must be manufactured under standards set by the Food and Drug Administration of the Department of Health, Education, and Welfare; the bacon must be inspected by the Department of Agriculture's Consumer and Marketing Service or must meet equivalent state standards; the eggs may have come from a box marked with a Department

[6] Motor Vehicle Safety Standards 104-3 (1969).

of Agriculture shield; the toast is made from bread that must by law be produced under sanitary conditions and comply with federal standards; and the coffee arrived in the United States under the eyes of both the Food and Drug Administration and the Bureau of Customs of the Department of the Treasury.

When a person drives a car, he is required by law to have a license issued by his state but conforming to federal standards. The car must also meet federal standards; automobiles manufactured in the United States after 1968 are required to have seat belts, shoulder belts, and head rests to reduce traffic injuries and fatalities.

A college student driving to class (perhaps over a highway built largely with federal funds) is expected to observe local traffic regulations. He may have to put a dime in a city parking meter. The classroom in which he sits may have been constructed with a federal grant. Possibly he is attending college with the aid of a federal loan or grant made available by the Higher Education Act of 1965. In fiscal 1971, for example, the Federal Government spent an estimated $1.7 billion on aid to 3.2 million college undergraduates.[7]

Clearly government's impact is real and far-reaching. An American normally must pay three levels of taxes—local, state, and federal. He attends public schools and perhaps public colleges. He draws unemployment insurance, welfare benefits, Medicare, and Social Security. He must either obey the laws or pay the penalty of a fine or imprisonment if he breaks them and is caught and convicted. His savings accounts and home mortgages are guaranteed by the Federal Government. His taxes support the armed forces, police, fire, health and sanitation departments. To hunt, fish, marry, drive, fly, or build he must have a government license. From birth certificate to death certificate, government accompanies the individual on his way. Even after he dies, the government is not through with him. Estate taxes must be collected and wills probated in the courts.

And in the United States, "government" is extraordinarily complicated. There are federal, state, and local layers of government, metropolitan areas, commissions, authorities, boards and councils, and quasi-governmental bodies. And many of these overlap.

The Impact of People on Government

Just as government affects people, people affect government. The American system of government is based on the concept that power flows from the people to the government. Jefferson expressed this eloquently when he wrote in the Declaration of Independence, "to secure these rights, Governments are instituted among men, deriving their just powers

[7] "Special Analysis I," in *Special Analyses, Budget of the United States, Fiscal Year 1971* (Washington, D.C.: U.S. Government Printing Office. 1970), p. 124.

from the consent of the governed." Abraham Lincoln expressed the same thought when he spoke in his Gettysburg Address of "government of the people, by the people and for the people."

These are ideals, statements embodying the principles of democracy. As we shall note at many points in this book, the principles do not always mesh with the practices. Yet, it remains true that if government in the United States has very real and often awesome powers over people, at the same time people, both individuals and the mass of citizens together, can have considerable power over the government.

The reciprocal nature of democratic power is a basic element of the American political system. As the late V. O. Key, Jr., the distinguished Harvard political scientist, has put it: "The power relationship is reciprocal, and the subject may affect the ruler more profoundly than the ruler affects the subject." [8] Described below are several ways that people influence government.

Voting. The first and most important power of the people in America is the right to vote in free elections to choose those who govern. At regular intervals, the people may, in the classic phrase of Horace Greeley, the nineteenth century journalist and politician, "turn the rascals out." The fact that a President, congressman, senator, governor, mayor, or school board member may want to stand for reelection influences his performance in office. The knowledge that he serves at the pleasure of the voters usually tends to make him sensitive to public opinion.

But isn't one person's vote insignificant when millions are cast? Not necessarily. That the individual's vote does matter even in a nation as big as the United States, can be dramatically illustrated by a look at some close presidential elections.

In 1960, John F. Kennedy, the Democratic nominee, defeated Richard M. Nixon, his Republican opponent, by 112,827 popular votes and 303 to 219 electoral votes. Presidents are elected by electoral votes, but these are normally cast by the electors in each state for the candidate who wins the most popular votes in the state. [9] A shift from Kennedy to Nixon of only 8,971 voters in Illinois and Missouri would have prevented either candidate from gaining a majority in the electoral college.

In 1968, Nixon defeated Humphrey by a popular margin of 499,704 and by 301 to 191 votes in the electoral college. A shift of slightly more than 150,000 voters in four states carried by Nixon—Illinois, Ohio, Missouri, and New Jersey—would have switched the electoral votes of those states and elected Humphrey as President.

[8] V. O. Key, Jr., *Politics, Parties, and Pressure Groups*, 5th ed. (New York: Crowell, 1964), p. 3.
[9] See the description of the electoral college in Chapter 9.

LUCIA PERRY: I was there . . . like helicopters had been buzzing in my dorm all night, and everywhere you went there were National Guard. . . . I went out and was standing on the veranda when the shooting took place. So I saw everything. I saw the men firing, and I saw the kids fall, and I looked out at the crowd and there were people crying, you know, people with blood all over them down the hill, and I just couldn't believe it. I've never seen people so mad and so horrified . . . as the kids in that crowd. Everything you could think of, those kids were shouting at those men: "You've killed them! You've killed them!" I don't know how, there's no way to describe the pain that I saw in people's faces or in their voices.

JEFFREY ZINK: In my home town—that's Canton, Ohio—people were saying, "Well, we ought to machine-gun them all. They should have killed them all right there." Or, "They deserved it. It's about time."

LUCIA: If this is a democracy, we're supposed to be involved in it, and frankly I feel about as alienated from my Government as you can get.

—*New York Times*, May 11, 1970.

History provides many more examples of the importance of an individual's vote. Charles Evans Hughes went to bed on election night in 1916 thinking he had been elected President of the United States. If 1,983 voters in California had shifted from Woodrow Wilson, he would have been right. In the disputed election of 1876, a shift of 116 votes in South Carolina would have elected Samuel J. Tilden as President instead of Rutherford B. Hayes.[10]

Party Activity. Political parties are basic to the American system of government because they provide a vehicle for competition and choice without which "free elections" would be meaningless. For the most part, the two-party system has predominated in the United States. Since candidates for public office, even at the presidential level, are usually selected by their parties, people can influence government, and the choice of who governs, by participating in party activities. Whether political campaigns offer meaningful alternatives on the issues depends in part on who is nominated. And that in turn may be influenced by how many people are politically active.

Political participation can take many forms, from ringing doorbells to running for local party committeeman, or for public office. We have already mentioned the college students who converged on New Hampshire in 1968 to work for Senator McCarthy.[11] There is little question that the

efforts of these students profoundly influenced the course of th[e] [presi]dential campaign in 1968 and set the stage for a power struggle w[ithin the] Democratic party.

In the spring of 1970, four students at Kent State University were shot and killed by national guardsmen, and at Jackson Stat[e] in Mississippi two students were killed by police. In reaction to th[ese] events, thousands of students resolved to make their voices heard [by par]ticipating in the political process. Some traveled to Washington [to take] part in a mass demonstration against the war in Vietnam, or to [lobby] Congress against the war; others took an active part in local con[gressional] campaigns, working for peace candidates or other candidates who[, basing] on such issues as civil rights and the environment appealed to th[em. Some] schools suspended classes for a time in the fall of 1970 to permi[t students] to participate in campaigns for the November elections.

By registering as a member of a political party, a citizen g[ains more] influence than a nonaligned voter. He can, for instance, take p[art in] primary elections that may determine party candidates in th[e general] elections.

Public Opinion. People may have an impact on governm[ent by ex]pressing opinions on public issues. Both candidates and elect[ed officials] are normally sensitive to what people are thinking. This has be[en particu]larly true since the Second World War with the development o[f sophisti]cated methods of political polling and statistical analysis. But a c[itizen need] not have to wait around to be polled. He can make his opini[ons felt in a] variety of ways: by participating in political activities, talkin[g to other] people, writing to his congressman, telephoning his city councilm[an, writing] to his newspaper, testifying at a public hearing.

---

[10] Neal R. Peirce, *The People's President* (New York: Simon and Schuster, 1968), pp. 317 ff.

[11] McCarthy did not win the New Hampshire primary popular vote. But he did win twenty of twenty-four elected delegates from that state to the Democratic National Convention, and his official showing of 42.2 percent of the Democratic preference vote in New Hampshire, against 49.4 percent for President Johnson, stunned the party and overnight turned McCarthy into a serious political force.

New York, 1970: Construction workers march in support of President Nixon's Vietnam policy.

Even by reading the newspapers and watching television news broadcasts (or by not doing those things) people may indirectly influence government. A citizen who carefully follows public issues in the news media and magazines of opinion may help to influence government, since a government is less likely to attempt to mislead when it knows it is dealing with an informed public.

Interest Groups. When people belong to groups that share common attitudes and make these views felt, or when they organize such groups, they may be influencing government. These private associations, or interest groups, may be unions, business and professional organizations, racial and religious groups, or organizations of such groups as farmers or veterans. An interest group does not have to be an organized body. Students, for example, constitute a highly vocal interest group, even when they do not belong to a formal student organization.

Direct Action. In the late 1960's and in the 1970's, as had happened before in American history, people sought to influence government by militant, sometimes violent action. Some civil rights leaders advocated "Black Power." Student activists practiced "the politics of confrontation." By whatever name, the idea of direct and often disruptive action to achieve political ends appeared to have grown in part out of the civil rights movement (beginning with peaceful "sit-ins" to desegregate lunch counters in the South) and in part out of the organized opposition to the war in Vietnam. Demonstrations, marches, sit-ins, campus strikes, picketing, and political heckling all may have an impact on government.

The political and social unrest of the late 1960's, characterized by militant forms of protest and direct action, alarmed many Americans and led to counterpressure for "law and order" and for greater police power to cope with demonstrators. The controversy cut deep into American society. The polarization and divisions were symbolized in 1970 by street battles between construction workers and peace demonstrators. People at both ends of the political spectrum were finding violent and often disturbing ways of influencing government.

WHAT IS GOVERNMENT?

The words "government," "politics," "power," and "democracy" ought to be clearly defined. The difficulty is that political scientists, philosophers, and kings have never been able to agree entirely on the meaning of these terms.

"Once upon a time there lived a little green elf in an old oak tree which had been condemned to make way for Interstate 95. The old oak tree stood by contaminated waters that ran along the edge of the strip mine just twenty-five miles from the heavily polluted air of the city. In spite of his emphysema he was a fairly happy elf . . ."

The ancient Greek philosopher Plato and his pupil Aristotle speculated on their meaning, and the process has continued up to the present day. Bearing in mind that no universal or perfect definitions exist, it is still possible to discuss the words and arrive at a *general* concept of what they mean.

Government

Even in a primitive society, some form of government exists. A headman or tribal chief emerges with authority over his fellows. He makes decisions, perhaps in consultation with other elders of the tribe. He is governing.

Government, then, even in a modern industrial state, can be defined on a simple level as the men, institutions, and processes that make the rules for society and possess the power to enforce them. But rules for what? To take an example, if private developers wish to acquire a wildlife preserve for commercial use, and environmental groups protest, government may be called upon to step in and settle the dispute. In short, government makes rules to decide who gets what of valued things in a society.[12] It attempts to resolve conflicts among individuals and groups.

David Easton, a political scientist at the University of Chicago, has written:

[12] A definition close to that suggested by the title of Harold D. Lasswell's *Politics: Who Gets What, When, How* (New York: McGraw-Hill, 1936).

18

Even in the smallest and simplest society someone must intervene in the name of society, with its authority behind him, to decide how differences over valued things are to be resolved.

This authoritative allocation of values is a minimum prerequisite of any society. . . . Every society provides some mechanisms, however rudimentary they may be, for authoritatively resolving differences about the ends that are to be pursued, that is, for deciding who is to get what there is of the desirable things.[13]

Easton's concept has come to be broadly accepted by many scholars today. In highly developed societies the principal mechanism for resolving differences is government. Government makes binding rules for society that determine the distribution of valued things.

Benjamin Disraeli, the nineteenth-century British Prime Minister and novelist, wrote in *Endymion* that "politics are the possession and distribution of power."

Politics

Disraeli's definition of *politics* comes very close to our definition of *government*. Disraeli was ahead of his time, for many political scientists today would agree in general with his definition, and they would add that there is little difference between politics and government.

For example, V. O. Key, Jr., equates politics with "the process and practice of ruling" and the "workings of governments generally, their impact on the governed, their manner of operation, the means by which governors attain and retain authority." [14]

Such a definition might be confusing to those Americans who tend to look at politics as the pursuit of power, and government as the exercise of power. In other words, the conventional notion is that people engage in politics to get elected. But, in fact, those who govern are constantly making *political* decisions. It is very difficult to say where government ends and politics begins. The two terms overlap and intertwine, even if their meanings are not precisely the same.[15]

Power is the possession of control over others. Men have sought for centuries to understand the basis of power, why it exists, and how it

Power

[13] David Easton, *The Political System, An Inquiry into the State of Political Science* (New York: Knopf, 1953), pp. 136–37.
[14] Key, *Politics, Parties, and Pressure Groups*, p. 2.
[15] Of course, the word "politics" can also refer to a process that occurs in a wide variety of nongovernmental settings—in fact, in every form of social organization where different people, with competing goals and differing objectives, interact. Thus, one sometimes speaks of politics in the local PTA, the politics of a ladies' garden club, or the politics in the newsroom of a campus newspaper. In this book, however, we are talking about politics as it is more commonly understood, in its governmental setting.

is maintained. Authority over others is a tenuous business, as many a deposed South American dictator can attest.

A century ago Boss Tweed, the leader of Tammany Hall, the Democratic party machine in New York City, reportedly expressed a simple, cynical philosophy: "The way to have power is to take it." But once acquired, power must be defended against others who desire it. For seven years Nikita Khrushchev appeared to be the unquestioned ruler of the Soviet Union. One day in October 1964, he was summoned back to Moscow from his Black Sea vacation retreat and informed by his colleagues in the Presidium of the Communist party that he was no longer Premier of the Soviet Union. It was reported that those who deposed him changed all the confidential government and party telephone numbers in Moscow, so that Khrushchev could not attempt to rally support among elements still loyal to him.[16] Khrushchev was helpless, cut off from the tremendous power that was his only twenty-four hours before.

It is a truism that power is often destructive of those who hold it. Lord Acton, nineteenth-century British peer and historian, said that "power tends to corrupt and absolute power corrupts absolutely." The eighteenth-century French philosopher Montesquieu expressed a similar idea in *The Spirit of the Laws:* "Every man who has power is impelled to abuse it."

As Key has observed, power is not something that can be "poured into a keg, stored, and drawn upon as the need arises." [17] Power, Key notes, is *relational*—that is, it involves the interactions between the man who exercises power and those whom his actions affect.

If man, even in a primitive state, finds it necessary to accept rulers who can authoritatively decide who gets what, then it follows that whoever governs possesses and exercises power in part because of his position. In other words, power follows office. To some extent, men accept the power exercised over them by others because of the need to be governed.

Democracy

Democracy is a word that literally defines itself. It comes from two Greek roots, *demos*, the people, and *kratia*, rule—taken together, rule by the people. The Greeks used the term to describe the government of Athens and other Greek city-states that flourished in the fifth century B.C. In his famous *Funeral Oration*, Pericles, the Athenian statesman, declared: "Our constitution is named a democracy, because it is in the hands not of the few, but of the many."

All governments make decisions about the distribution of valued things. As we have noted earlier, in a democratic government, power, in theory, flows from the people. This is one of the ideals upon which the

---

[16] *The Observer*, London, November 29, 1964.
[17] Key, *Politics, Parties, and Pressure Groups*, p. 2.

Something is very wrong in America. . . .

Growing numbers of our citizens are convinced that the American dream is a cruel illusion or a hypocritical nightmare. . . . They refuse to serve a System which, in their view, consistently fails to rise to its own rhetoric.

Black militant and white radical—the poor and the politically unorthodox—in varying degrees and for different reasons, all have lost faith in The System. They perceive the law as partisan or insensitive or vicious. And they are at least partially right. They are angry. And they should be.

The poor could have told us years ago about the inequities of criminal justice—but no one was willing to listen. . . .

It is difficult for blacks to believe in The System's fairness when bail for black defendants appears more severe than bail for white defendants. . . .

Worst of all, the archaic machinery of justice is remarkably resistant to change. Like every other bureaucratic institution, it is distant, impersonal, and even terrifying. . . .

The courts could change. They could be modern. . . . The problem is partially money. And that has to be repaired. But you can't use money as a cop-out. It is also true that The System stubbornly adheres to outworn patterns and traditions. It has not taken off the green eyeshades of a century ago. . . .

No society in the world has higher aspirations for individual freedom than ours. Inevitably, we fall short. Our task—your task and my task—is to make the reality equal to the promise. In peace, under law, we must go right on.

—Mayor John V. Lindsay of New York, address at the University of Pennsylvania, April 29, 1970.

American democracy was founded. The United States is too big for every citizen to take part in the deliberations of government, as in ancient Athens, so the distinction is sometimes made that America is a *representative* democracy rather than a direct one. Leaders are elected to speak for and represent the people.

Government by the people also carries with it the concept of *majority rule*. Everyone is free to vote, but whoever gets the most votes wins the election and represents *all* the people, including those who opposed him. But in a system that is truly democratic, minority rights and views are also recognized and protected.

Every schoolchild knows the phrase from the Declaration of Independence: "We hold these truths to be self-evident, that all men are created equal." The concept of *equality*—that all men are of equal worth, even if not of equal ability—is also basic to American democracy. So are basic *rights* such as freedom of speech, press, religion, assembly, the right to vote, and the right to dissent from majority opinion. The idea of *individual dignity* and the importance of each individual is another concept basic to American democracy. And, American government is *constitutional* —the power of government is limited by a framework of fundamental written law.

These are the ideals, noble, even beautiful, in their conception. But, this is not always how it really is. Blacks and other minorities in America are still struggling for full equality; a man may dissent from the dominant political view but lose his job as the price of nonconformity; the probing questions asked of a welfare recipient leave him with little individual dignity; in 1968, the Chicago police had their own views on freedom of assembly; and so on.

American democracy, like all the other dreams of men to order their lives, is far from perfect. "This is a great country," President John F. Kennedy once declared, "but it must be greater." [18] Every American has to judge for himself how far America falls short of fulfilling the principles on which it was founded. Nevertheless the ideas endure; the goals are there if not always the reality.

THE CONCEPT OF A POLITICAL SYSTEM

In today's electronic world, many people own or have listened to a stereo. Suppose for a moment that a visitor from outer space dropped in and asked you to describe a stereo set. You might say, "This is a turntable and record changer, this thing with all the tubes is an amplifier, and this big box over here is what we call a speaker." Perhaps you might take the trouble to describe the details of each component at some length. At the end of your elaborate explanation, the visitor from space would still not know what a stereo was.

A better way to describe the set would be to explain that it is a *system for the reproduction of sound*, consisting of several parts, each of which performs a separate function and relates to the others. Having said that, you might turn on the stereo and play a record. Now the visitor would understand.

A Dynamic Approach

In the same way, it is possible either to describe people, government, politics, and power as isolated, static elements, or to look at them as interacting elements in a *political system*. The concept of a political system may provide a useful framework, or approach, for understanding the total subject matter of this book. Just as in the case of the stereo system, a political system consists of several parts that relate to one another, each of which performs a separate, vital function. If we think in terms of a system, we visualize all the pieces in motion, acting and interacting, dynamic rather than static. In other words, something is happening—just as when the record is playing.

[18] "Remarks of Senator John F. Kennedy, Street Rally, Waterbury, Connecticut, November 6, 1960," in *The Speeches of Senator John F. Kennedy, Presidential Campaign of 1960* (Washington, D.C.: U.S. Government Printing Office, 1961), p. 912.

As Easton says, "we can try to understand political life by viewing each of its aspects piecemeal," or we can "view political life as a system of interrelated activities." [19] One of the problems of trying to look at a political system is that government and politics do not exist in a vacuum—they are embedded in, and closely related to, many other activities in a society. But it is possible to separate political activity from other kinds of activity, at least for purposes of study.

Just as the stereo is a system for the reproduction of sound, a political system also operates for a purpose: it makes the binding, authoritative decisions for society about who gets what.

We may carry the analogy of a stereo to a political system even further. A sound system has *inputs, outputs,* and sometimes a loud whistling noise called *feedback.* Those are precisely the same terms used by political scientists in talking about a political system.

Inputs, Outputs, and Feedback

The "inputs" of a political system are of two kinds: demands and supports.

Demands, as the word indicates, are what people and groups want from the system, whether it be Medicare for the aged, draft exemption for college students, equal opportunity for minorities, or higher subsidies for farmers.

Supports are the attitudes and actions of people that sustain and buttress the system at all levels and allow it to continue to work. They include everything from the patriotism drilled into schoolchildren to public backing for specific government policies.

The "outputs" of a political system are chiefly the binding decisions it makes, whether in the form of laws, regulations, or judicial decisions. Often such decisions reward one segment of society at the expense of another. The millionaire dowager on New York's Park Avenue may be heavily taxed to clothe slum children on the South Side of Chicago. The freeway that runs through an urban ghetto may speed white commuters from the suburbs but dislocate black residents of the inner city. These decisions are "redistributive" measures in that something of value is reallocated by the political system. Sometimes even a decision *not* to act is an output of a political system. By preserving an existing policy one group may be rewarded and another not.

"Feedback" in a political system describes the response of the rest

---

[19] David Easton, "An Approach to the Analysis of Political Systems," *World Politics,* Vol. 9 (April 1957), pp. 383–84. Our discussion of the concept of a political system relies chiefly on Easton's work, although it should not by any means be read as a literal summary of his approach. For example, the analogy to a stereo system is the authors' own; and Easton's analysis of a political system is both much more detailed and broader in scope than the outline presented here.

of society to the decisions made by the authorities. When those reactions are communicated back to the authorities, they may lead to a fresh round of decisions and new public responses.

The concept of a political system is simply a way of looking at political activity. It is an approach, an analytical tool, rather than a general theory of the type developed to explain the workings of scientific phenomena. It enables us to examine not only the formal structure of political and governmental institutions, but also how these institutions actually work.

Political Socialization
Every political system has certain mechanisms that serve to perpetuate it. One of the most important of these functions is *political socialization*, the process through which children and adults learn the prevailing mores and attitudes of the "political culture":

> Political socialization is the process of induction into the political culture. Its end product is a set of attitudes—cognitions, value standards, and feelings—toward the political system. . . . Thus in a modern Western political system such as the United States, family, church, peer group, community, school, work group, voluntary associations, media of communication, political parties, and governmental institutions all share in the function of political socialization, and the associations, relationships, and participations of adult life continue the process.[20]

In the Soviet Union, political indoctrination is highly organized. Kindergarten children sing songs and listen to stories designed to instill love for the Soviet system and its leaders. Formal indoctrination begins when the child is enrolled in the "little Octobrists" (named after the October Revolution). At the age of ten, he is eligible to join the Young Pioneers, and at fourteen he may qualify for admission to the Komsomol, the Soviet youth organization from which members of the Communist party and the future leaders of the Soviet Union are recruited.[21]

Political socialization in a democracy is more informal and less highly organized, but it serves the same end. A typical schoolchild in the United States is required at an early age to learn "God Bless America" and "The Star Spangled Banner" and to pledge allegiance to the flag. He is taught to respect the Founding Fathers and the government. He is told that everyone is equal, regardless of race, creed, or color. He absorbs these ideas almost unconsciously.

[20] Gabriel A. Almond, "A Functional Approach to Comparative Politics," in Gabriel A. Almond and James S. Coleman, eds., *The Politics of Developing Areas* (Princeton, N.J.: Princeton University Press, 1960), pp. 27–28.
[21] Merle Fainsod, *How Russia is Ruled* (Cambridge, Mass.: Harvard University Press, 1963), p. 293. See Chapter 9 of Fainsod's book for a fascinating and detailed account of the political socialization of Soviet youth.

Later on, it may come as a shock to discover that, in President Kennedy's words, "the practices of the country do not always conform to the principles of the Constitution." [22] When that discovery is made, the reaction may be violent.

In the wake of the violent social upheavals of the 1960's, including student protests, educators and politicians have become increasingly concerned about the nature of political socialization in America. Conservatives blame student dissent on "permissiveness" in the schools and homes; they argue that the trouble with the educational system is that it does not instill *enough* patriotism and respect for old-fashioned virtues.

Another, and we think much more persuasive, view has been advanced that "the schools have contributed to divisions within society by teaching a view of the nation and its political processes which is incomplete and simplistic, stressing values and ideals but ignoring social realities." [23]

Although the schools may ignore these realities,

> it is evident to many citizens that the picture of unity, equality, and freedom that is so often presented is distorted, oversimplified, and, to a degree, false. . . . The image of the United States . . . is one of a country which is an effective force for world peace, in which the laws are fair, justice prevails, people who break laws are usually apprehended, and what goes on in government is all for the best. This is the nature of the socialization that children receive both in the home and at school. Accompanied by feelings of strong attachment and loyalty, this image of the nation is designed to encourage pride in one's country and a desire to maintain it and support its policies. In transmitting this orientation to the political world, the school represents the convictions of the community. This view of the United States is both distorted and incomplete, and in the past few years these inaccurate representations have been seriously challenged, particularly by college students and other young adults. . . . The increasing volume of protest reflects the new realism; young people no longer find either government action or social and economic reality congruent with the national ideology and rhetoric of morality. . . . In short, the spirit of protest . . . is based on a feeling of having been misled.[24]

Family influence is an important factor in political socialization. If a child's parents are Republicans, he is less likely to be a Democrat. If the political atmosphere in the home is liberal, or conservative, that orientation may stay with the child in later life.

Children today are exposed to television before they can toddle. In a world of instant communication, in which TV and other outside influences compete with the classroom, children acquire greater social and political

[22] "Special Message to the Congress on Civil Rights," February 28, 1963, in *Public Papers of the Presidents of the United States, John F. Kennedy, 1963* (Washington, D.C.: U.S. Government Printing Office, 1964), p. 221.
[23] Robert D. Hess, "Political Socialization in the Schools," *Harvard Educational Review*, Vol. 38, No. 3 (Summer 1968), p. 531.
[24] Hess, "Political Socialization in the Schools," pp. 529–30.

sophistication, and at a much earlier age, than their parents did. They expect their teachers to provide a picture of America as it really is. The probability, therefore, is that political socialization in the schools will move toward a more balanced appraisal of American society, with emphasis not only on the considerable achievements of American democracy, but also on what has been left undone.

DEMOCRATIC GOVERNMENT AND A CHANGING SOCIETY

A political system relates to people, and the size of the population affects the outputs of the system. Of equal importance is the qualitative nature of the population: who they are, where they live, how they work, how they spend, how they move about. As society changes, the responses of government are likely to change. Government reacts to basic alterations in the nature of a society; it tries to tailor programs and decision-making to meet changing needs and demands. Population changes are also important politically; for example, the black migration out of the South has given black voters increased political power in the North.

200,000,000 Americans

On November 20, 1967, at 11:03 A.M., the census clock in the lobby of the Department of Commerce building in Washington registered 200,000,000 Americans. In the time it takes to read this page, the clock will click eight times, a relentless reminder that the population of the United States is increasing at a substantial rate.[25]

The Census Bureau estimates that by 1975 there may be 219,000,000 Americans. By the year 2000 the figure may soar beyond 300,000,000.[26] The American born in 1950, when the population was just over 150,000,000, can expect to see the size of the nation double in his lifetime.

At the same rate of increase, according to one study of population patterns in the United States, "we would have close to *one billion* people in the United States one hundred years from now." [27] Although the authors

[25] The census clock is tied to a computer and reflects a mathematical estimate of population increases, rather than actual changes. Nobody knows the *exact* moment at which the United States population exceeded 200,000,000. As of August 1970, the census clock operated on the computer's estimate that there is in the United States one birth every 9 seconds, one death every 16½ seconds, one immigrant each minute, and one emigrant every 23 minutes—for a net population gain of one person every 15½ seconds.

[26] U.S. Bureau of the Census, *Current Population Reports*, Population Estimates, Series P-25, No. 448 (Washington, D.C.: U.S. Government Printing Office, 1970), p. 1.

[27] Ben J. Wattenberg in collaboration with Richard M. Scammon, *This U.S.A.* (New York: Doubleday, 1965), p. 18.

of the study add that birth control and other factors make it unlikely that such a staggering total will be reached by that time, they estimate that the United States *could* support a population of one billion without people pushing one another into the ocean.

How the nation has expanded from a population of about 4,000,000 in 1790, and what the future may hold, can be charted with Census Bureau statistics and projections to the year 2000, as shown in Table 1-1.

TABLE 1-1

Profile of the United States Population, 1790–2000

| | Population (in millions) | | | | | | |
| | Actual | | | | Projected | | |
	1790	1870	1920	1960	1970	1980	2000
Total population	4	39	106	179	205	232	301
Urban	—[1]	10	54	125	NA[2]	NA	NA
Rural	4	29	52	54	NA	NA	NA
Nonwhite	1	5	11	20	25	31	NA
White	3	34	95	159	181	204	NA
Median age (years)	NA	20.2	25.3	29.5	27.5	28.7	NA
Primary and secondary school enrollment	NA	6.9	23.3	41.8	51.5	56.4	NA
College enrollment	NA	[1]	.6	3.2	7.4	11.2	NA

[1] Less than 200,000
[2] NA: Not Available

Sources: U.S. Bureau of the Census, *Historical Statistics of the U.S., Colonial Times to 1957* (Washington, D.C.: U.S. Government Printing Office); U.S. Bureau of the Census, *Historical Statistics of the U.S., Colonial Times to 1957; Continuation to 1962 and Revisions* (Washington, D.C.: U.S. Government Printing Office, 1965); U.S. Bureau of the Census, *Current Population Reports*, Population Estimates, Series P-25, Nos. 381, 388, 448 (Washington, D.C.: U.S. Government Printing Office, 1967, 1968, 1970).

This dramatic increase in numbers of people, often called the "population explosion," is taking place around the world. It raises questions, which governments must ponder. Will there be enough food to eat? Enough room to live? Enough natural resources to meet mankind's future needs? Will the environment be destroyed?

An interesting profile of the American public can be sketched with statistics that answer the question "Who are we?" (See Table 1-2.) A portrait of national origins can also be drawn. The great successive waves of immigration placed a stamp of diversity on America; even third and fourth generation Americans may think of themselves as "Irish" or "Italian." That there is still great pride, as well as sensitivity, over national origin was illustrated during the 1968 presidential race when Spiro T. Agnew, then the Republican candidate for Vice-President, referred to a newspaperman of Oriental descent as a "fat Jap," and to Polish-Americans as "Polacks." The storm he aroused was not dissipated when Agnew explained that he often used such terms humorously but not maliciously.

TABLE 1-2
Who Are We? [1]

104.8 million	females
101.2 million	males
18.7 million	under five years
19.6 million	sixty-five and over
180.7 million	white
25.3 million	nonwhite
111.8 million	married, divorced, or widowed
123.4 million	old enough to vote
7.4 million	in college
51.5 million	in other schools
37.9 million	white-collar workers
27.9 million	blue-collar workers
141.7 million[2]	urban dwellers
40.8 million	homeowners

[1] Based on projected population figures for 1970. The actual population total of 204.8 million in the 1970 census was slightly below these estimates.

[2] Projected for 1975. Data for 1970 not available.

Source: U.S. Bureau of the Census and U.S. Bureau of Labor Statistics.

Because the Census Bureau no longer asks the national origins of persons born in the United States of native-born parents, statistics about the famed "melting pot" are elusive. But unpublished Census Bureau estimates for 1960 based on past studies indicate that the national origin of the majority of Americans roughly breaks down this way: Great Britain, 39 percent; Germany, 16 percent; Ireland, 11 percent; Italy, 5 percent; Poland, 3 percent; and Russia, slightly under 3 percent. Figure 1-1 shows the origins of immigrants in the years 1820 to 1967.

FIGURE 1-1

Origins of Immigrants to United States, 1820–1967

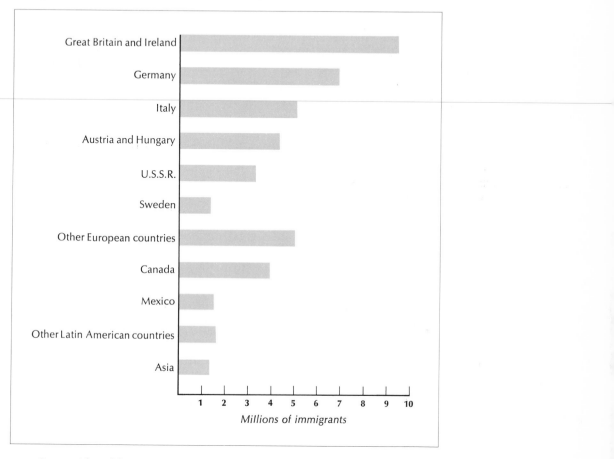

Source: Adapted from U.S. Bureau of the Census, *Pocket Data Book* (Washington, D.C.: U.S. Government Printing Office, 1969) p. 71.

The United States is also a nation of 69,000,000 Protestants, 46,000,000 Catholics, and 5,600,000 Jews.[28] Sometimes, prevailing notions about America's population are incorrect. For example, we are generally thought to be a nation of White, Anglo-Saxon Protestants. That group is influential in many areas of our national life. But as the national origin figures indicate,

[28] The Census Bureau does not ask the religion of Americans in the Decennial Census, which is taken every ten years in years that end in zero, but religious groups estimate their own membership. These are rounded figures based on the *Yearbook of American Churches, 1967.*

more than 60 percent of Americans stem from other than Anglo-Saxon stock.[29]

Although the accent in America is on youth, the median age of Americans is not eighteen or twenty-one but twenty-eight, and likely to go up as a result of a decline in the birth rate during the 1960's, combined with greater life expectancy.

The Mobile
Society

A political system reacts not only to shifts in population totals, but also to the *movement* of people, geographically, socially, and economically.

For example, farm population declined from 32,000,000 in 1920 to 12,000,000 in 1965. As the nation changed from a predominantly rural to an urban society (see Table 1-1) the importance of the "farm bloc" decreased. By 1970, Congress, although still concerned with price supports for wheat, was focusing more of its attention on mass transportation, housing, and the problems of the cities.

Americans move about a great deal. In 1964, California surpassed New York as the most populous state in the Union. As a result, presidential candidates now spend more time than they used to campaigning in California. Victory in the state's presidential primary is often crucial to a candidate; the prize of the state's large delegation to the party's national convention may help him win the nomination. Beyond that, he gains the psychological advantage of having demonstrated his strength in the most populous state of the union, one that is usually a key state in the general election.

Of the 22,000,000 black Americans in 1968, 40 percent lived in the North. In 1910, 91 percent of the nation's black population lived in the South and only 9 percent lived in the North. Between 1940 and 1966 more than 3.5 million blacks migrated from the South. Mostly, the blacks left hoping to escape segregation and to find better economic opportunities.

For the most part the migrants moved into the cities. By 1967, 15,000,000 blacks, or 69 percent of America's black population, lived in metropolitan areas. In 1960, Washington, D.C., became the first major American city in which blacks were a majority. By 1969 eight major cities were more than 30 percent black.

In 1966 blacks represented 11.1 percent of the total United States population. Because of the higher birth rate among blacks, it has been estimated that in 1972 one in every eight Americans will be black.[30]

[29] See Wattenberg and Scammon, *This U.S.A.*, pp. 45–46.
[30] Statistics on black population are from the Census Bureau and the *Report of the National Advisory Commission on Civil Disorders* (New York: Bantam Books, 1968), pp. 236–50. The commission, appointed by President Johnson following the Detroit riots of 1967, notes that figures on black population "are undoubtedly too low because the Census Bureau has consistently undercounted the number of Negroes in the U.S. by as much as 10 percent."

As whites moved to the suburbs, blacks for the most part moved into racially segregated neighborhoods in Northern cities. At the same time, the black voters gained a stronger political voice: national elections are won or lost in the populous states of the industrial North. Usually a national candidate does not feel that he can afford to ignore black voters in New York, Los Angeles, Philadelphia, Detroit, Chicago, and Cleveland, for example.

All of these shifts and changing population patterns affect the American political system. The migration of millions of black citizens to Northern cities resulted in the election of black mayors in three large cities by 1970, and in the election of more black members of Congress. The population shift from the cities to the suburbs increased the political power of suburbia. More congressmen and state legislators now represent suburban areas than in the past, because lawmakers are apportioned by population.

When a young couple moves to California from the East, or a retired worker moves to Florida, or a black man migrates from Georgia to New York, there is population movement. Another kind of population shift occurs with changes in economic and social status. For example, after the Second World War, blue-collar (factory) workers outnumbered white-collar (office) workers. Today, many millions more workers are white-collar. There has been a significant shift of workers from production lines to service industries, such as hotels, motels, laundries, dry cleaning stores, employment agencies, auto repair shops, entertainment, and recreation.

Americans, it is often said, are members of an "upward mobile" society. They constantly seek to make more money, to have two or three cars, and if possible, to move up to a higher social class.

In addition to the population explosion, America has experienced a knowledge explosion. The impact of science and technology, of computers, electronics, and high-speed communications is reshaping American society. Man has traveled to the moon and back. He has split the atom. He is deciphering the code of life. He listens for signals from other galaxies in outer space, and explores the inner space of the human brain. There appear to be no limits to man's technological potential—except his inability to control his own nature.

Technological Change

Technological change is soon reflected within the political system. Consider for a moment a single innovation of the electronic age: television. Prior to the Second World War, television did not exist for the mass of Americans. In 1946, for example, only 8,000 homes in the United States had TV sets. In 1969, 83,000,000 sets were in use in 95 percent of American homes. Today, political candidates spend millions of dollars to purchase television time. Presidential nominees deplore the "packaging" of political candidates by Madison Avenue, but they hire advertising agencies to do just that. Commercials are produced and Presidents sold just like detergents. The presence of TV mobile units may influence the actions of political

31

demonstrators. When students who clashed with police at the Democratic National Convention in 1968 chanted "The whole world is watching," they were absolutely right. The students, who grew up in the television age, understood this better than the police.

Much of the technology of the electronic age is the by-product of defense research and development. In his farewell address to the nation in 1961, President Eisenhower, although himself a career soldier, warned of the dangers to liberty and democracy of the "military-industrial complex." What Eisenhower feared was that the Pentagon and the defense contractors who produce weapons for the military would gain "unwarranted influence" in the political system. "The potential for the disastrous rise of misplaced power exists and will persist," he warned. As multibillion dollar defense budgets soared ever-higher in the decade that followed Eisenhower's warning, there seemed ample reason for Americans to share his concern. In recent years, the involvement of universities in defense research has been a major factor in student unrest on the campus.

In the view of economist John Kenneth Galbraith, there already exists a "close fusion of the industrial system with the state," and in time "the line between the two will disappear." As a result of the technological revolution, Galbraith contends, a few hundred huge corporations are shaping the goals of society as a whole, and "we are becoming the servants in thought, as in action, of the machine we have created to serve us." [31]

The technological explosion, in short, has raised moral and philosophical questions about the quality of American life. As the nation moves toward the last quarter of the twentieth century, the overriding question is not whether to adapt to the changing technology—because there can be no turning back to a simpler age—but to what end technological change should be put.

The Economy
Despite the external and internal tensions that beset America in the 1960's, the technological revolution brought unprecedented domestic prosperity during the decade. The annual Gross National Product—the yardstick that economists use to measure all the goods and services produced in the United States—passed the trillion mark in 1970.

Government was expected to help prevent either periodic economic recession or depression. Although economists argued over the best methods of managing the economy, they generally agreed that the government had the major responsibility in promoting prosperity and full employment. In large measure, this responsibility grew out of the Great Depression of the 1930's and the influence of British economist John Maynard Keynes, who

[31] John Kenneth Galbraith, *The New Industrial State* (Boston: Houghton Mifflin, 1967), pp. 7–9, 392–93.

argued that government must step in and spend to maintain economic stability if the private sector does not. His theories influenced the actions taken by economists in the New Deal and since then to cope with economic problems.

Beneath the pleasant exterior of prosperity in the late 1960's, there were problems and dangers as well. Rising consumer prices were bidding to outstrip higher incomes. Inflation diminished the value of savings. In November 1970, 4,600,000 Americans, 5.8 percent of the labor force, were unemployed. Recurring dislocations in the international monetary system threatened the value of the dollar.

Perhaps most disturbing of all is the specter of poverty in the midst of plenty. In his second inaugural address in January 1937, Franklin D. Roosevelt saw "one-third of a nation ill-housed, ill-clad, ill-nourished." It came as a shock to most Americans when Michael Harrington in his book *The Other America* estimated that in 1962, 25 percent of the nation was *still* living in poverty. Harrington argued that if poverty were defined as an income of less than $3,500 a year for an urban family of four, there were 50,000,000 poverty-stricken Americans.[32] "How long," he asked, "shall we ignore this underdeveloped nation in our midst? How long shall we look the other way while our fellow human beings suffer?"[33] The book influenced the Federal Government to launch what President Johnson called a "war on poverty." That effort, however, was only a beginning; poverty in America remains an urgent social problem.

A political system is influenced by the social and cultural environment in which it functions. This chapter began with an account of violence in Washington, and there could be no event or setting more symbolic of the rapid and revolutionary change taking place in American society. At almost every level, wherever one looks, the change is visible, in civil rights, in student power, in manners and morals, in the theater, in literature, and in the arts. In the political context, some of the rapid and ofttimes violent change has taken place because minorities and other Americans living in poverty have demanded entry into what John Kenneth Galbraith has called "the affluent society."[34]

Social Change

The Price of Affluence. A few years back, a motion picture called *The Graduate* drew large audiences and had a considerable impact on many

---

[32] Michael Harrington, *The Other America* (New York: Macmillan, 1962), p. 182. The Census Bureau, defining poverty as $3,743 or less a year for a nonfarm family of four, estimated there were 24.3 million poor Americans in 1969. Figures on poverty vary greatly depending on source, year, and the income level used.
[33] *Ibid*, p. 174.
[34] John Kenneth Galbraith, *The Affluent Society* (Boston: Houghton Mifflin, 1958).

Americans. In it, Dustin Hoffman played the part of a college graduate repelled by the materialism and social mores of the affluent, suburbanite world of his parents.

The movie's popularity reflected an interesting phenomenon of modern American life: Americans pursue wealth, but they are uneasy in their affluence.

Young people in particular have looked at the adult world with its pressures for conformity and said: there must be something better. But what? In the decade of the sixties, some young people "dropped out" of college and conventional society. They moved to San Francisco or to Greenwich Village in New York City. They let their hair grow long, wore beads, and became "hippies," espousing love, peace, and the beauties of nature. They turned within, experimenting with drugs such as LSD. Lack of communication and understanding between youth and age came to be called the "Generation Gap."

Sociologists saw in all this a manifestation of a broader problem of modern man: a sense of alienation, of being cut off from the rest of society. Possibly affluence itself had made Americans restless, rootless, and aimless, lacking national purpose.

Drawing by F. B. Modell
© 1961 The New Yorker Magazine, Inc.

"It's about time you realized, Harlan, that in life we
often have to do things that aren't our bag."

THE HONEYMOON IS OVER

Whatever a honeymoon visit to Niagara Falls was like in the days when Blondin was crossing on his tightwire, it's different now. Something new and unpleasant has been added. Sightseers boarding the famous *Maid of the Mist* excursion boat are likely to find themselves shrouded in a miasma that smells like sewage. That's what it is—coming over the American falls in the Niagara River and gushing out of a great eight-foot culvert beneath the Honeymoon Bridge. As the little boat plows through the swirling currents to a landing on the Canadian side, it has to navigate an expanse of viscous brown foam—paper-mill waste out of the culvert—that collects in a huge eddy across the river.

—Gladwin Hill, "The Great and Dirty Lakes," *Saturday Review*, October 23, 1965.

The Environmental Crisis. In the decade of the 1970's, increasing numbers of people were becoming concerned over the pollution of the natural environment that has accompanied technological advance. Many American cities are blanketed in smog. Rivers are polluted by industrial and human waste. Pesticides are killing our wildlife.[35] Oil spills from off-shore drilling are fouling our beaches. The gasoline engine, power plants, and other industries pour smoke into the atmosphere.

It is not only a matter of esthetics, of preserving the natural beauty of the land. Air and water pollution damages health and upsets the delicate balance of nature, the total relationship between man and his environment. It raises serious questions about whether man will be able to survive the damage he is inflicting upon the earth that sustains all life.[36]

Civil Rights and Black Power. To any white man who cared to listen, the message of the times was clear: the black man in America will wait no longer to obtain the equality and freedom that are rightfully his under the American political system. Of all the social changes at work in the United States, this is the most significant, with deep implications for the very survival of the democratic system.

Even before the death of Dr. Martin Luther King, Jr., black militants had become more visible in the civil rights movement, riding a wave of black frustration over the slow pace of nonviolent change. In the wake of the 1967 urban riots, some white housewives in the Midwest enrolled in classes in pistol-shooting, and fear between whites and blacks surfaced as a widespread national emotion. Threats of guerrilla warfare by black militants frightened and angered the white majority. Conversely, blacks feared repression.

After Dr. King's death, Stokely Carmichael, the black militant who popularized the phrase, "Black Power," declared at a news conference: "When white America killed Dr. King last night, she declared war on us.

[35] See Rachel Carson, *Silent Spring* (Boston: Houghton Mifflin, 1962).
[36] We shall examine the problem of environmental pollution in more detail in Chapter 15.

. . . The rebellions that have been occurring around these cities and this country is just light stuff to what is about to happen. We have to retaliate for the deaths of our leaders. The execution for those deaths will not be in the courtrooms. They're going to be in the streets of the United States of America." [37]

How did relations among Americans reach such a point? Opinions varied widely, but one view was voiced in 1968 by the Riot Commission, the panel named by President Johnson to investigate the 1967 disorders. As the commission saw it: "Race prejudice has shaped our history decisively; it now threatens to affect our future. White racism is essentially responsible for the explosive mixture which has been accumulating in our cities since the end of World War II." [38]

Youth and Dissent.   Students in Europe and Latin America have long been a volatile and powerful political force. In the 1960's, students and youth in America emerged in this role for the first time. They practiced "the politics of confrontation"—direct challenge to authority. According to a faculty leader of the 1964 Free Speech Movement at the Berkeley campus of the University of California: "The unique feature of the present situation in universities is the pervasive dislike and distrust of authority. Far more students in the Western democracies today—more than, say 10 years ago—hate their governments, police forces and university administrations." [39]

Some linked the new "student power" in America to the alienation of youth from the values of their parents. Others viewed student activism as the result of a mixture of opposition to the Vietnam war, disenchantment with the university as a tool of government and industry, and sympathy for the civil rights movement. Leaders of New Left organizations such as the Students for a Democratic Society made it clear that their goals went deeper: they sought to revamp the American political system completely.

The most militant of American youth went "underground" and re-

---

**THE TRIAL
OF THE 'CHICAGO SEVEN'**

ABBIE HOFFMAN: Are you asking if I had those thoughts or if I wrote that I had those thoughts? There's a difference.

MR. SCHULTZ: It's a convenient difference, isn't it, Mr. Hoffman?

ABBIE HOFFMAN: I don't know what you mean. I've never been on trial for my thoughts before.

—Excerpt from the trial, quoted in J. Anthony Lukas, "The Second Confrontation in Chicago," *New York Times Magazine,* March 29, 1970.

---

[37] Ben W. Gilbert and the staff of the *Washington Post, Ten Blocks From the White House, Anatomy of the Washington Riots of 1968,* pp. 60–61.
[38] *Report of the National Advisory Commission on Civil Rights* (New York: Bantam Books, 1968), p. 10.
[39] John R. Searle, "A Foolproof Scenario for Student Revolts," *New York Times Magazine,* December 29, 1968, p. 15.

sorted to bombings and other forms of violence. But a much larger number of students chose to work for change "within the system." This was the approach followed by the thousands of students who campaigned for peace candidates in the 1970 congressional elections, following the tragedy at Kent State.

One of the characteristics of a viable political system is that it adapts to change. Nearly 200 years after its creation, the ability of the American political system to adapt to relentless change was being severely tested. The goals and conditions of American society were being held up to the light, examined, and, in some cases, found wanting.

Adjusting to Change

Some of those engaged in violent political action wished to destroy the existing system and construct a new one. Often, however, the input of militant action created inequities. Demonstrators who block traffic are making a point at the expense of others. Revolutionaries who plant bombs may kill other human beings. Rioters who burn buildings may be destroying their neighbors' homes or stores. Students who shut down or disrupt a college may justify their actions as necessary in behalf of a crucial cause, but other students who want to attend classes may disagree.

An American in Vietnam

Even in 1968, there were signs of counterreaction to militant protest by a disturbed "silent majority." The presidential candidacy of George Wallace was directed against blacks, student "anarchists," liberals in general, and "pseudo-intellectuals." The country did not accept Wallace. But it turned to Richard Nixon, who appealed to the "forgotten Americans, the non-shouters, the non-demonstrators"—to the average citizen fed up with turmoil and longing for "law and order." It may be that President Nixon was elected principally because the voters were weary of the war in Vietnam and of President Johnson. But to some extent, Nixon's triumph also reflected the disenchantment of many Americans with urban riots, long-haired "hippies," "yippies," student demonstrators, and others who pushed beyond the limits of dissent acceptable to the "silent majority."

The reaction of the voters, however, could not make dissent disappear, because the underlying causes remained. And the right of dissent is essential in a democracy. Today's minority may become tomorrow's majority. The students and professors who demonstrated against the war in Vietnam in the 1960's helped to influence public opinion against the war, and that shift placed pressure on both the Johnson and Nixon administrations to seek an end to the conflict. As President Kennedy declared, in a speech at Amherst College in 1963, less than a month before his death, "men who create power make an indispensable contribution to the Nation's greatness, but the men who question power make a contribution just as indispensable." [40]

If the times did not permit consensus and total agreement, they did call for dialogue and understanding among Americans if government by the people was to endure. The challenge, in the words of Senator J. William Fulbright, was "to make certain that the major strand in our heritage, the strand of humanism, tolerance, and accommodation, remains the dominant one." [41] In the long afternoon shadows of the twentieth century, those qualities did indeed appear to offer the best hope for the survival in America of democracy, a system that Winston S. Churchill once described as "the worst form of government except all those other forms that have been tried from time to time." [42]

[40] John F. Kennedy, "Remarks at Amherst College," October 26, 1963, in *Public Papers of the Presidents of the United States, John F. Kennedy, 1963* (Washington, D.C.: U.S. Government Printing Office, 1964), p. 816.

[41] J. William Fulbright, *The Arrogance of Power* (New York: Random House, 1966), p. 254.

[42] *Parliamentary Debates*, House of Commons, Fifth Series, Vol. 444 (London: His Majesty's Stationery Office, 1947), pp. 206–07.

SUGGESTED READING

Almond, Gabriel A., and Coleman, James S., eds. *The Politics of the Developing Areas* (Princeton University Press, 1960). An influential book that explores and develops, among other topics, the concepts of "political culture" and "political socialization."

Easton, David. *The Political System: An Inquiry into the State of Political Science* (Knopf, 1953). An early statement of the systems approach to the study of politics developed by Easton. See also his *A Framework for Political Analysis* (Prentice-Hall, 1965) and *A Systems Analysis of Political Life* (Wiley, 1965).

Galbraith, John Kenneth. *The New Industrial State* * (Houghton Mifflin, 1967). A very readable account of changes in the nature and role of the large corporation in the modern state. These changes, Galbraith argues, have had a major effect on political and social life in highly industrialized countries such as the United States.

Greenstein, Fred I. *Children and Politics* * (Yale University Press, 1965). A study of the attitudes of young children toward politics and of how political attitudes are formed. Based on interviews with schoolchildren in New Haven, Connecticut.

Harrington, Michael. *The Other America* * (Macmillan, 1962). An absorbing account of the nature and extent of poverty in the United States in the early 1960's. The book helped focus public and governmental attention on the problem of poverty in America.

Helfrich, Harold W., Jr., ed. *The Environmental Crisis* (Yale University Press, 1970). Paperback. A series of essays, written by authorities in a variety of fields, examining problems of ecology, including air and water pollution and population growth.

Key, V. O., Jr. *Public Opinion and American Democracy* (Knopf, 1961). An important work in which the pre-1961 findings concerning public opinion and mass attitudes toward politics are analyzed in terms of their consequences for the actual workings of government.

Report of the National Advisory Commission on Civil Disorders (Bantam Books, 1968). Paperback. A comprehensive, provocative examination of the state of race relations in the United States in the mid-1960's. Discusses conditions in the inner-city and sets forth specific proposals for action at all levels of government.

Schattschneider, Elmer E. *The Semisovereign People* * (Holt, Rinehart and Winston, 1960). A lively and thoughtful analysis of the role of American interest groups and political parties in bringing public demands to bear on political officials.

Tocqueville, Alexis de. *Democracy in America*, Phillips Bradley, ed. (Vintage Books, 1945). Paperback (available in many editions). A classic analysis of American political and social life by a perceptive nineteenth-century French observer.

Walker, Daniel. *Rights in Conflict, Report of the Chicago Study Team to the National Commission on the Causes and Prevention of Violence* (Bantam Books, 1968). Paperback. A detailed, graphic, and controversial account of the violent confrontation between demonstrators and police in the streets of Chicago during the 1968 Democratic National Convention. This study, known as the Walker Report and conducted for a presidential commission on violence, concluded that a "police riot" had occurred in Chicago.

White, Theodore H. *The Making of the President 1968* * (Atheneum, 1969). The third in White's series of highly readable, knowledgeable accounts of American presidential campaigns. Discusses the retirement of President Johnson and the Wallace and McCarthy movements of 1968, as well as the Nixon-Humphrey campaign.

* Available in paperback edition

2

The Constitutional

Framework

At 10 o'clock each night in Washington, an unusual ceremony takes place in the great domed Exhibition Hall of the National Archives. There, beneath a gold eagle in the ornate hall, are displayed the Declaration of Independence, the Constitution, and the Bill of Rights. The faded parchments are sealed in protective bronze and glass cases containing helium and a small amount of water vapor for preservation.

The Fragile
Symbols

When the last visitor has left the building, a guard pushes a button. With a great whirring noise, the documents slowly sink into the floor. An electric mechanism gently lowers them into a "fireproof, bombproof vault" of steel and reinforced concrete twenty feet below. A massive lid clangs shut and the documents are safely put to bed for the night. The whole eerie process takes one minute.

Ideas, of course, cannot be preserved in a vault, but documents can. The documents, and the mystique that surrounds them, are part of what

41

Daniel J. Boorstin has called the "search for symbols."[1] The quest for national identity, in which such symbols play a role, is a continuing process in America.

But the Constitution is much more than a symbol. The Constitution established the basic structure of the American government; in its own words, it is "the supreme Law of the Land." But it is also a charter that has been continually adapted to new problems, principally through amendment and judicial interpretation by the Supreme Court.

Yet, today, the American political system is under sharp attack for what its critics see as a failure to respond to urgent national problems. Even though the Constitution is reinterpreted to meet changed conditions, does that process take place fast enough? Is the constitutional framework constructed in 1787 sufficiently flexible to meet the needs of a complex, urban society in the 1970's? Why, for example, did it take nearly one hundred years after the Civil War for the Supreme Court to apply the Constitution to outlaw racial discrimination in public accommodations?

We will be exploring these questions, and others: Who were the men who made the Constitution? What political ideas influenced them? What political bargains were struck by the framers? Why does the United States have a federal system of government, and what does that mean? How did the Supreme Court acquire its power to interpret the Constitution? How does the Constitution affect people's lives in the 1970's?

The
Constitution
in the 1970's

In June 1970, with the war in Vietnam still in progress, the Supreme Court of the United States ruled that Elliott Ashton Welsh II, a twenty-nine-year-old computer engineer from Los Angeles, could not be imprisoned for his refusal on ethical and moral grounds to serve in the armed forces. Welsh—and therefore other young Americans—the Court ruled, did not have to base his refusal on a belief in God or religious training. The government must exempt from military service, the Court declared, "all those whose consciences, spurred by deeply held moral, ethical, or religious beliefs, would give them no rest or peace if they allowed themselves to become part of an instrument of war."[2] The draft law, the Supreme Court ruled, did not exclude from draft exemption "those who hold strong beliefs about our domestic and foreign affairs or even those whose conscientious objection to participation in all wars is founded to a substantial extent upon considerations of public policy."[3]

The Court did not directly decide whether the draft law, allowing

[1] Daniel J. Boorstin, *The Americans: The National Experience* (New York: Random House, 1965), pp. 325 ff.
[2] *Welsh v. United States*, 398 U.S. 333 (1970).
[3] *Ibid.*

exemptions on grounds of "religious training and belief," violated the First Amendment to the Constitution, which bars establishment of a religion. But the case of Elliott Ashton Welsh II arose, and was decided, within the overall framework of the Constitution.

The Constitution gives the Congress power to "raise and support Armies." Acting under that power, Congress sets standards for conscription of men into the armed forces, which it did for the first time in the Civil War. The draft law exempted those with religious objections to war. Five years before the Welsh case, however, the Supreme Court ruled that a "sincere and meaningful" objection to war did not require a belief in a Supreme Being.[4] Congress sought to overrule the Court. It amended the law in an attempt to reestablish *religious* training or belief as the sole grounds for conscientious objection. But in its 1970 decision, the Court held to its earlier opinion—no religious basis was required. It remained up to the Selective Service system, an agency of the executive branch, to decide how to apply the law and the Court's ruling to individuals. The tug of war among Congress, the Court, and the executive branch over the draft law illustrates the dynamics of American constitutional government. It tells something as well about the checks and balances, and the continuing conflict, among the constitutionally separated branches of government.

When, in 1954, the Supreme Court outlawed officially supported segregation in the public schools, it did so on the grounds that "separate-but-equal" schools violated the Constitution.[5] But the enforcement of that constitutional decision is still being contested in the political arena and the courts in the 1970's.

Today, racial discrimination in most public facilities is prohibited by federal law. Congress passed a historic civil rights act in 1964 barring discrimination in public accommodations, such as hotels and restaurants, affected by interstate commerce, and in employment. The law was based upon the power of Congress, provided in the Constitution, "To regulate Commerce . . . among the several States." In two test cases, involving Ollie's Barbeque, a restaurant in Birmingham, Alabama, and the Heart of Atlanta Motel in Atlanta, Georgia, the Supreme Court ruled that the Constitution *did* give Congress the power to bar racial bias in such public accommodations.[6]

As these selected examples illustrate, constitutional government affects the quality of American society here and now, today and tomorrow. Yet it is a story that has been unfolding for two centuries; it began, as much as anywhere, in the city of Philadelphia, in June 1776.

---

[4] *United States v. Seeger,* 380 U.S. 163 (1965).
[5] *Brown v. Board of Education of Topeka, et al.,* 347 U.S. 483 (1954).
[6] *Katzenbach v. McClung,* 379 U.S. 294 (1964); *Heart of Atlanta Motel, Inc. v. United States,* 379 U.S. 241 (1964).

43

Early in May 1776, Thomas Jefferson rode down the mountain on horseback from Monticello, his Virginia home, and headed north to take his seat in the Continental Congress at Philadelphia. It had been just over a year since the guns blazed at Lexington and Concord, but the thirteen American colonies, although at war, were still under the jurisdiction of the British crown.

Independence was in the air, however, nourished by the words of an English corsetmaker only recently arrived in America. His name was Thomas Paine, and his pamphlet, *Common Sense*, attacked George III, the British monarch, as the "Royal Brute." Paine's fiery words stirred the colonies.

On June 7, Richard Henry Lee, one of Jefferson's fellow delegates from Virginia, introduced a resolution declaring that the colonies "are, and of right ought to be, free and independent states." Four days later, after impassioned debate, the Continental Congress appointed a committee of five including Jefferson, to "prepare a declaration."

At age 33, Jefferson was already known, in the words of John Adams of Massachusetts, as a man with a "peculiar felicity of expression," and the task of writing the declaration fell to him. Jefferson completed his draft in about two weeks. Sitting in the second-floor parlor of the house of Jacob Graff, Jr., a German bricklayer, Jefferson composed some of the most enduring words in the English language.

Jefferson's draft, edited somewhat by Benjamin Franklin and John Adams, was submitted on June 28. On July 2, the Continental Congress approved Richard Henry Lee's resolution declaring the colonies free of allegiance to the crown. The Declaration of Independence is not the official act by which Congress severed its ties with Britain. Lee's resolution did that. Rather the Declaration "was intended as a formal justification of an act already accomplished." [7]

[7] Carl L. Becker, *The Declaration of Independence* (New York: Vintage Books, 1942), p. 5.

Thomas Jefferson

Richard Henry Lee

Jefferson composed the first draft of the Declaration of Independence on this portable writing desk.

Jefferson's draft of the Declaration of Independence originally included an attack on slavery, and sought to blame that "execrable commerce" on King George III. But the Continental Congress cut the passage out of the final document. Had it remained in, the Declaration would have included these words:

he has waged cruel war against human nature itself, violating it's most sacred rights of life & liberty in the persons of a distant people who never offended him, captivating & carrying them into slavery in another hemisphere, or to incur miserable death in their transportation thither. this piratical warfare, the opprobrium of infidel powers, is the warfare of the Christian king of Great Britain. determined to keep open a market where MEN should be bought & sold. . . . suppressing every legislative attempt to prohibit or to restrain this execrable commerce . . . he is now exciting those very people to rise in arms among us, and to purchase that liberty of which he has deprived them, by murdering the people upon whom he also obtruded.

—Carl L. Becker, *The Declaration of Independence.*

For two days, Congress debated Jefferson's draft, making changes and deletions that Jefferson found painful. No matter; what emerged has withstood the test of time:

We hold these Truths to be self-evident, that all Men are created equal, that they are endowed by their Creator with certain unalienable Rights, that among these are Life, Liberty, and the Pursuit of Happiness—That to secure these Rights, Governments are instituted among Men, deriving their just Powers from the Consent of the Governed, that whenever any Form of Government becomes destructive of these Ends, it is the Right of the People to alter or to abolish it, and to institute new Government.

The Continental Congress approved the Declaration on July 4 and ordered that it be "authenticated and printed." Although the fact is sometimes overlooked, Jefferson and his colleagues produced and signed a treasonable document. They were literally pledging their lives.

Dr. Benjamin Rush of Philadelphia, one of the signers, asked John Adams many years later: "Do you recollect the pensive and awful silence which pervaded the house when we were called up, one after another, to the table of the President of Congress to subscribe what was believed by many at that time to be our own death warrants?"[8]

The solemnity of the moment was breached only once. It is said that Benjamin Harrison of Virginia, whom Adams once described as "an indolent and luxurious heavy gentleman of no use in Congress or committee," turned to Elbridge Gerry of Massachusetts, a skinny, worried-looking colleague, and cackled: "I shall have a great advantage over you Mr. Gerry, when we are all hung for what we are now doing. From the size and weight of my body I shall die in a few minutes, but from the lightness of your body you will dance in the air an hour or two."[9]

[8] David Hawke, *A Transaction of Free Men* (New York: Scribner's, 1964), p. 209.
[9] *Ibid.*

Although Jefferson later said he had "turned to neither book nor pamphlet" in writing the Declaration of Independence, he was certainly influenced by the philosophy of John Locke (1632–1704) and others, by his British heritage, with its traditional concern for the rights of man, and by the colonial political experience itself.

The Influence of John Locke

John Locke's philosophy of *natural rights* was political gospel to most educated Americans in the late eighteenth century. Jefferson absorbed Locke's writings, and some of the English philosopher's words and phrases emerged verbatim in the Declaration.[10]

Locke reasoned that man was "born free," and had possessed certain natural rights when he lived in a state of nature before governments were formed. Men contracted among themselves to form a society to protect those rights. All men, Locke believed, were free, equal, and independent, and no man could be "subjected to the political power of another, without his own consent."[11] These dangerous ideas—dangerous in an age of the divine right of kings—are directly reflected in the language of the Declaration of Independence, written nearly a century later.

Locke also believed in the separation of powers, in "balancing the Power of Government, by placing several parts of it in different hands."[12] This principle was to become a keystone of the American constitutional system. The French philosopher Montesquieu, in *The Spirit of the Laws* in 1748, also advocated a separation of powers, into legislative, judicial, and executive branches, and he, too, may have influenced Jefferson and the Founding Fathers.

John Locke

The English Heritage

The irony of the American Revolution is that the colonists, for the most part, rebelled because they felt they were being deprived of their rights as *Englishmen*. Many of the ideas of the Declaration of Independence in 1776, the Constitution, framed in 1787, and the Bill of Rights, added to the Constitution in 1791, evolved from their English heritage. The political and intellectual antecedents of the American system of government included such British legal milestones as the Magna Carta, issued by King John at Runnymede in 1215, in which the nobles confirmed that

[10] For example, the phrase "a long train of abuses."
[11] Peter Laslett, ed., *Locke's Two Treatises of Government* (Cambridge, England: Cambridge University Press, 1960), p. 348.
[12] *Ibid.,* p. 356.

the power of the king was not absolute; the Habeas Corpus Act (1679), and the Bill of Rights (1689).

From England also came a system of common law, the cumulative body of law as expressed in judicial decisions and custom, rather than by statute. The men who framed America's government were influenced by the writings of Sir Edward Coke, the great British jurist and champion of common law against the power of the king, and Sir William Blackstone, the Oxford law professor whose *Commentaries on the Laws of England* (1765–69) is still an indispensable standard reference work for law students and attorneys.

If the *ideas* embodied in the American system of government are to be found largely in the nation's English heritage, it is also true that American *institutions* developed to a great extent from colonial foundations. The roots of much of today's governmental structure can be found in the colonial charters.

Even before they landed at Plymouth in 1620, the Pilgrims—a group of English Puritans who had separated from the Church of England —drew up the Mayflower Compact. The Pilgrims had sailed from Holland, intending to settle in the area that is now New York City, but landed instead just north of Cape Cod. In the cabin of the *Mayflower*, forty-one male adults signed the compact, declaring that "we . . . doe by these presents solemnly & mutualy in the presence of God, and one of another, covenant & combine our selves togeather into a civill body politick."

The Colonial
Experience

The Mayflower Compact, as Samuel Eliot Morison notes, "is justly regarded as a key document in American history. It proves the determination of the small group of English emigrants to live under a rule of law, based on the consent of the people, and to set up their own civil government." [13]

A year earlier at Jamestown, Virginia, a group of settlers established the first representative assembly in the New World. Puritans from the Massachusetts Bay Colony and another group from London framed America's first written constitution in 1639—the Fundamental Orders of Connecticut. The Massachusetts Body of Liberties (1641) embodied traditional English rights, such as trial by jury and due process of law, which were later incorporated into the Constitution and the Bill of Rights.

The political forms established by the Puritans contributed to the formation of representative institutions. Beyond that, Puritanism shaped the American mind and left its indelible stamp on the American character. The English Puritans who came to America were influenced by the teach-

[13] Samuel Eliot Morison, "The Mayflower Compact," in Daniel J. Boorstin, ed., *An American Primer* (Chicago: University of Chicago Press, 1966), p. 1.

ings of John Calvin, the sixteenth-century French theologian of the Protestant Reformation. Theirs was a stern code of hard work, sobriety, and intense religious zeal. Even today, with rapidly changing, increasingly liberal sexual and moral codes, Americans do not seem to be able to enjoy their new freedom entirely. The Puritan heritage is not easily forgotten.

The Colonial Governments. The thirteen original colonies, some formed as commercial ventures, others as religious havens, all had written charters that set forth their form of government and the rights of the colonists. All had governors (the executive branch), legislatures, and a judiciary.

The eight *royal* colonies were New Hampshire, New York, New Jersey, Virginia, North Carolina, South Carolina, Georgia, and Massachusetts. They were controlled by the king through governors appointed by him. Laws passed by the colonial legislatures were subject to approval of the crown.

In the three *proprietary* colonies, Maryland, Delaware, and Pennsylvania, the proprietors (who had obtained their patents from the king) named the governors, subject to the approval of the crown. Only in the two *charter* colonies, Rhode Island and Connecticut, was there a measure of self-government. There, freely elected legislatures chose the governors, and laws could not be vetoed by the king.

Except for Pennsylvania, which had a unicameral legislature, the colonial legislatures had two houses. The members of the upper house were appointed by the crown or proprietor and the members of the lower house were elected by the colonists. Appeals from the colonial courts could usually be taken to the Privy Council in London.

The Paradox of Colonial Democracy. Colonial America was not a very democratic place by contemporary standards. For example, by the 1700's, every colony had some type of property qualification for voting. And, in 1765, the estimated population of the colonies was 1,450,000 whites and 400,000 blacks, almost all of them slaves. Consequently, "whatever political democracy did exist was a democracy of white male property-owners." [14]

In addition, more than a quarter of a million white persons were indentured servants during the colonial period. These were Europeans, including many convicts, who sold their labor for four to seven years in return for passage across the sea.

Even aside from slavery and indentured servitude, there was little social democracy. A tailor in York County, Virginia, in 1674 was punished

[14] Clinton Rossiter, *Seedtime of the Republic* (New York: Harcourt Brace Jovanovich, 1953), p. 35.

for racing a horse, since "it was contrary to law for a labourer to make a race, being a sport only for gentlemen." [15] In colonial New York, the aristocracy "ruled with condescension and lived in splendor." [16]

Nine of the thirteen colonies had an established, offical state church. And although the colonial press and pamphleteers developed into a powerful force for liberty, the first newspaper to appear in America, *Publick Occurrences*, was immediately suppressed.[17]

Democracy, in the modern sense, did not exist in colonial America. Rather, it has developed slowly and painfully, and it is still developing. The continuing struggle of minority groups for full equality, for example, illustrates that the process is far from complete.

The colonial governments provided an institutional foundation for what was to come. Certain elements were already visible: separation of powers, constitutional government through written charters, bicameral legislatures, free elections, and judicial appeal to London, which foreshadowed the role of the Supreme Court. Equally important, in their relationship with England, the colonies became accustomed to the idea of sharing powers with a central government, the basis of the federal system today. It was, in Clinton Rossiter's apt phrase, the "seedtime of the republic."

THE AMERICAN REVOLUTION

"The Revolution," John Adams wrote in 1818, "was effected before the war commenced. The Revolution was in the minds and hearts of the people." [18]

The American colonies existed chiefly for the economic support of England. Economic conflicts with the mother country, as well as political and social factors, impelled the colonies to revolt.

A Growing Sense of Injury

The British had routed the French from North America and provided military protection to the colonies; England in turn demanded that her subjects in America pay part of the cost. At the same time, the colonies were expected to subordinate themselves to the British economy; ideally they would remain agricultural, develop no industry of their own, and serve as a captive market for British manufactures.

The colonists had no representatives in the British parliament. They resented and disputed the right of London to raise revenue in America.

[15] *Ibid.*, p. 87.
[16] *Ibid.*, p. 88.
[17] The newspaper was published in Boston on September 25, 1690.
[18] In Charles Francis Adams, ed., *The Works of John Adams*, Vol. X (Boston: Little, Brown, 1856), p. 282.

Whether or not James Otis, the Boston patriot, cried "Taxation without representation is tyranny!"—and there is reason to think he did not—the words reflected popular sentiment in the colonies.[19]

A series of laws designed to give the mother country a tight grip on trade, restrict colonial exports, and protect producers in England were the economic stepping stones to revolution. In 1772, Samuel Adams of Massachusetts formed the Committees of Correspondence to unite the colonies against Great Britain. This network provided an invaluable political communications link among the colonies. Letters, reports, and decisions of one town or colony could be relayed to the next.

The committees resolved to hold the First Continental Congress, which met in Philadelphia in September 1774. The war began in April 1775. The Second Continental Congress met the following month and by July 1776, Thomas Jefferson was busily writing in the second-floor parlor of the bricklayer's house in Philadelphia.

The Articles
of Confederation
(1781–1789)

The Declaration of Independence had declared the colonies "free and independent states." During the war, all of the thirteen colonies adopted new constitutions or at least changed their old charters to eliminate references to the British crown. Seven of the new constitutions contained a Bill of Rights, but all restricted suffrage. All provided for three branches of government, but their dominant features were strong legislatures and weak executives. Governors were elected by the people or by legislatures, and their powers were reduced. For the first time, the colonies began to refer to themselves as "states."

When Richard Henry Lee offered his resolution for independence in June 1776, he had also proposed that "a plan of confederation" be prepared for the colonies. The plan was drawn up by a committee and approved by the Continental Congress in November 1777, a month before George Washington retired with his troops for the long hard winter at Valley Forge. The articles were ratified by the individual states by March 1, 1781, and so were already in effect when the war ended with the surrender of Cornwallis at Yorktown that October. The formal end to hostilities came with the conclusion of the Peace of Paris in February 1783.

Article III of the Articles of Confederation really established a "league of friendship" among the states, rather than a national government. There was no executive branch, no President, no "White House." Instead, Congress, given power to establish executive departments, created five: foreign affairs, finance, navy, war, and post office. Congress had power to declare

[19] Otis supposedly uttered his famous line in a speech to the Massachusetts Superior Court in 1761. But as Daniel J. Boorstin points out, the line does not appear in the original notes of the speech taken by John Adams. See Boorstin, *The Americans: The National Experience*, pp. 309, 360–61.

war, conduct foreign policy, make treaties, ask for—but not demand—revenues from the states, borrow and coin money, equip the Navy, and appoint senior officers of the Army, which was made up of the state militias. Congress was unicameral and each state, regardless of size had only one vote. The most important actions by Congress required the consent of nine states. There was no national system of courts.

While these were not inconsiderable powers, the most significant fact about the government created under the Articles was its weakness. Congress, for example, had no power to levy taxes or regulate commerce—the colonies had seen enough of these powers under English rule. Above all, Congress could not enforce even the limited powers it had. The functioning of government under the Articles depended entirely on the good will of the states. Because unanimous agreement of the states was required to amend the Articles, but in practice could never be obtained, there was no practical way to increase the powers of the government; the Articles were never amended.

Yet the Articles did represent the idea of some form of national government. As historian Merrill Jensen has emphasized, the Articles "laid foundations for the administration of a central government which were to be expanded but not essentially altered in function for generations to come." [20]

TOWARD A MORE PERFECT UNION

Under the inadequate government of the Articles of Confederation, the states came close to losing the peace they had won in war. They quarreled among themselves over boundary lines and tariffs. For example, New Jersey farmers had to pay heavy fees to cross the Hudson River to sell their vegetables in New York. With no strong national government to conduct foreign policy, some states even entered into negotiations with foreign powers. General Washington worried that Kentucky might join Spain.[21] There was real fear of military intervention by European powers. The thirteen colonies had concluded an "uneasy peace" but important political leaders in Britain "hoped to reopen the war." [22]

The Background

By 1786, severe economic depression had left many farmers angry and hungry. Debtor groups demanded that state governments issue paper money. The unrest among farmers and the poor alarmed the upper classes. There was fear, in today's terms, of a revolution of the Left. These

[20] Merrill Jensen, *The New Nation* (New York: Knopf, 1950), pp. 347–48.
[21] William H. Riker, *Federalism: Origin, Operation, Significance* (Boston: Little, Brown, 1964), pp. 18, 20.
[22] *Ibid.*

James Madison

Alexander Hamilton

political and economic factors, combined with fear of overseas intervention, generated pressure for the creation of a new national government.

Virginia, at the urging of James Madison, had invited all the states to discuss commercial problems at a meeting to be held at Annapolis, Maryland, in September 1786. The Annapolis conference was disappointing. Representatives of only five states turned up. But one of those delegates was Alexander Hamilton, a brilliant, thirty-one-year-old New York attorney who was one of a small group of men pushing for a convention to create a stronger government. There had been talk of such a meeting since 1780, when Hamilton wrote to his friend James Duane, listing the "defects of our present system."

At Annapolis, Hamilton and James Madison persuaded the delegates to call upon the states to hold a constitutional convention in Philadelphia in May 1787. In the interim, a significant event took place. In western Massachusetts late in 1786, angry farmers, unable to pay their mortgages or taxes, rallied around Daniel Shays, who had served as a captain in the American Revolution. They were seeking to stop the Massachusetts courts from foreclosing the mortgages on their farms. Armed with pitchforks, the farmers marched on the Springfield arsenal to get weapons. They were defeated by the militia. Fourteen ringleaders were sentenced to death, but all were pardoned or released after serving short prison terms. Shays escaped to Vermont.

Shays' rebellion, coming on the eve of the Philadelphia convention, had a tremendous effect on public opinion. Aristocrats and merchants were thoroughly alarmed at the threat of "mob rule." The British were amused at the American lack of capacity for self-government. The revolt was an important factor in creating the climate for a new beginning at Philadelphia.

The
Philadelphia
Convention

On February 21, 1787, Congress grudgingly approved the proposed Philadelphia convention "for the sole and express purpose of revising the Articles of Confederation." In May the Founding Fathers met and, disregarding Congress' cautious mandate, worked what has been called a "miracle at Philadelphia." [23]

The Men. Because the story of how a nation was born is in large part a story of men, it might be useful to focus briefly on some of the more prominent delegates who gathered at Philadelphia. First was George Washington, who had commanded the armed forces during the Revolution. A national hero, a man of immense prestige, Washington was probably the only figure who could have successfully presided over the coming struggle

[23] Catherine Drinker Bowen, *Miracle at Philadelphia* (Boston: Little, Brown, 1966).

in the convention. After Washington was Benjamin Franklin, internationally famous as a scientist-diplomat-statesman. Now eighty-one and suffering from gout, he arrived at the sessions in a sedan chair borne by four convicts from the Walnut Street jail. Alexander Hamilton was there, as a delegate from New York, but he took surprisingly little part in the important decisions of the convention. From Virginia came James Madison, often called the "Father of the Constitution." He had long advocated a new national government, and he helped to draft the Virginia Plan, the key proposals laid before the delegates. A tireless note-taker, Madison kept a record of the debates. Without him, there would be no detailed account of the most important political convention in the nation's history.

Gouverneur Morris

Gouverneur Morris, a colorful man who stumped about on a wooden leg, shatters the image of the Founding Fathers as stuffy patriarchs. His wit offended some, but his pen was responsible for the literary style and polish of the final draft of the Constitution. From Massachusetts came Elbridge Gerry and Rufus King, a lawyer with a gift for debating; from South Carolina, John Rutledge, a leading figure of the revolutionary period and later a justice of the Supreme Court, General Charles Cotesworth Pinckney, Oxford-educated war hero and aristocrat, and his elegant second cousin, Charles Pinckney, an ardent nationalist.

Twelve states sent delegates to Philadelphia. Only Rhode Island boycotted the convention.[24] Of the men who gathered in the State House (now Independence Hall), eight had signed the Declaration of Independence, seven had been chief executives of their states, thirty-three were lawyers, eight were businessmen, six were planters, and three were physicians. About half were college graduates.[25]

And it was a relatively young convention. Jonathan Dayton of New Jersey, at twenty-six, was the youngest delegate. Alexander Hamilton was thirty-two. Charles Pinckney was twenty-nine. James Madison was thirty-six. The average age of the delegates was just over forty-three. (At eighty-one, Ben Franklin pulled the average up.)

The Setting. The Convention of 1787 had many of the earmarks of a modern national political convention but for one factor: to preserve their freedom of debate, the delegates worked in strictest secrecy. No news reporters or members of the public were allowed in. In other respects, the setting would be a familiar one today: the weather was intolerably hot, the convention hall stuffy, and the speeches interminable. And just as in a modern convention, a plush tavern and inn, the Indian Queen, soon became a sort of informal headquarters.

[24] An agrarian party of farmers and debtors controlled the Rhode Island state legislature and feared that a strong national government would limit the party's power.
[25] Charles Warren, *The Making of the Constitution* (New York: Barnes & Noble, 1967), pp. 55–60.

The convention opened on May 14, 1787, but it was not until May 25 that a quorum of seven states had arrived in Philadelphia. The delegates gathered in the east room of the Pennsylvania State House, the same chamber where the Declaration of Independence had been signed eleven years before. "Delegates sat at tables covered in green baize—sat and sweated, once the summer sun was up. By noon the air was lifeless, with windows shut for privacy, or intolerable with flies when they were open." [26] For almost four months, the stuffy east room was to be home.

The Great Compromise.   On May 29, Edmund Randolph, the thirty-three-year-old governor of Virginia took the floor to present fifteen resolutions that stunned the convention. They went far beyond mere revision of the Articles—they proposed an entirely new national government. Randolph was moving swiftly to make the Virginia Plan, as his proposals are known, the main business of the convention.

Edmund Randolph

As John P. Roche has noted, the plan, drafted by James Madison and the Virginia delegation, "was a political master-stroke. Its consequence was that once business got underway, the framework of discussion was established on Madison's terms. There was no interminable argument over agenda; instead the delegates took the Virginia Resolutions—'just for the purposes of discussion'—as their point of departure." [27]

AN AMERICAN KING?

Charles Pinckney rose . . . to urge a "vigorous executive." He did not say a "President of the United States." It took the Convention a long while to come around to *President.* Always they referred to a chief executive or a national executive, whether plural or single. James Wilson followed Pinckney by moving that the executive consist of a single person; Pinckney seconded him.

A sudden silence followed. "A considerable pause," Madison wrote . . . *A single executive!*

There was menace in the words, some saw monarchy in them. True enough, nine states had each its single executive—a governor or president—but everywhere the local legislature was supreme, looked on as the voice of the people which could control a governor any day. But a single executive for the national government conjured up visions from the past—royal governors who could not be restrained, a crown, ermine, a scepter!

—Catherine Drinker Bowen, *Miracle at Philadelphia.*

[26] Bowen, *Miracle at Philadelphia,* p. 23.
[27] John P. Roche, "The Founding Fathers: A Reform Caucus in Action," *American Political Science Review,* Vol. 55, No. 4 (December 1961), p. 803.

The Virginia Plan called for:

1. A two-house legislature, the lower house chosen by the people and the upper house chosen by the lower.
2. A "national executive"—the make-up was not specified, so there might have been more than one President under the plan—to be elected by the legislature.
3. A national judiciary to be chosen by the legislature.

The convention debated the Virginia Plan for two weeks. As the debate wore on, the smaller states became increasingly alarmed. It had not taken them long to conclude that the more heavily populated states would control the government under the Virginia Plan.

On June 15, William Paterson of New Jersey, a lawyer, rose to offer an alternative plan. He argued that the convention had no power to deprive the smaller states of the equality they enjoyed under the Articles of Confederation. He proposed what became known as the New Jersey Plan, which called for:

1. Continuation of the Articles of Confederation, including one vote for each state represented in the legislature. Congress would be strengthened so it could impose taxes and regulate trade, and acts of Congress would become the "supreme law" of the states.
2. An executive of more than one person to be elected by Congress.
3. A Supreme Court, to be appointed by the executive.

The Paterson plan would have merely amended the Articles. The government would have continued as a weak confederation of sovereign states. But the delegates at Philadelphia were determined to construct a strong *national* government, and for this reason the Paterson plan was soon brushed aside. As both the weather and tempers grew warmer, the convention swung back to consideration of the Virginia Plan. But little progress was made.

The fact was that the convention was in danger of breaking up. "I *almost* despair," Washington, presiding over the deadlock, wrote to Hamilton in New York.

The impasse over the make-up of Congress was broken on July 16 when the convention adopted the Great Compromise, often called the Connecticut Compromise, because it had been proposed by Roger Sherman of that state. As adopted after much debate, the Connecticut Compromise called for:

1. A House of Representatives apportioned by the number of free inhabitants in each state plus three-fifths of the slaves.
2. A Senate, or upper house, consisting of two members from each state, elected by the state legislatures.

The plan broke the deadlock because it protected the small states by guaranteeing that each state would have an equal vote in the Senate. Only in the House, where representation was to be based on population, would the larger states have an advantage.

Catherine Drinker Bowen has suggested that the delegates might never have reached agreement "had not the heat broken." On Monday July 16, the day the compromise was approved, "Philadelphia was cool after a month of torment; on Friday, a breeze had come in from the northwest. Over the weekend, members could rest and enjoy themselves." [28]

With the large state versus small state controversy resolved by this compromise, the convention named a committee to draft a constitution. Then the convention adjourned for eleven days and General Washington went fishing.

On August 6, the convention resumed its work. The committee brought in a draft constitution that called for a "Congress," made up of a House of Representatives and a Senate; a "Supreme Court," and a "President of the United States of America."

The broad outline of the Constitution as it is today was finally clear. But much work remained. All through August and into September, the draft constitution was debated, clause by clause.

The Other Compromises. The convention made other significant compromises. Underlying the agreement to count three-fifths of all slaves in apportioning membership of the House of Representatives was a deep-seated conflict between the industrial North and the agrarian South, where the economy was based on slave labor. The men of the North argued that if slaves were to be counted in determining representation in the House, then they must be counted for tax purposes as well. In the end, the South agreed.

The slave trade itself was the subject of another complicated compromise. On August 22, George Mason of Virginia attacked "the infernal traffic" and its evil effect on both individuals and the nation. Slavery, he said, would "bring the judgment of heaven on a Country. As nations can not be rewarded or punished in the next world they must in

A REPUBLIC—IF YOU CAN KEEP IT

When the delegates to the Constitutional Convention at Philadelphia ended their long and difficult task in September of 1787 it is said that a lady approached Benjamin Franklin and asked:

"Well, Doctor, what have we got—a republic or a monarchy?"

"A republic," was the reply, "if you can keep it."

—Adapted from "Debates in the Federal Convention of 1787," in *Documents Illustrative of the Formation of the Union of the American States.*

[28] Bowen, *Miracle at Philadelphia*, p. 186.

this. By an inevitable chain of causes & effects providence punishes national sins, by national calamities." [29]

Charles Cotesworth Pinckney of South Carolina warned that his state would not join the union if the slave trade were prohibited. The issue was settled by an agreement that Congress could not ban the slave trade until 1808.[30] This compromise is contained in Article I of the Constitution, which obliquely refers to slaves as "other persons."

In yet another compromise, the South won certain trade concessions. Southerners were worried, with reason, that the Northern majority in Congress might pass legislation unfavorable to Southern economic interests. Because the South relied almost entirely on exports of its agricultural products, it fought for, and won, an agreement forbidding the imposition of export taxes. Even today, the United States is one of the few nations that cannot tax its exports.

We the People. On September 8, a Committee of Style and Arrangement was named to polish the final draft. Fortunately it included Gouverneur Morris. Morris, probably aided by James Wilson,[31] drafted the final version, adding a new Preamble that rivals Jefferson's eloquence in the Declaration of Independence: "We the People of the United States, in Order to form a more perfect Union, establish Justice, insure domestic Tranquility, provide for the common defence, promote the general Welfare, and secure the Blessings of Liberty to ourselves and our Posterity, do ordain and establish this Constitution for the United States of America."

On September 17, the long task was finished. The day was cold, and the trace of autumn in the air must have reminded the delegates of how long they had labored. Thirty-nine men signed the Constitution that afternoon. Benjamin Franklin had to be helped forward to the table, and it is said that he wept when he signed. According to Madison's notes, while the last members were signing, Franklin observed that often, as he pondered the outcome during the changing moods of the convention, he had looked at the sun painted on the back of Washington's chair and wondered whether it was rising or setting.

"But now at length I have the happiness to know," Franklin declared, "that it is a rising and not a setting sun." [32]

---

[29] In Carl Van Doren, *The Great Rehearsal* (New York: Viking Press, 1948), p. 153.
[30] Acting on President Jefferson's recommendation, Congress did outlaw importation of slaves in 1808. But the illegal slave trade flourished up to the Civil War. Perhaps 250,000 slaves were illegally imported to America between 1808 and 1860. The slavery issue was not settled until Appomattox and the ratification on December 18, 1865, of the Thirteenth Amendment, which declared that "neither slavery nor involuntary servitude, except as a punishment for crime whereof the party shall have been duly convicted, shall exist within the United States."
[31] Warren, *The Making of the Constitution*, pp. 687–88.
[32] In Van Doren, *The Great Rehearsal*, p. 174.

The Constitution was not perfect, but it represented a practical accommodation among conflicting sections and interests, achieved at a political convention. And the central fact of the Constitution is that it created a strong national government where none had existed before.

The Federal System. The structure of that government is deceptively simple at first glance, yet endlessly intricate. Article VI declares that the laws passed by Congress "shall be the supreme Law of the Land." This important Supremacy Clause means that federal laws are supreme over any conflicting state laws. But the states also exercise sovereignty within their borders over a wide range of activities.

The Constitution thus brought into being a *federal system,* in which the powers and functions of government are divided between the national government and the states.

The National Government. The Constitution divided the national government into three branches, legislative, executive, and judicial. It

FIGURE 2-1

The Government of the United States

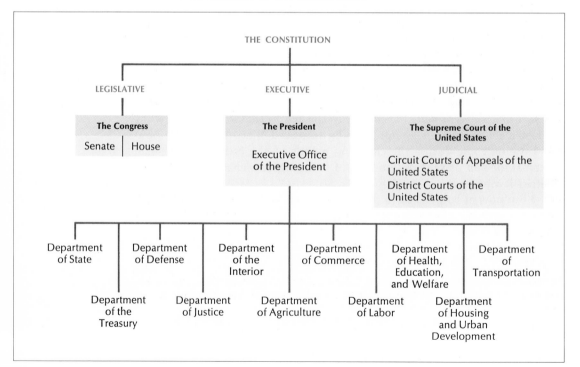

created a government, therefore, based on the principle of *separation of powers* and *checks and balances.* Each of the three branches is constitutionally equal to and independent of the other. In this way, the framers thought to prevent any single branch from becoming too powerful. (In fact, however, the twentieth century has seen the Presidency become the most powerful branch of the Federal Government, at least in the area of foreign affairs.)

Although the Constitution established institutional checks and separated powers, the United States is also a government of *shared powers.* The Constitution provided many ways in which the three branches would interact. For example, although Congress makes the laws, the President submits legislation to it, and he may convene Congress in special session. The President may also veto bills passed by Congress. Clearly, the President is involved in the legislative function.

Similarly, Congress is involved in the executive process through its power to create federal executive agencies, advise on and consent to the appointment of high-level federal officials, and by its watchdog functions. Since Congress appropriates money to run the Federal Government, it may delve deeply, through the committee system, into the operations of executive agencies.

Through the process of *judicial review,* the courts determine what the laws passed by Congress mean and whether they are constitutional. President Woodrow Wilson called the Supreme Court "a kind of Constitutional Convention in continuous session." The President participates in the judicial process through his power to nominate federal judges.

As we have noted, the notion of three separate-but-equal branches of government has been eroded by the pressures of the twentieth century. In the past, American Presidents have, at varying times, exercised great powers, as did Lincoln during the Civil War. But in modern times, power, especially military-diplomatic power, has been steadily concentrated in the hands of the President. The power of Congress to declare war, for example, has greatly diminished in importance since the Second World War. In 1970, President Nixon committed American forces to Cambodia without the approval of Congress. In a nuclear attack, the President would obviously have no time to consult Congress. But even in the case of Vietnam, a bitter and protracted struggle, Congress never declared war.

Today, the complex task of managing the economy has been delegated in part to independent regulatory commissions and agencies that do not fall neatly into any of the three categories—legislative, executive, and judicial—envisioned under the Constitution and in fact exhibit features of all three.

In sum, although the three branches of government are based upon separated powers, they also share powers. And among the three branches (as among human beings) there is a never-ending tug of war for dominance, a process that Alpheus T. Mason has called "institutionalized tension." [33]

The "Great Silences" of the Constitution. Some issues were so difficult and potentially divisive that the framers did not deal with them at all. Since they were trying to construct a political document that stated general principles, they chose to avoid some sensitive problems.

A vital moral and political issue ducked by the framers was whether to abolish slavery while forming "a more perfect union." Five southern states might not have ratified the Constitution had the issue been met head on. But the question of slavery, avoided at Philadelphia, led in time to a bloody Civil War. And the black man in America is still struggling two centuries later for the full freedom and equality denied to him by the Founding Fathers.

The framers also made no explicit statement in the Constitution defining the full scope of the powers of the national government. The history of the Supreme Court is the history of whether the Constitution is to be loosely or strictly interpreted.

But even the Supreme Court's power of judicial review is nowhere specifically provided for in the Constitution. The power of the Supreme Court to declare acts of Congress unconstitutional was not established until 1803, when the court ruled in the case of *Marbury v. Madison.*[34] Chief Justice John Marshall, in his historic opinion, argued that since the Constitution was clearly "superior" to an act of Congress, "It is emphatically the province and duty of the judicial department to say what the law is. . . . a law repugnant to the Constitution is void."

The Constitution says nothing whatever about how candidates for office shall be chosen. The development of political parties, nominating conventions, and primaries all occurred outside of the constitutional framework.

Similarly, the Cabinet is not specifically established in the Constitution, but has evolved through custom, beginning during Washington's first administration. As Richard F. Fenno, Jr., has noted, the Cabinet is "an extralegal creation," limited in power as an institution by the very fact that it has no basis in law.[35]

THE CONSTITUTION ACCORDING TO BOSS PLUNKITT

I know that the civil service humbug is stuck into the constitution, too, but, as Tim Campbell said: "What's the constitution among friends?"

—Boss Plunkitt (Tammany Hall ward leader),
quoted in William L. Riordon,
Plunkitt of Tammany Hall.

[33] Alpheus T. Mason, *The Supreme Court: Palladium of Freedom* (Ann Arbor, Mich.: University of Michigan Press, 1962), p. 8.
[34] *Marbury v. Madison,* 1 Cranch 137 (1803).
[35] Richard F. Fenno, Jr., *The President's Cabinet* (Cambridge, Mass.: Harvard University Press, 1959), pp. 19–20.

Motives of the Framers.   Were the Founding Fathers selfless patriots who thrust aside all personal interests to save America? Or were they primarily rich men who were afraid of radicals like Daniel Shays? Did they form a strong government to protect themselves and their property? In short, were they heroes, or men who today might be called "fat cats"?

The debate has raged among scholars, particularly since the publication by Charles A. Beard in 1913 of *An Economic Interpretation of the Constitution of the United States.* Beard analyzed in great detail the economic holdings of the framers and concluded that they acted to protect their personal financial interests. The Constitution, said Beard, was "an economic document drawn with superb skill by men whose property interests were immediately at stake." [36]

Later scholars, reacting to Beard, have reached opposite conclusions. Forrest McDonald asserts that of the fifty-five delegates "a dozen at the outside, clearly acted according to the dictates of their personal economic interests." He concludes that an "economic interpretation of the Constitution does not work" and that it is "impossible to justify" Beard's analysis. [37]

Similarly, Robert E. Brown has asserted that "we would be doing a grave injustice to the political sagacity of the Founding Fathers if we assumed that property or personal gain was their only motive." [38]

Was It Democratic?   The argument is sometimes advanced that the Constitution was framed to guard against popular democracy. "The evils we experience flow from the excess of democracy," Elbridge Gerry of Massachusetts told the convention.[39]

It is true that from a contemporary viewpoint some of the provisions of the Constitution appear highly undemocratic. For example, because the Constitution leaves voting qualifications to the states, persons without property, women, and many blacks were long disenfranchised. Until the passage of the Seventeenth Amendment in 1913, senators were elected by state legislatures, although by 1912 in at least twenty-nine states an attempt was made to reflect popular choice.[40] The framers had deliberately avoided

[36] Charles A. Beard, *An Economic Interpretation of the Constitution of the United States* (New York: Macmillan, 1960), p. 188.
[37] Forrest McDonald, *We The People* (Chicago: University of Chicago Press, 1958), pp. vii, 350, 415.
[38] Robert E. Brown, *Charles Beard and the Constitution* (Princeton, N.J.: Princeton University Press, 1956), p. 198.
[39] Elbridge Gerry, Edmund Randolph, and George Mason were the only three framers who refused to sign the Constitution. Much later, Gerry gave his name to a famous, but undemocratic, practice. While he was governor of Massachusetts in 1812, the legislature carved up Essex County to give maximum advantage to his party. One of the districts resembled a salamander. From then on, the practice of redrawing voting districts to favor the party in power became known as "gerrymandering." (See p. 458.)
[40] Edward S. Corwin, et al., eds., *The Constitution of the United States of America, Analysis and Interpretation* (Washington, D.C.: U.S. Government Printing Office, 1964), p. 1356.

direct election of senators, for the Senate was seen as a check upon the multitudes. Madison assured the convention that the Senate would proceed "with more coolness, with more system, and with more wisdom, than the popular branch." And, of course, the Constitution interposed an electoral college between the voters and the Presidency.

But to stress only these aspects of the Constitution would be to overlook the basically representative structure of the government it created and the revolutionary heritage of the framers. The Constitution perhaps originally reflected some distrust of popular rule, but it established a balanced, institutional framework within which democracy could evolve.

The Fight Over Ratification

The political contest over ratification of the Constitution lasted for more than two and a half years, from September 1787 until May 29, 1790, when Rhode Island finally joined the Union. But when the convention had finished its work, a successful outcome was by no means certain.

In the first place, the Articles of Confederation required that any amendment be approved by Congress and the legislatures of all thirteen states. No such unanimity could ever be achieved. In effect, this created a box from which the framers could not climb out. So they chose another route—they simply ignored the box and built an entirely new structure.

Article VII of the Constitution states that "ratification of the conventions of nine States shall be sufficient for the establishment of this Constitution." Why conventions and not legislatures? Since the Constitution took power away from the states, the framers reasoned that the state legislatures might not approve it. Secondly, if the Constitution was approved by popularly elected conventions, it would give the new government a broad base of legitimacy.

The great debate over the Constitution soon divided the country into two camps, the Antifederalists, who opposed it, and the Federalists. Although the debate was vigorous, relatively few people actually participated in the ratification process. The voters could not vote for or against the Constitution. Their choice was confined to selecting delegates to the state ratifying conventions. Moreover, only an estimated 160,000 persons voted for delegates to the ratifying conventions, out of a total population of about 4,000,000. While some scholars have argued that the property requirements excluded the bulk of potential voters, Robert E. Brown has estimated that perhaps as little as 5 percent were excluded by these requirements, since most men were middle-class farmers who owned property and were eligible to vote. The light turnout, he concludes, simply proves that "the Constitution was adopted with a great show of indifference." [41]

Some historians tend to pay more attention to the Federalists—since

[41] Brown, *Charles Beard and the Constitution*, pp. 170, 197.

It has been frequently remarked that it seems to have been reserved to the people of this country, by their conduct and example, to decide the important question, whether societies of men are really capable or not of establishing good government from reflection and choice, or whether they are forever destined to depend for their political constitutions on accident and force. If there be any truth in the remark, the crisis at which we are arrived may with propriety be regarded as the era in which that decision is to be made; and a wrong election of the part we shall act may, in this view, deserve to be considered as the general misfortune of mankind.

—Alexander Hamilton, *The Federalist*, No. 1.

they won—but the men opposed to the Constitution had a strong case. The convention, after all, had met in complete secrecy, in a "Dark Conclave," as the Philadelphia *Independent Gazetteer* termed it. What is more, the Constitution, as its opponents argued, was extralegal. The framers had clearly exceeded their mandate from Congress to revise the Articles of Confederation. Above all, the Constitution included no Bill of Rights.

The Federalists argued that the states faced anarchy unless they united under a powerful central government. The omission of a Bill of Rights was difficult to justify, however. The question had not been raised until near the end of the Philadelphia convention, and the weary delegates were not inclined to open a new debate. Furthermore, many delegates felt that a Bill of Rights would be superfluous, since eight states had bills of rights. Ultimately, as the price of winning support in the state conventions, the Federalists had to promise to enact a Bill of Rights as the first order of business under a new government.

Richard Henry Lee's *Letters of the Federal Farmer* was among the most effective of the various Antifederalist attacks circulated among the states. In New York, Hamilton, Madison, and John Jay, writing as "Publius," published more than seventy letters in the press defending the Constitution. Together in book form they are known today as *The Federalist*, the classic work explaining and defending the Constitution.

By January 9, 1788, a little over three months after the Philadelphia convention, five states had ratified the Constitution: Delaware, Pennsylvania, New Jersey, Georgia, and Connecticut. Massachusetts, a key and doubtful state, ratified next, thanks to the efforts of Sam Adams and John Hancock. Maryland and South Carolina followed suit, and on June 21, 1788, New Hampshire became the ninth state to ratify.

The Constitution was now in effect, but Virginia and New York were still to be heard from. Without those two powerful states no union could succeed. Washington, Madison, and Edmund Randolph, who finally decided to support the Constitution that he had not signed, helped to swing Virginia into camp four days later. In part because of *The Federalist* papers, New York ratified on July 26 by a narrow margin of three votes. North

John Jay

Carolina finally ratified in 1789 and Rhode Island in 1790. (See Table 2-1.) By that time George Washington was already serving as President of the United States of America.

TABLE 2-1

The Ratification of the Constitution

State	Date	Vote in the Ratifying Convention
Delaware	December 7, 1787	Unanimous
Pennsylvania	December 12, 1787	46–32
New Jersey	December 19, 1787	Unanimous
Georgia	January 2, 1788	Unanimous
Connecticut	January 9, 1788	128–40
Massachusetts	February 6, 1788	187–168
Maryland	April 28, 1788	63–11
South Carolina	May 23, 1788	149–73
New Hampshire	June 21, 1788	57–47
Virginia	June 25, 1788	89–79
New York	July 26, 1788	30–27
North Carolina	November 21, 1789	194–77
Rhode Island	May 29, 1790	34–32

AMERICA: A CASE STUDY IN NATION-BUILDING

"The United States was the first major colony successfully to revolt against colonial rule," Seymour Martin Lipset has written. "In this sense, it was the first 'new nation.' " [42]

The Declaration of Independence, and the success of the American Revolution, influenced the philosophers and political leaders of the French Revolution. Jefferson's words were translated into many languages, influencing liberals during the 19th century in Germany, Italy, and South America. Even today, the ideas expressed in the Declaration of Independence have relevance in a world in which millions of persons are groping toward political freedom.

Problems of a
New Nation

The turmoil that has accompanied the growth of the new countries of Africa and Asia demonstrates that independence does not necessarily bring political maturity and peace. From the Congo to Vietnam, as colonialism has given way to the forces of nationalism, political independence has often been accompanied by political instability. Yet America had a success-

[42] Seymour Martin Lipset, *The First New Nation* (New York: Basic Books, 1963), p. 2.

ful revolution. And, despite the Civil War, two world wars, a depression, Vietnam, and the issues that divide the nation in the 1970's, it has survived. How did the revolutionary leaders of America carve out an enduring new nation where none had existed before?

The process was slow and difficult. As Lipset observes:

> A backward glance into our own past should destroy the notion that the United States proceeded easily toward the establishment of democratic political institutions. In the period which saw the establishment of political legitimacy and party government, it was touch and go whether the complex balance of forces would swing in the direction of a one- or two-party system, or even whether the nation would survive as an entity. It took time to institutionalize values, beliefs, and practices, and there were many incidents that revealed how fragile the commitments to democracy and nationhood really were.[43]

The United States, in other words, went through growing pains similar to those of the new nations of Africa and Asia today. For example, some have criticized the emergence in new nations of charismatic leaders such as Kwame Nkrumah, the President of Ghana until his ouster in 1966. Yet a charismatic leader may be necessary in a nation with no past, for, in Lipset's words, "he legitimizes the state." Americans may forget that "in his time, George Washington was idolized as much as many of the contemporary leaders of the new states." [44] Americans hung portraits of Washington over their hearths, and he was regarded as more of a patron saint than President.

And, if some contemporary new nations have encountered difficulty in establishing political freedom and democratic procedures, so did America. The Federalists under President John Adams wanted no organized political opposition and used the Alien and Sedition Acts, passed in 1798, to suppress their opponents. At least seventy persons were jailed and fined under the Sedition Act, which made almost any criticism of the government, the President, or Congress, a crime.

Lucian Pye has conceived of the process of nation-building as a series of crises: identity, integration, penetration, participation, and distribution.[45]

The Process of Nation-Building

The first crisis in the making of a new nation, as Pye views it, is for a people to gain "a sense of common *identity* as either subjects or citizens

[43] *Ibid.*, p. 16.
[44] *Ibid.*, p. 18.
[45] Lucian W. Pye, "Transitional Asia and the Dynamics of Nation Building," in Marian D. Irish, ed., *World Pressures on American Foreign Policy* (Englewood Cliffs, N.J.: Prentice-Hall, 1964), pp. 154–72.

of a common political system."[46] For many years most colonists probably thought of themselves as Englishmen, or as New Yorkers or Virginians, rather than as Americans. And it took a number of important developments in colonial society, as well as a series of strains in colonial relations with the British government, and the passage of time, before a developing sense of American nationhood emerged.[47]

By this time the process of *integration* was also underway. Integration concerns the relationship of the social structure to the political system; that is, the way that minority groups and other elements in the nation relate to one another and to the national governmental system. In the pre-Revolutionary period, integration was taking place rather rapidly; the Committees of Correspondence, which enabled the colonists to coordinate their responses to the British, served as a significant integrating device.

Penetration is the ability of a government to reach all layers of society in order to carry out public policies, to act directly on the people. Since 1789 the scope and importance of the national government's penetration has increased greatly, as every individual who has submitted a federal income tax form is aware.

Participation, or bringing increasing numbers of people into the political process, began in the 1780's and has continued ever since. The proportion of the population who were actively involved in the enactment of the new Constitution, even the proportion who voted for delegates to the ratifying conventions, was fairly small. But it was sufficient to provide enough of a base of popular support for the new regime to meet eighteenth-century requirements. Since 1787, through successive broadenings of the franchise and other measures, the scope of popular participation in the national government has been enlarged substantially, though not always peacefully. Women, blacks, and other groups have often had to fight for the right to participate in the political system.

Distribution is concerned with the government's control over the outputs of the political process: "What are the rewards of the political system, and who is to receive them?"[48] When the Founding Fathers prohibited export taxes in the Constitution they were concerned with problems of distribution. Distribution lies at the very heart of the process of government and politics.

It is, of course, difficult to pinpoint just when a nation passes through these various crises. Nevertheless, all of the processes Pye has identified can be observed in the American experience. As a result, the historical development of the American nation—with all of its crises and problems—remains relevant to the emerging nations in today's world.

[46] *Ibid.,* p. 162.
[47] Richard L. Merritt, *Symbols of American Community* (New Haven, Conn.: Yale University Press, 1966).
[48] Pye, "Transitional Asia and the Dynamics of Nation Building," p. 167.

THE CONSTITUTION THEN AND NOW

Chief Justice John Marshall, in *McCulloch v. Maryland*, said of the Constitution that it was "intended to endure for ages to come and, consequently, to be adapted to the various crises of human affairs."[49] This opinion, delivered in 1819, embodied the principle of loose or *flexible construction* of the Constitution. That is, the Constitution must be interpreted to meet changing conditions.

The members of the Supreme Court have generally reflected the times in which they have lived. Successive Supreme Courts have read very different meaning into the language of the Constitution. But the Court is not the only branch of the government that interprets the Constiution. So does Congress, when it passes laws. So does the President when he makes decisions and takes actions. In addition, the Constitution has been amended twenty-five times. The inputs of the American political system have resulted in a continual process of constitutional change. (The Constitution is found on pages 681–89 of this book.)

The Legislative Branch.   Article I of the Constitution vests all legislative powers "in a Congress of the United States, which shall consist of a Senate and House of Representatives." This article spells out the qualifications and method of election of members of the House and Senate. It gives power of impeachment to the House, but provides that the Senate shall try impeachment cases. It empowers the Vice-President to preside over the Senate with no vote, except in the case of a tie.

What It Says

It provides that all tax legislation must originate in the House. It allows the President to sign or veto a bill and Congress to override his veto by a two-thirds vote of both houses.

Section 8 of this article gives Congress the power to tax, provide for the "general welfare" of the United States, borrow money, regulate commerce (the "commerce clause"), naturalize citizens, coin money, punish counterfeiters, establish a post office and a copyright and patents system, create lower courts, declare war, maintain armed forces, suppress insurrections and repel invasions, govern the District of Columbia, and make "all necessary and proper laws" (sometimes called the "elastic clause") to carry out the powers of the Constitution.

Section 9 provides certain basic protections for citizens against acts of Congress. For example, it says that the writ of *habeas corpus* shall not be suspended unless required by the public safety in cases of rebellion or

---

[49] *McCulloch v. Maryland*, 4 Wheaton 316 (1819).

"The executive Power shall be vested in a President of the United States of America . . ."

invasion. One of the most important guarantees of individual liberty, the writ is designed to protect against illegal imprisonment. It requires that a person who is detained be brought before a judge for investigation so that the court may literally, in the Latin meaning, "have the body."

The article also prohibits Congress or the states from passing a "bill of attainder"—legislation aimed at a particular individual—or "ex post facto" laws, imposing punishment for an act that was not illegal when committed. It provides that Congress must appropriate money drawn from the Treasury, a provision that is the single most important check on presidential power. The Article also outlaws titles of nobility in America.

The Executive Branch. Article II states that "The executive Power shall be vested in a President of the United States of America." The framers did not provide for direct popular election of the President. Rather, they established the electoral college, with each state having as many electors as it had representatives and senators. The electors choose the President and Vice-President. Alexander Hamilton argued that by this means the Presidency would be filled by "characters preeminent for ability and virtue." The electors, he thought, being "a small number of persons, selected by their fellow-citizens from the general mass, will be most likely to possess the information and discernment requisite." [50]

The election of 1800 was thrown into the House of Representatives because Jefferson and his vice-presidential running mate Aaron Burr, although members of the same party, each received the same number of electoral votes. On the thirty-sixth ballot, the House chose Jefferson as President. Afterward, the electoral system was modified by the Twelfth Amendment to provide that electors must vote separately for President and Vice-President.

The rise of political parties meant that in time the electoral college became largely a rubber stamp. As it works today, the voters in each state choose between slates of electors who run under a party label. All the electoral votes of a state normally go to the presidential candidate who wins the popular vote in that state; electors on the winning slate routinely vote for their party's candidates for President and Vice-President. But the electors do not *have* to obey the will of the voters. For a variety of reasons (discussed in Chapter 9), there has been pressure to modify or abolish the electoral college system. In 1969, the House approved a proposed constitutional amendment to abolish the electoral college and substitute a system of direct, popular election of the President. In the fall of 1970, the Senate debated the proposed constitutional amendment for direct election of the President, but its supporters were unable to break a filibuster and bring the proposal to a vote.

The Constitution makes the President Commander in Chief of the Armed Forces, gives him the right to make treaties "with the Advice and Consent" of two-thirds of a quorum of the Senate, to appoint ambassadors, judges, and other high officials, subject to Senate approval, and to summon Congress into special session. The Constitution also gives the President power to adjourn Congress (if the House and Senate disagree on when to adjourn), a power that no Chief Executive has exercised yet.

The Judiciary. Article III states that "The judicial Power of the United States, shall be vested in one supreme Court, and in such inferior Courts" as Congress may establish. It also provides for trial by jury. The Supreme Court's vital right of judicial review of acts of Congress stems from both the supremacy clause of the Constitution (see below) and Article III, which states that the judicial power applies to "all Cases . . . arising under this Constitution."

Other Provisions. Article IV governs the relations among the states and between the states and the Federal Government. Article V provides

[50] Alexander Hamilton, "The Federalist, No. 68," in Edward Meade Earle, ed., *The Federalist* (New York: Random House, Modern Library), pp. 441–42. **69**

methods for amending the Constitution and for ratifying these amendments. Article VI states that the Constitution, laws, and treaties of the United States "shall be the supreme Law of the Land." This is the powerful supremacy clause by which laws of Congress are supreme over any conflicting state laws. Article VII declares that the Constitution would be effective when ratified by nine states.

The Amendment Process

The framers knew that the Constitution might have to be changed to meet future conditions. It had, after all, been created because of the need for change. So they provided two methods of proposing amendments: by a two-thirds vote of both houses of Congress, or by a national convention called by Congress at the request of legislatures in two-thirds of the states.

Once proposed, an amendment, in order for it to become effective, must be ratified, either by the legislatures of three-fourths of the states or by special ratifying conventions in three-fourths of the states.

No amendment has ever been *proposed* by the convention method. But in the mid-1960's, the late Senator Everett McKinley Dirksen of Illinois, the Republican Senate leader, encouraged the states to petition Congress to call a constitutional convention. The general purpose was to amend the Constitution to overturn the Supreme Court's "one person, one vote" decisions that had forced the reapportionment of state legislatures.[51] Between 1963 and 1970, thirty-three state legislatures, only one short of the required two-thirds, had petitioned Congress to call a convention. But at least four of the petitions were open to challenge on various technical grounds. For example, most of the petitions were approved by legislatures that had not been reapportioned to conform to the Supreme Court's edicts. Several senators and other citizens have warned that a constitutional convention might run wild and make sweeping changes in the structure of the Federal Government, since there is no precedent for setting an agenda of such a convention were it to be called.

In 1965 and again in 1966, Dirksen led a fight in the Senate for the Dirksen Amendment, which would have empowered the states to apportion one house of their legislatures on a basis other than population. Although a majority of senators voted for the proposed constitutional amendment each year, the proposal fell short of the needed two-thirds majority.

Thirty-one amendments have been submitted to the states by Congress and twenty-five have been ratified. Only the Twenty-first Amendment, repealing Prohibition, was ratified by state conventions; the rest were ratified by state legislatures. Some of the amendments add to the Constitution; others supersede or revise the original language of the Constitution.

[51] See discussion in Chapter 9, pp. 358–61.

The amendments to the Constitution fall into three major time periods. The first twelve, ratified between 1791 and 1804, were remedial amendments designed to perfect the original instrument. The next three grew out of the great upheaval of the Civil War and were designed to deal with the new position of the blacks as free men. Amendments in the third group were all passed in the twentieth century and deal with a wide range of subjects, in part reflecting more recent pressures toward change in American society.

The Bill of Rights

The first ten amendments are the Bill of Rights.[52] The provisions of the first four are freedom of religion, speech, press, assembly, and petition (First Amendment); the right to bear arms (Second Amendment); protection against quartering of soldiers in private homes (Third Amendment); and protection against unreasonable search and seizure of people, homes, papers, and effects, and provision for search warrants (Fourth Amendment).

If there is any principle of the Constitution that more imperatively calls for attachment than any other it is the principle of free thought, not free thought for those who agree with us but freedom for the thought we hate.

—Justice Oliver Wendell Holmes, dissenting in *United States v. Schwimmer* (1929).

The Fifth Amendment provides that no person must testify against himself—a protection against self-incrimination often invoked before congressional investigating committees—or stand trial twice for the same crime. It also lists other rights of accused persons, including that of indictment by a grand jury for major crimes and the general provision that no person shall "be deprived of life, liberty or property, without due process of law." The Sixth Amendment calls for a speedy, public trial by jury in criminal cases as well as for other protections, including the right to have a lawyer.

The Seventh Amendment provides for jury trial in civil cases, and the Eighth Amendment bars excessive bail or fines, or cruel and unusual punishment. The Ninth Amendment provides that the enumeration of certain rights in the Constitution shall not deny other rights retained by the people and the Tenth Amendment reserves to the states, or to the people, powers not delegated to the Federal Government.

These ten amendments were designed to protect Americans against the power of the *Federal* Government. Nothing in the Constitution specifically provides that *state* governments must also abide by the provisions of the Bill of Rights. But in interpreting the Fourteenth Amendment, passed in 1866 after the Civil War, the Supreme Court has extended the protection of almost all of the Bill of Rights to the states.

[52] The Bill of Rights was passed by the First Congress on September 25, 1789 and went into effect when ratified by three-fourths of the states on December 15, 1791. The Bill of Rights is discussed in detail in Chapter 4.

The Eleventh Amendment (1798) [53] was added to guarantee that a sovereign state would never again be hauled into federal court by a private citizen or foreign citizen. In *Chisholm v. Georgia*,[54] the Supreme Court had ruled for two South Carolina citizens who had sued the state of Georgia on behalf of a British creditor to recover confiscated property.

The Twelfth Amendment (1804), as already discussed, was adopted after the deadlocked election of 1800. It provided that presidential electors vote *separately* for President and Vice-President.

The next three amendments resulted from the Civil War. The Thirteenth Amendment (1865) forbids slavery. It also outlaws involuntary servitude in the United States and its territories except as punishment for a crime. Its purpose was to free the slaves and complete the abolition of slavery in America. Lincoln's Emancipation Proclamation, which was issued during the war, applied *only* to areas in rebellion and under Confederate control and therefore freed not a single slave.

The Fourteenth Amendment (1868) was adopted to make the slaves citizens. But it has had other unintended and far-reaching effects. The amendment says that no state "shall abridge the privileges or immunities of citizens" nor "deprive any person of life, liberty or property, without due process of law"; nor deny anyone "the equal protection of the laws." The famous "due process" clause of the amendment has been used by the Supreme Court to protect the rights of individuals against the police power of the state in a broad spectrum of cases. The "equal protection of laws" provision was the basis for the landmark 1954 Supreme Court decision outlawing segregation in public schools.

The Fifteenth Amendment (1870) barred the Federal or state governments from denying any citizen the right to vote because of race, color, or previous condition of servitude. It did not stop some states from disenfranchising blacks, however, by means of restrictive voting requirements, such as literacy tests.

Forty-three years elapsed after the adoption of the Fifteenth Amendment in 1870 before another was ratified in 1913. The Sixteenth Amendment (1913) allowed Congress to pass a graduated individual income tax, based in theory on ability to pay. The tax is, of course, the largest single source of federal revenue.

The Seventeenth Amendment (1913) provided for direct election of senators by the people, instead of by state legislatures.

The Eighteenth Amendment (1919) established Prohibition by outlawing the manufacture, sale, or transportation of alcoholic beverages. It provides a classic instance of an output of government doomed to failure because ultimately the input of popular *support* was lacking. Prohibition led to the era of bathtub gin, "flappers," speakeasies, and bootlegging. It

---

[53] Date after each amendment refers to date of ratification.
[54] *Chisholm v. Georgia*, 2 Dallas 419 (1793).

Suffragettes parade, New York, 1912

was marked by widespread defiance of the law by otherwise law-abiding citizens and by the rise of organized crime, which quickly moved to meet public demand for illicit liquor. Partly as a result of Prohibition, organized crime remains entrenched in America today, exercising an unhealthy political influence in some areas of the country. Prohibition was repealed in 1933.

The Nineteenth Amendment (1920) gave women the right to vote. Many states permitted women to vote even before it was proposed, but

the amendment provided a constitutional guarantee. Even so, it may seem surprising today that female suffrage was not adopted until 1920, in time for that year's presidential election.

Under the Twentieth (or "lame duck") Amendment (1933), the terms of the President and Vice-President begin on January 20 and the terms of members of Congress on January 3. Prior to that time, congressmen defeated in November would continue in office for four months until March 4 (formerly the date also of presidential inaugurations). Injured by the voters, the defeated lawmakers sat like "lame ducks." [55] The amendment also provides alternatives in case of the death of the President-elect before Inauguration Day, or in case no President has been chosen.

The Twenty-first Amendment (1933) repealed Prohibition but permitted states to remain "dry" if they so desired.

The Twenty-second Amendment (1951) limits Presidents to a maximum of two elected terms. It was proposed after President Franklin D. Roosevelt had won a fourth term in 1944. Before then, through hallowed tradition established by George Washington, no President had been elected more than twice.[56]

The Twenty-third Amendment (1961) gives citizens of the District of Columbia the right to vote in presidential elections; they did so for the first time in 1964. When the amendment was adopted, the capital had a population of 800,000—larger than that of thirteen of the states.

The Twenty-fourth Amendment, adopted in 1964, abolished the poll tax as a prerequisite for voting in federal elections or primaries. It applied to only five Southern states that still imposed such a tax, originally a device to keep blacks (and in some cases poor whites) from voting.

The Twenty-fifth Amendment was spurred by President Dwight D. Eisenhower's 1955 heart attack and by the murder of President Kennedy in Dallas, Texas, on November 22, 1963. Ratified in February 1967, it defines the circumstances under which a Vice-President may take over the leadership of the country in case of the mental or physical illness or disability of the President. It also requires the President to nominate a Vice-President, subject to majority approval of Congress, when that office becomes vacant for any reason.

[55] The phrase apparently originated as London stock exchange slang. It was used to describe a stock jobber or broker who could not make good his losses and would "waddle out of the alley like a lame duck." Abraham Lincoln is sometimes credited with introducing the phrase in America. When a defeated senator called on Lincoln and asked for a job as Commissioner of Indian Affairs, Lincoln was quoted as saying afterward: "I usually find that a Senator or Representative out of business is a sort of lame duck." George Stimson, *A Book About American Politics* (New York: Harper & Row, 1952), pp. 527–28.

[56] In addition to George Washington and Franklin D. Roosevelt only eight Presidents have served two full terms.

"The Constitution belongs to the living and not to the dead,"
Thomas Jefferson wrote. He added:

> Some men look at constitutions with sanctimonious reverence and deem
> them like the ark of the covenant, too sacred to be touched. They ascribe
> to the men of the preceding age a wisdom more than human, and suppose
> what they did to be beyond amendment. . . . Laws and institutions must
> go hand in hand with the progress of the human mind. . . . As new dis-
> coveries are made, new truths disclosed, and manners and opinions change
> . . . institutions must advance also, and keep pace with the times.[57]

Through a variety of ways, including amendment and judicial review,
the oldest written, national constitution in the world remains the vital
framework of the American political system. But are constitutional principles enough? Today, many Americans are demanding change, renewal,
and reform of the political system and of American society. They are
demanding that America's institutions fulfill the promise of its ideals, and
that principles be translated into reality. Constitutional democracy was
born at Philadelphia, but, in a real sense, the work was only begun.

[57] "Letter to Samuel Kercheval, 1816," in Saul K. Padover, *The Complete Jefferson*
(New York: Duell, Sloan & Pearce, 1943), p. 291.

SUGGESTED READING

Beard, Charles A. *An Economic Interpretation of the Constitution of the
United States* * (Macmillan, 1913). The classic argument proposing that
delegates to the Philadelphia Convention were influenced primarily by
economic motives in framing the Constitution. A number of later scholars
have taken issue with Beard's interpretation.

Becker, Carl L. *The Declaration of Independence* * (Knopf, 1942). A perceptive discussion of the Declaration of Independence and the events leading
up to it.

Boorstin, Daniel J. *The Americans: The Colonial Experience* * (Random
House, 1958). An analysis of the impact of the colonial period on American political ideas and institutions.

Corwin, Edward S., et al., eds. *The Constitution of the United States of
America* (U.S. Government Printing Office, 1964). A comprehensive and
detailed line-by-line exposition of the Constitution. See also Corwin's
The Constitution and What It Means Today (Atheneum, 1963). Based
in part on the much longer *Constitution of the United States of America*,
this paperback is a useful guide to the Constitution, citing relevant
Supreme Court cases.

Earle, Edward Meade, ed. *The Federalist* (Random House, Modern Library).
A classic collection of essays written by Alexander Hamilton, James
Madison, and John Jay, prominent supporters of the proposed Constitu-

tion during the struggle over ratification. The Federalist papers were published in the press under the pseudonym *Publius;* they remain an important exposition of the structure of the Federal Government.

Farrand, Max. *The Framing of the Constitution of the United States* * (Yale University Press, 1926). A good general account of the Constitutional Convention, by the scholar who compiled in four volumes the basic documentary sources on the proceedings of the convention.

Kelley, Alfred H., and Harbison, Winfred A. *The American Constitution: Its Origins and Development,* 3rd ed. (Norton, 1963). A good general history of American constitutional development, beginning with the colonial period.

Lipset, Seymour Martin. *The First New Nation* * (Basic Books, 1963). An important historical and sociological study of America that seeks to trace the relationship between a nation's values and the development of stable political institutions. Compares the early American experience with that of today's emerging nations.

Rossiter, Clinton. *Seedtime of the Republic* * (Harcourt Brace Jovanovich, 1953). A penetrating analysis of American political and social history in the colonial and revolutionary periods, with emphasis on the political ideas that were to condition the formation of the American nation.

Rossiter, Clinton. *1787: The Grand Convention* * (Macmillan, 1966). A very readable account of the Philadelphia Convention, the battle for ratification of the Constitution, and the first years of the new Republic. Makes interesting observations on the personal characteristics and objectives of the framers of the Constitution.

* Available in paperback edition

3

The Federal System

It used to be said that the French Minister of Education could, by glancing at the clock in his office, tell at any given moment what book was being read by every schoolchild in France.

The tale may be a bit exaggerated, but no official in Washington could begin to perform the same feat. France has a centralized, unitary system of government. The nation is divided into administrative units called departments, uniformly administered from Paris. Educational and other policies are set by the *central government*.

In contrast, the United States has a *federal system* of government, in which power is constitutionally shared by a national government and fifty state governments. Within the states, of course, are thousands of local governments—and schools are controlled by local and state governments. The constitutional sharing of power by a national government and

The
Federal System:
What It Is

77

regional units of government (states in the case of the United States) characterizes and defines a federal system.

The terms "federalism" and "the federal system" are used interchangeably to describe the structure of government in the United States. (These terms should not be confused with "the Federal Government," which simply refers to the national government in Washington.)

To say that power in America is shared by the national and state governments may, at first glance, seem to be merely stating the obvious. Yet no principle of American government has been disputed more than federalism. Should anyone doubt that, he need only recall that more than 500,000 Americans died during the Civil War settling problems of federalism.

The question of *how* power is to be shared in the federal system is central to the political process in the United States. It is a subject of continuing political debate. It has been reflected in the most important decisions of the Supreme Court. The migrant worker in the citrus groves of Florida, the student facing a National Guard bayonet, the black family on welfare in New York, the West Virginia coal miner, the wife seeking a Nevada divorce, the murder suspect fighting extradition, the slum dweller hoping for an apartment in a federal housing project—none may think of their problems in terms of the federal system. Yet the relationship among national, state, and local governments vitally touches their lives. To a considerable extent, federalism affects who wins and who loses as a result of governmental decisions in American society.

Federalism is one answer to the problem of how to govern a large nation. Although there are all sorts of institutional arrangements in the more than 125 nations of the world, governments tend to be either centralized and unitary, or federated.

In the twentieth century, federalism has become a popular style of government. "In 1964, well over half the land mass of the world was ruled by governments that with some justification, however slight, described themselves as federalisms." [1] The list of federal systems includes the Soviet Union, Switzerland, Canada, Australia, Mexico, India, and West Germany. Unitary systems, in which all power is vested in a central government, include Britain, Israel, and South Africa.

Can Federalism Work?

Any large organization, such as a government bureaucracy or a big corporation, must decide whether it can accomplish its tasks best by centralizing or decentralizing its activities. If subordinate units exercise considerable local autonomy, the administrators at the center enjoy less

[1] William H. Riker, *Federalism: Origin, Operation, and Significance* (Boston: Little, Brown, 1964), p. 1.

power; but the tasks may be performed more efficiently. Although the analogy to the American governmental system is not exact, the argument can be made that a number of governments dealing directly with local problems, and accountable to local voters, may be more desirable, and may result in better performance, than decision-making by a single, remote bureaucracy.

Another argument advanced for a federal system of government is that it allows more levels of government, more points of access to the government, and as a result, more opportunities for political participation. Because Americans have a federal system they may vote at frequent intervals for mayors, councilmen, school boards, governors, other state officials, and congressmen and senators elected from the states.

In addition, advocates of federalism argue that it is well suited to the United States, a nation covering a large geographic area with a highly diversified population of more than 200,000,000 people.

But a federal system also has distinct disadvantages. Federalism may serve as a mask for privilege and economic or racial discrimination. In some areas of the South, the federal system has permitted state and local governments to repress blacks. Inequalities may occur when special interests exercise considerable influence on the politics and economy of a state or locality; for example, West Virginia, although the nation's leading coal producer, is a very poor state, a fact usually attributed in part to its heavy dependence on a single dominant industry. Along with abandoned strip mines and coal tipples, poverty and human despair scar the hillsides; in 1968, West Virginia ranked forty-sixth in the nation in per capita income.[2]

Critics argue that under the federal system, local or parochial interests —white supremacists in Mississippi, for example, or the automobile industry—have often been able to frustrate efforts to solve such national problems as race, poverty, pollution, and hunger. Because the Federal Government collects most of the taxes in America, it is argued as well that the system of federalism has left cities and states unable to pay for local services.

The relations between the states and the Federal Government are thus a source of continuing conflict and controversy in the American political system and raise a number of questions of fundamental importance. Who benefits and who loses under the federal system? Does federalism restrict progress in solving national problems? Do the advantages of federalism outweigh the price of fragmented government? Why does the United States have a federal system? What are the problems it has created? What are the consequences of federalism in American politics? In the performance of the states?

[2] U.S. Bureau of the Census, *Statistical Abstract of the United States 1969*, p. 320.

One does not decide on the merits of federalism by an examination of federalism in the abstract, but rather on its actual meaning for particular societies. . . .

The main beneficiary throughout American history has been the Southern whites, who have been given the freedom to oppress Negroes, first as slaves and later as a depressed caste. Other minorities have from time to time also managed to obtain some of these benefits; e.g., special business interests have been allowed to regulate themselves, especially in the era from about 1890 to 1936, by means of the judicial doctrine of dual federalism, which eliminated both state and national regulation of such matters as wage rates and hours of labor. But the significance of federal benefits to economic interests pales beside the significance of benefits to the Southern segregationist whites. The judgment to be passed on federalism in the United States is therefore a judgment on the values of segregation and racial oppression.

—William H. Riker, *Federalism: Origin, Operation, Significance.*

THE CHECKERBOARD OF GOVERNMENTS

The average American complains that he is being squeezed by high taxes on at least three levels of government—national, state, and local. He is confronted by a bewildering checkerboard of overlapping governments and local districts. One study of the federal system found that a resident of Park Forest, Illinois, paid taxes to eleven

The April 15th Nightmare

governmental units, starting with the United States of America and ending with the "South Cook County Mosquito Abatement District."[3]

The Census Bureau reported in 1967 that there were 81,299 governments in the United States: more than 3,000 counties, 18,000 municipalities, 17,000 townships, 21,000 school districts, 21,000 special districts (for fire protection, water supply, and other services), 50 states, and 1 national government.[4]

But knowing how many governments exist in America tells little about how the federal system operates—how the various levels of government relate to one another. One way to visualize the system as a whole was suggested by Morton Grodzins:

> The federal system is not accurately symbolized by a neat layer cake of three distinct and separate planes. A far more realistic symbol is that of the marble cake. Wherever you slice through it you reveal an inseparable mixture of differently colored ingredients. There is no neat horizontal stratification. Vertical and diagonal lines almost obliterate the horizontal ones, and in some places there are unexpected whirls and an imperceptible merging of colors, so that it is difficult to tell where one ends and the other begins. So it is with federal, state, and local responsibilities in the chaotic marble cake of American government.[5]

Cooperation —and Tension

Is the American federal system essentially cooperative—or is it competitive? In fact, federalism can be seen both as a rivalry between the states and Washington and as a partnership. A system of 81,299 governments could not operate without a substantial measure of cooperation, but a great tension is built into the system as well.

Three times in recent years the President of the United States has deployed armed federal troops in Southern states. In 1957, President Eisenhower sent troops into Little Rock, Arkansas, to enforce court-ordered integration of the previously all white Central High School. In the fall of 1962, two men were killed on the campus of the University of Mississippi at Oxford during rioting over the admission of James H. Meredith, a black student. President Kennedy deployed 16,000 federal troops in Mississippi to enroll Meredith and protect him as he attended classes. In June 1963, Governor George Wallace carried out a campaign pledge to "stand in the schoolhouse door" to try to prevent two black students from entering the University of Alabama. The Alabama governor read a statement to Nicho-

[3] Morton Grodzins, *The American System* (Chicago: Rand McNally, 1966), pp. 3–4.
[4] U.S. Bureau of the Census, "Census of Governments, 1967" Vol. I, *Governmental Organization* (Washington, D.C.: U.S. Government Printing Office, 1968), p. 1.
[5] Morton Grodzins, "Centralization and Decentralization in the American Federal System," in Robert A. Goldwin, ed., *A Nation of States* (Chicago: Rand McNally, 1963), pp. 1–4.

Federal troops escort students into Central High School in Little Rock, Arkansas
—September 1957

las deB. Katzenbach, Deputy Attorney General of the United States, charging "oppression of the rights, privileges and sovereignty of this state by officers of the Federal government." Wallace backed down after President Kennedy federalized the state's national guard to enforce the order of a federal court.

Although Presidents tend to use the rhetoric of cooperation when they talk about federal-state relations, there is clearly an underlying tension among competing levels of government. Sometimes the tensions arise from social issues, as in the armed confrontations over racial desegregation. Often, they are rooted in disagreements over how tax revenues should be shared.

There are political and ideological tensions as well—between those who look to the Federal Government to solve major national problems (chiefly Northern Democrats and liberal Republicans), and those who see the government in Washington as a threat to individual liberty and initiative and regard the states as a bulwark against an expanding federal "octopus" (chiefly Southern Democrats and conservative Republicans).

This division, while neat, does not give the whole picture. For example, some Southern advocates of "states' rights" actually look to the states as an instrument of inaction—of doing nothing—rather than as a guardian of individual liberty. This brand of "states' rights" may simply be a cloak for segregation. Conversely, many Northern liberals have become alarmed over the growth of the federal bureaucracy—traditionally a conservative concern—and in recent years have advocated community action programs and decentralization of schools and other government services.

The federal system has been viewed differently at different times. During much of the nineteenth century and until 1937, the concept of "dual federalism" was accepted, in which the Supreme Court saw itself as a referee between two competing power centers—the states and the Federal Government. The Federal Government and the states (and local governments) had clearly defined areas of responsibility in which they were autonomous; different functions were performed by separate levels of government.

The Changing
Federal
Framework

This orthodox view of the federal system prevailed until the New Deal of Franklin D. Roosevelt. During the 1930's, the Roosevelt administration responded to the Great Depression with a series of laws establishing social welfare and public works programs. In 1937, the Supreme Court began holding these programs constitutional. With the Federal Government thrust into an expanded position of power, a new view of federalism emerged, that of "cooperative federalism." In this view, the various levels of government are seen as related parts of a single governmental system, characterized more by cooperation and shared functions than by conflict and competition.

Although this concept is generally used to describe the federal system since the New Deal, Morton Grodzins and his associate, Daniel J. Elazar, have argued that, historically, the American federal system has always been characterized by shared functions at the federal, state, and local levels.[6] Even before the Constitution was written, for example, the central government gave land grants to the states for public schools.

President Johnson coined the term "creative federalism" to describe his own view of the relationship between Washington and the states. During his administration Congress enacted "Great Society" legislation that further expanded the role of the Federal Government. One of the criticisms of the federal system is that states, because they occupy a limited geographic area, are not equipped to deal with truly national problems that cut across state lines. In the legislation passed during the Johnson administration, Congress set certain national objectives and thrust the Federal Government directly into such community problems as public school education, poverty, law enforcement, and urban blight. The Economic Opportunity Act of 1964 and the Model Cities legislation of 1966 were examples of this approach in federal-state relations.

All of these changes in the patterns of federalism reflect the fact that the United States has gradually become a national society. People look to Washington to solve problems. In 1967, when racial disturbances erupted in many large cities, Americans did not consider these "local" problems; they turned to the President and the Federal Government for solutions.

[6] Grodzins, *The American System*; Daniel J. Elazar, *American Federalism: A View from the States* (New York: Crowell, 1966); Daniel J. Elazar, *The American Partnership* (Chicago: University of Chicago Press, 1962).

After a third of a century of power flowing from the people and the states to Washington it is time for a New Federalism in which power, funds and responsibility will flow from Washington to the states and to the people. . . .

For a third of a century, power and responsibility have flowed toward Washington—and Washington has taken for its own the best sources of revenue.

We intend to reverse this tide, and to turn back to the states a greater measure of responsibility—not as a way of avoiding problems, but as a better way of solving problems. Along with this should go a share of Federal revenues. I shall propose to the Congress that a set portion of the revenues from Federal income taxes be remitted directly to the states—with a minimum of Federal restrictions on how those dollars are to be used, and with a requirement that a percentage of them be channeled through for the use of local governments. . . .

After nearly 40 years of moving power from the states to Washington, we begin in America a decade of decentralization, a shifting of power away from the center whenever it can be used better locally.

—President Nixon in a television address to the nation, August 8, 1969.

The new look in the federal system during the 1960's did not resolve the larger question of how to make a federal system work. As one study viewed the problem,

> The basic dilemma . . . is how to achieve goals and objectives that are established by the national government, through the action of other governments, state and local, that are legally independent and politically may be hostile. Those state and local governments are subject to no federal discipline except through the granting or denial of federal aid. And that is not very useful, because to deny the funds is in effect to veto the national objective itself.[7]

During his first year in office, President Nixon proposed a "new federalism" that would introduce major changes in the nature of the federal system. Central to Nixon's program was his proposal for "revenue sharing," under which the Federal Government would turn billions of dollars of federal tax monies back to state and local governments. (The concept of revenue-sharing is discussed later in this chapter on page 102.) Nixon also proposed complete reform of the nation's welfare system, which he termed "a colossal failure."[8] (The welfare system and the President's proposals are discussed in Chapter 15.)

The 1970's could see new departures in the continually changing pattern of relationships within the federal system. The national government in Washington and the state and local governments may be groping toward greater accommodation in a system that, to begin with, was the result of a compromise among conflicting interests.

[7] James L. Sundquist with David W. Davis, *Making Federalism Work* (Washington, D.C.: The Brookings Institution, 1969), p. 12.

[8] President Nixon's radio and television address to the nation, *New York Times*, August 8, 1969, p. 10.

THE HISTORICAL BASIS OF FEDERALISM

In April 1787, a month before the Constitutional Convention opened at Philadelphia, James Madison set forth his thoughts on the structure of a new government in a letter to George Washington.

"A Middle Ground"

Madison argued that while the states could not each be completely independent, the creation of "one simple republic" would be "unattainable." "I have sought for a middle ground," Madison wrote, "which may at once support a due supremacy of the national authority, and not exclude the local authorities wherever they can be subordinately useful." [9]

Essentially, Madison had forecast the balanced and compromised structure that emerged five months later. The bargain struck at Philadelphia in 1787 was a federal bargain. The Constitutional Convention created the federal system, with its sharing of power by the states and the national government. The delegates to the convention agreed to give up some of the states' independence in order to achieve unity and create a nation. Yet, America probably got a federal system of government because no stronger national government would have been acceptable to the framers or to the states.

There are a number of reasons why a stronger central government would have been unacceptable. First, public opinion in the states almost certainly would not have permitted adoption of a unitary form of government. Loyalty to the states was strong. The Articles of Confederation showed just about how far people had been willing to go in the direction of a central government prior to 1787—which was not very far. The diversity of the American people, regional interests, even the state of technology —transportation was slow and great distances separated the colonies—all militated against the establishment of central government stronger than the one framed at Philadelphia. Finally, federalism was seen as an effective device for limiting national power by distributing authority between the states and the national government.

Pressures Toward Federalism

The collapse of European colonial empires since the Second World War confronted successful rebels in Africa and Asia with an urgent problem: how to organize their new nations. William H. Riker has suggested that emerging nations face two alternatives: they can unite under a

A Tool for Nation-Building

[9] Letter to George Washington, April 16, 1787.

central government, in which case they have "merely exchanged one imperial master for a lesser one," or they can join "in some kind of federation, which preserves at least the semblance of political self-control." He adds: "In this sense, federalism is the main alternative to empire as a technique of aggregating large areas under one government."[10]

The rationale of federalism is that it protects diversity of interests within regional units while allowing a national political system to develop. On the other hand, the terrible civil war in Nigeria, touched off in 1967 by Biafra's secession from the central government, is a reminder that a federal system does not guarantee political stability. And, it should not be forgotten that the United States also experienced a tragic civil war that threatened its federal system.

Yet the framework of federalism in the United States first permitted a disunited people to find a basis for political union and then allowed room for the development of a sense of national identity. As a result, "The United States of America" is not only the name of a country—to an extent, it is also a description of its formal governmental structure.

THE CONSTITUTIONAL BASIS OF FEDERALISM

Federal Powers:
Enumerated,
Implied,
and Inherent

The Constitution established the framework for the American federal system. Under it, the three branches of the Federal Government are granted certain specifically *enumerated powers*. In addition, the Supreme Court has held that the national government also has broad *implied powers*. These flow from its enumerated powers and the "elastic clause" of the Constitution, which gives Congress power to make all laws "necessary and proper" to carry out its enumerated powers. For example, the right of the United States to establish a national banking system is an implied power flowing from its enumerated power to collect taxes and regulate commerce.[11]

The Supreme Court has also held that the national government has *inherent powers* that it may exercise simply because it exists as a government. One of the most important inherent powers is the right to conduct foreign relations; since the United States does not exist in a vacuum, it must, as a practical matter, deal with other countries, even though the Constitution does not spell this out.

These various powers are complex concepts. They developed slowly as the nation grew and found it necessary to adapt the Constitution to changing conditions.

[10] Riker, *Federalism: Origin, Operation, Significance*, pp. 4–5.
[11] *McCulloch v. Maryland*, 4 Wheaton 316 (1819).

The Supreme Court serves as an arbiter in questions of state versus national power. The federal system could not function efficiently without an umpire.

The Court's attitude has changed radically over the decades; sometimes the Court has supported states' rights and sometimes it has supported expanded federal power. But in every period, the Court has served as a major arena in which important conflicts are settled within the federal framework.

The Division of Federal and State Power.   Under the Tenth Amendment, "The powers not delegated to the United States by the Constitution, nor prohibited by it to the States, are reserved to the States respectively, or to the people."

At first glance, this amendment might seem to limit the Federal Government to powers specifically "delegated" by the Constitution. But in deciding *McCulloch v. Maryland,* Chief Justice Marshall emphasized that the Tenth Amendment (unlike the Articles of Confederation) does not use the word "expressly" before the word "delegated."

This omission was not accidental. In 1789, during the debate on the first ten amendments, James Madison and others blocked the attempt of states'-rights advocates to limit federal powers to those "expressly" delegated.[12] During the debate Madison objected to insertion of the key word "because it was impossible to confine a Government to the exercise of express powers; [and because] there must necessarily be admitted powers by implication, unless the constitution descended to recount every minutia."[13]

The Supreme Court that followed the Marshall Court took a much narrower view of the powers of the Federal Government. Under Roger B. Taney, who served as Chief Justice from 1836 to 1864, the Court invoked the Tenth Amendment to protect the power of the states. In 1871, the Supreme Court ruled that the amendment meant that the Federal Government could not tax the salaries of state officials.[14]

In the twentieth century, the Court cited the Tenth Amendment in 1918 in striking down an act of Congress that barred the interstate transportation of goods produced by child labor. The Court reasoned in that case that the law had invaded powers reserved to the states under the

The
Supreme Court
as Umpire

[12] Alfred H. Kelly and Winfred A. Harbison, *The American Constitution* (New York: Norton, 1955), p. 176.

[13] In Walter Berns, "The Meaning of the Tenth Amendment," in Goldwin, *A Nation of States,* p. 138. For a spirited defense of the opposite view, see "The Case for 'States Rights,'" by James J. Kilpatrick in the same volume.

[14] *Collector v. Day,* 11 Wallace 113 (1871). This decision was overruled by the Supreme Court in 1939 in *Graves v. O'Keefe,* 306 U.S. 466 (1939).

amendment.[15] For two decades afterward, the Court leaned on the Tenth Amendment to invalidate a series of federal laws dealing with child labor and regulating industry and agriculture. And in 1935, the Court cited the amendment in declaring unconstitutional the National Industrial Recovery Act, a major piece of New Deal legislation designed to reduce unemployment.[16]

But in the watershed year of 1937, the Court swung around and upheld the Social Security program and the National Labor Relations Acts as valid exercises of federal power.[17] And in 1941 it specifically rejected the argument that the Constitution in any way limited the power of the Federal Government to regulate interstate commerce. The decision upheld the Fair Labor Standards Act. Speaking for the Court, Chief Justice Harlan Fiske Stone called the Tenth Amendment "a truism that all is retained which has not been surrendered." [18]

Thus, more than 120 years after *McCulloch v. Maryland,* the Supreme Court had finally swung back to John Marshall's view of the Constitution as an instrument that gave the Federal Government broad powers over the states and the nation.

Despite this prevailing interpretation, many advocates of a states'-rights position continue to rely on the Tenth Amendment as the constitutional foundation for their argument. In general, they see the Constitution as the result of a compact among the states. A forceful case can be made for a "states'-rights" interpretation, but the position has become weakened with the passage of time.

Certainly, outside of the South, advocacy of states' rights is a minority position. A more widely accepted view today is that the national government represents the *people,* not the states, and that sovereignty rests with "we the people," who created the Constitution and approved it.

Restrictions on the States

The Supremacy Clause of the Constitution (Article VI, Paragraph 2) makes it clear that the Constitution and the laws and treaties made under it are supreme over state constitutions or laws.

In addition, the Constitution places many restrictions on the states: they are forbidden to make treaties, coin money, pass bills of attainder or ex post facto laws, impair contracts, grant titles of nobility, tax imports or exports, keep troops or warships in peacetime, engage in war (unless invaded), or make interstate compacts without congressional approval. The

---

[15] *Hammer v. Dagenhart,* 247 U.S. 251 (1918).
[16] *Schecter Poultry Corporation v. United States,* 295 U.S. 495 (1935).
[17] *Steward Machine Co. v. Davis,* 301 U.S. 548 (1937); *National Labor Relations Board v. Jones & Laughlin Steel Corp.,* 301 U.S. 1 (1937).
[18] *United States v. Darby,* 312 U.S. 100 (1941).

Bill of Rights, as interpreted by the Supreme Court, and the Fourteenth and Fifteenth Amendments place additional restrictions on the states (see Chapter 4, pp. 137–38).

Local governments derive their powers from the states and are subject to the same constitutional restrictions as are the states. If a state cannot do something neither can a locality. And, "in a strictly legal sense it must be understood that all local governments in the United States are creatures of their respective states." [19]

The Constitution (in Article IV) defines the relations of the Federal Government to the states. For example, the United States must guarantee to every state "a republican form of government." In addition, the Federal Government must protect the states against invasion, and against domestic violence, on request of the governor or legislature. Under pressure of events, however, Presidents have on several occasions intervened in the states with force over the objections of the governor. President Eisenhower's dispatch of federal troops to Little Rock in 1957 was one well-known modern example. During the riots in Detroit in July 1967, there was much political fencing between President Johnson and Michigan Governor George Romney about whether and when to send in federal troops.[20] Behind all the careful maneuvering lay the fact that there is no more sensitive nerve in the American federal system than the use of force by the Federal Government within a state. The minuet between President Johnson and Governor Romney was undoubtedly even more elaborate than usual because they were potential opposing candidates for President in 1968.[21]

Congress may admit new states to the union, but the Constitution does not spell out any ground rules for their admission. In practice, a territory that desires statehood applies to Congress, which passes an "enabling act" allowing the people of the territory to frame a constitution. If Congress approves the constitution, it passes a joint resolution recognizing the new state. As the frontier expanded westward, new states were admitted steadily until 1912, when New Mexico and Arizona, the last contiguous continental territories, became states. The forty-eight states became fifty with the admission of Alaska and Hawaii in 1959—the only states of the union that do not border on another state.

Federal
Obligations
to the States

[19] Daniel J. Elazar, *American Federalism: A View from the States* (New York: Crowell, 1966), p. 164.
[20] See *Report of the National Advisory Commission on Civil Disorders* (New York: Bantam Books, 1968), pp. 95–97.
[21] As it turned out, Johnson chose not to run again, and Romney was eliminated early in the Republican race.

Article IV of the Constitution also requires the states to observe certain rules in their dealings with one another.

First, states are required to give "full faith and credit" to the laws, records, and court decisions of another state. In practice, this simply means that a judgment obtained in a state court in a civil (not a criminal) case must be recognized by the courts of another state. If, for example, a man in New York loses a lawsuit and skips to California to avoid paying the judgment, the courts there will enforce the New York decision without retrying the merits of the case.

Sometimes, particularly in divorce cases, states fail to meet their obligations to one another. A couple legally married in one state might not be legally married in another. In the famed *Williams v. North Carolina* cases [22] a man and a woman left their respective spouses in North Carolina, went to Nevada, got six-week divorces, and married each other. When they returned home, the state of North Carolina successfully prosecuted them for bigamy.

The Williams cases—the dispute went up to the Supreme Court twice —were decided during the Second World War. Despite the confusion of the divorce laws, the situation had improved somewhat since an earlier landmark case, *Haddock v. Haddock*.[23] In the words of one constitutional scholar: "The upshot [of that Supreme Court decision] was a situation in which a man and a woman, when both were in Connecticut, were divorced; when both were in New York, were married; and when the one was in Connecticut and the other in New York, the former was divorced and the latter married." [24] These examples are enough to suggest the complexity of the "full faith and credit" clause of the Constitution.

Second, the Constitution provides that the citizens of each state are entitled to "all privileges and immunities" of citizens in the other states. As interpreted by the Supreme Court, this hazy provision has come to mean that one state may not discriminate against citizens of another. But, in practice, states do discriminate against persons who are not legal residents. For example, a state university often charges higher tuition fees to out-of-state students. Usually, states charge nonresidents much higher fees for fishing and hunting licenses than they do residents.

Finally, the Constitution provides for extradition of fugitives who flee across state lines to escape justice. A state may request the governor of another state to return a fugitive, whether he is accused of committing a felony or a misdemeanor. Normally, the governor will comply with such a request. But in several instances, Northern governors refused to surrender blacks who had escaped from chain gangs or prisons in the South.

[22] *Williams v. North Carolina*, 317 U.S. 287 (1942), 325 U.S. 226 (1945).
[23] *Haddock v. Haddock*, 201 U.S. 562 (1906).
[24] Edward S. Corwin, et al., eds., *The Constitution of the United States of America, Analysis and Interpretation* (Washington, D.C.: U.S. Government Printing Office, 1964), p. 750.

One famous example is the Scottsboro case, which began in 1931 when nine black youths were pulled off a freight train in Alabama by a mob and accused of raping two white girls. There was considerable doubt that the crime had even been committed. The Supreme Court reversed death sentences imposed on eight of the defendants; one, Haywood Patterson was tried four times and ultimately sentenced to seventy-five years in prison. Three of the others drew life terms. In 1948, Patterson escaped from Kilby Prison in Alabama and fled north. In 1950, he was arrested in Detroit by the FBI at the request of the state of Alabama, which demanded his return. Governor G. Mennen Williams of Michigan refused to extradite him.[25]

The Constitution permits the states to make agreements with one another with the approval of Congress. These *interstate compacts* were of minor importance until the twentieth century, but the spread of metropolitan areas—and metropolitan problems—across state borders and the increasing complexity of modern life has brought new significance to the agreements.

Interstate Compacts

The Port of New York Authority was created by an interstate compact between New York and New Jersey and approved by Congress in 1921. The authority, powerful and quasi-independent, operates John F. Kennedy International Airport and La Guardia Airport in New York and Newark Airport in New Jersey. It also controls and runs the bridges and tunnels leading into Manhattan, and the world's largest bus terminal, near Times Square.

The Delaware River Basin Compact, the Interstate Oil Compact, the Crime Compact of 1934 (designed to improve parole supervision of ex-convicts), the Southern Regional Education Compact, and the Western Regional Education Compact, are other examples of interstate agreements. Air and water pollution, pest control, toll bridges, and transportation are items on which states have entered into agreements with one another, with varying degrees of success.

THE GROWTH OF STRONG NATIONAL GOVERNMENT

The late Senator Everett McKinley Dirksen of Illinois, a legislator noted for his Shakespearean delivery and dramatic flair, once predicted sadly that the way things were going, "The only people interested in state boundaries will be Rand McNally."[26]

---

[25] Patterson was later charged with stabbing a man, went to prison, and died there in 1953. The other Scottsboro prisoners were freed on parole by 1950.
[26] *New York Times*, August 8, 1965, Section IV, p. 2.

While this may be an exaggerated view of trends in the American federal system, Dirksen's remark reflected the fact that the national government *has* been gaining increased power. The formal structure of American government has changed very little since 1787, but the balance of power within the system has changed markedly.

The Supreme Court has played a vital role in the gradual expansion of the powers of the Federal Government. The decision of Chief Justice John Marshall in *McCulloch v. Maryland* in 1819, establishing the doctrine of implied powers, gave the Federal Government sanction to take giant steps beyond the literal language of the Constitution.

James W. McCulloch might otherwise not have gone down in American history. But as it happened he was cashier of the Baltimore branch of the National Bank of the United States, which had been established by Congress. The National Bank had failed to prevent a business panic and economic depression in 1819 and some of its branches were managed by what can only be termed crooks. As a result, several states, including Maryland, tried to force the banks out of their states. Maryland slapped an annual tax of $15,000 on the National Bank. McCulloch refused to pay, setting the stage for the great courtroom battle of the day. Daniel Webster argued for the bank, and Luther Martin, Attorney General of Maryland, for his state.

The first question answered by Marshall in his opinion for a unanimous court was the basic question of whether Congress had power to incorporate a bank. Marshall laid down a classic definition of national sovereignty and broad constitutional construction. "The government of the Union . . . is emphatically and truly a government of the people. In form and substance it emanates from them. Its powers are granted by them, and are to be exercised directly on them, and for their benefit."

Marshall conceded that the Constitution divided sovereignty between the states and the national government but said that "the government of the Union, though limited in its powers, is supreme within its sphere of action." Although the power to charter a bank was not among the enumerated powers of Congress in the Constitution, he said, it could be inferred from the "necessary and proper" clause. In short, Congress had "implied powers."

"Let the end be legitimate," Marshall wrote, "let it be within the scope of the Constitution, and all means which are appropriate, which are plainly adapted to that end, which are not prohibited, but consist with the letter and spirit of the Constitution, are constitutional." Congress, said Marshall, had the right to legislate with a "vast mass of incidental powers which must be involved in the Constitution, if that instrument be not a splendid bauble."

Chief Justice
John Marshall:
"Let the end
be legitimate . . ."

92

On the second question of whether Maryland had the right to tax the National Bank, Marshall ruled against the state, for "the power to tax involves the power to destroy." No state, he said, possessed that right because this implied that the Federal Government depended on the will of the states. Marshall ruled the Maryland law unconstitutional.

Thus, at a very early stage in the history of our nation, Marshall established the key concepts of implied powers, broad construction of the Constitution, and national supremacy. More than one hundred years were to pass before these powers were exercised fully, but the decision laid the basis for the future growth of national power.

A century ago, the Federal Government did not provide social security, medical insurance for 20,000,000 citizens, vast aid to public and private education, or billions of dollars in welfare payments. Nor did it have independent regulatory agencies to watch over various segments of the economy. Even in recent years, there was no Department of Health, Education, and Welfare, no Department of Transportation, and no Department of Housing and Urban Development at the Cabinet level.

The Rise of Big Government

As American society has grown more complex, as population has surged, the national government's managerial task has enlarged. People demand more services and government grows bigger in the process.

The power to tax and spend for the general welfare is a function of the national government that has expanded enormously in the twentieth century. The government's role in the regulation of interstate and foreign commerce has also vastly increased.

Much of the growth of big government and of federal social welfare programs took place during the New Deal in the 1930's. Although conservatives periodically attack these programs as "creeping socialism," they are so well established that no new administration in Washington is likely to attempt to abolish them. President Nixon, for example, proposed drastic reform of the welfare program, but he sought to enlarge the program, not to end it.

In the fiscal year 1970, the federal budget totaled almost $200 billion. Of that total, $79.4 was allocated for national defense—a staggering 40 percent of the total budget. An estimated $23.2 billion of the defense budget went to Southeast Asia, chiefly to support the war in Vietnam. Even excluding that portion, a defense budget of $56.2 billion would still have been the largest single item in the 1970 national budget. These figures illustrate how the nation's defense spending and war power have contributed to the rise of big government.

Big Government and Foreign Policy

Similarly, the responsibility of the Federal Government to conduct

93

foreign affairs in the nuclear age has increased the size of the national government. The State Department, the Central Intelligence Agency, the United States Information Agency, the National Security Agency, and related agencies have expanded along with the Pentagon.

THE IMPACT OF FEDERALISM
ON GOVERNMENT AND POLITICS

America's governmental institutions and its political system developed within a framework of federalism, and they reflect that fact. Federalism has also placed its stamp on a broad range of informal activities in American society, including the operations of many private groups.

Federalism
and Government

The nature of representation in Congress reflects the impact of federalism. Each state, no matter how small, has two senators who represent the constituents of their state. Members of the House represent districts within the states, but they also comprise an informal delegation from their states. Senators and representatives, when elected, must reside in the states they represent. In the event of a deadlock in the electoral college, the House of Representatives votes by state to select the President, with each state having one vote. Congress, in short, provides an institutional basis for federalism.

Federalism also affects the court system. State and local courts exist side by side with federal courts in the United States, and handle the vast majority of cases. But even the federal district courts and circuit courts are organized along geographic lines that take into account state boundaries. And, under the custom of "senatorial courtesy," before the President appoints a federal district or circuit court judge, he privately submits the name to the senator representing the home state of the nominee (when the state has a senator from the same party as the President). If the senator objects, the name is usually dropped.

Many powerful interest groups are in a sense federations of state associations and groups. This is true, for example, of the American Medical Association, the American Bar Association, and the American Federation of Labor-Congress of Industrial Organizations (AFL-CIO).

Federalism
and
American Politics

National political parties are organized along federal lines. The United States has no national party system as, say, the British do. Rather, there is a federation of fifty state parties, precariously held together by a national committee between presidential nominating conventions.

From the moment in 1787 when James Madison laid down his pen and the weary delegates to the Constitutional Convention departed from Philadelphia, there has existed in the United States a natural tension between the national government of the federal union and the still partially sovereign governments of the several states. Almost two centuries after the federal experiment began, the surprising fact is not that power has gradually shifted toward the national end of the balance, but that the states have succeeded in maintaining very considerable measures of independence and authority.

The persistent vitality of the states is derived not only from their roles in the functional work of government (which in recent years have fallen more and more under the influence of the federal bureaucracy) but also from their importance in the national political structure. In an age when armies, economies, religions, cultures, and almost everything else are organized on a national or international basis, the states remain the fundamental units of American politics.

—James Reichley, *States in Crisis.*

The governors' chairs in the fifty states are political prizes. As a result, there are fifty centers of political power in the states competing with the locus of national power in Washington.

To a party out of power nationally, the existence of state political machinery takes on special importance. By building up state parties and demonstrating leadership ability on the state level, the "out" party may consolidate its position and prepare for the next national election. Often a strong governor will emerge as a contender for the party nomination.

Although state political parties constitute basic political units in the United States, state political systems vary greatly. In some states there is lively competition between Democrats and Republicans. Other states are dominated by one party. The make-up of the electorate in the states may differ from that of the nation as a whole. For example, proportionately, there are fewer Democrats in Kansas and Nebraska than in the national electorate.

State governments also vary, in what they do and in the quality of their performance. How good are the schools in a state? Does the state have effective programs in the fields of health services, penology, welfare, law enforcement, pollution? As anyone who has driven across America knows, some states just look (and are) wealthier; they have better roads, for example. Some have adopted innovative social programs that have led the way for other states and the Federal Government.

Policy Outcomes in the States.   Since state governments do vary in quality, a question that arises is *whether the nature of a political system in a state affects the types of public policies that are adopted in the state.* In other words, does the politics of a state make a difference in the lives of the people of that state?

Political scientists have done a good deal of research on this question, and their answers have varied. Years ago, V. O. Key, Jr., suggested that states with active two-party competition were more likely to enact broad social welfare programs. As Key put it, "Politics generally comes down, over the long run, to a conflict between those who have and those who have less." [27] Where there were two active parties in a state, he theorized, those parties were likely to compete for votes by enacting programs for the state's "have-nots."

A study published in 1963, testing Key's theory, found that state taxing and spending for welfare programs did indeed vary with the level of competition between the state's political parties, but that socioeconomic factors (whether a state was rich or poor in per capita income), rather than political factors, seemed to account for most of these differences in state welfare spending. [28]

In 1966, Thomas Dye reported the results of his detailed study. He concluded that the economic development of a state shaped both its political system and its policies, and that differences in spending and taxing policies among the states were largely the result of varying socioeconomic levels rather than a direct result of differences in their politics. [29]

But a study published in 1970 concluded that if taxing and spending in a state were measured in terms of their *redistributive* impact—who gets what and who pays for it—then the politics of the state was considerably more important than its economics. Lower socioeconomic groups did fare better, for example, in states with certain political characteristics, such as higher levels of political participation. [30]

Thus, at least some researchers have concluded that politics *does* make a difference in the quality and type of government provided by the states. The fact that America has a federal system directly affects people's lives because it affects the performance of the states in which they live. Not only the structure of government, but the whole political process, is federalized.

FEDERALISM: 1970's STYLE

Aiding
the States
The *Budget of the United States Government, Fiscal Year 1970* is a blue-and-white covered volume approximately the girth and weight of the Washington, D.C. telephone book. It

[27] V. O. Key, Jr., *Southern Politics in State and Nation* (New York: Knopf, 1949), p. 307.
[28] Richard E. Dawson and James A. Robinson, "Inter-Party Competition, Economic Variables and Welfare Policies in the American States," *Journal of Politics*, Vol. 25 (1963), pp. 265–89.
[29] Thomas R. Dye, *Politics, Economics, and the Public: Policy Outcomes in the American States* (Chicago: Rand McNally, 1966), p. 293.
[30] Brian R. Fry and Richard F. Winters, "The Politics of Redistribution," *American Political Science Review*, Vol. 64 (June 1970), pp. 508–22.

contains 1,111 pages. To the nonexpert, it is a bewildering mass of statistics and gobbledygook, filled with phrases like "object classification" and "unobligated balance lapsing."

Buried in the budget's somewhat mysterious statistics are figures that add up to a substantial total of federal aid to state and local governments. For 1970, the amount was estimated at $25 *billion,* or 13 percent of the total federal budget.[31] The following figures show the sharp increase in federal aid to state and local governments since 1950:

1950: $ 2.5 billion
1960: $ 7.0 billion
1970: $25.0 billion

Any analysis of American government must take into account the huge sums of money flowing from people and corporations in the states to Washington in the form of taxes, and back again in the form of federal aid. It is here that federalism moves from the realm of theory into practical meaning in terms of dollars and cents.

Of the $25 billion budgeted by the Federal Government for state and local governments in 1970, 99 percent was in the form of "grants-in-aid." A federal grant-in-aid is "money paid or furnished to State or local

Shared Activities: Grants-in-Aid

WASHINGTON: COLORBLIND IN A BLIZZARD?

While a trivial matter, one example indicates the difficulty of keeping too many strings tied to the center nail, of seeking too much uniformity, or setting one pattern for all of the diverse nation. The state of Wyoming had a slight hassle with the U.S. Bureau of Public Roads over the color of paint to be used to mark the sides and center line of Wyoming highways. Wyoming had painted a solid yellow line to mark the shoulder of the road and an intermittent yellow line for the center. The Bureau of Public Roads said the lines must be standardized with the rest of the country, which meant white lines except in the no-passing stretches. After much haggling, Wyoming inevitably gave in, but with a parting comment: "Let them come out here and find one of their white lines during one of our blizzards." The highway engineers had found that in the blowing blizzards of Wyoming's winters drivers could see yellow lines, but not white ones. In this encounter they learned that yellow lines could not be seen from Washington.

—Terry Sanford, *Storm Over the States.*

[31] "Special Analysis O," in *Special Analyses, Budget of the United States, Fiscal Year 1970* (Washington, D.C.: U.S. Government Printing Office, 1969), p. 201.

Drawing by D. Fradon © 1969 The New Yorker Magazine, Inc.

"It's too bad you can't get federal matching funds, whatever they are."

governments to be used for specified purposes" [32] in ways spelled out by law or administrative regulations.

Normally, the states and local governments must meet *matching requirements*. That is, Washington requires the recipients to put up some of their own funds in order to get the federal money. On the average, state and local governments must raise $1 for every $2 received from the Federal Government.[33]

Communities and states that receive federal grants-in-aid match the federal money either in equal proportion, or under a formula that takes into account their ability to pay. This process of *equalization* is an important part of the overall program of federal aid. Poor states, in other words, put up relatively less matching money than rich states. In 1968, Connecticut, with an average per capita income of $4,256 ranked first in the nation.

[32] *Fiscal Balance in the American Federal System*, Vol. I, Advisory Commission on Intergovernmental Relations (Washington, D.C.: U.S. Government Printing Office, 1967), p. 137.
[33] "Special Analysis O," p. 209.

Mississippi, with an average per capita income of $2,081, ranked last.[34] In devising formulas for grants-in-aid, the Federal Government allows Mississippi to put up a smaller proportion of matching funds than Connecticut. The federal aid program thus has an equalizing and a redistributive effect among the states.

It is in the administration of grants-in-aid that the gears of national, state, and local governments mesh or collide. Federal fiscal aid is the primary means by which local, state, and federal governments interrelate. In dealing with such programs as slum clearance, education, or welfare services, mayors, governors, and lesser officials communicate with one another, and with the relevant officials in Washington. Because of the existence of these federally-financed programs, the lines of the federal system crisscross, linking various levels of government that must cope with common problems, from pollution to poverty. These relationships are characterized by both cooperation and conflict. For example, cities and states collaborate in a wide range of programs such as law enforcement and highway planning. But as a group, mayors tend to be distrustful of state governments; the mayors argue that the states are receiving too large a share of federal revenues at a time when the cities are desperate for funds.

How was the $25 billion in federal grants-in-aid spent in 1970? Budget Bureau estimates show that more than 90 percent of it was allocated to four categories: health and welfare, commerce and transportation, education and manpower, and community development and housing, in that order. Of the total, welfare payments and services to needy persons accounted for by far the biggest single item, amounting to $7.4 billion. (Figure 3-1 and Table 3-1 show where the money goes.)

Where the Money Goes

Increasingly, federal aid is going to the cities. In fiscal 1970, $16.7 billion, or more than two-thirds of the $25 billion total, was earmarked for urban areas. In 1964, only $5.6 billion, 55 percent of the total aid that year, was spent in urban areas.

As state and local authorities are quick to point out, state and local spending has been increasing at a faster rate than federal spending. For example, between 1948 and 1966 total federal spending rose from $36 billion to $143 billion, an increase of 301.8 percent. During the same period, state and local expenditures increased from $21 billion to $95 billion, an increase of 346.4 percent.[35] Yet, the Federal Government collects

Fiscal Headaches in the Federal System

---

[34] *Book of the States, 1970–71* (Lexington, Ky.: Council of State Governments, 1970), pp. 230–31.
[35] *Fiscal Balance in the American Federal System*, Vol. I, pp. 57–58.

FIGURE 3-1

Federal Aid to State and Local Governments, 1960–1970

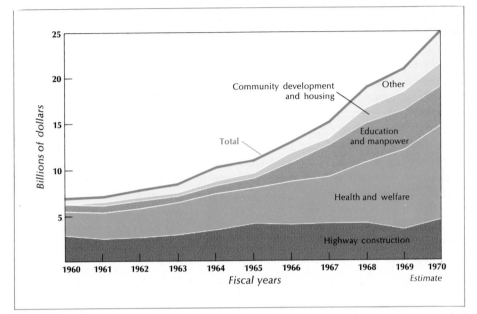

Source: "Special Analysis O," in *Special Analyses, Budget of the United States, Fiscal Year 1970* (Washington, D.C.: U.S. Government Printing Office, 1969), p. 202.

TABLE 3-1

Where the Money Goes: Federal Aid to State and Local Governments, 1970 (in billions of dollars)

Percent	Category	Total	Major items
40%	Health and welfare	10.1	Welfare and medical assistance
22	Commerce and transportation	5.6	Highways
18	Education and manpower	4.5	Aid to elementary and secondary education
11	Community development and housing	2.7	Urban renewal, Model Cities, Poverty Program, low-rent housing
7	Agriculture and natural resources	1.6	Farm surplus and water pollution control
2	Other	.5	
Total 100%		$25.0 billion	

Source: Based on "Special Analysis O," in *Special Analyses, Budget of the United States, Fiscal Year 1970.* Figures are rounded.

64 percent of all revenues in the United States, while state governments collect only 19 percent and local governments 17 percent. What is more, Washington collects 93 percent of the most important "growth" tax—the income tax. Revenues from income taxes directly reflect economic growth, providing the Federal Government with increased tax receipts in an expanding economy. By contrast, local governments rely mainly on real estate taxes, and state governments on sales taxes; both sources of revenue tend to grow less rapidly than the economy as a whole.

The states have been criticized for failing to tap the financial resources available to them. A report released in 1969 noted that fifteen states collected no income tax at all. "The personal income tax represents the last under-utilized major revenue source for many states," the study concluded. "About one-third of the states, including some in the most industrialized high-income sections of the country, do not tax personal incomes at all and one-third tax them at relatively low effective rates." [36]

THE FUTURE OF FEDERALISM

In 1967, the Advisory Commission on Intergovernmental Relations estimated there were 379 different grants-in-aid programs.[37] A Republican congressman, Representative William V. Roth, Jr., of Delaware, conducted his own survey in 1968 and concluded there were 1,091 grant-in-aid programs. The fact is, said Congressman Roth, "no one, anywhere, knows exactly how many federal programs there are." [38]

Efforts at Reform

Congress responded in 1968 to widespread criticism of the grants-in-aid program by passing the Intergovernmental Cooperation Act. Sponsored by Senator Edmund S. Muskie of Maine, it was designed to simplify grant-in-aid procedures. The bill as passed and signed into law, however, omitted provisions to consolidate related programs and thereby reduce the proliferation of federal grants.

In its report released in 1968, the Advisory Commission on Intergovernmental Relations called on the Federal Government to consolidate grants-in-aid, and make "block grants." [39] Block grants are broad, general grants designed to give state and local governments greater flexibility in meeting needs in functional areas. A grant-in-aid must be used

Block Grants

[36] *State and Local Finances, Significant Features, 1966 to 1969*, Advisory Commission on Intergovernmental Relations (Washington, D.C.: U.S. Government Printing Office, 1968), p. 101-1. In 1970, thirteen states had no income tax.
[37] *Fiscal Balance in the American Federal System*, Vol. I, p. 151.
[38] *Congressional Quarterly, Weekly Report*, August 16, 1968, p. 2198.
[39] *Fiscal Balance in the American Governmental System*, Vol. I, p. xxi.

for a specified purpose, but the recipient of a block grant has greater discretion in how the money is put to use. Although grants-in-aid remain the principal form of federal aid, block grants have been authorized in several instances by Congress, in the omnibus Crime Control and Safe Streets Act of 1968, for example.

Revenue
Sharing

When President Nixon proposed in 1969 that the Federal Government turn a share of its revenues back to the states "without Federal strings," he was endorsing a concept that had incubated for almost a decade. In June 1960, economist Walter W. Heller proposed the basic idea in a speech; later as a top economic adviser in the Kennedy and Johnson administrations, he restated his proposals. President Nixon embraced the plan, with some changes.

In a 1969 message to Congress, Nixon contended that Americans no longer supported continued expansion of the Federal Government. "No previous half decade had witnessed domestic Federal spending on such a scale," he said. "Yet, despite the enormous Federal commitment in new men, new ideas and new dollars from Washington, it was during this very period in our history that the problems of the cities deepened rapidly into crises." People, the President argued, had lost faith in the Federal Government and "are turning away from the central Government to their local and state governments to deal with their local and state problems." He added: "This proposal [revenue sharing] marks a turning point in Federal-state relations, the beginning of decentralization of governmental power, the restoration of a rightful balance between the state capitals and the national capital." [40]

As proposed by President Nixon, the Federal Government would turn tax revenues back to the states, starting at a level of $500 million the first year but rising to an annual level of $5 billion after five years. A "pass through" formula would guarantee that the states would have to pass on a portion of the money to the cities. In 1971, Nixon proposed an expanded plan of revenue sharing and broad grants totaling $16 billion a year.

The Nixon administration faced formidable obstacles in pushing the plan—the keystone of the President's "new federalism"—through Congress. Representative Wilbur Mills, Arkansas Democrat and powerful chairman of the House Ways and Means Committee, expressed reluctance to give up a share of federal taxing power. Organized labor was opposed to placing money in the hands of traditionally conservative state legislatures. And, in any event, unless the Federal Government had a surplus of tax revenues, there would be little money to share with the states and cities.

[40] *New York Times*, August 14, 1969, p. 24.

In the 1970's the grim prospect faced by many American cities was that they might become an inner core of ghetto slums and glass and concrete office buildings, surrounded by a belt of suburban bedrooms, plagued by crime, traffic jams, smog, power failures and lack of money to provide essential services. In short, a powderkeg of tension and a monument to the frustrations of urban living.

Federalism and the Cities

In a 1965 message to Congress, President Johnson declared: "In the remainder of this century—in less than 40 years—urban population will double, city land will double and we will have to build in our cities as much as all that we have built since the first colonist arrived on these shores. It is as if we had 40 years to rebuild the entire urban United States." [41]

It is a startling concept. Put another way, in 1964, America was a nation of a little over 190,000,000 Americans. By 1980, according to one government estimate, more than 190,000,000 people will be living in metropolitan areas alone.[42]

The vast problems of urban areas provide the greatest challenge yet

THE FEDERAL BULLDOZER

The federal urban-renewal program was aimed at clearing slums and building new housing—a program that grew out of the conviction that the way to improve the lives of poor people was to build new homes for them. The concept of asking the people living in the neighborhoods to be renewed how they felt about it was never really explored. It was simply assumed that those who had the power to plan and build knew what their "clients" wanted. . . . because of strict federal controls, the biases of those in power governed much of the program. Design was considered irrelevant; poor and middle-income people, the attitude was, should be grateful for any housing built. Thus, in many units there were no doors on closets, no play areas for children except for sterile playgrounds, and, of course, no places for people to gather, such as taverns, since that would have in effect been a federal endorsement of drinking liquor. The result was that the cities of America were afflicted with what one observer called "projectitis"—helter-skelter highrise apartments; little bits of ground space and large areas of asphalt divided by chain-link fencing, cheerless architecture. . . . They all look the same.

—John Lindsay, The City.

[41] President Johnson's message on housing and urban development, *1965 Congressional Quarterly Almanac* (Congressional Quarterly, Inc., 1966), p. 1400.
[42] *Metropolitan America: Challenge to Federalism*, Advisory Commission on Intergovernmental Relations (Washington, D.C.: U.S. Government Printing Office, 1966), p. 16.

to the American federal system. Some efforts have been made at new approaches. For example, increasing attention is being paid to solving problems on a metropolitan-area-wide basis. Many communities, especially in urban areas, have ignored traditional political jurisdictional lines to pool their efforts in attacking common problems (such as pollution) that respect no political boundaries, and in planning to take advantage of federal grants. Bills enacted by Congress such as the Urban Mass Transportation Act of 1970 represent federal legislation designed to assist and encourage area-wide solution to urban problems. New kinds of governmental structures may emerge along with new forms of revenue-sharing. For example, the Nixon administration established standard regional boundaries for five key federal agencies—the departments of Health, Education, and Welfare, Housing and Urban Development, and Labor, and the Office of Economic Opportunity and the Small Business Administration. In the past, each of these agencies divided the country into geographic regions that varied with each agency, but now all five have ten common regions, each with the same headquarters city. By September 1970, mayors and governors were able to talk with federal regional headquarters officials for all five agencies in a single trip to one city.

Yet serious dislocations continue to plague the federal system. Many critics of the federal structure question whether states are willing or able to meet their responsibilities. By contrast, defenders of the states, such as Governor Nelson Rockefeller of New York, have noted that most of the successful programs of the New Deal "had been anticipated, by experiment and practice, on the state level or by private institutions. The history of the years before 1932 tells this story plainly. Time and again, states like Massachusetts, Wisconsin, or New York acted on their own initiative to protect the health, safety, and welfare of the individual." [43]

The states, caught in a fiscal squeeze, may find it difficult to play such an innovative role today. The nation's cities are in financial difficulty at the very time that more city services are being demanded by the inner-city residents who are least able to pay for them. As it entered the decade of the seventies the federal system was moving ponderously, if at all, to reform its procedures for channeling tax revenues to the states and localities.

The Advisory Commission on Intergovernmental Relations has warned:

> America's federal system is on trial as never before in this century of crisis and change.[44]

[43] Nelson A. Rockefeller, *The Future of Federalism* (Cambridge, Mass.: Harvard University Press, 1962), p. 15.
[44] *Ninth Annual Report*, Advisory Commission on Intergovernmental Relations (Washington, D.C.: U.S. Government Printing Office, 1968), p. 13.

The crucial question of the day is whether the American federal system can survive the crisis that eddies and boils in the great cities of the nation or if only a centralized and unitary governmental system will be equal to the task.[45]

Thus, the problems that confront America in the 1970's raise the fundamental question of whether a federal system born in compromise almost two centuries ago can adapt itself to the needs of a technological, urban society in an age of onrushing change.

[45] *Urban America and the Federal System: Commission Findings and Proposals* (Washington, D.C.: U.S. Government Printing Office, 1969), p. 1.

SUGGESTED READING

Anderson, William. *The Nation and the States: Rivals or Partners?* (University of Minnesota Press, 1955). A thoughtful general survey of both the historical development and the more recent workings of America's federal system. The author served on the U.S. Commission on Intergovernmental Relations.

Elazar, Daniel J. *American Federalism: A View from the States* * (Crowell, 1966). A good general treatment of American federalism. The book emphasizes some of the problems and areas of controversy in contemporary intergovernmental relationships, and traces the historical roots of cooperation and shared functions among the various layers of government in the federal system.

Goldwin, Robert A., ed. *A Nation of States: Essays on the American Federal System* * (Rand McNally, 1963). A useful series of essays on various aspects of federalism written by specialists in the field.

Grodzins, Morton. *The American System* (Rand McNally, 1966). A comprehensive analysis of American federalism by a leading authority on the subject.

Macmahon, Arthur W., ed. *Federalism: Mature and Emergent* (Doubleday, 1955). A valuable series of essays on the federal system in the United States. A perceptive essay by David B. Truman treats the impact of American federalism on the dynamics of American politics.

Riker, William T. *Federalism: Origin, Operation, and Significance* (Little, Brown, 1964). Paperback. A historical and comparative analysis of federalism. Riker examines with great clarity the conditions that give rise to federalism and maintain it. He is sharply critical of certain aspects of American federalism, and argues that it has permitted the oppression of blacks.

Rockefeller, Nelson A. *The Future of Federalism* * (Harvard University Press, 1962). A series of lectures in book form in which the governor of New York State examines the federal system. Rockefeller stresses the creative role some states have played in developing and administering programs that later served as a model for federal programs.

Wheare, K. C. *Federal Government*, 4th edition (Oxford University Press 1964). A perceptive comparative analysis of federal governmental systems. Based primarily on a comprehensive examination of the workings of federalism in Australia, Canada, Switzerland, and the United States.

Wildavsky, Aaron, ed. *American Federalism in Perspective* (Little, Brown, 1967). Paperback. A useful general introduction to the subject. Includes essays by a number of scholars who have specialized in various aspects of the American federal system.

* Available in paperback edition

4

Civil Liberties

and Citizenship

A CASE OF FREE SPEECH

One day shortly before Christmas in 1965, Mary Beth Tinker, a dark-haired girl of thirteen, attended her junior high school class in Des Moines, Iowa, wearing a black armband. She mourned no personal loss but was protesting United States participation in the war in Vietnam. Several other students wore similar armbands to school.

The school authorities sent the students home and temporarily suspended them. Mary Beth Tinker took her case to court. Four years later, the Supreme Court of the United States ruled in the *Tinker* case.[1] The question, the Court began, was one of free speech. The school authorities claimed that they acted to avoid possible trouble, the Court noted.

> But in our system . . . apprehension of disturbance is not enough to overcome the right to freedom of expression. . . . Any word spoken, in class, in the lunchroom or on the campus, that deviates from the views of another

[1] *Tinker v. Des Moines School District et al.*, 393 U.S. 503 (1969).

person, may start an argument or cause a disturbance. But our Constitution says we must take this risk . . . and our history says that it is this sort of hazardous freedom—this kind of openness—that is the basis of our national strength. . . .

In our system, state-operated schools may not be enclaves of totalitarianism. School officials do not possess absolute authority over their students. Students in school as well as out of school are "persons" under our Constitution. . . . The Constitution says that Congress (and the States) may not abridge the right to free speech. This provision means what it says.

In winning the fight for her constitutional rights, Mary Beth Tinker made a much broader point for all students in America. For the Court concluded: "It can hardly be argued that either students or teachers shed their constitutional rights to freedom of speech or expression at the schoolhouse gate."

The first ten amendments to the Constitution comprise the Bill of Rights. The First Amendment provides that Congress shall make no law "abridging the freedom of speech." The Supreme Court has interpreted this to mean that speech cannot be abridged by state or lesser authorities, either.

Commencement protest at Brandeis University, June 1969

The Supreme Court does not operate in a vacuum, however. Its nine justices are human beings and actors in the drama of their time. As former Chief Justice Earl Warren once declared, "our judges are not monks or scientists, but participants in the living stream of our national life." [2] As it happened, the Court ruled in the *Tinker* case in the midst of widespread student protests on the nation's campuses. In this climate, many Americans might have disagreed with the right of public school students to wear anti-war armbands; in fact two justices of the Supreme Court did disagree. [3]

In a sharp dissent, Justice Hugo Black declared that after the Court's ruling, "students . . . will be ready, able, and willing to defy their teachers on practically all orders. This is the more unfortunate for the schools since groups of students all over the land are already running loose, conducting break-ins, sit-ins, lie-ins, and smash-ins." Students, Black declared, "will soon believe it is their right to control the schools. . . . I dissent."

The majority decision of the Supreme Court—not Black's dissent—became the law of the land. As always, the Court had judged a particular case. It is the great task of the Court to apply the Constitution and the Bill of Rights to specific disputes, even though its decisions have much wider application for society.

The *Tinker* case indicated that the Supreme Court, at least as of 1969, would uphold peaceful forms of protest and dissent. It seemed unlikely, however, that the Court would rule that violent actions or the seizure of buildings constituted free speech within the meaning of the First Amendment.

Evidence of this came early in 1969 when the Supreme Court declined to review the expulsion of ten students from Bluefield State College, West Virginia, for "riotous" behavior. [4] "The petitioners," the Court said, "were suspended from college *not* for expressing their opinions on a matter of substance, but for violent and destructive interference with the rights of others. . . . [They] engaged in an aggressive and violent demonstration, and not in peaceful, nondisruptive expression, such as was involved in *Tinker*." The language appeared to be an attempt to draw a clear line between peaceful and violent protest on the campus.

The Supreme Court also attempted to distinguish between speech and

---

[2] Earl Warren, "The Law and the Future," *Fortune*, November 1955, p. 107. Evidence of the truth of Warren's view was provided in May 1969 when Justice Abe Fortas, who wrote the Court's opinion in the *Tinker* case, resigned under fire amidst criticism of his outside financial dealings.

[3] Justice Hugo Black and Justice John Harlan. Public opinion polls showed that a majority of Americans disagreed with major goals of student demonstrators. For example, a Gallup Poll published in March 1969, less than a month after the decision on the *Tinker* case, indicated that only 25 percent of the general public felt students should have a greater say in the running of colleges; 70 percent said they should not and 5 percent had no opinion.

[4] *Barker v. Hardway*, 394 U.S. 905 (1969).

HAIR AND THE COURTS: NO

On September 7, 1966, Phillip Ferrell and Stephen Webb began the new school year at their Dallas high school by walking into the principal's office. Both students had let their hair grow long in order to perform in their rock and roll band, Sounds Unlimited. The principal told them to cut their hair. In the past, male students with long hair had been harassed by other students, obscene language had been used against them, and in one case, a fist fight had broken out. The two students refused to cut their hair and were not permitted to enroll in school. The boys and their parents went into federal district court, charging that their constitutional rights had been violated. They lost there, and they also lost their appeal in the circuit court which ruled: "The interest of the state in maintaining an effective and efficient school system is of paramount importance." The United States Supreme Court refused to consider the case. The lower court decision stood. Hair lost.

—Ferrell v. Dallas Independent School District, 392 F.2d 697 (1968).

HAIR AND THE COURTS: YES

In September, 1968, Thomas Breen and James Anton, students at a high school in Williams Bay, Wisconsin, were expelled for violating a ruled that read: "Hair should be washed, combed and worn so it does not hang below the collar line in the back, over the ears on the side and must be above the eyebrows. Boys should be clean shaven, long side-burns are out."

The students brought suit in federal district court and lost. But in their appeal to the 7th Circuit Court of Appeals, they won. The court held that the local board of education had no constitutional right to force students to cut their hair or face expulsion. It ruled that no court would uphold a law regulating the length of adults' hair, or the length of hair of adults taking night school courses, or the hair length of seventeen-year-olds who worked. Students, the court concluded, had the same right of free expression. In 1970, the United States Supreme Court declined to consider the case. Hair won.

—Breen v. Kahl, 296 F. Supp. 702 (1969).

action in the principal "draft-card burning" case.[5] David P. O'Brien had burned his draft card on the steps of a Boston courthouse in 1966 to protest the war in Vietnam. He was convicted under the 1965 law prohibiting such acts and sentenced to six years.[6] The Circuit Court of Appeals reversed his conviction as a violation of the First Amendment. In 1968, however, the Supreme Court upheld the conviction and the 1965 act and rejected David O'Brien's contention that the burning of his card was "symbolic speech" protected by the Constitution. Chief Justice Warren declared: "We cannot accept the view than an apparently limitless variety of conduct can be labeled 'speech.' "

[5] *United States v. O'Brien,* 391 U.S. 367 (1968).
[6] In November 1968, the six-year jail term was revoked and O'Brien was sentenced to three years probation with the condition that two years be spent working at Massachusetts General Hospital.

As these cases show, freedom of speech is a relative term, applied differently by the Supreme Court in different cases at different times. In *Tinker*, the Court agreed that wearing an antiwar armband in a public school was a form of expression protected by the free speech clause of the First Amendment. In *O'Brien*, it ruled that burning a draft card in violation of federal law was not a symbolic act protected by the First Amendment.

In February 1970, a federal jury in Chicago convicted five of the "Chicago Seven," the leaders of the protest demonstrations held during the Democratic National Convention. They were convicted of having crossed state lines with *"intent"* to incite a riot. (All seven defendants were acquitted of *"conspiracy"* to incite a riot.) Judge Julius J. Hoffman gave each of the five men, David Dellinger, Rennie Davis, Thomas Hayden, Abbie Hoffman, and Jerry Rubin, the maximum prison sentence of five years, and fined them $5,000 each. In addition, Hoffman imposed contempt sentences upon the lawyers for the defense and all the defendants, which totaled more than seventeen years. Did the leaders of the Chicago demonstrations, convicted in a federal court under a law passed by Congress, enjoy freedom of speech under the Constitution? Did the statute violate the First Amendment? Did the demonstrators clubbed by Mayor Daley's police enjoy the right of free speech? Were they attempting to exercise the right of peaceful assembly? Although the Supreme Court did not rule on the Chicago case in 1970, the trial and the law upon which it was based raised fundamental questions about the meaning of free speech in the United States.

In deciding cases under the Bill of Rights, the Supreme Court has the difficult task of attempting to balance the rights of the individual against those of society as a whole. The questions raised in this process are many and complex. Should freedom of expression be an absolute right under the First Amendment? What if free speech conflicts with the rights of others? What does the law say now about government wiretapping and "bugging"? What are the legal rights of student demonstrators? Can police enter your home or residence without a search warrant? Is it against the law to be a member of the Communist party? What are your rights if you are arrested? Will the federal Bill of Rights be of any help to you if you are arrested by state or local police? These are some of the questions we will explore in this chapter.

INDIVIDUAL FREEDOM AND SOCIETY

The various cases we have discussed are some examples of the role of the Supreme Court, the meaning of the Bill of Rights, and the practical application of the Constitution today.

Beyond that, the decisions illustrate the constant tension between liberty and order in a free society.

Freedom is not absolute, for as Supreme Court Justice Oliver Wendell Holmes once said, "the right to swing my fist ends where the other man's nose begins." But the proper balance in a democracy between the rights of one individual and the rights of society as a whole can never be resolved to everyone's satisfaction.

The rights of the individual should not always be viewed as competing with those of the community; in a free society, the fullest freedom of expression for the individual may also serve the interests of society as a whole. As John F. Kennedy observed, "the rights of every man are diminished when the rights of one man are threatened." [7]

The nineteenth-century British philosopher, John Stuart Mill, advanced the classic argument for diversity of opinion in his treatise, *On Liberty:* "Though the silenced opinion be an error, it may, and very com-

LIBERTY AND JUSTICE FOR ALL?

"The way they say it, it's as if there is liberty and justice, but there isn't."

Twelve-year-old Mary Frain sitting pensively on a wooden rocker in her Jamaica, Queens, home, gave this explanation yesterday as one of her reasons for objecting to the daily Pledge of Allegiance to the flag in school.

The crank calls and angry letters have almost disappeared from the life of the introverted seventh grader who, with a classmate, Susan Keller, won a Federal Court decision on Dec. 10 permitting students in city schools to remain in their seats during the flag-saluting ceremony.

Because of the pressure, Susan Keller soon transferred to another school. But Mary still refuses to stand in the morning when most of the children in her honors class at Junior High School 217 at 85th Avenue and 148th Street stand to recite the pledge.

At home, following a quick lunch, the youngster discussed the impact of the court case on her life.

"Like when we walked along the halls, the kids used to call us commies. We had phone calls. One was obscene. Some just laughed or breathed when you picked it up. But it's dying down now. . . ."

Mary persisted, she said, because of strong objections to the wording of the pledge.

"Liberty and justice for all?" she said. "That's not true . . . for the blacks and poor whites. The poor have to live in cold miserable places. And it's obvious that blacks are oppressed."

The girl would compromise her position if the pledge were rephrased to be spoken as a "goal." "Like if when you say it you're making a vow to make it liberty and justice for all" she explained.

—*New York Times,* January 31, 1970.

[7] John F. Kennedy, "Radio and Television Report to the American People on Civil Rights," June 11, 1963, in *Public Papers of the Presidents, John F. Kennedy, 1963* (Washington, D.C.: U.S. Government Printing Office, 1964), p. 468.

monly does, contain a portion of truth; and since the general or prevailing opinion on any subject is rarely or never the whole truth, it is only by the collision of adverse opinions that the remainder of the truth has any chance of being supplied." [8]

In American society, the Supreme Court is the mechanism called upon to resolve conflicts between liberty and order, between the rights of the individual and the rights of the many. In doing so, the Court operates within the framework of what James Monroe called that "polar star, and great support of American liberty," the Bill of Rights.

THE BILL OF RIGHTS

The supporters of the Constitution, it will be recalled, promised to pass a Bill of Rights in part so that they might win the struggle over ratification. Madison wrote to Jefferson in Paris that the critics of the Constitution believed the framers "had entered into a conspiracy against the liberties of the people at large, in order to erect an aristocracy for the rich, the wellborn, and the men of Education." [9]

The Constitution might have been ratified without a promise of a Bill of Rights, but in New York, Massachusetts, and particularly in Virginia, the contest focused on this great issue. When the First Congress met in 1789, James Madison successfully led the battle to pass the Bill of Rights.

Alpheus Mason, a leading constitutional scholar, has observed that the fundamental rights of a free society gained "no greater moral sanctity" by being written into the Constitution, "but individuals could thereafter look to courts for their protection. Rights formerly natural became civil." [10]

"Congress shall make no law respecting an establishment of religion, or prohibiting the free exercise thereof; or abridging the freedom of speech, or of the press; or the right of the people peaceably to assemble, and to petition the Government for a redress of grievances."

Freedom of Speech

These forty-five words are the First Amendment of the Constitution. Along with "due process of law" and other constitutional protections, these words set forth basic American freedoms. As the late Justice Benjamin N. Cardozo once wrote, freedom of thought and of speech is "the matrix, the indispensable condition, of nearly every other form of freedom." [11]

[8] John Stuart Mill, *On Liberty* (New York: Appleton-Century-Crofts, 1947), p. 52.
[9] In Alpheus T. Mason, *The Supreme Court: Palladium of Freedom* (Ann Arbor, Mich.: University of Michigan Press, 1962), p. 46.
[10] *Ibid.*, p. 58.
[11] *Palko v. Connecticut*, 302 U.S. 319 (1937).

Americans like to say to each other: "It's a free country, isn't it?" In fact, the courts have frequently placed limits on speech. In the process, the courts have attempted to define the point at which speech blends into action.

Several types of speech do not enjoy constitutional immunity from government regulation. These include fraudulent advertising, obscenity (which the courts have had vast difficulty in defining), libel, and, in some cases, street oratory. The Supreme Court, for example, has ruled that police are justified in arresting a sidewalk speaker if he is too effective in stirring his audience.[12] Three decades earlier, Supreme Court Justice Oliver Wendell Holmes, Jr., had established the classic "clear and present danger" test to define the point at which speech loses the protection of the First Amendment:

> The character of every act depends upon the circumstances in which it is done. . . . The most stringent protection of free speech would not protect a man in falsely shouting fire in a theater and causing a panic. . . . The question in every case is whether the words used are used in such circumstances and are of such a nature as to create a clear and present danger that they will bring about the substantive evils that Congress has a right to prevent.[13]

Holmes, speaking for a unanimous court, upheld the federal conviction of Charles T. Schenck, General Secretary of the Socialist Party, who had circulated leaflets urging young men to resist the draft in the First World War.

Later, in the *Gitlow* case, the Court went even further, ruling that some speech could be prohibited if it merely created a "dangerous tendency." [14] The Court's free speech yardstick shifted again during the New Deal and the Second World War, then appeared to swing back to the "clear and present danger" test in the 1950's. Thus, even so fundamental a right as free speech, while broadly protected by the Constitution, has been limited by the Supreme Court according to the circumstances and the times.

Preferred Freedoms and the Balancing Test. Different philosophies, often identified with particular justices, have emerged as the Supreme Court has struggled with problems of freedom of expression.

For example, Justices Hugo Black and William Douglas established themselves as advocates of the "absolute" position. Black argued that "there *are* 'absolutes' in our Bill of Rights" [15] that cannot be diluted by

[12] *Feiner v. New York*, 340 U.S. 315 (1951).
[13] *Schenck v. United States*, 249 U.S. 47 (1919).
[14] *Gitlow v. New York*, 268 U.S. 652 (1925).
[15] Hugo L. Black, "The Bill of Rights," *New York University Law Review*, Vol. 35 (April 1960), p. 867.

HOW MUCH FREE SPEECH? TWO OPPOSING VIEWS:

Whatever theoretical merit there may be to the argument that there is a "right" to rebellion against dictatorial governments is without force where the existing structure of the government provides for peaceful and orderly change. . . .

Overthrow of the Government by force and violence is certainly a substantial enough interest for the Government to limit speech. Indeed, this is the ultimate value of any society, for if a society cannot protect its very structure from armed internal attack, it must follow that no subordinate value can be protected.

—Chief Justice Fred M. Vinson, in *Dennis v. United States* (1951), upholding conviction of eleven leaders of the Communist party under the Smith Act.

Free speech has occupied an exalted position because of the high service it has given our society. Its protection is essential to the very existence of democracy. The airing of ideas releases pressures which otherwise might become destructive. When ideas compete in the market for acceptance, full and free discussion exposes the false and they gain few adherents.

. . . Some nations less resilient than the United States, where illiteracy is high and where democratic traditions are only budding, might have to take drastic steps and jail these men for merely speaking their creed. But in America they are miserable merchants of unwanted ideas; their wares remain unsold.

—Justice William O. Douglas, dissenting in *Dennis v. United States.*

judicial decisions. He maintained, for instance, that obscenity and libel are forms of speech and therefore cannot be constitutionally limited. Others on the Court took the position that the great rights of the First Amendment must be "balanced" against the competing needs of the community to preserve order, and to preserve itself. This view was championed by Justice Felix Frankfurter.

But, in performing this delicate balancing act, some members of the Court have argued that the basic freedoms should take precedence over other needs. Thus, Justice Harlan Fiske Stone argued that the Constitution had placed freedom of speech and religion "in a preferred position." [16]

Despite these mixed views, the Supreme Court, while reluctant to narrow the scope of basic liberties, has generally not hesitated to balance such freedoms against other constitutional requirements.

Closely tied to free speech, and protected as well by the First Amendment, is freedom of the press. The strong tradition of a free press in the United States rests on the principle, rooted in English common law, that in a democracy there must be no governmental "prior restraint" upon publications.

In a landmark decision, the Supreme Court ruled in 1931 that a Minneapolis weekly, the *Saturday Press,* could not be shut down because of

Freedom of the Press

[16] *United States v. Carolene Products Co.,* 304 U.S. 144 (1938).

articles attacking city officials as "corrupt" and "grafters." [17] The Court held that even though freedom of the press might be abused by "purveyors of scandal," the press was immune from "previous restraint."

In recent years, however, the Court has shown increasing concern over pretrial and courtroom publicity that may prejudice the fair trial of a defendant in a criminal case. The issue brings into direct conflict two basic principles of the Bill of Rights—the right of an accused person to a fair trial and the right of freedom of the press.

In several modern instances, the use of television has complicated the problem of a fair trial. In two cases, the Supreme Court struck down convictions in which the defendants' televised confessions of murder were presumed to have influenced the jury.[18]

In 1966, the Supreme Court reversed the conviction of Dr. Samuel H. Sheppard, a Cleveland, Ohio, osteopath found guilty in 1954 of bludgeoning his wife to death. The case had everything—sex, violence, tales of adultery, and a respectable defendant. During the trial, the press had a field day; when the jury visited the scene of the crime at Dr. Sheppard's home, reporters hovered overhead in a helicopter. The Supreme Court reversed the conviction because of the publicity that had surrounded the trial giving it the "atmosphere of a 'Roman holiday' for the news media." [19] The state of Ohio then retried Sheppard and a jury acquitted him in November 1966.

A year earlier, the Supreme Court upset the conviction of Billie Sol Estes, a Texas financial promoter, on a charge of swindling, partly because the judge had permitted live television coverage in the courtroom.[20]

Similar excessive courtroom publicity influenced the 1966 decision of the Texas Court of Criminal Appeals to reverse the conviction of Jack Ruby for the murder of Lee Harvey Oswald, the accused assassin of President Kennedy. Before Ruby could be retried, he died of illness in January 1967.

One solution to the problem of excessive publicity lies in increased voluntary restraint by police, lawyers, and prosecutors in commenting on the past criminal records of defendants and other aspects of pending cases.

Radio and television do not enjoy as much freedom as other segments of the press, because, unlike newspapers, they are licensed by the Federal Communications Commission. The FCC does not directly regulate news broadcasts, but stations are required to observe general standards of "fairness" in presenting community issues and to serve the public interest. Otherwise the FCC may revoke their licenses, although the commission, in the past, has seldom exercised its power to do so. Potentially, the Federal Gov-

[17] Near v. Minnesota, 283 U.S. 697 (1931).
[18] Irvin v. Dowd, 366 U.S. 717 (1961); Rideau v. Louisiana, 373 U.S. 723 (1963).
[19] Sheppard v. Maxwell, 384 U.S. 333 (1966).
[20] Estes v. Texas, 381 U.S. 532 (1965).

ernment has powerful leverage over the operations of the broadcasting industry.

In 1969, the Supreme Court specifically rejected the claim of the industry that the free-speech, free-press provisions of the First Amendment protected it from government regulation of programs. The Court did so in upholding the FCC's "fairness doctrine," which requires radio and television broadcasters to present both sides of important public issues. Justice Byron White ruled for the Court that "it is the right of viewers and listeners, not the right of the broadcasters, which is paramount"; a licensed broadcaster has no constitutional right under the First Amendment to "monopolize a radio frequency to the exclusion of his fellow citizens." [21]

Freedom of Information.   Freedom of the press would mean little if the news media were unable to obtain information from official agencies of government. Beginning in 1955, Congressman John E. Moss, a California Democrat, pushed for legislation to force the Federal Government to make more information available to the press and public. As a result, the "Freedom of Information Act" was signed into law by President Johnson in 1966. It requires federal agencies to make information available to newsmen and citizens unless it falls into one of several confidential categories. Exempted from disclosure, for example, are national security information, personnel files, investigatory records, and the "internal" documents of an agency. The law provides that individuals can go into federal district court to force compliance by the government.

Another complex question is whether news reporters should be compelled to testify about information they possess. The courts have generally held that the First Amendment's protection of freedom of the press does not exempt newsmen from testifying in criminal cases, but some reporters have gone to jail rather than comply. The press has contended that news sources will dry up if people come to believe that confidential information, and the identity of sources, will be disclosed in open court; the members of the press feel, therefore, that compelling newsmen to give evidence does abridge their First Amendment rights. The issue is particularly pertinent today because law enforcement agencies have sought to obtain information about the Black Panthers and other militant groups by subpoenaing reporters.

In 1969, movie theaters in American cities were packing in the crowds with a Swedish film called *I Am Curious (Yellow)*. The film, about two young lovers, included various scenes of sexual intercourse.

Obscenity

[21] *Red Lion Broadcasting Co., Inc. v. Federal Communications Commission,* 395 U.S. 367 (1969).

At about the same time, Broadway audiences were attending the musical *Hair* in which nude male and female actors appeared. At the top of the best-seller list was Philip Roth's novel *Portnoy's Complaint*, which examined the previously taboo subject of masturbation and described a sex orgy. Movie houses across America were showing the film, *The Killing of Sister George*, which dealt graphically with the subject of lesbianism.

All of this seemed a far cry from only a few years earlier, when the books of Edgar Rice Burroughs were almost removed from a Downey, California, elementary school library because of persistent reports that Tarzan and Jane were unmarried. (When it was established that the jungle king and his mate were in fact man and wife the books were left on the shelves.)

Changing standards of public morality have resulted in freer acceptance of sex in art, literature, and motion pictures by both the public and the Court. In general, when government officials and private groups have attempted to suppress allegedly obscene material, they have done so on the grounds that it may endanger community moral standards, lead to criminal conduct, or corrupt children. Opponents of moral censorship argue that the First Amendment prohibits *any* action against "obscene" or "pornographic" material.

In *Roth v. United States,* the Supreme Court held for the first time that "obscenity is not within the area of constitutionally protected speech or press." [22] Justice William Brennan, Jr., ruled for the Court that material that is "utterly without redeeming social importance" is not protected by the Constitution. Brennan went on to give his definition of obscene matter: "whether to the average person, applying contemporary community standards, the dominant theme of the material taken as a whole appeals to prurient interests." [23]

But the Court has had continued difficulty in defining obscenity. D. H. Lawrence, whose book, *Lady Chatterley's Lover*, was banned in the United States from 1928 until 1959, once said: "What is pornography to one man is the laughter of genius to another." [24]

Justice Potter Stewart, concurring in one Supreme Court decision, said he would not attempt to define "hard-core" pornography, "but I know it when I see it." [25] This somewhat subjective approach was further refined in the case of a book commonly known as *Fanny Hill* and first published in 1749. Justice Brennan, speaking for the Court, held that before a book can be banned as obscene, three elements must be present: the dominant theme

---

[22] *Roth v. United States* and *Alberts v. California,* 354 U.S. 476 (1957).
[23] Webster's New International Dictionary defines "prurient" as "itching; longing; uneasy with desire or longing; of persons, having itching, morbid, or lascivious longings; of desire, curiosity, or propensity; lewd."
[24] D. H. Lawrence, "Pornography and Obscenity," in Diana Trilling, ed. *The Portable D. H. Lawrence* (New York: Viking, 1947), p. 646.
[25] *Jacobellis v. Ohio,* 378 U.S. 184 (1964).

Drawing by Stevenson
© 1969 The New Yorker Magazine, Inc.

"No one could claim that Judge Walker doesn't approach these
obscenity hearings with an open mind."

of the material taken as a whole appeals to a "prurient interest in sex"; the
material is "patently offensive" to contemporary community standards; and
it is "*utterly* without redeeming social value." [26] The Supreme Court reversed a Massachusetts court that had found *Fanny Hill* obscene.

The result of these cases was to remove almost all restrictions on content of books and motion pictures, as long as the slightest "social value"
could be demonstrated. But in the *Ginzburg* case, the Supreme Court affirmed the federal conviction of publisher Ralph Ginzburg, who drew a
five-year sentence and a $28,000 fine for mailing allegedly obscene ma-
terial. The publications in question included *The Housewife's Handbook on
Selective Promiscuity* and the magazine *Eros.* The divided Court based its
5-4 decision not on the material itself, but on the way it had been advertised and exploited for "titillation" rather than "intellectual content." [27]
(For example, the publisher mailed 5,000,000 advertisements for *Eros* from
Middlesex, N.J., after failing to obtain mailing privileges from two Pennsylvania towns with more suggestive postmarks.)

[26] *A Book Named "John Cleland's Memoirs of a Woman of Pleasure" v. Attorney
General of Massachusetts,* 383 U.S. 413 (1966).
[27] *Ginzburg v. United States,* 383 U.S. 463 (1966).

As the foregoing cases might suggest, the Court has thus far been unable to resolve the difficult question of where art ends and obscenity begins.

Libel   If a person is defamed by a newspaper or other publication, he may be able to sue for libel and collect damages, for the First Amendment does not protect this form of "free speech." For example, some years ago a New York newspaper suggested that one Stanislaus Zbyszko, a wrestler, was built along the general lines of a gorilla. It ran a picture nearby of a particularly hideous-looking anthropoid. The New York State courts held this to be libelous.[28]

More recently, under the *New York Times rule*, the Supreme Court has made it almost impossible to libel a public official, unless the statement made is deliberately and recklessly false. In 1960, the *Times* published an ad accusing officials of Montgomery, Alabama, of mistreating black student protesters. The governor and four city officials filed libel suits totaling $3 million. Some of the statements in the ad were inaccurate, and a local jury awarded one plaintiff $500,000. But in 1964 the Supreme Court reversed the award, holding that in a free society "debate on public issues should be uninhibited, robust and wide-open, and . . . may well include vehement . . . attacks on government officials."[29] Later Court decisions have expanded the *New York Times rule* to include political candidates, some former public officials, and some persons in the public eye.

Freedom of Assembly   In addition to protecting free speech, the First Amendment protects "freedom of assembly." The Supreme Court has held this right to be "equally fundamental" to the right of free speech and free press.[30] The Supreme Court ruled in 1897 that a city can require a permit for the "use of public grounds."[31] But a city, in requiring licenses for parades, demonstrations, and sound trucks, must do so in the interest of controlling traffic and regulating the use of public streets and parks; it cannot—in theory—exercise its licensing power to suppress free speech.[32]

At the 1968 Democratic National Convention it was obvious that Mayor Daley and many of the Chicago police who cleared antiwar demonstrators from the streets and parks disliked both the protesters and the *nature* of their political views. The legitimate responsibility of public officials and police to control traffic or prevent a demonstration from growing

[28] Robert H. Phelps and E. Douglas Hamilton, *Libel* (New York: Macmillan, 1966), p. 62.
[29] *New York Times Co. v. Sullivan*, 376 U.S. 254 (1964).
[30] *De Jonge v. Oregon*, 299 U.S. 353 (1937).
[31] *Davis v. Massachusetts*, 167 U.S. 43 (1897).
[32] *Hague v. C.I.O.*, 307 U.S. 496 (1939).

into a riot may be used as a device to suppress free speech because there is a thin, and not always readily distinguishable, line between crowd control and thought control. This is especially true when police and students hold widely disparate political views and come from markedly different socio-economic backgrounds.

Student protests that began in the mid-1960's confronted the Supreme Court, Congress, university administrators, faculty, and students with a whole new set of questions concerning constitutional freedom of expression.

Starting with the "Free Speech" movement at the University of California at Berkeley in 1964, the student protest movement spread and grew steadily in strength. The expanding war in Vietnam provided it with a popular cause. The 1968 student uprising at Columbia University was soon followed by revolts at San Francisco State College and elsewhere. In subsequent years, protesting students seized buildings at Harvard, Cornell,

Campus Protests
and the
First Amendment

STUDENT PROTEST: THE VIEW FROM THE CAMPUS

We believe that we must speak out to make clear that much of the turmoil among young people and among those who are dedicated to humane and reasoned changes will continue.

It will continue until you and the other political leaders of our country address more effectively, massively, and persistently the major social and foreign problems of our society. Part of this turmoil in universities derives from the distance separating the American dream from the American reality.

. . . Until political leadership addresses itself to the major problems of our society—the huge expenditure of national resources for military purposes, the inequities practiced by the present draft system, the critical needs of America's 23,000,000 poor, the unequal division of our life on racial issues—until this happens, the concern and energy of those who know the need for change will seek outlets for their frustration.

—Communication to President Richard M. Nixon
by President Calvin H. Plimpton and the students of Amherst College, May 2, 1969.

STUDENT PROTEST: THE VIEW FROM THE WHITE HOUSE

The student who invades an administration building, roughs up the dean, rifles the files and issues "non-negotiable demands" may have some of his demands met by a permissive university administration. But the greater his "victory" the more he will have undermined the security of his own rights. . . .

The values we cherish are sustained by a fabric of mutual self-restraint, woven of ordinary civil decency, respect for the rights of others, respect for the laws of the community, and respect for the democratic process of orderly change.

The purpose of these restraints is not to protect an "establishment," but to establish the protection of liberty. . . .

To those intoxicated with the romance of violent revolution, the continuing revolution of democracy may seem unexciting. But no system . . . has ever 'turned on' man's energies, his imagination, his unfettered creativity the way the ideal of freedom has.

—President Nixon, speech on student revolt, June 3, 1969.

Black students leaving Willard Straight Hall at Cornell, 1969

Howard, and dozens of other institutions. Frequently, as the protests increased, so did the level of accompanying violence by police and students.

Where university administrators called in police or the National Guard, violent clashes often resulted. One of the most tragic episodes took place in May 1970 when National Guard troops killed four students at Kent State University and police killed two students at Jackson State College.

The reasons for campus unrest were many and varied. The students who participated in the protest movement of the 1960's were the first to come of age under the shadow of nuclear war, in a world in which mankind was hostage to ICBMs buried in the ground. The students, in the words of Professor George Wald of Harvard, comprised "a generation that is by no means sure that it has a future." [33]

Although the specific issues differed from campus to campus, students in general focused their protest on the war in Vietnam and the gap between the stated ideals of American society and the realities; they supported the demands of blacks and other minorities for full equality; they fought against pollution of the environment; they opposed university research for military and intelligence agencies; they sought a greater voice in the university community; and they rejected what they termed the "Establishment" values of the "power structure" in American society.

News photos of black students carrying guns as they left Willard Straight Hall at Cornell, after seizing it, shocked many Americans in the spring of 1969 and touched off congressional investigations as well as demands by the public, the White House, and members of Congress that colleges show "backbone" and "get tough" with rebelling students. Influential members of the academic community in turn warned that outside interference by federal authorities would simply make matters worse and threaten academic freedom.

In a reaction to the student protest movement, Congress between 1968 and 1970 passed ten laws designed to withdraw federal aid from students who disrupted college activities. Many of the laws overlapped, and their provisions created considerable confusion. Opponents of the laws argued that some of the legislation violated the free speech provisions of the First Amendment and would serve to intimidate lawful dissent. Many state legislatures passed similar laws designed to discourage campus demonstrations. Robert H. Finch, who was then Secretary of Health, Education, and Welfare, called for new federal legislation that would give college administrators, rather than Washington officials, the widest possible discretion in dealing with campus disorders. "The federal government is not equipped to be . . . a cop," he said.[34]

[33] *Washington Post*, March 30, 1969, p. B3.
[34] Congressional Quarterly, *Weekly Report*, April 25, 1969, p. 585.

Nevertheless, college administrators were turning increasingly to law enforcement authorities and the courts to deal with student demonstrators who "trespassed" on university property. In several instances, colleges obtained court injunctions to dislodge students from buildings they had seized.

The President's Commission on Campus Unrest warned in 1970 that polarization between students and the rest of American society could threaten the survival of the nation. The commission, headed by former Pennsylvania Governor William Scranton, condemned violence by students and law enforcement authorities and warned that continued violence could bring repression of individual rights.

Freedom
of Religion

President Jefferson wrote in 1802 that the freedom of religion clause of the First Amendment was designed to build "a wall of separation between Church and State." The wall still stands, but in several areas the Supreme Court has modified its contours.

Many of the American colonies were settled by groups seeking religious freedom, but intolerant of religious dissent. Gradually, however, religious tolerance increased. When the Bill of Rights was passed its first words were: "Congress shall make no law respecting an establishment of religion, or prohibiting the free exercise thereof."

Despite the constitutional separation between church and state, religion remains a significant factor in American life. Since 1865 the nation's coins have borne the motto "In God We Trust"; most major presidential speeches end with a reference to the Almighty; public meetings often open with invocations and close with benedictions; a chaplain opens the daily sessions of the United States Senate; ministers and divinity students are exempted from the draft; children are excused from public school on religious holidays; and so on.

Yet, hardly any subject generates more emotion than church-state relations. In 1962, the Supreme Court outlawed officially composed prayers in the public schools.[35] Then, in 1963, it outlawed daily reading of the Bible and recitation of the Lord's Prayer in the public schools.[36] These decisions by the Court brought down a tremendous storm of protest upon its marble pillars. Three years later, nearly 13 percent of the nation's schools—and almost 50 percent in the South—were openly defying the Court's prayer ban, according to one study.[37]

The "no establishment" clause of the First Amendment means, in the words of Justice Black, that "neither a state nor the Federal government can

[35] *Engel v. Vitale*, 370 U.S. 421 (1962).

[36] *Abington School District v. Schempp* and *Murray v. Curlett*, 374 U.S. 203 (1963).

[37] *New York Times*, March 26, 1969, p. 1, quoting Professor Richard B. Dierenfield of McAllister College.

set up a church. Neither can pass laws that aid one religion, aid all religions, or prefer one religion over another." [38] It was under the "no establishment" clause that the Court banned prayers in the public schools.

The initial school-prayer case arose after the Board of Regents of New York State composed a "nondenominational" prayer which it recommended local school boards adopt.[39] The parents of ten children in New Hyde Park, New York, objected and went to court. In ruling the prayer unconstitutional, Justice Black, speaking for the court, declared that the First Amendment means "that in this country it is no part of the business of government to compose official prayers for any group of the American people to recite as part of a religious program carried on by government." [40]

In 1967, Frederick Walz, a New York lawyer, purchased a small, weed-covered plot of land on Staten Island, taxed by the city at $5.24 a year. Walz then brought suit on the grounds that state tax exemption for churches raised his own tax bill and violated the constitutional barrier against "establishment of religion." But in 1970, the Supreme Court rejected his arguments.[41]

The "free exercise" clause in the First Amendment protects the right of each individual to worship or believe as he wishes, or to hold no religious beliefs. It also means that people cannot be compelled by government to act contrary to their religious beliefs, unless religious conduct collides with valid laws. In that difficult area, the courts have had to try to resolve the conflict between the demands of religion and the demands of law.

In the *Flag Salute Cases*, the Court initially ruled in 1940 that children of Jehovah's Witnesses could not be excused from saluting the American flag on religious grounds.[42] But three years later, the Court reversed itself and decided in favor of Walter Barnette, also a member of the Jehovah's Witnesses, whose seven children had been expelled from West Virginia schools for refusing to salute the flag.[43] Justice Robert H. Jackson, speaking for the Court, held that "the flag salute is a form of utterance" protected by the First Amendment. "If there is any fixed star in our constitutional constellation," Jackson said, "it is that no official, high or petty, can prescribe what shall be orthodox in politics, nationalism, religion or

[38] *Everson v. Board of Education*, 330 U.S. 1 (1947).
[39] "Almighty God, we acknowledge our dependence upon Thee, and we beg Thy blessings upon us, our parents, our teachers, and our country."
[40] *Engel v. Vitale* (1962). In a sharp dissent, Justice Potter Stewart pointed out that the fourth stanza of "The Star-Spangled Banner," which became the national anthem by act of Congress in 1931, contains the words, "And this be our Motto, in God is our Trust."
[41] *Walz v. Tax Commission of the City of New York*, 397 U.S. 664 (1970).
[42] *Minersville School District v. Gobitis*, 310 U.S. 596 (1940).
[43] *West Virginia Board of Education v. Barnette*, 319 U.S. 624 (1943).

other matters of opinion." Because the Court's decision rested on the "free speech" clause, it protects anyone who refuses to salute the flag for whatever reason.

In a modern case, a group of Navajo Indians were arrested in the California desert in 1962 for using peyote in a religious ceremony. Peyote, a variety of cactus containing the hallucinogenic drug mescaline, is a narcotic under California law. But in 1964, the California Supreme Court ruled that the state could not prohibit the religious use of the drug by the Navajos.[44] The case did not go as high as the United States Supreme Court.

Not every religious practice is protected by the First Amendment, however. During the nineteenth century, the Supreme Court outlawed polygamy.[45] In that case, although George Reynolds proved that as a Mormon he was *required* to have more than one wife, the Supreme Court sustained his conviction. The Court ruled that religious conduct could not violate the law, adding, rather gruesomely: "Suppose one believed that human sacrifices were a necessary part of religious worship?"

There are some 6,000,000 non-public school children in the United States, and 86 percent of these are Roman Catholic.[46] Should they be deprived of government educational assistance under the "no establishment" clause of the First Amendment? Obviously the question is politically explosive.

In 1947, the Supreme Court ruled as constitutional a New Jersey statute under which private and parochial school children were bused to school.[47] This was the celebrated *Everson* case.

In 1960, John F. Kennedy became the first Roman Catholic to be elected President. Politically, it would have been awkward for him to propose federal aid to church-supported schools. In 1961, Kennedy submitted a bill to aid elementary and high schools that *omitted* aid to parochial schools "in accordance with the clear prohibition of the Constitution." [48] The Catholic Church hierarchy attacked the bill, which went down to defeat in a tangle of religious controversy.

In 1965, Congress, under President Johnson, passed the first general bill authorizing federal aid to elementary and secondary schools. It provided aid, through the states, to children in both public and church-supported schools. By emphasizing assistance to children in low-income

[44] William Cohen, Murray Schwartz, and DeAnne Sobul, *The Bill of Rights: A Source Book* (New York: Benziger Brothers, 1968), pp. 267–68.

[45] *Reynolds v. United States*, 98 U.S. 145 (1878); *Davis v. Beason*, 133 U.S. 333 (1890).

[46] Adapted from *Statistics of Non-Public Elementary and Secondary Schools 1965–66*, Department of Health, Education, and Welfare (Washington, D.C.: U.S. Government Printing Office, 1968), p. 7.

[47] *Everson v. Board of Education* (1947).

[48] President Kennedy relied on *Everson* in reaching this conclusion.

areas it avoided much of the religious controversy that had surrounded previous attempts to pass an education bill.

Should those who would destroy the Bill of Rights enjoy its protection?

Loyalty and Security

This dilemma is at the heart of a great public debate that began with the end of the Second World War. In this area, two constitutional principles clash: freedom of expression and the right to protect national security.

The emergence of the Soviet Union as a rival power to the United States, the onset of the Cold War, and the division of the world during the 1950's into two armed nuclear camps created fear of communism at home and generated pressures to curb dissent and root Communists or "radicals" out of government posts.

Some political leaders, notably the late Senator Joseph R. McCarthy, a Wisconsin Republican, exploited public concern for political benefit. During the early 1950's, McCarthy's freewheeling investigations of alleged Communists in the State Department, the Voice of America, the Army, and other agencies injured many innocent persons, destroyed careers, and created a widespread climate of fear in the Federal Government and in the nation. Few dared to raise their voices against him. When he attacked the Army in 1954, a series of public hearings exposed McCarthy's methods to the blinding light of television and led to his censure by the Senate later that year. After that, McCarthy lost influence. He died in 1957.

Against this background, two opposing views crystallized in the Court and within American society. One view was that a nation, like an individual, has the right to self-preservation; it must take action against internal enemies, and it need not wait until the threat is carried out, for that may be too late. The other view was that the First Amendment guarantees free speech for everyone; that advocacy of communism is not the same as overt acts against the government; and that, in any event, if Americans have confidence in the democratic system they need not fear other ideologies or the clash of ideas.

The effort to suppress dangerous ideas did not begin with "McCarthyism." As early as 1798, the Alien and Sedition Acts had provided a maximum fine of $2,000 and two years in prison for "malicious writing" against the government of President John Adams. The first person to be convicted under the acts was Matthew Lyon, a Vermont congressman whose "crime" was to accuse President Adams of "a continual grasp for power . . . an unbounded thirst for ridiculous pomp, foolish adulation and selfish avarice." After Jefferson became President in 1801, the various Alien and Sedition Acts were repealed or permitted to expire.

In 1940, Congress passed the Smith Act, which made it unlawful for

127

any person to advocate "overthrowing or destroying any government in the United States by force or violence." In the 1951 case of *Dennis v. United States* [49] the Supreme Court upheld, by a decision of 6 to 2, the constitutionality of the Smith Act and the conspiracy conviction of Eugene Dennis and ten other principal leaders of the Communist party.

Chief Justice Fred M. Vinson argued that there is no "right" to rebellion "where the existing structure of the government provides for peaceful and orderly change." He found the Communist party to be a "highly organized conspiracy" and concluded that the danger was both clear and present. Justices Hugo Black and William Douglas dissented sharply. Douglas said of the Communist leaders, "the invisible army of petitioners is the best known, the most beset, and the least thriving of any fifth column in history."

In later decisions, the Supreme Court severely restricted the use of the Smith Act against the leaders and members of the Communist Party. [50] Although in the case of *Scales v. United States* the Supreme Court upheld the Smith Act provision making it a crime to be a *member* of the Communist party, [51] that case and subsequent rulings [52] established that a member of the party may not successfully be prosecuted unless it can be shown that he holds "active membership" and joined with "specific intent" of overthrowing the government.

Under the Internal Security Act of 1950, known as the McCarran Act, Communist "action" or "front" organizations are required to register with the Attorney General. The act also created a Subversive Activities Control Board to determine what groups came under the law. In 1961, the Supreme Court held that the Communist party could be compelled to register under the McCarran Act. [53] This created a paradox: under the McCarran Act, the Communist party was required to register, but an individual member who came forward to do so could be prosecuted under the Smith Act— and the Constitution bars self-incrimination under the Fifth Amendment. Because of this a federal court of appeals ruled in 1963 that the party could not be compelled to register. The Supreme Court in 1964 declined to review the case and let the lower court ruling stand. And in 1965, the Court ruled that to require *individual* Communists to register would also violate the Fifth Amendment. [54]

The vaguely worded Communist Control Act of 1954 was intended to outlaw the Communist party and deprive its candidates of a place on the

[49] *Dennis v. United States*, 341 U.S. 494 (1951).
[50] *Yates v. United States*, 354 U.S. 298 (1957).
[51] *Scales v. United States*, 367 U.S. 203 (1961).
[52] *Noto v. United States*, 367 U.S. 290 (1961); *Elfbrandt v. Russell*, 384 U.S. 11 (1966).
[53] *Communist Party v. Subversive Activities Control Board*, 367 U.S. 1 (1961).
[54] *Albertson v. Subversive Activities Control Board*, 382 U.S. 70 (1965).

ballot in local, state, or national elections. No political party had ever been outlawed in the United States and there is considerable doubt that the 1954 act accomplished this purpose. In 1954, a New Jersey court cited the act in denying the Communist party a place on the ballot, and in 1964, Connecticut ruled the party off the ballot. But in 1968, Mrs. Charlene Mitchell ran as the Communist party candidate for President of the United States (she received 1,052 votes in three states). In a key test, a federal court in Minneapolis declared that "grave doubts" existed as to the constitutionality of the 1954 act and ordered that Mrs. Mitchell be listed on the ballot in Minnesota as the Communist party candidate. The Federal Government did not oppose this; its brief took the position that the 1954 act did not deprive the nominee and the party of the right to appear on the ballot.

In sum, under various Supreme Court decisions narrowing the application of anti-Communist legislation, it was not a violation of federal law to be a member or official of the Communist party, and, whatever the intent of the 1954 act, fourteen years later a candidate was able to run for President under the party's label.

The anti-Communist actions of Congress during these years had their parallel in the executive branch. In 1947, President Harry S Truman issued an Executive Order establishing a federal loyalty program designed to screen out Communists and subversives from government service. Loyalty investigations were instituted for all federal employees and job applicants—a procedure still in force—and the question of "security risks" in the government became a controversial political issue. In 1953, President Eisenhower issued a new Executive Order expanding the loyalty-security program.

The Supreme Court, however, has limited the power of loyalty-security boards to dismiss federal employees, and has required that the government follow procedural "due process" of law in such cases. And in 1969, the Civil Service Commission, without publicity, informed all federal departments and agencies that new employees would no longer have to sign a loyalty oath stating that they were not Communists or Fascists and did not seek to overthrow the government. The Federal Government abolished the loyalty oath after Mrs. Roma Stewart, an applicant for a job as a teacher in the District of Columbia public schools, successfully challenged the oath in federal court.

The Communist party in the United States, heavily infiltrated by FBI agents, is today less widely regarded as a serious political force or internal menace. (In 1969, Gus Hall, general secretary of the party, estimated its membership at 12,000 to 13,000.) Those concerned about internal subversion have turned much of their attention to those radicals and revolutionaries of the left who employ violence.

As the postwar years have shown, the degree of freedom for "the thought we hate" has sharply varied with the political climate; even a "fixed star" may be viewed through a very different telescope in each decade.

Due Process
of Law

"The history of liberty," Justice Felix Frankfurter once wrote, "is largely the history of the observance of procedural safeguards." [55] A nation may have an enlightened system of government, but if the rights of individuals are abused, then the system falls short of its goals.

In the United States, the Fifth and Fourteenth Amendments to the Constitution provide for "due process of law," a phrase designed to protect the individual against the arbitrary power of the state. Sometimes, the distinction is made between *substantive due process* (laws must be reasonable), and *procedural due process* (laws must be administered in a fair manner).

Searches and Seizures. Due process begins at home, for the right of individuals to "be secure in their persons, houses, papers and effects, against unreasonable searches and seizures" is not only spelled out in the Fourth Amendment, but marks a fundamental difference between a free and totalitarian society.

In the United States, police are not authorized to search a home without a search warrant signed by a judicial officer and issued on "probable cause" that the materials to be seized are in the place to be searched. But police can lawfully enter a home without a warrant to make a valid arrest.

In 1970, after bitter and prolonged debate, Congress passed a crime bill for the District of Columbia containing a controversial "no knock" provision. The measure permitted police in Washington under certain circumstances to enter a home to search it and seize materials, or make an arrest, without knocking or otherwise announcing their presence. The "no knock" provision did not change the constitutional requirement for search warrants, however. Opponents of the bill charged that the measure was unconstitutional, invaded the privacy of individuals, and was a repressive measure aimed in part at blacks, who comprise some 70 percent of Washington's population.

Until 1969, police could search anywhere in a home without a warrant if the search was incident to a lawful arrest. But in June of that year, on the final decision day of the Warren era, the Court ruled that police lacking a warrant could not ransack a home but must confine their search to the suspect and his immediate surroundings.[56] The decision overturned the

[55] *McNabb v. United States,* 318 U.S. 332 (1943).
[56] *Chimel v. California,* 395 U.S. 752 (1969).

conviction of Ted Steven Chimel of California, who had been serving a five-year-to-life term for stealing rare coins—which police found after searching his home without a warrant.

Under other Court rulings, police may search an automobile without a warrant if they have probable cause to believe it contains illegal articles. And they may "stop and frisk" a suspect on the street if there is reasonable suspicion that a crime is about to be committed.

Cherished constitutional principles are usually established in cases involving criminals and people who are not pillars of the community. Sometimes, the circumstances are bizarre. In 1949, Los Angeles police, without a warrant, burst in on Antonio Richard Rochin. They spotted two morphine capsules in his room, but Rochin swiftly swallowed the evidence. The police tied him up, rushed him to a hospital, pumped out his stomach, and recovered the capsules. The Supreme Court decided that he had been deprived not only of the contents of his stomach but of due process. "This is conduct that shocks the conscience," said Justice Frankfurter. "They are methods too close to the rack and screw." [57]

A decade later, Cleveland police, also lacking a warrant, barged into the house of a lady with the melodious name of Dollree Mapp. They did not find the betting slips they were after, but seized some "lewd and lascivious books and pictures." She was tried and convicted for possession of these items. However, the Supreme Court ruled that a state could not prosecute a person with unconstitutionally seized evidence, a decision that protected not only Dollree Mapp but every American.[58]

The Uninvited Ear. The makers of the Constitution, Justice Brandeis wrote, sought to give Americans "the right to be let alone . . . the right

THE CONSTITUTION PROTECTS TELEPHONE BOOTHS

The Fourth Amendment protects people, not places. . . . No less than an individual in a business office, in a friend's apartment, or in a taxicab, a person in a telephone booth may rely upon the protection of the Fourth Amendment.

One who occupies it, shuts the door behind him, and pays the toll that permits him to place a call, is surely entitled to assume that the words he utters into the mouthpiece will not be broadcast to the world.

—Justice Potter Stewart, in *Katz v. United States* (1967).

[57] *Rochin v. California*, 342 U.S. 165 (1952).
[58] *Mapp v. Ohio*, 367 U.S. 643 (1961).

Listening devices

most valued by civilized men."[59] In the technological age, when the individual often seems hounded by forces beyond his control, the *right of privacy* becomes even more precious. This right has been threatened by the highly sophisticated wiretapping and eavesdropping devices that have come into widespread use.

In Washington, practically anyone of importance assumes, or at least jokes, that his telephone is tapped. (One leading columnist began his telephone conversations: "Hello, everybody.") As a Senate committee has demonstrated, even the olive in a martini may be an electronic bug. With infrared light, persons in a room may be photographed through the wall of an adjoining room. Infrared light may also be used to pick up speech as far as *thirty-four miles* away. A person who swallows a "radio pill" becomes for a time a human broadcasting station, emitting signals that enable an investigator to follow him from some distance away.[60]

Modern technology has made possible a new form of government intrusion into the private life of individuals, a threat that Justice Potter Stewart has called "the uninvited ear." Many prosecutors and law enforcement officials insist that wiretapping and electronic bugs are essential tools in cases involving espionage, kidnapping, and organized crime. When public concern over crime increases, so do pressures to employ wiretaps and electronic eavesdropping devices. In 1965, President Johnson directed that federal wiretapping be limited to national security cases with specific authorization of the Attorney General. But in the late 1960's "law and order" became a growing political issue. In 1968, Congress passed the Omnibus Crime Control and Safe Streets Act permitting court-authorized wiretapping and bugging by federal, state, and local authorities in a wide variety of cases. In one of his first official acts, President Nixon, as he had promised during his presidential campaign, authorized federal agents to use electronic surveillance against organized crime.

Despite the denunciation of wiretapping by Justice Holmes as a "dirty business," the Supreme Court for almost forty years (1928–1967) held that the practice did not violate the Fourth Amendment's protection against unreasonable search and seizure.[61] Section 605 of the Federal Communications Act of 1934 outlawed interception and divulgence of telephone conversations (a ban superseded by the 1968 Crime Control Act). The Supreme Court, in a series of decisions, held that wiretapping by anyone, including federal agents, was illegal, and that wiretap evidence could not be used in federal courts.[62] But the Justice Department interpreted the 1934 law to

[59] *Olmstead v. United States*, 277 U.S. 438 (1928).
[60] Alan F. Westin, *Privacy and Freedom* (New York: Atheneum, 1967), pp. 70, 87.
[61] *Olmstead v. United States* (1928).
[62] *Nardone v. United States*, 302 U.S. 379 (1937); *Benanti v. United States*, 355 U.S. 96 (1957).

mean that wiretaps could not be divulged *outside the Federal Government*, a view that permitted the FBI, the Internal Revenue Service, and other federal agencies to continue to tap. In 1966, the Court ordered a new trial for a lobbyist convicted on income tax violations when the Justice Department admitted that the FBI had eavesdropped on his conversations.[63]

Finally, in 1967, the Court caught up with modern technology by ruling that a conversation was tangible and could be seized electronically, and that placing a bug or tap did not have to involve physical "trespass" to violate the Fourth Amendment. And the Court ruled that police could not eavesdrop without a court warrant. The case involved Charles Katz, a Los Angeles gambler who made interstate telephone calls to bookmakers from a public phone booth to bet on college basketball games. Unknown to Katz, the FBI had taped a microphone to the top of his favorite phone booth on Sunset Boulevard. Since the FBI had no warrant, the Supreme Court held that Katz's constitutional rights had been violated and threw out his conviction.[64]

The 1968 Crime Control Act, while permitting government wiretapping on an unprecedented scale, did not mark the end of the vigorous debate over the use of taps and electronic eavesdropping devices in a democratic society. In 1969, several new developments added fuel to the controversy: the FBI disclosed that, with the approval of Attorney General Robert F. Kennedy, it had tapped the telephones of Dr. Martin Luther King, Jr.; extensive FBI wiretaps of organized crime were widely publicized and the Justice Department claimed it had power *without* court approval to tap domestic groups it considered to be a threat to internal security.

Rights of the Accused.   "Due process of law" may mean little to the average American—unless and until he is arrested. This is because most of the important procedural safeguards provided by the Constitution, as interpreted by the Supreme Court, concern the rights of accused persons.

Before anyone may be brought to trial for a serious crime, there must be a grand jury *indictment*, or (as is the case in most state trials) a criminal *information*, filed with the court by the prosecuting attorney. The Bill of Rights entitles a suspect or defendant to a lawyer, to be informed of his legal rights and of the charges against him, to a speedy and public trial by jury, to summon witnesses to testify in his behalf, to cross-examine prosecution witnesses, and to refuse to testify against himself. In addition, he may not be held in excessive bail, or subjected to cruel and unusual punishment or to double jeopardy for the same offense.

The Warren Court, in a series of split decisions in the mid-1960's,

[63] *Black v. United States,* 385 U.S. 26 (1966).
[64] *Katz v. United States,* 389 U.S. 347 (1967). *Katz* overruled the *Olmstead* decision.   **133**

"Quote. No person shall be held to answer for a capital, or otherwise infamous crime, unless on a presentment or indictment of a Grand Jury, except in cases arising in the land or naval forces, or in the Militia, when in actual service in time of War or public danger; nor shall any person be subject for the same offence to be twice put in jeopardy of life or limb; nor shall be compelled in any criminal case to be a witness against himself, nor be deprived of life, liberty, or property, without due process of law; nor shall private property be taken for public use, without just compensation. Unquote."

Drawing by Frascino
© 1970 The New Yorker Magazine, Inc.

greatly strengthened the rights of accused persons, particularly in the period immediately following arrest. It is in the station-house stage that police traditionally attempt to extract a confession from suspects. It is also the very time at which an accused person may be most disoriented, frightened, and uncertain of his rights. The Court came under severe political attack for these decisions, which many law enforcement authorities argued would hamper their ability to fight crime. The Warren Court rulings came at a time of rising violence and unrest in America. Many citizens, worried about "law and order," focused their criticism on the Court and on the judicial system, which was often accused of "coddling criminals." But supporters of the Warren Court decisions and of civil liberties argued that there is no better test of a democracy than the procedural safeguards it erects to protect accused persons from the police power of the state.

A landmark case of the Warren era began in Chicago on the night of January 19, 1960. A man named Manuel Valtierra was shot in the back and killed. Police picked up his brother-in-law, Danny Escobedo, a laborer of Mexican extraction. He was questioned, released, picked up ten days later, and interrogated again. He asked to see his lawyer, but the request was refused. During the long night at police headquarters, Danny Escobedo confessed. In 1964, by a vote of 5 to 4, the Supreme Court reversed his conviction, freeing him after four-and-a-half years in prison. Justice Arthur Goldberg ruled for the Court that under the Sixth Amendment a suspect is entitled to counsel even during police interrogation once "the process shifts from investigatory to accusatory." [65]

As far back as 1957, the Court had laid down the *Mallory rule*, requiring that a suspect in a federal case be arraigned without unnecessary delay.[66] In 1966, in *Miranda v. Arizona*, the Supreme Court further extended the protection it had granted to suspects with the *Escobedo* decision. Ernesto A. Miranda, an indigent twenty-three-year-old man, described by the Court as mentally disturbed, was arrested in March 1963, ten days after the kidnapping and rape of an eighteen-year-old girl near Phoenix. The girl picked Miranda out of a police line-up, and after two hours of interrogation—during which he was not told of his right to silence and a lawyer—he confessed. The Supreme Court struck down his conviction. In a controversial 5–4 decision, the Court ruled that the Fifth Amendment's protection against self-incrimination requires that suspects be clearly informed of their rights before they are asked any questions by police.

Chief Justice Earl Warren declared for the narrow majority that statements made by an accused person may not be used against him in court unless strict procedures are followed: "Prior to any questioning, the person must be warned that he has a right to remain silent, that any statement he does make may be used against him, and that he has a right to the presence of an attorney, either retained or appointed." [67] Although a defendant may knowingly waive these rights, Warren ruled, he cannot be questioned further if at any point he asks to see a lawyer, or indicates "in any manner" that he does not wish to be interrogated.

The Chief Justice, fully aware that *Miranda* went to "the roots of our concepts of American criminal jurisprudence," argued eloquently that the "compelling atmosphere" of a "menacing police interrogation" was designed to intimidate the suspect, break his will, and lead to an involuntary confession in violation of the Fifth Amendment. That is why, he concluded, "procedural safeguards" must be observed in the police station. In a strong dissent Justice John Harlan declared: "It's obviously going to mean a gradual disappearance of confessions as a legitimate tool of law enforcement."

The right of an indigent defendant to have a lawyer in a state court might seem basic, but in fact it was not established by the Supreme Court until 1963 in the celebrated case of *Gideon v. Wainwright*.[68]

[65] *Escobedo v. Illinois*, 378 U.S. 478 (1964).
[66] *Mallory v. United States*, 354 U.S. 449 (1957).
[67] *Miranda v. Arizona*, 384 U.S. 436 (1966).
[68] *Gideon v. Wainwright*, 372 U.S. 335 (1963).

The cases before us raise questions which go to the roots of our concepts of American criminal jurisprudence: the restraints society must observe consistent with the Federal Constitution in prosecuting individuals for crime.

. . . These precious rights were fixed in our Constitution only after centuries of persecution and struggle. . . .

In the cases before us today, given this background, we concern ourselves primarily with this interrogation atmosphere and the evils it can bring. . . .

It is obvious that such an interrogation environment is created for no purpose other than to subjugate the individual to the will of his examiner. This atmosphere carries its own badge of intimidation. To be sure, this is not physical intimidation, but it is equally destructive of human dignity. The current practice of incommunicado interrogation is at odds with one of our nation's most cherished principles—that the individual may not be compelled to incriminate himself.

—Chief Justice Earl Warren in *Miranda v. Arizona* (1966).

There can be little doubt that the Court's new code would markedly decrease the number of confessions. . . .

How much harm this decision will inflict on law enforcement cannot fairly be predicted with accuracy. . . . We do know that some crimes cannot be solved without confessions, that ample expert testimony attests to their importance in crime control, and that the Court is taking a real risk with society's welfare in im-

posing its new regime on the country. The social costs of crime are too great to call the new rules anything but a hazardous experimentation.

. . . confessions, and the responsible course of police action they represent, are to be sacrificed to the Court's own finespun conception of fairness which I seriously doubt is shared by many thinking citizens in this country.

—Justice John M. Harlan dissenting in *Miranda v. Arizona*.

Clarence Earl Gideon petitioned the Supreme Court in 1962 from the Florida State Prison at Raiford, where he was serving a five-year term for breaking into a pool room in Panama City, Florida, and allegedly stealing some beer, wine, and coins from a cigarette machine and a juke box. A drifter, a man whose life had more than the normal share of disasters, Gideon nevertheless had one idea fixed firmly in his mind—that the Constitution of the United States entitled him to a fair trial. And this, he insisted in his petition, he had not received. Clarence Earl Gideon had not been provided by the court with a lawyer. In 1942 the Supreme Court had ruled that the right of counsel was not a "fundamental right," essential to a fair trial in a *state* court and therefore guaranteed by the "due process" clause of the Fourteenth Amendment.[69] But in *Gideon*, two decades later, the Supreme Court changed its mind. Justice Black, for the majority, stated what might have been obvious long before: a person "who is too poor to hire a lawyer cannot be assured a fair trial unless counsel is provided for

[69] *Betts v. Brady*, 316 U.S. 455 (1942).

him." A few months later, Gideon won a new trial and this time—with the help of a lawyer—he was acquitted.

The Bill of Rights was passed as a bulwark against the new *Federal* Government. It did not apply to the *states*. Congress, in fact, rejected a proposal by James Madison to prohibit the states from interfering with basic liberties.

An Expanding
Umbrella
of Rights

Because America has a federal system of government, this created a paradox: the same constitutional rights established under the Federal Government were often meaningless within a state. It was as though the Bill of Rights were a ticket valid for travel on a high-speed train, but no good for local commuting. Not until 1925 did the Supreme Court systematically begin to apply the Bill of Rights to the states. By 1970, the process was virtually complete. But even today, there is no *written* provision in the Constitution requiring the states to observe the Bill of Rights.

In 1833, the Supreme Court ruled in *Barron v. Baltimore* that the provisions of the Bill of Rights did not apply to the state governments and "this Court cannot so apply them." [70] Near the end of the Civil War, Congress passed the Fourteenth Amendment, which for the first time provided that "No State shall . . . deprive any person of life, liberty, or property, without due process of law." Did Congress thereby mean to "incorporate" the entire Bill of Rights into the Fourteenth Amendment and apply the Bill of Rights to the states? The argument has never been settled, but the point—thanks to the decisions of the Supreme Court in this century —is rapidly becoming moot.

In the *Gitlow* case in 1925, the Court held that freedom of speech and press were among the "fundamental personal rights" protected by the Fourteenth Amendment from abridgment by the states. [71] The Court thus began a process of "selective incorporation" of the Bill of Rights. Two years later, the Court confirmed that freedom of speech was locked in under the Fourteenth Amendment. [72] In 1931, freedom of the press was specifically applied to the states. [73] In 1932, in the first of the *Scottsboro* cases, the Court partially incorporated the Sixth Amendment by requiring that a defendant in a capital case be represented by a lawyer. [74] Two years later, it applied freedom of religion to the states. [75]

In 1937, freedom of assembly was held to apply to the states. [76] Later

[70] Chief Justice John Marshall in *Barron v. Baltimore*, 7 Peters 243 (1833).
[71] *Gitlow v. New York* (1925).
[72] *Fiske v. Kansas*, 274 U.S. 380 (1927).
[73] *Near v. Minnesota* (1931).
[74] *Powell v. Alabama*, 287 U.S. 45 (1932).
[75] *Hamilton v. Regents of the University of California*, 293 U.S. 245 (1934).
[76] *De Jonge v. Oregon* (1937).

that same year came the landmark incorporation decision of *Palko v. Connecticut*.[77] Frank Palko had been sentenced to life imprisonment for killing two policemen. Under an unusual Connecticut statute, the state could appeal and did; a new trial resulted in a death sentence. Palko appealed to the Supreme Court, contending that the second trial had placed him in double jeopardy in violation of the Fifth Amendment. Justice Cardozo ruled that the Fourteenth Amendment *did* require the states to abide by the Bill of Rights where the rights at stake were so fundamental that "neither liberty nor justice would exist if they were sacrificed." But Cardozo added that while procedural rights such as the immunity against double jeopardy were important, "they are not of the very essence of a scheme of ordered liberty," and therefore not binding on the states. The distinction was small help to Frank Palko; he was executed.

In 1947, the *Everson* case "incorporated" the principle of separation of church and state, and in 1961, Dollree Mapp, however unlikely a constitutional heroine, established that the Fourth Amendment applied to the states. In 1962, the Court seemingly carried the Eighth Amendment's protection against cruel and unusual punishment to the states.[78] In rapid succession, other rights were applied to the states: the Fifth Amendment's protection against self-incrimination,[79] and the Sixth Amendment's rights to counsel,[80] to a speedy trial,[81] to confrontation of an accused person by the witnesses against him,[82] to compulsory process for obtaining witnesses,[83] and to trial by jury in all serious criminal cases.[84]

In 1969, on Chief Justice Warren's final day, the Court, in *Benton v. Maryland*,[85] finally applied the Fifth Amendment's prohibition of double jeopardy to the states; it ruled that John Dalmer Benton should not have been tried twice for larceny. The Court thus overruled Justice Cardozo's decision in the *Palko* case.

The process of selective incorporation had in effect come full circle in the twenty-two years between *Palko* and *Benton*. Of the portions of the Bill of Rights that could apply to the states, every significant provision—with the exception of the Fifth Amendment's right to indictment by grand jury for major crimes—had been applied. Thus, through the slow and shifting process of "selective incorporation," the Supreme Court has brought the states almost entirely under the protective umbrella of the Bill of Rights.

[77] *Palko v. Connecticut* (1937).
[78] *Robinson v. California*, 370 U.S. 660 (1962).
[79] *Malloy v. Hogan*, 378 U.S. 1 (1964).
[80] *Gideon v. Wainwright* (1963).
[81] *Klopfer v. North Carolina*, 386 U.S. 213 (1967).
[82] *Pointer v. Texas*, 380 U.S. 400 (1965).
[83] *Washington v. Texas*, 388 U.S. 14 (1967).
[84] *Duncan v. Louisiana*, 391 U.S. 145 (1968).
[85] *Benton v. Maryland*, 395 U.S. 784 (1969).

At a time when democracy is under pressure, when the American political system is being tested to determine whether it can meet the problems of an urbanized, complex, and changing society, the Bill of Rights is more important than ever.

The Bill of Rights and the Supreme Court remain a buffer between popular emotion and constitutional principle. For it is precisely in times of stress and upheaval that fundamental liberties require the most protection. As Justice Jackson put it so eloquently, freedom to differ over "things that do not matter much" is a "mere shadow" of freedom. "The test of its substance is the right to differ as to things that touch the heart of the existing order." [86]

Fear of communism characterized the 1950's. Yet, the Court, often acting in the face of public opinion, gradually narrowed the scope of anti-Communist legislation to conform to the First Amendment. A decade later, crime, and fear of the local criminal, had replaced communism as a major public concern. Yet, during this same period, the Warren Court, often going against popular opinion, broadened the rights of suspects.

While the Court may at times be more zealous than other institutions in protecting civil liberties, it is by no means insensitive to public pressure. As John P. Frank has noted: "The dominant lesson of our history . . . is that courts love liberty most when it is under pressure least." [87] It is not enough, therefore, to leave the protection of fundamental liberties to the courts. Public awareness of, and support for, civil liberties is a vital factor in the preservation of those liberties.

It is in the field of civil liberties and civil rights, in the whirlpool of public pressure brought upon all three branches of the government, that some of the most sensitive demands and supports (inputs) are fed into the political system. For example, in weighing the rights of defendants versus the suppression of crime by society, the Federal Government is making some highly important allocations of values (outputs). The civil rights movement, and the broad spectrum of government response to its demands, is another example of the functioning of the political system. And in Supreme Court decisions such as school desegregation, reapportionment, the rights of suspects, and school prayers, the public reaction (feedback) is formidable.

In balancing the claims of individual rights versus those of society, the Supreme Court in applying the First Amendment generally moved during the 1960's in the direction of freer expression, reflecting the attitudes of a more permissive society.

However, the Warren Court's decisions on the rights of defendants collided with a public alarmed over crime. Under Chief Justice Warren

[86] *West Virginia Board of Education v. Barnette* (1943).
[87] In Mason, *The Supreme Court: Palladium of Freedom*, p. 171n.

Burger, named by President Nixon in 1969, some observers thought the Court might shift away from the *Miranda* philosophy. This conclusion was based upon statements made by Judge Burger before his elevation to the high court. In its 1969–70 term, Burger was on the minority side in several Court decisions dealing with criminal justice. He dissented from a number of rulings that limited the methods police and prosecutors might use against suspects. In the initial term of the Burger Court, the justices did not overturn any of the landmark cases of the Warren Court dealing with the rights of suspects.

In the area of student protests, sit-ins, and direct action, the Court was charting new waters, again against a background of strong public sentiment. The delicate balance between liberty and order is constantly shifting, from issue to issue and from one decade to the next. Even with the Constitution as ballast, this will always be so.

THE RIGHTS AND RESPONSIBILITIES OF CITIZENSHIP

Who Is a Citizen?

Although the Constitution as framed in 1787 uses the phrase "citizen of the United States," the term was not defined until the adoption of the Fourteenth Amendment in 1868. It provides that: "All persons born or naturalized in the United States . . . are citizens of the United States and of the State wherein they reside."

The amendment rests on the principle of *jus soli* (right of soil) which confers citizenship by place of birth. Congress by law has also adopted the principle of *jus sanguinis* (right of blood) under which the citizenship of a child is determined by that of his parents. All persons born in the United States, except for the children of foreign diplomats, are citizens. But in addition, children born abroad of American parents, or even of one American parent, may become American citizens if they and their parents meet the complex and varying legal requirements.

An immigrant who wishes to become a citizen may become "naturalized" after residing in the United States continuously for five years, or three years in the case of the spouse of a citizen. (Aliens who serve in the United States Armed Forces for three years can become citizens immediately if they meet other provisions of law.) The oath of citizenship is administered by a federal judge but the processing of applications for citizenship is handled by the Immigration and Naturalization Service of the Department of Justice. The minor children of naturalized citizens normally derive their American citizenship from their parents. Generally speaking, naturalized citizens enjoy the same rights as native-born Americans, although no naturalized citizen may be elected President or Vice-President.

Although it is sometimes believed that a person loses his citizenship if imprisoned for a year and a day, this is not so; the laws of most states deprive persons convicted of certain crimes of the right to vote, but no *state* may deprive an American, native-born or naturalized, of his citizenship. In general, the Supreme Court has barred congressional attempts to deprive natural-born Americans of their citizenship as punishment for crimes. For example, in 1958, the Court ruled that desertion from the Armed Forces during wartime was not grounds for deprivation of citizenship, because such a penalty would constitute "cruel and unusual punishment" forbidden by the Eighth Amendment.[88] In 1963, the Supreme Court struck down a law that provided automatic loss of citizenship for leaving the country in wartime to evade the draft.[89] As a result, at least during the Warren Court era, loss of citizenship was not among the penalties faced by the many young men who went to live in Canada during the late 1960's to avoid military service in the Vietnam war. But persons who left the United States to avoid the draft were subject upon return to the regular penalties for draft evasion.

In 1964, the Court held that naturalized citizens enjoyed the same rights as native-born Americans.[90] It struck down the law that had provided that a naturalized person lost his citizenship for living three years in his country of national origin.

In 1967, in the landmark case of *Afroyim v. Rusk*,[91] the Court ruled that Congress had no power to take away American citizenship unless it is freely renounced. An American, the Court said, had "a constitutional right to remain a citizen in a free country unless he voluntarily relinquishes that citizenship." Specifically, the Court held that Beys Afroyim, a naturalized citizen, could not be deprived of citizenship for voting in an election in Israel. With voting in a foreign election no longer grounds for loss of citizenship, similar provisions of law were likely to be challenged as unconstitutional. Among these were the provisions that citizenship is forfeited for serving in the armed forces of another country and accepting employment in a foreign state of a sort open only to nationals of that state.

The McCarran-Walter Act, passed in 1952 over President Truman's veto, preserved the "national origins" system of immigration quotas first imposed by Congress in the 1920's to curb the wave of immigration that followed the First World War. Opponents of the national origins quota system argued that it was based on racial prejudice and designed to favor

Loss
of Citizenship

A Nation
of Immigrants

[88] *Trop v. Dulles*, 356 U.S. 86 (1958).
[89] *Kennedy v. Mendoza-Martinez*, 372 U.S. 144 (1963).
[90] *Schneider v. Rusk*, 377 U.S. 163 (1964).
[91] *Afroyim v. Rusk*, 387 U.S. 253 (1967).

white, northern Europeans in preference to immigrants from southern and eastern Europe. For example, in 1965, before the system was changed, the quota for all countries totaled 158,503. Of this, 108,931 (70 percent) was allotted to three countries—Great Britain, Ireland, and Germany. Italy, where thousands of young men desired to come to the United States, had a quota of 5,666. India had a quota of 100, as did most of the Asian and African nations. (From 1917 until 1952 Chinese and all other Asians were completely excluded.)

The immigration reform bill passed in 1965 (Immigration Act of 1965) abolished the national origins quota system and substituted a new annual ceiling of 120,000 immigrants from the Western Hemisphere and 170,000 from other nations, with a limit of 20,000 persons from any one nation. The new law gives preference to members of the immediate family of United States citizens, to immigrants with special work skills, and to political refugees.

Working for Change

The Bill of Rights, discussed earlier in this chapter, is really a list of promises by the government to the people. There is no similar list of constitutional obligations of the people to the government. Nevertheless, for a democracy to work, there must be concerned citizens who participate in the political process.

ON FREEDOM OF THOUGHT

If there is any fixed star in our constitutional constellation, it is that no official, high or petty, can prescribe what shall be orthodox in politics, nationalism, religion, or other matters of opinion or force citizens to confess by word or act their faith therein. If there are any circumstances which permit an exception, they do not now occur to us.

—Justice Robert H. Jackson,
in *West Virginia Board of Education v. Barnette*, 319 U.S. 624 (1943)

During the Kennedy administration, thousands of young Americans joined the Peace Corps and served overseas, helping people in less developed nations. A few years later, many others volunteered to work at home in the Poverty Program, established during the Johnson administration. During the 1960's, thousands of young men died in Vietnam. Thousands of others felt that by actively opposing the war and participating in demonstrations against it, they were also serving their country.

Freedom to dissent is an important aspect of a democratic system. In fact, it may be argued that one of the *responsibilities* of citizenship is to exercise the rights protected by the Constitution, including that of free speech and dissent.

The students in the 1970's who worked for a better environment, or supported political candidates, were making tangible contributions to their society. When Americans speak out or organize on public issues, whether they dissent from established policy or support it, they are fulfilling an obligation of citizenship.

SUGGESTED READING

Abraham, Henry J. *Freedom and the Court: Civil Rights and Liberties in the United States* * (Oxford University Press, 1967). A detailed examination of the Bill of Rights. Analyzes how the Supreme Court, through decisions in specific cases, has gradually enlarged the area of constitutional freedom in the United States.

Berns, Walter. *Freedom, Virtue and the First Amendment* * (Louisiana State University Press, 1957). A provocative analysis that takes sharp issue with some of the major court decisions designed to protect freedom of expression in the United States.

Jackson, Robert H. *The Supreme Court in the American System of Government* * (Harvard University Press, 1955). A very useful general discussion of the Supreme Court's role in the American political system. Jackson was an associate justice of the Supreme Court.

Lewis, Anthony. *Gideon's Trumpet* * (Random House, 1964). A detailed and readable account of the Supreme Court case that established the right of a poor man to have a lawyer when charged with a serious criminal offense in a state court. Sheds light on the role of the Supreme Court in safeguarding the rights of defendants.

Mason, Alpheus T. *The Supreme Court: Palladium of Freedom* (University of Michigan Press, 1962). A concise discussion of the Supreme Court's place in the American political system by a distinguished scholar of constitutional law. Emphasizes the Bill of Rights and the Court's role in protecting minority views.

Mill, John Stuart. *On Liberty* (Appleton-Century-Crofts, 1947). Paperback. (Originally published in 1859.) A classic examination of the problem of balancing individual rights and the rights of the community.

Pritchett, C. Herman, and Westin, Alan F., eds. *The Third Branch of Government: Eight Cases in Constitutional Politics* * (Harcourt Brace Jovanovich, 1963). A series of detailed studies of civil liberties cases providing useful insights into how such cases arise and are actually handled. Contains a valuable general introduction by the editors.

Roche, John P. *Courts and Rights: The American Judiciary in Action* * (Random House, 1961). A concise examination of the role of the courts in civil rights and civil liberties. Summarizes the major trends in judicial decision-making in these areas.

Westin, Alan F. *Privacy and Freedom* (Atheneum, 1967). A discussion of how technological developments, such as electronic eavesdropping devices, have affected individual privacy in a modern society. Traces some of the practical problems posed for the courts in this area, and sets forth specific proposals for safeguarding privacy in the face of the new technology.

* Available in paperback edition

5

The Struggle

for Equal Rights

The rights set forth in the Declaration of Independence and the Constitution are not enjoyed equally by all Americans. For many minority groups, the equality promised by these fundamental American charters has been an elusive goal rather than an achieved fact, a vision of a possible future rather than a description of the often bleak present.

Equality for Whom?

Despite the civil rights laws enacted by Congress in the 1960's, and the landmark decisions of the Supreme Court, even today many of the 23,000,000 black Americans do not enjoy full social and economic equality. Blacks, it is true, have made demonstrable economic gains in recent years. But, nearly one out of three blacks in the United States is poor—by official definition of the Federal Government—as opposed to one out of ten whites.[1]

[1] U.S. Bureau of the Census, *Current Population Reports*, Population Characteristics, Series P-20, No. 204, July 13, 1970, p. 6. Data for 1969.

145

Selma, Alabama

Economic gains registered by blacks were little comfort in the 1970's to the black veteran who returned from Vietnam to be frozen out of a construction job by a white union, to a black youth caught in a system of criminal justice that was often harshest on the poor, or even to a middle-class black seeking to move into a hostile white suburb.

President Kennedy once tried to sketch for whites the obstacles faced by a black man in the United States:

> The Negro baby born in America today, regardless of the section of the Nation in which he is born, has about one-half as much chance of completing high school as a white baby born in the same place on the same day, one-third as much chance of completing college, one-third as much chance of becoming a professional man, twice as much chance of becoming unemployed, about one-seventh as much chance of earning $10,000 a year, a life expectancy which is 7 years shorter, and the prospects of earning only half as much.[2]

[2] "Radio and Television Report to the American People on Civil Rights," June 11, 1963, *Public Papers of the Presidents of the United States, John F. Kennedy, 1963*, pp. 468–69.

A MISSISSIPPI MEMORY

The earliest memory of my life is of an incident which occurred when I was three-and-a-half years old in Holly Springs, Mississippi. My father was registrar and professor of religion and philosophy at Rust College, a Negro Methodist institution there.

One hot summer day, my mother and I walked from the college campus to the town square, a distance of maybe half a mile. I remember it as clearly as though it were a few weeks ago. I held her finger tightly as we kicked up the red dust on the unpaved streets leading to the downtown area. When we reached the square she did her shopping and we headed for home. Like any other three-and-a-half-year-old on a hot day, I got thirsty.

"Mother," I said, "I want a Coke." She replied that we could not get Cokes there and I would have to wait until we got home where there was lots of Coke in the icebox.

"But I want my Coke now," I insisted. She was just as insistent that we could not get a Coke now. "Do as I tell you," she said, "wait 'til we get home; you can have a Coke with plenty of ice."

"There's a little boy going into a store!" I exclaimed as I spied another child who was a little bigger than I. "I bet he's going to get a Coke." So I pulled my mother by the finger until we stood in front of what I recall as a drugstore looking through the closed screen doors. Surely enough, the other lad had climbed upon a stool at the counter and was already sipping a soft drink.

"But I told you you can't get a Coke in there," she said. "Why can't I?" I asked again. The answer was the same, "You just can't." I then inquired with complete puzzlement, "Well, why can *he?*" Her quiet answer thundered in my ears. "He's white."

We walked home in silence under the pitiless glare of the Mississippi sun. Once we were home she threw herself across the bed and wept. I walked out on the front porch and sat on the steps alone with my three-and-a-half-year-old thoughts.

—James Farmer, Former National Director of CORE, in *Esquire*, May 1969.

President Kennedy's dramatic statistical portrait did not sketch in the daily indignities, the rebuffs, the humiliations and defeats that many black Americans face, a fact of life that led James Baldwin to write: "The brutality with which Negroes are treated in this country simply cannot be overstated, however unwilling white men may be to hear it." [3]

Today, the black citizen in many cases remains on the outside of American society, looking in. He has an excellent chance of being born in a ghetto. If so, he lives in crowded, substandard slum housing, often paying high rent to a white landlord. His school may still be segregated if it is located in a black neighborhood, since the 1954 Supreme Court decision outlawed only official, government-backed segregation of public schools. And his school may also be old, overcrowded, and below the standards of public schools in white neighborhoods.

[3] James Baldwin, *The Fire Next Time* (New York: Dial Press, 1962), p. 82.

He may well become a high school dropout. If he does not succumb to rats, crime, heroin, and other soul-destroying forces of the ghetto, perhaps he will obtain work. But most likely the work will be menial, and low-paying. He may have to buy shoddy merchandise at high credit rates from neighborhood merchants. The food he purchases at the local supermarket may be of poorer quality and priced higher than the same items at the chain's branches in white neighborhoods.[4] If he is sick, he may have to stand in line for hours at a clinic to get the treatment he needs—provided he can find a clinic with room to take him. If he raises a family his children may face the same bleak future, continuing the cycle of poverty and despair.

Even if he climbs out of the ghetto, gets a job as a skilled worker, or goes to college and becomes a professional man, his troubles are not over. On moving to a white neighborhood, he may encounter social ostracism. Under the best of economic circumstances, he must still face the problem of explaining to his children the divisions in American society between white and black.

But it is not only blacks who are struggling for equal rights in the United States. Many of the approximately 1.5 million Americans of Puerto Rican descent suffer discrimination and poverty, and are locked in the *barrios*, or slums, of the great cities. And for 650,000 American Indians, the rhetoric of equality has a particularly ironic sound. Often living in poverty, with an unemployment rate at least ten times the national average, the Indian is an outcast in a land that once was his own.

As one observer has noted, "American Indians have been oppressed and brutalized, deprived of their ancestral lands and denied the opportunity to control their own destiny." Those are the words of President Nixon.[5]

Some 5 million Mexican Americans, or *chicanos*, comprise another group that has been denied full equality in American society. Although Mexican Americans make up a sizable population bloc in five southwestern states, they are underrepresented politically. Many are migrant workers living in abysmal conditions. In 1970, Cesar Chavez and his United Farm Workers were victorious in a five-year strike against grape growers in central California. Chavez' effort, aided by a nationwide boycott of table

[4] A House Government Operations subcommittee headed by Representative Benjamin Rosenthal, D., N.Y., reported in 1968 that supermarket chainstores in inner-city areas of Washington, D.C., New York City, and St. Louis had sold to low-income customers "food items of lower quality than are available in outlets located in middle-and-upper income areas." A staff report of the Federal Trade Commission in 1969 found that the poor pay more for food in chain stores in slum areas. The study estimated that some inner-city residents paid as much as 10 percent more in supermarkets because twice as many advertised "specials" were unavailable in chain stores in low-income areas as were missing from the stores in more affluent neighborhoods. See *Economic Report on Food Chain Selling Practices in the District of Columbia and San Francisco* (Washington, D.C.: U.S. Government Printing Office, 1969), pp. 3–5.
[5] President Nixon's message to Congress on Indian affairs, *New York Times*, July 9, 1970, p. 18.

With the help of Senator Robert F. Kennedy, Cesar Chavez ends a 23-day fast, undertaken to dramatize the union leader's efforts to win higher wages for California grapeworkers.

grapes by housewives in sympathy with the strike, helped to focus national attention on "La Causa," as the grape workers called their movement, and on "La Raza," the Mexican Americans themselves. The contracts signed by the union gave the workers $1.80 per hour, plus 20 cents for each box picked. Before the strike began, workers received about $1.10 per hour.[6]

The Women's Liberation movement of the 1970's reflected the growing awareness that women, although constituting a majority of the population, were another "minority group." Discrimination based on sex is built into many public and private institutions. A presidental task force reported in 1970, for example, that the median income of white men was $7,396, and of black men $4,777, while that of white women was $4,279 and that of black women was $3,194.[7]

Many other minorities have suffered discrimination. Jews have been widely accepted in many areas of American society, but are still unwelcome in some private clubs, in the executive suites of some corporations, and in some residential areas. Prejudice against Catholics was a major issue as recently as John F. Kennedy's 1960 presidential campaign. Poles, Italians, Chinese, Japanese, Filipinos, and other groups are still victims of racial slurs and discrimination.

All these inequalities, but particularly the divisions between blacks and whites, cast a long shadow over the future of America. By 1970, the nonviolent civil rights demonstrations of the past two decades had turned at times into something akin to urban guerrilla warfare in a number of cities, as police officers and blacks shot and killed one another. Racial

[6] *New York Times*, July 30, 1970, p. 19.
[7] *A Matter of Simple Justice*, The Report of the President's Task Force on Women's Rights and Responsibilities (Washington, D.C.: U.S. Government Printing Office, April 1970), p. 18.

polarization in American society was also reflected in the nation's politics, as George Wallace's appeal had indicated. Social tension and racial protest put increasing pressure on American institutions.

Would the nation respond by supporting repression of minorities, or would it mobilize its energies to remove some of the causes of racial unrest—poverty, hunger, discrimination, slums, powerlessness, and unemployment? What is the history of the struggle for equal rights in America? How have governments and private institutions contributed to discrimination? How did the civil rights movement of the postwar decades evolve? What steps has government taken to ensure the civil rights of minorities? Can blacks and other minority groups achieve integration only at the cost of losing their ethnic and cultural identity? These are some of the problems we will explore in examining the continuing American struggle for equality.

SOME MINORITIES IN PROFILE

American
Indians

Who is an Indian? Since there is no accepted legal definition, an Indian is whoever tells the census-taker that he is one. In 1970, the Interior Department's Bureau of Indian Affairs estimated there were 650,000 Indians in America, of whom more than 450,000 lived on reservations. The total included about 60,000 Alaskan Indians, Aleuts, and Eskimos. But a private organization, Americans for Indian Opportunity, estimated that there were 1,000,000 Indians in the United States, of whom half lived in urban areas.

Indians are American citizens (Congress conferred citizenship on all Indians in 1924) and there is no requirement that an Indian live on a reservation, an area of land "reserved" for Indian use and held in trust by the Federal Government. There are 282 reservations in the United States, varying in size from small settlements in California of only a few acres, to the 14-million-acre Navajo reservation spreading through Arizona, New Mexico, and Utah.

The Federal Government spends about $500 million a year on aid to Indians. But the Bureau of Indian Affairs does not have responsibility for assisting Indians who are living off the reservation. Of American Indians dwelling in urban areas, approximately three-fourths are living in poverty.[8] And the plight of the reservation Indian is no better.

President Nixon has declared: "The first Americans—the Indians—are the most deprived and most isolated minority group in our nation. On virtually every scale of measurement—employment, income, education,

---

[8] President Nixon's message to Congress on Indian Affairs, *Congressional Record*, July 8, 1970, p. H6440.

. . . Civil Rights bills passed during and after the Civil War systematically excluded Indian people. For a long time an Indian was not presumed capable of initiating an action in a court of law, of owning property, or of giving testimony against whites in court. Nor could an Indian vote or leave his reservation. Indians were America's captive people without any defined rights whatsoever.

Then one day the white man discovered that the Indian tribes still owned some 135 million acres of land. To his horror he learned that much of it was very valuable. Some was good grazing land, some was farm land, some mining land, and some covered with timber.

Animals could be herded together on a piece of land, but they could not sell it. Therefore it took no time at all to discover that Indians were really people and should have the right to sell their lands. Land was the means of recognizing the Indian as a human being. It was the method whereby land could be stolen legally and not blatantly.

—Vine Deloria, Jr., *Custer Died For Your Sins.*

health—the condition of the Indian people ranks at the bottom. . . . This condition is the heritage of centuries of injustice." [9]

The average American can expect to live to seventy years; the life expectancy of the reservation Indian is forty-six. Few reservations can support their Indian population; unemployment among Indians ranges as high as 80 percent on the poorest reservations and averages 40 percent nationally. An estimated 90 percent of Indians live in shacks, adobe huts, crude shelters, even abandoned automobiles. Incidence of illness and disease is significantly higher among Indians than among the white population; for example, in 1968, tuberculosis was nearly six times more prevalent among Indians than among other Americans. Unsanitary housing, unsafe water, and malnutrition all contribute to ill health among Indians.

Only 58 percent of Indian children attended school in 1968. More than half drop out before completing high school, and Indians under federal supervision average less than six years of school (other Americans average 11.2 years). Indian literacy rates are among the lowest in the nation.

Under these conditions, it is not surprising that the suicide rate among Indians is twice as high as that of all Americans, and among Indian teenagers, three times as high as the national average. The rate of alcoholism among reservation Indians is often high.

The Federal Government has been deeply involved in the history of the white man's broken promises to the Indians. Until 1871, the Federal Government treated Indian tribes as separate, sovereign nations. After that, the government stopped making treaties with the tribes and adopted a policy of breaking down the tribal structure. The Dawes Act of 1887 divided reservations into small allotments; but the land not distributed to

[9] *Ibid.*, p. H6438.

individual Indians was put up for public sale. Between 1887 and 1934, some 90 million acres of land were removed from Indian hands in one way or another. When the Indian Reorganization Act of 1934 ended the practice of breaking up the reservations, the tribes regained some of their vitality.

In 1953, Congress adopted a policy declaration designed to end the special trustee relationship between the Federal Government and Indians. This policy of "forced termination" was almost unanimously opposed by the Indians, who feared that without federal protection their lands and cultural identity would vanish. Although the policy was curtailed in 1958, the congressional declaration stood. In his message to Congress in 1970, President Nixon called on Congress to renounce the termination policy and "explicitly affirm the integrity and right to continued existence of all Indian tribes and Alaska native governments."[10]

Beset by poverty, disease, illiteracy, substandard housing, and the threat of forced cultural assimilation, the Indian felt he had long overdue claims on the American political system. In the 1960's, Indians added their voices to the protests of other minorities. In 1969, seventy-eight Indians invaded the abandoned federal prison on Alcatraz Island in San Francisco Bay and claimed it as their own. A group of Indians in the state of Washington closed off fifty miles of seashore reservation lands to protest littering of their beaches by whites. Indians in Maine began charging motorists for driving through their reservation. And early in 1970, Indians staged a series of raids on Fort Lawton, an Army post near Seattle, Washington, contending that it was located on Indian land. Alaskan natives laid claim to 90 percent of the land of Alaska. They argued that the United States did not purchase the land from Russia in 1867, but merely bought the right to tax and govern the territory.

Much of the Indian militance was directed at the Bureau of Indian Affairs, which makes decisions affecting the lives of Indians but is controlled by white executives. President Nixon named an Indian to head the bureau, and many more Indians were named to top jobs in the bureau. In his proposals to Congress in 1970, President Nixon urged that Indians be empowered to take over the control or operation of federal Indian programs administered by the Interior Department and the Department of Health, Education, and Welfare. Slowly, and only after years of neglect, the Federal Government was beginning to respond to the demands of "Indian Power."

Mexican Americans

Like American Indians, Mexican Americans must contend with the twin problems of discrimination and poverty.

The majority of the 5,000,000 or more Mexican Americans in the

---

[10] President Nixon's message to Congress on Indian affairs, *Congressional Record*, July 8, 1970, p. H6438.

152

United States live in five states of the southwest, where they comprise the largest single minority group. In 1970, California, with some 2.2 million Mexican Americans, had the largest population, followed by Texas with more than 1.6 million. Other Mexican Americans were concentrated in smaller numbers in New Mexico, Arizona, and Colorado.

The 1960 census showed that 35 percent of all Mexican American families in the southwest had incomes of less than $3,000; unemployment was almost double that of the rest of the population and education completed averaged 7.1 years, well behind that of the nation as a whole. The migrant Mexican American worker has a life expectancy of forty-eight years. His birth rate is double the national average, as is his infant mortality rate.

Between 1951 and 1964, hundreds of thousands of Mexican migrant laborers entered the United States temporarily as farm workers under the "bracero" program enacted by Congress. Others have entered the country illegally to join the ranks of the migrants.

Many migrants live and work under the most difficult conditions. They perform backbreaking stoop labor in the fields under the hot sun, risking injury from insecticides used to protect the crops. Often, they must

AMERICA THE BEAUTIFUL

For a child born with brown skin in one of the southern tier of states, of farm-migrant parents who speak a different language from most Americans, the future is already charted.

The young Chicano—or Mexican-American— migrant will move with his parents through the citrus groves of Florida or California, stoop over the beans and tomatoes in Texas, hoe sugarbeets in western Kansas, crawl through the potato fields of Idaho or Maine and pick cherries in Michigan, moving with the season and the harvests.

He will sleep, crowded with his family in shells of migrant housing without heat, refrigeration or sanitary facilities. He will splash barefoot through garbage-strewn mud infested with internal parasites and drink polluted water provided in old oil drums.

By the age of 12 he will have the face of an adult and his shoulders will form in a permanent stoop. He will acquire the rough dry skin and the pipestem arms and legs that indicate a lack of vitamins and proteins. He will be surrounded by children infected with diseases of the intestines, blood, mouth, eyes and ears and thus condemned to poor learning records at school—when they are able to attend school at all.

That was the picture of the Chicano's life painted at a Senate subcommittee hearing last week. Dr. Raymond M. Wheeler, a Southern physician who had served on a team studying health conditions of the migrants, told the Senators: "The children we saw have no future in our society. Malnutrition since birth has already impaired them physically, mentally and emotionally."

—New York Times, July 26, 1970.

live in shacks without electricity or running water, their health endangered by open sewage and other unsanitary conditions. Farm workers are not covered by the National Labor Relations Act, and they have encountered great obstacles in organizing labor unions. Cesar Chavez' victory in winning contracts for the grape workers of California was widely publicized in part because it was the exception, not the rule.

The percentage of Mexican Americans in the general population is not reflected in the makeup of Congress. In California, where Mexican Americans make up about 11 percent of the population, none of the thirty-eight congressmen serving in 1970 were Mexican Americans. Only in New Mexico, where the Mexican American population numbers about 25 percent, was there both a representative and a senator of Mexican descent.

The *chicanos*, as many Mexican Americans proudly call themselves, have in recent years joined the ranks of other minority groups fighting for full equality in American society. Chavez was not the only example. In Texas, such leaders as José Angel Gutiérrez were attempting to weld Mexican American voters into a powerful political force.

In the summer of 1967, Gutiérrez led farm workers on a 400 mile march from the fields along the Rio Grande to the state capital at Austin, where they demanded a minimum wage of $1.25 an hour. In the aftermath of that march, Gutiérrez organized "La Raza Unida"—the United People— to press Mexican American demands for higher wages, better housing, and integrated schools. La Raza Unida also demonstrated that in some areas of south and west Texas, it was a potent third political party; its candidates elected officials in Crystal City, Carrizo Springs, and Cotulla, all in the southwest part of the state. By 1970, the state's candidates for governor and senator were carefully wooing Mexican American voters.

Puerto Ricans

Puerto Rico has commonwealth status and Puerto Ricans are American citizens, with a nonvoting Resident Commissioner in the United States House of Representatives. Yet many of the island's residents who come to the mainland seeking a better life encounter not only a language barrier, but economic and racial discrimination as well. In 1970, there were approximately a million Puerto Ricans in New York City, and large Puerto Rican communities in Chicago, Philadelphia, Newark, and Bridgeport and Hartford, Connecticut. As in the case of many other minorities, the per capita income of Puerto Ricans was much lower than that of other Americans, and the unemployment rate often eight times as high.

Like other minority groups, Puerto Ricans in the United States have evidenced growing cultural pride and political awareness in recent years. In several cities, Puerto Rican citizen groups have organized to work for such goals as better education and employment. In addition to such moderate groups, the Puerto Rican protest movement includes an activist organization, the Young Lords. In 1970, Herman Badillo, a New Yorker born in Puerto Rico, was elected to the United States House of Representatives.

"Equality of rights under the law shall not be denied or abridged by the United States or by any state on account of sex." Although this proposed amendment to the Constitution, designed primarily to eliminate discrimination against women, had been introduced in the House every year since 1923, it did not pass the House until August 10, 1970. The Senate amended but did not approve the proposal in 1970, however.

Women

Congressional debate on the equal rights amendment was a reflection of the growing effort in the 1970's to assure women equal rights and responsibilities in American society. The equal rights amendment was aimed at state laws that discriminate against women in marriage, property ownership, and employment. For example, some state laws have excluded women from state universities, and others have required longer prison sentences for women than for men for the same offense. The equal rights amendment, on the other hand, would also nullify certain laws favoring women; for instance, it would require that women assume equal responsibility for child support and alimony in divorce actions. Opinions varied on whether the amendment as passed by the House would make women liable for military service. One of the amendments added to the measure

A GOVERNMENT OF MEN?

What goes largely unexamined, often even unacknowledged (yet is institutionalized nonetheless) in our social order, is the birthright priority whereby males rule females. Through this system a most ingenious form of "interior colonization" has been achieved. It is one which tends moreover to be sturdier than any form of segregation, and more rigorous than class stratification, more uniform, certainly more enduring. However muted its present appearance may be, sexual dominion obtains nevertheless as perhaps the most pervasive ideology of our culture and provides its most fundamental concept of power.

This is so because our society, like all other historical civilizations, is a patriarchy. The fact is evident at once if one recalls that the military, industry, technology, universities, science, political office, and finance—in short, every avenue of power within the society, including the coercive force of the police, is entirely in male hands. As the essence of politics is power, such realization cannot fail to carry impact.

—Kate Millett, *Sexual Politics.*

Women demanding equal rights march together down New York's Fifth Avenue in August 1970.

in the Senate stated that Congress could exempt women from compulsory military service. Proponents of the constitutional amendment argued that many laws designed to protect women—such as those limiting the number of hours a woman may work—have, in fact, deprived women of economic benefits, including overtime pay.

In 1969, 30.5 million women workers in the United States comprised 38 percent of the labor force. Yet, women held more than two-thirds of all clerical jobs and earned only 58 percent of the median earnings of male workers. Only 3 percent of working women but 28 percent of working men earned $10,000 or more in 1968.[11] These statistics reflected the fact that most companies do not promote women to executive-level jobs. And even when women are hired in professional and executive positions, they earn considerably less than their male counterparts. (See Figure 5-1.)

Although the last legal barriers to equal employment of women by the Federal Government were removed in 1962, the bureaucracy is not ex-

[11] *Background Facts on Women Workers in the United States*, Women's Bureau, U.S. Department of Labor (Washington, D.C.: U.S. Government Printing Office, 1970), pp. 1–4.

empt from the bias toward employment of women that prevails in private industry. In 1968, for example, women comprised 34 percent of federal white-collar workers, but they held only 3.7 percent of the jobs that paid $14,409 and up. [12]

In 1970, the Department of Justice filed suit against Libbey-Owens-Ford, a major glass manufacturer, and the United Glass and Ceramic Workers union, charging that both had barred women workers at some of the firm's Toledo plants, and that women who did get hired were assigned to the lowest-paying and least desirable jobs. The suit was brought under the 1964 Civil Rights Act, which outlawed discrimination in employment because of race, color, religion, national origin, or sex. Libbey-Owens-Ford

[12] *Study of Employment of Women in the Federal Government 1968*, U.S. Civil Service Commission, Manpower Statistics Division (Washington, D.C.: U.S. Government Printing Office, 1969), pp. 4, 235.

FIGURE 5-1

Why Women Complain

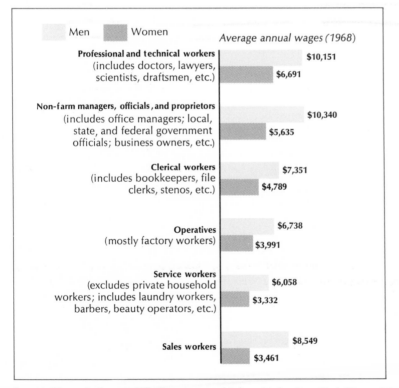

Source: Women's Bureau, U.S. Department of Labor, in the *New York Times*, July 26, 1970. © 1970 by the New York Times Company. Reprinted by permission.

employed 5,400 people in Toledo, but only 200 women. Ohio law barred the women from working more than eight hours a day or more than six days a week and from lifting more than twenty-five pounds. Although such laws were passed at the turn of the century to protect the "weaker" sex, many lawyers and advocates of women's rights argued that when these laws are used to discriminate against women workers, they violate the 1964 Civil Rights Act.

"So widespread and pervasive are discriminatory practices against women they have come to be regarded, more often than not, as normal," a presidential task force reported in 1970. "American women are increasingly aware and restive over the denial of equal opportunity, equal responsibility, even equal protection of the law. An abiding concern for home and children should not, in their view, cut them off from the freedom to choose the role in society to which their interest, education, and training entitle them." [13]

BLACK AND WHITE: AN AMERICAN DILEMMA

What is it like to be born with black skin in America? In his prophetic book, *The Fire Next Time*, author James Baldwin tried to tell:

> Long before the Negro child perceives this difference, and even long before he understands it, he has begun to react to it, he has begun to be controlled by it. . . . He must be "good" not only in order to please his parents and not only to avoid being punished by them; behind their authority stands another, nameless and impersonal, infinitely harder to please, and bottomlessly cruel. And this filters into the child's consciousness through his parents' tone of voice as he is being exhorted, punished, or loved; in the sudden, uncontrollable note of fear heard in his mother's or his father's voice when he has strayed beyond some particular boundary. He does not know what the boundary is, and he can get no explanation of it.[14]

Another writer, Ralph Ellison, explained that the black adult is unseen by the white world. "I am an invisible man," he wrote. "I am a man of substance, of flesh and bone, fiber and liquids—and I might even be said to possess a mind. I am invisible, understand, simply because people refuse to see me." [15]

[13] *A Matter of Simple Justice*, The Report of the President's Task Force on Women's Rights and Responsibilities, p. iii.
[14] Baldwin, *The Fire Next Time*, p. 40.
[15] Ralph Ellison, *The Invisible Man* (New York: Modern Library, 1952), p. 3.

Ellison wrote those words in 1952. If the black man in America is visible today, it is because a revolution in civil rights has taken place since that time. Yet, the black American still has not reached the goal of full equality in American society.

It is paradoxical, and tragic as well, that a nation founded on the principle that all men are created equal should have "a race problem." It is this paradox that the Swedish sociologist Gunnar Myrdal termed the "American Dilemma" in his classic study more than a quarter of a century ago.[16] "The American Negro problem is a problem in the heart of the American," Myrdal wrote. "The American Dilemma . . . is the ever-raging conflict between, on the one hand, the valuations preserved on the general plane which we shall call the 'American Creed,' where the American thinks, talks, and acts under the influence of high national and Christian precepts, and on the other hand . . . group prejudice against particular persons or types of people."[17]

As Myrdal perceived so clearly, the conflict between black and white Americans is not only a problem for the black citizen, who is still seeking his rightful place in American society, but a problem for all Americans, a moral dilemma that strikes at the roots of American democracy. Two decades after Myrdal had summarized his views, the "fire next time" predicted by James Baldwin had already visited American cities, and social conflict threatened the future of the nation as it had at no time since the Civil War.

The unprecedented migration of blacks from the South to northern cities in the years after the Second World War helped to create explosive ghetto conditions in those cities. And the poverty of the inner-city exists in the midst of an affluent society. Blacks in America, Charles Silberman notes, are "an economic as well as a racial minority." No matter how "assimilated" the black American becomes, because of his skin color, "he cannot lose himself in the crowd. He remains a Negro . . . an alien in his own land."[18]

THE HISTORICAL BACKGROUND

"The Negro," Gunnar Myrdal has observed, "was brought to America for the sake of the white man's profit. He was kept in slavery for generations in the same interest."[19]

[16] Gunnar Myrdal, *An American Dilemma: The Negro Problem and Modern Democracy* (New York: Harper & Row, 1962). Originally published in 1944.
[17] *Ibid.*, p. lxxi.
[18] Charles E. Silberman, *Crisis in Black and White* (New York: Random House, 1964), pp. 43–44.
[19] Myrdal, *An American Dilemma: The Negro Problem and Modern Democracy*, p. lxxvi.

159

The
Afro American

Unlike most other immigrants, who came to these shores seeking freedom, the black man came in slavery. His was a forced immigration. While the Irish American, the Italian American, or other Americans might regard their forebears' country of national origin with pride, until the 1960's, few black Americans identified with African culture or the term Afro American. In part this was because black Americans absorbed the white man's concept of Africa as a land of jungles and savages. It has been only in relatively recent years that substantial numbers of scholars have explored the history and culture of West Africa, focusing on the large and flourishing medieval empires of Ghana, Mali, and Songhai. According to one study: "Modern scholarship places the western Sudan among the important creative centers in the development of human culture." [20]

It was here, south of the Sahara in the western Sudan, that the majority of the slaves brought to America were captured, to be transported across the sea under cruel conditions. The slaves, chained together and lying on their backs, were packed in layers between the decks in spaces that sometimes measured less than two feet. Often, only a third survived the voyage "and loss of half was not at all unusual." [21]

It was not surprising that the slaves sometimes mutinied during the voyages. The most famous instance took place in 1839 aboard the *Amistad*, a Spanish slave ship. The vessel was outbound from Havana for another Cuban port when the fifty-three slaves aboard rebelled and killed the captain and crew, sparing one crewman to sail the ship. The *Amistad* was picked up by the United States Navy off Long Island and taken to New Haven, Connecticut. Spain demanded that the slaves be returned for trial. The case went to the United States Supreme Court. With former President John Quincy Adams as their lawyer, the slaves won and were set free and returned to Africa. But death or prison was the more usual reward for slaves who mutinied.

[20] August Meier and Elliott M. Rudwick, *From Plantation to Ghetto* (New York: Hill and Wang, 1966), p. 5.
[21] *Ibid.*, p. 33.

No one knows how many slaves were brought to North and South America and the West Indies between the sixteenth and the mid-nineteenth centuries, but the figure has been conservatively estimated at 15 million. It may easily have been twice that.

Interest in the cutural heritage of the Afro American was accompanied in the 1960's by new studies of the role of black Americans in the nation's history. In the 1950's, a white or black schoolchild reading a textbook in American history would scarcely have realized that the black man was a significant part of the American past—and not just a slave on the plantation.

A
Black American
Heritage

Perhaps the first person to fall in the American Revolution was a black man, Crispus Attucks. A twenty-seven-year-old runaway slave, he was the first of five men killed by British soldiers in the Boston Massacre of 1770, five years before the Revolutionary War began.[22] Black Americans took part in the battles of Lexington, Concord, and Bunker Hill; they were with Washington at Valley Forge. About 5,000 blacks served in the Continental Army. And 186,000 blacks served in the Union ranks during the Civil War.

Black explorers, soldiers, scientists, poets, writers, educators, public officials—the list of such men who made individual contributions is long and distinguished; moreover, black Americans as a group have contributed to the culture of America and participated in its historical development. Yet, from the start, the role of the black man was overlooked or neglected.

"We hold these truths to be self-evident," the Declaration of Independence says, "that all men are created equal." But that soaring language was not meant to include the black American, who was recognized by the Founding Fathers at Philadelphia as only "three-fifths" of a person. The

[22] John Hope Franklin, *From Slavery to Freedom* (New York: Knopf, 1967), p. 128. Originally published in 1947.

American dilemma, even as the Republic began, was engraved in the new nation's Constitution but had scarcely touched its conscience.

Dred Scott,
Reconstruction,
and Jim Crow
Citizens of a state automatically are "citizens of the United States" under the Constitution. But until after the Civil War, this in reality meant free white persons. The citizenship status of free blacks—there were almost 100,000 in the early 1800's—remained a subject of political dispute. The Supreme Court ruled on the question in the famous Dred Scott decision of 1857.

Dred Scott was a slave who had lived in the North for four years. Antislavery forces sought to bring Scott's case before the Supreme Court on the grounds that his residence on free soil had made him a free man. To sue for freedom, Scott first had to prove he was a citizen. But Chief Justice Roger B. Taney ruled that Dred Scott and black Americans "are not included, and were not intended to be included, under the word 'citizens' in the Constitution." [23]

It took a civil war and a constitutional amendment to reverse Taney's decision. In 1865, eight months after the surrender at Appomattox, the states ratified the Thirteenth Amendment, abolishing slavery. The Fourteenth Amendment, ratified in 1868, reversed the Dred Scott decision by making citizens of the freed slaves. The Fifteenth Amendment, ratified in 1870, was designed to give former slaves the right to vote.

During the Reconstruction era (1863–1877) Congress passed a series of civil rights measures, of which the last, the Civil Rights Act of 1875, was the strongest. The law was aimed at providing equal public accommodations for blacks. But this postwar trend toward equality for black Americans was short-lived. In the *Civil Rights Cases* of 1883, the Supreme Court struck down the 1875 Civil Rights Act, decreeing that the Fourteenth Amendment protected citizens from infringement of their rights by the *states* but not by *private individuals*. Discrimination by one citizen against another citizen was a private affair, the Court held.

Thus, less than two decades after the Civil War, the Supreme Court had seriously weakened the Fourteenth Amendment and neutralized the efforts of Congress to pass civil rights laws to protect black citizens. The Court decisions were also a sign of what was to come.

After 1883, the atmosphere was ripe for the rise of segregation and of "Jim Crow" laws designed to give legal recognition to discrimination.[24] Segregation, the separation of black and white Americans by law, became

[23] *Dred Scott v. Sandford*, 19 Howard 393 (1857).
[24] In 1832, Thomas D. "Daddy Rice," a minstrel, had introduced a song and dance about a slave named Jim Crow ("Weel a-bout and turn a-bout/And . . . jump Jim Crow") and the term came to be applied to the antiblack laws of the 1890's.

the new way of life in the South. "Jim Crow" was accompanied by lynchings and terror for the black man.[25]

In 1896, the Supreme Court put its official seal of approval on segregation in America. The great constitutional test of legal discrimination began on a June day in 1892, when Homer Adolph Plessy bought a ticket in New Orleans, boarded an East Louisiana Railroad train, and took his seat—in a coach reserved for whites. He was asked to move, refused, and was arrested.

Plessy was chosen for this test by opponents of the state's Jim Crow railroad law, which required equal but separate accommodations for white and black passengers. The Supreme Court ruled that the Louisiana statute did not violate the Fourteenth Amendment, any more than did existing separate-but-equal schools in Boston or Washington.

Yet, *Plessy* is remembered as well for the ringing dissent of a single justice, a former slaveholder from Kentucky, John Marshall Harlan. Shocked by the activities of the Ku Klux Klan, Harlan had become a champion of civil rights for the black man. He declared: "Our Constitution is color-blind and neither knows nor tolerates classes among citizens. . . . The thin disguise of 'equal' accommodations for passengers in railroad coaches will not mislead anyone nor atone for the wrong this day done."[26]

Despite Harlan's eloquent dissent, the doctrine of "separate but equal" remained the law of the land for fifty-eight years, until 1954, when the Supreme Court finally ruled that it had no place in American life.

Plessy v. Ferguson

In the city of Topeka, Kansas, more than half a century after *Plessy*, Oliver Brown, a black man and a welder by trade, was disturbed by the fact that his eight-year-old daughter, Linda Carol, attended an elementary school twenty-one blocks away from her home. The school was all black, for Topeka elementary schools were segregated by local option under state law. To go the twenty-one blocks to Monroe Elementary School, Linda Carol caught a school bus each morning at 7:40 a.m. The difficulty was that the bus arrived at the school at 8:30 am., but the doors of the school did not open until 9 a.m. Often, it meant that the children had to wait outside in the cold. To get home in the afternoon, she had to walk past the railroad tracks and cross a busy and dangerous intersection. Oliver Brown tried to enroll his children at Sumner Elementary School, which was only seven blocks from the Brown home. He was unable to do so. Sumner

A Girl Named Linda Carol Brown

[25] There were about 100 lynchings a year in the 1880's and 1890's; 161 lynchings took place in 1892.
[26] *Plessy v. Ferguson*, 163 U.S. 537 (1896).

was a school for white children. With the help of the National Association for the Advancement of Colored People (NAACP), Oliver Brown took his case to court.

On May 17, 1954, Chief Justice Earl Warren delivered the unanimous opinion of the Supreme Court in the school desegregation case. There were actually several similar cases before the Court, from Kansas, South Carolina, Delaware, Virginia, and the District of Columbia. The Kansas case lent its name to the historic decision because it happened to be listed first: *Brown v. Board of Education of Topeka, Kansas*.[27] The decision marked the start of a new era in civil rights in the United States.

The issue before the Supreme Court was very simple: The Fourteenth Amendment guarantees equal protection of the laws. The plaintiffs argued that segregated schools were not and could never be equal, and were therefore unconstitutional.

Chief Justice Warren declared:

In approaching this problem, we cannot turn the clock back to 1868 when the amendment was adopted, or even to 1896 when *Plessy v. Ferguson* was written. . . .

We come then to the question presented: Does segregation of children in public schools solely on the basis of race, even though the physical facilities and other "tangible" factors may be equal, deprive the children of the minority group of equal educational opportunities? We believe that it does.

Such segregation of children, the Chief Justice added,

may affect their hearts and minds in a way unlikely ever to be undone. . . . We conclude that in the field of public education the doctrine of 'separate but equal' has no place. Separate educational facilities are inherently unequal. Therefore, we hold that the plaintiffs . . . are, by reason of the segregation complained of, deprived of the equal protection of the laws guaranteed by the Fourteenth Amendment.[28]

The Supreme Court did not attempt in 1954 to implement its decision. The Court, as Justice Robert Jackson pointed out, "is dependent upon the political branches for the execution of its mandates, for it has no physical force at its command." It was this truth that supposedly led President

[27] Thurgood Marshall headed the team of NAACP attorneys who argued the school desegregation cases. Marshall later became the first black man to serve on the United States Supreme Court; he was appointed by President Johnson in 1967.
[28] *Brown v. Board of Education of Topeka, Kansas*, 347 U.S. 483 (1954).

"We are for speedy compliance, bearing in mind that there's been only fifteen years to desegregate these schools."

© Copyright 1969 by Herblock in The Washington Post

Andrew Jackson to declare of his Chief Justice: "John Marshall has made his decision—*now let him enforce it!*"[29]

Much of the South reacted to the *Brown* decision by adopting a policy of massive resistance. How would the Court's ruling be implemented? In May 1955, the Supreme Court itself faced the problem, unanimously ordering local school authorities to comply with the decision "with all deliberate speed."[30]

In a series of cases in succeeding years, the Court continued to prod local school districts to desegregate. But compliance was very slow and in some instances there were direct armed confrontations between federal and state power.

In September 1957, nine black children attempted to enter the previously all-white Central High School in Little Rock, Arkansas, under a federal court order. Governor Orval Faubus called out the National Guard to block integration of the school, but the troops were withdrawn by direction of the court. Accompanied by Mrs. Daisy Bates, president of the state branch of the NAACP, the black students braved a screaming mob of whites.

Little Rock,
Oxford,
and Alabama

[29] In Robert H. Jackson, *The Supreme Court in the American System of Government* (Cambridge: Harvard University Press, 1955), p. 11.
[30] *Brown v. Board of Education of Topeka, Kansas,* 349 U.S. 294 (1955). John Marshall Harlan, grandson of the justice who dissented in *Plessy v. Ferguson,* was by this time a member of the Supreme Court and participated in the second *Brown* decision.

President Eisenhower reluctantly dispatched federal paratroopers to Little Rock to quell the violence. Central High was (and is) integrated—although Governor Faubus closed all the high schools in Little Rock for the 1958–59 school year.

Violence continued to flare in the South during the Kennedy administration. When James Meredith, a black student, enrolled in the University of Mississippi at Oxford in 1962, two men were killed and several injured in the rioting that took place on the campus. President Kennedy dispatched federal marshals and ordered 16,000 troops to restore peace and protect Meredith.

The following year, Alabama's Governor George Wallace attempted to block the enrollment of two black students at the University of Alabama at Tuscaloosa. Wallace backed down only after Kennedy federalized the Alabama National Guard.

The School
Decision:
Aftermath

Ten years after the *Brown* decision, only 2 percent of black public school students in eleven Southern states were attending school with whites. In 1969, fifteen years after the Warren Court ruled that "separate education facilities are inherently unequal," a survey by the Department of Health, Education, and Welfare found that only 20.3 percent of black students in the eleven states of the South attended integrated public schools (defined by HEW as at least 50 percent white). Of 2,551,790 black students, only 518,607 were integrated. Nearly 80 percent, in other words, continued to attend segregated schools.[31]

Faced with continued defiance, the Supreme Court ruled unanimously in October 1969 that school districts must end segregation "at once" and operate integrated systems "now and hereafter." [32] It was the first major Supreme Court decision presided over by the new Chief Justice, Warren Burger.

How would the Nixon administration, elected with Southern support, carry out the new Supreme Court mandate? Earlier in 1969, the administration had appeared to vacillate, partly as a result of internal policy differences. These differences revolved around the personalities and policies of Robert Finch, then Secretary of Health, Education, and Welfare, and John Mitchell, the influential Attorney General.

In August 1969, the administration asked federal courts in Mississippi for a three-month delay in desegregation of public schools there to avoid "chaos." The NAACP accused the administration of abandoning the rights of black children for the first time since 1954. In ruling that desegregation must take place "at once," the Supreme Court specifically rejected the re-

[31] Congressional Quarterly, *Weekly Report*, January 24, 1969, p. 154.
[32] *Alexander v. Holmes County Board of Education*, 396 U.S. 19 (1969).

quest of the Nixon administration for a delay in the desegregation of the Mississippi school districts.

Early in 1970, Leon Panetta, director of HEW's Office of Civil Rights, resigned, charging that the administration was catering to the states of the Deep South. In March, President Nixon issued a statement of policy on school desegregation. It said the administration would move to end officially sanctioned school segregation, but would not take action against "de facto" segregation (resulting from residential patterns) and would not require busing of pupils to achieve racial balance in schools.

Over the summer, however, the administration moved to try to bring all Southern school districts into compliance for the 1970–71 school year. The Justice Department sued Mississippi and individual school systems in three other Southern states in an effort to force desegregation in those areas. The firmer administration stance on public school desegregation threatened to cost Nixon some of his Southern support. Senator Strom Thurmond, Republican of South Carolina, a staunch Nixon backer in 1968, denounced the administration's moves. And George Wallace, reelected governor of Alabama in 1970, warned Nixon that he might run for President again in 1972 "if you don't give us back our schools." [33]

Public school segregation was by no means confined to the South. In the cities of the North, school segregation often resulted not by law but because of patterns of residential segregation that created black neighborhoods and, along with them, black schools. In some cases, school boards gerrymandered school districts to make certain that white schools stayed white. Often, black schools received less money per pupil.

The 1964 Civil Rights Act did not require schools to eliminate "racial imbalance"—de facto segregation resulting from residential patterns. However, a United States Appeals Court judge ruled in 1967 that de facto segregation in Washington, D.C. was illegal. And in 1970, a judge of the Los Angeles Superior Court ordered the city to integrate its public school system. In the fall of 1970, the Supreme Court heard several school desegregation cases in an effort to clarify such questions as whether the Constitution required busing and other measures to achieve racial balance. The cases originated in Charlotte, North Carolina, Mobile, Alabama, and Clarke County, Georgia. At issue, among other problems, was the validity of state "antibusing" laws.

In Northern cities, such as New York and Boston, efforts to correct racial imbalance through busing of children to more distant schools created intense political controversy and school boycotts. The movement of large numbers of whites to the suburbs, leaving many of the Northern inner-city public schools with heavily black enrollments, only exacerbated the desegregation problem.

[33] *New York Times*, June 4, 1970, p. 1.

A typical northern case was that of Pasadena, California. HEW investigators charged in 1968 that the city's local school board had violated the 1964 Civil Rights Act by refusing to assign white students to schools with large black enrollments and by gerrymandering school boundaries. By 1969, an HEW official estimated that the South had overtaken the North in integrating its schools.[34] It became very clear in the years following the *Brown* decision that racial problems were not confined to any one section of the nation.

But even as these developments were taking place, some black Americans had come to feel that integration was irrelevant, or at least secondary to the larger question of how to obtain good schools, with adequate teachers and modern classrooms. In a number of cities, the pressures for community control of schools in black neighborhoods had replaced demands for integration.

THE CIVIL RIGHTS MOVEMENT: FREEDOM NOW

The Montgomery Bus Boycott

On the evening of December 1, 1955, Rosa Parks, a forty-three-year-old seamstress, boarded a bus in Montgomery, Alabama, as she did every working day to return home from her job at a downtown department store. When half a dozen whites got on at a bus stop, the driver asked black passengers near the front of the bus to give up their seats to the whites and move to the rear. Three other black passengers got up; Rosa Parks did not. She was arrested and fined $10, but her quiet refusal launched a boycott of the Montgomery bus line by a black population that had had enough. It was a remarkable year-long protest, and it catapulted to national fame the twenty-seven-year-old Baptist minister who led it. His name was Dr. Martin Luther King, Jr.

During the boycott King went to jail, and his home was bombed, but he won. The boycott ended in November 1956 as a result of a federal court injunction prohibiting segregation of buses in Montgomery. The victory set the pattern for other boycotts and for direct action throughout the South.

Martin Luther King, who led the civil rights movement and remained its symbolic head until his assassination in 1968, was an apostle of nonviolence, an eloquent man who attempted, with considerable success, to stir the American conscience.

King grew up in comfortable middle-class surroundings in Atlanta, where his father was pastor of the Ebenezer Baptist Church. And it was

[34] *New York Times*, April 7, 1969, p. 33.

in Atlanta in 1957, following the Montgomery boycott, that King formed the Southern Christian Leadership Conference (SCLC) as a vehicle for his philosophy of nonviolent change, in which he had been influenced by the teachings of Gandhi.

Until then, the principal black organization in the United States had been the NAACP, which stressed legal action in the courts as the road to progress. It was a lawyer's aproach and it had won many important struggles. King's battleground was the streets, rather than the courts, and he sought through nonviolent confrontation to dramatize the issue of civil rights for the nation and the world.

The civil rights movement came of age at a time when many blacks were growing impatient with the pace of "gradual" change. Their desire was for "freedom now"—rather than at some unspecified time in the future. Against this background, new groups emerged—not only Martin Luther King's SCLC, but the Congress of Racial Equality (CORE), founded during the Second World War and active under James Farmer in the 1960's, and the Student Nonviolent Coordinating Committee (SNCC), formed in 1960 and led first by Stokely Carmichael and later by H. Rap Brown.

In February 1960, Joseph McNeill and three other black students from the Agricultural and Technical College at Greensboro, North Carolina, sat down at a lunch counter at Woolworth's and asked politely for cups of coffee. They were refused service. They continued to sit for the rest of the morning. They came back the next day, and the next. Soon other students, white and black, joined them. They were spattered with mustard and ketchup and spat upon and cursed by whites. But at Greensboro the sit-in movement was born.

Sit-ins and Freedom Rides

It spread to seven other states within four weeks and led to the formation of SNCC. The new tactics were a success. Within six months, not only the Woolworth's in Greensboro but hundreds of lunch counters throughout the South were serving blacks. In 1961 the sit-in technique was adapted to test segregation in interstate buses and terminals. Black and white Freedom Riders, organized by CORE, rode into Alabama, where they were savagely beaten, slashed with chains, and stoned in attacks by whites. One bus was burned. But

A BLACK MAYOR SPEAKS

They have beat us, cussed us, killed our brothers and our friends, but we keep on coming. All we got to do now is lock arms, blacks and whites, and let the black and white extremists know that we gonna make America work. So if our country is not going to work then where do we go? What do we do? We got to make it work.

—Charles Evers, campaigning for mayor of Fayette, Mississippi, 1969.

the Freedom Riders succeeded in publicizing the fact that segregation on interstate transportation, although outlawed by the Supreme Court, was still a reality.

Birmingham
and the Dream

In the spring of 1963, Dr. King organized mass demonstrations against segregation in industrial Birmingham, Alabama. When arrests failed to stop the demonstrators, who included many schoolchildren, the authorities used high pressure fire hoses, police dogs, and cattle-prods. The demonstrators sang "We Shall Overcome," and continued to march. News photos of the police dogs unleashed by Birmingham Police Commissioner Eugene "Bull" Connor went out on the wires. Another photo showed five patrolmen sitting on a black woman. The scenes outraged much of the nation and the world.

King was arrested and wrote his memorable "Letter from a Birmingham Jail." In the letter, King argued that progress in civil rights had never been achieved without nonviolent pressure. The purpose of nonviolent direct action, he said, was to create sufficient tension through confrontation to force a community to negotiate the issues in question. The letter became a classic statement of the civil rights movement.

The violence in Birmingham continued throughout the summer. Late in August, however, Martin Luther King led a massive, peaceful "March

The police dogs of Birmingham, 1963.

Dr. Martin Luther King at the March on Washington, August 1963:
"I have a dream . . ."

LETTER FROM A BIRMINGHAM JAIL

One may well ask, "How can you advocate breaking some laws and obeying others?" The answer is found in the fact that there are two types of laws: There are *just* laws and there are *unjust* laws. I would be the first to advocate obeying just laws. One has not only a legal but moral responsibility to obey just laws. Conversely, one has a moral responsibility to disobey unjust laws. I would agree with Saint Augustine that "An unjust law is no law at all."

Now what is the difference between the two? How does one determine when a law is just or unjust? A just law is a man-made code that squares with the moral law or the law of God. An unjust law is a code that is out of harmony with the moral law. To put it in the terms of Saint Thomas Aquinas, an unjust law is a human law that is not rooted in eternal and natural law. Any law that uplifts human personality is just. Any law that degrades human personality is unjust. All segregation statutes are unjust because segregation distorts the soul and damages the personality. . . .

I hope you can see the distinction I am trying to point out. In no sense do I advocate evading or defying the law as the rabid segregationist would do. This would lead to anarchy. One who breaks an unjust law must do it *openly, lovingly* . . . and with a willingness to accept the penalty. I submit that an individual who breaks a law that conscience tells him is unjust, and willingly accepts the penalty by staying in jail to arouse the conscience of the community over its injustice, is in reality expressing the very highest respect for law.

—Martin Luther King, Jr., April 16, 1963.

on Washington for Jobs and Freedom." Some 200,000 Americans, black and white, jammed the Mall between the Lincoln Memorial and the Washington Monument. The nationally televised, orderly demonstration had a powerful effect on the nation, but even more powerful were the words of Dr. King, who articulated the vision of what America could be and might become:

> I have a dream that one day this nation will rise up and live out the true meaning of its creed. . . .

> I have a dream . . . that my four little children will one day live in a nation where they will not be judged by the color of their skin but by the content of their character. . . .

> So let freedom ring. . . . From every mountainside, let freedom ring . . . to speed up that day when all of God's children, black and white men, Jews and Gentiles, Protestants and Catholics, will be able to join hands and sing in the words of that old Negro spiritual, "Free at last! Free at last! Thank God Almighty, we are free at last!" [35]

In Birmingham, eighteen days later, a bomb was thrown into the Sixteenth Street Baptist Church on a Sunday morning. Four black girls attending Bible class died in the explosion. But from the agony of Birmingham that summer, from the impressive March on Washington, and from the powerful words of Dr. King, there emerged the strongest civil rights legislation since Reconstruction.

The Legislative Breakthrough

During the Eisenhower administration, Congress had passed the Civil Rights Act of 1957, the first such legislation since 1875. It created a United States Commission on Civil Rights, strengthened the civil rights section of the Justice Department, and authorized the Attorney General to seek federal court injunctions against interference with the right to vote. The Civil Rights Act of 1960 provided federal voting referees to enroll voters where local officials denied them the right of suffrage.

Both laws proved to be of limited value. The 1957 act had been watered down as the price of passage, and the 1960 law was not protecting black voters in the Deep South.

The Civil Rights Act of 1964. During the "long hot summer" of 1963, President Kennedy proposed a comprehensive civil rights measure, including a section to outlaw discrimination in public accommodations. Five days after Kennedy's assassination, President Johnson, in his first address

---

[35] *The Negro in American History*, Vol. 1, *Black Americans 1928–1968*, with an introduction by Saunders Redding (Chicago: Encyclopaedia Britannica Educational Corporation, 1969), pp. 175–76.

to Congress, urged passage of the civil rights measure as the best possible memorial to his predecessor.

The House passed the Civil Rights bill in February after nine days of debate, but Southerners in the Senate staged a fifty-seven day filibuster. On June 10, the Senate invoked cloture to cut off debate—the first time it had ever done so on a civil rights bill (see Chapter 12, pp. 479–81). On July 2, President Johnson signed the Civil Rights Act of 1964 into law. The principal provisions would:

1. Prohibit racial or religious discrimination in public accommodations that affect interstate commerce, including hotels, motels, restaurants, cafeterias, lunch counters, gas stations, motion picture houses, theaters, and sports arenas.
2. Prohibit discrimination because of race, color, sex, religion, or national origin by employers or labor unions.
3. Bar voting registrars from adopting different standards for white and black applicants.
4. Permit the Attorney General to bring suit to enforce desegregation of public accommodations; and allow individuals to sue for their rights under the act.
5. Permit the executive branch of the Federal Government to halt the flow of funds to public or private programs that practice discrimination.
6. Extend the life of the Civil Rights Commission; create a Community Relations Service to conciliate racial disputes and an Equal Employment Opportunity Commission to enforce the fair employment section of the act.

Hotels, restaurants, and other public accommodations have largely complied with the 1964 act, but job discrimination remains a serious roadblock to racial progress. "Denial of equal employment opportunity to Negroes is the major underlying cause of black unrest," Stephen J. Pollak, former Assistant Attorney General in charge of the Civil Rights Division of the Justice Department, wrote in 1969. "We have had, and in major part still have, a caste system where blacks have provided the hottest, dirtiest, toughest manual labor and the most menial services." [36]

The 1964 act did not cover violence directed at black Americans or at civil rights workers, white or black. Two days after President Johnson signed the bill into law the bodies of three young civil rights workers were found in a shallow grave near Philadelphia, Mississippi. In 1967, seven men were convicted of conspiracy against the slain civil rights workers under an 1870 federal statute. Because the murders of the rights workers did not constitute a federal crime, the conspiracy statute was the only weapon available to the Justice Department. The seven, including an Imperial Wizard of the Ku Klux Klan and the deputy sheriff of Neshoba County, were given prison sentences ranging from three to ten years.

[36] *Washington Post*, June 15, 1969, p. B3.

In a civil rights act passed in 1968, Congress provided criminal penalties for injuring or interfering with civil rights workers or any person exercising his civil rights. If the injury results in death, the maximum penalty is life imprisonment. The 1968 law also made it a federal offense to cross state lines with intent to incite a riot—the statute under which the "Chicago Seven" were tried.

The act provided the first federal open housing law in the twentieth century. On January 1, 1970, when the law went fully into effect, it prohibited discrimination in the rental or sale of all privately owned single-family houses rented or sold through real-estate agents or brokers. Private individuals who sold their houses without an agent were not subject to the law, but approximately 80 percent of all housing was covered.

The Voting Rights Act of 1965. During the Reconstruction era, state governments in the South were controlled by Northern radical Republicans. After the white South regained control over its governments, particularly in the 1890's and thereafter, the black man was systematically disenfranchised. What the Ku Klux Klan could not accomplish by intimidation, a broad range of other obstacles did. These included literacy tests rigged to keep black voters from the polls, the all-white primary (which rested on the theory, rejected by the Supreme Court in 1944, that political parties were private clubs), the poll tax, and gerrymandering of election districts. All of these devices were deliberate attempts to keep black voters in the South from gaining political power and challenging or changing the existing order. In short, the Fifteenth Amendment was being systematically flouted.

Only 12 percent of black Americans of voting age were registered in the eleven Southern states in 1948. And, although the figure rose to 43.3 percent by November 1, 1964, it was still far below the 73.2 percent white registration in the same states.[37] (See Table 5-1.)

In other words, despite the passage of the 1964 Civil Rights Act, less than half of the black citizens of voting age in the Southern states were registered. In Dallas County, Alabama, exactly 335 blacks out of a black population of 15,115 were registered to vote at the start of 1965. Martin Luther King chose Selma, the county seat, as the place he would dramatize the voting rights issue. Dr. King organized and led a fifty-mile march from Selma to Montgomery, the state capital. But state troopers acting under orders of Governor Wallace used tear gas, whips, and night sticks to break up the march. After President Johnson federalized the National Guard, the march resumed under protection of the troops. Through the heat, the mud, and the rain, their ranks swelling in numbers and in pride, the marchers walked on until they reached the steps of the Alabama capitol building.

[37] Southern Regional Council data in *1965 Congressional Quarterly Almanac*, p. 537.

President Johnson, addressing a special joint session of Congress, urged the passage of new legislation to assure black Americans the right to vote. Congress responded with a second landmark civil rights measure.

The Voting Rights Act of 1965, passed after the Senate once again invoked cloture to crush a filibuster, was aimed at roughly one hundred counties in Alabama, Georgia, Louisiana, Mississippi, North Carolina, South Carolina, and Virginia. Through an automatic "triggering" formula, the act suspended literacy tests in areas where less than half the voting-age population had registered for, or had actually voted in, the 1964 election. It gave the Civil Service Commission power to appoint federal examiners to require enrollment of qualified voters in such areas. Even outside of such areas, the Attorney General could go into federal court to seek the appointment of examiners. The bill also provided criminal penalties of up to five years in jail and a $5,000 fine for intimidating voters or interfering with voting rights.

The effect of the Voting Rights Act was immediate. The efforts of federal examiners were supplemented by the voter registration drives of the Southern Regional Council. According to a study released by the United States Commission on Civil Rights in May 1968, black registration increased by more than 1,280,000 in the eleven states of the South after passage of the Voting Rights Act. Black registration in Mississippi jumped from 6.7 percent of eligible voters to 59.8 percent. What is more, in 1967, approximately 1,000 blacks sought party, state, and local offices in the South and nearly 250 were elected.[38] The Southern Regional Council estimated that by the summer of 1968, black registration in the South had increased from the 43.3 percent registration of 1964 to 62 percent.[39]

TABLE 5-1

Voter Registration in the South
Before and After the Voting Rights Act of 1965

Percent of Voting-Age Population Registered

	1964	1968
Black	43.3%	62.0%
White	73.2%	78.1%

Sources: Southern Regional Council data in *1968 Congressional Quarterly Almanac*, pp. 772, 1055, and in Congressional Quarterly, *Revolution in Civil Rights*, p. 70.

[38] United States Commission on Civil Rights, *Political Participation*, May 1968, pp. 171, 222.
[39] Southern Regional Council, *Voter Registration in the South*, Summer, 1968.

FIGURE 5-2

Increase of Black Voters in the Seven Southern States
Covered by the 1965 Voting Rights Act

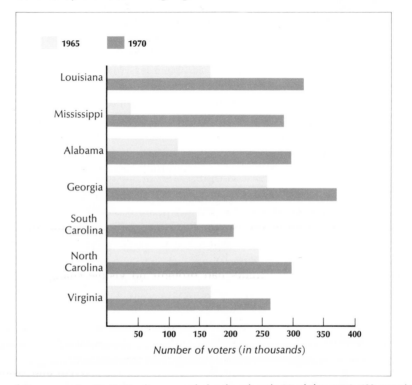

Number of voters (*in thousands*)

¹ Figures are for North Carolina as a whole, though only 39 of the state's 100 counties
are covered by the act.
Source: *New York Times,* March 8, 1970, p. 12. © 1970 by the New York Times Company.
Reprinted by permission.

Despite these remarkable increases, many problems remained for
black voters in Mississippi and other states of the Deep South. Southern
states adopted various devices to dilute the effect of increased black registration, such as redrawing the boundaries of legislative districts and holding
at-large elections. In 1966, the year after passage of the Voting Rights Act,
the Mississippi legislature passed twelve bills and resolutions to alter the
state's election laws to the disadvantage of blacks. The Civil Rights Commission reported incidents of harassment, bomb threats, and voter intimidation in several areas of Mississippi during the local elections of May
1969.[40]

[40] United States Commission on Civil Rights, Staff Report, *May 13, 1969, Municipal
Elections in Mississippi,* pp. 2, 3.

Black registration drives in the South following passage of the Voting Rights Act also spurred new white registration. As a result, despite the greater percentage increase in black registration, in actual numbers, there were more new white voters in the South than new black voters.

In 1970, the Voting Rights Act (which would otherwise have expired that year) was extended to August 1975, and its provisions broadened. The "triggering" formula was amended to extend the law to areas of Alaska, Arizona, California, Idaho, Oregon, and parts of New York City. In addition, the use of literacy or "good character" tests was suspended in all states for five years. (Other provisions to lower the voting age to eighteen, and to ease residence requirements for voters in presidential elections, are discussed in Chapter 9.)

Even as the major civil rights laws of the mid-1960's were taking effect, black protest in America entered a new phase with far-reaching social and political consequences. By 1965, the migration of blacks from the South to the cities of the North, combined with the exodus of whites from the inner-city to suburbia, had created scores of black, urban ghettos. The great expectations aroused by "the Movement" and action by Congress in the field of civil rights had brought no visible change of status to the millions of black Americans in city slums. Frustration and poverty characterized the ghettos. Combined with summer heat and police incidents, the mixture proved volatile and tragic.

The
Urban Riots

Los Angeles was sweltering in a heat wave on the night of August 11, 1965, when a highway patrolman stopped a young black driver for speeding and arrested him. A crowd gathered, more police arrived, and trouble flared. By the time the police had left, the residents of the city's black ghetto were in an angry mood. Two days after the incident, arson, looting, and shooting broke out. The Watts riot had begun. Cries of "Burn, baby, burn!" filled the air. When it was all over, thirty-four persons were dead, hundreds had been injured, and $35 million in damage had been done.

The Watts explosion was the most dramatic event in a pattern of major violence that was to afflict dozens of American cities. Watts was followed by disorders in Chicago and Cleveland in 1966, and by even more destructive riots in Newark and Detroit in 1967. Outbreaks occurred in Washington and in more than one hundred other cities after the assassination of Martin Luther King in 1968.

One result of the violence was the polarization of race relations in the United States. Viewed from the ghetto, white police and National Guard troops symbolized white repression and white power. Conversely, many whites feared violence by the black community; some whites kept guns in their homes. And in some areas of the country, self-appointed armed vigilantes patrolled the streets.

177

During the 1967 Detroit riot, President Johnson went on nationwide television to plead for calm and to announce the appointment of a National Advisory Commission on Civil Disorders. "The looting, arson, plunder, and pillage which have occurred are not part of a civil rights protest," Johnson insisted. Yet, in the same address, the President recognized that in a very real sense the urban riots *were* bound up in the civil rights protest, for he added: "The only genuine, long-range solution for what has happened lies in an attack—mounted at every level—upon the conditions that breed despair and violence." [41]

The President's Riot Commission reported back in March 1968.

> Our nation is moving toward two societies, one black, one white—separate and unequal.

> . . . certain fundamental matters are clear. Of these, the most fundamental is the racial attitude and behavior of white Americans toward black Americans.

> Race prejudice has shaped our history decisively; it now threatens to affect our future.

> White racism is essentially responsible for the explosive mixture which has been accumulating in our cities since the end of World War II. [42]

To meet these problems, the Riot Commission recommended a massive national effort to eliminate racial barriers in employment, education, and housing. It urged such steps as the creation of 2,000,000 new jobs in three years. The findings of the Riot Commission were controversial—many Americans disagreed with the emphasis on white racism as the cause of the urban riots. Few could disagree, however, that the problems underscored by the explosions in the ghettos threatened the future of America.

Black Power

Violence, according to black militant H. Rap Brown, is "as American as cherry pie." [43]

By the late 1960's, advocates of direct, aggressive action had to a considerable extent drowned out the voices of more moderate black leaders. Well before his death, Martin Luther King was struggling to maintain the leadership of the civil rights movement in America against mounting pressure from more militant rivals. Black Power advocates and Black Panthers

[41] *Report of the National Advisory Commission on Civil Disorders* (New York: Bantam Books, 1968), pp. 538–39.
[42] *Ibid.*, pp. 1, 10.
[43] Jerome H. Skolnick, *The Politics of Protest*, Staff Report to the National Commission on the Causes and Prevention of Violence (Washington, D.C.: U.S. Government Printing Office, 1969), p. 7.

often found it easier to capture the attention of the public and the press than did the moderates. And the assassination of King and other leaders committed to nonviolence weakened the position of the moderates.

Stokely Carmichael, who popularized the phrase "Black Power" during James Meredith's march through Mississippi in June 1966, has defined the term as "a call for black people in this country to unite, to recognize their heritage, to build a sense of community." [44]

While there were various definitions of Black Power in the late 1960's, and considerable disagreement on what the term meant, a common theme was the need for black Americans to exercise political control of black communities, both in the urban ghettos and in rural areas of the South. Economically, Black Power was tied to the creation of independent, black-owned and black-operated businesses. Spiritually, Black Power meant racial pride; it also gave rise to slogans such as "Black is Beautiful," and to the emphasis on "soul" and "soul-brothers."

The shift from nonviolent confrontation to Black Power and black militancy marked a major turning point in the civil rights movement. By 1969, armed clashes between police officers and blacks were increasing both in frequency and intensity.

The Black Panther party, the most publicized black militant group, was founded in Oakland, California in 1966 by Huey P. Newton and Bobby Seale. Armed with two guns and a lawbook, they began shadowing police in the city's black community to see that the rights of black citizens were not abused. Eldridge Cleaver joined the party in 1967. Within two years, it had spread from Oakland to more than thirty cities.

Sharply conflicting views of the Black Panthers soon emerged. The Panthers saw themselves as a self-defense organization, resorting to violence, they claimed, only when attacked. The party viewed blacks in America as an oppressed colony and police as the armed forces of the oppressor. To most police officials, on the other hand, the Panthers were a dangerous, armed, revolutionary organization. FBI director J. Edgar Hoover, reflecting the prevailing view of law enforcement officials, called the Black Panther party the "most dangerous and violence-prone of all extremist groups." [45]

Panthers and local police were killed in a series of "shootouts" in several cities. Police claimed that their raids on party offices were necessary to seize illegal caches of guns and ammunition. Panthers, in turn, contended that police had regularly harassed them since the party's early days in Oakland. The most widely publicized clash came on December 4, 1969, when Chicago police raided an apartment at 4:40 A.M., allegedly in a search

[44] Stokely Carmichael and Charles V. Hamilton, *Black Power* (New York: Random House, 1967), p. 44.
[45] *New York Times*, July 14, 1970, p. 21.

> We shall have our manhood. We shall have it or the earth will be leveled by our attempts to gain it.
>
> —Eldridge Cleaver in *Soul on Ice*.

for weapons, and shot to death Fred Hampton, chairman of the Illinois Black Panther party and Mark Clark, a party organizer in Peoria. Police claimed that there had been a wild exchange of gunfire; but a federal grand jury found that police had fired between eighty-two and ninety-nine shots into the apartment, while only one shot could be attributed to the Panthers.[46] The jury also found that a series of false statements had been made by police and other officials in Chicago in an attempt to cover up the truth. However, the grand jury did not indict any of the fourteen police who participated in the raid; the jury said it was unable to bring indictments because the surviving Panthers had refused to testify on the grounds that the grand jury consisted of only one black out of twenty-three persons, and was not, therefore, a jury of their peers.

Many Americans were dismayed by police excesses against Panthers and by episodes such as the Chicago police raid, but deeply disturbed as well by the existence of an armed militant group like the Black Panthers. There was widespread concern over the increasing use of violence to gain political objectives.

A task force of the National Commission on the Causes and Prevention of Violence has argued that violence is "politically defined," that is, "prescribed or condoned through political processes and decisions. The violence of the warrior in the service of the state is applauded; that of the rebel or insurgent against the state is condemned." The report added: "Official violence is frequently overlooked." [47] The study group also noted that blacks do not constitute the first group in American history to employ violence or militant action to win political goals. The American colonists used violence, the report observed, as did Appalachian farmers, the Ku Klux Klan, the Native American party of the 1840's, and the Molly Maguires, the anthracite-coal workers in western Pennsylvania in the 1870's. The task force concluded that some black Americans were turning to violent action because peaceful efforts had failed to bring social change.[48]

Many of the black militants of the 1960's and 1970's identified with the success of anticolonial movements after the Second World War. They sought to draw a parallel between the successful revolt of blacks in Africa and of Asians against colonial powers and the struggle of American blacks. Some alienated blacks advocated an alliance of black Americans with "third

[46] *New York Times,* May 23, 1970, p. 12.
[47] Jerome H. Skolnick, *The Politics of Protest,* pp. 4–5.
[48] *Ibid.,* pp. 6–14, 127.

180

world" liberation movements in other parts of the globe. Others contended that the future of the black man in America lay in rejecting integration into the white community, perhaps even in forming a black enclave in one or more states within the United States.

Thus, at the end of the sixties, some black leaders were urging a new form of segregation or separation. Most black Americans, however, still preferred to seek equality as part of the larger United States society. A *Newsweek* magazine poll of black Americans conducted by the Gallup Organization in 1969 indicated that 21 percent of those polled believed there should be a separate nation in the United States for blacks but 69 percent opposed the idea. The same poll showed that 74 percent of the blacks surveyed would rather live in an integrated neighborhood and only 16 percent would not; 78 percent would rather send their children to an integrated school and only 9 percent would not.[49]

In sum, although the voices of the militants commanded a wide audience, the majority of black Americans sought full social and economic equality and dignity *within* the American system rather than apart from it. Along with many white Americans, they still believed in Martin Luther King's dream.

[49] *Newsweek*, June 30, 1969, p. 20. Percentage of undecided omitted.

EQUAL RIGHTS:
A BALANCE SHEET FOR THE 1970'S

In 1963, Medgar Evers, state chairman of the NAACP in Mississippi, was murdered by a sniper in Jackson. In 1969, his brother Charles Evers was elected mayor of Fayette, Mississippi. The two events, separated by six turbulent years, were a sign that at least in the political arena black Americans were moving toward greater equality.

By the time Charles Evers was elected mayor, a black American had served in the Cabinet, and another sat on the Supreme Court. There were nine black members of the House of Representatives, a black senator, and approximately 800 black elected officials throughout the nation. There were several black mayors: Carl Stokes in Cleveland, Richard Hatcher in Gary, Indiana, and Walter Washington in Washington, D.C. A black city councilman, Thomas Bradley, won 46.7 percent of the vote for mayor in Los Angeles that year, even though the city's population was only 15 percent black. And in 1970, Kenneth Gibson was elected as the first black mayor of Newark. The American political system, in the civil rights legislation passed in the mid-1960's, had demonstrated its ability to respond to peaceful pressures for change. Federal law protected black voters in the South, who were coming to the polls in increasing numbers. Public accommodations were finally, by federal law, open to all Americans. And the nation was acutely aware that 23,000,000 black Americans would no longer wait.

But these gains reflected only part of the picture. The ghettos of the nation still existed. In jobs, housing, education, and income, the black man or woman still sat, figuratively, in the back of the bus. A Census Bureau Survey published in 1970 showed median family income for blacks was $5,999 in 1969 compared to $9,794 for whites. Those figures alone told much of the story. The same survey showed that 31 percent of black Americans were below the poverty line compared to 10 percent of whites.[50] The unemployment rate for nonwhites was 6.5 percent in 1969 compared to 3.2 percent for whites. For nonwhite teenagers, the unemployment rate was 24.4 percent, compared to 10.8 percent for whites.[51]

But there were some encouraging economic gains registered during

[50] U.S. Bureau of the Census, *Current Population Reports*, Population Characteristics, Series P-20, No. 204, July 13, 1970, pp. 4–6.
[51] *The Social and Economic Status of Negroes in the United States, 1969*, Joint report of the Bureau of the Census and the Bureau of Labor Statistics (Washington, D.C.: U.S. Government Printing Office, 1970), pp. 14, 17, 29, 30.

the 1960's. For example, a Census Bureau study showed that percentage income gains for blacks were considerably higher than for whites. In 1957, only 10 percent of nonwhite families had incomes of $8,000 or more; the *—adjust due to inflation* percentage had more than tripled to 32 percent in 1968. During the same period the percentage of white families with such incomes had less than doubled, from 32 to 58 percent. Despite these gains, the median income of black families in 1969 was only 61 percent of the median income for white families.[52]

The urban riots, and the growing militancy of black leaders, had alienated large numbers of whites. Although racial prejudice existed among many groups in American society, it was often somewhat stronger among low-income whites, for it was this group that felt most immediately threatened by blacks, economically and socially. Belatedly, in 1970, more attention began to be focused both in and out of government on the problems of low-income whites and blue-collar workers.

Low-income whites were often the group that reacted most strongly against urban disorders. But substantial numbers of black Americans, however much they disapproved of violence, concluded that the urban riots, on balance, had aided the black cause. The 1969 *Newsweek* poll by the Gallup Organization indicated that 40 percent of blacks polled thought the riots, whether justified or not, had helped more than they had hurt, and 31 percent thought the riots were "justified." (However, of those polled, 63 percent felt that blacks could win rights without violence.) [53]

In 1969, two nonprofit groups issued a study, entitled *One Year Later,* analyzing developments since the publication of the Riot Commission Report. Their gloomy conclusion was that "the nation in its neglect may be sowing the seeds of unprecedented future disorder and division. For a year later, we are a year closer to being two societies, black and white, increasingly separate and scarcely less unequal." [54]

Yet this picture showed signs of change as well. A study published in 1970 suggested that in the late 1960's, blacks began migrating from the central cities to the suburbs in significant numbers. The study, by David L. Birch, discerned "a continuous and sharply increasing black migration into suburban towns." [55]

Birch adds: "It is not at all clear, therefore, that black concentrations in central cities will continue to rise." At the same time, Birch found that suburban blacks, by most social and economic indicators, "are increasingly better off than their central-city counterparts." Gains in education and

[52] U.S. Bureau of the Census, *Current Population Reports,* July 13, 1970, p. 4.
[53] *Newsweek,* June 30, 1969, p. 23.
[54] *One Year Later* (Washington, D.C.: Urban America, Inc. and the Urban Coalition, February 27, 1969), p. II-d.
[55] David L. Birch, *The Economic Future of City and Suburb* (New York: Committee for Economic Development, 1970), p. 30.

opportunity among blacks were increasingly reflected in higher incomes, with an accompanying rise in family stability. Many black couples in their early twenties, the Birch study added, were leaving the city with their children for suburban life.[56]

On the other hand, racial polarization in America was reflected in greater political support for candidates who adopted a hard line on crime, urban disorders, and sometimes by implication, black militancy. President Nixon stressed law and order during his 1968 campaign, and "law and order" candidates won elections in a number of cities in 1969.

Despite political and economic gains by blacks, serious racial divisions remained, and substantial numbers of blacks remained outside the mainstream of American affluence. More than a century after the Civil War, black Americans were still struggling for equality and justice. In an address to the nation in 1963, President Kennedy declared: "This is not a sectional issue. . . . We are confronted primarily with a moral issue. It is as old as the scriptures and is as clear as the American Constitution." America, he said, "will not be fully free until all its citizens are free." [57]

How America responds to this moral issue may well decide its future. No greater domestic problem faced the nation in the last third of the twentieth century. No greater challenge tested its political system and the minds and hearts of the American people.

[56] *Ibid.*, pp. 30–33.
[57] "Radio and Television Report to the American People on Civil Rights," June 11, 1963, *Public Papers of the Presidents of the United States, John F. Kennedy 1963*, p. 469.

SUGGESTED READING

Baldwin, James. *The Fire Next Time* * (Dial Press, 1962). A leading black writer explains what it means to be a black man in America. Baldwin argues for "total liberation" of blacks and maintains that the black man is the key to America's future.

Carmichael, Stokely, and Hamilton, Charles V. *Black Power* * (Random House, 1967). The political definition of Black Power. Carmichael is the black leader who popularized the term, and Hamilton is a political scientist. They urge black Americans to seek community control and utilize other such political tools.

Clark, Kenneth B. *Dark Ghetto: Dilemmas of Social Power* * (Harper and Row, 1965). A study of the black ghetto in Harlem by a noted black social psychologist. Clark views the ghetto as an economic colony exploited by whites.

Ellison, Ralph. *The Invisible Man* * (Random House, 1952). In this novel a black writer describes the identity problem of blacks in a white society. The "invisible man" cannot be seen because whites refuse to acknowledge his existence.

Franklin, John Hope. *From Slavery to Freedom* * (Knopf, 1967). (Originally published in 1947). A classic study of black history in America written by a distinguished black historian.

Franklin, John Hope, and Starr, Isidore, eds. *The Negro in 20th Century America* (Vintage Books, 1967). Paperback. An excellent, wide-ranging collection of readings on the role of the black man in America, past and present. Includes selections from the civil rights movement of the 1960's, as well as an assessment of the effectiveness of that movement.

Grier, William H., and Cobbs, Price M. *Black Rage* * (Basic Books, 1968). A study of black anger and emotional conflicts by two black psychiatrists. Based on case studies of black children and adults, the book argues that white Americans have never freed themselves of the attitudes toward blacks learned during the era of slavery.

Lewis, Anthony, and the staff of the *New York Times. Portrait of a Decade: The Second American Revolution* * (Random House, 1964). A readable account of the civil rights movement born in the 1950's. Compiled from and based upon daily newspaper stories that appeared in the *New York Times.*

Meier, August, and Rudwick, Elliott M. *From Plantation to Ghetto* (Hill and Wang, 1966). Paperback. A history of blacks in America with emphasis on black protest movements, particularly in the twentieth century. Includes a discussion of the African heritage of American blacks.

Myrdal, Gunnar. *An American Dilemma: The Negro Problem and Modern Democracy* (Harper and Row, 1962). Paperback. (Originally published in 1944.) A classic and comprehensive study of race relations in the United States until the time of the Second World War. Traces the history of blacks in America and stresses the gap between the American creed of equality for all and the actual treatment black Americans have received. This book, by an eminent Swedish sociologist, has had a major influence on American thought about race relations.

Report of the National Advisory Commission on Civil Disorders (Bantam Books, 1968). Paperback. A detailed study, by a commission named by President Johnson, of the riots that erupted in the black ghettos of America in the mid-1960's. Analyzes the causes of black protest and urges a massive federal effort to provide remedies.

Silberman, Charles E. *Crisis in Black and White* * (Random House, 1964). A detailed analysis of the racial problems in contemporary America. Particularly useful in relating black history in the United States to the current struggle for equal rights.

Skolnick, Jerome H. *The Politics of Protest,* * A Task Force Report submitted to the National Commission on the Causes and Prevention of Violence (U.S. Government Printing Office, 1969). An analysis by a study panel of a presidential commission of protest and the politics of confrontation in America, with a section on the black protest movement. Argues that police and government authorities sometimes employ "official violence" in suppressing dissent.

* Available in paperback edition

185

PART TWO

Politics U.S.A.

6

Public Opinion

and Interest Groups

When Marie Antoinette responded to the bread shortage in France by remarking, "Let them eat cake," she was showing an unwise disregard for public opinion. In due course, her head was cut off in the guillotine.

After Lyndon Baines Johnson sent half a million men to fight in Vietnam, he discovered that public opinion had turned against him. In due course, he announced that he would not run again and retired to his ranch in Texas.

All governments are based, to some extent, on public opinion. Even dictators must pay some attention to public opinion, if only in order to repress it.

In a democracy public opinion is often described as a controlling force.

Public Opinion

"Public opinion stands out, in the United States," James Bryce wrote, "as the great source of power, the master of servants who tremble before it."[1]

In fact, the role of public opinion in a democracy is extremely difficult to define. Who is the public? What is public opinion? Does a person's opinion matter? Should government leaders try to follow public opinion or their own judgment? What influence should, or does, public opinion have on government? On policy-making? Who governs? These are questions that continue to divide philosophers, politicians, pollsters, and political scientists.

Although people usually speak about "the public," students of public opinion have discovered that the phrase is not very useful because there are very few questions on which every citizen has an opinion. The concept of "special publics" was developed by political scientists "to describe those segments of the public with views about particular issues."[2] There are, in short, many publics.

Not all opinions held by the public are public opinion. People have opinions on many subjects—music, women's fashions, and movies, for example. But only opinions about public matters constitute public opinion. In Key's view, it is "those opinions held by private persons which governments find it prudent to heed."[3] Under a broader definition, however, *public opinion is the expression of attitudes relevant to government and politics.* Private opinions become public when they relate to government and politics. The phrase *political opinion* is sometimes used to refer to opinions on political issues—a choice among candidates or parties, for example.

Political Socialization

How is public opinion formed?

A baby is born. Eighteen years later, he may be working sixteen hours a day as a volunteer in a presidential campaign. Somewhere along the way, he has acquired a set of political attitudes and has formed opinions about social issues. He has undergone *political socialization.*

In Chapter 1, we cited a definition of political socialization as "the process of induction into the political culture."[4] We also noted that when the lofty ideals that a child is taught through this process fall short of actual practice, he may be disillusioned and may sometimes react violently when he matures and forms his own view of reality.

[1] James Bryce, *The American Commonwealth*, Vol. I (New York: Putnam, Capricorn Books, 1959), p. 296.
[2] V. O. Key, Jr., *Public Opinion and American Democracy* (New York: Knopf, 1961), p. 10.
[3] *Ibid.*, p. 14.
[4] Gabriel A. Almond, *A Functional Approach to Comparative Politics*, in Gabriel A. Almond and James S. Coleman, eds., *The Politics of Developing Areas* (Princeton, N.J.: Princeton University Press, 1960).

The Family. "The family incubates political man," in the view of Robert E. Lane.[5] And the "crucial period" of a child's political, social, and psychological development is between the ages of nine and thirteen.[6] Yet, even before this age, the child is learning that he can make his voice felt within the family unit. If he makes enough racket, he may be allowed to stay up a few minutes past his bedtime. He has something to say in such decisions as what TV program the family watches.

Through watching television, children acquire rudimentary ideas about politics at an early age. One study demonstrated that 63 percent of fourth-graders identified with a political party. Almost every one of the children interviewed thought of party affiliation as a family characteristic: "All I know is *we're* not Republicans." [7] Children may acquire not only party preferences from their parents, but "an orientation toward politics" and a

[5] Robert E. Lane, *Political Life* (New York: Free Press, 1959), p. 204.
[6] Fred I. Greenstein, *Children and Politics* (New Haven, Conn.: Yale University Press, 1965), p. 1.
[7] *Ibid.*, pp. 71–73.

set of "basic values and outlooks, which in turn may affect the individual's views on political issues long after he has left the family fold."[8] Naturally, this is not true in every case. A conservative Republican who voted for Barry Goldwater in 1964 may be horrified to discover a decade later that he has reared a radical son. The generation gap has its political aspects.

The Schools. Schools also have a part in the political socialization of children. Every country indoctrinates its schoolchildren with the basic values of its political system. An American child salutes the flag in school, sings patriotic songs, learns about George Washington's cherry tree (an invention of a literary charlatan named Parson Weems), and acquires some understanding of democracy and majority rule. In high school, he is required to take "civics" courses. His political socialization continues in college, and not only in the political science courses he may take. He also learns from the political environment on the campus. The high degree of political involvement, conflict, and controversy that characterized many American campuses in the 1960's obviously had some influence on the political opinions of college students, whether or not they participated personally in the protest demonstrations.

Social Class. Differences in social class, occupation, and income also appear to affect people's opinions on public matters. For example, one study indicates that people who identify with the working class are more likely to favor federal social welfare programs than are people who identify with the middle class.[9] Another survey demonstrates that community leaders are more tolerant of Communists, atheists, and nonconformists than are people of lower social and economic status.[10]

One study of political learning suggests that children brought up in homes of lower economic status are taught to accept authority more readily than children reared in upper-class homes. This study found that upper-class children are therefore more likely to criticize political authority, that they receive more political information from their parents, and that they are more likely to become politically active.[11]

Religion and Ethnic Factors. Religion, race, and ethnic background also may influence the opinions that people hold. To influence and attract

[8] Key, *Public Opinion and American Democracy*, pp. 301, 305.
[9] Lloyd A. Free and Hadley Cantril, *The Political Beliefs of Americans* (New Brunswick, N.J.: Rutgers University Press, 1967), p. 216. See also extensive data of the Survey Research Center, University of Michigan, 1956, quoted in Key, *Public Opinion and American Democracy*, Chapter 6.
[10] Samuel A. Stouffer, *Communism, Conformity and Civil Liberties* (Gloucester, Mass.: Peter Smith, 1963).
[11] Greenstein, *Children and Politics*, pp. 155–56.

voters from ethnic groups, political parties in New York and other large cities customarily run a "balanced ticket"—one that includes an Irish candidate, an Italian candidate, and a Jewish candidate. In the primary election for mayor of New York City in June 1969, the victorious Democratic candidate, Controller Mario Procaccino, repeatedly emphasized that he was once an immigrant boy from Bisaccia, Italy. In a sentence that reached artistic perfection in its wide-ranging ethnic appeal, he told the crowds: "I couldn't get a job on Wall Street because my name was Procaccino and I was a Catholic, and my father was a shoemaker right in the heart of black Harlem."

Although Americans like to think that they form their opinions without reference to race, creed, or color, studies of their political behavior have demonstrated that this has not been the case in years past. (See Table 6-1.) No Catholic was elected President until 1960.

TABLE 6-1

How Race and Religion Influence Voter Attitudes

Nationwide surveys taken by the Gallup Poll have shown that voter prejudice against blacks, Jews, and Catholics in politics has declined dramatically in recent years.

Beginning in 1958, the Gallup Poll asked voters this question, in part: "If your party nominated a generally well-qualified man for President and he happened to be a Negro, would you vote for him?"

Following are the answers received in selected years:

	Yes	No	No Opinion
1958	38%	53%	9%
1965	59%	34%	7%
1969	67%	23%	10%

Voters were also asked whether they would vote for a Jew for President. Following are the answers received in selected years:

	Yes	No	No Opinion
1937	46%	46%	8%
1958	62%	28%	10%
1969	86%	8%	6%

Voters were also asked whether they would vote for a Catholic for President. Following are the answers received in selected years:

	Yes	No	No Opinion
1937	64%	28%	8%
1958	68%	25%	7%
1969	88%	8%	4%

Source: Adapted from the Gallup Poll, April 2, 1969. By permission of the American Institute of Public Opinion (The Gallup Poll).

In one survey, 65 percent of the Jews questioned and 63 percent of the Roman Catholics identified themselves as Democrats, compared to 45 percent of the Protestants.[12] Jewish and black voters questioned were more inclined to support government social welfare programs than were other groups.[13]

Religious affiliation may affect public opinion on specific issues—Quakers may favor disarmament; Jews may support aid to Israel; and Catholics may oppose United States support of birth control programs in underdeveloped nations. Similarly, ethnic identification may help to shape public opinion on certain issues—Americans of Italian descent may be offended by the depiction of fictional gangsters with Italian names on publicly licensed television stations; black Americans may respond favorably to the slogan "Black Power."

Geographic Factors. A person's opinions are sometimes related to where he lives. Democrats have traditionally been more numerous in the South and the big cities of the North; Republicans have been stronger in the Midwest and rural areas. Yet sectional and geographic differences among Americans are often exaggerated; although the South resisted public school desegregation more firmly than did the North, resistance existed in many Northern cities and elsewhere in the country. On some broad questions of foreign policy, sectional variations today are likely to be minimal. To a great extent, differences in outlook between the cities and suburbs have replaced the old sectional divisions.

Group Influence. The shape of a person's opinions on public questions is initially influenced by the family, but in later life other groups, friends, associates, and peers influence his views. In numerous experiments psychologists have discovered that people tend to "go along" with the decision of a group even when it contradicts the evidence before their own eyes. For example, Solomon Asch, a psychologist at Swarthmore College, placed subjects among groups of college students whose members, unknown to the subjects, deliberately responded incorrectly when they were asked to match up black lines of varying lengths on white cards. Influenced by the group's false judgments, the subjects gave incorrect answers 37 percent of the time.[14]

Two types of groups may influence people. A group whose views serve as guidelines to an individual's opinion is known as a *reference group.* For many people, a political party serves as a reference group; because the Democratic party stands for expansion of social welfare programs, the

[12] Free and Cantril, *The Political Beliefs of Americans*, pp. 147.
[13] *Ibid.*, p. 148.
[14] S. E. Asch, *Psychology Monograph*, Vol. 70, No. 416 (1956).

individual Democrat may find it easy to adopt this view as his own. Groups that people come into face-to-face contact with in everyday life—friends, office associates, and a local social club—are more likely to be *primary* groups, for their influence is direct.

Walter Lippmann, in his classic study of public opinion, observed that each individual, in viewing distant events, tends to form a "picture inside his head of the world beyond his reach." [15] And as Lippmann noted, the mental snapshots do not always correspond with reality.

The Qualities of Public Opinion

Up to now, we have been discussing how the "pictures" are formed and how they may be influenced by such factors as family, school, social class, occupation, income, religion, race, ethnic background, geography, and group membership. But opinions also have identifiable *qualities*. Like pictures, they may be sharp or fuzzy, general or detailed—and they may fade. In analyzing the qualities of opinions, political scientists speak of *direction, intensity,* and *stability.*

There was a time when political scientists would describe people as being "for" or "against" something. But after the Second World War, when public opinion polling evolved into a more exact science, pollsters and analysts discovered that simple "yes" or "no" answers sometimes masked wide gradations in opinion on a given subject. In other words, it is possible to measure opinions in *direction* along a scale.[16] For example, one person may favor government control of all medical programs; another may prefer federal health programs that are limited to the aged and needy; a third person may favor wholly private health care; and a fourth person may be undecided.

Public opinion varies in *intensity* as well as direction. A person may have mild opinions or deeply felt views. A secretary may be mildly in sympathy with the women's liberation movement. The partisans who cheered George Wallace during the 1968 presidential campaign held strong opinions. Some of the students who battled police on the nation's campuses in the 1960's were New Left radicals who also had strong opinions. Robert E. Lane and David O. Sears have suggested that there may be "something congenial" about extreme views and intensity of opinion "which suggests a mutual support." [17] That is, people well to the left or right may hold their political opinions more fiercely than others.

Another quality of public opinion is its degree of *stability.* Opinions change sometimes slowly, sometimes rapidly and unpredictably, in response

[15] Walter Lippmann, *Public Opinion* (New York: Free Press, 1965), pp. 18–19. Originally published in 1922.
[16] Key, *Public Opinion and American Democracy,* p. 11.
[17] Robert E. Lane and David O. Sears, *Public Opinion* (Englewood Cliffs, N.J.: Prentice-Hall, 1964), p. 106.

to new events or personalities. In January 1965, two months after President Johnson's landslide victory, the Gallup Poll showed his popularity at 71 percent. By October 1968, during the last months of his Presidency, Johnson's popularity had plummeted to 42 percent. By then the President's public image had worn thin, and Americans were upset about city riots, crime, and the war in Vietnam.

Public opinion may be measured and its qualities analyzed. The measuring tool is the political poll.

Political
Polls

As a principal aide to Senator John F. Kennedy, Theodore Sorensen had an insider's view of Kennedy's drive for the 1960 Democratic presidential nomination. Sorensen wrote several years later,

> Kennedy sought help from the science of opinion polling—not because he felt he must slavishly adhere to the whims of public opinion but because he sought modern tools of instruction about new and unfamiliar battlegrounds. Tens of dozens of private polls were commissioned at great expense to probe areas of weakness and strength, to evaluate opponents and issues, and to help decide on schedules and tactics. Showings of strength in a particular state were often shared with the leaders of that state. States with Presidential primaries were polled more than once before he would decide on his entry, and usually many more times once he entered.[18]

Kennedy had enough confidence in opinion polling to pay Louis Harris, his chief pollster, a minimum guaranteed fee of $100,000. According to Sorensen, Kennedy and the man who became his Republican opponent, Richard M. Nixon, quietly agreed to swap the results of their private

THE LIMITS OF POLITICAL POLLS

All polls have their limitations. They can be most helpful in determining a rough comparison of relative strength between two well-known candidates as of the day of the survey. They can indicate how well and how favorably a candidate and his opponent are known among various voter groups. But they cannot be as precise as they pretend, provide protection against wide fluctuations or predict the final choice of the undecided. The weight of their answers often varies with the wording of their questions.

—Theodore C. Sorensen, *Kennedy.*

[18] Theodore C. Sorensen, *Kennedy* (New York: Harper & Row, 1965), p. 106.

opinion surveys. The polls were "surreptitiously exchanged" by the candidates' administrative assistants.[19]

Sorensen's account gives an insight into the use of polls by modern, working politicians. But over the years politicians have discovered that the data gathered by political polls are not always reliable.

In 1948, the Gallup and Roper polls predicted that Governor Thomas E. Dewey of New York, the Republican candidate, would defeat President Harry S Truman. "I never paid any attention to polls myself," Mr. Truman later wrote in his typically direct style. "The 1948 election proved the pollsters and forecasters so wrong and unreliable that to this day their reputations have not been fully restored." [20]

The art of political polling has come a long way since 1948, and the margin of error has been greatly reduced. Even so, polls may still be wrong or in conflict with one another. Just before the 1968 Republican National Convention at Miami, two major polling organizations issued presidential preference polls that seemed to disagree. According to a Gallup Poll, Nixon ran 2 to 5 percentage points stronger than Rockefeller in tests against Humphrey or McCarthy. But a Harris poll showed Nixon trailing Humphrey by 5 points, and Rockefeller ahead of Humphrey, 40 to 34 percent.

When two of the major polling organizations disagree on the eve of a presidential nominating convention it is embarrassing and bad for the polling business. On August 1, 1968, Harris and Gallup issued an extraordinary joint statement denying any conflict in their polls on the basis that the Gallup Poll had been taken several days earlier than the Harris survey.

In 1969, Thomas Bradley, a black Los Angeles city councilman, ran

[19] *Ibid.*, p. 107.
[20] Harry S. Truman, *Memoirs by Harry S. Truman: Years of Trial and Hope*, Vol. II (Garden City, N.Y.: Doubleday, 1956), pp. 177, 221.

"Undecided! Do you mean to tell me that despite the extraordinary and clear-cut differences between the candidates and between their policies this year, you—an adult American—can't make up your mind?"

Drawing by Stevenson
© 1969 The New Yorker Magazine, Inc.

for mayor against the conservative incumbent, Sam Yorty. Mervin D. Field and Don M. Muchmore, respected California poll-takers, both reported Bradley leading Yorty. (Discounting undecided voters, Muchmore reported Bradley leading 53 to 36 percent; Field reported Bradley ahead by 43 to 38 percent.) On election day, Yorty won with 53 percent of the vote. "I feel like George Gallup did in 1948," Mr. Muchmore declared.

Despite such well-publicized errors, political polls are substantially accurate more often than not, and often useful as a guide to voter sentiment. Politicians are convinced of their value.[21] Today, polls—before, during, and even after election day—are a standard part of political campaigns. More than 200 polling organizations were in business in 1968.[22] An estimated $6,000,000 was paid to pollsters in that presidential election year.

How Polls Work. A political polling organization may question only 1,500 people to measure public opinion on a given issue or to determine which candidate leads in a campaign.[23] Many people find it difficult to ac-

[21] Louis Harris estimated in 1968, for example, that 80 percent of all candidates for the U.S. Senate used polls.
[22] Congressional Quarterly, *Weekly Report*, May 3, 1968, p. 992. Major political polling organizations include the American Institute of Public Opinion (the Gallup Poll) and Louis Harris & Associates, Inc. (the Harris Survey), which publish their findings in newspapers and magazines. Pollsters who take private polls for political clients include John F. Kraft, Inc., Oliver A. Quayle and Co., Inc., and Opinion Research Corp. In addition, there are many smaller regional polls as well as polls conducted by newspapers.
[23] The Gallup Poll normally uses a national sample of 1,500 persons. Louis Harris interviews 1,600 people.

cept the idea that public opinion in an entire nation may be measured from such a small sample. Behind some of the skepticism is the belief that each individual is unique, and that his opinions and thoughts cannot be so neatly categorized by computers. If only 1,500 Americans are polled in a population of 200,000,000, each person questioned is, in effect, "speaking for" 133,333 people. How, it may be asked, can the views of one individual represent the opinions of so many fellow citizens?

The answer lies in the mathematical law of *probability*. Toss a coin 1,000 times and it will come up heads about 500 times. The same principle of probability is used by insurance companies in computing life expectancy. And it is used by pollsters in measuring opinion. Because the group to be measured, known as the *population* or the *universe*, is usually much too large to be polled individually on every issue, the poll-taker selects at *random* a *sample* of the population. The random sample must be representative of the universe that is being polled. When the *Literary Digest* polled owners of automobiles and telephones in 1936—a time when many Americans had neither—it was not sampling a representative group of Americans. As a result, its prediction that Franklin Roosevelt would lose the presidential election proved incorrect. If the sample is properly selected at random, the law of probability will operate, and the results will usually be accurate within a 4 percent margin of error.

Suppose, for example, that one out of every four Americans has blue eyes. For the same reason that the flipped coin comes up heads half the time, the probability is that a random sample will catch in its net the same percentage of blue-eyed persons as exists in the whole population. Using this technique, we can estimate the number of blue-eyed Americans from a random sample; similarly, we can estimate the number of Americans who support the space program or who oppose "socialized medicine."

The desirable size of the sample does not depend very much on the size of the population being measured, and beyond a certain point increasing the number of persons polled reduces the sampling error only slightly.

Because it would be difficult to select, locate, and interview 1,500 persons at random from all over the United States, and to locate and interview them all at once, polling organizations select geographical or political units at random and then interview persons at random within those units. Though not so precise as a true random sample, this modified sampling still preserves the principle of probability.

A less reliable method of polling is based on the *quota* sample. For example, an organization that wanted to test ethnic opinion would instruct its staff to interview blacks, Italians, Jews, Poles, Irishmen, and so on, in proportion to their percentage in the population as a whole. Because this method does not employ the rules of probability, it is less useful than the true random sample as a method of sampling political opinion.

The method of selecting the sample is not the only factor that may affect the reliability of a poll. The way in which questions are phrased, the personality of the interviewer, and the manner in which poll data are interpreted may all affect the result. Perhaps 10 to 20 percent of the people interviewed refuse to answer or answer only reluctantly. Gallup and Harris polls taken just before the 1968 election showed 5 to 7 percent "undecided" —a fairly normal percentage of persons in this flexible category. How this undecided vote is interpreted and allocated can drastically affect the accuracy of a political poll.

Political polls do not necessarily predict the outcome of an election. A poll only measures opinion at the moment the survey is taken. A poll taken four days before an election, for example, will not always match the vote on election day. As matters turned out in 1968, Dr. Gallup's final poll—which was taken from October 31 to November 2 and released on November 3, three days before the election—was very near the mark; it gave Nixon 42 percent of the vote. On November 6, Nixon was elected President with 43.4 percent of the vote.

An intriguing question today is whether there is a danger that the political polls will themselves influence the outcome of an election. Do some voters or convention delegates, out of a desire to be with the winner, jump on the bandwagon of the candidate who is leading in the polls? Such a conclusion, based on present evidence, is debatable, but the subject merits exploration.[24]

In any event, polls today are a permanent part of the political landscape and an important tool of the "new politics."

What
Americans
Believe

Do Americans agree on anything? Some people say that there is an underlying consensus in America, a basic agreement among all citizens on fundamental democratic values and processes, that permits democracy to flourish. But the supposed consensus often melts away and disappears upon closer examination. For example, Americans say they believe in fair play and justice, but they may not stick by those principles when their own interests are threatened. A white home-owner may know that it is "fair" for a black man to buy the house next door, but he may oppose the sale because he believes that the value of his property may go down if the neighborhood becomes racially mixed.

Nor is there a consensus about specific issues. On July 20, 1969, the Apollo 11 astronauts made man's first moon landing. But not all Americans approved of the cost of that historic feat. Many argued that the $24 billion that it cost to put a man on the moon would have been better spent in urban ghettos. The moon landing was booed by blacks in Harlem. One black resident declared: "There ain't no brothers in the program. . . .

[24] For a pollster's view of the question, see Dr. George H. Gallup, "Polls and the Political Process," *Public Opinion Quarterly*, Vol. 29 (Winter 1965–66), p. 546.

The whole thing uses money that should be spent right here on earth and I don't like them saying 'all good Americans should be happy about it'—I damn sure ain't happy about it." [25]

V. O. Key, Jr., has identified some attitudes on which Americans do seem to agree. For example, Americans seem to hold "an attitude of suspicion of authority" combined with admiration for the "lone hero"; on the whole they seem to be pragmatic, approaching each issue as it comes up and judging it on its merits. Most Americans do not have a fixed, coherent set of political beliefs. "Ideology, in the sense of a systematic ordering of specific issues in terms of general beliefs, seems to be limited to a small fraction of the electorate." [26]

Despite the conventional belief that America is a nation of "moderates," "conservatives," and "liberals," research on mass attitudes has shown that the great bulk of the public cannot be so neatly classified. People may have ideological preferences on specific issues, but often their convictions are not interrelated. A voter who is "liberal" on one issue may be "conservative" on another—for example, the white auto worker in Detroit who is a strong supporter of social welfare measures but is opposed to civil rights programs.

[25] *New York Times*, July 27, 1969, Sec. 4, p. 6.
[26] Key, *Public Opinion and American Democracy*, pp. 42–44, 49.

Studies have indicated, in fact, that many Americans hold ambivalent views on specific issues. Free and Cantril have reported that a majority of Americans are *operationally* liberal and *ideologically* conservative. They concluded that from the New Deal days to the present a majority of Americans have agreed that "at the operational level of Government programs, the Federal Government should act to meet public needs" in such fields as education, medical care, public housing, urban renewal, unemployment, and poverty.[27] This is being "operationally liberal."

But when the same Americans are asked questions about their general concepts of the proper role of government, they are "pronouncedly conservative." For example, of those with an opinion, a clear majority agreed with the statement: "The government has gone too far in regulating business and interfering with the private enterprise system." And, when asked to respond to the statement "We should rely much more on individual initiative and not so much on governmental welfare programs," 79 percent of those questioned agreed, 12 percent disagreed, and 9 percent did not know.[28]

This "split" personality of Americans is summed up by the salesman in Oregon who said he desired that "something be done for the poor, for the elderly and for people on relief." A few minutes later, however, he added that he feared "the Government will keep on spending over their income. If this doesn't end, we'll all be taxed to death." [29]

Party Identification

In any campaign, voters are influenced by a candidate's personality and appearance, and by the nature of the issues that arise. But how they vote, and what they think about public issues, are also closely linked to their political party affiliation. Political scientists distinguish, therefore, among *candidate* orientation, *issue* orientation, and *party* identification.[30] Of the three factors, the voter's attachment to a particular political party has traditionally been a very important influence on his thinking.

More than two-thirds of adult Americans identify with one of the two major parties. What is more, many voters maintain the same party allegiance for long periods of time. As we have noted, a child often identifies with his parents' political party by the time he has reached the fourth grade. Party loyalty tends to be passed on from one generation to the next.

Political Participation

In 1968, the Census Bureau estimated that 120,006,000 people in the United States were old enough to vote. Of that total, according to an Associated Press survey, 90,141,438 were registered to vote. Of these, on

[27] Free and Cantril, *The Political Beliefs of Americans*, p. 13.
[28] *Ibid.*, pp. 24, 26, 30.
[29] *Ibid.*, p. 39.
[30] Angus Campbell, Philip E. Converse, Warren E. Miller, and Donald E. Stokes, Survey Research Center, University of Michigan, *The American Voter* (New York: Wiley, 1960).

election day, November 6, 1968, 73,211,562 actually cast their ballots for President. That means that slightly more than 60 percent of the population of voting age actually voted.[31]

In off-year, nonpresidential elections, it is not unusual for less than half of the voting-age population to go to the polls to vote for senators and congressmen. In 1966, for example, 45.6 percent cast their ballots for members of the House of Representatives.

These figures, not uncommon for American elections, raise important questions about the nature of "government by the people."

"Every regime lives on a body of dogma, self-justification, glorification and propaganda about itself," E. E. Schattschneider has written.[32]

> In the United States, this body of dogma and tradition centers about democracy. The hero of the system is the voter who is commonly described as the ultimate source of all authority. The fact that something like forty million adult Americans are so unresponsive to the regime that they do not trouble to vote is the single most truly remarkable fact about it. . . . What kind of system is this in which only a little more than half of us participate? Is the system actually what we have been brought up to think it is? [33]

Some people do not vote because they may feel the system holds no benefits for them, or because they feel there is little difference between the candidates. Others are nonvoters because they are apathetic about politics and political issues.

Americans not only fail to participate fully in the political system, they are often poorly informed about government and many public issues. In 1964, a study conducted by the Survey Research Center of the University of Michigan showed that one-fourth of the American people were not aware that mainland China was ruled by a Communist government.[34] Another study also found only 26 percent of the American public "well informed" on specific questions dealing with international affairs (such as the identity of four major world leaders).[35]

Public knowledge about many specific questions concerning domestic politics is equally limited. A 1954 Gallup Poll reported that only 19 percent

[31] Of the nearly 40 percent who did not vote, some were barred from doing so for various reasons: 5,590,000 failed to meet state residence requirements, 1,078,000 were in correctional and mental institutions, and 2,704,000 were resident aliens, who cannot vote by law. When these categories of nonvoters are excluded, the percentage of voters goes up. For example, in 1968, 61.8 percent of the voting-age population voted, but the turnout as a percentage of those actually eligible to vote was 66.2 percent. And these figures on nonvoters, compiled by the Census Bureau, do not take into account persons who were ill on election day, or traveling. Source: U.S. Bureau of the Census, *Current Population Reports*, Population Estimates, Series P-25, No. 406, October, 4, 1968.
[32] E. E. Schattschneider, *The Semisovereign People* (New York: Holt, Rinehart and Winston, 1960), p. 99.
[33] *Ibid.*, pp. 99–100.
[34] Free and Cantril, *The Political Beliefs of Americans*, p. 59.
[35] *Ibid.*, p. 61.

of Americans interviewed could name the three branches of the Federal Government, and 51 percent did not know that each state has two United States senators.[36] A 1964 study showed that 37 percent of Americans could not identify Earl Warren, who at that time was serving his tenth year as Chief Justice of the United States.[37]

Schattschneider has concluded, "an amazingly large number of people do not seem to know very much about what is going on." [38] One effect of the lack of public knowledge is to give government officials wide latitude in making policy decisions—since they may assume that the public will neither know nor care very much about the results of those decisions.

Some scholars have argued that apathy is no real case for concern and that *too much* political participation may actually pose dangers to democracy.[39] They point out that Germany in the three years before Hitler came to power had an exceptionally high rate of political participation, and voting participation in Louisiana under demagogue Huey Long rose to 65 percent in the mid-1930's.[40] However, as Robert E. Lane notes, the risks to a democratic society of nonparticipation may be greater than the risks of participation.[41]

Complete political participation cannot be achieved in any society, nor is it necessary in order for democracy to function. But for a political system to be democratic, the number of players in the game cannot be limited except by individual choice.

Violence

The United States has a violent past. The American Revolution, the Civil War, the frontier, racial lynchings, and the Ku Klux Klan are some examples. Clearly, assassination and violence are not new forms of American political behavior. Four American Presidents have been assassinated—Lincoln, Garfield, McKinley, and Kennedy—and serious attempts have been made against the lives of four others—Jackson, Theodore Roosevelt, Franklin Roosevelt, and Truman.

But political assassination and violence occurred with tragic frequency during the 1960's. The assassination of President Kennedy in 1963, of his brother, Robert Kennedy, a presidential candidate, in 1968, and of Dr. Martin Luther King, Jr., that same year, all had dramatic impact upon the political process. So did the racial violence in America's cities.

Most political assassinations in American history appear to have been

[36] Gallup Poll, March 3, 1954.
[37] Free and Cantril, *The Political Beliefs of Americans*, p. 199.
[38] Schattschneider, *The Semisovereign People*, p. 132.
[39] For the pros and cons of this argument, see Lane, *Political Life*, Chapter 22.
[40] *Ibid.*, p. 350.
[41] *Ibid.*, p. 344.

November 22, 1963: President Kennedy is assassinated while riding in a motorcade in Dallas. Five years later, in 1968, similar violence claimed the lives of his brother Robert and Dr. Martin Luther King, Jr.

the acts of unbalanced men venting their rage and frustration on the national leader. Such purposeless acts differ in motivation from the planned assassination of a political leader by conspirators or revolutionists. Planned assassinations may be viewed as an attempt to go *outside* the political system. They are not a form of "participation" in the political system, but rather a rejection of that system.

As a Presidential study panel reported, "Assassination, especially when the victim is a President, strikes at the heart of the democratic process. It enables one man to nullify the will of the people in a single, savage act. It touches the lives of all the people of the nation." The study added: "The evidence from American history is overwhelming: no presidential assassination, with the exception of an abortive attempt on the life of President Truman, has been demonstrated to have sprung from a decision of an organized group whose goal was to change the policy or the structure of the United States government." [42]

Urban riots are another form of violence. But they are more clearly linked to the demands of a specific deprived group, the ghetto blacks. The riots of the 1960's affected the political system in contradictory ways. On the one hand, by bringing the mass of white Americans to a new and sharp awareness of the grievances of black Americans, they brought about efforts by the government and by private citizens to improve conditions in the inner-city. At the same time, they gave rise to a white "backlash" and to the political slogan "law and order."

Violence became so widespread in American society in the 1960's

[42] "Assassination," *To Establish Justice, To Insure Domestic Tranquility*, Final Report of the National Commission on the Causes and Prevention of Violence (Washington, D.C.: U.S. Government Printing Office, 1969), pp. 120, 122.

that President Johnson found it necessary to appoint three commissions to deal with various aspects of violence: the Warren Commission to study the murder of President Kennedy, the National Advisory Commission on Civil Disorders to study the urban riots, and the National Commission on the Causes and Prevention of Violence. The last panel was appointed after the assassination of Robert Kennedy; both its creation and its title reflect the political climate and the bewilderment of the 1960's.

A study group of scholars appointed by this commission noted that violence, urban mobs, lynchings, labor wars, and vigilantism are part of the nation's history, however much Americans may choose to ignore that fact. The study group added that the question of whether or not the United States today is a "violent society" cannot be answered in abstract terms but only by comparison with the American past or with other nations.[43] The study concluded that the United States was probably less violent in the turbulent 1960's than it had been in the nineteenth century, and that it had enjoyed relative stability in its political institutions despite the fact that, since 1948, it has ranked "among the half-dozen most tumultuous nations in the world." [44]

It would be a mistake, however, to minimize the danger of violence to American institutions or to gloss over the causes of violent political expression. In a sense, the level of violence is an index of a society's ability to cope with its problems, meet the demands of its people, and ensure its own survival.

Mass Opinion in a Democracy

Suppose that the President of the United States could push a button every morning and receive, along with his scrambled eggs and coffee, a punch card that would summarize the precise state of public opinion on a given spectrum of issues during the preceding twenty-four hours. And suppose that he tried to tailor his policies to this computerized intelligence. Would that be good or bad?

Good, one person might respond. After all, democracy is supposed to be government by the people, and if the President knows just what people are thinking he can act in accordance with the popular will.

Bad, another might answer. The President is elected to lead the nation, not to follow the shifting winds of public opinion. After all, if the people are not satisfied with a President's leadership and judgment, they may elect a new one every four years.

Both arguments have merit. A President or a congressman usually tries to lead public opinion and at the same time to follow it. No President can

---

[43] Hugh Davis Graham and Ted Robert Gurr, *Violence in America: Historical and Comparative Perspectives* (New York: Bantam Books, 1969), p. 798.
[44] *Ibid.*

totally ignore public opinion during the four years between elections. But if our hypothetical President did try to rule according to his computer punch cards, he would soon find there was no way to please everybody. He would also discover that if the policies suggested by his punch cards failed to work, those policies—and he—would soon become highly unpopular.

The truth is that the role of public opinion in a democracy has never been satisfactorily defined. The people, Walter Lippmann has argued, "can elect the government. They can remove it. They can approve or disapprove its performance. But they cannot administer the government. They cannot themselves perform. . . . A mass cannot govern." [45]

Certainly the public does not possess nearly so much information as the President, who daily receives a massive flow of data from all over the globe to aid him in his decision-making. On the other hand, as E. E. Schattschneider has pointed out, *nobody knows enough to run the government. Presidents, senators, governors, judges, professors, doctors of philosophy, editors and the like are only a little less ignorant than the rest of us.*" [46]

The unstated premise of opinion polls, Schattschneider adds, is that "the people really do decide what the government does on something like a day-to-day basis." [47] Obviously, that is rarely the case. It is reasonable to assume, however, that Presidents and legislators, because they hope to be reelected, do take public opinion into consideration in reaching major policy decisions. (In addition, they try to influence public opinion to win support for the decisions they make.)

Public opinion in a democracy, then, may be seen as a broad but flexible framework for policy-making, setting certain outer limits within which government may act. As Key has observed, "Unless mass views have some place in the shaping of policy, all the talk about democracy is nonsense." [48]

MASS MEDIA AND PUBLIC OPINION

In a modern society, the public forms its opinions largely on the basis of what the mass media—newspapers, television, radio, and magazines—present to it. Consequently, the quality of the mass media, the amount of time and space they devote to public affairs, their editorial stands, ownership patterns, and objectivity are all matters of interest.

[45] Walter Lippmann, *Essays in the Public Philosophy* (Boston: Little, Brown, 1955), p. 14.
[46] Schattschneider, *The Semisovereign People*, p. 136.
[47] *Ibid.*, p. 133.
[48] Key, *Public Opinion and American Democracy*, p. 7.

With 83,000,000 television sets in American homes, the potential for creating an informed public through TV is vast. Entertainment is the economic heart of the television industry, however, and news and public affairs programs occupy only a small part of the broadcast day. The three major networks, CBS, NBC, and ABC, dominate the industry. In 1968, for example, 51.9 percent of all television revenues went to the three networks and their fifteen wholly owned TV stations.[49] The networks sell popular packaged shows to affiliates across the nation, and charge large fees for airing sponsors' commercials during "prime" time—the after-dinner hours when millions of persons are tuned in to network programs. For example, on a typical weeknight during the prime time of 9 to 10 P.M. sponsors pay almost $1,000,000 to the three networks for six minutes of advertising time on each network.[50]

Audience rating figures are the controlling statistics in the broadcast industry. On an evening in February 1970, a weekly average of 32,812,620 Americans were watching *Laugh-In* on NBC. Earlier the same evening, an average of only 17,700,000 Americans watched the NBC evening news; 18,217,500 persons watched CBS news.[51]

In spite of these figures, the networks have expanded their news programs in recent years. Sunday panel shows like *Meet the Press* continue to air political issues, and the networks broadcast a wide range of news documentaries. The networks and many local stations maintain their own news staffs. Because television reaches so many homes, news programs have a strong influence on public opinion. Certainly news reports of the fighting in Vietnam, by bringing that conflict into American living rooms night after night, were a major factor in swinging public opinion against the war. Television coverage of political debates and conventions convey an immediacy and have an impact that no other medium can approach.

A farmer in Nebraska and an attorney in Manhattan may both read newspapers, but the treatment of news about government and politics may be very different in the pages they read. The attorney probably reads the *New York Times*, which places heavy emphasis on national and international news gathered by its own reporters. The farmer may read a small-town daily that concentrates on crop reports, wheat prices, and local events and that relies on the wire services for sketchy reports about national and world events.

There are a number of excellent newspapers in the United States. A partial list would include the *New York Times*, the *Washington Post*, the

[49] Congressional Quarterly, *Weekly Report*, September 26, 1969, p. 1801.
[50] Hyman H. Goldin, "The Television Overlords," *Atlantic*, July 1969, p. 88.
[51] *National Nielsen TV Ratings*, two weeks ending February 8, 1970.

St. Louis Post-Dispatch, the *Christian Science Monitor*, the *Wall Street Journal*, the *Los Angeles Times*, the *Chicago Sun-Times*, and the *Minneapolis Tribune*. But for a majority of Americans, who live outside the circulation area of such publications, the outstanding fact about their newspaper is often not its excellence but how limited is its coverage of national and world news.

Moreover, daily papers are disappearing. In 1909, there were 2,600 dailies in the United States. By 1955 there were 1,785, and by 1967, only 1,749.

As a result, more and more cities have no competing newspapers—either there is only one newspaper, or else all the papers are controlled by one owner. By 1967, there was no competition in an estimated 97 percent of cities with daily papers; and 752 daily newspapers, or 44 percent of all

FIGURE 6-1

Decline in United States Daily Newspaper Competition

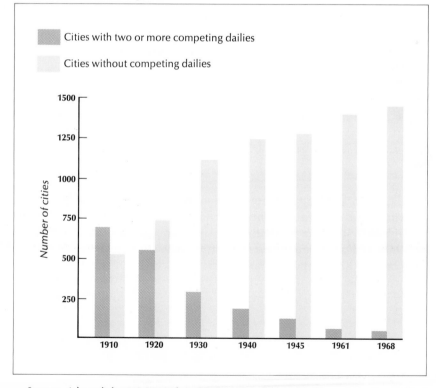

Source: Adapted from Raymond B. Nixon, "Trends in U.S. Newspaper Ownership," American Newspaper Publishers Association reprint, 1969.

FIGURE 6-2

Audiences Reached by Leading Media

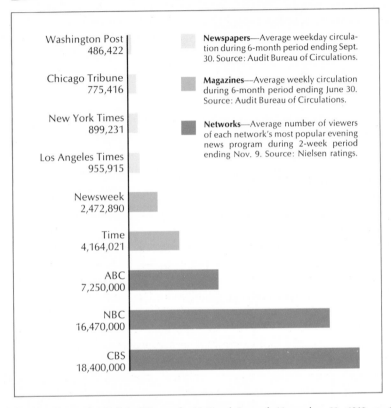

Washington Post 486,422

Chicago Tribune 775,416

New York Times 899,231

Los Angeles Times 955,915

Newsweek 2,472,890

Time 4,164,021

ABC 7,250,000

NBC 16,470,000

CBS 18,400,000

Newspapers—Average weekday circulation during 6-month period ending Sept. 30. Source: Audit Bureau of Circulations.

Magazines—Average weekly circulation during 6-month period ending June 30. Source: Audit Bureau of Circulations.

Networks—Average number of viewers of each network's most popular evening news program during 2-week period ending Nov. 9. Source: Nielsen ratings.

Source: Center for Political Research, *National Journal,* November 22, 1969, p. 186. Courtesy of *National Journal* (copyright 1969).

the dailies in the United States were controlled by chains.[52] Because of a growing trend toward concentrated ownership of all media, in 1967 there were seventy-three communities in which one person or company owned or controlled all the local newspaper and television and radio outlets.[53] This means that the public has less and less choice in selecting its sources of information. This has proved dramatically true in New York City, for example, which had eight newspapers in 1948 and three in 1968.

Magazines

The citizen who feels that his local newspaper and broadcast outlets fail to provide him with enough news on public issues may, of

[52] *Hearings,* Senate Judiciary Committee, Subcommittee on Antitrust and Monopoly, U.S. 90th Congress, Vol. 243, Part I, p. 202.
[53] The editors of the *Atlantic,* "The American Media Baronies, a modest Atlantic Atlas," *Atlantic,* July 1969, p. 83.

course, subscribe to a weekly newsmagazine. Less than 5 percent of the population does so, however. The circulation of *Time* is 4,137,697; *Newsweek*, 2,540,867; and *U.S. News and World Report*, 1,812,936. By contrast, the circulation of the *Reader's Digest* is 17,586,127, and a mass pictorial magazine such as *Life* has a circulation of 8,560,647. Smaller magazines that comment on public affairs have relatively tiny circulations: *Harper's*, 382,863; the *Atlantic*, 344,141; and the *New Republic*, 143,955.[54]

In short, Americans do not read much about public affairs. How much they retain is still another question. According to one study of newspaper reading habits, 47 percent of the people interviewed said they just read the headlines; fully 20 percent said the part of the newspaper they were most interested in was the comic strips.[55]

The Press in a Democratic Society

Despite its shortcomings, the free press in the United States is essential to the functioning of a democracy and a vital link between the public and the government. Public opinion is formed on the basis of what the media present to the public. Democratic government rests broadly on public opinion and presupposes a reasonably well-informed public. American governments have always had to worry about adverse public judgments on the quality of their performance in office. In the course of four years, opinions *are* formed about the merits of a President and his staff.

Aside from its role of informing the general public, the American press—particularly the quality newspapers, magazines, and television news programs—does an excellent job of informing those who are politically aware—politicians, opinion leaders, political scientists, lawyers, journalists, teachers, college students, and others who are attuned to politics.

Information about public affairs, in other words, is available to those who want it. There is nothing about democracy that guarantees an alert, educated public. Like voting and other forms of political participation, knowledge of public affairs—the basis of intelligent public opinion—is largely up to the individual.

INTEREST GROUPS IN A PLURALIST SOCIETY

Who governs in a democracy? Three different answers are possible. It can be said that "the people" govern through political leaders elected as candidates of political parties.

Who Governs?

Another view is that a "power elite," a "power structure," or an "establishment" actually runs things. This was the view advanced by sociologist C. Wright Mills in *The Power Elite*. Mills argued that a small group,

[54] Magazine circulation figures as of August 11, 1970.
[55] Lane, *Political Life*, pp. 284–85.

"possessors of power, wealth and celebrity" occupy the key positions in American society.[56] Political writer Richard H. Rovere, in a semi-humorous vein, describes the "American Establishment" as a loose coalition of leaders of finance, business, the professions, and the universities who hold power and influence in the United States regardless of what administration occupies the White House.[57]

Although elites do exist in almost every field of human activity, many scholars reject the concept that a single economic and social elite wields ultimate political power. In his classic study of community power in New Haven in the late 1950's, Robert A. Dahl provided a third answer to the question of "Who Governs?" He examined several specific public issues and traced the process by which decisions were made on those issues. He concluded that the city's economic and social "notables" did not run New Haven. Some individuals and groups were particularly influential in the making of one type of decision—educational policy, for example. But in other policy areas, very different individuals and groups often played the most important role. The city was dominated by many different sets of leaders: "It was, in short, a pluralist system."[58]

Some have criticized Dahl's approach on the grounds that the wielders of power cannot always be identified by examining key decisions. For example, truly powerful men might prevent certain issues from ever reaching the public arena.[59]

Nevertheless, the *pluralist* character of American democracy is widely recognized. Pluralism exists when many conflicting groups within the community have access to government officials and compete with one another in an effort to influence policy decisions. Pluralism supposes, of course, that individuals are active in many groups and associations to advance their interests, and that these multiple interests and memberships overlap and, in many cases, conflict. For example, the same man who favors new school construction as a member of the PTA may oppose higher taxes as a member of a neighborhood association. As we shall see, however, many groups have been badly underrepresented or left out of the pluralist system.

Interest Groups: A Definition

Public opinion, as we have seen, is the expression of attitudes on public questions. When people organize to express attitudes held in common and to influence the government to respond to those attitudes, they become members of *interest groups.*

[56] C. Wright Mills, *The Power Elite* (New York: Oxford University Press, 1959), pp. 8, 13.
[57] Richard H. Rovere, *The American Establishment* (New York: Harcourt Brace Jovanovich, 1962), p. 6.
[58] Robert A. Dahl, *Who Governs?* (New Haven, Conn.: Yale University Press, 1961), p. 86.
[59] See Peter Bachrach and Morton S. Baratz, "Two Faces of Power," *American Political Science Review*, Vol. 56, No. 4 (December 1962).

In the nineteenth century, political cartoonists were fond of drawing pot-bellied men in top hats and striped pants to represent Big Business. Muckrakers assailed oil, steel, and railroad barons as members of interest groups in league against the public welfare. Partly as a result of this muckraking tradition, many people tend to regard all "interest groups" as evil, business-dominated organizations that are plotting against the common weal.

Most political scientists today consider interest groups a normal and vital part of the political process, conveyors of the demands and supports that are fed into the political system. David B. Truman defines an interest group as "a shared-attitude group that makes certain claims upon other groups in the society" by acting through "the institutions of government." [60]

Whether such groups are called "interest groups," or "pressure groups," or "lobbies"—and there is some disagreement over which label is best—their purpose is much the same. Interest groups are listened to because they are considered legitimate representatives of segments of American society. These groups should not be confused with political parties, which also seek to influence government—but by electing candidates to office. As we noted in Chapter 1, the members of some interest groups—college students, for example—may not be formally organized as a group.

The tendency of Americans to come together in groups was noticed in the early nineteenth century by Alexis de Tocqueville. "In no country of the world," he observed, "has the principle of association been more successfully used or applied to a greater multitude of objects than in America." [61]

Who Belongs?

There are more than 100,000 clubs and associations in the United States. Not everyone belongs to a group, however. Just as some 40 percent of the population does not vote, a like percentage belongs to no organizations. Not all organizations are interested in influencing government, and so only a minority of Americans belong to interest groups. One survey reported that only 31 percent of the population belonged to groups that sometimes take a stand on housing, better government, school problems, or other public issues.[62] The fact that well over one-third of Americans belong to no groups at all raises basic questions about pluralist democracy that will be discussed later in this chapter.

[60] David B. Truman, *The Governmental Process* (New York: Knopf, 1951), p. 37.
[61] Alexis de Tocqueville, *Democracy in America*, Vol. I, Phillips Bradley, ed. (New York: Vintage Books, 1945), p. 198.
[62] Lane, *Political Life*, p. 75.

In 1968, according to Congressional Quarterly, 266 organizations reported spending $4.2 million to influence Congress.[63] The breakdown shows that business spent the most, then labor groups and citizens' organizations. Farm groups ranked next, followed by professional associations and military and veterans' organizations. (See Table 6-2.)

TABLE 6-2

Lobby Spending, 1968

Type of Organization	Number of Groups Reporting	Reported Expenditures
Business	141	$1,498,161
Employee and Labor	31	1,082,655
Citizens	52	849,143
Farm	17	438,951
Professional	19	274,135
Military and Veterans	6	155,117

Source: Adapted from Congressional Quarterly, *Weekly Report,* June 27, 1969, p. 1136.

What were these groups lobbying about? Who were they? Here is a look in capsule form at some of these organizations and their activities during 1969:

The American Security Council, sponsored by contributions from industry and private sources, is a Chicago-based organization that lobbies in the field of foreign and military policy. In 1969, with contributions from three large defense contractors engaged in the Anti-Ballistic Missile program (ABM)—Motorola, Inc., General Electric, and the Lockheed Aircraft Corporation—the council lobbied heavily in favor of the ABM. It distributed 20,000 copies of a book favoring the ABM to members of Congress, journalists, and Pentagon officials. Congress narrowly approved the construction of the first two ABM sites in 1969.

The National Association of Manufacturers, a major business interest group, represents 14,000 companies. It is highly conservative and has generally opposed the efforts of organized labor. Its main concern in 1969 was the Tax Reform Act. Among the various sections of the bill that it fought were an increase in personal income tax exemptions, a reduction in the oil depletion allowance, and an increase in the tax on capital gains, all of which were passed in the version of the bill enacted into law.

[63] Congressional Quarterly, *Weekly Report*, June 27, 1969, p. 1128. Because of loopholes in the Federal Regulation of Lobbying Act of 1946, these figures fall short of reflecting the actual number of groups that lobby and what they spend.

The AFL-CIO, an aggressive and often effective interest group, represents 14,000,000 members. In 1969, it fought against the nomination to the United States Supreme Court of a Southern conservative, Clement Haynsworth, Jr., of South Carolina. The Senate rejected the Haynsworth nomination.

The American Automobile Association (AAA) represents 12,000,000 motorists in all fifty states. In 1969, as it had in 1968, the AAA lobbied against a bill that would have allowed bigger and heavier trucks on the nation's highways. The measure died in a house committee.

The Urban Coalition Action Council is the lobbying arm of the Urban Coalition, an organization that represents business, labor, civil rights, and citizens groups interested in urban problems. The council lobbies for increases in the amount of funds appropriated by Congress for urban needs. In 1969, it was only moderately pleased with the size of the increases voted for Model Cities, urban renewal, and public housing.

The Sierra Club, representing 85,000 members, lobbies to protect the environment. Among its activities in 1969, the club urged the appropriation of $1 billion for clean water programs. Congress approved $800 million.

Although interest groups vary tremendously in size, goals, budget, and scope of interest, they often employ the same techniques to accomplish their objectives. Some of these techniques are described below.

How They Operate

Mass Propaganda. One of the ways in which interest groups try to influence government is through mass publicity campaigns. Using television, magazine, and newspaper advertising, and direct mailings to the general public and specialized audiences, interest groups seek to create a favorable climate for their goals. With the aid of a public relations firm, an interest group can mount a short- or long-range campaign to further its cause, utilizing all the latest techniques of Madison Avenue's idea merchants. But it takes a great deal of ballyhoo to influence public opinion enough to create a response from government, and only affluent interest groups can afford programs for the mass manipulation of public opinion.[64]

An example of an apparently successful campaign by an affluent group was the lobbying effort by the American Automobile Association to force the trucking bill off the road in 1968. The AAA ran newspaper advertisements showing a triple-trailer truck with a huge boar's head devouring the highway as John Q. Motorist sat helplessly by, trapped in a monstrous traffic jam. The ad urged that the bill be defeated for reasons of safety, and "because of the irreparable damage bigger trucks will do to

[64] V. O. Key, Jr., *Politics, Parties, and Pressure Groups*, 5th edition (New York: Crowell, 1964), p. 130.

our highways and bridges." With the public alarmed and the nation's bridges in apparent danger of imminent collapse, Congress abandoned the trucking bill. Presumably the AAA's publicity barrage influenced this outcome.

In 1962 alone, the American Medical Association is reported to have spent between $7,000,000 and $12,000,000 to fight Medicare. By its own account, $1,300,000 of that total went for a single item—public relations.[65]

Lobbying. By far the most powerful technique of interest groups is lobbying, the direct attempt to influence legislation through contact with the legislators. Originally, the term "lobby-agent" was used to describe someone who waited in the lobbies of government buildings to buttonhole lawmakers. The term "lobbying" first came into use in the New York State capital at Albany and was being used in Washington by the early 1830's.

In its broadest sense, lobbying is not confined to efforts to influence the legislative branch. Lobbyists also seek to influence officials of the executive branch. For this reason Lester Milbrath prefers to define lobbying as communication by someone other than an ordinary citizen *"directed to a governmental decision-maker with the hope of influencing his decision."* [66]

One way that a lobbyist influences an official is simple: he gets to know him. By paying personal visits to Congressmen and government officials, by attending hearings of congressional committees, government agencies, and regulatory commissions, and by forming friendships with staff members and bureaucrats, the lobbyist makes his presence felt. Milbrath found that more than half of the Washington lobbyists felt that the personal presentation of viewpoints was the most effective way of reaching congressmen.[67]

Senators and representatives are busy men—often the lobbyist's chief value is that he presents carefully researched background material that may help a congressman decide how to vote on a complex bill. According to Washington lobbyist Scott Lucas, a former Democratic senator from Illinois, "The important thing is the research work done in your office. . . .

[65] James Deakin, *The Lobbyists* (Washington, D.C.: Public Affairs Press, 1966), p. 222.
[66] Lester W. Milbrath, *The Washington Lobbyists* (Chicago: Rand McNally, 1963), p. 8.
[67] *Ibid.*, pp. 212–13.

216

off and on, I may spend three or four weeks on research for a 10 or 15 minute appointment with a Senator. I could have a lot of time with that Senator because I'm a former Senator, but I don't want to take up that good man's time. So I brief myself thoroughly before I go up—that's where the work comes." [68]

Money is another useful tool for the lobbyist. The public often thinks of the lobbyist as someone who hands out money to buy the votes of legislators. That may happen. A direct bribe, however, is a violation of federal law. Under a 1962 statute, a person who bribes a congressman or a congressman who takes "anything of value" in exchange for his vote may be fined $20,000 and imprisoned up to fifteen years. The language of the statute is broad enough to cover any kind of valuable favor, not just money. Instances of bribery are probably relatively infrequent for two reasons. First, bribery is illegal and risky. Second, there are better, legal ways to channel money to legislators. For example, lobbyists for interest groups can exert influence by means of campaign contributions and fund-raising.

In the six years prior to 1969, the American Medical Political Action Committee, the AMA's political arm, raised more than $1.8 million for distribution to candidates for the House and Senate and state and local offices. [69] In 1968 alone, AMPAC handed out $681,000 to political candidates. Many of the recipients were conservative Republicans.

Many large interest groups like the AMA are deeply involved in poli-

[68] Deakin, *The Lobbyists*, p. 186.
[69] *Washington Star*, June 29, 1969, p. 1.

"There's getting to be a lot of dangerous talk about the public interest."

From *The Herblock Gallery* (Simon & Schuster, 1968)

A number of the modern lobbies operating in Washington are of the highest quality. With plenty of money to spend, they spend it on qualified analysts and advocates and provide Congressional committees with lucid briefs and technical documentation in support of their positions. Nothing is more informative and helpful to a legislative committee than to hear the views of competent well-matched advocates on the opposite sides of a legislative issue.

—Congressman Emanuel Celler,
in Lester W. Milbrath, *The Washington Lobbyists.*

tics. They not only make campaign contributions to the candidates they favor; they publicly endorse and assist them as well. An example is the AFL-CIO Committee on Political Education (COPE). COPE contributes money to candidates, runs voter registration drives, publicly endorses candidates, publishes their voting records for union members, and often provides volunteers to assist in political campaigns. Although ostensibly nonpartisan, COPE in fact has mainly aided Democrats, just as the AMA and the NAM are Republican-oriented.

During the battle between the AAA and the trucking industry, the *Des Moines Register* disclosed that the American Trucking Association had contributed $83,000 to political campaigns in two years, mostly to members of Congress serving on committees that affect the trucking industry. The contributions included $1,000 to the chairman of the House Public Works Committee and $3,000 to the chairman of the Roads Subcommittee, both Democrats. Two ranking Republicans also received substantial contributions from the truckers.

Lobbyists are expected to purchase tickets or whole tables of tickets to fund-raising dinners for political parties and candidates. A lobbyist may take a senator to lunch at an expensive restaurant in Washington. He may arrange a weekend on a yacht or a free trip to a resort. Christmas may bring the legislator a ham, a case of Scotch, or a pair of gold cufflinks.

But lunches and small favors are only minor props in the drama of influencing lawmakers. Many members of Congress are practicing lawyers, insurance agents, bankers, and businessmen. For example, 315 members of the Ninetieth Congress were lawyers. It is not difficult for interest groups with nationwide chapters and members to channel legal or insurance fees or bank loans to members of Congress. Unless such payments can be shown to be outright bribes, they are legal; in any event, they are difficult to trace.

The popular image of a Washington lobbyist as a glamorous figure who entertains powerful senators and dines at the best places is overdrawn, however. As most lobbyists are quick to point out, the bulk of their work consists of solid research, long hours of committee hearings, and conversations with congressmen in their offices.

After a careful study of Washington lobbyists, Milbrath concluded

Most people do not write to their congressman, but interest groups may inspire a letter-writing campaign.

that the process is "remarkably clean," and added: "It is virtually impossible to steal or buy a public policy decision of any consequence in Washington." [70] Nevertheless, lobbyists and their techniques, including the powerful weapon of the campaign contribution, do have a substantial influence on political decision-making.

Grassroots Pressure. Although lobbyists prefer direct contact with legislators, most interest groups and their lobbyists employ various forms of grassroots pressure. To influence a senator, for example, an interest group might persuade a powerful banker in the senator's state to telephone him in Washington. A lobbyist may ask a close personal friend of the senator's to get in touch with him. Or the lobbyist may try to get great numbers of a legislator's constituents to write or wire him.

Members of Congress are well aware that interest groups may be behind a sudden flood of postcards or letters on a pending bill. In addition the legislator knows that, since most people do not write letters to their congressmen, the mail he receives reflects the feelings of only a small percentage of his constituents. One 1964 study showed that only 17 percent of the general public writes letters to members of Congress.[71] Furthermore, if interest groups on opposite sides of an issue stimulate their members to write to their congressmen, the letters tend to cancel each other out. Nevertheless, grassroots pressure remains a popular form of lobbying, in part because lobbyists, never certain which techniques are the most effective, tend to try them all.

Still other weapons are available to interest groups, as we know from our discussion of the civil rights movement in Chapter 5. For example, interest groups may use court litigation to influence government, they may practice peaceful protest, or, as in the case of some militant groups, they may turn to violence.

[70] Milbrath, *The Washington Lobbyists*, p. 304.
[71] Donald Devine, *The Attentive Public* (Chicago: Rand McNally, 1969), p. 119.

On January 15, 1969, five days before President Nixon's inauguration, the incoming Secretary of Health, Education, and Welfare, Robert H. Finch, summoned Dr. John H. Knowles to Washington and offered him the post of Assistant Secretary for Health and Scientific Affairs, the nation's top health post. "I accept," said Dr. Knowles.[72]

Dr. Knowles, a young, personable man and an outstanding physician and scientist, had for eight years served successfully as chief administrator of Massachusetts General Hospital. His credentials were excellent, and there seemed no reason to doubt that his appointment would be announced in due course and would receive the necessary Senate approval.

A few days later Dr. Knowles was informed of a slight hitch—but everything, he was assured, would be cleared up and the President would announce his appointment. The slight hitch, as matters developed, was the powerful American Medical Association, which considered Dr. Knowles too liberal on the question of the role of the Federal Government in health care programs and related matters. For example, Dr. Knowles favored more government aid to the poor and the aged, programs that the AMA opposed.

Despite the AMA's campaign against the Knowles appointment, it was widely assumed that President Nixon would approve it, partly because Secretary Finch was one of his closest friends and oldest political advisers. But the AMA gained a powerful ally in the person of Senator Everett M. Dirksen, the Republican leader of the Senate. Representative Bob Wilson of California, chairman of the Republican Congressional Campaign Committee, which raises campaign funds for Republican House members, also opposed Knowles. In 1968, the AMA's political arm (AMPAC) had contributed $681,000 to political races. House Republican Leader Gerald R. Ford pointed out that many of these contributions had helped Republican congressmen, and that Republicans, in turn, "support their friends."

Nevertheless, on June 19, President Nixon announced at a press conference that he would support whomever Finch recommended for the health post. So confident was Finch of the appointment that he told a newspaper reporter that Nixon would "have to find another Secretary" of HEW if Dr. Knowles' name was not sent to the Senate for confirmation.

But the President then came under intense pressure from Republican conservatives, whose votes he needed to pass an income tax surcharge bill that was before Congress. And the AMA was continuing to lobby against Dr. Knowles. On June 26, Finch called Dr. Knowles at his vacation home in Massachusetts.

"I have bad news," he said. "The President says 'no soap.' "

The next day, Finch announced that he had "reluctantly and regretfully" decided to drop his six-month fight for Dr. Knowles. The following

---

[72] This summary of the Knowles affair is based on contemporary newspaper accounts in the *New York Times*, the *Washington Post*, and the *Washington Star*.

"Actually, Dr. Knowles, I was calling about some trouble I've been having with my back."

Copyright 1969 by Herblock in The Washington Post

day, Nixon chose Dr. Roger Egeberg of California for the post, and Finch introduced the new Assistant Secretary to reporters. Dr. Egeberg was a jolly, cherubic sort of man, wrote columnist Mary McGrory, but his patient, Robert H. Finch, "was in such pain that there was little that science and skill could do for him." Finch (who was transferred from HEW to the White House less than a year later) was politically scarred by his unsuccessful battle, and the AMA had proven itself one of the most formidable interest groups in America.

Because the Constitution protects free speech and the right to petition the government, the efforts of interest groups to influence Congress are constitutionally protected. Nevertheless, public concern over lobbying abuses led Congress some years ago to try to impose legal controls on interest groups. The first such bills were introduced in 1907, but Congress did not pass even limited legislation to control lobbying until 1935 and 1936. A bill that was enacted soon afterward, the Foreign Agents Registration Act of 1938, requires lobbyists for foreign governments to register with the Justice Department. Not until 1946, however, did Congress pass a general bill that attempted to control lobbying.

The Federal Regulation of Lobbying Act of 1946 requires individuals and groups to register with the Clerk of the House and the Secretary of

Regulating Interest Groups

the Senate if they solicit or collect money or any other thing of value "to be used principally to aid . . . the passage or defeat of any legislation by the Congress of the United States." In 1954, the Supreme Court narrowed the scope of the act by exempting grassroots lobbying aimed at the public. Because of this decision and the loose wording of the statute, many interest groups simply do not register, on the grounds that lobbying is not their "principal purpose." The NAM is such a group. Moreover, although the law contains penalties, it has no enforcement provision. As a result, there have been few prosecutions since its enactment in 1946.

In 1956, Senator Francis Case, a South Dakota Republican, speaking on the floor of the Senate, revealed that a lobbyist for the natural gas bill had tried to give him a $2,500 "campaign contribution." A Senate committee was appointed to investigate. Meanwhile, President Eisenhower vetoed the gas bill because of "arrogant" lobbying. Later two attorneys for the Superior Oil Company of California, and the Company itself, pleaded guilty and were fined for offering the money to Case without having registered as lobbyists. On the whole, however, the Lobbying Act does not effectively regulate lobbying of Congress. And, of course, it does not apply at all to lobbying of the executive branch or the independent regulatory commissions.

The Uses and Abuses of Interest Groups

The view persists in American politics that interest groups are undemocratic, and that they work for narrow goals against the general welfare. It may be more realistic to view these groups simply as one part of the total political process. Citizens, after all, have every right under the Con-

---

THE SUPREME COURT ON LOBBYING

Present day legislative complexities are such that individual members of Congress cannot be expected to explore the myriad pressures to which they are regularly subjected. Yet full realization of the American ideal of government by elected representatives depends to no small extent on their ability to properly evaluate such pressures. Otherwise the voice of the people may all too easily be drowned out by the voice of special interest groups seeking favored treatment while masquerading as proponents of the public weal. This is the evil which the Lobbying Act was designed to help prevent.

Toward that end, Congress has not sought to prohibit these pressures. It has merely provided for a modicum of information from those who for hire attempt to influence legislation or who collect or spend funds for that purpose. It wants only to know who is being hired, who is putting up the money, and how much.

—Chief Justice Earl Warren,
delivering the majority opinion in *U.S. v. Harriss*, 347 U.S. 612 (1954).

stitution to organize to influence their government. Interest groups compete for the government's attention and action—but so do individual voters, political parties, and the press; this is the nature of a pluralist society.

On many major issues, there are likely to be interest groups arrayed on opposite sides. Those who accept democratic pluralism and the politics of interest groups believe that out of these conflicting pressures some degree of balance may be achieved, at least much of the time.

Interest groups perform functions in the American political system that cannot be performed as well through the conventional structures of government, which are based largely on geographic representation.

Interest groups provide a kind of *representation* that supplements the representation provided by Congress. And they may permit the *resolution of intergroup conflicts.* In collective bargaining, for example, differences between two powerful interest groups—management and labor—are resolved. Interest groups also perform a *watchdog* function; they can sound the alarm when new government policies threaten to injure the interests of their members. Finally, interest groups perform the function of *idea initiating,* that is, they generate new ideas that may become government programs. So important are these functions, Lester Milbrath has concluded "if we had no lobby groups and lobbyists we would probably have to invent them." [73]

Some very serious criticisms can be leveled at interest groups, however. Perhaps the most comprehensive criticism of interest group politics has been formulated by Theodore J. Lowi.[74] Lowi questions the assumption of many scholars and political leaders that the interest group process in a pluralist society provides a desirable, or satisfactory, way for the American governmental system to work. He also argues that there is no assurance that the "pulling and hauling among competing interests" will result in policy decisions that are adequate to meet the social and political problems now facing the United States. In Lowi's view, interest group pluralism has not resulted in "strong, positive government" but in "impotent government." And, he adds, "Government that is formless in action and amoral in intention (i.e., *ad hoc*) is government that can neither plan nor achieve justice." [75]

As we have seen, most Americans do *not* belong to interest groups. Those who do, tend to come from the better-educated, middle- or upper-class backgrounds that produce citizens with a high degree of political motivation. "The flaw in the pluralist heaven," E. E. Schattschneider has observed, "is that the heavenly chorus sings with a strong upper-class

[73] Milbrath, *The Washington Lobbyists,* p. 358.
[74] Theodore J. Lowi, *The End of Liberalism: Ideology, Policy, and the Crisis of Public Authority* (New York: Norton, 1969).
[75] *Ibid.,* p. x.

223

The poor are powerless because they are a minority of the population, are often difficult to organize, and are not even a homogeneous group with similar interests that could be organized into an effective pressure group. . . .

Although every citizen is urged to be active in the affairs of his community and nation, in actual practice participation is almost entirely limited to organized interest groups or lobbies who want something from government.

As a result, legislation tends to favor the interests of the organized: of businessmen, not consumers, even though the latter are a vast majority; of landlords, not tenants; doctors, not patients. . . . while the American political structure often satisfies the majority, it also creates *outvoted minorities* who can be tyrannized and repressed by majority rule, such as the poor and the black, students, migrant workers and many others. . . . The only other source of power left to outvoted minorities is *disruption,* upsetting the orderly processes of government and of daily life so as to inconvenience or threaten more powerful groups. . . .

Clearly, disruption is not the ideal way for outvoted minorities to achieve their demands.

Nevertheless, disruption has become an accepted political technique, and may be used more widely in the nineteen seventies, as other groups who feel they are being short-changed by American democracy begin to voice their demands. Consequently, perhaps the most important domestic issue before the country today is whether outvoted minorities—in the cities and elsewhere—must resort to further disruption, or whether more peaceful and productive ways of meeting their needs can be found.

—Herbert J. Gans, "We Won't End the Urban Crisis Until We End 'Majority Rule,' " *New York Times Magazine,* August 3, 1969.

accent. Probably about 90 percent of the people cannot get into the pressure system." [76]

Disadvantaged groups—the poor, blacks, Mexican Americans, slum dwellers, migrant workers—often have neither the knowledge nor the money to organize to advance their interests. Interest group politics, in other words, is biased against minorities and in favor of business organizations and other affluent groups in American society.

The ordinary American consumer is also largely unrepresented in interest group politics. The average American who drives to work in a costly but possibly unsafe car, is assailed by noisy commercials, sits in front of a color TV set that emanates harmful X-rays, swims at a beach polluted by oil, inhales pesticides and smog-filled air, and eats food enhanced with dangerous additives may be forgiven if he wonders what interest group represents *him.*

In 1969, there were hundreds of business groups represented in Washington, but less than half a dozen consumer organizations. One reason is that the interest of consumers is so general that it does not lend itself to organized expression as readily as the narrower interest of a special group, such as physicians or truckers. And as Mancur Olson, Jr.,

[76] Schattschneider, *The Semisovereign People,* p. 35.

has pointed out, unless the number of individuals in a group is very small, or unless there is coercion or some special incentive to make individuals work together in their mutual interest, many people will not organize or act to achieve common or group interests through the political process.[77]

Even organized, active interest groups do not represent all they claim to represent. The leaders of an interest group tend to formulate policy positions for the group as a whole. Consequently, the public stance of an interest group often represents the views of an oligarchy rather than the views of the rank and file. The AMA, for example, is more conservative than are many of its 213,000 members. Moreover, at least 100,000 of the nation's physicians do not even belong to the AMA.

Despite all their flaws, interest groups do supplement formal channels of representation and allow for the expression of public opinion in an organized manner. But the nation's legislators must find new ways to heed the voice of the poor, the black, the alienated, and the powerless, groups that are much less likely to have a steel and glass office building and a team of registered lobbyists to speak for them in Washington.

[77] Mancur Olson, Jr., *The Logic of Collective Action: Public Goods and the Theory of Groups* (Cambridge, Mass.: Harvard University Press, 1965), p. 2.

SUGGESTED READING

Bryce, James. *The American Commonwealth* (Putnam, 1959). Paperback. (Originally published in 1888.) A classic general analysis of the American political system in the late nineteenth century. Bryce was a British statesman and man of letters who at one time served as ambassador to the United States.

Dahl, Robert A. *Who Governs?* * (Yale University Press, 1961). An influential and detailed exploration of the nature of political power, based on a study of political decision-making in New Haven, Connecticut. Dahl maintains that there is a pluralism of power—rather than a single "power elite"—in the United States.

Free, Lloyd A., and Cantril, Hadley. *The Political Beliefs of Americans* * (Rutgers University Press, 1967). A comprehensive study of the political attitudes of the American public, including both opinions on specific issues and more general attitudes toward government and politics. Free and Cantril based their study on extensive public opinion polling.

Graham, Hugh Davis, and Gurr, Ted Robert. *Violence in America: Historical and Comparative Perspectives* (Bantam Books, 1969). Paperback. An analysis by a study group of the National Commission on the Causes and Prevention of Violence that attempts to place violence in contemporary America in historical perspective, and to compare the level of violence in the United States with that of other countries.

Key, V. O., Jr. *Public Opinion and American Democracy* (Knopf, 1961). A detailed analysis of public attitudes concerning government and politics and their relation to the way government operates.

Lane, Robert E. *Political Life* * (Free Press, 1959). A comprehensive summary of political participation and public attitudes toward politics in the United States. Analyzes the factors that encourage and discourage political participation by the public.

Lane, Robert E., and Sears, David O. *Public Opinion* (Prentice-Hall, 1964). Paperback. A useful, concise study of the nature of public opinion and its relationship to government and politics. Includes an analysis of the way political attitudes are learned and changed.

Lippmann, Walter. *Public Opinion* (Free Press, 1965). Paperback. (Originally published in 1922.) A basic work on how public opinion operates. As a distinguished political columnist, Lippmann helped to mold American public opinion for half a century.

Lowi, Theodore J. *The End of Liberalism: Ideology, Policy, and the Crisis of Public Authority* * (W. W. Norton, 1969). A stimulating analysis of the theory and practice of interest group politics in the United States. Lowi is strongly critical of the consequences of the interest group bargaining process as it has developed since the New Deal.

Milbrath, Lester W. *The Washington Lobbyists* (Rand McNally, 1963). An empirical and generally sympathetic study of the role of lobbyists and lobbying in the American political system. Based on interviews with lobbyists and those whom they seek to influence.

Mills, C. Wright. *The Power Elite* * (Oxford University Press, 1956). One of the best known statements of the view that there is a unified "power elite" in the United States. In Mills' view, wealth, prestige, and power in America are concentrated in the hands of a hierarchy of corporate, government, and military leaders.

Olson, Mancur, Jr. *The Logic of Collective Action: Public Goods and the Theory of Groups* * (Harvard University Press, 1965). An important analysis of the role of groups in the American political process. Based on an application of economic analysis to the relationships between individual self-interest and group membership and activity. Examines the consequences these relationships have for politics.

Truman, David B. *The Governmental Process* (Knopf, 1951). An influential study of interest groups in the United States. Develops and modifies a general theory of groups and applies it to American politics.

* Available in paperback edition

7

Political Parties

THE REVOLT OF 1968

As the presidential election year 1968 approached, millions of Americans were disenchanted with the Democrats and President Lyndon Baines Johnson. Among the most vocal dissenters were thousands of college students. Others might be angered and frustrated by the rising casualty rates in Vietnam and by the higher taxes imposed by Congress to pay for the war. But it was the students, and other young Americans, who faced the reality of being drafted and sent to Southeast Asia to fight a war in which many of them did not believe.

America had two major political parties. But, many students could argue that the two parties offered little choice; that there was, as presidential candidate George Wallace was repeatedly to tell his campaign crowds in 1968, "not a dime's worth of difference" between the Democrats and Republicans.

It had long been an axiom of American politics that a President in

227

power could not be denied renomination by his party.[1] And not since Herbert Hoover's defeat in 1932 had an incumbent President been rejected by the electorate. In 1968 it could be expected, therefore, that the big city bosses, the power brokers of the Democratic party, would meet in a smoke-filled room and nominate Lyndon Johnson. And very possibly he would be elected. Clearly, the system was stacked against anyone who opposed its policies.

At least one man disagreed with this assessment. Allard K. Lowenstein, a New York attorney, was, at age thirty-eight, a perennial student leader who had kept in close contact with political movements on the American campus. He had an idea that the President of the United States could be forced out of the White House. The idea seemed slightly ridiculous, especially since Lowenstein's name was unknown in national politics.

In September 1967, Lowenstein began touring America calling for a political revolt: "I must have spoken to twenty Senators or Congressmen. Some thought I was a kook. Some of them listened. No one defended Lyndon Johnson or the war. I told them we had the strength. I told them there was a base in the student movement. But no major figure would take the lead—I couldn't find a trigger or a fuse." [2]

In October of 1967, Lowenstein found the fuse he sought. Senator Eugene J. McCarthy of Minnesota, a strong Democratic opponent of the war, indicated to Lowenstein that he was ready to challenge President Johnson in the primaries. In November, McCarthy announced his candidacy. Early in 1968, thousands of college students descended on New Hampshire to work for McCarthy in that state's primary, a crucial one because it was the first in the nation. Theodore H. White, the distinguished political observer, has described the students in action: "They knew what they were doing. They were skilled. They were organized ('*Happiness*,' read one sign, '*is a nine o'clock staff meeting that starts at nine o'clock*'). And they were happy. Girls with sleek Ivy League blond hair bustled in and out, smiling, laughing, but precise. Booted in black shiny leather, as was the style that year, their mini-skirts and plaids flickering over their pretty legs, they might have arrived for a ski weekend. But they had come to stop the war." [3]

---

[1] By 1968 no incumbent President had been rejected by his party for eighty-four years; the last such instance had occurred in 1884 when the Republicans declined to nominate President Chester A. Arthur. Only four other incumbent Presidents had been denied renomination; John Tyler in 1844, Millard Fillmore in 1852, Franklin Pierce in 1856, and Andrew Johnson in 1868. And only Pierce had been elected President in his own right.

[2] Theodore H. White, *The Making of the President 1968* (New York: Atheneum, 1969), p. 72.

[3] *Ibid.*, p. 85.

McCarthy's students canvassed the length and breadth of New Hampshire, talking to voters and distributing literature. Male students even cut their long hair so as not to offend the sensibilities of the New Hampshire townspeople. On March 12, primary day, Senator McCarthy won a surprising 42.2 percent of the Democratic vote. On March 16, Senator Robert F. Kennedy jumped into the presidential race. On March 31, Lyndon Johnson told a nationwide TV audience that he had restricted the bombing of North Vietnam; then in a peroration that took the nation by surprise, he announced that he would not run for reelection.

The unbelievable had happened, and the students had helped to make it happen. Eugene McCarthy did not win the Democratic nomination in 1968, but his campaign had a major impact on the party and on the course of American politics. Following President Johnson's actions, peace talks opened in Paris. In November, the American people elected a Republican President who—regardless of whether he proved successful—had, at least, publicly pledged to end the war in Vietnam.

In retrospect the events of 1968 seemed fantastic. On the face of it, at least, an argument could be made that a few thousand college students, two senators, and someone named Allard K. Lowenstein had helped to alter the course of an American presidential election.[4]

The drama of 1968 provided one set of answers to the recurring questions about American political parties: Are they truly responsive and responsible instruments of democracy? Or are they boss-controlled elitist organizations closed to outsiders? Do they offer a genuine choice on the major issues facing the nation? Do they nominate the most able men to run the nation and its states and communities in the nuclear age? Are national conventions a farce, or useful tools of representative government? In discussing the role, history, organization, and performance of American political parties, we shall explore all these questions.

EUGENE McCARTHY ON A THIRD PARTY

The two-party system can be defended only if the parties themselves are responsive to the needs of the country and if they give the people a choice and a voice on major issues affecting the country. . . .

Even without the emergence of a clear issue or position on issues, growing dissatisfaction with party processes themselves, with current political procedures and institutions could be expressed in a move to establish a new party which would provide for more open and more effective participation by those who are affected by political decision.

—New York Times Magazine, June 7, 1970.

[4] Lowenstein was elected in 1968 as a Democratic congressman from Nassau County in New York. He was defeated in 1970. In the interim, the lines of his congressional district had been redrawn by the Republican-controlled state legislature.

"As there are many roads to Rome and many ways to skin a cat," Frank J. Sorauf has written, "there are also many ways to look at a political party." [5]

A political party is Mayor Richard Daley packing the galleries of the Democratic National Convention at Chicago in 1968 so that his ward-heelers might cheer their leader on national television and wave "WE LOVE MAYOR DALEY" placards. It is the leaders of the House and Senate having a private breakfast at the White House with the President to discuss the administration's legislative proposals. It is the delegates to a national political convention exploding in a carefully planned frenzy of noise, emotion, confetti, and balloons after the name of their candidate for President is placed in nomination. It is the disaffected students demonstrating outside the hall. It is the millions who vote on election day.

As Sorauf has concluded, the nature of a political party is somewhat in "the eye of the beholder." [6] Nevertheless, it is possible to identify some of the elements that make up a major political party. There are the *voters*, most of whom consider themselves Democrats or Republicans; the *party leaders outside of government*, who frequently control the party machinery and usually have important power bases; the *party activists*, who ring doorbells, serve as delegates to county, state, and national conventions and perform the day-to-day, grassroots work of politics; and finally, the *party leaders in the government*, including the President, the leaders in Congress, and party leaders in state and local governments.

When someone speaks of "the Democratic party" or "the Republican party" he may really mean any one of these diverse elements—or all of them. Because a political party is like a big circus tent, encompassing so many different acts, it is as difficult to define in a shorthand way as it would be to define a circus. But, in very general terms, a major political party is a broadly-based coalition that attempts to gain control of the government by winning elections, in order to exercise power and reward its members.

The Role of Political Parties

The best way to look at political parties is not in terms of what they are but in terms of what they do.

One of the major problems of governments has been the manage-

---

[5] Frank J. Sorauf, *Political Parties in the American System* (Boston: Little, Brown, 1964), p. 1.
[6] *Ibid.*

ment of the transfer of power. In totalitarian governments, power, once seized, is seldom peacefully relinquished. Usually the change comes unexpectedly. We have already noted how, in 1964, Premier Khrushchev returned from vacation to find his colleagues had removed him as Premier of the Soviet Union. To find a parallel, it would be as though President Nixon returned from a weekend at Key Biscayne to find that Vice-President Spiro T. Agnew had staged a *coup d'état*.

A democracy provides orderly institutional arrangements for the transfer of power. In the United States, a President, running as the nominee of a political party, is elected every four years. American political parties thus perform "an essential function in the management of succession to power." [7] They serve as a vehicle for choice, offering the electorate competing candidates for public office and, often, alternative policies. The element of choice is absolutely vital to democratic government. Where the voters cannot choose, there is no democracy. The parties operate the machinery of choice: nominations, campaigns, and elections.

Within the framework of a political system (the concept discussed in Chapter 1), political parties help to mobilize the demands and supports that are fed into the system and participate as well in the authoritative decision-making, or outputs, of the government.

In a presidential election, the party in power traditionally defends its record, while the party out of power suggests that it is time for a change. For example, in 1960, Nixon, the Republican nominee, had to defend President Eisenhower's record, but John F. Kennedy campaigned effectively on the slogan, "it is time to get this country moving again." By seeking to mobilize mass opinion behind their slogans and policies, political parties channel public support for, or against, the government. In so doing, they serve as an essential bridge between the people and the government. They provide a powerful means for the public's voice to be heard—and politicians must listen if they wish to survive in office. Parties help to hold officials accountable to the voters. They also help to recruit candidates for public office.

Because a political party consists of people expressing attitudes about government, it might seem to fit the definition of an interest group. But a political party runs candidates for public office. It is therefore much more comprehensive than an interest group. Instead of seeking to *influence* government on a narrow range of issues, it attempts to win elections and *gain control* of the government.

Political parties try to form "winning coalitions" by maneuvering "to create combinations powerful enough to govern." [8] In the process, they may serve to reconcile the interests of conflicting groups in society. The

[7] V. O. Key, Jr., *Politics, Parties, and Pressure Groups*, 5th edition (New York: Crowell, 1964), p. 9.
[8] Key, *Politics, Parties, and Pressure Groups*, p. 167.

political party can fill the natural role of broker or mediator among interest groups, organized or not, because in order to win elections, it usually tries to appeal broadly to many groups of voters.

Parties also play a key role in the governmental process. When the Nixon administration succeeded the Johnson administration in January 1969, Washington real estate agents were happy; it meant that Democrats would be selling their houses and Republicans would be buying them. Following a presidential election, the White House staff, the cabinet, and the more important policy-makers and officials of the various departments of the executive branch are for the most part appointed from among members of the President's party. To the victors belong the White House limousines.

Political parties play a vital role in the legislative branch as well. The President appeals to party loyalty through his legislative leaders in order to get his programs through Congress (although he may face a Congress controlled by the opposition party). Because political parties are involved in the governmental process, they serve to link different parts of the government: the President communicates with party leaders in Congress; the two houses of Congress communicate in part through party leaders; and relationships among local, state, and national governments depend to a considerable degree on ties among partisan officials and leaders.

Yet political parties do not control the government in the United States, as the Communist party does, for example, in the Soviet Union. Because the President is leader of his party, the party in power is subordinate to the President.

In sum, political parties perform vital functions in the American political system. They (1) manage the transfer of power, (2) offer a choice of rival candidates and programs to the voters, (3) serve as a link between government and people by helping to hold elected officials accountable to the voters, (4) help to recruit candidates for office, (5) may serve to reconcile conflicting interests in society, (6) staff the government and help to run it, and (7) link various branches and levels of government.

THE DEVELOPMENT OF AMERICAN POLITICAL PARTIES

The framers of the Constitution created the delicately balanced machinery of the Federal Government, and provided for regular elections of a President and Congress, but they said not a word about political parties. The reason was simple: in the modern sense, they did not exist.

Yet, James Madison, the "father of the Constitution," foresaw that Americans would group together in factions. In *The Federalist* No. 10, he predicted that the task of regulating conflicting economic interests would involve "the spirit of party and faction in the necessary and ordinary operation of the government."

In his farewell address, George Washington warned against "the baneful effects of the spirit of party." His Vice-President, John Adams, had declared: "There is nothing I dread so much as the division of the Republic into two great parties, each under its leader." [9] Yet, the American party sytem began to take just such a shape in the 1790's during Washington's administration.

The Federalists, organized by Alexander Hamilton, Washington's Secretary of the Treasury, were the first national political party in the United States. The Federalists stood for strong central government, and their appeal was to banking, commercial, and financial interests.

Federalists and Democratic-Republicans

Thomas Jefferson built a rival coalition that became known as the Republican party, or Democratic-Republicans.[10] It was primarily an agrarian party of small farmers, debtors, Southern planters, and frontiersmen. Being a practical politician, Jefferson sought to expand his coalition; in 1791 he made a famous trip to New York State, allegedly on a "butterfly hunting" expedition but actually to form an alliance with Aaron Burr and the Sons of Tammany, the political organization that was to dominate New York City. In the partnership of rural America and the cities, the Democratic party was born.

Jefferson's triumph in the election of 1800 inaugurated a twenty-eight-year period of ascendancy by the Jeffersonian Democratic-Republicans. In fact, the Federalists never put forward another candidate for the Presidency after 1816 when James Monroe, the Democratic-Republican candidate, was overwhelmingly elected. Monroe's victory launched the brief Era of Good Feelings, in which there was little partisan activity.

By 1824, the Democratic-Republicans had split into several factions and the first phase of party government in the United States came to an end. The election in 1828 of Andrew Jackson, the hero of the War of 1812, opened a new era of two-party rivalry, this time, between Democrats and Whigs. Jacksonian Democracy soon came to symbolize popular rule and the aspirations of the common man.

Democrats and Whigs

[9] Wilfred E. Binkley, *American Political Parties* (New York: Knopf, 1965), p. 19.
[10] The name tends to be confusing to the student attempting to trace the origins of the American party system. Today's Democratic party, the oldest political party in the world, claims the Jeffersonian Republican, or Democratic-Republican, party as its political and spiritual ancestor, a fact that Democratic orators remind us of endlessly and annually at Jefferson-Jackson Day dinners. Today's Republican party invokes Abraham Lincoln, not Jefferson.

The rival Whigs, led by Henry Clay, William Henry Harrison, and Daniel Webster, were a coalition of bankers, merchants, and Southern planters held together precariously by their mutual distaste for Jacksonian Democracy. The Whigs won two presidential elections between 1840 and 1854, and the two-party system flourished.[11] As Clinton Rossiter has noted, "Out of the conflict of Democrats and Whigs emerged the American political system—complete with such features as two major parties, a sprinkle of third parties, national nominating conventions, state and local bosses, patronage, popular campaigning, and the Presidency as the focus of politics."[12]

During the 1850's, the increasingly divisive issue of slavery caused the Democratic party to split between North and South. The Whigs, crushed by Democrat Franklin Pierce's landslide victory in 1852, were equally demoralized. The nation was about to be torn apart by civil war and the major political parties, like the Union itself, were disintegrating.

Democrats and Republicans

The Republican party was born in 1854 as a party of protest against the extension of slavery into the territories. The Kansas-Nebraska Act, passed that year, permitted slavery to move westward with the frontier and aroused discontent in the North and West.

In February 1854, a group of Whigs, Free-Soilers, and antislavery Democrats gathered in a church at Ripon, Wisconsin, to recommend the creation of a new party to fight the further expansion of slavery.[13] The name "Republican party" was suggested at the meeting. The political organization that resulted from the meeting took the place of the Whigs as the rival party of the Democrats, but it was a new party and not merely the Whigs masquerading under another label.

The first Republican presidential candidate, John C. Fremont, the "Pathfinder of the Rockies," was unable to find the trail that led to the White House in the election of 1856. In 1860 the Republicans nominated Abraham Lincoln. By that time, the Democratic party was so badly divided over the issue of slavery that its Northern and Southern wings each nominated separate candidates for President. The split enabled Lincoln to win with only 39.8 percent of the popular vote. His election was a rare

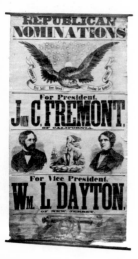

[11] Four Whig Presidents occupied the White House. Only two were *elected*, however—William Henry Harrison in 1840 and General Zachary Taylor in 1848. Both died in office and were succeeded by their Vice-Presidents, John Tyler and Millard Fillmore.

[12] Clinton Rossiter, *Parties and Politics in America* (Ithaca, N.Y.: Cornell University Press, 1960), pp. 73–74.

[13] The party birthplace is also claimed by Jackson, Michigan, where the Republicans held their first state convention five months later.

fusion of the man and the times. Lincoln preserved the Union; in the process, he insured the future of the Republican party. By rejecting slavery, the Republicans had automatically become a sectional party, representing the North and West. And North and West meant Union, emancipation, and victory. The Democrats and the South meant slavery, secession, and defeat. Having been on the losing side of the bloody and tragic Civil War, the Democrats were a long time in recovering; the party was trapped and tangled in the folds of the Confederate flag.

For twenty-five years after 1860, the Republicans consolidated their strength and ruled America. But by 1876 the Democrats had recovered sufficiently to give the Republicans spirited two-party competition for two decades. Twice, in 1884 and 1892, the Democrats elected Grover Cleveland as President.

America was changing. After the Civil War, the nation gradually became industrialized; railroad tracks pushed westward, spanning the continent; immigrants from Europe poured in. As the rail and steel barons amassed great fortunes, small farmers found themselves squeezed economically and outnumbered by workingmen. Agrarian discontent was reflected in the rise of minor parties like the Grangers, the Greenbackers, and the Populists.

The Populists, or People's party, were a protest party of Western farmers. In 1892, their presidential candidate, James B. Weaver, showed surprising strength. By 1896, the spirit of Populism had captured the Democratic party, which nominated William Jennings Bryan for President. Bryan, running on a "free silver" platform, lost to Republican William McKinley, who defended the gold standard and conservative fiscal policies. The election resulted in a major realignment of the parties from which the Republicans emerged stronger than ever as a coalition of Eastern business interests, urban workers, midwestern farmers, and New England Yankees.

Theodore Roosevelt held the coalition together while he was President from 1901–1909, but his attempt to move the Grand Old Party in a more progressive direction alarmed its conservative business wing. In 1912, the Republican party split apart. The conservative wing renominated William Howard Taft, who had been Roosevelt's hand-picked successor. The Progressive ("Bull Moose") party nominated Roosevelt. The Republican split resulted in victory for Woodrow Wilson, the Democratic nominee.

Wilson's two terms proved to be a short Democratic interlude. A nation weary of the First World War chose to "return to normalcy" in the 1920's with the Republican administrations of Warren G. Harding and

235

Until 1964, preconvention politics had been a matter of winning over county and state leaders in the hope that they would back your man. . . .

But the new Goldwater-style of preconvention politics did not waste time on winning over county and state organizations, but concentrated on actually taking over the county and state organizations by an inundation of the Goldwater volunteers. It was indeed a revolutionary doctrine. It meant that the Goldwater delegates sent to San Francisco would be not merely the run-of-the-mill party workers under the command and the bidding of regular party leaders. Here was a new breed of delegate, most of whom had never been to a national convention before. They were going not as a reward for faithful service, not to see the sights of San Francisco, and certainly not to ride the bandwagon of a winner. They were going there for one purpose: to vote for Barry Goldwater. To woo them away to another candidate would be as difficult as proselytizing a religious zealot.

—Robert D. Novak, *The Agony of the G.O.P. 1964.*

Calvin Coolidge, two of the least distinguished Presidents ever to occupy that office. Big Business dominated; it was the era of the Teapot Dome scandal, flappers, bathtub gin, and the Prohibition "speakeasy." In 1928, Republican Herbert Hoover defeated Al Smith, the first Roman Catholic nominee of a major party. A year later, the market crash and the onset of the Great Depression dealt the Republican party a blow comparable to the effect of the Civil War on the Democrats.

The result of these events was the election of Franklin D. Roosevelt in 1932, the New Deal, and twenty years of uninterrupted Democratic rule under Roosevelt and his successor, Harry S Truman. Roosevelt put together a new, grand coalition composed of the white South, the big cities of the North, labor, immigrants, blacks, and other minority groups.

In 1952, in the midst of the Korean War, the Republicans nominated General Eisenhower and recaptured the Presidency. But the Eisenhower magic could not be transferred to Richard Nixon, who narrowly lost the Presidency to John F. Kennedy in 1960. The "New Frontier" seemingly opened a new era of Democratic supremacy. But Kennedy died when, as Theodore H. White has put it, he was only "half way across his bridge of dreams." [14] In 1964, Barry Goldwater, a conservative from Arizona, captured control of the GOP from its long-dominant, Eastern, internationalist wing. The result was Republican disaster. Lyndon Johnson, who had succeeded to the Presidency after Kennedy's death, was elected in his own right by the greatest popular vote landslide in history.

But American political parties, as Rossiter has pointed out, have extraordinary resiliency: "Each one is a citadel that can withstand the impact of even the most disastrous national landslide and thus provide elements of obstinacy and stability in the two-party pattern." [15] This ability of American political parties to survive adversity and rise again, rests in

[14] White, *The Making of the President 1968*, p. 66.
[15] Rossiter, *Parties and Politics in America*, p. 7.

part on the fact that many areas of the country and many congressional districts are dominated by one party; even when a party is defeated nationally, it will still have durable pockets of power across the nation. This remains true despite the spread of two-party politics to more states in recent years.

The Republican party survived the Goldwater debacle. It regrouped around the more moderate, familiar figure of Richard Nixon, who accurately gauged the temper of the nation in 1968. Lyndon Johnson, unable to hold the Democratic coalition together in the face of war and urban riots, did not choose to run. With the Democrats divided into at least three camps, Nixon triumphed, thereby not only restoring the Republican party to power but demonstrating anew the remarkable strength of the American two-party system.

THE TWO-PARTY SYSTEM

Under the two-party system, to become the nominee of one of the two major parties is at least half the battle; in areas where one party dominates, it is equivalent to election.

Throughout most of the nation's history, two major political parties have been arrayed against each other. The Democrats, in one guise or another, have endured. During successive eras, they have been challenged by the Federalists, the Whigs, and the Republicans. Minor or third parties have joined the struggle, with greater or lesser effect, but the main battle has, historically, been a two-party affair. As Allan P. Sindler has observed, "From 1828 to the present with few exceptions the two parties together have persistently polled upward of 90 percent of the national popular vote—that is, there has been little multi-partyism." [16]

In 1968, Eugene McCarthy and Robert Kennedy sought the Presidency *within* the framework of the two-party system. George Wallace, who formed the American Independent party and ran *outside* the framework, received only 13.5 percent of the popular vote. In the states and in many local communities, one party may dominate, as the Democrats did for decades in the Solid South, and the Republicans did in Kansas and Vermont. But, on the whole, America has been a two-party nation.

Why this should be so is a subject of mild dispute because there is no wholly satisfactory, simple answer. Among the explanations that have been offered are these:

1. *Tradition and history.* The debate over ratification of the Constitution split the country into two groups. Dualism, therefore, is as old as the nation itself. And, once established, human institutions tend to per-

[16] Allan P. Sindler, *Political Parties in the United States* (New York: St. Martin's Press, 1966), p. 15.

WHY FRANCE HAS A MULTI-PARTY SYSTEM: ONE EXPLANATION

How can one conceive of a one-party system in a country that has over 200 varieties of cheeses?

—Charles De Gaulle,
New York Times Magazine, June 29, 1958.

petuate their original form. To some extent, Americans accept the two-party system because it has almost always been there.

2. *The electoral system.* The major features of the American political system appear compatible with the existence of two major parties. In the United States, the single-member district system prevails in federal elections; for example, only one congressman may be elected from a congressional district, no matter how many seek that honor—it is a case of winner-take-all. The same is true of a presidential election; normally in each state the candidate who receives the most popular votes wins all of the state's electoral votes. Under such a system, minor parties lacking a strong geographical base have little chance of poaching on the two-party preserve; they tend to lose and, having lost, to disappear.[17] (By contrast, a system of proportional representation with multimember districts, as in West Germany, encourages the existence of many parties by allotting seats to competing candidates according to the percentage of votes that they win.)

3. *Patterns of belief.* A majority of the American voters stand somewhere near the middle ground on many issues of American politics. Ideological differences among Americans have in the past normally not been strong enough to produce minor parties representing gradations of political opinion, as is the case in many Western European nations.

During the 1968 campaign, candidate Nixon predicted "a victory that will be bigger than a party, a victory that will bring to our ranks Democrats, Independents."[18] There are more Democratic than Republican voters in America, but neither party enjoys the support of a majority of the electorate and both must therefore look outside their own ranks for victory. To put together a winning coalition, a presidential candidate must appeal to the great mass of voters in the ideological center. As a result, it sometimes appears that there is very little difference between the two major parties. As Clinton Rossiter has put it: "In some important respects there is and can be no real difference between the Democrats and the Republicans, because the unwritten laws of American politics demand that the parties overlap substantially in principle, policy, character, appeal, and purpose—or cease to be parties with any hope of winning a national election."[19]

[17] The two parties need not be the same in all areas of the country, however. In some states, historically, minor parties have competed successfully with one of the two major national parties. For example, in Minnesota during the 1920's and 1930's, the Farmer-Labor party—not the Democratic party—was the chief competitor with the Republican party in state and congressional elections.

[18] White, *The Making of the President 1968,* p. 325.

[19] Rossiter, *Parties and Politics in America,* p. 108.

"How would you like me to answer that question? As a member of my ethnic group, educational class, income group, or religious category?"

Drawing by D. Fradon
© 1969 The New Yorker Magazine, Inc.

Since both parties woo the same voters, it is not surprising that, to an extent, they look alike. But they have important differences as well, differences of substance and of style. One study has found that the opinion of Democratic and Republican leaders diverge sharply on many important issues.[20] What is more, these opinions were found to conform to party images: Republican leaders identified with "business, free enterprise, and economic conservatism in general" and Democrats were friendly "toward labor and toward government regulation of the economy."[21] The differences of opinion among members of the rank and file of the two parties were found to be much less sharp than differences among party leaders, however.[22]

A good way to perceive the differences between the two major parties is to examine their images. The "typical" Democrat lives in a big city in the North. He is a Catholic, a Jew, a black, a Pole, an Italian, a Mexican, a Puerto Rican, or a member of some other minority group. He drinks beer, eats pizza, blintzes, or other ethnic fare, belongs to a union, goes bowling, and has a fairly low income.

Genus Republican's habitat, by contrast, is the hedge-trimmed sub-

The Democrats

[20] Herbert McClosky, Paul J. Hoffmann, and Rosemary O'Hara, "Issue Conflict and Consensus Among Party Leaders and Followers," *The American Political Science Review*, Vol. 54, No. 2 (June 1960), pp. 425–26.
[21] *Ibid.*, pp. 415–16.
[22] *Ibid.*, p. 426.

urbs. He lives in a split-level house with a picture window, commutes to the city, and belongs to a country club that has no members from minority groups. He is almost certainly a white Protestant. He drinks martinis and eats white bread. His wife drives a station wagon. He owns his own company or works for IBM. He golfs on weekends. He is rich, or at least comfortable, equally at home in the board room or the locker room.

Like any caricature, these portraits are overdrawn. Plenty of Democrats live in the suburbs, own companies, play golf, and have money. Two recent Democratic Presidents, John F. Kennedy and Lyndon Johnson, were millionaires. Many Catholics and Jews vote Republican, and so on. Nevertheless, the image of each party, and of individual Democrats and Republicans, comes remarkably close to mirroring reality: numerous studies have demonstrated that the Democrats enjoy greater support from labor, Catholics, Jews, blacks, minorities, men, young people, and persons who have not attended college, who have low incomes, and who live in the cities (and in the South). Republicans are more likely to be Protestant, white, suburban, rural, wealthy, older, college educated, women, and professional or business men.

Since 1932, the Democratic party has, in spirit, been the party of Franklin D. Roosevelt. The vast social welfare programs launched by the New Deal changed the face of America and gave the Democratic party an identity that has changed little with the passage of time. Truman's "Fair Deal," Kennedy's "New Frontier," and Johnson's "Great Society" were all patterned on Roosevelt's New Deal. All sought to harness federal funds and federal energies to solve national problems.

Despite the success of Roosevelt's grand coalition, the Democratic party continues to display some of the characteristics of a bivalve, with two distinct halves. The Southern, rural, conservative wing of the party bears little resemblance to the Northern, urban, liberal wing. Thus, the Democrats are at once the party of Richard B. Russell of Georgia and James Eastland of Mississippi; and of Edward Kennedy of Massachusetts and Hubert Humphrey of Minnesota. Normally, the overriding desire for power and electoral victory is the muscle that holds the two halves together. Sometimes, the muscle fails. In 1948, Southern Democrats walked out of the national convention over the civil rights issue. The dissident Dixiecrats, forming a third party, nominated Senator Strom Thurmond of South Carolina for President. And in 1968 the dissident Democrats included many liberal supporters of Senator Eugene McCarthy.

For decades, the Democrats could count on the eleven states of the Old Confederacy as a solid Democratic bloc. But the South is no longer a one-party enclave. Since 1952, when Eisenhower captured Virginia, Florida, Tennessee, and Texas, every Republican presidential candidate has carried some Southern states. In 1964, five of the six states carried by Goldwater were in the Deep South. The South was a vital element in Nixon's victory

TABLE 7-1

Republican Inroads in the Solid South, 1950–1970

Year	Number of Congressmen		Number of Senators		Number of Governors		Number of States Voting for Presidential Nominee	
	D	R	D	R	D	R	D	R
1950	103	2	22	0	11	0		
1952	99	6	22	0	11	0	7	4
1954	99	7	22	0	11	0		
1956	99	7	22	0	11	0	6	5
1958	99	7	22	0	11	0		
1960	99	7	22	0	11	0	8^1	2
1962	95	11	21	1	11	0		
1964	89	17	21	1	11	0	6	5
1966	83	23	19	3	9	2		
1968	80	26	18	4	9	2	1	5^2
1970	79	27	16 (1)^3	5	9	2		

[1] Eight Mississippi electors voted for Harry Byrd.

[2] George Wallace won five states on the American Independent ticket.

[3] Harry Byrd, Jr., was elected in Virginia as an independent.

Source: House, Governor and President figures in Congressional Quarterly, *Politics in America 1945–1966* (Washington, D.C.: Congressional Quarterly Service, 1967), pp. 101, 123, 117–121. Senate figures in Richard Scammon, *America Votes 7* (Washington, D.C.: Governmental Affairs Institute, 1968), pp. 12, 31, 74, 82, 147, 205, 289, 357, 371, 379, 404. 1968 figures in Congressional Quarterly, *Weekly Report*, November 8, 1968, p. 3072. 1970 figures from the *New York Times*, November 5, 1970, p. 43.

in 1968. With the support of Strom Thurmond (who switched from the Democratic to the Republican party in 1964) Nixon carried five Southern states. (See Table 7-1.)

On the whole, Democrats, as Republicans like to remind them, are "spenders," much more willing to appropriate federal funds for social action. As a result of this political reality, the Democratic party was from 1933 into the 1960's the party of Social Security, TVA, Medicare, and federal aid to education. It has, in short, often been the party of social innovation. Programs of this sort tend to get "locked in" to American society; they gain such widespread acceptance that the Republicans, although they may oppose them initially, have no choice in the end but to accept them.

In addition to differences of substance, the two parties show perceptible differences in style. Democrats tend to be uninhibited and occasionally raucous, fighting among themselves; Republicans are normally more sedate. Although the Goldwater conservatives at the 1964 national convention booed and hissed and sounded almost like Democrats, by 1968 the party had reverted to its traditional ways—the Republican National Convention

"Democrats tend to be uninhibited . . ." Floor demonstration during the 1968 Democratic National Convention at Chicago.

in Miami was as dull as a convention of dentists. The 1968 Democratic National Convention at Chicago turned into a street brawl.

"A gathering of Democrats *is* more sweaty, disorderly, offhand, and rowdy than a gathering of Republicans," Clinton Rossiter has noted; "it is also more likely to be more cheerful, imaginative, tolerant of dissent, and skillful at the game of give-and-take. A gathering of Republicans *is* more respectable, sober, purposeful, and businesslike than a gathering of Democrats; it is also likely to be more self-righteous, pompous, cut-and-dried, and just plain boring." [23]

The Democratic donkey brays, snorts, kicks up its heels, balks, fusses, and is a very different animal in appearance, substance, and temperament from the Republican elephant.

The Republicans

"Fundamentally," Theodore H. White has written, "the Republican Party is white, middle-class and Protestant. . . . Two moods color its thinking. One is the old Protestant-Puritan ethic of the small towns of America. . . . The other is the philosophy of private enterprise, the sense that the individual, as man or corporation, can build swifter and better for

[23] Rossiter, *Parties and Politics in America*, p. 117.

"Republicans are normally more sedate . . ." Delegates at the 1968 GOP Convention in Miami.

common good than big government. From middle-class America the Republicans get their votes; from the executive leadership and from the families of the great enterprises they get their funds." [24]

Despite its success in 1968, the Republican party has, since the New Deal, enjoyed the support of only a minority of American voters. People who identify themselves as Democrats have, in recent decades, outnumbered people who say they are Republicans by 3 to 2, or more at times. In the 1964 Republican disaster, Goldwater lost by almost 16,000,000 votes. In the face of such figures, the Republican party's constant task is to broaden its popular appeal and turn its minority into a majority, or at least a plurality.

The familiar Democratic charge that "the Republican party is the party of Big Business" is essentially accurate, just as it is true that, nationally, the Democrats have traditionally been the party of organized labor. For example, the American business community never felt comfortable when President Kennedy was in the White House; the rollback in steel prices that he forced in 1962 merely confirmed the suspicions that business interests already held.

The preference of business for the Republican party may be measured

[24] White, *The Making of the President 1968*, p. 33.

by analyzing campaign contributions. A Senate study showed that in 1956, during the height of the Eisenhower era, the Republicans received 94.6 percent of gifts of $500 or more contributed by the officers and directors of the 225 largest corporations in America (see Figure 7-1). Out of a total of $1,900,000, more than $1,800,000 supported Republican campaigns.

During the Eisenhower years, federal regulatory agencies were markedly friendly to the broadcasting networks, airlines, and other businesses they were supposedly regulating. It can be argued that "it does make a difference to the television industry, the railroads, or the stock exchanges whether Democrats or Republicans have a majority in the independent commissions." [25]

Like the Democrats, the Republicans have a split personality. The scar left when Theodore Roosevelt bolted the party in 1912 has never entirely healed; in modern times the battle of Republican conservatives (the

[25] Rossiter, *Parties and Politics in America*, p. 131.

John A. Ruge
© 1966 Saturday Review, Inc.

"Roger and I have stayed in the Republican Party because of the children."

FIGURE 7-1

Share of Campaign Gifts of $500 or More from Officers and Directors
of the 225 Largest Corporations in America in 1956

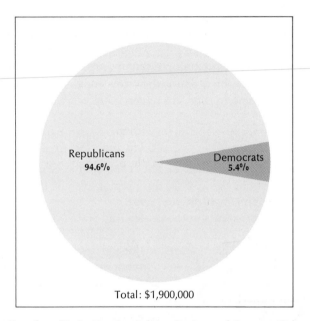

Republicans
94.6%

Democrats
5.4%

Total: $1,900,000

Source: Data from V. O. Key, Jr., *Politics, Parties, and Pressure Groups,* 5th edition
(New York: Crowell, 1964), p. 495. Copyright © 1964 by The Thomas Y. Crowell Company.

political heirs of William Howard Taft) against Republican liberal-
moderates (the heirs of Theodore Roosevelt) continues as fiercely as ever.

The struggle broke out afresh in 1952 in the convention battle between Senator Robert A. Taft of Ohio (the son of William Howard Taft)
and General Eisenhower, who was backed by the Eastern liberals. Then, in
1964, Goldwater and the conservative wing won control of the party from
the Eastern Establishment led by Nelson Rockefeller. In 1968, the ideological split was still highly visible, with liberals Rockefeller and Romney on
one side, Governor Ronald Reagan of California at the conservative end of
the spectrum and Richard Nixon near the center.

It was doubtful that a cleavage that ran so deep would soon disappear.
Despite the lesson of the 1964 election, the right wing of the Republican
party remained a strong force within the GOP, ready to recapture the party
if it could. Some analysts thought that the Republican split would be
cemented over in a new party alignment signaled by Nixon's victory in
1968. Kevin P. Phillips, a young Nixon conservative, has predicted such a
major restructuring of the American political system. In *The Emerging*

245

Republican Majority, Phillips theorized that the new, conservative Republican majority was centered in the "Heartland" (or middle America), the South, and the "Sun Belt," stretching from Florida across Texas and Arizona to Southern California. The Democrats, he predicted, would remain powerful only in the cities of the Northeast, in the Pacific Northwest, and among black voters in the North and the South.[26]

Unless the Republican party can forge some form of durable coalition —not necessarily conservative in nature—the elephant may continue to be a ponderous, dignified, solid, and rather slow-moving beast who visits the White House from time to time but never stays very long.

Minor Parties

Minor parties have been active throughout most of the nation's history, from the Anti-Masons of the 1830's, and the Barnburners of the 1840's, to the Know-Nothings of the 1850's, the Greenbackers of the 1880's, the Populists of the 1890's, the Progressives of the 1920's, and the American Independents in 1968.

In 1968 the combatants in the center ring were Nixon and Humphrey, but a number of sideshows took place as well. The third party movement of Alabama's George Wallace scared major party supporters because of the possibility that Wallace would carry enough states to prevent either major party candidate from gaining a majority of electoral votes. He would then be in a position to bargain for his electoral votes, or to throw the outcome into the House of Representatives.

Although Wallace appeared on the ballot in every state, usually as the candidate of the American Independent party, in the end he carried only Mississippi, Alabama, Louisiana, Georgia, and Arkansas. His 46 electoral votes were not enough to deadlock the presidential election. And his 13.5 percent of the popular vote was considerably less than the 21.1 percent received by the Know-Nothings [27] in 1856, the 27.4 percent polled by Theodore Roosevelt's Bull Moose party in 1912, or the 16.6 percent received by Robert La Follette's Progressives in 1924. On the other hand, Wallace did better than the 2.4 percent that Strom Thurmond and Henry Wallace each polled in 1948. And George Wallace's candidacy, unlike Thurmond's Dixie-

---

[26] Kevin P. Phillips, *The Emerging Republican Majority* (New Rochelle, N.Y.: Arlington House, 1969). Although at the time the book was published Phillips was an administration official, President Nixon was careful to disassociate himself from the book. "I believe the Republican party should be a national party," he said. "I don't believe in writing off any section of the country. I have attempted to make our appeal nationally—to the South, to the North, the East, the West, and to all groups within the country. To the extent that the book advocates theories that are inconsistent with that principle, of course I would disagree with it." (President's news conference, September 26, 1969, *New York Times,* September 27, 1969, p. 14.)

[27] The anti-Catholic, anti-Irish Native American party was so secret that its members pretended ignorance of party affairs; as a result editor Horace Greeley dubbed it the Know-Nothing party.

FIGURE 7-2

Minor Party Vote, 1880–1968 [1]

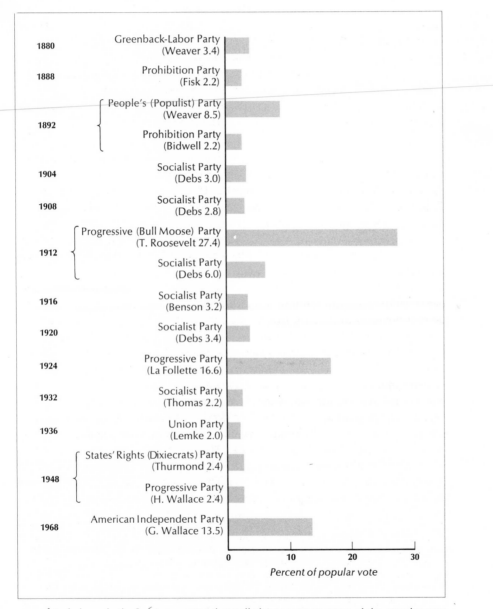

1880	Greenback-Labor Party (Weaver 3.4)	
1888	Prohibition Party (Fisk 2.2)	
1892	People's (Populist) Party (Weaver 8.5)	
	Prohibition Party (Bidwell 2.2)	
1904	Socialist Party (Debs 3.0)	
1908	Socialist Party (Debs 2.8)	
1912	Progressive (Bull Moose) Party (T. Roosevelt 27.4)	
	Socialist Party (Debs 6.0)	
1916	Socialist Party (Benson 3.2)	
1920	Socialist Party (Debs 3.4)	
1924	Progressive Party (La Follette 16.6)	
1932	Socialist Party (Thomas 2.2)	
1936	Union Party (Lemke 2.0)	
1948	States' Rights (Dixiecrats) Party (Thurmond 2.4)	
	Progressive Party (H. Wallace 2.4)	
1968	American Independent Party (G. Wallace 13.5)	

0   10   20   30

Percent of popular vote

[1] Includes only those minor parties that polled 2 percent or more of the popular vote

Source: Donald B. Cole, *Handbook of American History* (New York: Harcourt Brace Jovanovich, 1968), pp. 304–05; Neal R. Peirce, *The People's President* (New York: Simon and Schuster, 1968), pp. 306–07.

crat movement in 1948, was not just a sectional effort. Wallace won votes in every state; he polled 487,270 votes in California and 467,495 in Ohio, for example.

Seven other parties ran candidates for President in 1968.[28] Unlike Wallace's American Independent party, which was a serious factor in the 1968 presidential campaign, the other minor parties had no hope of electing a President.

V. O. Key, Jr. has suggested that minor parties fall into two broad categories, "those formed to propagate a particular doctrine" and "transient third-party movements" that briefly appear on the American scene and then disappear. The Prohibition party and the Socialist party are examples of doctrinal parties that "have been kept alive over long periods by little bands of dedicated souls."[29] Among the transient third-party movements, Key perceived two types: parties of economic protest, such as the Populists, the Greenbackers, and the Progressives of 1924, and "secessionist parties" that have split off from one of the major parties, such as the Progressives in 1912 and the Dixiecrats in 1948.

Sometimes minor parties have a strong nativist streak; just as the Wallace campaign played upon white fears of black Americans, more than a century ago, the Know-Nothings, or Native American party, exploited fear of Irish immigrants and other "foreigners." The party platform in 1856, when Millard Fillmore ran as the Know-Nothing candidate warned: "Americans must rule America."

In certain states minor parties have gained a powerful position. The Liberal party and the Conservative party in New York sometimes hold the balance of power in elections in that state. In 1970, James Buckley, a Conservative party candidate, was elected senator from New York, defeating the Republican incumbent, Charles Goodell. Nationally, however, minor parties have never consistently enjoyed much power or influence. On some occasions they have influenced the politics of the major parties—as when Populism captured the Democratic party in 1896.

"One of the persistent qualities of the American two-party system," Clinton Rossiter has concluded, "is the way in which one of the major parties moves almost instinctively to absorb (and thus be somewhat reshaped by) the most challenging third party of the time. In any case it is a notable fact that no third party in America has ever risen to become a major party, and that no major party has ever fallen to become a third party."[30]

[28] Prohibition party: E. Harold Munn, Sr.; Peace and Freedom party: Eldridge Cleaver; Socialist-Labor party: Hennings Blomen; Socialist Worker party: Fred Halstead; New party: Eugene McCarthy; New party: Dick Gregory; Communist party: Charlene Mitchell.
[29] Key, Politics, Parties, and Pressure Groups, p. 255.
[30] Rossiter, Parties and Politics in America, pp. 5–6.

PARTY STRUCTURE

On the day before Hubert H. Humphrey was nominated for President in 1968, Theodore White strolled into the Chicago hotel room of Joseph Napolitan, a Humphrey aide and professional campaign manager, and found Napolitan in shirt sleeves, furiously banging away at a typewriter: "The normally affable and friendly Napolitan had no time at all to talk. 'I'm writing the campaign plan,' he said. 'Do you know there isn't *any* campaign plan? I have to get this ready by tomorrow!' " [31]

National Parties

This story shatters any illusions one might have of the national Democratic party in 1968 as a well-oiled, highly-organized machine, ready to swing into action as soon as it had a nominee for President. The truth was very different.

At three A.M. on the final day of the convention, Vice-President Humphrey summoned Lawrence O'Brien, his convention manager, to his hotel suite "and poured out his emotions: he was desperate; he had neither campaign plan nor campaign manager; he had to face the Democratic Natitonal Committee that day and announce to them his choice of [a] new National Chairman. 'Larry,' said Humphrey, 'I've just got to have you.' And O'Brien consented." [32]

Although one could draw a neat organizational chart of a major political party, with the national chairman and national committee at the top of the pyramid, and state and local party machinery arrayed below, it would be highly misleading. In fact, the national party exists more on paper than in reality, in theory more than in fact.

American political parties are *decentralized* and only loosely organized. Rather than a pyramid, with all power flowing from the top down, party structure, as Key has observed, "may be more accurately described as a system of layers of organization. Each successive layer—county or city, state, national—has an independent concern about elections in its geographical jurisdiction." [33]

A national political party is somewhat like a sports trophy that a team may win and retain for a time but must return eventually so that it may be awarded to a new team. Thus, Barry Goldwater captured the Republican party in 1964, but after his defeat, he was obliged to give up control of the party machinery. Four years later, it belonged to Richard Nixon.

[31] White, *The Making of the President 1968*, p. 338.
[32] *Ibid.*
[33] Key, *Politics, Parties, and Pressure Groups*, p. 316.

On paper, the party's quadrennial *national convention* is the source of all authority. The convention nominates the party candidates for President and Vice-President; it writes a platform, settles disputes and writes rules, and elects the members of the national committee.

The *national chairman* is elected by the members of the national committee. In practice, as the Humphrey-O'Brien anecdote illustrates, he is chosen by the party presidential nominee at the end of the national convention.[34]

The *national committee* consists of one man and one woman from each state, the District of Columbia, Puerto Rico, and some of the territories. In addition, since 1952, the Republicans have included in the national committee state party chairmen from states that voted Republican in the last national or state election. Within each state, members of the national committee are selected under state law by state party convention, by the state delegation to the national convention, by state committees, or in primary elections. The national convention formally "elects" the members of the national committee, but in fact it simply ratifies the choices of each state.

Committee members meet rarely; the national committee, in practice, is little more than the permanent offices in Washington housing the national chairman and the committee staff. Between elections, the chief functions of the staff of the national committee are public relations, patronage, research, and fund-raising.

As a rule, a presidential nominee either largely ignores the machinery of the national committee and builds a personal organization to run his campaign, or he takes over the national committee machinery and makes it his own. In theory the national chairman's main job is to manage the presidential campaign; in practice, however, the candidate's real campaign manager is seldom the party chairman. In 1960, for example, Robert F. Kennedy —not the Democratic national chairman—ran his brother's presidential campaign.

Independent of the national committees, and serving as further evidence of the decentralization of American party politics, are the *congressional and senatorial campaign committees*. Both major parties have campaign committees in the House and Senate; their members are chosen by party members in each branch of Congress. The congressional committees channel money, speakers, advice, and assistance to party members who are up for election.

In both the Republican and Democratic parties there is normally a good deal of conflict between the party leaders in Congress and the leaders

[34] The national chairman may or may not serve a full four years, however. For example, following the 1964 Republican defeat, Dean Burch, Barry Goldwater's choice as GOP national chairman, was forced out by leaders of the party's moderate and liberal wings who replaced him with Ray Bliss of Ohio.

of the more presidentially-oriented national party organization, a built-in tension often reflected in rivalry and jealousy between the congressional campaign committees and the national committees.

Party organization and election laws vary tremendously in the states, with the result that one can find kaleidoscopic variety in almost any given phase of American politics below the national level.

State and Local Parties

Just as the national party in power is controlled by the President, the state party is usually dominated by the governor, or in the case of some large Northern industrial states, by the mayor of a large city. Some state party organizations are the fiefdom of a single party boss—either an elected official or a party leader outside government. For example, the rival Democratic candidates for the presidential nomination in 1968 knew that the Illinois Democratic party was controlled by one man—Mayor Richard J. Daley of Chicago, the boss of Cook County. Yet in California and New York, the most populous states in the Union, no single figure controlled the Democratic party.

Republicans or Democrats may consistently dominate within a state; or power may be divided between the two parties. After studying party competition on the state level, Austin Ranney concluded that half the states have two-party systems; eight states have one-party systems and the remaining seventeen have modified one-party systems.[35]

But even within one party, there are great variations in party politics from state to state. The Democratic party in Alabama is very different from that of Michigan. In both parties, liberals may control one state, conservatives another. And these local differences tend to make American political parties decentralized, fragmented, and weak.

State politics often reflects geographic cleavages. In New York, the Democratic party traditionally controls New York City while Republicans dominate "upstate," the areas outside of the city. In Illinois, the Democrats, strong in Cook County, must contend with a heavy downstate Republican vote. In Michigan, Democrats are strong in Detroit, but Republicans dominate most other areas of the state.

The state parties are bound together within the national political party by a mutual desire to have a "winner" at the head of the national ticket. Often (although not always), a strong presidential candidate will sweep state and local candidates into office on his coattails. A Mayor Daley may be more interested in electing a Democratic governor in Illinois than a Democratic President; but he knows that victory in the State House may depend on victory in the White House.

---

[35] Austin Ranney, "Parties in State Politics," in Herbert Jacob and Kenneth Vines, eds., *Politics in the American States* (Boston: Little, Brown, 1965), p. 66.

George Washington (Boss) Plunkitt, a political leader in New York City at the turn of the century, explained his philosophy for attracting votes:

What holds your grip on your district is to go right down among the poor families and help them in the different ways they need help. I've got a regular system for this. If there's a fire in Ninth, Tenth, or Eleventh Avenue, for example, any hour of the day or night, I'm usually there with some of my election district captains as soon as the fire engines. If a family is burned out I don't ask whether they are Republicans or Democrats, and I don't refer them to the Charity Organization Society, which would investigate their case in a month or two and decide they were worthy of help about the time they are dead from starvation. I just get quarters for them, buy clothes for them if their clothes were burned up, and fix them up til they get things runnin' again. It's philanthropy, but it's politics, too—mighty good politics. Who can tell how many votes one of these fires brings me?

—Boss Plunkitt in William L. Riordon, *Plunkitt of Tammany Hall.*

The layer of party organization below that of the national committees is the state committees. As in the case of national committeemen, members of the state committees are chosen in many different ways, including county conventions and direct primaries.

At the grassroots of each major political party is a third layer of party organization, consisting of the county committees, county chairmen, district leaders, precinct or ward captains, and party workers. The local party organization is held together in part by the paste of patronage—the rewarding of party faithfuls with government jobs. The old-style big-city political machines depended almost entirely on patronage; even today a substantial portion of party workers may be found on town, city, and county payrolls.

Although big-city machines still exist, the cigar-chomping derby-hatted political "boss" of the late nineteenth and early twentieth centuries has in most areas enjoyed his "last hurrah." At one time Frank Hague, the Democratic boss of Jersey City, could blatantly declare: "I am the law." Edward J. Flynn, the boss of the Bronx, could rise to considerable power within the national Democratic party. Carmine De Sapio, the leader of Tammany Hall, was able to dominate New York City politics in the 1950's. But, Frank J. Sorauf has suggested, "the defeat of Carmine De Sapio and the Tammany tiger by the reformers in the fall of 1961 may stand as one of the great turning points in American politics." [36]

The urban machines drew their power from the vast waves of immigrants to America's cities. The machines offered all sorts of help to these newcomers—from food baskets to city jobs. In return, all the boss demanded was the newcomer's vote. Each ward captain knew precisely how many votes he could deliver—the captain who did not would soon find he was no longer a municipal inspector of sewers. Since the 1930's, social

[36] Sorauf, *Political Parties in the American System,* p. 53.

security, welfare payments, unemployment benefits, and general prosperity have cut the ground out from under the city machines: the social services formerly provided by the party clubhouse now flow from the impersonal bureaucracy in Washington. And the establishment of the direct primary has, in some cases, impaired the power of the bosses to control nominations of candidates.

The local party organization can still find a city job for a loyal worker. It can award a municipal construction contract to a party activist or financial contributor. But people participate in politics at the grassroots level today for a variety of reasons other than economic motives. The students ringing doorbells and tramping through the snow in New Hampshire in 1968, and those who worked for congressional candidates in 1970, did so because they believed in peace, and for the sheer excitement of being involved and committed. A precinct captain may be active in politics because he enjoys the added prestige he acquires in the eyes of his neighbors (he is the man who can get a new street light put in, or prevent the new high-rise apartment building from going up). He may even be a party worker because he likes to attend the party's national convention as a delegate every four years.

The number of political activists at any level is fairly small, however. Perhaps slightly more than 10 percent of the population could be classified as "politically involved." A 1964 study reported that 4 percent of persons sampled belonged to a political club or organization; 11 percent had given money, bought tickets for fund-raising affairs, or otherwise contributed to one of the parties or candidates that year; 8 percent had attended political meetings, rallies, or dinners; and 5 percent had worked for one of the candidates or parties. (See Table 7-2.) If we apply these percentages to the

TABLE 7-2

Political Participation

	1952	1956	1960	1964
Do you belong to any political club or organization?	2%	3%	3%	4%
Did you give any money or buy tickets or do anything to help the campaign for one of the parties or candidates?	4%	10%	11%	11%
Did you go to any political meetings, rallies, dinners, or things like that?	7%	7%	8%	8%
Did you do any other work for one of the parties or candidates?	3%	3%	5%	5%

Source: Survey Research Center, University of Michigan, in William H. Flanigan, *Political Behavior of the American Electorate* (Boston: Allyn and Bacon, 1968), p. 96.

1964 voting age population of 113,800,000 [37] we find that in round numbers only 4,600,000 Americans belonged to political clubs, 12,500,000 contributed to parties or candidates, 9,100,000 attended political gatherings or functions and 5,700,000 did political work for parties or candidates. Since a member of a political club is also likely to attend political rallies, many of these were the same people.

THE NATIONAL CONVENTIONS

Television has brought American politics into the living room. Perhaps nowhere is this more apparent than in the spectacle of the presidential nominating convention. Viewers at home may have a better and closer view of a national convention than the delegates. Network television reporters, sprouting antennae and electronic gear and looking like Martians in button-down collars, roam the convention floor interviewing political leaders and generating excitement. Faceless TV directors, sitting in darkened rooms just off the convention floor, follow the action on glowing monitors. They bark crisp orders; the camera cuts to Dan Rather of CBS or John Chancellor of NBC. The latest gossip, the newest floor rumor is fed back, in living color, to millions of American homes.

True, the television viewer will miss some of the drama of the convention hall, the actual feel of the crowd, the vast size of the amphitheater. On the other hand, he can sit back in comfort in his home, beer in hand, and watch democracy in action as the Democrats and Republicans choose their candidates for the most powerful office in the world.

But is that really what he is seeing? Are the delegates actually choosing the nominee, or merely ratifying what has been a foregone conclusion for weeks or months? Do the delegates have meaningful power, or are they puppets taking orders from the political bosses? Is the convention rigged, or does it have a mind of its own? Would it perhaps be better, after all, to watch *Laugh-In?*

The answers to these questions depend entirely on what convention, what delegation, and which delegates one has in mind. Depending on the year and the circumstances, one can accurately answer "yes" or "no" to each question.

The national convention has been roundly denounced as a carnival and a bore, and vigorously defended as the most practical method of choosing political candidates in a democracy. It may be all three.

The national nominating convention evolved slowly in American politics. Until 1824, nominations for President were made by party caucus

[37] U.S. Bureau of the Census, Population Estimates, *Current Population Reports,* Series P-25, No. 406, October 4, 1968.

THE NATIONAL NOMINATING CONVENTIONS: CORN PONE AND APPLE PIE

The national nominating convention is something unknown to the Constitution and undreamed of by the founding fathers. It is an American invention, as native to the U.S.A. as corn pone or apple pie. A Democratic or a Republican national nominating convention, once it gets going, emits sounds and lights that never were on land or sea. . . . At different hours of the day or night, it has something of the painted and tinselled and tired gaiety of a four-ring circus, something of the juvenile inebriety and synthetic fraternal sentiment of a class reunion, something of the tub-thumping frenzy of a backwoods camp meeting. . . . What goes on beneath the surface and behind locked doors is something both realistic and important. For it is here, unexposed to the public eye, that the deals and bargains, the necessary compromises are arranged—compromises designed to satisfy as well as possible all of the divergent elements within the party.

—Carl Becker, "The Will of the People," *Yale Review*, March 1945.

in Congress. As a presidential aspirant that year, Andrew Jackson knew he did not have enough strength in the congressional caucus to gain the nomination; so his supporters boycotted the caucus. The Tennessee legislature nominated Jackson, who received the most popular and electoral votes. But he lost the election when the House chose John Quincy Adams as President. Jackson's efforts, however, successfully dethroned "King Caucus"; in the election of 1832, presidential candidates of all political parties were nominated by national conventions for the first time.

The early conventions provided no surprises, but in 1844, on the eighth ballot, the Democrats chose a "dark horse," James K. Polk, who won the election and proved an able President. Polk's nomination "marked the coming of age of the convention as an institution capable of creating as well as of ratifying consensus within the party." [38]

Today, national party conventions normally take place over four days in July or August. The convention city is invariably hot and overcrowded; delegates spend long hours waiting for elevators and attempting to do such simple things as ordering breakfast in a hotel coffee shop, or placing an outgoing phone call. Rival candidates set up headquarters in hotel suites. As the convention opens, rumors fly of deals and of switches by key delegations. There are press conferences, television interviews, parades, bands, pretty girls, and other forms of confusion and diversion.

Nominating a Presidential Candidate

As the 1968 Democratic National Convention proved, there may also be violence and tragedy. The bloody confrontation between police and young antiwar protesters at Chicago overshadowed the events inside the

[38] Key, *Politics, Parties, and Pressure Groups*, p. 398.

convention hall and proved that under some circumstances what happens in the streets may become more significant than the formal proceedings. During the presidential campaign, Humphrey did not succeed in dispelling the image of a badly divided party or the memory of the bloodshed at Chicago.

Even at a peaceful political convention, major decisions are made outside the convention hall. Behind the scenes, presidential candidates and their lieutenants apply a combination of carrot and stick to party leaders and delegates, alternately pleading and pressuring for their support. The candidates know that state delegations seek to provide the winning margin of victory to a nominee, thereby earning his gratitude, and, hopefully, future rewards. The psychological pressure on delegates is always the same: hop aboard this or that bandwagon before it is too late to matter.[39]

The convention, on its first day, normally hears the report of its credentials committee, the body that decides what delegates shall be seated. Often, rival delegations claim to represent the party in a state, or one faction may charge irregularities in the selection of delegates. The credentials committee must decide these disputes, subject always to the approval of the convention. In the evening the keynote speaker fills the air with the customary rhetoric. On the second day, the party platform is debated and voted upon. The outcome of these lesser struggles over credentials and the platform often signals which party faction has the votes to win the nomination for its candidate.

On the third day, the nominations and balloting for presidential nominee usually begin. Traditionally, a candidate's name is not mentioned until the very end of the nominating speech ("I give you the name of the next President of the United States ———————— ———————— ————————!"). The name is a signal for a carefully planned "spontaneous" demonstration on the floor, often employing professional demonstrators and organized to the split second by experts armed with walkie-talkies and stopwatches.

Despite time limits on oratory, the nominating and seconding speeches go on to the near limits of delegate endurance. Then the roll of states is called in alphabetical order for the balloting. In both parties, the candidate who wins a simple majority of the convention votes is nominated. Front-runners attempt to win on the first ballot. Lesser candidates and dark horses naturally hope that nobody wins on the first ballot; they may then have a chance of picking up increased delegate strength on the second, third, or subsequent ballots.

It is the traditional privilege of the presidential nominee to select his

[39] Political candidates have a way of remembering who was for them when. Early backers enjoy a special status; for example, during the era of the New Frontier, the Kennedy administration knew very well what states and individuals were "FKBLA"—"For Kennedy Before Los Angeles" (the site of the 1960 convention).

Chicago, 1968: Troops of the Illinois National Guard outside the convention hall where Democrats nominated Hubert Humphrey for President.

choice for vice-presidential nominee.[40] The fourth day of the convention is devoted to the routine nomination of and balloting for the Vice-President, the acceptance speeches of both candidates, and their climactic appearance with their families before the cheering delegates. This moment of high personal and political drama underscores the fact that a national convention

[40] In 1956, Adlai Stevenson, the nominee of the Democratic National Convention, threw open the choice of a vice-presidential candidate to the delegates. In the floor balloting, Senator Estes Kefauver of Tennessee narrowly defeated Senator John Kennedy to become Stevenson's running mate.

Richard Nixon and Spiro Agnew appear with their families before a cheering Republican National Convention in 1968 after being nominated as their party's candidates for President and Vice-President.

also serves the function of a party pep rally, generating enthusiasm for the ticket and, in effect, kicking off the presidential campaign.

Beneath the hoopla and ballyhoo of a national party convention, serious business has taken place. Rival political leaders have clashed and fought, differences on issues within the party have been publicly aired, and a major political party has produced its nominees for the highest offices in the land.

The Delegates   Who are the few thousand men and women formally entitled to select the presidential nominees of the two major parties? In general, they represent a cross section of the party, but an affluent cross section, since the cost of travel to a convention city, of hotels and meals, mounts up to hundreds of dollars. The delegates usually include governors, senators, congressmen, mayors, state legislators, state party officials, and activists and contributors at the grassroots level.

Delegates to national party conventions are chosen by a variety of methods. In 1968, fourteen states and the District of Columbia held presidential primaries in which voters expressed their preference for a presidential nominee and, except in the case of Wisconsin and Indiana, also chose all or some convention delegates. In some instances, the results of the primaries were binding on the delegates; in others, the delegates went to the conventions unpledged to any particular candidate. Although most public attention tends to focus on the drama of the primaries, which are heavily covered by the media, many more delegates are chosen in the majority of states that do *not* hold presidential primaries. In 1968, 937 regular delegates to the Democratic National Convention were elected in the primaries; but 2,052 delegates, more than two-thirds, were chosen by other methods—district conventions, state conventions, and, in a few cases, by state committees.

These methods are not always democratic. For example, in some Southern states, blacks have been systematically excluded from Democratic party delegations to national conventions. When the all-white Mississippi delegation was challenged at the convention in 1964 by the largely black Mississippi Freedom Democratic party, the convention voted to eliminate all racial barriers in party affairs. But this action did not prevent new disputes over the racial make-up of several Deep South delegations in 1968. As a result, reform elements within the Democratic party sought means to democratize the delegate-selection process. Their efforts led the Democrats, in 1968, to establish a Commission on Party Structure and Delegate Selection to recommend methods for choosing convention delegates "by procedures open to public participation." Party reformers warned that unless delegate selection and other party procedures were opened up to include all Democrats, dissident groups, such as Eugene McCarthy's supporters in 1968, would desert the party ranks. Senator Harold E. Hughes of Iowa, a leader of the fight for reform, warned: "It is no secret that we are in trouble, especially with significant groups that have traditionally been identified with the Democratic Party. . . . for much too long now, national conventions have largely been the private domain of the rich, the white and the party regular." [41]

The Democratic reform commission reported in 1970 that in at least twenty states there were no adequate rules for selection of delegates to the 1968 convention, "leaving the entire process to the discretion of a handful of party leaders." It reported that more than one third of the delegates had, in effect, been selected prior to 1968—before issues and possible candidates were clear. The report added that "secret caucuses, closed slate-making, widespread proxy voting—and a host of other procedural irregularities—

---

[41] Congressional Quarterly, *Weekly Report*, March 7, 1969, p. 330.

were all too common at precinct, county, district, and state conventions." It concluded that the costs of being a delegate were discriminatory, and that delegates were substantially wealthier than the general population. And it found representation of minorities far below the proportion of such groups in the population: blacks comprised only 5 percent of the delegates, women only 13 percent, and a majority of delegations had no more than one delegate under thirty years of age.[42] The commission issued a set of eighteen guidelines designed to eliminate such abuses, but it had no authority to enforce its recommendations on state and local party organizations.

Both major parties apportion delegates under complicated formulas based on population and party strength within each state. The Republican National Convention of 1968 had 1,333 regular delegates, each casting one vote, and an equal number of alternates. Since 1952, the Republicans have allotted a bonus of six delegates to each state that votes Republican in the preceding presidential, senatorial, or gubernatorial race. Republican election gains in the South since 1952 resulted in a marked increase in Southern delegate strength between the 1952 and 1968 Republican national conventions. (See Table 7-3.)

The Democrats also allot a bonus of extra delegates to states carried by the party's presidential nominee in the last election; the effect of this formula has been to erode Southern strength at Democratic national conventions. Under the Democratic formula, the number of delegates at the

TABLE 7-3

Regional Strength at the Republican National Conventions, 1952–1968

	1952	1960	1964	1968
East[1]	372(30.8%)	386(29.0%)	355(27.1%)	355(26.6%)
South[2]	299(19.0)	329(24.7)	325(24.8)	356(26.7)
Midwest	372(30.8)	372(28.0)	364(27.8)	352(26.4)
West[3]	229(19.0)	242(18.2)	256(19.6)	262(19.7)
Totals[4]	1,206	1,331	1,308	1,333

[1] Includes Washington, D.C. delegation.

[2] South defined to include the 11 states of the old Confederacy plus Oklahoma and Kentucky.

[3] Includes Alaska and Hawaii.

[4] Totals include Puerto Rico and Virgin Islands, not included in regional breakdown.

Source: Congressional Quarterly, *Weekly Report*, June 7, 1968, p. 1312.

[42] *Mandate for Reform, Report of the Commission on Party Structure and Delegate Selection to the Democratic National Committee* (Washington, D.C.: Democratic National Committee, 1970), pp. 10–11.

1968 national convention mushroomed to an unmanageable 5,611 (2,989 regular delegates, 2,512 alternates, and 110 members of the Democratic National Committee). Because there were more delegates than the maximum number of convention votes (2,622) some delegates cast only half votes.

Delegates who are chosen by state and local party organizations are often under the control of party leaders. Although it is popular, and sometimes accurate, to depict delegates as puppets, there is a wide range of difference in the degree of boss control over delegations. A study of the 1952 conventions found that while some delegations were tightly knit and carefully rehearsed, many others were fragmented and subdivided into rival factions.[43] The study concluded that at the Democratic National Convention, "individual delegates by the hundreds made their own assessments" and drifted toward Adlai Stevenson: "The result was a gathering consensus that showed little evidence of dictation or overwhelming influence from any single power center." [44] Most of the time, it remains true, however, that "a relatively few party leaders control the decisions of a large proportion of the delegates to conventions." [45]

ON REFORMING POLITICAL PARTIES: ONE VIEW

The key word in the lexicon of the New Politics is "Participation." Real political power in both parties has too often rested disproportionately in the hands of a few party officials and contributors, nearly all of them white, male, affluent, Establishment-oriented and over 50, many of them more concerned about keeping their places on the political ladder than solving the national and urban crises surrounding them.

The frustrating sense of powerlessness that many Americans feel toward remote, impersonal institutions applies to political parties as well. . . . We must formulate procedures to redistribute political power to achieve the broadest possible participation in the exercising of that power. Precinct meetings open to all must have an effective voice in the formulation of policy and in the selection of both party leaders and candidates. The notion that a few men should successfully choose the party nominee for any important office regardless of whether he reflects the will of the voters is shocking.

—Theodore C. Sorensen, "Did Chappaquiddick Finish the Democrats?"
Look, November 4, 1969.

[43] Paul T. David, Ralph M. Goldman, and Richard C. Bain, *The Politics of National Party Conventions*, Kathleen Sproul, ed. (New York: Vintage Books, 1964), p. 252. A paperback condensation of the study originally published by the Brookings Institution.
[44] *Ibid.*, p. 256.
[45] Nelson W. Polsby and Aaron B. Wildavsky, *Presidential Elections* (New York: Scribner's, 1968), p. 78.

Until 1968, the Democrats followed one form or another of the unit rule, which allowed the majority of a state delegation to cast the state's entire vote if so instructed by the state convention. The opponents of this system argued that it made boss rule easier. In 1968, the Democrats voted to drop the unit rule at all party levels for the 1972 convention. Thus, another tool of the "old politics" has fallen by the wayside; with delegates free to vote their choice, party bosses may find it more difficult to control their state delegations.

Do Conventions
Decide?

Despite the tumult and the shouting, the results of many recent national conventions have been unsurprising. So the question remains: Are national conventions real arenas of democratic decision or mere rubber stamps?

In 1960, the Brookings Institution, an independent research organization, published a study of national nominating conventions. Analyzing sixty-five conventions from 1832 to 1960, the study identified five types of nominations: [46]

1. *Confirmation.* An existing President or party titular leader is confirmed as the party's choice.
2. *Inheritance.* A political understudy or previous leader inherits the party mantle.
3. *Innergroup selection.* Dominant party leaders get together and agree on the nominee.
4. *Compromise in stalemate.* A deadlocked convention turns to a dark horse or unexpected candidate.
5. *Factional victory.* One of several competing factions within the party succeeds in nominating its candidate.

Although twenty-two conventions have been "confirming," fully nineteen, the second highest number, fell into the category of "factional victory," evidence that genuine competition has characterized national nominating conventions a substantial share of the time. (See Table 7–4.) Only three of the nineteen conventions—those nominating McKinley in 1896, Dewey in 1944, and Kennedy in 1960—had outcomes that were generally anticipated in advance of the convention.[47]

The struggle for nomination at a convention can, of course, take many different shapes. The phrase "smoke-filled room," often used to describe the selection of a candidate by political bosses operating in secret, grew out of the 1920 GOP convention. There, a group of Republican leaders met in a room of Chicago's Blackstone Hotel and ended a conven-

[46] David, Goldman, and Bain, *The Politics of National Party Conventions*, Chapter 7.
[47] *Ibid.*, p. 286.

TABLE 7-4

Patterns in Major-Party Presidential Nominations
Since 1832

| | Number of Presidential Nominations | | | | | |
| | Democratic | | Republican[1] | | Major-Party Total | |
Type of Nomination	1832–1892	1896–1960	1832–1892	1896–1960	1832–1892	1896–1960
Confirmation	4	8	3	7	7	15
Inheritance	1	1	2	3	3	4
Innergroup selection	5	1	2	2	7	3
Compromise in stalemate	3	1	2	1	5	2
Factional victory	3	6	6	4	9	10
Total	16	17	15	17	31	34

[1] Includes National Republican and Whig parties.

Source: Paul T. David, Ralph M. Goldman, and Richard C. Bain, *The Politics of National Party Conventions,* Kathleen Sproul, ed. (New York: Vintage Books, 1964), p. 138. By permission of the Brookings Institution.

tion stalemate by selecting Warren G. Harding of Marion, Ohio, who *looked* like a President but was otherwise a mediocre chief executive. The Democrats set a record at their 1924 convention in New York, the longest ever held. The weary delegates finally chose John W. Davis, a New York lawyer, on the 103rd ballot; but America preferred the Republican candidate, Calvin Coolidge.

Franklin D. Roosevelt led the field at the Democratic National Convention in 1932, but he was not nominated until the fourth ballot. In 1940, with the galleries chanting "We Want Willkie," the Republicans nominated Wendell L. Willkie, Wall Street lawyer and a true dark horse. The Taft-Eisenhower convention battle in 1952 reflected the greatest split in the Republican party since 1912.

Since 1960, however, national conventions have filled more of a ratifying than a selecting function. For example, John F. Kennedy was the front-runner in advance of the Democratic National Convention at Los Angeles in 1960. In 1964, Barry Goldwater had a firm grip on the Republican nomination well before the delegates assembled in San Francisco. In 1968, it was generally anticipated that Nixon would emerge from the Miami convention with the Republican nomination. A joint Rockefeller-Reagan pincerlike movement to block Nixon never developed sufficient strength. Despite the bloodshed in the streets at the 1968 Democratic convention in Chicago, Vice-President Humphrey's nomination at no point seemed seriously endangered.

This "ratifying" trend since 1960 does not mean that conventions have lost all power to decide or that vigorous battles will not take place

in the future. But two factors have combined to diminish the decisional role of the convention in recent years.

First, preconvention campaigns by presidential hopefuls have gained in intensity and length. Fifteen months before the 1960 convention John Kennedy mounted a smoothly-organized campaign to win the Democratic nomination. The Goldwater forces concentrated on electing their own supporters as delegates to the 1964 Republican National Convention in an organizational effort that began a year and a half before the delegates met in San Francisco. The Nixon organization was stirring in 1966, two years before the Republican convention at Miami.

Second, extensive coverage by television and other media has focused national attention on these preconvention campaigns and increased their importance. Consequently, they have become, to some extent, elimination races. In 1960, for example, Kennedy's victory in the West Virginia primary on May 10 eliminated Hubert Humphrey from the race and sent the Kennedy bandwagon rolling at top speed. Democratic party leaders, the press, and the public were impressed by the fact that Kennedy, a Catholic, had won in a heavily Protestant state. In 1968, George Romney's difficulties with the media removed him from contention early in the year. The press had a field day with Romney's remark that he had been "brainwashed" by the administration on Vietnam; his ratings in the polls dropped drastically and he withdrew from the race for the Republican nomination even *before* the New Hampshire primary.

As a result of the intense coverage now given to presidential primaries and to preconvention campaigning, one or another candidate has tended to gain a clear lead before the convention in the public mind, in the political polls, and often, within the rank and file of the party. The Brookings Institution study concluded: "Much of the struggle that used to occur in the conventions has been shifted to the preconvention period, and with the great modern access to information about delegate commitments and intentions, most of the losers in recent times have probably known that they were beaten before the convention opened." [48]

Nevertheless, as long as the institution of the national convention remains, the potential exists for a sharply contested battle for the nomination if two or more candidates enter the arena with roughly equal support and resources.

The Future of the Convention System

From time to time, various proposals have been made to revamp the national nominating convention or even replace it with some presumably more representative or more dignified procedure. One of the recurrent proposals is for a national presidential primary, in which the voters

[48] David, Goldman, and Bain, *The Politics of National Party Conventions*, p. 324.

could directly choose the presidential candidates of the major parties. The plan has some drawbacks, however: for example, its critics have argued that if too many candidates entered the primary, no single candidate might gain a majority of the votes.

In any event, the convention system, having survived since 1832, is not likely to disappear in the television age, at a time when it has grown into a sort of political Super Bowl. Nor is it at all clear that the national convention should be replaced. The Brookings Institution study concluded: "The continuing contributions made by the conventions to the survival and stability of the American political order are unique, indispensable, and, granted our form of Constitution, probably irreplaceable. . . . The services of the convention as a general conclave for the selection and recognition of top leadership in each party, and for its replacement when necessary, could be abandoned only at serious national peril." [49]

POLITICAL PARTIES AND DEMOCRATIC GOVERNMENT

At best, Americans have always had a somewhat ambivalent attitude toward politics and politicians. "Politics," Clinton Rossiter has noted, "is sin, and politicians, if not sinners, are pretty suspicious fellows." [50]

In 1952, General Eisenhower enjoyed the support of many voters who felt he was "above politics" or "not a politician." The same was true of Ronald Reagan when he ran for governor of California for the first time in 1966 in a campaign that emphasized his nonprofessional political status. Among many voters, the image of the politician as an unprincipled opportunist persists.

Since political parties are vital to the functioning of American democracy, it is somewhat paradoxical that politics and politicians—especially with their access to the image-making resources of Madison Avenue—do not enjoy greater prestige.

The truth about politics and its practitioners may lie somewhere between Aristotle's view that "the good of man" is the object of politics and the classic statement of Simon Cameron, the Republican boss of Pennsylvania, that "an honest politician is one who, when he is bought, will stay bought."

Possibly Americans would have a more generous view of the craft of politics if it were more widely understood that parties and democracy are mutually dependent. Competition among political parties is the essence of democracy. Political parties in America, as we have seen, provide a vehicle

---

[49] David, Goldman, and Bain, *The Politics of National Party Conventions*, p. 339.
[50] Rossiter, *Parties and Politics in America*, p. 34.

of political choice, manage the transfer of power, help to hold politicians accountable to the voters, recruit candidates, staff and link branches of the government, and may sometimes resolve social conflict.

The rest of the world also has a vital stake in the politics of American democracy; certainly the man nominated by his party and chosen by the electorate to be President has greater power than any other leader in history. How an American President uses that power, including the nuclear weapons under his control, is of direct concern to all other nations, as well as to the voters at home.

The "brokerage" role of political parties in mediating among interest groups, whether such groups are organized or not, and in resolving social conflict, is of tremendous importance in a democracy under pressure. Both major political parties try to form a broad base by appealing to diverse groups in society. As a result, when one party loses power and another wins the Presidency, the change tends to be accepted, or at least tolerated, by the voters. In this way, parties help to keep conflict manageable, for if substantial numbers of voters violently opposed the election results, the political system could not work.

A Choice,
Not an Echo?

In his classic complaint about the similarity of American political parties, James Bryce concluded that "neither party has any principles, any distinctive tenets." The similarities of American parties are often lamented, but, as our discussion of the characteristics of American political parties pointed out, there are significant differences as well.

While it is true that American parties are not sharply ideological, it is also true that many American voters are not sharply ideological. The argument is often made that the major parties should offer a more pronounced choice on issues, and not merely a choice between candidates, but it is by no means clear that extreme polarization of the parties on issues that divide American society is desirable. "The difference between Democrats and Republicans," Max Lerner has observed, "while it is more than the difference between Tweedledum and Tweedledee, is not such as to split the society itself or invite civil conflict. . . . The choices between the two are usually substantial choices but not desperate ones."[51]

Are Parties
Accountable
to the Voters?

When Americans go to the polls, they do not elect parties; they elect officials who usually run as the candidates of political parties. By its very nature, the American political system holds these officials accountable to the voters and the parties only indirectly accountable.

Nevertheless, the most frequent criticism of the American party sys-

[51] Max Lerner, *America As a Civilization*, Vol. 1 (New York: Simon and Schuster, 1967), pp. 389–90.

tem is that the parties are not "responsible" to the electorate, that there is no way to make them keep the promises outlined in their platforms, and that, in any event, they lack the internal discipline to whip their programs through Congress.[52] One difficulty, as the Brookings Institution study noted, is that party platforms "are written for use in *presidential* campaigns, yet they consist mainly of proposals for legislation that will be meaningless unless there is congressional action." [53]

In a parliamentary system of government, such as that in Great Britain, political parties are more closely linked to the popular will because the voters choose a majority party that is responsible for the conduct of both the executive and legislative branches of government. Since few critics of the American party system advocate parliamentary democracy for the United States, party accountability in America is likely to remain a matter of degree.

Many political scientists do not agree on the need for or desirability of greater party responsibility. For example, party cohesion strong enough to pass programs in Congress could only be achieved by reducing the importance and independence of individual legislators. But advocates of strong, responsible parties point to several ways that party responsibility can be strengthened, short of adopting the British system of parliamentary democracy: greater discipline within parties, rewarding cooperative members with campaign funds, electing the chairmen of congressional committees on the basis of party loyalty rather than seniority.

To an extent, however, a broad measure of party responsibility already exists. When American parties embark on courses of action that displease large numbers of voters, the voters may retaliate. In 1964, Barry Goldwater, the Republican candidate, was the "hawk" who advocated "total victory" over Communism. President Johnson, on the other hand, presented himself as a "dove," promising: "We are not about to send American boys nine or ten thousand miles away from home to do what Asian boys ought to be doing to protect themselves." Many of Johnson's supporters felt misled a few years later when it turned out that they had voted for a "dove" and elected a "hawk." But in the election of 1968 the nation sent a Republican to the White House. The fact that Johnson, an incumbent President, found it prudent not to run for reelection is further evidence that a measure of accountability is not wholly lacking in American politics.

Attempting to predict the future of American political parties is a perilous business. Like life itself, politics is often unpredictable; A Look Ahead

[52] See, for example, *Toward a More Responsible Two-Party System*, Report of the Committee on Political Parties of the American Political Science Association (New York: Holt, Rinehart and Winston, 1950).
[53] David, Goldman, and Bain, *The Politics of National Party Conventions*, p. 344.

those who forecast the eclipse of the Republican party in 1964 were required to watch the elephant ride into the White House in 1968.

One fact seems clear. In a time of ferment and great social upheaval, of tension and conflict, political parties must respond to the pressures for, or against, change, or pay the price of defeat. And it seems likely that in times of acute social stress in America, minor parties of the right and left will continue to arise. Possibly, even "non-party" candidates will seek the Presidency. Yet, in one form or another, the two-party system has flourished since the beginning of the Republic and will probably survive.

Some changes in political parties are already discernible. In America of the 1970's, the nomination of a black man on the national ticket of one or both of the major parties is no longer impossible. The new political awareness of students and the participation of youth in the front lines of American politics are likely to have a continuing impact on both parties, just as they did in 1968.

Although in the presidential year 1968 most students participating in politics did so at the national level, by 1970, many concerned students had plunged into local campaigns. After four students demonstrating against the Vietnam war were killed at Kent State, students in some areas began working for congressional peace candidates in the primary and general elections. They passed out campaign literature, talked to voters, and performed dozens of routine campaign tasks. They were not always successful, but in the process many discovered that it is on the local level, in the grinding job of reaching the voters, that individuals can participate most directly in the political process.

How well did the students do in the 1970 elections? According to a Congressional Quarterly study, of thirty-eight candidates for the House of Representatives who had significant student support, nineteen won and nineteen lost. Although the turnout of student workers fell far short of what had been generally anticipated in the spring, an estimated 75,000 students did participate.[54] The student support was coordinated by the Movement for a New Congress, based at Princeton University, with more than 450 chapters at colleges and universities across the country. Baltimore Democrat Parren Mitchell, a black candidate elected to the House, credited his success to his student workers. James Buckley, the Conservative elected to the Senate from New York, said 5,000 young workers had been active in his campaign.

Behind this effort was a belief by most students that the political system can be made to respond in time to public demands. A Louis Harris poll taken in July 1970 showed that 89 percent of college students agreed that, eventually, government policy can be altered by public pressure; 63

[54] Congressional Quarterly, *Weekly Report*, November 6, 1970, p. 2763.

percent believed the democratic process can work; and 65 percent thought that working to elect better public officials was a very effective way of improving American society.[55]

The increased importance of television and of preconvention campaigns probably makes the selection of a "dark horse" candidate by a national convention less likely than in the past. Candidates may be expected to rely more on television, which can reach millions of people, than on old-fashioned stump campaigning. Professional campaign managers skilled in media techniques have begun to play a major role in campaigns. So have political polls.

Political parties mirror the society in which they function. Their future is America's future. As in the case of so many other institutions in America, political parties are under strong pressure for change. If they are to serve as meaningful instruments of democracy, they must open their own doors to accommodate blacks and other minorities, women, and students. If government can be made more responsive to public pressure, political parties will be a vital part of that process, for they are uniquely situated to translate the hopes of the American people into action by the American government.

[55] Harris Survey, *Washington Post*, July 20, 1970, p. 3.

SUGGESTED READING

Binkley, Wilfred E. *American Political Parties,* 4th edition (Knopf, 1965). A comprehensive treatment of the historical development of the American party system. Emphasizes the building of coalitions by American political parties.

Committee on Political Parties of the American Political Science Association. *Toward a More Responsible Two-Party System* (Holt, Rinehart and Winston, 1950). Statement of the case for stronger, more disciplined, and more centralized political parties in the United States. This report, by sixteen authorities on political parties, initiated a lively debate among political scientists over the nature of American political parties.

Costikyan, Edward N. *Behind Closed Doors: Politics in the Public Interest* * (New York: Harcourt Brace Jovanovich, 1966). An inside examination of the workings of politics in New York City by a reform Democrat and former party leader. Includes detailed explanation of primaries, conventions, campaigns, and the job of local political leaders.

Cotter, Cornelius P., and Hennessy, Bernard C. *Politics Without Power* (Atherton Press, 1964). A study of the two major-party national committees. Analyzes the role of the national chairman and the development of national committee staffs.

David, Paul T., Goldman, Ralph M., and Bain, Richard C. *The Politics of National Party Conventions* (Washington, D.C.: The Brookings Institution, 1960). (A condensation edited by Kathleen Sproul is available in paperback.) A detailed examination of the historical development of national party conventions. Stresses the functions that the national conventions perform in the American party system.

Duverger, Maurice. *Political Parties: Their Organization and Activity in the Modern State* * (Wiley, 1955). An influential comparative analysis of political parties in a number of countries. Among other topics, Duverger, a French political scientist, examines the nature of party organization in different types of parties, and explores the relationship between the electoral system in a country and the type of party system that flourishes there.

Eldersveld, Samuel J. *Political Parties: A Behavioral Analysis* * (Rand McNally, 1964). A detailed empirical analysis of local party organization in Michigan. Provides revealing insights into the attitudes, patterns of communication, and actual behavior of party activists.

Epstein, Leon D. *Political Parties in Western Democracies* (Praeger, 1967). Paperback. A useful comparative study of political parties in various countries, with special stress on those in Great Britain and the United States. Examines the historical development of parties, recruitment of party leaders, and the contribution of the parties to governing.

Key, V. O., Jr. *Politics, Parties, and Pressure Groups*, 5th edition (Crowell, 1964). A comprehensive analysis of political parties and interest groups. The extensive footnotes serve as a useful guide to much of the scholarly work on political parties and interest groups up to 1963. Examines the nature of the American party system, party structure and procedures, the relations between parties and the voters, and the impact of parties on government.

Mandate for Reform, Report of the Commission on Party Structure and Delegate Selection to the Democratic National Committee (Washington, D.C.: Democratic National Committee, 1970). Paperback. Analyzes procedures for selecting delegates to the Democratic National Convention, giving specific proposals for reform. Prepared by a commission appointed after the 1968 Democratic National Convention in response to pressures for broadening participation in party affairs.

Rossiter, Clinton. *Parties and Politics in America* * (Cornell University Press, 1960). A concise, readable summary of the historical development and the more recent characteristics and functions of political parties in the United States. Contains a useful comparison of the Democratic and Republican parties.

Sindler, Allan P. *Political Parties in the United States* * (St. Martin's Press, 1966). A general overview and analysis of the American party system.

Sorauf, Frank J. *Party Politics in America* (Little, Brown, 1968). A comprehensive analysis of political parties in the United States. Examines political party organization, the behavior of party supporters in the mass electorate, the role of parties in contesting elections, and the impact of parties on government. For a shorter statement of Sorauf's views on political parties, see his *Political Parties in the American System* (Little, Brown, 1964), which is available in paperback.

* Available in paperback edition

8

Political Campaigns

and Candidates

AND NOW, A WORD FROM OUR PRESIDENT . .

Americans watching an adventure program on NBC television one night in September 1968 saw an unusual commercial. It was not the typical advertisement for a detergent, a dentifrice, or a floor wax. Rather, it sought to sell the voters the Republican candidate for President of the United States. It was not, of course, the first time that a presidential candidate had advertised his qualifications in a television commercial; during election campaigns, political parties compete for network exposure. The commercial went like this:

VIDEO	AUDIO
Wounded Americans and Vietnamese.	RICHARD NIXON: Never has so much military, economic, and diplomatic power been used as ineffectively as in Vietnam.

NIXON: And if after all this time and all of this sacrifice . . .

there is still no end in sight, then I say the time has come for the American people . . .

to turn to new leadership not tied to the policies and mistakes of the past.

I pledge to you we will have an honorable end to the war in Vietnam.

ANNOUNCER: This time vote like your whole world depended on it.

Montage of facial CU's [close-ups] of Americans and Vietnamese natives with questioning, anxious, almost perplexed attitudes.	RN: And if after all of this time and all of this sacrifice and all of this support there is still no end in sight, then I say the time has come for the American people to turn to new leadership—not tied to the policies and mistakes of the past.
Proud faces of Vietnamese peasants . . . helmet of American G.I. and pull back to reveal his face.	RN: I pledge to you we will have an honorable end to the war in Vietnam.
	Music up and out
Fadeout . . . face in still of Richard Nixon	ANNOUNCER: This time vote like your whole world depended on it.

For an instant, through the medium of television, the consciousness of millions of viewers had been touched by a political message. It should not be surprising in the television age that a candidate for political office tries to sell himself on TV. Once nominated by his party, a candidate must make his appeal to the voters. The campaign is often concentrated in a period of no more than nine weeks, and television offers the surest means of reaching the largest number of voters.

As a result, television has revolutionized American political campaigns since 1948. The day is long past when a William McKinley could campaign from his front porch in Canton, Ohio. Today's candidate hires a Madison Avenue advertising agency to prepare one or two minute commercial "spots." He may debate his opponent on television, or appear in carefully staged, televised question-and-answer sessions designed to display his warm personality and firm grasp of the issues. Or, he may buy an expensive half-hour of prime TV time for a sincere talk to the American people.

Television, in short, is very much a part of a modern political campaign. For every candidate, between nomination and election, there stands the campaign. In American politics, the campaign is the battleground of power, and victory may depend on how well the battle is fought.

Mostly because of the wide use of television, campaigns are expensive: in 1968 candidates at all levels spent an estimated $300,000,000. But political candidates do not always have equal financial and creative resources. In the era of electronic mass media, disturbing questions have arisen. Will the candidate with the best "image"—the cleverest television advisers, the smoothest packaging—win the election? Do Americans vote for the carefully sanitized "image" of the candidate, rather than the man? Does the candidate with the most money always win? Should candidates have to depend on big contributors to whom they may feel obligated?

Should one candidate enjoy a financial advantage over another in a democracy? If not, what can be done about it? Above all, amid the hoopla, the oratory, and the television commercials, can the voters make a reasonable choice for themselves and for the nation?

These questions have no easy answers. And yet, however imperfect campaigns may be, however raucous and divisive, they are a vital part of the American political system. Campaigns, in the words of the historian Henry Adams, are "the dance of democracy."

HOW CAMPAIGNS ARE ORGANIZED

Campaigns are organized chaos. On a national level, large numbers of people, professionals and volunteers, are thrown together for a relatively short period of time to mount an incredibly complex effort to elect a President. The candidate is rather like a man in the eye of a hurricane; as he jets around the country—stumping, speechmaking, and handshaking—the crowds and cameramen, the press and the voters, local politicians and aides swirl around him. He may arise

at 5 A.M. and not get to sleep until 2 A.M. the next morning, with a dozen cities and thousands of miles traversed in between. Physically exhausted, his hands cut and bruised from the crowds, he is expected to keep smiling throughout his ordeal and to remain alert, ready to respond instantly to any new issue or crisis. In some remote cornfield of Iowa, he may be asked to comment on a sudden and complicated development in Moscow or Peking. He worries that an inappropriate word or phrase might, at any time, cost him the election. An assassin may lurk in the hotel kitchen. In the jet age, the pressures on the candidate are constant and cruel.

The candidate, jetting about the country at 500 miles an hour, obviously must have an elaborate campaign organization behind him with a headquarters staff to plan and coordinate the total effort. His ultimate success may depend on many variables—his charisma, his TV make-up, his advertising agency, his experience, the issues, the number of registered Democrats, a sudden foreign policy crisis, his wife's taste in clothes, the weather on election day—but not the least of these factors is the quality of his campaign organization.

Lawrence O'Brien, John Kennedy's director of campaign organization in 1960, wrote a "Democratic Campaign Manual" for party workers that has been revised in subsequent presidential election years. A few of the chapter titles and subheadings of the slim volume, which has become a sort of campaign classic, suggest the wide range of problems faced in organizing a campaign: "Campaign Director," "Methods of Raising Money," "Research Chairman," "Importance of Women in the Campaign," "Conduct a Registration Drive," "Public Opinion Surveys," "Instructions for Addressing Envelopes," "Distribution of Bumper Stickers," "Coffee Parties and Receptions," "Sound Trucks," "Television," "The Telephone Campaign," and "Voter Transportation."[1]

A presidential candidate must have a campaign manager and a small group of top-level aides to give overall direction to the campaign. He must have someone in charge of fund-raising, for a national campaign costs millions of dollars. He needs a media team to handle advertising and television, a press secretary, advance men to handle the details of his personal appearances, speechwriters, regional and state coordinators, and citizens groups to enlist volunteer support. He must attempt to coordinate the work of national, state, and local party organizations.

Nixon's campaign organization in 1968 was widely regarded as a model of controlled efficiency. To run it, the Republican nominee chose his law partner—John Mitchell, who had no previous formal political experience. Mitchell directed the Nixon-Agnew Campaign Committee from headquarters on Park Avenue in New York. Another Nixon law partner,

---

[1] *Victory '68, Democratic Campaign Handbook 1968* (Washington, D.C.: Democratic National Committee, 1968).

HOW TO WIN AN ELECTION: DEMOCRATIC VERSION

The following are excerpts from the official handbook of instructions for Democratic party workers.

Methods of Raising Money

Direct Solicitation. The best method of raising money, bar none, is to ask people for it. Many Democrats will make a campaign contribution, if someone will ask them to do so. . . .

Testimonial Dinners and Receptions. . . . a fund raising dinner doesn't require a tab of $100 or $50 and $25 or even $10 to be successful. If someone can cook up a few pots of spaghetti, contribute some grated cheese, hot peppers, and fresh bread, finance people may be able to parlay this into a tidy campaign profit even if tickets are sold for only $5 a head.

Research Chairman

The Research Director should place someone on the opponent's mailing list during the campaign, so he can obtain the complete text of any statement he issues.

Public Opinion Surveys

Polls are useful. If a contest is in doubt, and the budget can stand it, a poll should be taken.

The polling firm should be politically oriented, have worked for Democratic candidates before, be able to document its success, and speak the candidate's political language. The Democratic National Committee can provide names of reputable polling firms.

Coffee Parties and Receptions

There is a point of no return at coffee hours; the candidate should shake hands, smile, make his remarks, answer a few questions—and get out while everyone is happy and before he is cornered by an argumentative individual.

Sound Trucks

A touring sound truck should never pass through a residential neighborhood after 7:30 p.m. It is a sure way to lose votes.

Meetings and Debates

During the campaign a candidate will appear at many meetings, rallies, and perhaps some debates.

At all of these there should be sufficient numbers of volunteer workers and friends to make a good impression. . . . when the candidate enters the hall he should be greeted by cheers and clapping. . . . when he makes a point in his speech it should be applauded. . . . he should be asked the type of question which will give him an opportunity to present an effective portion of his program. . . . his opponent should be asked specific, pointed questions that he might prefer not to have asked.

Television

Always try to videotape or film the candidate's television appearances; that way if he makes a slip of the tongue or the photography isn't particularly good, the sequence can be junked and shot over again.

Voter Transportation

One of the surest ways to earn votes is to take voters to the polls. A well-organized Transportation Committee is vital. . . . If sufficient workers are available, they may be used as "hoppers" or "jumpers." These are volunteers who go from door to door asking people if they would like transportation to the polls. . . . High school and college students make good "hoppers" during the late afternoon when they are needed most.

—Democratic National Committee, *Victory '68, Democratic Campaign Handbook* 1968.

Leonard Garment, directed the extensive media campaign. Maurice Stans headed the Republican National Finance Committee, the chief fund-raising arm of the campaign. The party's national chairman, Ray Bliss, ran the Republican National Committee, the "Truth Squad" (to answer Democratic campaign oratory), and a voter registration drive.

Charles Rhyne, a law school classmate of Nixon's, headed United

HOW TO WIN AN ELECTION: REPUBLICAN VERSION

The following are excerpts from a publication of the Republican National Committee.

On Campaigns. And believe me, in a campaign you're not looking for a mandate. All you want to do is win. It really doesn't matter where the votes come from.

I don't care who tells you what is an issue— you decide what it is. . . . If your opponent says, "My opponent is a thief." Even if you are, and you don't think you should join the issue, don't. Talk about his possible thievery, but don't join your own thievery. I say dance to your own tune. Dance to the beat of your own drums. Don't let anybody set the issues for you. [William E. Roberts, p. 60.]

On Polls. Most of the surveys that we make personally for the campaign are very rarely made public. Only if there was a particular psychological reason for doing so. Because it cuts both ways. If you're winning, you have a tendency for your finance group to sit down on the job, and if you're behind, it has a tremendously bad reaction with your troops and discourages them. . . . I think, all things being equal, I would not make survey information public. Because the chances are you're privy to a little more information than your opponents are, and you should keep it to yourselves. [William E. Roberts, p. 63.]

On Broadcasting. If you get something out to a radio station before the noon broadcast hour so that they can have it and insert it into their programming, you know you're going to

get it on the noon broadcast, the 6 p.m. broadcast, and almost invariably the 11 o'clock broadcast that evening. In a newspaper, a story is carried only once; that's all. If a guy misses it, that's it. But, if he doesn't hear a noon broadcast, maybe he'll hear another one later.

There's another valuable asset in this thing. In getting such extensive radio station response, we've indirectly applied a little blackjacking to the newspapers. A newspaper editor who once might have just tossed out a news release from us without even opening the envelope now looks at it twice and generally puts it in the paper because he's afraid the radio stations are going to have something on it at noon and he's got to protect himself. [Hugh Humphrey, p. 44.]

On Ghostwriting. A good speech has to be tailored to the audience. . . . If your candidate is addressing . . . the Harvard faculty . . . a prosy speech, with long, convoluted sentences that give a thoughtful mood, deliberately avoiding the oratory and dramatic, should be the product sought by the writer.

But if it is a political rally or a plowing contest—a speaking situation in which your man faces a raucous throng of happy-go-lucky citizens, crying children, bleating sheep, roaring tractors and barking dogs, and has to shout his message against a 30-knot wind—then the short crackling sentence, the uncomplicated thought, and the verbal whammies need to be assembled, else things like eggs or tomatoes or boos or, worst of all, a cold, stony silence and a dwindling crowd will be the lot of our hero. [Bryce Harlow, p. 218.]

—Republican National Committee, *The Art of Winning Elections* (1967).

Citizens for Nixon-Agnew, the committee designed to lure Democrats, independents, and volunteers to the Republican nominee's cause. Governor John Volpe of Massachusetts headed the committee's Nationalities Division, with sections such as Italian-Americans, Polish-Americans, Eastern Europeans, Spanish-Americans, and Mexican-Americans for Nixon-Agnew. Specialized citizens groups included Celebrities/Athletes for Nixon-Agnew, Barbers for Nixon-Agnew, Dentists for Nixon-Agnew, Ham Radio Operators for Nixon-Agnew, Jewelers for Nixon-Agnew, Pilots for Nixon-Agnew, Senior Citizens for Nixon-Agnew, and Service Station Attendants for Nixon-Agnew.

Some sense of the smoothness of the Nixon operation can be gleaned from Theodore H. White's description of the staff jet, the *Tricia*:

> Control radiated from the staff plane. Two open-circuit ground-to-air phones; seven internal phone circuits; six ground-to-ground press phones and four for staff, hooked up instantly when the plane alighted; a radio-receiving Xerox machine; an airborne teletype, receiving or sending at 100 words a minute; fifteen walkie-talkie machines with air-to-air or air-to-ground radii of five miles—all combined to create a web of invisible communication about the plane, whether in flight or at rest, that made every input from New York headquarters or around the country instantly available, made question and answers a matter of minutes.[2]

Vice-President Humphrey's campaign was organized along lines similar to the Nixon campaign. But because it was hastily thrown together when Humphrey received the Democratic nomination and because it suffered grievously from lack of money, it never achieved the smooth efficiency of the Nixon effort. "In 1968," White has written, "one left the Nixon tour to join the Humphrey tour as if leaving a well-ordered and comfortable mansion for a gypsy encampment."[3]

CAMPAIGN STRATEGY

Studies have shown that many voters are committed to one candidate or another in advance of the campaign. For example, in 1964, almost half of a sample of voters reported they had made up their minds *before* the campaign got underway; 26 percent decided during the campaign or even in the last two weeks, and 25 percent did not recall when they made up their minds. (See Table 8-1.) As Nelson Polsby and Aaron Wildavsky have noted, "For the vast majority of citizens

Aiming for
the Undecided

[2] Theodore H. White, *The Making of the President 1968* (New York: Atheneum, 1969), p. 327.
[3] *Ibid.*

TABLE 8-1

A Presidential Election: When the Voter Decides

Question: "How long before the election did you decide to vote the way you did?"

1964	Percentage
Knew all along	13
Before the conventions, when knew candidates would run	17
At the time of the conventions	19
During the campaign	16
In the last two weeks	10
Don't remember, not ascertained	25
Total:	100%

Source: Adapted from data compiled by the University of Michigan Survey Research Center.

in America, campaigns do not function so much to change their minds as to reinforce their previous convictions."[4]

Nevertheless, the votes of the 26 percent of the people who *do* make up their minds during a campaign may well determine the outcome. If 75,000,000 votes are cast in a presidential election, 26 percent translates into 19,500,000 votes, a sizable bloc by any standards. The undecided hold the key to victory in any close election.

Since more than two-thirds of all American voters identify with one of the two major parties, political candidates try to preserve their party base—to hold on to their natural constituency—while winning over voters from the other party, the waverers, the independents, and the undecided.

As one analyst has suggested, campaigns may influence "a small but crucial proportion of the electorate. . . . It seems clear that professional politicians drive themselves and their organizations to influence every remaining undecided voter in the hope and expectation that they are providing or maintaining a winning margin."[5]

Which Road to the White House?

Long before he can get into a general election campaign, the aspiring presidential candidate must decide whether to enter the bruising arena of the primaries. What makes the decision so difficult is that victory in the primaries does not guarantee the candidate his party's nomination. Senator Estes Kefauver won twelve of the fourteen presidential primaries in 1952, but Adlai Stevenson got the nomination. On the other hand, John

[4] Nelson W. Polsby and Aaron B. Wildavsky, *Presidential Elections* (New York: Scribner's, 1964), p. 123.
[5] William H. Flanigan, *Political Behavior of the American Electorate* (Boston: Allyn and Bacon, 1968), p. 98.

Kennedy's victory in the West Virginia primary in 1960 was a crucial step on the road to his nomination.

For an underdog or a relatively unknown candidate, the primary route may prove an attractive means of demonstrating his strength and gaining nationwide exposure in the media. For a presidential aspirant who is far out in front, however, entering the primaries may hold more dangers than advantages. Each candidate attempts to calculate the potential advantages and disadvantages of taking the primary route.

With preconvention campaigns growing in importance, a candidate may find it necessary to have a well-financed campaign organization already in operation long before the national convention. In 1968, for example, the preconvention campaign organization of Senator Robert F. Kennedy was hardly distinguishable in size and efficiency from that of a major-party nominee in a general election. Today, few politicians would agree with President Truman's 1952 observation that primaries are nothing but "eyewash."

Once nominated, a candidate or his managers must decide how and where his precious time (and money) can most profitably be spent. In 1960, Richard Nixon pledged to become the first candidate to take his presidential campaign to all fifty states. He did, but at great physical and political cost. The 65,000 miles that he traveled in carrying out the commitment exhausted him. In retrospect, Nixon recognized that the decision was a mistake. Had he followed the advice of his campaign manager, he wrote later, "I would not have had to put myself through such a brutal schedule before the first radio-television debate and, in addition, would have had more time to spend in some of the critical states than eventually was possible." [6]

By contrast, in 1968, Nixon moved at a relatively serene pace that preserved his physical energies. He concentrated on ten populous "battleground states," on those states in the South that might be captured from George Wallace, and on the border states.[7] This time, he won.

In general, presidential candidates of both parties have tended to spend more time stumping in the pivotal big states, such as California, New York, Pennsylvania, Illinois, Ohio, Texas, and Michigan, where the votes are.

The pattern of future campaigning may be influenced, however, by a combination of two factors—the threat of political violence and the advantages offered by television in reaching large numbers of voters. In 1969, the National Commission on the Causes and Prevention of Violence rec-

Where and How
to Campaign

---

[6] Richard M. Nixon, *Six Crises* (New York: Doubleday, 1962), p. 329.
[7] White, *The Making of the President 1968*, pp. 326–333.

ommended that presidential candidates make greater use of television as the safest way to reach the most voters. Although the commission recognized that an incumbent President, or candidates for that office, could not and should not be confined to television studios, it urged that greater emphasis be placed on indoor rallies "to which access is carefully controlled" and where "the risk of assassination can be significantly reduced." [8]

In the light of the assassinations of President Kennedy and Robert Kennedy, precautions would seem sensible; yet candidates are under great pressure to mingle with the voters and to show themselves in person. "Rightly or wrongly, presidential candidates judge that they must be personally seen by audiences throughout the country, through such rituals as motorcades, shopping-center rallies and whistle-stop campaigns." [9] The atmosphere of political violence creates a subtle, additional pressure on candidates to go out among the people and demonstrate their personal courage. As a result, candidates will probably continue to feel it necessary to mix conventional campaign trips and television appearances.

Timing
and "Peaking"

Political candidates also worry about such factors as timing, "peaking," and overexposure in a campaign. Generally speaking, candidates attempt to gear their campaign to a climactic windup in the last two weeks; late in a campaign, voters are bombarded with more political "spot" commercials and broadcasts than at the outset. President Nixon, in particular, has become identified with the view that a political campaign has a certain "pace" and flow, and that it is essential not to "peak" too soon.

Political campaigns help to weld political parties together; campaign rallies generate enthusiasm among partisan workers and volunteers. Candidates are concerned about maintaining their momentum and a certain level of excitement, not only with the voters, but for the sake of their own party organization as well.

The President
as Candidate

An incumbent President, of course, normally enjoys a tremendous advantage over his opponent in a presidential campaign. Not only do the prestige and power of his office follow him on the hustings, but all the visible trappings go along as well: Air Force One, the gleaming presidential jet, lands for an airport rally, the band plays "Hail to the Chief," and the voters are enveloped by the aura and mystique of the Presidency. Moreover, the incumbent President already has a huge organized staff and all

---

[8] "Assassination," in *To Establish Justice, To Insure Domestic Tranquility*, Final Report of the National Commission on the Causes and Prevention of Violence (Washington, D.C.: U.S. Government Printing Office, 1969), pp. 131, 132.
[9] *Ibid.*, p. 132.

the advantages of White House communications and facilities, including advance men and established press arrangements. An incumbent President may be in such a strong position that he will decide to restrict his campaigning, allow the dignity of his office to work for him, and, in effect, campaign from the White House. He may adopt "the lofty, nonpartisan pose."[10]

In 1948, Harry Truman, although an incumbent President, was the underdog and could not rely on such tactics. He launched a vigorous, "give 'em hell" whistle-stop campaign that defeated Republican Thomas E. Dewey. In 1956, President Eisenhower in announcing his candidacy for reelection, declared: "I shall, in general, wage no political campaign in the customary pattern." Eisenhower had suffered a serious heart attack five months earlier, but this, he later wrote, was not a factor in his decision: "Doctors' orders or no, I would not have conducted the same sort of campaign in 1956 as I had in 1952. Because I was President I was determined not to go 'whistle-stopping' or 'barnstorming.' "[11]

Until 1968, the President-as-candidate enjoyed another advantage: he had the Secret Service to plan his movements and provide security. Candidates other than a President (or Vice-President) had to move through the crowds unprotected, or at best with a private, and often amateur, bodyguard or a few local police. After Robert Kennedy was fatally shot during

[10] V. O. Key, Jr., *Politics, Parties, and Pressure Groups*, 5th edition (New York: Crowell, 1964), p. 471.
[11] Dwight D. Eisenhower, *The White House Years, Waging Peace 1956–1961* (New York: Doubleday, 1965), pp. 4–5.

President Theodore Roosevelt campaigning.

the preconvention campaign of 1968, President Johnson assigned Secret Service agents to all the candidates, a practice that Congress speedily made law.[12]

usually expressed in a slogan (that rhymes)

THE ISSUES

Political candidates in most cases develop a central theme for their campaign. Sometimes it emerges as the battle progresses; often it is well thought out in advance. Candidates attempt to choose their terrain, staking out certain issues that they believe will give them the advantage over their opponents.

But to a great extent the campaign theme is shaped by the candidate's status—incumbent President, political heir to an incumbent, or candidate of the "out" party. For example, when John Kennedy promised in 1960 "to get this country moving again," he was taking the offensive, charging that America had stagnated during the eight Eisenhower years. Nixon, as Eisenhower's Vice-President, could scarcely promise to outdo Kennedy in getting America moving—for that might seem an admission that Kennedy was correct. Nixon was forced instead to defend the Eisenhower record.[13]

For many voters in 1964, Barry Goldwater was *the* issue. An advocate of a hard-line policy of "total victory" against communism, Goldwater at one point seemed to suggest the use of nuclear weapons in Vietnam;[14] he had not quite done so, but the net effect of his pugnacious "image" was to frighten away many voters. President Johnson took full advantage of this fear during the campaign, stressing that the nation needed responsible, sober leadership in an age when a President could "push the button" of nuclear disaster.

In the 1968 campaign, Vice-President Hubert Humphrey was saddled with accountability for the Vietnam war and urban disorders. As a member of the administration in power, he could not disavow Johnson. Midway in

[12] The law authorizes Secret Service protection, unless declined, for "major presidential or vice presidential candidates." The Secretary of the Treasury, after consultation with an advisory committee that includes leaders of Congress, decides who qualifies as a candidate under this definition. The law does not specifically provide protection for preconvention candidates, but the precedent was set in 1968 when the Secret Service guarded a total of twelve candidates, six presidential candidates before the conventions and the six party nominees (for President and Vice-President).
[13] See Nixon, *Six Crises*, p. 338, for Nixon's own comments on this point.
[14] Appearing on ABC's *Issues and Answers*, May 24, 1964, Senator Goldwater said, "I don't think we would. . . . But defoliation of the forests by low-yield atomic weapons could well be done. When you remove the foliage, you remove the cover." It was widely assumed that Goldwater was advocating such action, but in a press conference two days later he clarified his position: "I outlined the low-yield defoliation idea which had been talked of and talked of and talked of by the highest levels in the Pentagon. This is nothing new, and I made it perfectly clear, I thought, that this was not a suggestion of mine."

the campaign, in a speech at Salt Lake City, Humphrey moved slightly away from the administration's Vietnam policy, and his popularity increased in both the Gallup and Harris polls. But Humphrey was unable to overtake Nixon.

As Polsby and Wildavsky have noted, "One of the most difficult positions for a candidate is to try to succeed a President of his own party. . . . No matter how hard he tries to avoid it he is stuck with the record made by the President of his own party."[15]

There is evidence that some incumbent Presidents are a bit reluctant to expend their prestige on behalf of the heir apparent—who may not always want help. President Eisenhower did not campaign for Nixon in 1960 until the last eight days, a delay that may have cost Nixon votes and possibly even the election. In 1968, President Johnson's attitude toward Humphrey seemed ambivalent at first, although in the end he publicly supported him.

Peace and pocketbook issues have tended to dominate presidential campaigns. On domestic issues, the Democrats are often on firm ground, for they can point to a wide range of social legislation passed during Democratic administrations. Not all of these programs have worked equally well, and some, such as the welfare program, have been widely criticized. Nevertheless, Democratic candidates since the New Deal have been able to campaign on the party's efforts toward achieving social prog-

Bread and Butter Issues

[15] Polsby and Wildavsky, *Presidential Elections*, p. 129.

"I should like to ask the man who threw that whether he enjoyed paying 79 cents a dozen!"

Ed Fisher
© 1969 Saturday Review, Inc.

ress at home. And, perhaps remembering the Great Depression that began in 1929 under a Republican President, voters tend to associate prosperity with Democrats. (See Figure 8-1.) Occasionally, the Democrats are helped by a Republican candidate like Barry Goldwater, who threatened to sell TVA and make Social Security voluntary.

Foreign Policy Issues

In the area of foreign affairs, the Republicans often have an advantage. (See Figure 8-2.) Because the Democrats were in power during the First World War, the Second World War, Korea, and Vietnam, the Republicans have been able to tag the Democrats, fairly or not, as the "war party." In 1952, General Eisenhower promised a nation weary of the

FIGURE 8-1

Political Party Rated Best for Prosperity

Question: "Looking ahead for the next few years, which political party—the Republican or the Democratic—do you think will do the best job of keeping the country prosperous?"

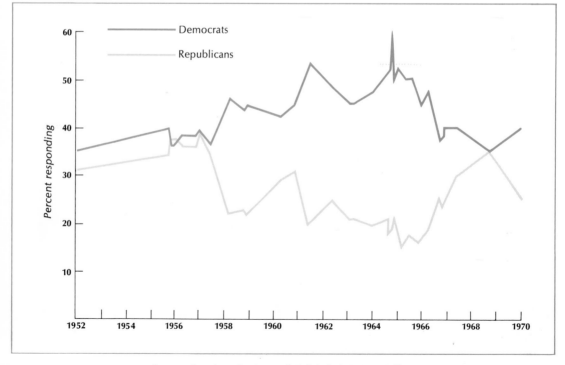

Source: American Institute of Political Opinion, *Gallup Opinion Index*, Report No. 17, October 1966, pp. 12–13; 1968 figures in Report No. 39, September 1968, p. 12. 1970 figures from Gallup Poll, September 16, 1970.

Korean conflict that if elected, "I shall go to Korea," a pledge that helped him win the election. Similarly, Richard Nixon in 1968 was able to promise new leadership to bring an end to the war in Vietnam.

The Republican advantage in foreign affairs is not always decisive, however. In 1960, Nixon, who had recently engaged in a finger-pointing debate with Soviet Premier Nikita Khrushchev, stressed his ability to handle the Russians. He repeatedly assailed Kennedy for suggesting that the United States might have "apologized" for the U-2 spy flight over Soviet territory; he accused Kennedy of willingness to "slice off a bit of freedom" by abandoning the Nationalist Chinese offshore islands of Quemoy and Matsu, and he attacked Kennedy's suggestion that the United States assist Cuban rebels against Fidel Castro. "I think when you look at these three

FIGURE 8-2

Political Party Rated Best for Peace

Question: "Which political party do you think would be more likely to keep the United States out of World War III—the Republican party or the Democratic party?"

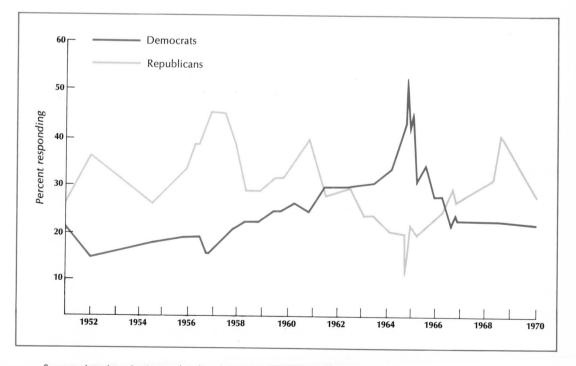

Source: American Institute of Political Opinion, *Gallup Opinion Index*, Report No. 17, October 1966, pp. 10–11; 1968 figures in Report No. 39, September 1968, p. 12. 1970 figures from Gallup Poll, September 16, 1970.

episodes," Nixon declared, "that this should convince many Americans that they could not rest well at night with a man with such a total lack of judgment as Commander in Chief of our Armed Forces in this critical period." As President, Nixon warned, Kennedy's views could only lead "to war or surrender." [16] By placing such heavy emphasis on foreign policy issues in 1960, Nixon sought to exploit his opponent's lack of "experience." But this strategy failed to win the Presidency for the Republican nominee.

The Imponderables

A sudden foreign policy crisis, a personal scandal, a chance remark—these are among the many imponderables that may affect the outcome of political campaigns.

In 1884, when Grover Cleveland was the Democratic nominee, his Republican opponents chanted:

Ma, Ma, where's my Pa?
Gone to the White House,
Ha, ha, ha.

The slogan was a gleeful reference to the illegitimate child that Cleveland was accused of fathering.[17] It was soon overshadowed, however, by another slogan. A few days before the election, a Protestant minister supporting James G. Blaine, the Republican candidate, referred to the Democrats as the party of "rum, Romanism, and rebellion." The insult to Roman Catholics may have cost Blaine New York State and thereby the election.

In 1948, Dewey's campaign train, the "Victory Special," lurched backwards into the crowd while the Republican nominee was orating at Beaucoup, Illinois. "Well, that's the first lunatic I've had for an engineer," snapped Dewey. The remark was widely publicized and did not sit well with the railroad unions, or for that matter with Dewey's engineer, a Democrat. Overnight, "Lunatic Engineers for Truman" and similar groups

---

[16] Speech of the Vice President at Muhlenburg College Gymnasium, Allentown, Pa., October 22, 1960," in *The Speeches of Vice President Richard M. Nixon, Presidential Campaign of 1960* (Washington, D.C.: U.S. Government Printing Office, 1961), pp. 709, 712.

[17] The story broke during the campaign in a Buffalo newspaper, under the headline: "A Terrible Tale—A Dark Chapter in a Public Man's History." Ten years earlier, Maria Crofts Halpin, an attractive widow, had given birth to a son, whom she named Oscar Folsom Cleveland, charging Cleveland with its paternity. Cleveland said he was not certain he was the father, but he had assumed full responsibility for supporting the child; when the scandal broke he telegraphed his friends in Buffalo: "Tell the truth." Because of his open attitude, Cleveland managed to minimize the damage to his presidential campaign. After Cleveland's election, the Democrats celebrated their first presidential victory in twenty-eight years by singing:
Hurrah for Maria,
Hurrah for the kid,
We voted for Grover,
And we're damned glad we did!

sprang up to plague the Republican candidate along the right-of-way of the "Victory Special."

In 1952, Richard Nixon's place as the vice-presidential candidate on the Republican ticket was endangered when newspapers reported the existence of the "Nixon fund," some $18,000 contributed by a group of California businessmen to meet Nixon's political expenses as a United States senator. When the storm broke, Eisenhower, the Republican presidential nominee, was on a campaign train in the Midwest. Eisenhower called in newsmen on his train and remarked that his crusade against corruption in Washington meant little unless the Republicans were "clean as a hound's tooth." [18]

Nixon's future, indeed the Republican chances in 1952, hung in the balance. Nixon went on nationwide television and, in his famed "Checkers" speech, defended his use of the $18,000 fund, listed his personal finances, noted that his wife, Pat, wore a "respectable Republican cloth coat," and announced that, come what may, his family intended to keep a black-and-white cocker spaniel named Checkers, which had been given to his two children. [19]

Although the speech was a patently emotional appeal for which Nixon was often assailed by later critics, it turned the tide of public opinion and impressed Eisenhower. In a reunion at Wheeling, West Virginia, the General publicly reaffirmed his confidence in his running mate, declaring: "You're my boy."

Eight years later, a chance remark by Eisenhower haunted Nixon during the 1960 campaign. At a press conference, Eisenhower was asked to name the major decisions of his administration in which Nixon had participated. "If you give me a week, I might think of one," Eisenhower responded. No amount of advance planning can deal with difficulties of this sort.

Grover Cleveland's troubles, or Nixon's difficulties in 1952, are not unusual occurrences in American politics. Mudslinging and charges of corruption are common in campaigns. Under the unwritten rules of the seamier side of American politics, a candidate may attempt to "get something" on his opponent. (The information might not be publicized, however, if the other side possesses equally damaging information, or if it is felt that the opponent can cry "smear" and turn the charges to his own

[18] Earl Mazo and Stephen Hess, *Nixon, A Political Portrait* (New York: Harper & Row, 1968), p. 119.

[19] Checkers died in September, 1964 and is buried at Westhampton, Long Island. He was not the first canine to gain fame in a presidential campaign. Running for a fourth term in 1944, Franklin D. Roosevelt ridiculed the Republicans for charging that he had sent a destroyer to fetch his dog: "The Republican leaders have not been content to make personal attacks upon me—or my wife—or my sons—they now include my little dog, Fala. . . . I am accustomed to hearing malicious falsehoods about myself but I think I have a right to object to libelous statements about my dog." See Robert E. Sherwood, *Roosevelt and Hopkins* (New York: Harper & Row, 1948), p. 821.

The following is an excerpt from a publication of the Republican National Committee that advises GOP candidates on campaign techniques.

Researching Scandals in the Democratic Party

With proper research and publicity, exposure of scandals can serve as a public service and as a source of votes. Historically, incumbent administrations are turned out very frequently for mismanagement and abusing the public trust.

Most scandals evolve from "tips," usually coming from newsmen, victims of the "scandal," public reports such as those of the State Auditor, or abused factions within or on the fringes of the wrongdoers' organization. Persons in the same business, social friends of the opposition, and anonymous sources can also provide leads to a possible scandal. . . .

Publicizing the Scandal. A "believable" springboard from which to break the scandal must be found. A newsman, a disenchanted insider, or a local prosecutor are possible means for breaking the scandal to the public.

A word of caution: care must be exercised in the timing of the release to the public.

Anticipate the type of reaction you might expect from the opposition. Common reactions are: (a) denial, (b) belittlement, (c) claimed disbelief, (d) counterclaims, (e) claims of "smear," (f) claims of appropriate steps having been or about to be taken, (g) admission with or without extenuating circumstances.

Once the public has been informed that a scandal in fact does exist, it must be kept continually aware that its trust has been violated. Convince newsmen that the scandal is worthy of their coverage. Supply *facts* to editorial writers, and to your supporters in the field. Question the principals of the opposition at every opportunity—at public gatherings as well as in the press. Convince third parties to view the scandal with alarm and to vocalize about it. In other words, take advantage of every possible form of publicity—and be sure to cry, SCANDAL!

—Republican National Committee, *Research Techniques for Republican Campaigns* (1969).

advantage.) Because mudslinging, rumors, and scandals presumably influence some voters, their use in political campaigns persists. It is often near the end of a campaign that a candidate's supporters try to leak such stories to the newspapers to damage his rival.

In 1960, opponents of Nixon let it be known that his brother Donald had received a controversial $205,000 loan from the Hughes Tool Company, a firm controlled by the mysterious industrialist, Howard Hughes. The loan was prominently publicized in Nixon's unsuccessful campaign for Governor of California in 1962. In the midst of the 1964 presidential campaign, it was revealed that Walter Jenkins, President Johnson's top aide, had twice been arrested on morals charges. Whispers about the mental stability, sex life, or integrity of presidential candidates are not at all unusual.

Mudslinging is a fairly old American institution (and sometimes there is truth buried in the mud). As long as the voters expect politicians to adhere to higher moral standards than the rest of the population, political figures will remain vulnerable to such charges.

Sometimes a sudden development in a campaign offers a candidate an unexpected opening. During the 1960 campaign, Martin Luther King was arrested in Georgia. Kennedy placed a long-distance telephone call to Mrs. King to assure her of his interest and concern; his brother Robert telephoned the judge who had sentenced Dr. King and pleaded successfully for his release. Martin Luther King's father endorsed Kennedy, declaring, "I've got a suitcase of votes, and I'm going to take them to Mr. Kennedy and dump them in his lap." [20] Some observers speculated after the election that the episode won the Presidency for Kennedy; certainly it influenced many black voters.

World crises that suddenly erupt during a campaign are another category of imponderables that may affect election results. In general, foreign policy crises tend to help the party in power because of voter reluctance to "change horses in midstream." The Suez invasion and the Hungarian revolt both occurred just before the 1956 election; President Eisenhower already enjoyed a clear lead over his opponent, Adlai Stevenson, but the crises abroad probably increased his margin of victory. The Tonkin Gulf crisis of 1964, about which many details are disputed, created an atmosphere of wartime tension that, in the short run, may have benefited the reelection campaign of President Johnson. (On the other hand, a foreign crisis that leads to a prolonged, and eventually unpopular overseas commitment, as in Korea or Vietnam, may erode the strength of the party in power and lead to retribution at the polls.)

CAMPAIGN TECHNIQUES

The little girl in the television commercial stood in a field of daisies, plucking the petals and counting, as birds chirped in the background. Then, as the little girl reached number ten, a doomsday voice began a countdown. When the voice reached zero, there was a rumbling explosion and a huge mushroom cloud filled the screen. As it billowed upward, President Lyndon Johnson's voice boomed out: "These are the stakes. To make a world in which all of God's children can live or to go into the dark. We must either love each other or we must die." A message was then flashed on the screen, reading: "Vote for President Johnson on November 3."

Millions of Americans saw the famous "Daisy Girl" commercial during the 1964 campaign. To many, it seemed to suggest that Barry Goldwater, the Republican candidate, might lead the nation into nuclear war. As White has noted, "The film mentioned neither Goldwater nor the Republicans specifically—but the shriek of Republican indignation fastened the bomb message on them more tightly than any calculation could have expected." [21]

Television and Politics

"Ten, nine, eight, seven . . .

. . . six, five, four, three . . .

[20] Theodore H. White, *The Making of the President 1960* (New York: Atheneum, 1961), p. 323.
[21] Theodore H. White, *The Making of the President 1964* (New York: Atheneum, 1965), p. 322. Because of protests, the film was shown only once.

... two, one ...

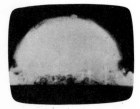

... These are the stakes. To make a world in which all of God's children can live ...

... or to go into the dark. We must either love each other, or we must die ...

VOTE FOR PRESIDENT JOHNSON ON NOVEMBER 3.

... The stakes are too high for you to stay home."

Without doubt, the "Daisy Girl" was the most famous political commercial of all time. It was produced for the Democrats by their advertising agency, Doyle Dane Bernbach. (President Kennedy had originally chosen Doyle Dane as the Democrats' agency because he was impressed by one of its ads showing a photograph of a Volkswagen under the headline: "Think Small.") [22]

The marriage of television and politics took place in 1948, the first year in which substantial numbers of Americans viewed parts of the national nominating conventions on TV.[23] Since less than 200,000 homes had television sets in 1948, however, the real impact of television was not felt until the 1952 and 1956 Eisenhower-Stevenson campaigns. By 1956, almost 35,000,000 homes had TV sets. In 1960, of America's 53,000,000 households, 46,600,000, or 88 percent, had television sets. By this time, television was playing a central role in an American presidential campaign.

The Kennedy-Nixon Debates: A Case Study. In 1960, the major party candidates were able to reach vast audiences in a series of televised debates. These debates were widely credited with providing John Kennedy with his narrow margin of victory over Richard Nixon.

Congress made the debates possible. Under Section 315 of the Federal Communications Act a broadcaster who permits any "legally qualified" candidate to use his facilities must provide "equal opportunities" to all other candidates. Broadcasters protested that this "equal time" provision, which applies to both free and paid broadcasts, was unfair because it required them to make air time available to marginal candidates as well. Congress in 1960 temporarily suspended the "equal time" provision of the law. This cleared the way for the "great debates" of 1960, because it meant that the networks could put the major party candidates on television without having to give equal time to minor candidates. CBS and NBC offered free time to Kennedy and Nixon. The four debates were held on September 26 and October 7, 13, and 21.

As Vice-President, Nixon was better known than Kennedy at the start of the 1960 campaign. "Looking at the problem from a purely political standpoint, Kennedy had much more to gain from joint appearances than I did," Nixon later wrote. But, he added, "Had I refused the challenge, I would have opened myself to the charge that I was afraid to defend the Administration's and my own record." [24]

But, as Theodore Sorensen notes, "Nixon also had reason for self-

[22] Pete Hamill, "When the Client Is a Candidate," *New York Times Magazine*, October 25, 1964, p. 31.
[23] 1948 was not the first year in which the national conventions were televised. But because very few people owned TV sets in the 1940's, less than 100,000 persons saw television broadcasts of the 1940 and 1944 conventions.
[24] Nixon, *Six Crises*, p. 323.

confidence. He had launched his political career in 1946 by outdebating an able congressman. His "Checkers" speech in 1952, defending his private political fund, was generally regarded as the most skillful use of television in the campaign that sent him to the Vice-Presidency. His impromptu 'kitchen debate' with Chairman Khrushchev in Moscow had measurably improved his ratings in the polls." [25]

Tension was high when the two candidates met in a Chicago television studio for the first debate. Recently recovered from a stay in the hospital for an infected knee, Nixon had lost weight and looked pale. Moreover, his heavy beard, a favorite subject of political cartoonist Herblock, was not very well covered by an application of "Lazy Shave" powder before the telecast. By contrast, Kennedy, looking tanned and vigorous, presented a much more telegenic image to the public.

The millions of voters watching the first debate may have remembered little of what the candidates said, but they noticed that Nixon did not *look* as pleasing as Kennedy. As White put it, "Probably no picture in American politics tells a better story . . . than that famous shot of the camera on the Vice-President as he half slouched, his 'Lazy Shave' powder faintly streaked with sweat, his eyes exaggerated hollows of blackness, his jaw, jowls, and face drooping with strain." [26]

applicable to Trudeau in 1968

HEY, LOOK HIM OVER: BIRCH BAYH'S SENATE CAMPAIGN

A part of Bayh's being a novice in statewide politics, and the most crippling part, was that people had trouble pronouncing his name. He was being called "Bah," "Bay," "Baha," "Bee," everything. It was hurting. With about six weeks left in the campaign, Mary Lou Conrad, the campaign manager's wife, solved the problem. In about 10 minutes, she put together a campaign ditty to the tune of "Hey, Look Me Over." It went:

Hey, look him over,
He's your kind of guy.

His first name is Birch,
His last name is Bayh.

Poetry lovers will pale at the thought of being subjected to that on radio and television for six weeks of heavy exposure, but politics lovers will recognize it for the smasher it was. Mary Lou won an award for the outstanding locally produced television commercial, and her husband, even discounting for normal bias, was accurate in saying: "It just changed everything overnight. We zonked our money into it on radio. Kids went crazy over it. Birch was like a movie star."

—Robert Sherrill, "Birch Bayh Isn't a Household Word—Yet," *New York Times Magazine*, February 15, 1970.

[25] Theodore C. Sorensen, *Kennedy* (New York: Harper & Row, 1965), p. 196.
[26] White, *The Making of the President 1960*, p. 289.

In the Kennedy-Nixon debates of 1960, television played a central role in an American presidential campaign for the first time. Millions of voters watched the four debates between the Democratic and Republican nominees.

Nixon had, in the public mind, lost the first debate.[27] He realized how bad he looked when his mother called from California to ask if he was "feeling all right." [28] Fattened up on a rich milk shake diet, Nixon recovered in the remaining three debates, but many Americans never lost their initial impression of the Republican candidate. "I spent too much time . . . on substance and too little time on appearance," Nixon concluded. "I paid too much attention to what I was going to say and too little to how I would look." [29] It was a mistake that he was not to repeat in 1968.

Although the 1960 debates may not have added much to public understanding of the issues, they did expose the personalities of the two men to the American public and did give some indication of how they behaved under stress. Since Kennedy performed well, his participation in the televised debates weakened Nixon's argument that, as Vice-President, he was more experienced and better informed than his Democratic rival. In addition, the debates brought the candidates into the living room, providing the sort of close-up portrait that a voter can seldom get, even if he is one of the few to shake the hand of a presidential candidate at a political rally.

Estimates are that from 85,000,000 to 115,000,000 persons watched one or all of the debates.[30] Perhaps 20,000,000 more Americans watched the first debate than watched any of the later ones, a fact that worked to Nixon's disadvantage in view of his physical appearance during that first debate.

Nothing in the 1960 campaign matched the impact of the TV debates. An Elmo Roper poll for CBS concluded that 57 percent of the voters thought the debates had influenced their decisions. The survey indicated that more than 4,000,000 voters made their final decision based on the debates alone, and these voters decided 3 to 1 on Kennedy. As White concluded, "since Kennedy won by only 112,000 votes, he was entirely justified in stating on the Monday following election, November 12th: 'It was TV more than anything else that turned the tide.' " [31]

---

[27] After the first debate, a Gallup Poll indicated that 43 percent of respondents considered Kennedy to have done best, 23 percent gave the edge to Nixon, 29 percent considered the results even, and 5 percent were undecided. Source: *ibid.*, p. 294.

[28] Nixon, *Six Crises*, p. 341.

[29] *Ibid.*, p. 422.

[30] White, *The Making of the President 1960*, p. 293. By contrast, a total of about 78,400 persons watched the seven Lincoln-Douglas debates of 1858; an average of 11,200 persons saw each debate. Source: Carl Sandburg, *Abraham Lincoln: The Prairie Years*, Vol. II (New York: Harcourt Brace Jovanovich, 1926), pp. 144–51.

[31] White, *The Making of the President 1960*, p. 294.

As for subsequent elections, President Johnson showed little interest in debating Goldwater in 1964 (since this would have made Goldwater familiar to more voters) and Congress did not suspend the "equal time" provision that year or in 1968. Had Congress done so in 1968, Humphrey and Nixon would have come under pressure to appear with George Wallace, the third-party candidate. During the campaign, Humphrey invited his opponents to appear in a three-way televised debate, but Nixon declined to take part in any debate that included Wallace. Congress in 1970 sought to suspend permanently the "equal time" provision for presidential and vice-presidential candidates, an action that would have permitted debates in 1972. But President Nixon vetoed a bill limiting campaign TV spending, which had included the "equal time" suspension. Televised debates may be desirable from the voter's standpoint, but whether or not they take place will probably continue to depend on whether the candidates want them.

Madison Avenue: The Packaging of the President. By 1969, there were 83,000,000 television sets in almost 58,000,000 homes in America; 95 percent of all American homes had TV sets—more than had bathtubs or telephones. The ability of political candidates to reach increased numbers of voters through television was reflected in a dramatic rise in campaign spending for TV broadcasts. In 1964, the cost of all political broadcasts totalled $34.6 million, of which $12.8 million was spent on the presidential and vice-presidential elections. In 1968, the total figure soared to $58.9

million, of which $18.7 million was spent on the presidential and vice-presidential campaigns.

If Nixon's defeat in 1960 was due in part to his poor showing on television, his election in 1968 may have been due in part to his expert use of the medium. The television aspects of the Nixon campaign in 1968 were managed by a group of professionals that included Harry Treleaven, a vice-president of J. Walter Thompson advertising agency; Frank Shakespeare, a vice-president of CBS; and Roger Ailes, a young TV producer. Nixon's television team worked out a highly successful format in which the Republican candidate answered questions from a selected panel of voters before a carefully screened, partisan audience. The format provided a controlled forum for exposing the candidate under favorable conditions, and it was used in many cities during the campaign.

MOTHER: He's so adorable. I wonder what he'll be like . . .

A book published after the campaign quoted Ailes on the importance of panel shows:

> Let's face it, a lot of people think Nixon is dull. Think he's a bore. . . . They look at him as the kind of kid who always carried a bookbag. Who was forty-two years old the day he was born. They figure other kids got footballs for Christmas. Nixon got a briefcase and he loved it. He'd always have his homework done and he'd never let you copy.
>
> Now you put him on television, you've got a problem right away. He's a funny-looking guy. He looks like somebody hung him in a closet overnight and he jumps out in the morning with his suit all bunched up and starts running around saying, "I want to be President." I mean this is how he strikes some people. That's why these shows are important. To make them forget all that.[32]

when he grows up. (Continuing hesitantly) There's so much violence now . . .

In contrast to Nixon's extensive television advertising campaign in 1968, the Humphrey TV effort suffered from lack of funds. White reports that the Democratic National Committee "barely scraped together the necessary $100,000" to pay for Humphrey's first nationwide telecast—his important position statement on Vietnam. After his speech, Humphrey's standing in the polls improved and more money began to flow into the campaign. The Democrats were finally able to surpass Nixon's spending for network TV advertising in the last two weeks of the 1968 campaign. (See Figure 8-3.) Humphrey apparently felt the money came too late: "It's not the amount of money you get, it's when you get it," he said.[33]

ANNOUNCER: Hubert Humphrey has said every American has . . .

The increasing use of television and Madison Avenue techniques has, of course, raised the question of whether political candidates can be merchandised and packaged like toothpaste. To some extent the answer must

Vote Humphrey Muskie Nov. 5th

Paid for by Citizens

a right to a comfortable and safe neighborhood.

[32] Joe McGinniss, *The Selling of the President 1968* (New York: Trident Press, 1969), p. 103.
[33] White, *The Making of the President 1968*, pp. 340, 354–57, 357n.

FIGURE 8-3

Weekly Expenditures on Network Television
in the Humphrey and Nixon Campaigns, 1968

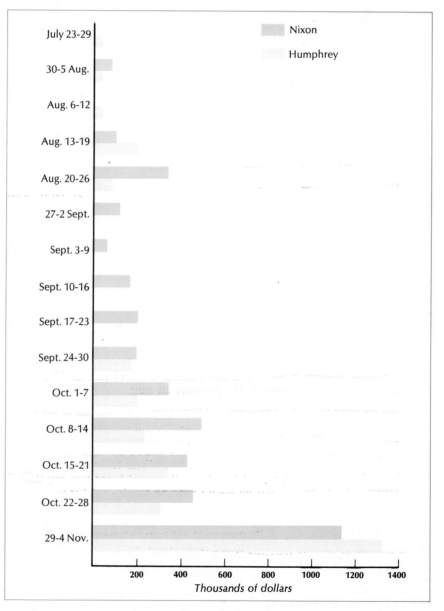

Source: *Voters' Time, Report of the Twentieth Century Fund Commission on Campaign Costs in the Electronic Era* (New York: Twentieth Century Fund, 1969).

We finally got about five or six million dollars, all in all . . . if we'd finally gotten ten million dollars, we could have licked Nixon. And that scares me. The old tradition of sleeves-rolled-up volunteers may work in the primaries; but in a campaign there has to be more and more reliance on the fat cats who put up the money for the media, not on the volunteers. The impact of the media . . . is the Democratic Party's major problem in the future, just the fantastic cost of the media. If we hadn't been able to match Nixon dollar for dollar in the last two weeks, this would have been the debacle everyone predicted. If you figure that by setting up a twenty-five-million-dollar media budget, and making a game of who gets the best time slots and who hires the most creative media talent—and if you elect a President that way, what the Hell's the country coming to?

—Lawrence F. O'Brien, 1968 Humphrey campaign manager, in Theodore H. White, *The Making of the President 1968.*

be yes; certainly many of the advertising men who handle political "accounts" think in just those terms.

For example, in 1966, Governor Nelson Rockefeller of New York faced an uphill battle in his reelection campaign. His chief adviser, William Ronan, hired an advertising agency, Jack Tinker & Partners: "We liked their different approach. It was offbeat and it had been successful in restoring some products." [34]

Myron McDonald, of the Tinker agency, has explained what happened next:

The agency I work for, as you know, is a consumer goods agency. We peddle Alka-Seltzer, Buick automobiles, Coca-Cola, and so forth. And until 13 or 14 months ago none of us had any political experience. We looked at the Governor in the only way we knew how to look at him; that is as a consumer product. Now, if you don't like to think of him as Alka-Seltzer, why think of him as a Buick. It's perfectly all right.

But we went to our first meeting and they gave us the results of the current poll, and we all went back home feeling as though we had been appointed purser on the Titanic because the first poll showed that 21 per cent of the people would vote for Governor Rockefeller and 79 per cent would vote for someone else. It is not apocryphal that the pollster told the Governor that he couldn't be elected dog-catcher. I was there and heard him say that. Of course we're fortunate that he wasn't running for dog-catcher. [35]

Because the Tinker agency thought Rockefeller looked awkward on television, McDonald added, "we professionally decided that we would keep him off as long as possible. What we decided in the case of Governor

---

[34] James M. Perry, *The New Politics* (New York: Clarkson N. Potter, 1968), pp. 112–13. For an excellent account of the use of television in the Rockefeller campaign, see Chapter 5 of Perry's book.

[35] Public Broadcast Laboratory interview, November 10, 1967

Rockefeller, therefore, was not to run the Governor in the campaign but to run his record." [36]

This was done through a series of imaginative commercials that extolled Rockefeller's accomplishments without putting the governor on camera. One spot starred a talking fish puppet (VIDEO: Simulated interview with large-mouth bass) that gave a first-person account of how Rockefeller had attacked water pollution in New York State.

Despite the increased profits of the advertising and television industries from political commercials, some industry sources have, publicly at least, deplored the trend. For example, one Madison Avenue executive has declared: "I think it's dangerous when the electorate is asked to decide which candidate has the most creative agency." [37]

The impact of television on American politics since 1952 should not be underestimated, but it is easy to exaggerate the influence of Madison Avenue and "the tube." The idea that a few advertising men in New York can manipulate the mass of voters ignores other important factors—such as party identification, or the voter's personal economic circumstances—that affect how voters cast their ballots. Millions of persons did *not* vote for Nixon in 1968 despite the skilled efforts of his television advisers. As V. O. Key, Jr., has noted, the advertising industry does not always discourage exaggerated estimates of its abilities: "As a group at bottom professionally dedicated to the dissemination of falsehood (we need not blink [at] so obvious a fact), the advertising fraternity had few inhibitions against the propagation of myths that inflated its own capabilities." [38]

Arie Kopelman of Doyle Dane Bernbach, the young account supervisor for Humphrey's preconvention campaign in 1968, has suggested that Madison Avenue has its limitations: "In the end, communications skills alone can't do it. I don't think it's possible to merchandise a vegetable. I think that eventually the man must show himself." [39]

With the increased importance of television, however, there is at least a danger that a candidate with more money, or more skilled media men, will enjoy an unfair advantage in resources over his rival. Moreover, with access to an audience of millions of voters through the electronic media, a political candidate may be tempted to display an "image" that masks the real man, to present the issues in capsulized, simplistic form, and to become a performer rather than a leader. But the candidate who goes too far in this direction takes the risk that the voters may "see through" the slickness and, in effect, switch channels—by voting for his opponent. There are, in short,

[36] *Ibid.*
[37] Fred Papert, of Papert Koenig Lois, in *Newsweek*, May 27, 1968, p. 106.
[38] V. O. Key, Jr., *Public Opinion and American Democracy* (New York: Knopf, 1961), p. 6.
[39] McGinniss, *The Selling of the President 1968*, p. 130.

"Eventually the man must show himself . . ." Despite the increased importance of television, political candidates still like to get out among the voters. Here Senator Jacob K. Javits, R., New York, campaigns among the salamis and sausages in a New York delicatessen.

limits to the ability of Madison Avenue and the media men to package and sell a candidate.

In the spring of 1965, when Ronald Reagan was thinking about running for governor of California, he approached the Spencer-Roberts political management firm to see whether it would handle his campaign. Such was the reputation of the California firm that aspirants for political office sought out Spencer-Roberts rather than vice versa. George Christopher, the former mayor of San Francisco (who eventually opposed Reagan in the primary), had also approached Spencer-Roberts. After meeting with Reagan, the political management firm "accepted" him as a client.[40]

Spencer-Roberts managed Reagan's successful campaign against incumbent Governor Edmund "Pat" Brown, providing a wide range of public relations and other professional services. For example, because Reagan was an actor, some voters felt he was simply playing the part of a candidate and memorizing his speeches. Spencer-Roberts advised Reagan to hold question-and-answer periods after each of his speeches, to demonstrate to the voters that he had a real grasp of the issues. The firm's advice helped elect Reagan governor.

The role of Spencer-Roberts in the 1966 California gubernatorial campaign was not unusual. Increasingly, at all levels of politics, candi-

Professional
Campaign
Managers

[40] Perry, *The New Politics*, pp. 25–26.

dates have turned to professional campaign managers and consultants. The firms earn large fees for their varied services, which include advertising, public relations, research on issues, public opinion sampling, fundraising, telephone solicitations, computer analysis, and speechwriting.

From its beginnings in California in the 1930's, campaign management has rapidly grown to the status of being a profitable nationwide industry. Its first practitioner was the San Francisco firm of Whitaker and Baxter, which became a formidable force in California politics. From 1933 to 1955, Whitaker and Baxter managed seventy-five political campaigns in the state and won seventy.

Spencer-Roberts came into being in 1960; William Roberts was a television dealer and Stuart Spencer a suburban recreation director when they met and set up business in the back room of a travel agency. By 1964, they were managing Nelson Rockefeller's California primary fight against Barry Goldwater. Although Rockefeller lost, the contest was close and the firm's reputation was assured. According to one writer, "A Spencer-Roberts fee runs between 10 and 20 percent of the outlay for a campaign. In the Reagan campaign it was reported to be $150,000." [41]

Both firms, Whitaker and Baxter and Spencer-Roberts, handle only Republican candidates. Many other firms specialize in managing Democrats, including Joseph Napolitan Associates, Inc., and Publicom, Inc., both based in Washington. Almost inevitably, public relations firms that have branched out into campaign management have evolved from technicians giving advice on press releases to strategists helping candidates make major campaign policy decisions. As Stanley Kelley, Jr., has observed: "It is hard to see why the same trends which have brought the public relations man into political life will not also push him upward in political decision making. His services are valuable because effective use of the mass media is one of the roads to power in contemporary society, and it is difficult clearly to separate strategic and tactical considerations in that use." [42]

The Polls

Public opinion polls, as Chapter 6 pointed out, are essential tools in political campaigns. Political candidates are always concerned over their standing in the published "popularity" polls, but the use of public opinion surveys has become much more sophisticated than a simple comparison of the relative standing of competing candidates. A politician may order a confidential poll to be taken well before a campaign in order to gauge his potential strength; he may decide whether to run on the basis

[41] Gladwin Hill, *Dancing Bear: An Inside Look at California Politics* (Cleveland: World, 1968), p. 199.
[42] Stanley Kelley, Jr., *Professional Public Relations and Political Power* (Baltimore: The Johns Hopkins Press, 1956), p. 212.

of the findings. Once the candidate is committed to running in a primary or running in a general election campaign, he may commission private polls to test voter sentiment; these assist him in identifying the issues and planning his campaign strategy. After the campaign is underway, additional private polls are taken to measure the success of the candidate's personal appeal and his handling of the issues; he may adjust his style and his positions on the issues accordingly.

For example, in becoming the first black candidate to be popularly elected to the Senate, Edward W. Brooke of Massachusetts relied heavily on polling data in his 1966 campaign. Surveys indicated early in the campaign that his standing had dropped because he failed to speak out on Black Power and urban riots. Brooke went on television and staked out a moderate racial position, attacking both black and white extremists; his lead in the polls immediately increased, and he defeated his Democratic opponent, former Governor Endicott Peabody.[43]

Candidates or political parties sometimes commission confidential post-election polls to find out what went wrong—or right. If elected, the candidate may rely on polls to measure voter reaction to his performance in office. During the mid-1960's, President Johnson customarily pulled private-poll data out of his pockets to impress visitors with his popularity in general or on specific issues. When the data began to reflect a sharp decline in public approval of the President, he displayed his confidential polls less often.

As the reader may have suspected, there is a close interrelationship among the various tools and techniques of "the new politics": the image the candidate tries to project on television may be tailored to the advice provided by professional campaign managers, who in turn rely on polls they have taken or commissioned. Many of these expensive, interlocking, and highly professionalized services were relatively new in the campaigns of the 1960's; in the 1970's they are taken for granted.

The Press

After he lost the governor's race in California in 1962, Richard Nixon held a famous news conference in which he declared: "You won't have Nixon to kick around any more, because, gentlemen, this is my last press conference. . . ."

The press, Nixon added, should recognize "that they have a right and a responsibility, if they're against a candidate, to give him the shaft, but also recognize if they give him the shaft, put one lonely reporter on the campaign who will report what the candidate says now and then." [44]

---

[43] John F. Becker and Eugene E. Heaton, Jr., "The Election of Senator Edward W. Brooke," *Public Opinion Quarterly*, Vol. 31, No. 3 (Fall 1967).

[44] Mazo and Hess, *Nixon, A Political Portrait*, p. 282.

Nixon was exhausted and upset when he made these remarks, but his comments reflected his feeling after the 1960 presidential campaign and the 1962 California contest that he had been treated unfairly by newsmen. The complaint was not a new one; as far back as 1807, President Jefferson lamented "the falsehoods of a licentious press."

Modern candidates for political office can ill afford to ignore the press. In 1960, a mutual hostility developed between the press and Nixon, who allowed himself to be interviewed only by a few, favored correspondents. By contrast, Kennedy and his staff cultivated the friendship of the reporters assigned to his campaign, and a friendly atmosphere prevailed on his press plane. Determined not to repeat his mistake, Nixon in 1968 paid great personal attention to the creature comforts of the reporters traveling with him; his staff was available to the press and conspicuously affable.[45]

Until 1964, when many normally Republican publishers failed to back Barry Goldwater, "most newspapers supported Republican candidates in their editorials and (to some extent) in their news columns." On the other hand, "most reporters assigned to cover the candidates . . . are inclined to support Democrats, and this may show in their stories."[46] However, the personal politics of news reporters may not be reflected in their stories, since many newsmen attempt to adhere to professional standards of fairness in covering the candidates.

National political correspondents and columnists play an influential role in interpreting political developments and even in recruiting candidates. Speculation in the press about who may or may not become a candidate, and published analyses of the relative strength and abilities of rival contenders may affect what happens at the conventions and the polls.

In contrast, editorial support of political candidates by newspapers has little demonstrable effect in presidential campaigns. (See Table 8-2.) During the New Deal years, Roosevelt was consistently opposed by one-half to two-thirds of the nation's daily newspapers; Harry Truman in 1948 and John Kennedy in 1960 were endorsed by only 15 percent of the daily papers but both won.

Recently, there has been some tendency by candidates to attempt to bypass the written press through the medium of television. Frank Shakespeare, a top Nixon adviser in 1968, has been quoted as saying bluntly: "Without television, Richard Nixon would not have a chance. He would not have a prayer of being elected because the press would not let him get through to the people. But because he is so good on television he will get through despite the press. The press doesn't matter any more."[47]

[45] See White, *The Making of the President 1960*, pp. 336–38, and *The Making of the President 1968*, p. 327.
[46] Polsby and Wildavsky, *Presidential Elections*, p. 144.
[47] McGinniss, *The Selling of the President 1968*, p. 58.

TABLE 8-2

Political Division of Daily Newspapers
in Presidential Elections, 1932–1968[1]

Year	Republican	Democratic	Independent or Neutral	Wallace
1932	55.5%	38.7%	5.8%	
1936	60.4	34.5	5.1	
1940	66.3	20.1	13.6	
1944	60.1	22.0	17.9	
1948	65.2	15.4	19.4	
1952	67.3	14.5	18.2	
1956	59.0	17.0	24.0	
1960	54.0	15.0	31.0	
1964	34.7	42.4	22.9	
1968	60.8	14.0	24.0	1.2

[1] Figures represent percentages of total number of papers responding to questionnaires. Coverage varied from year to year. In most cases the participating newspapers represented about 80 percent of total daily circulation.

Source: In William B. Dickinson, Jr., "Politicians and the Press," in Richard M. Boeckel, ed., *Editorial Research Reports,* Vol. 2, No. 2 (September 2, 1964), p. 659. Data on 1964 and 1968 from *Editor & Publisher,* October 31, 1964 and *Editor & Publisher,* November 2, 1968, respectively.

Despite the emphasis on television, there are some 62,000,000 daily newspaper readers in the United States, and the impressions they receive in political campaigns are formed in part by what they read. As a result, candidates must include the written press in their calculations of campaign techniques and strategy, even if they rely on television for direct mass appeal to the electorate.

CAMPAIGN FINANCE

When Abraham Lincoln ran for Congress in 1846, it cost him 75 cents: "I made the canvass on my own horse; my entertainment, being at the houses of friends, cost me nothing; and my only outlay was 75¢ for a barrel of cider, which some farm-hands insisted I should treat to." [48]

Clearly, times have changed. The rising cost of American political campaigns can be seen at a glance from these figures, which are rough estimates of spending at all levels in presidential years since 1952: [49]

[48] Sandburg, *Abraham Lincoln: The Prairie Years,* Vol. I, p. 344.
[49] Herbert E. Alexander, *Financing the 1964 Election* (Princeton, N.J.: Citizens' Research Foundation, 1966), p. 13. 1968 estimate from Congressional Quarterly, *Weekly Report,* September 12, 1969, p. 1701.

$140 million in 1952
$155 million in 1956
$175 million in 1960
$200 million in 1964
$300 million in 1968

"Money," as California Democratic leader Jesse Unruh has remarked, "is the mother's milk of politics."

Money is also a subject cloaked by a good deal of secrecy, and a vast amount of confusion. Over the years Congress has attempted to control the sources, amounts, and reporting of campaign expenditures, but the overlapping and largely ineffective legislation on the subject has resulted in more loophole than law.

No politician or political scientist accepts the officially reported campaign spending figures as more than a token of the actual political campaign costs. Of the iceberg that is campaign finance, very little shows above the surface. (See Figure 8-4.) Partly as a result, an atmosphere of public cynicism and mistrust tends to surround the subject of money and

FIGURE 8-4

Political Campaign Expenditures, 1952–1968

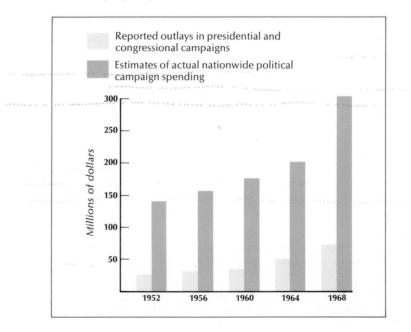

Reported outlays in presidential and congressional campaigns

Estimates of actual nationwide political campaign spending

Source: Congressional Quarterly, *Weekly Report*, January 21, 1966, back cover; and *Weekly Report*, December 5, 1969, p. 2433. Reprinted with permission.

politics. Voter attitudes on the subject are reflected in such knowing statements as: "money wins elections," "politicians can be bought," or "politics is a rich man's game."

Money *is* important. It did not, however, win the Democratic nomination for Averell Harriman in 1956, nor did it put Nelson Rockefeller in the White House in 1960, 1964, or 1968—and neither man lacked money. Since the Second World War, the Republicans have generally spent more than the Democrats on national campaigns. Therefore, if money *alone* determined the result of presidential elections, the Democrats could not win. Obviously in some elections, Democratic votes have proved more powerful than Republican dollars.

In many states, it costs $100,000 or more to run for Congress. To run for the United States Senate, a candidate may spend over $1,000,-000 in a large state like New York or California. James Buckley and Richard Ottinger each reported spending of about $2,000,000 in the 1970 Senate race in New York.[50]

How Much Does it Cost?

Running for President is vastly more expensive: in 1968, Republican committees for Nixon-Agnew reported spending a total of $29.6 million; Democratic committees for Humphrey-Muskie reported spending $12.6 million; George Wallace reported expenditures of $7.2 million. Thus, reported spending by the three main candidates in the 1968 presidential election totaled $49.4 million.[51] The price tag for presidential elections, like campaign costs in general, has gone up in succeeding election years. (See Figure 8-5.)

Alexander Heard, author of an authoritative study of campaign finance, has concluded that money is particularly important in "the shadow land of our politics" where it is decided who shall be a nominee of a political party: "Cash is far more significant in the nominating process than in determining the outcome of elections."[52]

Preconvention and primary campaigns can reach staggering totals. The cost of John Kennedy's drive for the Democratic nomination in 1960 has been estimated at more than $1,000,000.[53] (One of his chief opponents, Hubert Humphrey, was severely handicapped in his campaign for

[50] *New York Times*, November 28, 1970, p. 24. The third candidate, Charles Goodell, reported spending of about $1,000,000. Even a Senate primary fight may cost $1,000,000 in a state like California; Max Rafferty spent that amount in defeating Senator Thomas Kuchel for the Republican Senate nomination in California in 1968. Source: *New York Times*, November 5, 1968, p. 30.

[51] Congressional Quarterly, *Weekly Report*, December 5, 1969, p. 2435.

[52] Alexander Heard, *The Costs of Democracy* (Chapel Hill, N.C.: University of North Carolina Press, 1960), pp. 14, 35.

[53] Herbert E. Alexander, *Financing the 1960 Election* (Princeton, N.J.: Citizens' Research Foundation, 1964), p. 16.

FIGURE 8-5

Major Party Campaign Spending at National Level, 1952–1968

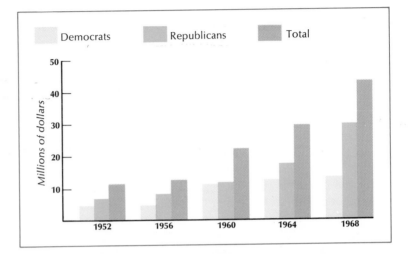

Source: 1952 and 1956: Alexander Heard, *The Costs of Democracy* (Chapel Hill, N.C.: University of North Carolina Press, 1960), p. 20; 1960 and 1964: Herbert E. Alexander, *Financing the 1960 Election* (Princeton, N.J.: Citizens' Research Foundation, 1964), p. 10; Herbert E. Alexander, *Financing the 1964 Election* (Princeton, N.J.: Citizens' Research Foundation, 1966), p. 3; 1968: Congressional Quarterly, *Weekly Report*, December 5, 1969, p. 2435. Reprinted with permission.

the nomination by a chronic lack of funds.) In 1964, six candidates for the Republican nomination spent at least $9,568,000. It was estimated that Senator Goldwater spent $5.5 million to win the nomination in 1964; Rockefeller's unsuccessful effort cost between $3.5 and $5 million.[54]

Which party spends more? The answer varies from one campaign to the next. Between 1952 and 1968, the Republicans outspent the Democrats on the national level (see Figure 8-5). In the 1960 campaign, however, the gap in spending between the two major parties was not significant, in fact, if spending by labor committees of $2.3 million is added to the Democratic total—and most labor money went to support Democrats—spending by the Democrats actually exceeded that by the Republicans. But in 1968, as already noted, Humphrey's campaign suffered from lack of funds and the Republicans outspent the Democrats more than 2 to 1.

Where Does
the Money Go?

Today, radio and television costs are by far the biggest single item in campaign spending. Of the roughly $300,000,000 spent on all political campaigns in 1968, almost $59,000,000, or just under 20 percent,

[54] Alexander, *Financing the 1964 Election*, pp. 18, 23, 30.

was spent on political broadcasting. Of the $18.7 million spent on political broadcasting at the national level in 1968, the Nixon-Agnew camp spent $12.6 million and Humphrey-Muskie ticket spent $6.1 million. Overall, an FCC study found TV accounted for 64.5 percent of political broadcasting in 1968. Spot announcements—commercials—account for 70 to 80 percent of political broadcast costs. And spots are expensive: network TV political spots cost an average of $23,193 each in 1968.[55]

Political committees also spend money on other forms of publicity and advertising. They must pay for polls and data processing, printing costs, telephone bills, headquarters costs, and salaries of party workers. A great deal of money is spent on election day to pay poll workers, to provide transportation to get the voters to the polls—and, sometimes, illicitly, to pay voters. Alexander Heard has estimated that election-day spending accounts for "as much as one-eighth of the total election bill in the United States."[56]

Underlying some of the public suspicion over campaign contributions are the widespread assumptions that (1) a few wealthy "fat cats" provide most of the money for political campaigns and (2) political contributors expect something in return for their investment. The idea that a handful of "fat cats" provide most of the money for campaigns has little foundation in fact. As to the reasons why people give money to campaigns, these vary widely. Some contributors simply believe in a party or a candidate and wish to express their support. Others do give because they do expect some tangible benefit or reward from the winning candidate. Others hope to buy access to a public official; for some who long for social recognition, an invitation to a White House dinner may be reward enough.[57]

With few exceptions, candidates of both major parties in the last several presidential elections have relied on contributions of $500 or more for the bulk of their funds. (See Figure 8-6.) And substantial gifts are increasing: 4,000 individuals gave $500 or more in 1960; by 1964 the number had grown to 6,700. But large gifts do not always account for the bulk of campaign funds; for example, in 1964, 50 percent of individual gifts to the Republicans were under $100.[58]

Between 1960 and 1964, there occurred a dramatic switch in "fat cat" giving—the contributions by donors of $10,000 or more. As Figure 8-7 shows, in 1960 the Democrats received only 30.3 percent of all gifts of

Where Does
the Money
Come From?

[55] Congressional Quarterly, *Weekly Report*, September 12, 1969, pp. 1701–02.
[56] Heard, *The Costs of Democracy*, p. 394.
[57] For a discussion of the complex motives for campaign giving, see Heard, *The Costs of Democracy*, Chapter 4.
[58] Alexander, *Financing the 1960 Election*, p. 57, *Financing the 1964 Election*, pp. 84–86.

FIGURE 8-6

Campaign Gifts of $500 or More

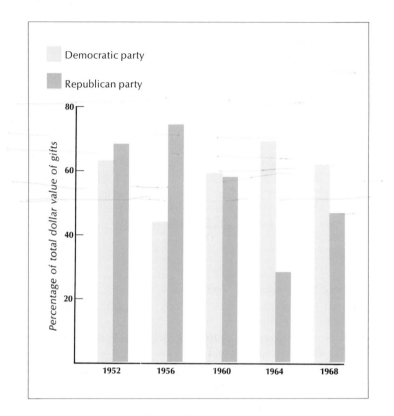

Source: Congressional Quarterly, *Weekly Report*, January 21, 1966, back cover; reprinted with permission. 1968 data from Citizens' Research Foundation, Princeton, N.J.

$10,000 or more; after four years in power, the Democrats' percentage of such gifts rose to 57.4 percent.

Yet, the total number of big contributors and the total percentage of their gifts are surprisingly small. In 1964, 130 persons made reported gifts of $10,000 or more; these gifts totaled $2.2 million, or less than 8 percent of the $29.2 million that the major parties reported spending at the national level.[59] A gift of $10,000, in other words, puts the donor in the category of a very substantial party angel.

Some contributors hedge their bets and give to both major parties; in 1964, 80 individuals contributed $500 or more to *both* the Democrats and the Republicans.[60]

Some of America's wealthiest families contribute heavily to political campaigns, although the totals of such gifts declined markedly between 1956 and 1964. The bulk of the contributions from these families—whose

[59] Adapted from Alexander, *Financing the 1964 Election*, pp. 86–88.
[60] *Ibid.*, p. 90.

FIGURE 8-7

The "Fat Cat" Givers: Party Receipts from Donors of $10,000 or More

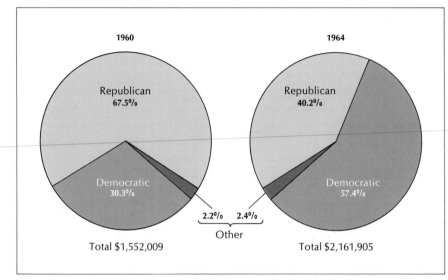

1960

Republican
67.5%

Democratic
30.3%

2.2%   2.4%
Other

Total $1,552,009

1964

Republican
40.2%

Democratic
57.4%

Total $2,161,905

Source: Congressional Quarterly, *Weekly Report*, January 21, 1966, back cover. Reprinted with permission.

wealth is rooted in the oil, steel, auto, railroad, and other large industries—goes to the Republican party. (See Table 8-3.)

Both major parties rely on a variety of sources to raise money: individual contributions from the public, $100-a-plate and even $1,000-a-plate

TABLE 8-3

Campaign Contributions of Eleven Prominent Families, 1968

Name	Number of Members Contributing[1]	Total Contributions	Contribution Breakdown Republican	Democratic	Miscellaneous
duPont	32	$ 107,000	$ 99,800	$ 1,700	$ 5,500
Field	4	39,000	2,000	17,000	20,000
Ford	8	109,750	57,750	52,000	—
Harriman	2	17,500	16,500	—	500
Lehman	7	51,000	2,500	48,500	—
Mellon	22	298,962	278,962	17,000	3,000
Olin	7	70,000	70,000	—	—
Pew	11[2]	213,549	207,898	—	5,651
Rockefeller	21	1,714,375[3]	1,700,875	13,500	—
Vanderbilt	2	12,000	11,000	—	1,000
Whitney	6	133,500	133,500	—	—
	122	$2,766,136	$2,580,785	$149,700	$35,561

[1] In this analysis, husbands and wives were counted separately.

[2] The Estate of J. N. Pew Deceased was counted as one contributing member.

[3] Total does not include the $356,000 contribution made by Nelson Rockefeller for his own campaign.

Source: Herbert E. Alexander, Preliminary Analysis, Princeton, N.J.: Citizen's Research Foundation, 1970.

dinners, direct mail solicitation, televised appeals, contributions from members of labor unions and corporation executives, and corporate advertising in convention programs and political booklets.

An unadvertised source of campaign funds is the underworld. In some communities close ties exist between organized crime and politics; elected officials may take graft to protect criminal operations, and sometimes the payoffs take the form of campaign contributions. Heard has guessed that perhaps "15 percent of political campaign expenditures at state and local levels" comes from the underworld.[61]

The Democrats received several million dollars—and some unfavorable publicity—in the 1960's from a fund-raising device known as the President's Club. The club, whose members paid $1,000 apiece to join, was formed in 1961 under President Kennedy and expanded to a reported 4,000 members in 1964 under President Johnson; its president was Arthur B. Krim, motion picture executive and Democratic fund-raiser. The members, whose names were not made public, were invited to exclusive receptions in Washington and other cities where the President would shake hands and chat with them. The press was barred from these meetings. Special arrangements were made for members to attend the 1964 convention, the Inaugural Gala, and even White House briefings and seminars. Because its members appeared to be buying special access to the President—a questionable procedure in a democracy—the club drew some criticism.

Regulating
Campaign
Finance

Federal laws governing campaign finance have sought to require disclosure of receipts and expenditures and to limit the amounts spent, the size of individual gifts, and the sources of campaign funds. For many years, however, the patchwork of campaign legislation has fallen far short of achieving these objectives. As a result, "There prevails a widespread cynicism toward the legal regulation of campaign finance. This cynicism springs in part from statutory regulations that have proved inadequate or are impossible to enforce."[62]

The Corrupt Practices Act of 1925 requires national political committees operating in two or more states to file reports of receipts and expenditures with the Clerk of the House of Representatives or the Secretary of the Senate. The reports must list receipts of $100 or more and expenditures exceeding $10. But the law does not cover spending for presidential campaigns on the state and local levels and its provisions have been virtually unenforced.

For example, the 1925 law limited campaign spending to $5,000 by

---

[61] Heard, *The Costs of Democracy*, p. 163.
[62] *Financing Presidential Campaigns, Report of the President's Commission on Campaign Costs* (Washington, D.C.: U.S. Government Printing Office, April 1962), p. 21.

a candidate for the House and $25,000 by a candidate for the Senate. Candidates traditionally evade these ceilings by interpreting the law to cover only their "personal" expenditures. So committees working for the candidate can spend as much as they want, and if they operate within one state they are not required to report to Congress. In 1968, seven senators reported that it cost them *nothing* to be elected. In documents filed with the Secretary of the Senate, they listed "none" under the heading for "expenditures." (The seven senators were Barry Goldwater, R., Arizona; J. W. Fulbright, D., Arkansas; Alan Cranston, D., California; Herman Talmadge, D., Georgia; George McGovern, D., South Dakota; George Aiken, R., Vermont; and Robert Dole, R., Kansas.) But even those who listed expenditures seldom gave totals that provided a realistic picture. For example, Senator Richard S. Schweiker, a Pennsylvania Republican, reported "personal" spending of $5,736 in his successful campaign for the Senate in 1968. But state records in Pennsylvania indicate that the Schweiker campaign actually cost $664,614.[63]

The Hatch Act of 1940 prohibits contributions of more than $5,000 in one year to a candidate for federal office, or to a national political committee. In practice, the limitation is meaningless; anyone may give $5,000 to each of any number of national political committees and there is no limit in most states to the number and value of gifts a person may donate to state and local party committees. The Hatch Act also limits spending by each interstate political committee in federal elections to $3,000,000 during a calendar year. The parties evade the law by forming several committees under different names, each of which may spend up to $3,000,000. (The Hatch Act also prohibits federal employees from actively participating in political campaigns.) Forty-three states have campaign financial reporting laws, but they vary greatly and few are stringent.

As far back as 1907, Congress prohibited corporations from contributing to candidates for office in federal elections. The Taft-Hartley Act of 1947 bars gifts by labor unions or corporations to federal election campaigns; the ban also applies to national conventions and primary elections to choose candidates for federal office. The unions are free, however, to spend regular union funds for get-out-the-vote drives and to contribute to state and local elections, and many corporations place advertisements in political journals. Finally, the law does not bar "voluntary" contributions to any campaign by members of labor unions or by corporation executives. Often, such contributions are voluntary in name only: union members may be pressured to donate, and corporations get around the law by giving executives special "bonuses," which are then passed on as campaign contributions.

Despite a federal law prohibiting loans by national banks to political

---

[63] Congressional Quarterly, *Weekly Report*, December 5, 1969, pp. 2436, 2454–56.

campaigns, some banks do lend money for this purpose. Nor do existing laws prevent political contributions by partnerships such as law firms and insurance agencies and brokerage houses; in 1968 Wall Street brokerage houses contributed almost $150,000 to members of Congress who were influential in securities legislation.[64]

In 1962, a presidential study commission recommended a series of reforms, including measures designed to encourage greater citizen contributions to campaigns. It proposed tax incentives for campaign giving and repeal of the meaningless $3,000,000 ceiling on spending by interstate political committees and the $5,000 limit on individual gifts. The commission also recommended that the Federal Government pay the transition costs of a President-elect between election day and Inauguration Day.[65] In 1964 Congress passed a law providing a maximum of $900,000 for transition costs. None of the other recommendations was acted upon.[66]

The Senate in 1967 passed a comprehensive campaign finance reform bill that would have set new and stricter reporting requirements for spending by candidates in presidential and congressional elections. The House, however, failed to act on the measure.

Members of Congress and some private organizations had for several years proposed various laws to reduce the high cost of television broadcasts in political campaigns.[67] In 1970, Congress passed the Campaign Broadcast Reform Act, which for the first time would have set ceilings on campaign spending for radio and television broadcasts in federal elections and state elections for governor and lieutenant governor. The measure would have limited spending on radio and TV to 7 cents for each vote cast in the previous election, or $20,000, if greater. It also sought to require broadcasters to sell time to political candidates at the lowest rate charged to commercial advertisers. The measure, which was to have gone into effect after the 1970 elections, was vetoed by President Nixon on the grounds that it was not the best way to deal with the problem of regulating campaign spending. Democrats charged that the bill was vetoed because Republicans, who generally spend more in campaigns than Democrats, wanted

---

[64] Walter Pincus, "Campaign Spending: The Public Isn't Let in on Many Secrets," *Washington Post,* December 9, 1968.

[65] *Financing Presidential Campaigns, Report of the President's Commission on Campaign Costs,* 1962.

[66] In 1966, Congress did enact a law allowing taxpayers to check a box on their income tax returns if they wished to contribute $1 of their income tax to presidential campaigns, with the money divided equally between both major parties. But implementation of the measure, sponsored by Senator Russell B. Long, D., La., was suspended after a bitter debate in 1967, in which opponents charged that the law contained no guidelines on how the money should be spent.

[67] See *Voters' Time, Report of the Twentieth Century Fund Commission on Campaign Costs in the Electronic Era* (New York: Twentieth Century Fund, 1969).

no ceiling on TV expenditures. The Democratic-controlled Congress was unable to pass the measure over the President's veto.

Campaigns cost a great deal of money. Once a candidate is nominated by a political party, the financial resources of the party and its supporters become available to him to some extent; but this is not true of preconvention campaigns to obtain a nomination. As a rule, challengers are more in need of money than incumbents. One danger is that only wealthy men will be able to afford to enter primary contests and preconvention campaigns.

Campaigns, Money, and Democracy

Most suggestions for reforming campaign finance seek to provide meaningful public disclosure of campaign gifts and spending (in place of the present laws that invite evasion), to allow candidates equal access to the public airwaves, and to broaden the base of campaign giving—by direct appeal to small contributors, through tax incentives, or through government subsidies. Many of these proposals are based on the belief that candidates should not have to depend on big contributors to whom they may become obligated, and that roughly equal resources should be available to candidates for public office.

An even more compelling reason for meaningful reform of campaign finance is that inadequate controls only serve to reinforce voter cynicism about politics. The inequalities in the financial resources of candidates, the abuses surrounding campaign finance, and the trend toward slick packaging of candidates for public office, all tend to undermine public confidence in the political process. And campaigns are a vital part of that process, for, within limits, they give the voters a chance to decide who shall govern.

SUGGESTED READING

Alexander, Herbert E. *Financing the 1960 Election* (Citizens' Research Foundation, 1964). Paperback. A detailed examination of costs in the 1960 election. Includes data on sources of campaign contributions and comparative analyses of income and spending by the major parties. Alexander has also made detailed studies of campaign financing in subsequent election years.

Financing Presidential Campaigns, Report of the President's Commission on Campaign Costs (U.S. Government Printing Office, 1962). A comprehensive study of the problems of financing presidential campaigns. Contains specific policy recommendations.

Heard, Alexander. *The Costs of Democracy* * (University of North Carolina Press, 1960). A comprehensive and useful analysis of the relationships between money and politics. Examines the motives for campaign contributions, who contributes, techniques for raising money, efforts to regulate campaign financing, and some of the political consequences of current campaign financing practices. Makes specific policy recommendations.

Kelley, Stanley, Jr. *Professional Public Relations and Political Power* (Johns Hopkins Press, 1966). Paperback. (Originally published in 1956.) An influential early analysis of the use of public relations techniques on behalf of candidates for public office and in campaigns focused on specific political issues. Kelley traces the rise of professional public relations firms extensively involved in politics, examines the political role of the public relations man, and assesses the consequences this role is likely to have in American politics.

Kessel, John H. *The Goldwater Campaign: Coalitions and Strategies* * (Bobbs-Merrill, 1968). A detailed study of the Republican and Democratic campaign strategies in the 1964 presidential election.

McGinniss, Joe. *The Selling of the President, 1968* * (Trident Press, 1969). A critical, behind-the-scenes description of Richard Nixon's use of television in the 1968 presidential campaign. By a writer who had extensive access to the advertising, television, and political advisers of the Republican candidate.

Perry, James M. *The New Politics* (Clarkson N. Potter, 1968). A readable study of how today's candidates use television and modern polling techniques. Includes detailed case studies and some sample scripts of television political commercials.

Polsby, Nelson W., and Wildavsky, Aaron B. *Presidential Elections,* * 2nd edition (Scribner's, 1968). An excellent, concise analysis of the basic strategic considerations affecting the conduct of presidential election campaigns.

Voters' Time, Report of the Twentieth Century Fund Commission on Campaign Costs in the Electronic Era (The Twentieth Century Fund, 1969). Paperback. An analysis of the rising costs of political broadcast time and advertising, and the implications for the democratic process. Contains specific proposals for making the airwaves more accessible to candidates during campaigns.

White, Theodore H. *The Making of the President 1968* * (Atheneum, 1969); *The Making of the President 1964* * (Atheneum, 1965); *The Making of the President 1960* * (Atheneum, 1961). Colorful, detailed accounts of American presidential campaigns, set against the background of the social and cultural forces at work in American society. White is a leading political analyst who has access to many of the political figures he writes about.

---

* Available in paperback edition

9

Voting Behavior

and Elections

There comes a moment in every campaign when the bands are silent and the cheering stops. The candidate has given his last speech, made his last promise, answered his last question in the election-eve telethon, smiled at the red light on the TV camera for the last time. He boards his campaign plane to fly home and await the verdict of the voters.

There is a certain majesty and mystery in this moment, for no one—not the candidates, the voters, the poll-takers, the news reporters, not even the computers blinking and buzzing in the control centers of the television networks—knows what the outcome will be.

In a democracy, the people choose who shall govern, and that choice is expressed in the voting booth. Although the right to vote is basic to the American political system, it is not as common elsewhere as might be thought. Only about 25 percent of the world's countries hold regular, free elections in which the people may choose among rival candidates.

315

It was quiet on the plane, and remained so as dusk settled.

It was somewhere between Mississippi and Indiana that the dark began to fall—the checkerboards of the flat Midwestern plains all so neat and clean. "You could almost feel the mood changing," remembers Len Garment, "as the darkness came over the land. There was a TV set in the staff compartment, and they were starting to give accounts—from Kansas and New Hampshire, and places like that. It was like inviting people to a party and then waiting to see who would come. I felt like an observer for the first time in a year. Everything had been done, and now I had a front seat at a drama. . . . And down below there was this twinkling of lights from the towns that were beginning to light up, like a stage-setting just before the action begins. It was all so moving and beautiful. And people in the plane, drawing apart in their thoughts, leafing through magazines and papers, doing their own thing. It was very quiet in the last hour." Someone else remembers Nixon looking down as the plane passed into dusk over Indiana, absolutely still, as "if by looking down and concentrating he could pull in more votes."

—Theodore H. White, *The Making of the President, 1968.*

In Chapter 1, we discussed the reciprocal nature of power in a democracy: government makes authoritative, binding decisions about who gets what in society, but derives its power from the people. People may influence government in a number of ways—by taking part in political activity, by the opinions they hold, by belonging to interest groups, by direct action. But a fundamental way that people influence government is through the ballot box; voting is a very powerful "input" in the political system. As one political scientist declared: "The most effective weapon of popular control in a democratic system is the capacity of the electorate to throw a party from power."[1]

Not only do voters have great political power; they also exercise formidable economic power over public officials. For many politicians, politics is a livelihood, and elections determine whether or not they are out of work.

In the federal system that exists in the United States, the voters choose at all levels of government. In a presidential year, for instance, the voters select many of the more than 520,000 local, state, and federal elected officials, including the President and Vice-President, 435 members of the House, one-third of the Senate, and about 20 state governors.

American voters normally may choose among two or more *competing* candidates for the same office. In a democracy, voting is an act of choice among alternative candidates, parties, and, depending on the election, alternative policies.

Under a democratic form of government, then, the voter is theoretically supreme. Yet, as we have seen, there is often a gap between demo-

[1] Arthur Maass, in V. O. Key, Jr., *The Responsible Electorate* (Cambridge, Mass.: The Belknap Press of Harvard University Press, 1966), p. xii.

cratic theory and practice. For example, minority groups may not be fully represented in a pluralist democracy; political parties, in managing the nomination of presidential candidates, may be closed elites rather than broadly based structures; and candidates for public office may compete with vastly unequal financial resources. Many problems of democratic practice are directly relevant to voters and voting. To take one example, some voters may be unenthusiastic about the nominees of *both* major parties and may believe that their choice is for the lesser of two evils; they may easily come to feel that, for them, voting is a waste of time.

In this chapter, we shall examine some central questions about voting in a democratic society: Do enough people vote? How do voters make up their minds? What do elections mean in a democracy—do voters speak in a voice that can be understood by those whom they elect? Do their votes influence government policies?

WHO VOTES?

The voter may have the final say in the United States—but how many people vote? To those who hold an idealized view of representative democracy, the statistics are bound to be disappointing.

More than half of Americans of voting age have voted for President in each election since 1928. But in nonpresidential election years, considerably less than half have bothered to vote for members of Congress. In the presidential elections between 1952 and 1968, an average of 62.3 percent cast their ballots for President; in the four off-year congressional elections during the same period, an average of only 44.7 percent voted.[2] (See Figure 9-1.)

FIGURE 9-1

Voter Participation
in Presidential and House Elections, 1952–1968

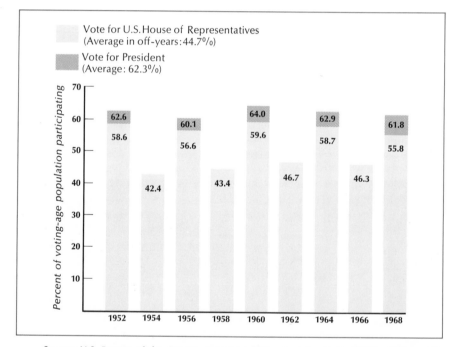

Source: U.S. Bureau of the Census, *Statistical Abstract of the United States 1969*, p. 368.

Although twentieth-century Americans have made great technological progress, their forebears in the horse-and-buggy era scored much higher in voting participation. A much larger proportion of voters took part in presidential elections in the 1890's than in the 1960's. In the election of 1896, for example, almost 80 percent of the voting-age population cast their ballots (in contrast to 61.8 percent in the Nixon-Humphrey-Wallace

[2] Based upon *Statistical Abstract of the United States 1969*, p. 368.

FIGURE 9-2

Voter Participation in Presidential Elections, 1880–1968

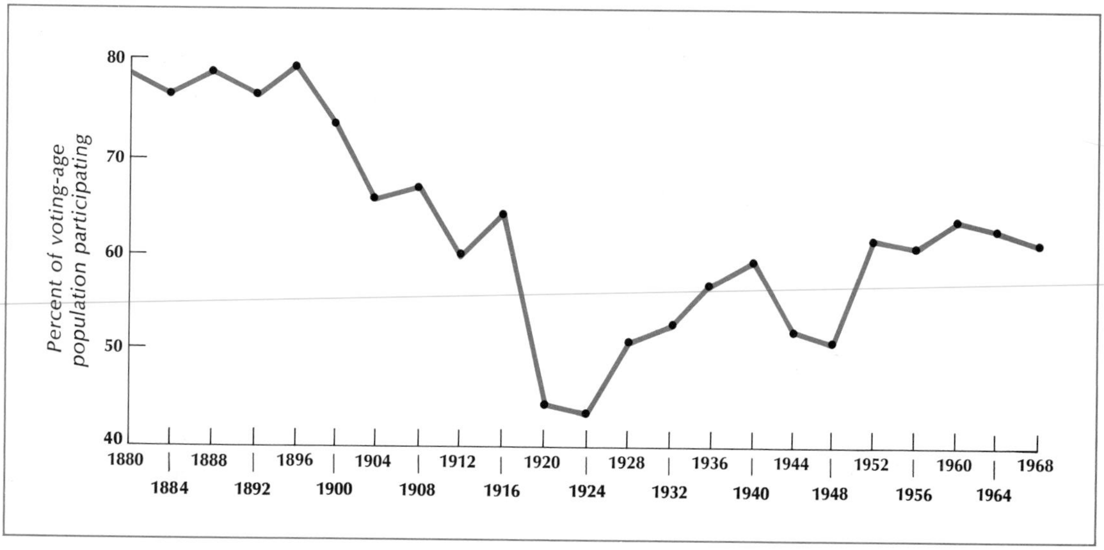

Sources: Figures for 1880 to 1916 in Robert E. Lane, *Political Life* (New York: The Free Press, 1965), p. 20; figures for 1920 to 1968 in the U.S. Bureau of the Census, *Statistical Abstract of the United States 1969*, p. 368. Reprinted with permission of The Macmillan Company from *Political Life* by Robert E. Lane. © The Free Press, a Corporation, 1959.

contest of 1968). The drop in turnout is often attributed to the fact that the adoption of women's suffrage in 1920 brought into the electorate a large new group unaccustomed to voting. But the decline in voter participation had begun well before then. After voter turnout dipped to a low point in the 1920's, it began moving on a generally upward curve (see Figure 9-2). Despite this trend, voting participation in the United States is substantially lower than it is in many other countries of the world, including Great Britain, Denmark, Norway, West Germany, France, and

TABLE 9-1

Voter Participation in Other Countries

Country	Year	Turnout
Canada	1968	75.7%
Denmark	1968	89.3
France	1968	80.0
West Germany	1969	86.8
Great Britain	1970	72.0
Norway	1969	82.5

Source: Walter Dean Burnham and Richard Scammon in the Freedom to Vote Task Force Report, *That All May Vote* (Washington, D.C.: Democratic National Committee, December 1969), App. VIII. Data for Great Britain from the *New York Times*, June 20, 1970, p. 12.

Canada (see Table 9-1). Because other nations calculate voter turnout in varying ways, however, the comparison with the United States is not precise.

Socioeconomic Factors. It is clear that who votes varies with factors of geography, age, sex, education, ethnic background, religion, income, social class, and occupation. This does not mean that people vote or do not vote *because* of such social, demographic, and economic factors; it merely means that these factors often coincide with higher or lower voting participation.[3]

Regional differences in voter participation may be associated with social and economic factors in those areas, the degree of two-party competition, and, in some cases, differences in the election laws governing registration and voting.

Middle-aged people vote more than the young or the very old. Although college students and young people were noticeably active in the 1968 election, poll data indicate that 49 percent of Americans in their

TABLE 9-2

Voter Turnout by Group and Region, 1968

Voting Groups	*Percent Voting*
College educated	83.1%
White collar	81.6
$10,000 and above	80.4
High school educated	72.5
Nonagricultural industrial workers	71.2
North and West	71.0
Farm workers	70.7
Male	69.8
White	69.1
Metropolitan area	68.0
Nonmetropolitan area	67.3
Female	66.0
65 years and above	65.8
Manual workers	64.7
Service workers	64.3
Grade school educated	62.4
South	60.1
Black	57.6
Below $3,000	55.0
21–24 years	51.1

Source: U.S. Bureau of the Census, *Current Population Reports, Population Characteristics,* P-20, No. 192, December 2, 1969; *Statistical Abstract of the United States 1969,* p. 371.

[3] See Lester W. Milbrath, *Political Participation* (Chicago: Rand McNally, 1965), for detailed citations of studies of political participation.

twenties did not register to vote in 1968.[4] In general, studies have shown that voting and political participation increase slowly with age, peak in the mid-forties, and decline after age sixty.[5]

Men vote more than women. College graduates vote more than people with high school or grade school educations. One survey found that 83.1 percent of college-educated Americans reported that they voted in the 1968 presidential election; but only 72.5 percent of those with four years of high school and 62.4 percent of those with grade school educations said they voted.[6] Of all factors, voter turnout seems to vary most sharply with education.

Income, education, social class, and occupation are closely related; in general, the higher the level in all these categories, the more likely a person is to vote. (See Table 9-2.)

Jews vote more than Catholics, and Catholics vote more than Protestants. Churchgoers are more likely to vote than nonchurchgoers, a phenomenon perhaps associated with the willingness of the churchgoer to participate in organized activity and the inclination of some religious groups to get involved in politics. Blacks vote less than whites—but historically black voters in the South have been prevented from voting by legal subterfuge, violence, or intimidation. As we have noted in Chapter 5, the number of black registered voters in the South increased dramatically after passage of the Voting Rights Act of 1965.

THE VOTER

is more likely to be . . .

A Midwesterner
Middle-Aged
Male
College graduate
City dweller
Affluent
Professional man
Upper class
Party loyalist
Politically concerned

Voter Attitudes. Voter turnout does vary with demographic and social differences, but other research has identified additional factors that seem to influence participation at the polls. This research has focused on voter *attitudes.*[7]

For example, a strong Democrat or a rock-ribbed Republican is more

[4] Gallup Poll, August 29, 1968.
[5] V. O. Key, Jr., *Politics, Parties and Pressure Groups,* 5th edition (New York: Crowell, 1964), p. 587 and Milbrath, *Political Participation,* p. 134.
[6] U.S. Bureau of the Census, *Current Population Reports,* Population Characteristics, Series P-20, No. 192, p. 17.
[7] Angus Campbell, Philip E. Converse, Warren E. Miller, and Donald E. Stokes, *The American Voter* (New York: Wiley, 1965), pp. 96–101. Our discussion of voter attitudes is based on Chapter 5 of this landmark study of voting conducted at the Survey Research Center, University of Michigan.

likely to get out and vote than a citizen whose party loyalties are casual. The higher the *intensity of partisan preference*, the more likely it is that the person will vote. Similarly, the *degree of interest* a person has in the campaign and his *concern over the election outcome* appear to be related to whether he votes. If a person thinks the election is close, he is more likely to vote, because he may feel his vote will count. And, if a person thinks he can understand and influence politics, he is more likely to vote than someone who regards politics and government as distant and complicated. The greater a person's *sense of political effectiveness*, the greater the chance that he will vote. Americans, moreover, are indoctrinated with the importance of voting, long before they are old enough to do so, so the voter's *sense of civic duty* also bears upon whether he goes to the polls.

The Nonvoter

Some 40 percent of Americans do not vote in presidential elections. Who are they? Why don't they vote?

The preceding section indicated that the nonvoter is more likely to be less educated, rural, nonwhite, Southern, female, very young or very old, a person "whose emotional investment in politics . . . is on the average much less than that of the voter." [8] Although a rough portrait of the nonvoter can be sketched in these terms, the picture does not answer the question of *why* he does not vote.

As noted in Chapter 6, 61.8 percent of the voting-age population voted in the 1968 election; but if persons disqualified from voting for various legal reasons are subtracted from the voting-age population, the number of nonvoters drops from 47 to 38 million, and the turnout of voters rises to 66.2 percent. After the 1968 election, the Gallup Poll published the following breakdown of "eligible" nonvoters (with the percentages from the sample projected into numbers of people):

15 million were registered but were disinterested or did not like the candidates.
10 million could have registered but did not.
7 million were sick or disabled.
3 million were away from home.
3 million said they could not leave their jobs.
1 million did not obtain absentee ballots.[9]

Obviously this total includes at least 10 million people with apparently valid reasons for staying away from the polls; if these are excluded, the voter turnout in 1968 was actually 73 percent.

Even taking into account the fact that some people had good reasons for not voting, a nation with some 38 million persons who do not turn out in a presidential election would seem to fall somewhat short of the idealized

[8] Campbell, Converse, Miller, and Stokes, *The American Voter*, p. 111.
[9] Gallup Poll, December 10, 1968.

is more likely to be . . .

A Southerner
Young, or old
Female
Grade school educated
Rural
Poor
Blue-collar worker
Lower class
Nonwhite
Politically apathetic

model of popular democracy. But some political scientists believe that what might work in the simple, agrarian society does not apply in a modern, highly industrialized society such as the United States today.[10] The harassed housewife with five young children may find it difficult to get to the polls on election day. Most people spend more time worrying about money, sex, illness, crime, the high cost of living, automobile repairs, and a host of other things than they do worrying about politics and public issues.

So if we ask whether enough people vote in the United States, we must also ask "How much is enough?" A turnout of 61 percent in a presidential election may not meet classic standards of democracy, but it may be the best that can be expected in the United States today. In any event, it is reality; it is what we have.

One overall pattern that emerges from all of these data about the voter and the nonvoter in the United States is that those who are more advantageously situated in the social system vote more than the have-nots or less advantaged. There is, therefore, an upper-class bias in voting. If the members of all social groups in the United States voted in equal proportions, candidates might have to offer programs that appealed more to the disadvantaged groups that do not now come to the polls. In short, if everybody voted, the candidates and policies of the American political system might be somewhat different from what they are today.

HOW THE VOTER DECIDES

We have an idea of who votes and who does not. The question now is: why do people vote the way they do? How people make up their minds to vote for one candidate instead of another is obviously of great interest to politicians, campaign managers, advertising executives, and pollsters. But the question also has much broader implications for all citizens and for democratic government; the kind of society in which we live depends in part on whether voters flip a coin in the voting booth or choose on a somewhat more rational basis—satisfaction or dissatisfaction with the incumbent administration, for example.

Although the American voter has been extensively analyzed, we still do not know *precisely* why he behaves the way he does. We do not know which of many factors ultimately causes a person to stay home or to vote

[10] Milbrath, *Political Participation*, p. 143.

the way he does. To say, for example, that many Catholics are Democrats does not mean that a person is a Democrat *because* he is a Catholic. And, although party loyalty appears to be related to voting habits, we do not know, for example, that a Vermont farmer votes Republican *because* he identifies with the Republican party. Psychologists know that it is extremely difficult to judge people's motives from their behavior; even asking voters to explain their actions may not produce satisfactory answers.

So there are limits to the ability of political science to interpret the behavior of voters. Even allowing for these limits, however, a great deal has been learned about voting habits in recent decades.

Two basic approaches have been followed in studying how the voters decide:

1. *Sociological.* This method focuses on the social and economic background of the voter, his income, class, ethnic group, education, and similar factors, and attempts to relate these factors to how he votes.

2. *Psychological.* This method attempts to go beyond socioeconomic factors and find out what is going on inside the mind of the voter, to measure his *perception* of parties, candidates, and issues. This second approach is based on the premise that how the voter responds depends less on *static* factors, such as social class, than on *dynamic* changing factors of issues and politics; in short, voting behavior may change as the issues and candidates change.

The difference between these two approaches is not as great as might seem at first glance: how a voter currently perceives the issues may well be shaped by his social and economic background. The social psychologists who followed the second approach in the 1950's built on the foundations laid by the political sociologists in the 1940's.

The
Sociological
Factors

The first of two classic voter studies was conducted in 1940 by Paul F. Lazarsfeld and his associates.[11] They chose a sample of 600 residents of Erie County, Ohio. The Ohio county was chosen because it was small and because, until then, it had reflected national voting trends in every presidential election in this century.

The researchers' method was new; instead of tabulating results after an election they attempted to probe "votes in the making." Grouping the 600 Ohio residents by socioeconomic status, the study found that: "The wealthier people, the people with more and better possessions, the people with business interests—these people were usually Republicans. The poorer people, the people whose homes and clothes were of lower quality, the self-

[11] Paul F. Lazarsfeld, Bernard Berelson, and Hazel Gaudet, *The People's Choice* (New York: Columbia University Press, 1968). Originally published in 1944.

Reprinted with permission from the Chicago Daily News.
Cartoon by John Fischetti.

"Presidents ain't my bag, man."

acknowledged laboring class—they voted Democratic. Different social characteristics, different votes." [12] But the voter is a member of several groups simultaneously. Sometimes the claims of one group conflict with those of another; for example, the study concluded that rich people are more likely to vote Republican, Catholics are more likely to vote Democratic. What of wealthy Catholics? Such persons are said to be "cross-pressured" because their social affiliations are pulling them in opposite directions. The study found that these voters were more likely than others to delay their decision and change their minds during a campaign.

In 1948, the same research method was used in a study of how 1,000 voters in Elmira, New York, made up their minds during the Truman-Dewey campaign.[13] This more detailed study also concluded that social class influenced voting behavior. It also found that voters who liked a candidate tended to think that the candidate's stand matched their own. Moreover, only about one-third of the voters were very accurate in their understanding of where the candidates stood on the issues.[14]

From these and many other studies, it is possible to draw a picture of the American voter in terms of his social class and other sociological factors. (A breakdown of how different groups have voted in presidential elections is summarized in Table 9-3.)

[12] *Ibid.*, p. 21.
[13] Bernard R. Berelson, Paul F. Lazarsfeld, and William N. McPhee, *Voting* (Chicago: University of Chicago Press, 1966). Originally published in 1954.
[14] *Ibid.*, Chapter 10.

TABLE 9-3

Votes by Groups in Presidential Elections, 1952–1968

	1952		1956		1960		1964		1968		
	Dem.	Rep.	Dem.	Rep.	Dem.	Rep.	Dem.	Rep.	Dem.	Rep.	Wallace
National	44.6%	55.4%	42.2%	57.8%	50.1%	49.9%	61.3%	38.7%	43.0%	43.4%	13.6%
Men	47	53	45	55	52	48	60	40	41	43	16
Women	42	58	39	61	49	51	62	38	45	43	12
White	43	57	41	59	49	51	59	41	38	47	15
Nonwhite	79	21	61	39	68	32	94	6	85	12	3
College education	34	66	31	69	39	61	52	48	37	54	9
High school education	45	55	42	58	52	48	62	38	42	43	15
Grade school education	52	48	50	50	55	45	66	34	52	33	15
Professional and Business men	36	64	32	68	42	58	54	46	34	56	10
White-collar workers	40	60	37	63	48	52	57	43	41	47	12
Manual workers	55	45	50	50	60	40	71	29	50	35	15
Union Members	61	39	57	43	65	35	73	27	56	29	15
Farmers	33	67	46	54	48	52	53	47	29	51	20
Under 30	51	49	43	57	54	46	64	36	47	38	15
30-49 years	47	53	45	55	54	46	63	37	44	41	15
Over 49	39	61	39	61	46	54	59	41	41	47	12
Protestants	37	63	37	63	38	62	55	45	35	49	16
Catholics	56	44	51	49	78	22	76	24	59	33	8
Republicans	8	92	4	96	5	95	20	80	9	86	5
Democrats	77	23	85	15	84	16	87	13	74	12	14
Independents	35	65	30	70	43	57	56	44	31	44	25

Source: Gallup Poll, November 30, 1968, and December 7, 1968.

Social Class, Income, and Occupation. Upper-class and middle-class voters are more likely to be Republicans than are lower-class voters, who tend to be Democrats.

Business men and professional men are more likely to be Republicans than to be Democrats. For example, with the exception of 1964—when Republicans in droves deserted Goldwater for Johnson—business men and professional men voted overwhelmingly Republican in the five elections between 1952 and 1968. (See Table 9-3.) Among persons making $10,000 a year or over, there are more Republicans than Democrats. Manual workers tend to vote Democratic, and 55 percent of a national sample of persons with incomes of under $5,000 identified themselves as Democrats.[15] Of

FIGURE 9-3

How the Voters See the Parties

Question: "Which political party—the Republican or Democratic—do you think best serves the interest of people like yourself?"

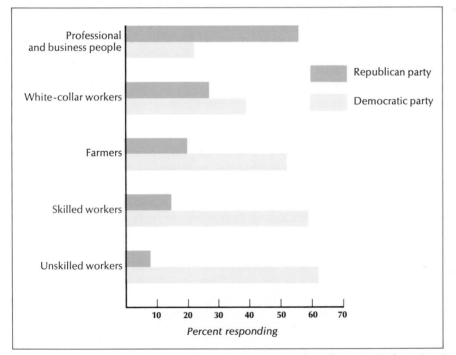

Source: Gallup Poll, February 1965, in Lloyd A. Free and Hadley Cantril, *The Political Beliefs of Americans* (New Brunswick, N.J.: Rutgers University Press, 1967), p. 144.

[15] Lloyd A. Free and Hadley Cantril, *The Political Beliefs of Americans* (New Brunswick, N.J.: Rutgers University Press, 1967), pp. 144, 233.

various categories of voters, only the business and professional group thinks the Republican party serves its interest best. (See Figure 9-3.) These sociological factors in voting represent trends as measured in many past elections. That does not mean that they hold true in a given election. A construction worker who voted Democratic in past years might vote Republican in 1972, for example.

Education. In the past, at least, college graduates have tended to be Republicans rather than Democrats. College-educated voters were solidly in the ranks of the GOP during the elections of Eisenhower, Kennedy, and Nixon between 1952 and 1968. Although Nixon averaged 43.4 percent of the popular vote in 1968, he received 54 percent of the votes of college graduates; by contrast, only 33 percent of voters with grade school education voted for Nixon. (See Table 9-3.)

Religion and Ethnic Background. In a 1964 survey, 65 percent of Jews, 63 percent of Catholics, but only 45 percent of Protestants said they favored the Democratic party.[16] In 1960, Jews, Catholics, and Protestants voted 81, 78, and 38 percent, respectively, for Kennedy. Because Kennedy was the first Roman Catholic to be elected President, the 1960 election was carefully analyzed to assess the effect of his religion on the result. The Michigan Survey Research Center concluded that Kennedy won a "bonus" from Catholics of 4.3 percent of the two-party vote (2,900,000 votes) but lost 6.5 percent (4,400,000 votes) from Protestant Democrats and Independents. His religion cost him a net loss of 2.2 percent, or 1,500,000 popular votes.[17] On the other hand, the heavy Catholic vote in big northern industrial states probably helped him win in the electoral college.[18] It cannot be demonstrated, however, that Kennedy won *because* he was a Catholic. The 1960 election provides an excellent illustration of the relationship of voting and religion.

Various studies have shown that voters of Irish, Italian, Polish, Eastern European, and Slavic descent often favor Democrats. Black Americans who generally had voted Republican until the New Deal shifted away from the party of Lincoln to give approximately 94 percent of their votes to the Democrats in 1964 and 85 percent in 1968. (See Table 9-3.)

Primary Groups. In addition to conventional social groups, voters are influenced by personal contacts with much smaller "primary" groups,

[16] Free and Cantril, *The Political Beliefs of Americans*, p. 234.
[17] Angus Campbell, Philip E. Converse, Warren E. Miller, and Donald E. Stokes, "Stability and Change in 1960: A Reinstating Election," *American Political Science Review*, Vol. 55, No. 2 (June 1961), pp. 269–80. Actual votes were obtained by applying percentages to the 1960 total two-party vote.
[18] See Ithiel de Sola Pool, Robert P. Abelson, and Samuel L. Popkin, *Candidates, Issues, and Strategies* (Cambridge, Mass.: Massachusetts Institute of Technology Press, 1964), pp. 68, 117–18.

such as families, co-workers, and friends. Sometimes these influences may change a voter's mind. However, because people of similar social background tend to associate with one another, primary groups often merely reinforce the political views already held by the voter.

Geography. In general, the Democrats still draw their strength from the big cities of the North and East. Outside the South, voters in rural areas are more likely to be Republicans. In spite of the rural vote, the Democrats can no longer count on the South; from 1952 to 1964 only 49.8 percent of the voters in the South voted Democratic.[19] In 1968, the Republican presidential ticket outpolled the Democrats in the South, 34.6 percent to 30.9 percent, and even ran slightly ahead of George Wallace, who received 34.3 percent of Southern votes.[20]

The suburbs, originally Republican strongholds after the Second World War, are today more of a mixture of Democrats and Republicans. Democratic strength has grown in suburbia as lower-class and middle-class whites have left the cities, but Republicans still dominate many suburbs.

Sex. In the long run, whether voters are men or women does not seem to have a significant influence on how they vote. One study has concluded that women voted Republican 3 to 5 percent more than men during the Eisenhower era.[21] Another survey, however, shows that in 1968 more women voted for Humphrey than for Nixon, and that some women voters shifted to the Democratic candidate at the last minute.[22]

Age. Younger voters are much more likely to be Democrats than to be Republicans. Older voters seem to find the GOP attractive. In presidential elections from 1952 to 1968, the Democrats consistently received a higher proportion of their votes from voters under 30 than from those 50 and over. (See Table 9-3.)

It would be wrong to give too much weight to sociological factors in determining how voters behave. To do so would be to ignore the very important question of people's changing attitudes toward politics. After the

The Psychological Factors

[19] Bureau of the Census, *Statistical Abstract of the United States 1953, 1957, 1961, 1969.* Vote totals are for the eleven states of the Old Confederacy: Alabama, Arkansas, Florida, Georgia, Louisiana, Mississippi, North Carolina, South Carolina, Tennessee, Texas, and Virginia.

[20] *The 1968 Elections* (Washington, D.C.: Research Division, Republican National Committee, 1969), p. 27.

[21] Campbell, Converse, Miller, and Stokes, *The American Voter*, p. 493.

[22] Theodore H. White reports in *The Making of the President 1968* (New York: Atheneum, 1969) that poll-taker Louis Harris detected the women's vote slipping away from Nixon over the peace issue after the Democratic administration ordered a bombing halt in Vietnam six days before the election.

Second World War, a group of scholars at the Survey Research Center of the University of Michigan conducted new studies of voting behavior, concentrating on the psychology of voting—on how individuals perceive and evaluate politics.

The Michigan researchers noted that social characteristics of the population change only slowly over a period of time. The percentage of Catholics or Jews in the United States does not change overnight, for example. Yet, the electorate may behave very differently from one election to the next. Long-term factors such as social class did not seem adequate to explain such sudden shifts; candidates and issues, which change in the short term, provided a more likely explanation: "It seemed clear that the key to the finer dynamics of political behavior lay in the reactions of the electorate to these changes in the political scene." [23]

In measuring voter attitudes, the Survey Research Center team identified three powerful factors: *party identification, candidates, and issues.*

Party Identification. Americans display persistent loyalties to the Democratic or Republican parties. Voters form an attachment to one party or the other and many do not change. Most presidential and congressional elections have taken place within the framework of this basic division in the electorate.

Since the late 1930's there have been substantially more Democrats than Republicans in the United States. (See Table 9-4.) In fact, in 1964, Democrats outnumbered Republicans by *more* than 2 to 1. In 1964, when a sample of adults was asked whether they considered themselves Republicans, Democrats, or Independents, about half identified themselves as

TABLE 9-4

Party Identification Among the American Electorate, 1940–1969

| Year | Percentage of Voters Identifying Themselves as: | | |
	Democrats	Republicans	Independents
1940	42%	38%	20%
1950	45	33	22
1960	47	30	23
1964	53	25	22
1966	48	27	25
June 1968	46	27	27
July 1969	42	28	30

Source: *Gallup Opinion Index,* Report No. 28, October 1967, for data for 1940 through 1966; Congressional Quarterly, *Weekly Report,* August 23, 1968, for data for June, 1968; Gallup Poll, July 18, 1969, for data for July 1969.

[23] Campbell, Converse, Miller, and Stokes, *The American Voter,* p. 17.

Democrats, one-quarter as Republicans, and about one-quarter as Independents. Since 1964, the Democratic edge over the GOP seems to have narrowed.

Scholars at the Survey Research Center have concluded from their analyses of modern election returns, that in the absence of any strong pro-Republican or pro-Democratic short-term factors, a Democratic candidate could expect a "normal vote" of about 53-54 percent of the two-party vote.[24]

Although party identification remains a key factor in American politics, there are some signs that it may be growing somewhat less important. As shown in Table 9-4, the number of people who identified with either of the two major parties dropped from 80 percent in 1940 to 70 percent in 1969, as the number of Independents rose from 20 to 30 percent. Disenchantment with both major parties was widespread in the 1968 election, particularly among college students, but apparently among the general public as well, a Gallup Poll released May 26, 1968, indicated that 42 percent of Americans thought it made "no difference" which party handled the problems facing the nation.

The Candidates. Given the "normal" Democratic advantage and the much higher percentage of those who identify with the Democratic party, how has the Republican party ever won? In 1968, for example, with Democrats outnumbering Republicans 46 to 27 percent, it seemed on paper that Humphrey was likely to beat Nixon.

The answer is that although people may identify with a party, and frequently vote for its candidates, they do not always vote that way. Short-term factors, such as changes in candidates or issues, may cause enough voters to switch from the party they normally favor to have a decisive impact on the outcome of the election. In 1968, Humphrey was associated in the minds of the voters with President Johnson, whose popularity was then very low. Nixon was a known quantity from his years as Vice-President and his 1960 campaign against Kennedy. In addition, the Democrats were split by the preconvention candidacies of Eugene McCarthy and Robert Kennedy. These and other factors combined to override the influence of party identification: a quarter of the Democrats and more than two-thirds of the Independents voted for Nixon or Wallace. And a smaller percentage of Democrats than Republicans voted. The result was victory for the GOP.

Similarly, in 1952 and 1956 Eisenhower easily defeated Stevenson, a Democrat. Eisenhower's personal appeal, his smile, his image as an outstanding military hero of the Second World War, and—in the second election—his popularity as President all helped to offset normal party loyalties.

[24] Campbell, Converse, Miller, and Stokes, *Elections and the Political Order* (New York: Wiley, 1966), pp. 9–39, 86.

Clearly, the personal impression that a candidate makes on the voters may influence the election returns. Thus, dour Calvin Coolidge looked like he had been "weaned on a pickle." Dewey, in the classic phrase of Mrs. Alice Roosevelt Longworth, resembled "the bridegroom on a wedding cake." Stevenson, some thought, was "an egghead." Nixon remained "Tricky Dick" to many strong Democratic partisans. Humphrey "talked too much." Appearance, personality, and popularity of the candidates obviously bear some relation to the number of votes they receive.

The Issues. Two central questions should be asked about the role that issues play in a political campaign: Do voters vote according to their opinions about public issues? If so, do their policy preferences later affect the direction of the government? Both points will be discussed later in this chapter.

For now, it is enough to note that a voter must be aware of the existence of an issue and must have an opinion about it if he is to be motivated by it. Yet, the Michigan researchers concluded that one of the greatest limits on political participation is "sheer ignorance" of major social and economic problems.[25]

If an issue is to affect voting behavior, a voter must not only recognize the issue and have a minimum degree of feeling about it, he must also come to think that one candidate or the other is closer to his own position. Research shows, however, that human beings are highly selective in accepting political messages. If they do not happen to be tuned in to the proper "wavelength," the messages may be received only as so much noise. Increasing the volume may only make the voter flick the "off" switch; like mechanisms that control the body's blood pressure and temperature, this mental fuse "seems to protect the individual citizen from too strenuous an overload of incoming information."[26] Even among voters who do hold opinions on public issues, only 40 to 60 percent can perceive differences between the parties on those issues.[27]

On certain *major* issues, or on issues that affect them directly, the voters do seem to "tune in" and form definite party preferences. We noted in Chapter 8 that most of the time people think the Democrats are more likely to preserve prosperity and the Republicans more likely to keep the peace.

When one group of voters is directly affected by a political issue, its members listen carefully to the political debate. For example, in 1964, Barry Goldwater voted against the first major civil rights bill since Recon-

---

[25] Campbell, Converse, Miller, and Stokes, *The American Voter*, p. 170.
[26] *Ibid.*, pp. 171–72.
[27] *Ibid.*, p. 180.

struction. Because black voters seemed to know in general where Goldwater stood on civil rights, they turned out in unprecedented numbers to vote for Johnson.

VOTING PATTERNS

Although the act of voting represents an individual decision, the result of an election is a group decision. On election day as the sun moves west across the continent's four time zones, the tides and patterns of electoral choice are already beginning to form. The polls have closed in the East as voters in California and along the Pacific coast are still casting their ballots. The results from first precincts in New England trickle in, then more, and as the night wears on, the decision takes shape much as a photograph slowly gains definition in the developing trays of a darkroom.

Sometimes the resulting picture is sharp and its meaning clear; other times it is as blurred as an impressionist painting. Yet, the trained eye analyzing the result of American elections can detect patterns and trends, interrelationships, currents, sectional nuances, and sometimes national meaning.

For national political parties, the prize is control of the Presidency. But party success or failure is measured in terms of states won or lost. Broad voting patterns on the national level can easily be seen by comparing political maps in presidential years, such as those in Figure 9-4 (pp. 334–35). Some political results are geographically dramatic—for example, Franklin D. Roosevelt's 1936 landslide, in which the map is solidly Democratic except for Maine and Vermont.

Control

Bedrock GOP strength in the Midwest is illustrated by the maps of the elections of 1940, 1944, and 1948; in each case the Plains states are a Republican island in a Democratic sea. Or look for a moment at the maps of Republican victories in 1928 and 1952; they bear a strong resemblance to each other because in each case the losing Democratic candidates, Smith and Stevenson, carried a hard core of Southern states. Then look at the 1964 map; it looks a good deal like the other two, but this one charts a Republican defeat. In this election it was Goldwater, the Republican candidate, who carried five states of the Old Confederacy.

The landslide of popular votes in the Roosevelt, Eisenhower, and Johnson victories swept all before it, leaving behind a rather homogeneous map. But the "checkerboard" effect of 1960 and 1968 reflects the fact that the nation was narrowly divided in those elections.

FIGURE 9-4   **Presidential Elections, 1928–1968**

1928

Electoral votes

Smith (D) 87

Hoover (R) 444

1932

Electoral votes

Roosevelt (D) 472

Hoover (R) 59

1936

Electoral votes

Roosevelt (D) 523

Landon (R) 8

1940

Electoral votes

Roosevelt (D) 449

Willkie (R) 82

1944

Electoral votes

Roosevelt (D) 432

Dewey (R) 99

1948

Electoral votes

Truman (D) 303

Dewey (R) 189

Thurmond (States Rights) 39

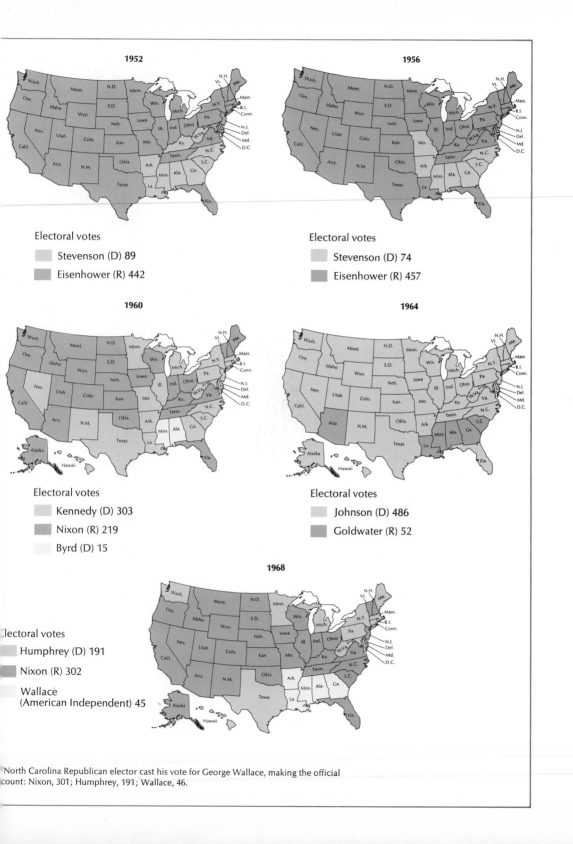

1952

Electoral votes

Stevenson (D) 89

Eisenhower (R) 442

1956

Electoral votes

Stevenson (D) 74

Eisenhower (R) 457

1960

Electoral votes

Kennedy (D) 303

Nixon (R) 219

Byrd (D) 15

1964

Electoral votes

Johnson (D) 486

Goldwater (R) 52

1968

Electoral votes

Humphrey (D) 191

Nixon (R) 302

Wallace
(American Independent) 45

North Carolina Republican elector cast his vote for George Wallace, making the official count: Nixon, 301; Humphrey, 191; Wallace, 46.

Coalitions

The broad outline of the national vote can be shown on a map, but much that is politically significant is less visible. Electoral victories are built not merely on simple geographic foundations; they are also formed by alliances of segments of the electorate, of interest groups and unorganized masses of voters who coalesce behind the winner. Politicians and political scientists are interested, therefore, in *coalitions* of voters.

Roosevelt's New Deal brought together a coalition of the South, the urban North, minority groups, and labor unions. Nixon's winning coalition in 1968 included part of the South, most of the Midwest, the West, whites, Protestants, businessmen, and white-collar workers. Long-term trends in American politics can be traced by analyzing the make-up of winning and losing coalitions.

Congress

In analyzing these alignments, however, congressional as well as presidential voting patterns should be considered. Although, as will be

FIGURE 9-5

Presidential and House Vote, 1928–1968

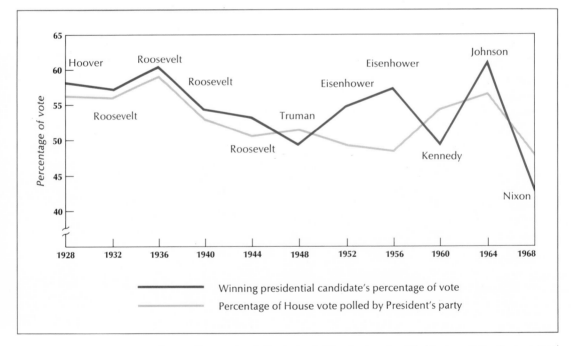

Source: Congressional Quarterly, *Politics in America* (Washington, D.C.: Congressional Quarterly Service, May 1969), p. 41. Reprinted with permission.

shown, the two are linked, in most presidential elections since the New Deal days, the Democratic party has been stronger in congressional elections than in contests for the Presidency. In the period from 1932 to 1970, Republican presidential nominees were elected to three four-year terms in the White House. Yet, during that same period the Republicans controlled Congress for a total of only four years (1947–48 and 1953–54). In presidential election years since the 1940's, the Democratic presidential nominee has run behind the Democratic congressional ticket as a whole in every presidential election except that in 1964.

The entire House of Representatives and a third of the Senate are elected every two years. In a presidential election year, the vote for President usually affects the vote for Congress and may have a powerful effect on state and local offices.

Coattails

The interrelationship between the vote for President and for members of the House is illustrated in Figure 9-5. Although some individual con-

TABLE 9-5

Major Party Lineup: President and Congress, 1932–1970 [1]

Election Year[2]	President and Party		Congress	House	Senate	President's Popular Vote Percentage
				D R	*D R*	
1932	Roosevelt	D	D	313–117	59–36	57.4%
1934	Roosevelt	D	D	322–103	69–25	
1936	Roosevelt	D	D	333– 89	75–17	60.8
1938	Roosevelt	D	D	262–169	69–23	
1940	Roosevelt	D	D	267–162	66–28	54.7
1942	Roosevelt	D	D	222–209	57–38	
1944	Roosevelt	D	D	243–190	57–38	53.4
1946	Truman	D	R	188–246	45–51 *R*	
1948	Truman	D	D	263–171	54–42	49.6
1950	Truman	D	D	234–199	48–47	
1952	Eisenhower	R	R	213–221	47–48 *R*	55.1
1954	Eisenhower	R	D	232–203	48–47	
1956	Eisenhower	R	D	234–201	49–47	57.4
1958	Eisenhower	R	D	283–154	66–34	
1960	Kennedy	D	D	263–174	64–36	49.5
1962	Kennedy	D	D	259–176	68–32	
1964	Johnson	D	D	295–140	67–33	61.1
1966	Johnson	D	D	248–187	64–36	
1968	Nixon	R	D	243–192	58–42	43.4
1970	Nixon	R	D	255–180	54–44	

[1] Does not include independents and minor parties.

[2] Presidential years appear in boldface.

Source: Adapted from Congressional Quarterly, *Politics in America* (Washington, D.C.: Congressional Quarterly Service, 1969), pp. 121–22; 1970 data from Congressional Quarterly, *Weekly Report*, November 6, 1970, p. 2743.

gressmen are strong enough to withstand the tides of presidential voting, usually a President carries into office with him a majority of his own party in the House.

The fortunes of presidential and senatorial candidates are also frequently linked, especially in the more competitive two-party states. The party that wins the White House can usually expect to hold on to its Senate seats in the states carried by its presidential candidate.

In this century only two Presidents have been elected along with a Congress controlled by the opposition party in both wings of the Capitol— Eisenhower in 1956 and Nixon in 1968 (see Table 9-5).

As Table 9-6 shows, the President's party generally loses strength in midterm congressional elections. In off-year elections since 1920, the party in power has lost an average of thirty-five seats in the House; in some of these election years, the party's losses were well above average, as in 1922 and 1938. In unusual circumstances, the party in power may actually gain a few seats or suffer only minor losses.

Why the voters normally reduce the strength of the party of the President they elected two years earlier has been the subject of some scholarly

TABLE 9-6

Midterm Loss in House of Representatives of Party in Control of Presidency, 1922–1970

Size of Loss (Average loss: 35 seats)	Number of Seats Lost or Gained Since Previous Election	Year	Incumbent President
Massive	−75	1922	Harding
	−71	1938	Roosevelt
Above average	−55	1946	Truman
	−49	1930	Hoover
	−47	1958	Eisenhower
	−47	1966	Johnson
	−45	1942	Roosevelt
Below average	−29	1950	Truman
	−18	1954	Eisenhower
	−12[1]	1970	Nixon
	−10	1926	Coolidge
	− 4	1962	Kennedy
	+ 9	1934	Roosevelt

[1] Republicans lost three House seats in special elections in 1969; their net loss on election day in 1970 was nine seats.

Source: Adapted from Congressional Quarterly, Weekly Report, November 6, 1970, p. 2779.

research. It is clear that many less voters turn out in off-years. (See Figure 9-1.) Angus Campbell has suggested that in presidential elections that stimulate a high degree of public interest, the normally "less involved peripheral voters" tend to turn out and vote for the winner, as do many independents and people who switch from the opposing party. In the mid-term elections, the peripheral voters tend to "drop out," and many independents and party-switchers move back to their usual positions. The result is a decline in the proportion of the vote for the President's party.[28]

While the "coattail" effect in presidential voting exists, it can be overstated. In most elections, many candidates of the party that loses nationally are able to survive. This is because voters are selective: some do not vote for all candidates on the ballot; others pick and choose and split their tickets. Sometimes, the "coattail" effect may work in reverse, as when a local candidate runs ahead of the national ticket.[29]

Presidential coattail voting occurred in 1964 when Lyndon Johnson swept into office with an overwhelmingly Democratic Congress. His party made a net gain of thirty-eight seats in the House and two in the Senate. The Republicans were reduced to 140 seats in the House. Yet, because of the ticket-splitters, an extraordinary number of Republicans were able to withstand the Johnson tide. If the congressional voting had exactly paralleled the presidential results, the GOP would have elected only sixty members of Congress. Instead, "In about one district in every four, the voters elected a Republican candidate while returning a Democratic majority in the presidential race. In all, 113 of the 140 Republicans elected to the House won despite a Johnson victory in their district."[30]

Candidates for governor may also ride into the statehouse on a sufficiently long presidential coattail, for there is a relationship between national and state election results in presidential election years. "The great tides of presidential politics," Key observes, "tend to engulf the affairs of states and often to determine the results of state elections."[31] In 1964, after the Johnson triumph, the Democrats controlled thirty-three of the nation's statehouses. By 1968, after Nixon's election, the line-up was thirty-one Republicans and nineteen Democrats. The swings in party control at the gubernatorial level are shown in Table 9-7. Just as voting for members of

[28] Angus Campbell, "Surge and Decline: A Study of Electoral Change," in Campbell, Converse, Miller, and Stokes, *Elections and the Political Order*, pp. 44–45, 59, 61–62.
[29] For an additional discussion of the coattail phenomenon, see Warren E. Miller, "Presidential Coattails: A Study in Political Myth and Methodology," *Public Opinion Quarterly*, Vol. 19, No. 1 (Spring 1955), pp. 353–68.
[30] Milton C. Cummings, Jr., "Nominations and Elections for the House of Representatives," in Milton C. Cummings, Jr., ed., *The National Election of 1964* (Washington, D.C.: The Brookings Institution, 1966), p. 229.
[31] Key, *Politics, Parties, and Pressure Groups*, p. 304.

TABLE 9-7

Party Control of Governorships

Following elections of[1]	Democrats	Republicans
1946	23	25
1948	30	18
1950	23	25
1952	18	30
1954	27	21
1956	28	20
1958	35	14
1960	34	16
1962	34	16
1964	33	17
1966	25	25
1968[2]	19	31
1970	29	21

[1] Presidential years appear in boldface.

[2] The Republican total includes Gov. Agnew of Maryland who was elected Vice-President. Following his resignation, a Democrat was elected by the state legislature to succeed him, making the new line-up: Democrats 20; Republicans 30.

Source: Congressional Quarterly, *Politics in America* (Washington, D.C.: Congressional Quarterly Service, 1969), p. 69; 1970 data from Congressional Quarterly, *Weekly Report*, November 6, 1970, p. 2743.

Congress falls off in midterm elections, voting in gubernatorial contests drops dramatically in off-years.

One reason for the relationship between presidential and gubernatorial voting is that many voters find it convenient to vote a straight

TABLE 9-8

How the Governors Are Elected (as of 1971)

Four-year Term	
Election in presidential years	10
Election in even-numbered years at midterm	26
Election in odd-numbered years	4
Louisiana election held in February of presidential years	1
Total, four-year terms	41
Two-year Term	
Election in even-numbered years	9
Total, all states	50

Source: *Book of the States, 1970–71* (Lexington, Ky.: Council of State Governments, 1970, p. 145.

party ticket by making a single mark or pulling a single lever (in the states where they are permitted to do so). Even so, ticket-splitting between candidates for President and governor is common, particularly in states where there is strong two-party rivalry. In 1968, for example, eight out of thirteen successful Democratic candidates for governor survived a Nixon victory in their state.

A growing number of states have scheduled gubernatorial elections in off-years to insulate themselves from the tides of national presidential politics. (See Figure 9-6.) In 1968, a presidential year, twenty-one governors were elected; but in 1970, an off-year, thirty-five governors were elected. This separation of gubernatorial and presidential elections often helps the candidates of the party that is out of power nationally.

FIGURE 9-6

States Scheduling Gubernatorial Elections
in Nonpresidential Years [1]

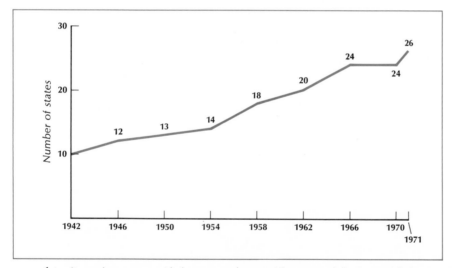

[1] Applies only to states with four-year gubernatorial terms and does not include states that hold elections for Governor in odd-numbered years.

Source: Adapted from Congressional Quarterly, *Politics in America* (Washington, D.C.: Congressional Quarterly Service, May 1969), pp. 148–55. Reprinted with permission.

PRESIDENTIAL '68: A CASE STUDY

The 1968 election amounted to a repudiation of the incumbent Democratic administration, although President Johnson himself was not a candidate. The results were:

	Popular Vote	Electoral Vote	Popular Vote Percentage
Richard M. Nixon (R)	31,785,480	301	43.4%
Hubert H. Humphrey (D)	31,275,165	191	42.7
George C. Wallace (AIP)	9,906,473	46	13.5
Total: [32]	73,211,562	538	99.6%

Nixon's popular vote plurality over Hubert Humphrey was 510,315 votes, or less than 1 percent of the total vote, but his victory represented a dramatic turnabout from 1964 when the American electorate gave Johnson the largest number of votes in history—43.1 million—and the biggest share of the popular vote—61 percent. Nixon carried thirty-two states, Humphrey thirteen, plus the District of Columbia, and Wallace five. In addition to winning the Presidency the Republican party made a net gain of five Senate seats, four congressional seats, and five governorships, and added four more state legislatures to the sixteen they already controlled.

Nixon built his victory with three big states—Ohio, Illinois, and California—but he carried much of the Midwest and the border states and won decisively in the prairie states and the Rocky Mountain states. Humphrey carried New York, Pennsylvania, Michigan, and Texas—but the latter was

[32] Nixon carried states with a total of 302 electoral votes, but one Republican elector in North Carolina voted for Wallace. Popular vote total includes 244,444 votes cast for minor party candidates. Source: Congressional Quarterly, *Weekly Report*, June 6, 1969, back cover.

the *only* Southern state he won. George Wallace carried five states of the Deep South.

These data, however, do not reflect the political crosscurrents at work behind the bare statistics. For example, a major factor in the 1968 election was the third-party movement of George Wallace. Wallace pulled many votes away from both parties by polling the highest percentage of popular votes of any third party candidate since the Progressive candidate who ran in 1924.

Almost 49 percent of Wallace's total vote of 9.9 million came from *outside* of the South. Who were the Wallace voters? Those groups that voted most heavily for Wallace in the 1968 election may be ranked in this order:

Independent voters (25%)
Farmers (20%)
Men (16%)
Protestants (16%)
Whites (15%)
Manual workers (15%)

A fuller breakdown of the groups that voted for Wallace is shown under the Wallace column in Table 9-3.

Which candidate lost the most votes to Wallace—Nixon or Humphrey? One post-election analysis found that in the South, 68 percent of Wallace voters considered themselves nominal Democrats, and 20 percent considered themselves Republicans. Outside the South, the proportions were

46 percent Democratic and 34 percent Republican.[33] It might appear that Humphrey, the Democratic nominee, lost the most votes to Wallace. On the other hand, many Wallace voters might have voted for Nixon if Wallace had not been in the race. As a Michigan Survey Research Center analysis concluded, it is dubious that the Wallace candidacy "by itself changed the major outcome of the election." [34]

Probing beneath the returns in 1968, the Michigan researchers made some interesting discoveries. For example, although Eugene McCarthy's supporters were generally thought of as "doves" opposed to the war in Vietnam, the survey found that among the voters for McCarthy in the New Hampshire primary, those unhappy with the Johnson administration for not pursuing a *harder* line against North Vietnam outnumbered those in favor of withdrawal by nearly 3 to 2.[35]

The war was a major factor in 1968 but so was white reaction to black urban riots. According to the analysis of the Michigan researchers, 97 percent of black voters cast their ballots for Humphrey but only 35 percent of white voters did so. "Thus the presidential vote must have been as sharply polarized along racial lines as at any time during American history." [36]

The study found a further erosion of traditional sectional voting in 1968. Humphrey carried only one state of the "Solid South"; Nixon carried five.

It is reasonable to assume that in 1968 Americans voted against urban riots, crime, and the war in Vietnam. But they also seemed to vote against demonstrators and protesters—those who opposed the Vietnam war *and* sympathized with war protesters made up less than 3 percent of the electorate.[37] In a sense, the voters registered their displeasure with turbulence in any form, both at home and abroad. At the same time, they rejected the wares of George Wallace and remained emphatically within the two-party framework. Above all else, however, in 1968 the American voter exercised his ultimate weapon and turned out the party in power.

THE ELECTORAL SYSTEM

The act of choice performed by the American voter on election day takes place within a legal and structural framework that strongly influences the result.

[33] Philip E. Converse, Warren E. Miller, Jerrold G. Rusk, and Arthur G. Wolfe, "Continuity and Change in American Politics: Parties and Issues in the 1968 Election," *American Political Science Review*, Vol. 63 (December 1969), p. 1091.
[34] *Ibid.*, p. 1092.
[35] *Ibid.*
[36] *Ibid.*, p. 1085.
[37] *Ibid.*, p. 1088.

The electoral system in the United States is not neutral—it affects the dynamics of voting all along the way. Before the voter can step into the voting booth, he must meet a number of legal requirements. The candidates whose names appear on the ballot must have qualified under state law. The form of the ballot may influence the voter's decision—if he is allowed to pull a single lever, for example, he is more likely to vote a straight party ticket than if he must pull many levers to vote that way. How his vote counts in a presidential election is controlled by custom, state law, and the Constitution, for all three affect the workings of the electoral college. In short, the structure, details, and workings of the electoral system affect the people's choice.

The Constitution provides for popular election of members of the House of Representatives, a provision extended to the election of senators by the Seventeenth Amendment, ratified in 1913. In electing a President, the voters in each state actually choose electors, who meet in December of election year and elect the chief executive. In 1969, the House passed a proposed constitutional amendment to abolish the electoral college and provide for direct popular election of the President. The change to direct election would become law only if approved in the Senate and ratified by three-fourths of the states.

Suffrage

Voting is a basic right provided for by the Constitution. Under the Fourteenth Amendment, it is one of the privileges and immunities of national citizenship that the states may not abridge, and that Congress has the power to protect by federal legislation. The *states*, however, set many requirements for voting. State laws in part govern the machinery of choice —residence and other voting requirements, registration, primaries, and the form of the ballot. And state laws regulate political parties.

Until the age of Jackson, voting was generally restricted to men who owned property and paid taxes. Since then, suffrage has gradually been broadened. Most states lifted property requirements in the early nineteenth century. In 1869 Wyoming became the first state to grant women's suffrage, and three other Western states did so in the 1890's. In 1917, the suffragettes began marching in front of the White House; they were arrested and jailed in scenes that foreshadowed the clashes between police and demonstrators in the 1960's. In 1919, Congress passed the Nineteenth Amendment, giving women the vote. It was ratified by the states in time for women to vote in the presidential election of 1920.

The long struggle of black Americans for the right to vote is described in Chapter 5. As we have seen, even though the Fifteenth Amendment specifically gave black citizens the right to vote, it was circumvented when the South regained political control of its state governments following Reconstruction. Poll taxes, all-white primaries, phony literacy tests,

In July 1968, a local civil rights volunteer [in Mississippi] took a crippled black woman and four other black persons (two to register, and two to help the crippled woman) to the clerk's office. The clerk refused to allow the crippled woman to sit while she was registering, instead forcing her to walk from table to table for different parts of the registration process. This took about 15 minutes, the clerk asserting that, after all, the woman would have to stand while voting. . . .

A black candidate . . . in Hinds County was unable to qualify for election because she was unaware of the proper procedures to follow. She allegedly filed her papers to run for office with the town clerk before the filing deadline. Someone, however, told her that she had to take the papers to the Mayor. She returned to the town clerk, obtained her papers from him and took them to the Mayor who informed her that he had nothing to do with the election. She then went back to the clerk's office, but he had left. She returned the next day and gave the papers to the clerk, but was told that she was one day past the deadline and, therefore, the clerk refused to put her on the ballot.

—United States Commission on Civil Rights, *Staff Report,*
May 13, 1969 Municipal Elections in Mississippi.

intimidation, and violence were all effective in disenfranchising blacks in the South. In 1964, the Twenty-fourth Amendment eliminated the last vestiges of the poll tax in federal elections.[38] But blacks still faced many of the other barriers to voting; only 44 percent of voting-age black citizens in the South voted in the 1964 presidential election. The Voting Rights Act of 1965, which was modified and extended in 1970 for another five years, sought to throw the mantle of federal protection around these voters. It was followed by a dramatic increase in blacks voting in the South: 51.6 percent of the black voting-age population took part in the election of 1968. (See Table 9-9.)

Despite the Voting Rights Act, abuses continued, as we pointed out in Chapter 5.[39] Reports by voter-registration workers in the South "show that among blacks there is a deep fear of having welfare checks cut off or being fired from their jobs if they try to vote." [40]

As long as members of any minority group are discouraged from voting anywhere in America, universal suffrage remains a goal rather than a reality.

[38] Only five southern states still imposed a poll tax as a requirement for voting in federal elections when the Twenty-fourth Amendment went into effect on January 23, 1964. Under the Voting Rights Act of 1965, the United States Attorney General filed lawsuits against four of the twenty-seven states still imposing poll taxes in state and local elections. In 1966, the United States Supreme Court ruled in *Harper v. Virginia State Board of Elections*, 383 U.S. 633, that any state poll tax violated the Fourteenth Amendment. The decision outlaws poll taxes at any level of election anywhere in the United States.

[39] See United States Commission on Civil Rights, *Political Participation*, May 1968, and *Staff Report, May 13, 1969 Municipal Elections in Mississippi.*

[40] Congressional Quarterly, *Weekly Report*, August 1, 1969, p. 1413.

TABLE 9-9

The Voting Rights Act of 1965

*Percentage of Voting Age Population
in the South Who Reported Voting
Before and After Passage of the Act*

	1964	*1968*
Black[1]	44.0%	51.6%
White	59.5	61.9

[1] The comparison between 1964 and 1968 figures is not exact because the Census Bureau took the percentage of "Negro" voters in 1968 and of "nonwhite" voters in 1964; the latter is a broader category including American Indians and Asians. However, the difference in 1968 between reported voters in the two categories is only two-tenths of 1 percent.

Source: Adapted from U.S. Bureau of the Census, *Current Population Reports*, Population Characteristics, Series P-20, No. 172, May 3, 1968, p. 3; and No. 192, December 2, 1969, pp. 13, 14.

Residence Requirements. Although progress has been made toward broadening the franchise in the United States, more than 5,000,000 people, or over 5 percent of the voting-age population, were prevented from voting in 1968 by state residence requirements. For the 1968 election, thirty-three states required voters to have lived in the *state* for one year, fifteen states required six months residence, two required three months, and Mississippi required two years. Most states had *county* and *precinct* residence requirements as well.

By 1968, however, thirty states had special rules that often permitted new residents to vote for President and Vice-President even though they failed to meet normal state residence requirements.[41] Then, in 1970, when Congress extended the Voting Rights Act, it included a provision permitting voters in every state to vote in presidential elections after living in the state for thirty days. This uniform federal standard was designed to override state statutes. The law also required states to permit absentee registration and voting.

Literacy and Character Tests. In extending the Voting Rights Act in 1970, Congress suspended the use of literacy and "good character" tests in all states.[42] Historically, literacy tests were used to keep recent immigrants

[41] Of these, eight states had no minimum residence requirements to vote for President and Vice-President. Source of data on residence requirements: U.S. Bureau of the Census, *Current Population Reports*, Population Estimates, Series P-25, No. 406, October 4, 1968.

[42] The provision expires August 6, 1975, unless extended by Congress.

347

and blacks from voting. In 1963, a presidential commission recommended that all states abolish literacy tests as a voting requirement.[43] Two years later, the Voting Rights Act of 1965 suspended literacy tests in the six Southern states and a number of North Carolina counties where less than half the voting-age population had registered or voted in the 1964 election. The law also suspended in those areas tests requiring voters to prove "good moral character."

The 1970 amendments to the Voting Rights Act extended the ban against literacy and character tests to all states. Prior to passage of the law, twelve states—including California and New York—still listed literacy as a requirement for voting. Two states, Idaho and Connecticut, had "good character" tests. Idaho law barred from voting prostitutes, their customers, madams, bigamists, persons of Chinese or Mongolian descent, and persons who "lewdly or lasciviously cohabit together." [44] And Connecticut had a law on its books requiring that voters be of "good moral character."

Although these anachronistic character tests were suspended along with literacy tests by the 1970 act, a number of states retained other odd barriers to voting on the statute books. The laws of nine states, for example, disqualified paupers, and Louisiana law disqualified parents of illegitimate children. The laws of seven states disqualified persons engaging in duels. Such oddities were not affected by the Voting Rights Act or its extension, but they were generally not enforced by the states anyway.

Most states bar insane or mentally incompetent persons and inmates of prisons from voting. Persons convicted of certain types of crimes lose the right to vote under the laws of forty-six states. Some states restore the right to vote upon release from prison, or after a set number of years of imprisonment, or by executive or legislative clemency.

Age. In the same statute that extended the Voting Rights Act of 1965 Congress lowered the voting age to eighteen in all federal, state, and local elections after January 1, 1971. But in December 1970, the Supreme Court ruled that Congress had power to lower the voting age only in *federal* elections. This decision created a dilemma for most states; either they would have to provide two sets of ballots for younger voters—to permit persons between eighteen and twenty-one to vote for President and members of Congress—or they would have to lower the voting age to eighteen in state and local elections. Alternatively, Congress and the states could amend the Constitution to lower the voting age to eighteen in all elections.

With young Americans fighting and dying in Vietnam—but denied

[43] *Report of the President's Commission on Registration and Voting Participation* (Washington, D.C.: U.S. Government Printing Office, 1963), p. 40.
[44] Elizabeth Yadlosky, *Election Laws of the Fifty States and the District of Columbia,* Legislative Reference Service of The Library of Congress, June 5, 1968, p. 305.

the right to vote—pressure to lower the voting age to eighteen built up in the late 1960's. During the Second World War (in 1943), Georgia lowered its voting age to eighteen. By 1970, the voting age was also eighteen in Kentucky and Alaska, and twenty in Hawaii. On November 3, 1970, the voters in four more states—Maine, Nebraska, Montana, and Massachusetts —approved lowering the voting age below twenty-one. In all other states the legal voting age was twenty-one years old and over. Efforts to amend the Constitution to allow people to vote at age eighteen failed to pass Congress in the 1950's and 1960's.

In 1970, support mounted in Congress for lowering the voting age by statute. Opponents of the proposal argued that the Constitution, in Article II, Section 1, left voting age up to the states. But sponsors of a statutory change, relying on a memorandum prepared by Harvard Law Professor Archibald Cox, argued that recent Supreme Court decisions made it clear that Congress could legislate the vote for eighteen-year-olds.[45] Their rationale was this: although the Constitution gives the states general authority to set voting qualifications, in doing so they must not violate the Fourteenth Amendment's bar against state actions that deny people equal protection of the laws. Since persons aged eighteen to twenty-one pay taxes and are subject to military service, Congress could declare that persons in that age bracket were denied equal protection of the laws in states where the voting age was twenty-one. Congress made such a finding in extending and amending the Voting Rights Act in 1970.

While the political effect was unclear, it was estimated that the law would enfranchise approximately 10.5 million persons between the ages of eighteen and twenty-one in time to vote in the 1972 presidential elections. An addition of so large a group of young voters could have an impact on the political system. For example, many students were estranged from the policies of the Nixon administration; a Gallup Poll released late in 1969 reported that 50 percent of college students who were surveyed approved of the President's policies in Vietnam, but 44 percent disapproved.[46] And, according to a Gallup Poll of June 1970, only 18 percent of college students identified themselves as Republicans; 30 percent said they were Democrats, and 52 percent considered themselves independents.[47] But other factors suggested that the lower voting age might not result in dramatic political change. Younger voters have had a low rate of turnout, most of the 10.5 million potential new voters are *not* in college, and party identification is often influenced by parents. Thus the political effects of the lower voting age remained uncertain. A profile of the potential voter between the ages of eighteen and twenty-one is shown in Figure 9-7.

[45] In particular, Professor Cox's argument rested on *Katzenbach v. Morgan*, 384 U.S. 641 (1966).
[46] Gallup Poll, December 17, 1969.
[47] Gallup Poll, the Gallup Opinion Index, Report No. 60, June 1970.

349

FIGURE 9-7

Profile of the Eighteen- Through Twenty-Year-Old Potential Voter

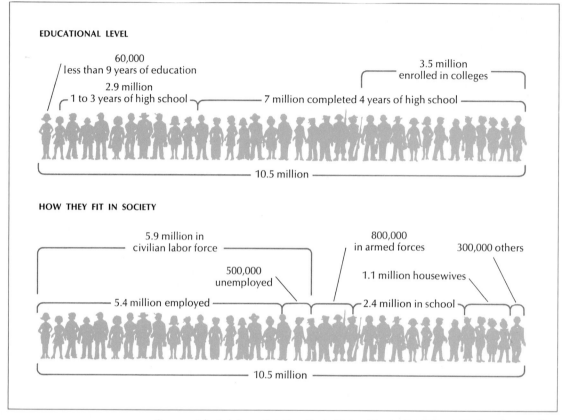

Source: Adapted from the *New York Times,* March 15, 1970, p. E2, based on Gallup Poll data. © 1970 by The New York Times Company. Reprinted by permission.

Citizenship. Only United States citizens can vote. This was not always the case, however. In the nineteenth century, twenty-two states and territories gave aliens the right to vote; the last state to abolish alien voting was Arkansas, in 1926. As a result, the presidential election of 1928 was the first in which only United States citizens could vote. Almost 3,000,000 United States residents could not vote in 1968 because they were not American citizens.

The Nominating Process: Primaries and Conventions

Voting requirements restrict the number of people who can step into the voting booth. The nominating process restricts choice, since the voter is effectively limited to those candidates nominated by parties and placed on the ballot. (Write-in votes, where permitted, seldom elect anyone.)

State laws govern the nominating process and the selection of party leaders. Although the Constitution provides for election of members of Congress and the President, it makes no direct mention of how they shall be nominated and placed on the ballot. In the nineteenth century, candidates for public office were chosen by back-room caucuses of politicians or by local or state conventions. The abuses of that manner of selection led to demands for reform. By 1900, two-thirds of the states had some kind of law providing for primary elections to choose candidates for the general elections. Today, every state but Indiana has provisions for primary elections to choose some candidates who run in statewide contests. Party officials may also be chosen in primaries.

Currently, forty-four states hold direct primaries to nominate candidates for the House and Senate. In the six other states, nominations are by convention, party committee, or by a combination of methods. In states using primaries, the most common form is the closed primary, in which only registered members of a party or persons declaring their affiliation with a party, can vote. Seven states use the open primary, in which any voter may participate and vote for a slate of candidates of one political party. Two states, Washington and Alaska, use the blanket or jungle primary, in which voters can pick and choose among two or more party slates, crossing back and forth to select nominees for each office.

Political parties still hold conventions to nominate candidates for President and Vice-President. As noted in Chapter 7, fourteen states held presidential preference primaries in 1968. But most states choose delegates to national nominating conventions by conventions and committees.

The old Tammany Hall slogan, "Vote Early and Vote Often," still brings nostalgic smiles to the faces of political leaders in New York. But the use of "repeaters" to vote more than once, and of "tombstone" voters (using the names of deceased voters), and similar devices is made much more difficult—although by no means impossible—by modern systems of voter registration.

Voter Registration

Before voters can vote, they must register. Under state laws, when the voter registers, his name is entered on a list of people qualified to vote. He may, if he wishes, declare his party affiliation when he registers. On election day, the registration list may be checked for each voter who comes to the poll to ensure that he is qualified to cast his ballot.

Permanent registration, under which the voter registers only once in his district, prevails in all but a few states. *Periodic* registration, under which the voter must register every year or at other stated intervals, is used in only six states. Two states, North Dakota and Alaska, require no registration.

Like other forms of election machinery, registration procedures can affect the political result. For example, in Idaho door-to-door canvassers remind people to register to vote (the canvassers receive 50 cents per registration); in the 1960 election, 81 percent of adults voted in Idaho, and the figure remained above 70 percent in 1964 and 1968. No doubt other factors were at work in Idaho, but, as a presidential commission concluded: "The average American is far more likely to vote if few barriers stand between him and registration." [48]

Ballots

The secret, so-called Australian, ballot was not adopted by every state in the United States until 1950. Early in American history, the voter often orally announced his vote at the polling place. After the Civil War, this method was replaced by ballots printed by each political party; since the ballots were often of different colors, it was easy to tell how someone voted. Concern over voter intimidation and fraud led to pressure for secret ballots printed by public authorities. By 1900, a substantial number of states had adopted the secret ballot. This ballot has two chief forms:

1. The *party-column ballot*, or Indiana ballot, used in a majority of states, lists the candidates of each party in a row or column, beside or under

[48] *Report of the President's Commission on Registration and Voting Participation*, p. 32.

GENERAL ELECTION 1968

NATIONAL and STATE OFFICES

STRAIGHT PARTY LEVERS
PULL TO RIGHT TILL BELL RINGS

Party	1 For PRESIDENTIAL ELECTORS	2 For United States Senator	3 For Governor	4 For Lieutenant-Governor	5 For Secretary of State	6 For Auditor of State	7 For Treasurer of State	8 For Attorney General	9 For Superintendent of Public Instruction	10 For Reporter of the Supreme and Appellate Courts	11 For Judge of the Supreme Court First District	12 For Judge of the Supreme Court Third District	13 / 14 For Judge of the Appellate Court First District (Vote for two only)		15 / 16 For Judge of the Appellate Court Second District (Vote for two only)	
REPUBLICAN	1A RICHARD M. NIXON / SPIRO T. AGNEW	2A WILLIAM D. RUCKELSHAUS	3A EDGAR D. WHITCOMB	4A RICHARD E. FOLZ	5A WILLIAM N. SALIN	6A TRUDY ALABY ETHERTON	7A JOHN K. SNYDER	8A THEODORE L. SENDAK	9A RICHARD D. WELLS	10A MARILOU WERTZLER	11A NORMAN F. ARTERBURN	12A RICHARD M. GIVAN	13A JOE W LOWDERMILK	14A PATRICK D. SULLIVAN	15A GEORGE R. HOFFMAN, JR.	16A ALLEN SHARP
DEMOCRATIC	1B HUBERT H. HUMPHREY / EDMUND S. MUSKIE	2B BIRCH BAYH	3B ROBERT L. ROCK	4B JAMES W BEATTY	5B STEPHEN W CRIDER	6B BETTY SHEEK	7B EUGENE M. BRINER	8B JOHN J. DILLON	9B WEARLE R. DONICA	10B HELEN COREY	11B ADDISON M. BEAVERS	12B THOMAS J. FAULCONER	13B JONATHAN J. ROBERTSON	14B HARRY L. ZERBE	15B FREDERICK C. WORK	16B ALAN E. YERGIN
GEORGE C. WALLACE	1C GEORGE C. WALLACE / S. MARVIN GRIFFIN	2C	3C	4C	5C	6C	7C	8C	9C	10C	11C	12C	13C	14C	15C	16C
PROHIBITION	1D E. HAROLD MUNN, SR. / ROLLAND E FISHER	2D L. EARL MALCOM	3D MELVIN E. HAWK	4D JAMES C. HARKLESS	5D GLENN DECKARD	6D A. TERRY CRALL	7D A.J. YOUMANS	8D	9D MARTHA SHELLEY	10D W. KENDRICK GRIFFIN	11D	12D	13D	14D	15D	16D
SOCIALIST-WORKER	1E FRED HALSTEAD / PAUL BOUTELLE	2E RALPH LEVITT														

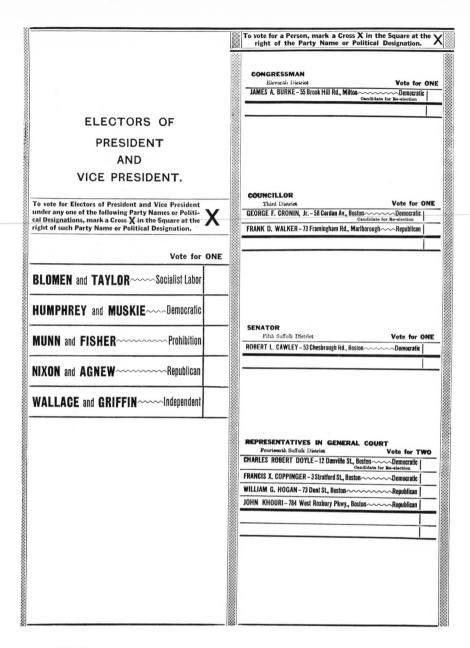

To vote for a Person, mark a Cross **X** in the Square at the right of the Party Name or Political Designation. **X**

ELECTORS OF

PRESIDENT

AND

VICE PRESIDENT.

To vote for Electors of President and Vice President under any one of the following Party Names or Political Designations, mark a Cross **X** in the Square at the right of such Party Name or Political Designation. **X**

Vote for ONE

BLOMEN and **TAYLOR**~~~~Socialist Labor

HUMPHREY and **MUSKIE**~~~~Democratic

MUNN and **FISHER**~~~~Prohibition

NIXON and **AGNEW**~~~~Republican

WALLACE and **GRIFFIN**~~~~Independent

CONGRESSMAN

Eleventh District — Vote for ONE

JAMES A. BURKE – 55 Brook Hill Rd., Milton~~~~Democratic
Candidate for Re-election

COUNCILLOR

Third District — Vote for ONE

GEORGE F. CRONIN, Jr. – 58 Cerdan Av., Boston~~~~Democratic
Candidate for Re-election

FRANK D. WALKER – 73 Framingham Rd., Marlborough~~~~Republican

SENATOR

Fifth Suffolk District — Vote for ONE

ROBERT L. CAWLEY – 53 Chesbrough Rd., Boston~~~~Democratic

REPRESENTATIVES IN GENERAL COURT

Fourteenth Suffolk District — Vote for TWO

CHARLES ROBERT DOYLE – 12 Danville St., Boston~~~~Democratic
Candidate for Re-election

FRANCIS X. COPPINGER – 3 Stratford St., Boston~~~~Democratic

WILLIAM G. HOGAN – 73 Dent St., Boston~~~~Republican

JOHN KHOURI – 784 West Roxbury Pkwy., Boston~~~~Republican

FIGURE 9-8

Sample Ballots

Above: The office-column, or Massachusetts ballot, groups candidates by office, making straight-ticket voting impossible. Shown is a paper ballot used in Massachusetts in the 1968 election.
Left: The party-column, or Indiana ballot, used in most states, lists candidates alongside the party emblem. Usually, the arrangement allows a person to vote a straight ticket by pulling a single lever—in this case, the large handle at left. Illustration shows face of an Indiana voting machine in 1968.

the party emblem. In most cases, the voter can make one mark at the top of the column, or pull one lever, and thus vote for all the party's candidates for various offices. This ballot encourages straight-ticket voting.

2. The *office-column ballot*, or Massachusetts ballot, groups candidates according to the office for which they are running—all the presidential candidates of all the parties appear in one column or row, for example.

Research has demonstrated that the form of the ballot may influence the vote. Among independent voters, one study found that a party-column ballot increased "straight ticket" voting by 60 percent.[49]

The first voting machine was used in 1892 by the city of Lockport, New York. By the presidential election of 1960, an estimated 50 percent of votes were recorded by machine. By 1968, twenty-one states used machines statewide or in most areas, twenty-six states used voting machines in some areas, and only three states continued to use only paper ballots.

Counting the Votes

On election night, the results in each state are tabulated by state and local election officials and reported to the nation through the News Election Service, a cooperative pool of the three major television networks and the Associated Press and United Press International, the two major wire services.

The drama of election night is in a sense entirely artificial. As the night wears on, one candidate appears to lead, then fall behind and perhaps forge ahead again. Actually, once the polls close, the popular vote result is already recorded inside the ballot boxes and voting machines.

In recent years the nation has no longer had to wait until the votes were actually counted to know the results of some elections, because the television networks have developed systems of *projecting* the vote with the aid of electronic computers. CBS used its Vote Profile Analysis (VPA) for the first time in the 1964 election and NBC used a similar system. NBC predicted a victory for President Johnson at 6:48 P.M. EST, with only 2 percent of the vote counted. In 1968, however, the election was so close that neither the computers nor the commentators were willing to make any predictions for many hours. In some instances the computers have predicted the wrong winners in state contests.

The computerized vote projection systems are based on analysis of key precincts in selected areas; past election data about the sample precincts is coded and stored in the computers and compared with actual returns as they come in on election night. As it processes the data flowing in, the computer is able to make a statistical forecast of the probable outcome. Some candidates have complained that televising election projections

---

[49] Campbell, Converse, Miller, and Stokes, *The American Voter*, p. 285.

I know every man, woman, and child in the Fifteenth District, except them that's been born this summer—and I know some of them, too. I know what they like and what they don't like, what they are strong at and what they are weak in, and I reach them by approachin' at the right side.

For instance, here's how I gather in the young men. I hear of a young feller that's proud of his voice, thinks that he can sing fine. I ask him to come around to Washington Hall and join our Glee Club. He comes and sings, and he's a follower of Plunkitt for life. Another young feller gains a reputation as a baseball player in a vacant lot. I bring him into our baseball club. That fixes him. You'll find him workin' for my ticket at the polls next election day. . . . I don't trouble them with political arguments. I just study human nature and act accordin'.

—Boss Plunkitt, in William L. Riordon, *Plunkitt of Tammany Hall*

while the polls are still open on the West Coast or other areas may influence the voters, although little concrete evidence of this has yet come to light.

With so much at stake on election night, it is not surprising that from time to time there are charges of electoral fraud, even in presidential elections.

Fraud

In 1960, after John Kennedy's narrow popular-vote victory over Richard Nixon, some Republicans charged that there had been election frauds in Cook County, Illinois and in Texas; if Kennedy had failed to carry these two states, Nixon would have won in the electoral college. Kennedy carried Illinois by a mere 8,858 votes, but his margin in Texas was much larger, 46,257 votes. Nixon himself did not ask for an investigation or a recount.

It may well be that in the age of the computer, some form of electronic voting system will be developed so that votes can be recorded and tallied quickly with a minimum possibility of tampering.

The Constitution does not provide for the popular election of the President.[50]

The Electoral College

Instead, it provides that each state "shall appoint, in such manner as the legislature thereof may direct," electors equal in number to the representatives and senators that each state has in Congress. Instead of voting directly for President, an American in casting his ballot votes for a slate of electors that is normally pledged to the presidential candidate of the

---

[50] At this writing, the proposed constitutional amendment to provide for direct, popular election of the President and Vice-President had not been approved by both houses of Congress and ratified by three-fourths of the states. Were this to occur, of course, the electoral college machinery discussed in this section would be abolished.

voter's choice. Many voters are unaware that they are voting for electors because their names do not even appear on the ballot in thirty-five states. The slate that receives the most votes meets in the state capital in December of a presidential election year and casts its ballots. Each state sends the results to Washington, where the electoral votes are officially counted in a joint session of Congress on January 6. The candidate with a majority of the electoral votes is elected President. If no one receives a majority, the House of Representatives must choose the President, with each state delegation in the House having one vote. If there is no majority vote for Vice-President, the Senate makes the choice.[51]

Custom, not the Constitution, is the reason that electors are chosen in each state by popular vote. In the first four presidential elections, state legislatures chose the electors in most cases. South Carolina was the last state to switch to popular election, in 1860. Although there is hardly any possibility that a state would discontinue popular election of electors, legally, a state may select them any way it wishes.[52]

The framers of the Constitution had great difficulty in agreeing on the best way to elect the President. Some favored direct election, but others thought this would give an advantage to the more populous states. The provision for presidential electors represented a compromise between the big and little states. Furthermore, "only a few delegates to the Constitutional Convention felt that American democracy had matured sufficiently for the choice of the President to be entrusted directly to the people." [53]

Over the decades, the electoral college has been severely criticized as an old-fashioned device standing between the people and their choice of a President. The criticism may be summarized as follows:

1. The "winner-take-all" feature of the electoral college means that if a candidate carries a state by even one popular vote, he wins *all* of the state's electoral votes, distorting the will of the voters because the minority votes cast within a state count for nothing. As a result, a President may be elected who has lost the popular vote. This actually happened in the elec-

[51] The House chose the President twice, after the election of 1800, when it elected Jefferson, and following the election of 1824, when it elected John Quincy Adams. The Senate chose the Vice-President only once, when it elected Richard M. Johnson of Kentucky to that office in 1837. In the case of a tie in the presidential balloting in the House that is not resolved by Inauguration Day, January 20, the Vice-President-elect becomes acting President. Since the Senate chooses the Vice-President in the event of an electoral vote deadlock, the Senate, in effect, would elect the new President. On Inauguration Day, if no President or Vice-President is qualified, the Presidency would go to the Speaker of the House, or next to the president pro tempore of the Senate, or down through all the Cabinet posts under the Presidential Succession Act.
[52] In fact, in 1969 Maine changed its system of choosing presidential electors; under a new state law, two electors are chosen at large and two are chosen from Maine's two congressional districts. Previously, all states elected electors on a statewide basis.
[53] Neal R. Peirce, *The People's President* (New York: Simon and Schuster, 1968), p. 41.

tions of John Quincy Adams in 1824, Rutherford B. Hayes in 1876, and Benjamin Harrison in 1888.

2. The system, with its winner-take-all feature, gives an advantage to the populous, Northern, and generally liberal states that have many electoral votes and to minority groups that constitute powerful voting blocs within those states. At the same time, very small states are overrepresented because every state has a minimum of three electoral votes.

3. Electors are not constitutionally bound to vote for the candidate to whom they are pledged. In 1968, Dr. Lloyd W. Bailey, an ophthalmologist from Rocky Mount, North Carolina, voted for George Wallace even though he was a Nixon elector. Since 1820 nine electors have defected in similar fashion.

In 1968, major party supporters feared that George Wallace would receive enough electoral votes to deprive Nixon or Humphrey of a majority; the third-party candidate might then be in a position to win concessions in return for his electoral votes, or to force the election into the House of Representatives, where he might strike further bargains.

The closeness of the 1960 election, the Wallace campaign in 1968, and other factors, all combined to create new pressures for electoral college reform. Past debates had centered on plans to choose presidential electors by district (as congressmen are chosen), or to award each candidate electoral votes in proportion to his share of the popular vote within each state. In the 1960's, however, the idea of *direct election* of the President gained in popularity. It seemed closest to the principle of "one man, one vote," enunciated by the Supreme Court.

Direct Election of the President

In September 1969, the House passed a proposed constitutional amendment to abolish the electoral college and substitute direct election of the President and Vice-President. Under the amendment, if no candidate received 40 percent of the popular vote, a runoff election would be held between the top two presidential candidates. Congress was authorized to set the date for the election and for any runoff. The states would continue to run the election machinery, but Congress reserved the right to set uniform nationwide residence requirements for voting in presidential elections. Although the states would still set the qualifications for candidates to appear on the ballot, Congress for the first time would have the power to override and change the relevant state laws. This provision was included to ensure that candidates of major parties would appear on the ballot in every state—if only to avoid the threat of intervention by Congress. As under the present system, however, minor parties could find it difficult to qualify for the ballot in many states.

357

There is no official, national popular-vote count under the electoral college system.[54] Under the direct-election amendment, Congress would by law set the time, the place, and the way in which the presidential vote would be totaled and the result officially announced. Finally, Congress would have power to provide by law for replacing candidates for President and Vice-President who died before election, before a runoff, or after their election.

Critics of the direct-election plan argued that it would encourage the growth of splinter parties. The result, they warned, could be fragmentation of American politics and destruction of the two-party system.[55] And the two-party system, these critics have contended, is a vital instrument in resolving social conflict and managing the transfer of power.

Those opposed to direct election also argued that the electoral college is compatible with the federal system and that direct election would (1) increase the temptation of fraud in vote-counting, leading to prolonged recounts and chaos, (2) rob minority groups of their influence in big electoral-vote states, and (3) tempt states to ease voter qualification standards in order to fatten the voter rolls. In 1970, a filibuster by opponents of direct election prevented the Senate from voting on the proposal.

One Man,
One Vote

During the 1960's, the Supreme Court ruled in a series of *reapportionment* decisions that each person's vote should be worth as much as another's. Yet, the decisions were controversial, for they upset the balance of political power between urban and rural areas in the United States. The result was a concerted but unsuccessful effort in Congress and the states to amend the Constitution to overturn the Supreme Court rulings.

The State Legislatures. All votes are equal when each member of a legislative body represents the same number of people. In the United States, however, successive waves of immigration and the subsequent growth of the cities resulted by the turn of the century in glaring inequalities in the population of urban and rural state legislative districts. The 1920 census showed that for the first time more Americans lived in urban than in rural areas. The rural state legislators, representing sparsely populated districts, passed state laws to maintain their advantage over the cities. By 1960, in every state, the largest legislative district was at least twice as populous as the smallest district.

[54] The Constitution and federal law provide only for the counting of *electoral* votes. Every four years, the secretaries of state certify each state's popular vote for President and Vice-President and forward the totals to the Clerk of the House, who publishes the figures for the convenience of Congress. The total is in no way a legal or official count of the national popular vote.
[55] See, for example, Irving Kristol and Paul Weaver, "A Bad Idea Whose Time Has Come," *New York Times Magazine*, November 23, 1969.

In Tennessee that year, the smallest district in the lower house had a population of 3,400 and the largest 79,000. Obviously, the people in the biggest district were not equally represented with the voters in the smallest. Because the legislature had refused to do anything about it, a group of urban residents, including a county judge named Charles W. Baker, sued Joe C. Carr, Tennessee's secretary of state. The case went to the United States Supreme Court, which in 1946 had refused to consider a case involving malapportionment in Illinois (*Colgrove v. Green*). Justice Felix Frankfurter, in that earlier opinion, ruled that the Supreme Court "ought not to enter this political thicket." [56]

But in 1962, in *Baker v. Carr*,[57] the Supreme Court ruled in favor of the voters who had challenged the established order in Tennessee. In 1964, in *Reynolds v. Sims*,[58] the Supreme Court made it clear that the Fourteenth Amendment requires that seats in *both* houses of a state legislature be based on population. Second, the Court ruled that although legislative districts might not be drawn with "mathematical exactness or precision" they must be based "substantially" on population. The Court had laid down the principle of "one man, one vote."

The reapportionment decisions had an immediate effect on the political map of America. The legislature of Oregon had reapportioned on the basis of population in 1961; between the *Baker v. Carr* ruling in 1962 and 1970, the other forty-nine states took similar steps.

Conservative and rural forces reacted strongly to the Supreme Court rulings. In 1965 and 1966, the late Senator Everett M. Dirksen proposed a constitutional amendment to allow a state to apportion one house of its legislature on a basis other than population. Although the "Dirksen amendment" received majority support in the Senate both years, it fell short of the needed two-thirds majority. Undaunted, Dirksen and his backers encouraged the states to petition Congress for a constitutional convention, an alternate method of amending the Constitution that has never been used (see Chapter 2). On April 30, 1969, Iowa became the thirty-third state to pass a resolution requesting a constitutional convention, one short of the necessary two-thirds of the states. Because of doubt over the legality of many of the state petitions and widespread concern over what changes a convention might make in the Constitution, there was powerful opposition to the effort to convene what would be the first constitutional convention since the one that took place in Philadelphia in 1787.

Congressional Districts. It was not just the state legislatures that were malapportioned prior to the mid-1960's. Although the *average* con-

[56] *Colgrove v. Green*, 328 U.S. 549 (1946).
[57] 369 U.S. 186.
[58] 377 U.S. 533.

gressional House district had a population of 410,000 in the 1960's, the actual population of these districts varied greatly. For example, in Georgia, one rural district had 272,000 people, but the Fifth Congressional District (Atlanta and its suburbs) numbered 823,000 people. In 1964, in the case of *Wesberry v. Sanders*,[59] the Supreme Court ruled that this disparity in the size of Georgia congressional districts violated the Constitution. Within two years, twenty-seven states with a total of 258 congressional districts had redistricted to conform to the Court ruling.

Under the Constitution and federal law, Congress determines the total *size* of the House of Representatives, which grew from 65 members in 1790 to 435 in 1912. Congress has kept the House membership at 435 since then, although it could change that semipermanent figure.[60] After each ten-year census, federal law requires that the *number of representatives for each state* be reapportioned on the basis of population. If a state gains or loses congressmen, the state legislature *redistricts* by drawing new boundary lines for its House districts.[61] By 1972, for example, California would gain a total of five seats as a result of the 1970 census, making its House delegation the largest in the nation. Previously New York was the largest. The average population of House districts will rise to around 470,000 in the early 1970's.

As a result of the reapportionment revolution of the 1960's, rural areas had been expected to lose power to the cities. But because of the population exodus from the cities, the *suburbs* have proved to be the areas that have gained the most from reapportionment of state legislatures and congressional districts. As far back as 1965, an official of the National Municipal League noted that almost half of the big cities in the United States had less population than their suburbs: "No center city contains the necessary 50 percent of the people to dominate the state. . . . The U.S. is an urban nation, but it is not a big-city nation. The suburbs own the future." [62]

Because the suburbs have grown much faster than the nation as a whole, in the 1970's, for the first time, there are expected to be more members of the House of Representatives from the suburbs than from the cities.

As the political battle shifts to the suburbs, Gerald Pomper has predicted, "Suburban power will influence the way both politics and government are conducted." [63] In New York and New Jersey, Pomper observes,

---

[59] *Wesberry v. Sanders*, 376 U.S. 1 (1964).
[60] The membership of the House increased only briefly, to 436 in early 1959 and to 437 from late 1959 through 1962, as a result of the admission to statehood of Hawaii and Alaska.
[61] In a few instances, the new lines have been drawn by federal courts.
[62] William J. D. Boyd, in Congressional Quarterly, *Weekly Report*, November 21, 1969, p. 2342.
[63] Gerald M. Pomper, "Census '70: Power to the Suburbs," *Washington Monthly*, May 1970, p. 23.

FIGURE 9-9

Population Trends in Rural, City, and Suburban Areas

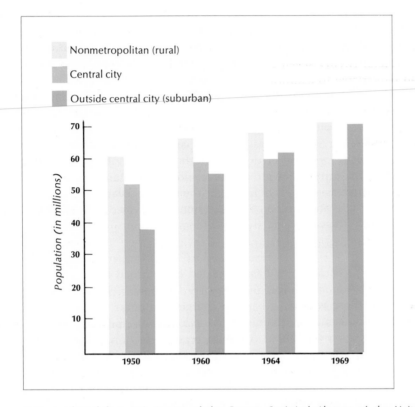

Source: Adapted from U.S. Bureau of the Census, *Statistical Abstract of the United States 1969*, p. 18, and Congressional Quarterly, *Weekly Report*, November 21, 1969, p. 2346. Reprinted with permission.

suburban-oriented legislatures have turned down programs to aid city dwellers. The New York State legislature, for example, declined to provide significant help to the New York City subway system, which carries 2 million riders a day, but underwrote the losses of the Long Island Railroad, which carries 100,000 suburban commuters each day.

One result of the decline in rural power in state legislatures through reapportionment has been a liberalization of many state abortion and divorce laws and of obscenity and pornography statutes, as well as abolition of the death penalty in more states. But thus far, the chief impact of reapportionment has been to reward suburbia. Combined with population trends, reapportionment means that the suburbs will continue to gain political representation at the expense of the central cities and rural areas.

Who Won the Election?

Who won the election? In the United States, with its federal system, the question must be asked on all levels— national (the Presidency, Congress), state (state houses and state legislatures), and local (county and city governments). Since candidates of both major parties win these offices, the outcome of American elections is mixed. Which party won or lost is not as simple as it might appear. In 1968, for example, the Republicans captured the White House and a majority of the state houses, but the Democrats retained control of both houses of Congress and a majority of seats in the state legislatures. In 1970, the Democrats regained a majority of the governors' chairs while retaining control of Congress and increasing their numbers in the state legislatures.

Yet, there are differences in elections; the voice of the voter speaks more clearly in some years than in others.

Types of Elections

V. O. Key, Jr., has suggested three broad types of presidential elections.[64] A *landslide* for the out-party "expresses clearly a lack of confidence in those who have been in charge of affairs." Or, the voters may approve an incumbent administration in a vote of confidence that amounts to a *reaffirmation* of support. A third type of election, a *realignment*, may return a party to power, but with the support of a new coalition of voters. When the realignment within the electorate is "both sharp and durable," Key suggests that a "critical" election has taken place, one that results in "profound readjustments" in political power.[65]

Angus Campbell and his associates have classified presidential elections in somewhat similar fashion: they relate the election returns to the basic pattern of party identification. They speak of *maintaining elections,* which reflect the standing party identification of the voters; of *deviating elections,* in which the majority party (according to party identification) is defeated in a temporary reversal; and of *realigning elections,* which may lead to a basic shift in the party identification of the electorate.[66]

The Meaning of Elections

Much of our discussion in this chapter has focused on the wide variety of reasons, sociological and psychological, that may cause different voters to vote for the same political candidate. Regardless of these indi-

[64] Key, *Politics, Parties, and Pressure Groups,* pp. 520–36.
[65] V. O. Key, Jr., "A Theory of Critical Elections," *Journal of Politics,* Vol. 17 (February 1955), pp. 3–18.
[66] Campbell, Converse, Miller, and Stokes, *The American Voter,* pp. 531–38.

vidual reasons, the overall election verdicts have broad meaning for the political system as a whole.

First of all, elections decide which individuals shall govern. Voters may not be sharply ideological, but the leaders of the two major parties often do hold very different opinions on public issues. Who wins can make a difference—in the philosophy and caliber of men appointed to the Supreme Court by the President and approved by Congress, to take but one example.

Second, elections can have important consequences for the broad direction of public policy. Naturally, many specific questions are not settled by elections, but 1936 was rather clearly a broad approval of the New Deal, just as 1964 was a repudiation of extremely conservative Republicanism. The series of four Democratic presidential victories from 1936 to 1948 ("maintaining elections" in Angus Campbell's terminology, "reaffirmations of support" in Key's classification) served to ensure that most of the policy innovations of the New Deal would become established public programs.

The voice of the people is not always so clear. The meaning of a particular election, the "mandate" of the people to the President on specific issues, may be subject to varying interpretations. As we have noted, many different people vote for the same candidate for different reasons; this candidate, once elected, may make decisions that cause some of his voters to feel misled. For example, in 1964, Americans voted for a President who seemed to promise, among other things, to avoid an Asian war, but did not.[67] In 1968, some voters retaliated by voting Republican.

Elections do leave elected officials with a great deal of flexibility in governing. Yet, elections also often set broad guidelines within which decision-makers must stay—or risk reprisal by the voters.

It is true that most American elections tend to be fundamentally centrist, or middle-of-the-road in character. Parties and candidates compete for the center ground in American politics because that is where the parties believe that the majority of voters are.[68] For this reason candidates do not as a rule endorse radical programs of social change. Yet, the New Deal marked a considerable departure in government's approach to America's problems. Since 1932, government has intervened in the social and economic

Continuity
and Change

[67] See Chapter 7, p. 267. At the start of the 1964 campaign there were 16,000 American troops in Vietnam as "advisers." Three months after his election, President Johnson ordered the bombing of North Vietnam. By June of 1965, U.S. troops were admittedly fighting, not advising. By 1968, more than 500,000 American troops were in Vietnam.
[68] For a detailed statement of the view that elections are won and lost "in the center," see Richard M. Scammon and Ben J. Wattenberg, *The Real Majority* (New York: Coward-McCann, 1970). The Scammon-Wattenberg book may have influenced the electoral strategy of some political candidates in 1970, particularly Democrats but also some Republicans, and campaign planning for the 1972 presidential election.

363

order to an unprecedented extent. Its role as social regulator has been approved by the voters in elections over four decades. Elections do at times set broad parameters for change.

"The people," Key has observed, "may not be able to govern themselves but they can, through an electoral uprising, throw the old crowd out and demand a new order, without necessarily being capable of specifying exactly what it shall be. An election of this type may amount, if not to revolution, to its functional equivalent." [69]

Besides establishing a framework for change, elections also provide continuity and a sense of political community, for they are links in a chain that bind one generation of voters to the next. Every four years, the voters come together in an act of decision that is influenced by the past and present, but designed to shape the future.

[69] Key, *Politics, Parties, and Pressure Groups*, pp. 522–23.

SUGGESTED READING

Berelson, Bernard R., Lazarsfeld, Paul F., and McPhee, William N. *Voting: A Study of Opinion Formation in a Presidential Campaign* * (University of Chicago Press, 1954). An influential study of how voters decide for whom they will vote. Based on a series of interviews with about 1,000 residents of Elmira, New York, during the Truman-Dewey presidential contest of 1948.

Campbell, Angus, Converse, Philip E., Miller, Warren E., and Stokes, Donald E. *The American Voter* (Wiley, 1960). (An abridged paperback edition was published in 1964.) A landmark study of voting behavior, based on interviews with national samples of the American electorate conducted by the Survey Research Center of the University of Michigan. Among other topics, the book analyzes relationships between political attitudes and the vote, the nature and patterns of party identification in the electorate, and social and economic factors that may affect the vote.

Campbell, Angus, Converse, Philip E., Miller, Warren E., and Stokes, Donald E. *Elections and the Political Order* (Wiley, 1966). Scholars at the University of Michigan Survey Research Center present additional research on American voting behavior. Several chapters analyze how voters' behavior is related to the functioning of the political system generally.

Flanigan, William H. *Political Behavior of the American Electorate* (Allyn and Bacon, 1968). Paperback. Useful, concise analysis and summary of research on how and why Americans vote.

Key, V. O., Jr. *The Responsible Electorate* * (Harvard University Press, 1966). An examination of American voting behavior in presidential elections, based primarily on an analysis of Gallup Poll data from 1936 to 1960. Key argues that the voters' views on issues and government policy are quite closely related to how they vote in presidential elections.

Key, V. O., Jr. *Southern Politics in State and Nation* * (Knopf, 1949). A classic study of the politics of the South. Analyzes why the Democratic party dominated that region for nearly three generations after the Civil War, and what the political consequences were.

Lazarsfeld, Paul F., Berelson, Bernard, and Gaudet, Hazel. *The People's Choice: How the Voter Makes Up His Mind in a Presidential Campaign* * (Columbia University Press, 1968). (Originally published in 1944.) A classic in the study of voting behavior, based on a series of interviews with potential voters in Erie County, Ohio, during the Roosevelt-Willkie presidential contest of 1940. The book stresses the relationship between the voters' socioeconomic status and how they voted.

Lubell, Samuel. *The Hidden Crisis in American Politics* (W. W. Norton, 1970). An examination of American politics and political attitudes at the beginning of the 1970's, based on extensive interviewing of American voters by the author, supplemented by analysis of precinct election returns. Includes discussions of voter support for George Wallace in 1968 and the political consequences of the growing black urban population.

Milbrath, Lester W. *Political Participation: How and Why Do People Get Involved in Politics* * (Rand McNally, 1965). A comprehensive general analysis of who participates in politics and why.

Peirce, Neal R. *The People's President* * (Simon and Schuster, 1968). A detailed study of the history of the electoral college and its effect in past presidential elections. Argues the case for abolishing the electoral college and electing the President directly by popular vote.

Phillips, Kevin P. *The Emerging Republican Majority* * (Arlington House, 1969). A controversial study of recent voting trends. Argues that a new Republican party coalition is likely to replace the Democratic party coalition as majority party in national elections following 1968.

Scammon, Richard M., and Wattenberg, Ben J. *The Real Majority* (Coward-McCann, 1970). A lively analysis of current American political attitudes and voting patterns. Argues that the majority of American voters are "unyoung, unpoor, and unblack," and contends that candidates who take moderate positions on issues—close to the "political center"—are more likely to be elected than candidates who take more extreme positions, on either the right or the left.

* Available in paperback edition

PART THREE

The Policy Makers

10

The President

The day before he took the oath of office as thirty-fifth President of the United States, John F. Kennedy called upon President Eisenhower at the White House.

"There are no easy matters that will ever come to you as President," Eisenhower told the younger man. "If they are easy, they will be settled at a lower level."

The accuracy of this parting advice had come home to President Kennedy when he told the story almost two years later during an interview over the three major television networks.[1] Kennedy's conversation with three newsmen in his Oval Office provided an unusual insight into the dimensions and perspectives of the American Presidency. When asked how the job had matched his conception of it, Kennedy replied:

[1] "After Two Years—a Conversation With the President," Television and Radio Interview, December 17, 1962, in *Public Papers of the Presidents of the United States, John F. Kennedy, 1962* (Washington, D.C.: U.S. Government Printing Office, 1963), pp. 889–904.

"Well, I think in the first place the problems are more difficult than I had imagined they were. Secondly, there is a limitation upon the ability of the United States to solve these problems."

Although Kennedy was speaking of world problems, the same tone was apparent in his remarks about the President's domestic power. "The fact is," he said, "I think the Congress looks more powerful sitting here than it did when I was there in the Congress. . . . when you are in Congress you are one of a hundred in the Senate or one of 435 in the House, so that the power is so divided. But from here I look at a Congress, and I look at the collective power of the Congress . . . and it is a substantial power."

In addition, Kennedy, an activist President, impatient to get things done, fumed at the bureaucracy: "You know, after I met Mr. Khrushchev in Vienna and they gave us an *aide-mémoire*, it took me many weeks to get our answer out through the State Department. . . . this is a constant problem in various departments. . . . you can wait while the world collapses."

As Kennedy was well aware, an American President bears enormous responsibility in the nuclear age. In the event of an atomic war, Kennedy observed in the interview, "that is the end, because you are talking about Western Europe, the Soviet Union, the United States, of 150 million fatalities in the first 18 hours. . . . one mistake can make this whole thing blow up."

This candid discussion of the Presidency illuminated both the power and limits of the office. It pointed up the fact that the President is not merely the symbolic and actual leader of more than 200,000,000 Americans,

A PRESIDENT LOOKS TO THE FUTURE

It is not by any means the sole task of the Presidency to think about the present. One of the chief obligations of the Presidency is to think about the future. We have been, in our one hundred and fifty years of constitutional existence, a wasteful nation, a nation that has wasted its natural resources and, very often, wasted its human resources.

One reason why a President of the United States ought to travel throughout the country and become familiar with every State is that he has a great obligation to think about the days when he will no longer be President, to think about the next generation and the generation after that.

—Franklin D. Roosevelt,
in Arthur Bernon Tourtellot, *The Presidents on the Presidency*.

sworn to "preserve, protect and defend" the Constitution—but also a world leader, whose decisions may affect the future of 3.5 billion inhabitants of the globe.

Kennedy's dual sense of his power and its limits illustrates the paradox of the modern Presidency. A classic question, often asked, is: Has the American Presidency grown too powerful? Are there enough checks and controls over presidential power? The paradox, however, is that the opposite question may also be asked: Is the office of the Presidency adequate to cope with the awesome demands placed upon it? Does the President have enough control over the executive branch and policy formation, and enough influence upon Congress, to solve the problems placed before him?

The core of the dilemma is that the technology of the nuclear age and the growth of government in a modern, industrial society have combined to concentrate great power in the hands of a chief executive in some policy areas while restricting his options in others.

A President can bring us to the brink of nuclear disaster, as in the Cuban missile crisis of 1962, or involve us in war, as in Southeast Asia, almost entirely by his own decisions and actions. Yet he may not be able to get an education bill through Congress, reduce poverty in our affluent society, or cope with the racial conflict that threatens to tear the nation apart.

The Presidency is both an institution and a man. The *institution* is the office created by the Constitution, custom, cumulative federal law since 1789, and the gradual growth of formal and informal tools of presidential power. The *man* is a human being, powerful yet vulnerable, compassionate or vain, ordinary or extraordinary. To the institution, he brings the imprint of his personality and style. Under the Twenty-second Amendment, the man must normally change at least once every eight years. The Presidency is, then, both highly institutionalized and highly personal.

George Washington assumed the office feeling not unlike "a culprit who is going to the place of his execution." William Howard Taft thought it "the loneliest place in the world." Harry Truman declared that "being a President is like riding a tiger. A man has to keep on riding or be swallowed." Warren Harding thought the White House "a prison." And Lyndon Johnson spoke of "the awesome power, and the immense fragility of executive authority," both of which he experienced.

The strands of power have come together in the person and the institution of the modern Presidency. When the President speaks to the nation, millions listen. His words are instantly transmitted around the globe by satellite and high-speed communications. When he pulls his beagle's ears, as Lyndon Johnson did, the bark of dog-lovers is heard round the world. If he cancels a subscription to a newspaper, as John Kennedy did, a thousand thunderous editorials denounce him. Is his daughter dating a movie star? His wife spending too much on her clothes? His kitten ill? His chef disloyal? Does he have a cold? Are his suits custom-made? Does he take tranquilizers? Does he eat cottage cheese with ketchup? No detail in the life of a modern President (and these are real examples) escapes the eye of the media, which provide such information to a public apparently hungry for more.

Public disclosure of intimate details of a President's life is not limited to the press, or to the literary endeavors of White House cooks, seamstresses, and bottlewashers. His own distinguished, high-level staff assis-

> I can't make a damn thing out of this tax problem. I listen to one side and they seem right, and then God! I talk to the other side and they seem just as right, and there I am where I started. I know somewhere there is a book that would give me the truth, but hell, I couldn't read the book. . . . God, what a job!
>
> —Warren G. Harding, in
> Richard F. Fenno, Jr., *The President's Cabinet.*

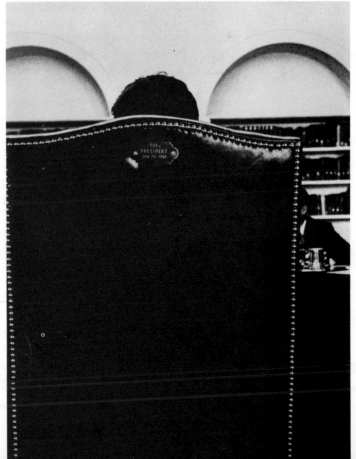

"The Presidency is both an institution and a man . . ."

tants may be secret diarists, scribbling away nights for the sake of posterity, the best-seller lists, and *Life* magazine. Indeed, Presidents themselves write books, not only for money but to give their own version of events and, hopefully, to secure their place in history. Truman, Eisenhower, and Johnson all published memoirs after they left the White House (in Johnson's case reportedly for a fee in excess of $1,000,000).

The intense public interest in the person and office of the President is a reflection of how the job has become magnified through the prism of the twentieth century. The immense pressures on the human being who occupies the office of President have intensified, because the institution of the Presidency has evolved and grown with the nation.

THE EXPANDING PRESIDENCY

"We Never Once Thought of a King"

The framers of the Constitution who met at Philadelphia toiled in the greatest secrecy. No television cameras invaded their privacy in 1787. Yet even in that preelectronic age, the Founding Fathers felt it necessary to issue a press release (their only one) to counteract rumors that were circulating around the country. The statement was leaked to the *Pennsylvania Herald* in August: "Tho' we cannot, affirmatively, tell you what we are doing; we can, negatively, tell you what we are not doing—we never once thought of a king." [2]

The men who made the American revolution were, perhaps understandably, prejudiced against kings. At the same time, the difficulties encountered under the Articles of Confederation had exposed the shortcomings of legislative government and demonstrated the need for a strong executive. But how strong?

James Wilson and Gouverneur Morris championed a single, powerful chief executive, and James Madison eventually adopted that view. Many of the framers considered legislatures to be dangerously radical; the blessings of liberty could best be enjoyed, they felt, if popular government was checked by a strong executive branch that could protect wealth, private property, and business. Support for a powerful, single President was by no means unanimous, however; some of the framers had specifically proposed a plural executive, and some wanted the President chosen by Congress.

Out of the debates emerged the basic structure of the Presidency as we know it today: a single President heading one of three separate branches of government, elected independently for a four-year term. The great authority given to the President by the framers was limited by the separation of

[2] Carl Van Doren, *The Great Rehearsal* (New York: Viking Press, 1948), p. 145. Alexander Hamilton, however, did propose a virtual monarchy in the form of a lifetime Chief Executive, but his plan won no support.

powers among three branches of government, by the checks and balances engraved in the Constitution, by the federal system, and, in time, by other, informal controls generally unforeseen in 1787—the rise of political parties and mass media, for example.

"I prefer to supervise the whole operations of the government myself . . . and this makes my duties very great," President James Polk wrote in his diary in 1848.[3]

The Growth of the American Presidency

So great had those duties become in the twentieth century, that by fiscal 1971 President Nixon presided over a federal budget of approximately $200 billion and a bureaucracy of 2,900,000 civilians and 2,900,000 members of the armed forces. He would not have dreamed of attempting to "supervise the whole operations of the government" by himself.

Great crises and great Presidents have contributed to the growth of the Presidency since 1789. George Washington, Andrew Jackson, Abraham Lincoln, Theodore Roosevelt, Woodrow Wilson, and Franklin Roosevelt all placed their personal stamp on the Presidency. When a President strengthens and reshapes the institution, the change may endure even after he leaves. The modern Presidency, for example, is rooted in the style and approach of Franklin D. Roosevelt.

Although Presidents and events have played a decisive role in the development of the Presidency, several broad historical factors, discussed below, have combined to create a powerful Chief Executive today.

[3] In Richard F. Fenno, Jr., *The President's Cabinet* (Cambridge, Mass.: Harvard University Press, 1959), p. 217.

Franklin D. Roosevelt influenced the modern Presidency more than any other Chief Executive.

The Nuclear Age. The United States and the Soviet Union each possess nuclear missiles that could destroy the other country in half an hour; given the time factor, the President, rather than Congress, has of necessity become the man who must decide whether to use such hideous, and ultimately irrational, weapons. (As Clinton Rossiter has noted, the next wartime President "may well be our last." [4]) The constitutional power of Congress to declare war has become eroded in the twentieth century by the power of the President to use nuclear weapons, to commit United States forces to meet sudden crises, and to fight so-called "limited" wars. As a result of the war in Southeast Asia, Congress has sought to regain some of its control over the use of American national power (see Chapter 14). But the President remains the dominant figure in responding to crisis with military force.

Foreign Affairs. The President, under the Constitution, has the prime responsibility for conducting the foreign affairs of the United States.

LYNDON JOHNSON LEAVES THE WHITE HOUSE

Of course I miss it. . . . President Nixon said to me, "How did you feel when you weren't President any more?" And I said, "I don't know whether you'll understand this now or not, but you certainly will later. I sat there on that platform and waited for you to stand up and raise your right hand and take the oath of office, and I think the most pleasant words . . . that ever came into my ears were 'So help me God' that you repeated after that oath. Because at that time I no longer had the fear that I was the man that could make the mistake of involving the world in war, that I was no longer the man that would have to carry the terrifying responsibility of protecting the lives of this country and maybe the entire world, unleashing the horrors of some of our great power if I felt that that was required. But that now I could ride back down that avenue, being

concerned about what happened, being alarmed about what might happen, but just really knowing that, I wasn't going to be the cause of it. . . . The real horror was to be sleeping soundly about three-thirty or four or five o'clock in the morning and have the telephone ring and the operator say, "Sorry to wake you, Mr. President," . . . there's just a second between the time the operator got me on the line until she could get Mr. Rostow in the Situation Room, or Mr. Bundy in the Situation Room, or maybe Secretary Rusk or Secretary McNamara, Secretary Clifford. And we went through the horrors of hell that thirty seconds or minute or two minutes. Had we hit a Russian ship? Had an accident occurred? We have another *Pueblo?* Someone made a mistake—were we at war? Well, those experiences are gone."

—Lyndon B. Johnson. Excerpts from a CBS Television News Special, "LBJ: Why I Chose Not to Run," December 27, 1969.

[4] Clinton Rossiter, *The American Presidency*, rev. ed. (New York: Harcourt Brace Jovanovich, 1960), p. 25.

From its isolationism before the Second World War, the United States emerged in the post-war period as one of the two major world powers. During the Eisenhower administration, when John Foster Dulles exercised a powerful influence as Secretary of State, the United States embraced the principle of collective security to "contain" communism and entered into a series of military alliances with other nations for this purpose. The wisdom of the role of the United States as a "world policeman" has been seriously questioned since the late 1960's, when the United States became bogged down in the Vietnam war. Nevertheless, the United States remains one of the two most powerful nations in the world, making the President inevitably a world leader as well as a national leader.

Domestic Affairs. The great increase in presidential power in recent decades has taken place in the domestic field as much as in foreign affairs. Roosevelt's New Deal, as Edward S. Corwin has pointed out, brought "social acceptance of the idea that government should be active and reformist, rather than simply protective of the established order of things." [5]

With the tremendous growth of government-as-manager, the President directs a steadily expanding bureaucracy. Modern government is expected to solve social problems, from racial discrimination to health care, and the President has become the chief problem-solver.

The Mass Media. Television and the other news media have helped to magnify the person and the institution of the Presidency. All the major networks, newspapers, magazines and wire services have correspondents assigned full time to covering the President. These "White House regulars" accompany the Chief Executive wherever he travels, sending out a steady flow of news about his activities.

When a President wants to talk to the people, the networks (whose stations are licensed by the Federal Government) customarily make available free prime time. Presidential news conferences are often televised live. People identify with a President they see so often on television; his style and personality help to shape the times and the national mood. Man and myth blend in the mystique of the modern Presidency.

THE IMPOSSIBLE BURDEN: THE MANY ROLES OF THE CHIEF EXECUTIVE

President Kennedy was having breakfast in the White House on October 16, 1962 when McGeorge Bundy, his national security adviser, informed him that U-2 reconnaissance pho-

[5] Edward S. Corwin, *The President, Office and Powers 1787–1957* (New York: New York University Press, 1957), p. 311.

tographs had disclosed the existence of medium-range Soviet missiles in Cuba. For the next seven days, while the President and his assistants debated in the utmost secrecy how the United States should respond, the President deliberately went about his routine duties to maintain an air of normalcy. He gave a luncheon for Crown Prince Hasan al-Rida al-Sanusi of Libya. He observed National Cultural Center Week. He signed a bill to establish a National Institute of Child Health. He flew to Connecticut, Cleveland, and Chicago to campaign for Democratic congressional candidates. He presented the Harmon International Trophies to a group of outstanding aviators. He vetoed a bill that would have amended the tariff classification of lightweight bicycles. He took astronaut Walter Schirra and his family out on the White House lawn to see his daughter Caroline's ponies. Then, on October 22, he went on television, revealed that the United States and the Soviet Union were locked in a nuclear confrontation, and announced the naval quarantine of Cuba. The President had ordered that his advisers debate American options in secret so that the Soviet Union would not have the advantage of knowing the United States response in advance. He knew, perhaps better than anyone else, that the best way to accomplish this was to continue to devote his attention to the routine, often ceremonial, and sometimes trivial duties that are a regular part of every President's job while conferring in secret with his assistants.

Kennedy's public, "cover" activities during the first week of the Cuban missile crisis, and the numerous decisions he made in private, demonstrate the astonishing scope of the Presidency. The President is one man but he fills many separate roles: Chief of State, Chief Executive, Commander-in-Chief, Chief Diplomat, and Chief Legislator. All of these are required of him by the Constitution; in addition, he is Chief of Party, Voice of the People, Protector of the Peace, Manager of Prosperity, and World Leader.[6]

It would be a mistake to think of the President as a man rapidly changing hats as he goes about filling these varied roles. Many of the presidential roles blend and overlap; some of the roles may collide with others. Being a vigorous party leader, for example, will often conflict with playing the role of Chief of State, of being President of all the people.

For purposes of analysis, however, it is convenient to separate out the principal roles of the President. When we do so, we discover that the "awesome burden" has identifiable parts.

Chief of State

The President of the United States is the ceremonial and symbolic head of state, as well as head of government. In many countries, the two jobs are distinct; a figurehead King, Queen, or President is head of state,

[6] Rossiter, *The American Presidency*, pp. 16–41.

but the Premier or Prime Minister is head of government and exercises the real power. It is because the two functions are combined in the person of the American President that he finds himself declaring National Codfish Week or solemnly toasting the Grand Duchess of Luxembourg at a state dinner.

The distinction between head of state and head of government may seem trivial—of interest only to protocol officers and society columnists—but it is not. Much of the awe and mystery, the power and dignity that surround the Presidency are due precisely to the fact that the President is more than a Prime Minister; he is a symbol of nationhood as well as a custodian of the people's power. In Theodore Roosevelt's famous phrase, he is almost both "a king and a prime minister." [7]

As a result, when a President dies in office, people often react as though they have suffered a great personal loss. Even the radio announcers wept as they told of Franklin Roosevelt's death. After President Kennedy's assassination, the nation went through a period of mourning; 250,000 people braved cold weather to line up to pass his bier in the Capitol rotunda; 100 million people watched the funeral on television. Social scientists studying the effect of the assassination on children and adults found definite physical and psychological affects. For example, among adults, one study found that "the assassination generally evoked feelings similar to those felt at the death of a close friend or relative." [8] Of a sample of the adult population, 43 percent said they did not feel like eating, 29 percent smoked more than usual, 53 percent cried, 48 percent had trouble sleeping, and 68 percent felt nervous and tense.[9] And children also "mourned, grieved, and participated in the general sense of bereavement after the death of President Kennedy." [10]

"The executive power shall be vested in a President of the United States of America." So reads Article II of the Constitution, which also states: "He shall take Care that the Laws be faithfully executed."

Under this simply worded but powerful grant of executive authority, the President runs the executive branch of the government. As of fiscal 1971, President Nixon headed a federal establishment with a combined payroll of $47 billion. With federal income running over $200 billion a year, the government's revenues were larger than that of the top thirty-six

Chief Executive

[7] Letter to Lady Delamere, March 7, 1911.
[8] Paul B. Sheatsley and Jacob J. Feldman, "A National Survey on Public Reactions and Behavior," in Bradley S. Greenberg and Edwin B. Parker, eds., *The Kennedy Assassination and the American Public* (Stanford, Calif.: Stanford University Press, 1965), p. 168.
[9] *Ibid.*, p. 158.
[10] Roberta A. Sigel, "Television and the Reactions of Schoolchildren to the Assassination," in Greenberg and Parker, p. 199.

United States corporations combined. No executive in private industry has responsibilities that match the President's. The President receives $200,000 a year, plus $50,000 in expenses (both taxable), and $40,000 in travel expenses (tax-free) as well as handsome retirement benefits. There are few legal qualifications for the office; the Constitution requires only that he be a "natural-born" citizen, at least thirty-five, and fourteen years a resident of the United States.[11]

Obviously, there would be more than enough work in the President's in-basket to keep him busy if he did nothing else but administer the government. And, in fact, Presidents do find themselves bogged down under a mountain of paper. Most Presidents work at night to try to keep up; the sight of Franklin Roosevelt, a polio victim, being wheeled to his office at night, preceded by wire baskets full of paperwork, was a familiar one to White House aides during the New Deal era. President Eisenhower tried to solve the paperwork problem by ordering his staff to prepare memos no more than one page long. Lyndon Johnson took a swim and nap each afternoon, then began a second working day at 4 P.M., often summoning weary aides for conferences at the end of *their* working day.

Because administering the government is only one of six major presidential roles, the President cannot spend all of his time in the executive sandbox. He has a White House staff, other agencies in the Executive Office of the President, and his Cabinet to help him. He tries to confine himself to *presidential* decisions, such as resolving major conflicts within the bureaucracy, or among his own advisers, and initiating and approving major programs and policies.

Beneath the President in the executive branch are the eleven Cabinet departments and, as of 1970, fifty-two major independent agencies, boards, and commissions. (See Figure 11-3, pp. 422–23.) These are of two main types: *executive agencies* and *regulatory agencies*. The independent executive agencies are units of government under the President within the executive branch, but not part of a Cabinet department. They are, therefore, "independent" of the departments, not of the President. The members of the eight regulatory agencies are appointed by the President from both major parties to staggered, fixed terms but do not report to him. The regulatory agencies, which exercise quasi-judicial and quasi-legislative powers, are administratively independent of both the President and Congress (although politically independent of neither).

The neat organizational charts do not show the overlapping and intricate real-life relationships among the three branches of government.

[11] A citizen born abroad of American parents might well be regarded as "natural-born." The question arose in 1968 because George Romney, a Republican hopeful, had been born in Mexico. The requirement of fourteen years residence apparently does not mean that a President must have resided in the United States for fourteen successive years immediately prior to the election, since Herbert Hoover had not.

Nor do they give any hint of the difficulties a President faces in controlling his own executive branch and in making the bureaucracy carry out his decisions.

President Truman understood the problems that Eisenhower would have as an Army general elected President: "He'll sit here," Truman would remark (tapping his desk for emphasis), "and he'll say, 'Do this! Do that!' *And nothing will happen.* Poor Ike—it won't be a bit like the Army. He'll find it very frustrating." [12]

Despite his vast constitutional and extraconstitutional powers, the President is as much a victim of bureaucratic inertia as anyone else. "I sit here all day," Truman said, "trying to persuade people to do the things they ought to have sense enough to do without my persuading them. . . . That's all the powers of the President amount to." [13]

Richard Neustadt agrees with Truman that "Presidential *power* is the power to persuade." [14] In persuading people, however, the President can draw upon a formidable array of tools, not the least of which is his power to appoint and remove officials from their jobs. Under the Constitution, the President, "with the advice and consent of the Senate" appoints ambassadors, Supreme Court judges, and a total, under present law, of about 2,000 upper-level federal officials. The Constitution leaves it up to Congress to decide whether the President, the courts, or the department heads should appoint "inferior" officers of the government. Under the law, the great bulk of the 2,900,000 federal employees are appointed by department heads through the civil service system.

The Constitution does not specifically give the President the power to remove government officials, but the Supreme Court has ruled that Congress cannot interfere with the President's right to fire officials whom he has appointed with Senate approval. [15] During Franklin Roosevelt's administration, the Court held that the President did *not* have the right to remove officials serving in administratively independent "quasi-legislative or quasi-judicial agencies." [16] Even though commissioners of regulatory agencies are thus by law and judicial decision theoretically immune from removal by presidential power, in practice, they may not be. In 1958, Richard A. Mack "voluntarily" resigned from the FCC when a House investigating subcommittee disclosed that he had voted to award a Miami television channel to an applicant whose attorney had paid him several thousand dollars. The White House did not deny that it had asked for Mack's resignation, and President Eisenhower called the commissioner's decision "wise." In 1960, a newspaper revealed that John C. Doerfer, the chairman of the

[12] In Richard E. Neustadt, *Presidential Power* (New York: Wiley, 1960), p. 9.
[13] *Ibid.,* pp. 9–10.
[14] *Ibid.,* p. 10.
[15] *Myers v. United States,* 272 U.S. 52 (1926).
[16] *Humphrey's Executor v. United States,* 295 U.S. 602 (1935).

FCC, had cruised aboard the yacht of a broadcaster whose licenses were subject to his jurisdiction. The incident embarrassed President Eisenhower; within a week Doerfer resigned.

To the task of bureaucrat-in-chief, therefore, the President brings powers of persuasion that go beyond his formal, constitutional, and legal authority. By the nature of his job, he is the final decision-maker in the executive branch. As the sign on Harry Truman's desk said: "The buck stops here."

Commander-in-Chief

When President Kennedy died at Parkland Hospital in Dallas on November 22, 1963, an Army warrant officer named Ira D. Gearheart, armed but dressed in civilian clothes, picked up a locked briefcase known as the "football," or "black box," and walked down a hospital corridor to a small room where President Lyndon Johnson was being guarded by secret service agents. The man who carries the "football" must be near whoever is the President. He guards "a national security portfolio of cryptographic orders the President would send his military chiefs to authorize nuclear retaliation. The orders can be dispatched by telephone, teletype or microwave radio." [17]

In effect, the warrant officer has custody of the "nuclear button," which is not a button, but a set of coded orders. That such a person and such machinery exist is a reminder of the fact that, regardless of his other duties, the President is at all times Commander-in-Chief of the armed forces of the United States.

Although a President normally delegates most of this authority to his generals and admirals, he is not required to do so. During the Whiskey Rebellion of 1794, President Washington personally led his troops into Pennsylvania. During the Civil War, Lincoln often visited the Army of the Potomac to instruct his generals. Franklin Roosevelt and Prime Minister Winston Churchill conferred on the major strategic decisions of the Second World War. Truman made the decisions to drop the atomic bomb on Japan in 1945 and to intervene in Korea in 1950. Kennedy authorized the invasion of Cuba at the Bay of Pigs by Cuban exiles armed and trained by the Central Intelligence Agency. Johnson personally approved bombing targets in Vietnam. President Nixon made the decision to send American troops into Cambodia in 1970.

The principle of *civilian supremacy* over the military is embodied in the clear constitutional power of the President as supreme commander of the armed forces. The principle was put to a severe test during the

[17] Bob Horton, Associated Press Staff Writer, "The Job of Guarding the President's Code Box," *Washington Star*, November 21, 1965. See also William Manchester, *The Death of a President* (New York: Harper & Row, 1967), pp. 62, 321.

Korean War when General Douglas MacArthur repeatedly defied President Truman's orders. The hero of the Pacific theater during the Second World War, MacArthur enjoyed personal prestige to rival the President's and had a substantial political following of his own. As Truman's memoirs make clear, the President and his advisers dealt gingerly with MacArthur during this crucial period, almost as though he were another head of state rather than a subordinate general. Truman finally dismissed MacArthur in April 1951. Secretary of Defense George C. Marshall, after reviewing the record, concluded that "MacArthur should have been fired two years ago."[18] Nevertheless, in the most dramatic conflict in modern times between the military and the President, the President prevailed.

The Constitution declares that "Congress shall have the power . . . To declare War," but Congress has not done so since December 1941, when it declared war against Japan and Germany following the Japanese attack on Pearl Harbor.[19] In the intervening years the President has made the decision to go to war. By 1970, however, Congress was trying to regain some of its control over the war power. Congress repealed the Tonkin Gulf resolution, which it had passed to support President Johnson's Vietnam policy as of 1964, and it passed an amendment originated by Senator John Sherman Cooper of Kentucky and Senator Frank Church of Idaho restricting President Nixon's future use of American troops in Cambodia.

Congress is also empowered by the Constitution to "raise and support Armies" and to appropriate money for the military. The chairman and members of the Senate and House Armed Services and Appropriations committees in particular jealously guard this power and constitute a strong counterbalance to the President's influence over the Pentagon.

The "military-industrial complex"—the term often used to describe the ties between the military establishment and the defense-aerospace industry—is another limit upon the President's power as Commander-in-Chief. For example, a President may find it difficult to cancel a fighter plane, a bomber, an aircraft carrier, or some other weapons system that enjoys the strong support of the Joint Chiefs of Staff, Congress, and private industry.

Despite these limits, Presidents have claimed and exercised formidable "war powers" during emergencies. In the ten weeks after the fall of Fort Sumter in April 1861, Lincoln called out the militia, spent $2,000,000 without authorization by Congress, blockaded Southern ports, and suspended the writ of habeas corpus in certain areas. Lincoln declared: "I felt that measures otherwise unconstitutional might become lawful by becoming

[18] Harry S. Truman, *Memoirs by Harry S. Truman: Years of Trial and Hope*, Vol. II (Garden City, N.Y.: Doubleday, 1956), p. 448.
[19] Congress has declared war five times: in the War of 1812, the Mexican War, the Spanish-American War, the First World War, and the Second World War. It did not declare war in Korea or Vietnam.

indispensable to the preservation of the Constitution through the preservation of the nation. Right or wrong, I assumed this ground and now avow it." [20]

During the Second World War, Franklin Roosevelt exercised extraordinary powers over food rationing and the economy, only partly with congressional authorization. And in 1942, with the consent of Congress, he permitted the removal of 112,000 persons of Japanese descent—most of them native-born citizens of the United States—from California and other Western states to concentration camps called "relocation centers" in the interior of the country.

During the Korean War, Truman seized the steel mills in the face of a strike threat, but the Supreme Court ruled he had no constitutional right to do so, even as Commander-in-Chief,[21] President Johnson expanded American forces in Vietnam after Congress passed the Tonkin Gulf resolution, empowering the President to take "all necessary measures" in Southeast Asia. The President contended, however, that he did not need congressional approval to fight the war in Vietnam.

Chief Diplomat

"I make American foreign policy," President Truman declared in 1948.

By and large, Presidents do make foreign policy; that is, they direct the relations of the United States with the other nations of the world. The Constitution does not *specifically* confer this power on the President, but it does so indirectly. It authorizes him to receive foreign ambassadors, to appoint ambassadors, and to make treaties with the consent of two-thirds of the Senate. Because it requires that the President share some foreign policy powers with Congress, the Constitution has been called "an invitation to struggle for the privilege of directing American foreign policy." [22]

In this struggle the President usually enjoys the advantage. Because the State Department, the Pentagon, and the CIA report to him as part of the executive branch, the President—or so it is usually assumed—has more information about foreign affairs available to him than do members of Congress. But senators and representatives also have sources of information—official briefings, unofficial "leaks" from within the bureaucracy, and friends in the press and the universities. A President, therefore, does not have a monopoly of information. Much of the information he does receive is conflicting, because it represents different viewpoints within the bureaucracy; and even with the best intelligence reports, a President may

[20] In Arthur Bernon Tourtellot, *The Presidents on the Presidency* (Garden City, N.Y.: Doubleday, 1964), p. 311.
[21] *Youngstown Sheet and Tube Co. v. Sawyer*, 343 U.S. 579 (1952).
[22] Corwin, *The President, Office and Powers 1787–1957*, p. 171.

make decisions that prove to be misguided. Nevertheless, the information that flows in daily is a substantial source of power for the President.

Those who lack the information that the President has, or is presumed to have, including senators and representatives, find it difficult to challenge the President's actions. Over a period of time, however, Congress can chip away at a President's power in foreign affairs; during the height of the Vietnam war, for example, the Senate Foreign Relations Committee under Chairman J. William Fulbright, strongly criticized Johnson's war policies. The committee held a series of televised hearings that aired the Vietnam issue and may have helped to turn the tide of public opinion against the war.

The President has sole power to negotiate and sign treaties. The Senate may veto a treaty by refusing to approve it, but seldom does so. In 1920, however, it did refuse to ratify the Treaty of Versailles and its provision for United States membership in the League of Nations. Sometimes a President does not submit a treaty to the Senate because he knows it will not be approved; or he may modify the treaty to meet Senate opposition.

Since 1900, *executive agreements*, which do not require Senate approval, have been employed by the President in the conduct of foreign affairs more often than treaties. Some executive agreements are made by the President with the prior approval of Congress. For example, until its expiration in 1967, the President negotiated tariff agreements with other countries under the Trade Expansion Act of 1962, which superseded the Reciprocal Trade Agreements Act of 1934.

Because a President can sign an executive agreement with another nation without the necessity of going to the Senate, the use of this device has increased enormously. This has been particularly true since the Second World War, as the United States' role in international affairs has expanded. Today, in a single year, a President may sign literally hundreds of executive agreements.

Alarmed by this growing aspect of presidential power, a group of senators led by John Bricker, an Ohio Republican, attempted in 1954 to amend the Constitution to curb the President's treaty power and give Congress control over executive agreements. The measure failed to get the necessary two-thirds approval in the Senate by only one vote.

The President also has sole power to recognize or not recognize foreign governments. The United States did not recognize the Soviet Union until November 1933, sixteen years after the Russian Revolution. Since Wilson's day, Presidents have used diplomatic recognition as an instrument of American foreign policy.

In acting as Chief Diplomat, the President, as Commander-in-Chief, can back up his diplomacy with military power. Both the arrows and the olive branch depicted in the Presidential seal are available to him, a good example of how presidential roles overlap.

"He shall from time to time give to the Congress Information of the State of the Union, and recommend to their Consideration such Measures as he shall judge necessary and expedient." With this statement in Article II, "the Constitution puts the President right square into the legislative business," as President Eisenhower observed at a 1959 press conference.

Today, Presidents often use their State of the Union address, delivered to a joint session of Congress in January, as a public platform to unveil their annual legislative program. The details of proposed legislation are then filled in through a series of special presidential messages sent to Capitol Hill in the months that follow.

This was not always the case. Active presidential participation in the legislative process is a twentieth century phenomenon, and the practice of Presidents sending a comprehensive legislative package to Congress developed only after the Second World War during the Truman administration.[23]

The success of the President's role as Chief Legislator depends on the cooperation of Congress. A Republican President faced with a Democratic Congress (as was Eisenhower during most of his two terms), or a Democratic President blocked by a coalition of Republicans and Southern Democrats (as in Kennedy's case), may find his role as Chief Legislator frustrating. As President Kennedy observed ruefully: "It is very easy to defeat a bill in the Congress. It is much more difficult to pass one. . . . They are two separate offices and two separate powers, the Congress and the Presidency. There is bound to be conflict."[24]

Every President has staff assistants in charge of legislative liaison. Their job is to pressure Congress to pass the President's program. The senator or representative who wants the administration to approve a new federal building, or dam, or public works project in his state or district may discover that the price is his vote on a bill that the President wants passed. There are other, more subtle pressures. When Senator Fulbright opposed Lyndon Johnson's foreign policies, he found he was not being invited to White House social functions. Often, on an important measure, the President himself takes charge of the "arm-twisting"—telephoning members of Congress in their offices, or inviting them to the White House for a chat about the merits of his program.

As Chief Legislator, the President is not limited entirely to the arts of persuasion. He has an important constitutional weapon in the *veto*. The President, if he approves a bill, may sign it—often in front of news photographers and with much fanfare and handing out of pens. If he disapproves, however, he may veto the bill and return it with his objections

[23] Richard E. Neustadt, "Presidency and Legislation: Planning the President's Program," *American Political Science Review*, Vol. 49, December 1955, p. 981.
[24] "After Two Years—a Conversation with the President," p. 894.

to the branch of Congress in which it originated. By a vote of two-thirds of each house, Congress may pass the bill over the President's veto. If the President does not sign or veto a bill within ten working days after he receives it, the measure becomes law without his signature. If Congress adjourns during this ten-day period, the President can exercise his *pocket veto* and kill the bill by taking no action. Except for joint resolutions, which are the same as bills, resolutions of Congress do not require presidential action since they are expressions of sentiment, not law.

Because Congress normally finds it difficult to override a presidential veto, merely the threat of a veto is often enough to force Congress to tailor a bill to conform to administration wishes. Only about 3 percent of presidential vetoes have been overridden by Congress. (See Table 10-1.)

Table 10-1

Presidential Vetoes, 1789–1970

	Regular Vetoes	Pocket Vetoes	Total Vetoes	Vetoes Overridden
Washington	2	–	2	–
Madison	5	2	7	–
Monroe	1	–	1	–
Jackson	5	7	12	–
Tyler	6	3	9	1
Polk	2	1	3	–
Pierce	9	–	9	5
Buchanan	4	3	7	–
Lincoln	2	4	6	–
A. Johnson	21	8	29	15
Grant	45	49	94	4
Hayes	12	1	13	1
Arthur	4	8	12	1
Cleveland	304	109	413	2
Harrison	19	25	44	1
Cleveland	43	127	170	5
McKinley	6	36	42	–
T. Roosevelt	42	40	82	1
Taft	30	9	39	1
Wilson	33	11	44	6
Harding	5	1	6	–
Coolidge	20	30	50	4
Hoover	21	16	37	3
F. Roosevelt	372	261	633	9
Truman	180	70	250	12
Eisenhower	73	108	181	2
Kennedy	11	9	21	–
L. Johnson	16	14	30	–
Nixon[1]	6	3	9	2
Total	1,299	955	2,255	75

[1] As of December 31, 1970.

Source: Senate Library, *Presidential Vetoes* (New York: Greenwood Press, Publishers, 1968), p. iv. Originally published by U.S. Government Printing Office. Data for Kennedy and L. Johnson from *Congressional Quarterly Almanac*, 1963, 1968 (Washington, D.C.: Congressional Quarterly Service, 1963, 1968), p. 1020, p. 23. Data for Nixon from Congressional Quarterly, Inc.

The presidential veto power is limited by the fact that unlike the governors of most states the President does not possess the item veto, the power to disapprove particular parts of a bill. As a result, Congress is encouraged to pass *riders,* provisions tacked on to a piece of legislation that are not relevant to the bill. Sponsors of riders know that the President must swallow the legislation whole or veto the entire bill—he cannot veto just the rider.

As Chief Legislator, the President may call Congress back into session. He may also adjourn Congress if the House and Senate should disagree about when to adjourn, although no President has exercised this constitutional power.

The Supreme Court has held that Congress may not delegate legislative authority to the President, but Congress has in some cases passed legislation setting broad guidelines within which the President may act. Under such laws the President may be authorized, for example, to reduce tariffs. And since 1939, Congress has passed a series of Reorganization Acts that permit the President to restructure federal agencies under plans that he must submit to Congress. Unless Congress *disapproves* the plans within sixty days, they go into effect.

The President's real ability to persuade Congress often rests on his personal popularity rather than on his formal or informal powers. The veto, arm-twisting, threats to withhold a public works project, and social ostracism of a congressman or senator are, over the long run, less important than the ability of a President to enlist public support for his programs and the extent of his prestige with both Congress and the electorate.

Chief of Party

"No President, it seems to me, can escape politics," John Kennedy said in 1960 when he sought the Presidency. "He has not only been chosen by the Nation—he has been chosen by his party." [25]

Not every President has filled the role of party chief with the same enthusiasm that Kennedy brought to it. President Eisenhower, a career Army officer for most of his life, displayed a reluctance to engage in the rough and tumble of politics. As he told a press conference in 1955: "In the general derogatory sense . . . I do not like politics . . . the word 'politics' as you use it, I think the answer to that one, would be, no. I have no great liking for that." [26]

Whether or not a President enjoys his partisan role, he is chief of his party. The machinery of the national committee reports to him; he can install his own man as national chairman; he can usually demand his party's renomination and stage-manage the convention that acclaims him.

[25] *Congressional Record,* January 18, 1960, pp. 710–12.
[26] In Neustadt, *Presidential Power,* p. 166.

The President, among his various roles, is chief of his political party.

Since his success as Chief Legislator depends to a considerable degree on the political make-up of Congress, he may find it to his advantage to campaign for congressional candidates in off-year elections.

Given the decentralized nature of American political parties, a President's influence may not extend to state and local party organizations in every case. Nor does it prevail at all times with members of his party in Congress. In fact, his own leaders in Congress may not always bow to his political wisdom or his policy wishes. A dramatic example occurred in 1969, when Hugh Scott of Pennsylvania, the Senate Republican leader, voted against Judge Haynsworth, President Nixon's nominee to the Supreme Court.

In Chapter 1, we defined politics as the pursuit or exercise of power. When a President makes decisions, he is, in the broadest sense, engaging in politics. A successful President must lead and gauge public opinion, he must be sensitive to change, and he must have a sure sense of the limits of the possible. All of these are *political* skills. As Chief of Party, the President is also the nation's Number 1 professional politician. And, as Neustadt has suggested, "The Presidency is no place for amateurs." [27]

[27] *Ibid.*, p. 180.

The President, it must be emphasized again, fills all six presidential roles at once. The powers and duties of his office are not divisible. The roles conflict and overlap; and in performing one role the President may incur political costs that make it more difficult for him to perform another. In short, the Presidency is a balancing act.

In addition to the six basic roles, Americans expect the President to take on many other roles. In the event of a major civil disturbance, he is expected to act as a policeman and restore domestic tranquillity. As the manager of the economy he is expected to prevent a recession, ensure prosperity, and hold down the cost of butter and eggs. He is expected to set an example as a model husband and father—and woe unto the President who drives too fast, or is photographed too often with a highball glass in his hand. He is expected to be a teacher, to educate the people about great public issues. In some mysterious way, the President is expected to speak for all the people and to give voice to their deepest aspirations and ideals. "The Presidency," Franklin Roosevelt said, "is not merely an administrative office. That is the least of it. It is pre-eminently a place of moral leadership." [28]

THE TOOLS OF PRESIDENTIAL POWER

In the exercise of power, the President of the United States has available to him an awesome list of tools, money, and manpower. In ever-widening circles, this last category includes the White House staff (his own secretaries and advisers), the Executive Office of the President (a conglomerate of presidential substaffs), the Vice-President, the Cabinet, the eleven Cabinet departments, the many other agencies of the executive branch, and the nearly 6,000,000 employees of the federal bureaucracy and the military.

He has almost unlimited personal resources, as well. When President Johnson had reviewed the Marines in California on one occasion and was walking back to a helicopter, he was stopped by an officer who pointed to another helicopter and said, "That's your helicopter over there, sir." Johnson replied, "Son, they are all my helicopters." [29]

When the President travels, he has at his disposal not only helicopters, but a fleet of jets; aboard Air Force One, he can communicate with his aides or with the military anywhere in the world. If he flies to Kansas City to deliver a speech, a special switchboard, manned by a Pentagon communications unit that travels with the President, connects him with the White House.

In addition to the formal machinery of government at the President's command, he has other, informal resources—his reputation, his personality

[28] In Rossiter, *The American Presidency*, p. 148.
[29] In Hugh Sidey, *A Very Personal Presidency* (New York: Atheneum, 1968), p. 98.

and style, his ability to arouse public opinion, his political party, and his informal advisers and friends. Yet, as we have already seen, there are limitations upon presidential power at almost every turn. Indeed, one of the measures of his power is how well he can use the tools at his command.

A month after his election, President Nixon, acting as master of ceremonies, unveiled his Cabinet to a nationwide television audience. While the format of the program had certain elements of a Miss America contest, it nevertheless served to give the voters a close-up look at the "team" assembled by the new President.

The Cabinet

The Cabinet consists of the President, the Vice-President, and the men who run the eleven executive departments of the government. In his 1971 State of the Union address, President Nixon proposed to reduce the number of Cabinet departments from eleven to eight by absorbing the Departments of Agriculture, Commerce, Labor, Transportation, Interior, HUD, and HEW into four new super-departments: Community Development, Natural Resources, Human Resources, and Economic Development.

TABLE 10-2

The President's Cabinet

The Executive Departments in Order of Formation[1]

State	1789
Treasury	1789
Interior	1849
Justice[2]	1870
Agriculture[3]	1889
Commerce[4]	1913
Labor[4]	1913
Defense[5]	1947
Health, Education, and Welfare	1953
Housing and Urban Development	1965
Transportation	1966

[1] The Office of Postmaster General, created in 1789, received Cabinet rank in 1829 and was made a Cabinet department in 1872. In 1970, Congress abolished the Post Office as a Cabinet department and replaced it with the United States Postal Service, an independent federal agency.

[2] The Office of Attorney General, created in 1789, became the Department of Justice in 1870.

[3] Originally created in 1862 and elevated to a Cabinet department in 1889.

[4] The Department of Commerce and Labor, created in 1903, was divided into two separate departments in 1913.

[5] The Department of War (the Army), created in 1789, and the Department of Navy, created in 1798, were consolidated along with the Air Force under the Department of Defense in 1949.

A tool of the Presidency—President Nixon's Cabinet.

The Constitution speaks of "the principal Officer in each of the executive Departments" and of "Heads of Departments." The Twenty-fifth Amendment, ratified in 1967, allows for the possibility of the department heads acting as a group in case of presidential disability. But the Cabinet as an organized body is nowhere specifically provided for by law or in the Constitution.

The President, Richard F. Fenno points out, "is not required by law to form a Cabinet or to keep one" and the Cabinet has become "institutionalized by usage alone." [30] Perhaps because the Cabinet is entirely a creature of custom, it is a relatively weak institution. Each President is free to use it as he sees fit. The weakness of the Cabinet under a strong President is often illustrated by the story of how Lincoln counted when the entire Cabinet was opposed to him: "Seven nays, one aye—the ayes have it."

Among the modern Presidents, Franklin Roosevelt made little use of the Cabinet as an advisory group. Meetings tended to wander, skipping from one subject to another. Roosevelt enjoyed and encouraged conflict and competition among his subordinates, and sometimes he by-passed Cabinet officers to talk directly to lower-level officials.

Eisenhower, who favored a more orderly approach, created the post of Cabinet Secretary to formulate an agenda for Cabinet meetings. During his administration, department heads arrived at weekly meetings with a "Cabinet notebook," containing background briefs for each item on the agenda. But a Cabinet member, with or without an agenda, may not be competent to discuss problems of a general nature, for "beyond his imme-

[30] Fenno, *The President's Cabinet,* p. 19.

diate bailiwick, he may not be capable of adding anything to the group conference." [31] For this reason, President Kennedy thought that Cabinet meetings were "a waste of time." [32]

Lyndon Johnson met regularly with his Cabinet, but his own personality was so forceful that he overshadowed its members. The conduct of the war in Vietnam was normally discussed not in the Johnson Cabinet, but at regular Tuesday luncheon meetings of the President and selected officials. When he became President, Nixon, who had participated in the Eisenhower Cabinet, sought to revitalize the Cabinet as a formal advisory body. After his initial television spectacular, however, relatively little was heard of the Cabinet as an organized advisory body. In fact, in 1970 Interior Secretary Walter Hickel criticized Nixon for his inaccessibility to Cabinet members in a letter that became a *cause célèbre* after it was leaked to the press.

Although the Cabinet is often considered to be a device to assist the President, it also limits his power to some extent. "The members of the Cabinet," Vice-President Charles G. Dawes said, "are a President's natural enemies." [33] In part, this is because a Cabinet member after a time tends to adopt the parochial view of his own department. He may become a narrow advocate of the programs and needs of his bureaucracy, competing with other Cabinet members for bigger budgets and presidential favor. "His formal responsibilities extend both upward toward the President and downward toward his own department." [34]

What is more, since Congress creates or approves the departments headed by the members of the Cabinet, and appropriates the funds with which the departments operate, the legislative branch competes with the President for control of the bureaucracy.

ADVICE TO CABINET MEMBERS

Officials, bless them, love to talk, especially on television, and very few of them have mastered the art of saying nothing gracefully.

Engine Charlie Wilson, who was President Eisenhower's first Secretary of Defense, bounced out of General Motors right into the same kind of trouble when he arrived in Washington, but he didn't grieve too much about it and he even passed on a useful conclusion.

"Every Cabinet member," he said, "should learn the lesson of the whale: The only time you get harpooned is when you're up on the surface spouting."

—James Reston, *New York Times,* December 20, 1968.

During the 1960 campaign, Harry Robbins (Bob) Haldeman served as candidate Richard Nixon's chief advance man; among his other duties were to make sure that buses and baggage reached their destinations.

The White House Staff

---

[31] *Ibid.,* p. 137.
[32] *Conversation Between President Kennedy and NBC Correspondent Ray Scherer,* broadcast over NBC Television Network, April 11, 1961, Stenographic Transcript, p. 17.
[33] In Neustadt, *Presidential Power,* p. 39.
[34] Fenno, *The President's Cabinet,* p. 218.

After Nixon lost, Haldeman went to work for the J. Walter Thompson advertising agency in Los Angeles, handling the Disneyland, 7-Up, and Diaper Sweet accounts. After Nixon won in 1968, Haldeman moved into the White House as a chief aide. It soon became clear that the former advertising executive was one of the most powerful men in Washington, and for a simple reason: it was Haldeman who decided who would see the President of the United States and who would not.

The role of Haldeman in the Nixon White House exemplified the formidable power wielded by the men around the President, some of whom rise from relative obscurity to great influence. Wilson had his Colonel House, Franklin Roosevelt his Harry Hopkins, Eisenhower his Sherman Adams, Kennedy his Theodore Sorensen, Johnson his Bill Moyers. All modern Presidents have come to rely on their advisers, and in every case, some aides have emerged as more important than others.

The power of the President's assistants, however, flows from their position as extensions of the President. Seldom possessing any political prestige or constituency of their own, they depend entirely on staying in the President's good graces for their survival. Their power is derivative, though nonetheless real—it is not uncommon in the White House to see a Cabinet member waiting to confer with a member of the President's staff.

In recent administrations, the President's assistant for national security affairs has taken a central role in foreign policy formation and crisis management. With access to the President and the White House "Situation Room," the downstairs office into which all military, intelligence, and diplomatic information flows, the "man in the basement" may emerge as a powerful rival to the Secretary of State. Under President Kennedy, McGeorge Bundy, the White House adviser for national security, often seemed to exercise more policy influence than Dean Rusk, the cautious and self-effacing Secretary of State.

During much of the Johnson administration, Bundy's successor, Walt Rostow, played an influential role in advising the President on policy in Vietnam. Henry A. Kissinger took the post in the Nixon administration and quickly emerged as a powerful White House adviser.

A President may delegate too much power to an assistant. In 1958, it was disclosed that Sherman Adams, Eisenhower's laconic, powerful chief of staff, had accepted more than $6,000 in hotel hospitality, and gifts—including a celebrated vicuna coat—from Boston industrialist Bernard Goldfine, for whom he intervened with two federal regulatory agencies. The public storm that broke eventually forced Adams to resign, despite an extraordinary plea by Eisenhower: "I need him."

The President does indeed need his staff. He needs them because they fill a variety of functions that are essential to presidential decision-making. Some act as gatekeepers and guardians of the President's time. Others deal almost exclusively with Congress. Still others serve as links with the executive departments and agencies, channeling problems, and conflicts among the departments, to the President. Some advise the President on political questions, patronage, and appointments. Others may write his speeches. The press secretary issues presidential announcements on matters large and small and fences with correspondents at twice-daily press briefings.

Presidents use their staffs differently. Eisenhower had a tight, formal system, with Adams, as chief of staff, screening all problems and deciding what the President should see. Kennedy favored a less structured arrangement, regarding his staff as "a wheel and a series of spokes" with himself in the center.[35]

The federal budget for 1971 listed 548 persons under "The White House Office," and a budget of $8,500,000. Of these presidential staff members, perhaps only a dozen occupied top-ranking positions of policy influence.

Inevitably, the Chief Executive's vision, to a degree, is filtered through the eyes of these men. An Eisenhower or a Nixon, with a rigid staff system, may become isolated in the White House. A Lyndon Johnson, with an overpowering, demanding personality, may surround himself with deferential yes-men. In short, the President's staff may not let him hear enough, or it may tell him only what he wants to hear. Like all presidential instruments, the White House staff is a double-edged sword.

The White House staff is only a small part of the huge presidential establishment that has burgeoned since Franklin D. Roosevelt's day. Under the umbrella of the Executive Office of the President, there are more than half a dozen key agencies serving the President directly, with a combined budget in 1971 of $45 million and a total staff of 4,600.[36] (See Figure 10-1.) Most of these employees have offices in the Executive Office Building just west of the White House.

President Roosevelt established the Executive Office of the President in 1939, by executive order, after a committee of scholars had reported to him: "The President needs help." Since that time, the office has grown steadily. Its major components are described below.

The National Security Council. When the United States emerged as a major world power after the Second World War, no central machinery existed to advise the President and help him coordinate American military and foreign policy. The National Security Council (NSC) was created under the National Security Act of 1947 to fill this gap. Its members are the Presi-

The
Executive Office
of the President

---

[35] *Conversation Between President Kennedy and NBC Correspondent Ray Scherer*, p. 3.
[36] This total includes some 2,700 employees of the Office of Economic Opportunity, not a Presidential staff agency. A more realistic total of employees in the Executive Office of the President, therefore, would be 1,900.

FIGURE 10-1

Executive Office of the President

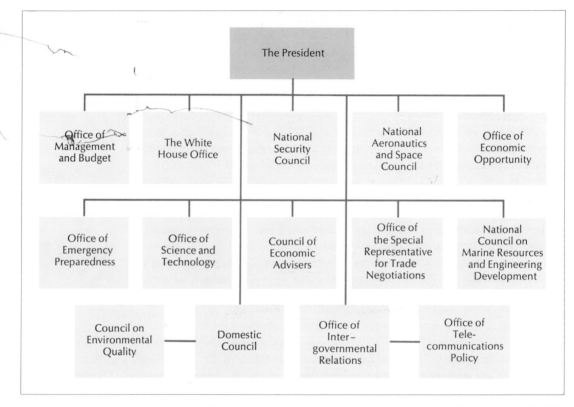

Source: Adapted from the *United States Government Organization Manual, 1970–1971* (Washington D.C.: U.S. Government Printing Office, 1970).

dent, the Vice-President, the Secretaries of State and Defense, and the Director of the Office of Emergency Preparedness.

Like the Cabinet, the NSC has been put to vastly different use by different Presidents. Eisenhower used the NSC extensively, and during his administration a substructure of boards and committees mushroomed beneath it. During one period, Eisenhower personally attended forty-three of forty-five consecutive NSC meetings.[37]

Kennedy abolished the NSC substructure but utilized the council staff under McGeorge Bundy to plan and coordinate policy. During the Cuban missile crisis, Kennedy established an informal body known as the Execu-

[37] Harry Howe Ransom, *Can American Democracy Survive Cold War?* (Garden City, N.Y.: Doubleday, 1963), pp. 33–34.

tive Committee of the National Security Council. Much larger than the statutory membership of the NSC, it consisted of some sixteen top officials and advisers in the foreign policy, military, and intelligence fields whom the President felt it appropriate to consult. Johnson also used the NSC informally. Nixon, an NSC member during the Eisenhower administration, sought as President to restore the NSC and its staff to its former place in the White House policy machinery. Although he has made greater use of the NSC than either of his two predecessors did, he has not used that body as rigidly as some had predicted at the start of his administration. Before making the controversial decision to send combat forces into Cambodia, for example, Nixon met with the NSC, but he also held a series of conferences with such White House staff aides as Robert Haldeman and John Erlichman, and other advisers outside the NSC structure.

Domestic Council. In 1970, President Nixon created a Domestic Council to advise the President "on the total range of domestic policy." [38] In the field of domestic affairs, the council occupies a position equivalent to that of the NSC in the national security field.

The Domestic Council was established under a reorganization plan sent to Congress by Nixon. Its creation had been recommended by an Advisory Commission on Executive Organization appointed by the President in 1969. The council's members are the President, who serves as chairman, the Vice-President, members of the Cabinet (excluding the secretaries of State and Defense), three counselors to the President, the director and deputy director of the Office of Management and Budget, and the director of the Office of Economic Opportunity. Nixon appointed his top assistant, John Ehrlichman, as executive director of the council, with substantial influence over its operations.

As an advisory body, the council has no responsibility for administering programs, but since it includes the majority of the Cabinet, most of its members do have responsibility for carrying out the council's recommendations. Nixon described the council's chief functions this way: to assess national needs, to identify alternative ways to achieve national goals, to respond rapidly on urgent domestic problems, to help establish national priorities for the allocation of available resources, and to maintain a check on existing programs.[39] Like the NSC, the council has a separate staff under its executive director.

Office of Management and Budget. The Office of Management and Budget (OMB) was created by President Nixon in 1970 under the same

---

[38] President Nixon's message to Congress on reorganizing the Executive Office, *New York Times*, March 13, 1970, p. 18.
[39] *Ibid.*

reorganization plan that established the Domestic Council. A successor agency to what had been called the Bureau of the Budget, OMB was designed to tighten presidential control over the federal bureaucracy and improve its performance.

Nixon described OMB as "the President's principal arm for the exercise of his managerial functions." He added: "The Domestic Council will be primarily concerned with what we do: the Office of Management and Budget will be primarily concerned with how we do it, and how well we do it." [40]

The OMB has two overlapping functions: preparing the federal budget, and serving as a management tool for the Chief Executive. The director of the office advises the President on the allocation of federal funds, and he attempts to resolve the competing claims of the departments and agencies for a larger share of the federal budget. The task of preparing and administering the annual budget gives OMB enormous power within the government. At the same time, because of OMB's monitoring of federal spending, it serves as a valuable instrument of presidential control over the executive branch. Subject to congressional action, of course, OMB helps the President control the purse strings.

In establishing the office, Nixon placed great emphasis on OMB's second function as a managerial tool. The office has responsibility for evaluating the performance of federal agencies to ascertain which programs "are actually achieving their intended results." [41] OMB also is responsible for improving government organization, developing information and management systems, and creating programs for the recruitment and training of federal career executives.

As in the case of its predecessor, OMB reviews legislation for its potential impact on the budget and supervises all federal statistical information. Its director advises the President on economic policy as a member of an informal group that includes the Secretary of the Treasury, the chairman of the Council of Economic Advisers, and the chairman of the Federal Reserve Board.

Council of Economic Advisers. Since the Great Depression of the thirties, the President has taken on the role of Chief Economist; he is expected to manage the nation's prosperity. Because few Presidents are economic experts, the President, since 1946, has relied upon a three-man council of economists to assist him in the formation of national economic policy. Should the Federal Government institute wage and price controls to stem inflation? Should taxes be increased, or federal spending reduced? What level of unemployment can the administration risk in formulating its

[40] *Ibid.*
[41] *Ibid.*

economic programs and policies? For help in answering these complex questions, the President may turn to the Council of Economic Advisers.

The three members, one of whom is designated chairman by the President, are subject to Senate confirmation. The council is expected to give impartial, professional advice, but since its members are also part of the President's administration, they perform a difficult task. Before an election, for example, the council may express optimism about the economy even though the cost of living and unemployment are rising. As in the case of other presidential advisers, the council operates within a political framework.

Council on Environmental Quality. The council was created by an act of Congress signed into law by President Nixon in 1970. Its purpose is to advise the President on how the Federal Government can attempt to control pollution of the environment in a technological society. The creation of a council directly under the President reflected the increasing public concern over this issue in the 1970's. The council has three members who are appointed by the President and approved by the Senate. The principal task of the council is to review and clear any project of a federal department or agency affecting the environment. It also conducts research on problems relating to the environment—air pollution by automobiles, for example—and assists the President in the preparation of an annual report on the state of the environment.

Other Presidential Units. Several other important units are located in the Executive Office of the President. The *Office of Emergency Preparedness* was created in 1968 as the successor to a series of civil defense agencies. It assists the President in planning to cope with disasters, both military and natural, and in stockpiling critical materials. The *Office of Science and Technology*, created in 1962, advises the President on science policy, in both the national security and domestic fields. The *Office of Intergovernmental Relations* was also created in 1969 by Nixon to act as a clearinghouse for problems involving the relationships among federal, state, and local governments. The *Office of Economic Opportunity*, better known as the Poverty Program, was created in 1964 under President Johnson and extended during the first year of the Nixon administration.

"I am Vice President," said John Adams. "In this I am nothing, but I may be everything." [42]

The remark is apt, even today. Under the Constitution, the Vice-President's only duties are to preside over the Senate, to vote in that body

The Vice-President

[42] Donald Young, *American Roulette: The History and Dilemma of the Vice Presidency* (New York: Holt, Rinehart and Winston, 1965), p. 10.

399

in case of a tie, and (under the Twenty-fifth Amendment) to help decide whether the President is disabled, and, if so, to serve as Acting President.

If the President dies, resigns, or is removed from office, however, the Vice-President becomes President. Up to 1970, this had occurred eight times as the result of the death of a President. In four of those cases, the President had been assassinated.

Traditionally, the candidate for Vice-President is chosen by the presidential nominee to "balance the ticket," to add geographic or other strength to the campaign. Thus, Kennedy, a Northerner, selected Lyndon Johnson, a Southerner, even though his decision was initially opposed by labor and big city party leaders in the North. Similarly, Nixon chose Spiro Agnew of Maryland, a relatively obscure governor, in an effort to strengthen the national ticket's appeal in Southern and border states.

Agnew quickly emerged as a controversial political figure. He attacked leaders of the protest against the Vietnam war as an "effete corps of impudent snobs" and assailed network news commentators who had been critical in their analyses of a presidential address to the nation on Vietnam. It appeared that Nixon had found in his Vice-President a useful political instrument to woo Southern and conservative voters away from George Wallace. In addition, Agnew served as a political lightning rod, drawing some criticism away from the President.

In the twentieth century, four Vice-Presidents have succeeded to the Presidency through the death of an incumbent President. These statistics

SOME VICE-PRESIDENTS VIEW THEIR OFFICE

JOHN ADAMS

My country has in its wisdom contrived for me the most insignificant office that ever the invention of man contrived or his imagination conceived.

THOMAS JEFFERSON

The second office of this Government is honorable and easy, the first is but a splendid misery.

JOHN NANCE GARNER

The vice-presidency isn't worth a pitcher of warm spit.

HARRY TRUMAN

Look at all the Vice-Presidents in history. Where are they? They were about as useful as a cow's fifth teat.

THOMAS R. MARSHALL

Like a man in a cataleptic state [the Vice-President] cannot speak; he cannot move; he suffers no pain; and yet he is perfectly conscious of everything that is going on about him.

SPIRO AGNEW

Now I know what a turkey feels like before Thanksgiving.

—In Donald Young, *American Roulette;* Spiro Agnew quoted in the Los Angeles Times *West Magazine,* June 22, 1969.

would seem to recommend that Vice-Presidents be carefully selected on merit rather than solely for political considerations.

From time to time, Presidents appoint *ad hoc* "blue ribbon" commissions of prominent citizens to study special problems. Such panels can be helpful to a President by dealing with a major crisis, providing influential support for his programs, or by deflecting political pressure from the White House. Conversely, they may cause him headaches by criticizing his administration or by proposing remedies he does not favor.

Presidential
Commissions

After President Kennedy's assassination, the nation was torn by doubt and speculation over the facts of his death. President Johnson convinced the prestigious Chief Justice Earl Warren to head the investigating commission. The detailed, 888-page report of the Warren Commission concluded that Lee Harvey Oswald, "acting alone," had shot the President. At first, this conclusion seemed to reassure much of the public that no conspiracy existed, but in the months and years that followed, the Warren Commission's conclusions were widely attacked by many critics who refused to accept the shooting as the act of one person.

After the urban riots of 1967, Johnson named a presidential commission headed by Governor Otto Kerner of Illinois to study the problem. The Riot Commission largely blamed "white racism" for the protests in the ghettos, and called for massive federal programs to improve conditions in the inner-city. But the commission failed to praise Johnson for what his administration had accomplished in the field of civil rights, and thereby won only a lukewarm endorsement from the President. When the National Commission on Obscenity and Pornography, which had been appointed by President Johnson, suggested in 1970 that restrictions on pornography be eased, President Nixon publicly denounced the recommendations as "morally bankrupt" and rejected the report.

Other factors affect the President's ability to achieve his objectives. The President is the chief actor on the Washington stage. He is carefully watched by bureaucrats, members of Congress, party leaders, and the press. The decisions he makes affect his professional reputation among these groups. In turn, his effectiveness as President depends upon this professional reputation.[43]

The Informal
Tools of Power

In the exercise of presidential power, in the process of reputation-building, the President has available to him not only the formal tools of the office, but a broad range of *informal techniques*. Many Presidents since Andrew Jackson have had a "kitchen cabinet" of informal advisers who

[43] Neustadt, *Presidential Power*, Chapter 4.

hold no official position on the White House staff. Theodore Roosevelt had his "tennis cabinet," Warren Harding his "poker cabinet," and Herbert Hoover, who liked exercise, his "medicine ball cabinet." More recently, President Johnson often called on friends such as Washington attorneys Abe Fortas, James H. Rowe, and Clark Clifford for advice.

With the development of electronic mass media, Presidents can make direct appeals to the people. Roosevelt began the practice with his famous "Fireside Chats" over radio. Today, the President may schedule a live, televised speech or press conference to publicize his policies. He may call a White House Conference to dramatize a major issue, such as hunger, education, or civil rights. He may flatter key members of Congress by inviting them to cruise down the Potomac on the presidential yacht. He bargains with congressional leaders at weekly White House breakfasts, an informal institution that pays presidential homage to the importance of the leaders and incidentally allows them to make statements for the television cameras as they emerge from the Executive Mansion.

The President
and the Press

One of President Nixon's first moves was to install Herbert G. Klein as his "Communications Director," in order, it was claimed, to eliminate the "credibility gap" that had plagued Johnson. The phrase had been used to describe public mistrust, at times, of statements by the Johnson administration. Nixon pledged an "open" Presidency and Klein promised that "truth will become the hallmark of the Nixon administration," but gaining public confidence in government pronouncements is not a simple task. Administrations normally conceive it in their self-interest to suppress embarrassing information. Mistakes, errors in judgment, poorly conceived or badly executed policies, are seldom brought to light unless discovered by the press or congressional investigators. Even then, White House spokesmen try to minimize unfavorable events. In describing military or intelligence operations, in particular, government sometimes tends to conceal or distort. If the truth later becomes known, public confidence may be undermined.

Yet today, a President's credibility is a very important measure of his power to persuade and to lead. And that credibility rests in large part on what he and his administration tell the press, and on how the presidential "image" is reflected in the news media.

Most Presidents grant private interviews with a few syndicated columnists and influential Washington correspondents. They hope in that way to gain support for their views in the press and among readers. But the presidential press conference is a more direct device used by the Chief Executive to reach the public. Wilson began the practice by inviting reporters into his office. Harding, Coolidge, and Hoover accepted only written questions, and their press conferences were generally dull. Roosevelt held regular news conferences, canceled the requirement for written questions, and played the press like a virtuoso. Truman moved the press conference from his office to the Executive Office Building, establishing a more formal atmosphere.

Since Wilson's day, reporters could not quote the President directly without permission, but Eisenhower changed this, allowing his news conferences to be filmed and released to television after editing. Kennedy instituted "live," unedited TV press conferences in the modern auditorium of the State Department, and he dazzled the press with his skill in fielding questions. But Kennedy was also accused of "news management," of manipulating events to preserve the administration's image; and he drew unfavorable reaction by canceling his subscription to the *New York Herald Tribune* when its coverage irritated him. Johnson had some full-dress press conferences but often preferred to answer questions from newsmen while loping rapidly around the White House south lawn. President Nixon, agile in answering questions, reverted to formal, televised press conferences, usually in the White House East Room.

PRESIDENTIAL DISABILITY AND SUCCESSION

Twice in American history, Presidents were incapacitated for long periods. Garfield lived for eighty days after he was shot in 1881. Wilson never fully recovered from the illness that struck him in September 1919; yet he remained in office until March 1921. To a considerable extent, Mrs. Wilson was President. President Eisenhower suffered three serious illnesses, including a heart attack in 1955 that incapacitated him for four days and curtailed his workload for sixteen weeks. Sherman Adams and Press Secretary James Hagerty ran the executive branch machinery during this period.

Eisenhower's heart attack in 1955 raised anew the question of Presidential disability. The Constitution was exceedingly vague on the subject. It spoke of Presidential "inability" and "disability" but left it up to Congress to define those terms and to decide when and how the Vice-President would take over when a President was unable to exercise his powers and duties. If a President became physically or mentally ill, or disappeared, or was captured in a military operation, or was under anesthesia in the hospital, what was the Vice-President's proper role? Did he become President or only assume the "powers and duties" of the office? And for how long? Eisenhower and Nixon sought to cover these contingencies with an unofficial written agreement, a practice followed by Kennedy and Johnson and Johnson and Humphrey.

But suppose a President was unable or unwilling to declare that he was disabled? Who would then decide whether he was disabled or when

If the President is disabled. . . . When Woodrow Wilson was incapacitated by a stroke in 1919, his wife, Edith Bolling Galt Wilson, virtually acted as President for seventeen months, until his term expired. The Twenty-fifth Amendment was designed to cope with this problem by permitting the Vice-President to act when the President is disabled.

he might resume his duties? Could a scheming Vice-President, with the help of psychiatrists, somehow have a perhaps temporarily unstable President permanently removed from office?

The Twenty-fifth Amendment, ratified in 1967, sought to settle these questions. It provides that the Vice-President becomes *Acting President* if the President informs Congress in writing that he is unable to perform his duties. Or, the Vice-President may become Acting President if he and a majority of the Cabinet, or of some "other body" created by Congress, decide that the President is disabled. The President can reclaim his office at any time unless the Vice-President and a majority of the Cabinet or other body contend that he has not recovered. Congress would then decide the issue. But it would take a two-thirds vote of both houses within three weeks to support the Vice-President; anything less and the President would resume office.

Kennedy's assassination in 1963 focused attention on two related problems. First, there was no constitutional provision for replacing a Vice-President when that office became vacant.[44] Second, under the Presidential Succession Act of 1947, after Johnson was sworn in as President in 1963, those next in line for the Presidency were House Speaker John McCormack, then 72, and the President pro tempore of the Senate, Carl Hayden, then 86.

[44] The nation has been without a Vice-President 16 times for a total of 37 years.

We arrived at Love Field in Dallas, as I remember, just shortly after 11:30 a.m.

. . . the President and Mrs. Kennedy walked along the fence, shaking hands with people in the crowd that had assembled. . . .

Mrs. Johnson, Senator Ralph Yarborough, and I then entered the car which had been provided for us in the motorcade. . . . We were the second car behind the President's automobile. . . .

As we drove closer to town, the crowds became quite large. . . .

After we had proceeded a short way down Elm Street, I heard a sharp report. . . .

I was startled by the sharp report or explosion, but I had no time to speculate as to its origin because Agent Youngblood turned in a flash, immediately after the first explosion, hitting me on the shoulder, and shouted to all of us in the back seat to get down. I was pushed down by Agent Youngblood. Almost in the same moment in which he hit or pushed me, he vaulted over the back seat and sat on me. I was bent over under the weight of Agent Youngblood's body. . . .

When we arrived at the hospital, Agent Youngblood told me to get out of the car, go into the building, not to stop, and to stay close to him and the other agents. . . .

In the hospital room to which Mrs. Johnson and I were taken, the shades were drawn—I think by Agent Youngblood. . . .

Agent Youngblood told me that I could not leave the room, and I followed his direction. . . .

It was Ken O'Donnell who, at about 1:20 p.m., told us that the President had died. I think his precise words were "He's gone." . . .

I found it hard to believe that this had happened. The whole thing seemed unreal—unbelievable. A few hours earlier, I had breakfast with John Kennedy; he was alive, strong, vigorous. I could not believe now that he was dead. I was shocked and sickened.

—Statement of President Lyndon B. Johnson to the Warren Commission, July 10, 1964.

So the Twenty-fifth Amendment also provided that the President shall nominate a Vice-President, subject to the approval of a majority of both houses of Congress, whenever that office becomes vacant. The provision virtually nullifies the possibility of presidential succession by the House Speaker or the Senate President, or by Cabinet members, except in the event that the President and Vice-President died simultaneously.

THE SPLENDID MISERY: PERSONALITY AND STYLE IN THE WHITE HOUSE

Thomas Jefferson conceived of the Presidency as "a splendid misery." Others, like Franklin Roosevelt and Kennedy, brought great vigor and vitality to the job; they seemed to *enjoy* being President.

The personality, style, and concept of the office that each President brings to the White House affect the nature of his Presidency. William Howard Taft expressed the classic, restrictive, view of the Presidency: "The President can exercise no power which cannot be fairly and reasonably traced to some specific grant of power." [45] Theodore Roosevelt ad-

[45] Tourtellot, *The Presidents on the Presidency*, p. 426.

hered to the "stewardship" theory. He saw the Chief Executive as "a steward of the people" and believed that "it was not only his right but his duty to do anything that the needs of the Nation demanded unless such action was forbidden by the Constitution or by the laws." [46] Lincoln and Franklin Roosevelt went even further, contending that in great emergencies the President could exercise almost unlimited power to preserve the nation.

Louis W. Koenig has classified Presidents as "literalist" (Madison, Buchanan, Taft, and, to a degree, Eisenhower) and "strong" (Presidents such as Washington, Jackson, Lincoln, Wilson, and the Roosevelts), adding that many Chief Executives fall somewhere in the middle. A literalist President, as defined by Koenig, closely obeys the letter of the Constitution; a strong President, who generally flourishes in times of crisis and change, interprets his constitutional powers as liberally as possible.[47]

A President's personality and approach to the office may leave a more lasting impression than his substantive accomplishments or failures. We think of Teddy Roosevelt shouting "Bully!"; Wilson, austere and idealistic, in the end shattered by events; Franklin D. Roosevelt in a wheel chair, cigarette holder tilted at a jaunty angle, conquering paralysis with élan. We think of Eisenhower's golf, Kennedy's glamour, Johnson's cowpuncher image, Nixon's polished use of television—all say something about how they occupied the office of President.

James David Barber has tentatively attempted to systematize the study of presidential behavior by analyzing how childhood and other experiences may have molded a President's character and style. He has proposed four broad, general character types into which Presidents may be grouped, and has suggested that from such an analysis it might ultimately be possible to theorize about future presidential behavior.[48] Thus, Barber contends that Eisenhower reluctantly ran for President because he was "a sucker for duty" as a result of his background; that Johnson ruled through "social manipulation"; and that there is a danger that Nixon, who makes decisions in "lonely seclusion," may "commit himself irrevocably to some disastrous course of action." [49] Barber attempts to support his conclusions by searching out patterns in the histories of the leaders he studies. In Johnson's case, for example, Barber contends that as far back as his college days, Johnson used social manipulation to gain prominence in the college he attended. Barber analyzes Nixon's book *Six Crises*, and reports in the press since Nixon became President, to draw his conclusion that Nixon makes his decisions in isolation.

[46] *Ibid.*, pp. 55–56.
[47] Louis W. Koenig, *The Chief Executive* (New York: Harcourt Brace Jovanovich, 1968), pp. 10–12.
[48] James David Barber, "The President and His Friends," paper prepared for delivery at the American Political Science Association Annual Meeting, New York, September 1969. The four types that Barber identified are active-positive, active-negative, passive-positive, passive-negative.
[49] *Ibid.*, pp. 28, 37, 41.

A President's personality and style leave their imprint: Lyndon Johnson issues orders to a doubtful steer on his Texas ranch; and William Howard Taft, who weighed 332 pounds, displays a graceful follow-through.

While such speculation is fascinating, some observers would contend that Presidents may decline to act in ways that psychological analysis of their lives from afar might suggest.[50]

THE AMERICAN PRESIDENCY: CENTER OF AMERICAN DEMOCRACY

President Kennedy, seeking the Presidency in 1960, viewed it as "the vital center of action in our whole scheme of government." The problems of America, he said, "demand a vigorous

[50] It is interesting to note in this connection that before President Kennedy met in Vienna in 1961 with Soviet Premier Khrushchev, he had access to an assessment of Khrushchev's character prepared for the CIA by a panel of psychiatrists and psychologists. See Bryant Wedge, "Khrushchev at a Distance—A Study of Public Personality," *Trans-Action*, October 1968.

John F. Kennedy viewed the Presidency as a "vital center of action."

proponent of the national interest—not a passive broker for conflicting private interests," a President who will "place himself in the very thick of the fight." [51]

In 1968, Richard Nixon expressed much the same view. "The days of a passive Presidency belong to a simpler past," he said. "The next President must take an activist view of his office. . . . He must lead." [52]

Yet, as Koenig has noted, the President may *not* be able to solve the worst problems that confront him. [53] He cannot, singlehandedly, end the racial conflict that threatens America's future in the 1970's. Nor can he easily use the nation's nuclear power in foreign policy crises—to prevent the seizure of an American vessel by a smaller power, for example. Koenig has suggested the concept of "the imagined Presidency," which is "vested in our minds with more power than the Presidency really has." [54] The dif-

[51] *Congressional Record*, January 18, 1960, p. 711.
[52] Richard Nixon, "The Nature of the Presidency," speech broadcast over NBC and CBS Radio Networks, September 19, 1968.
[53] Koenig, *The Chief Executive*, Chapter 1.
[54] *Ibid.*, p. 3.

ference between the real and the imagined Presidency, he contends, may lead to public frustration over presidential performance.

Although the great power of the Presidency tends to overshadow its limitations, we have seen how, in many spheres, that power is circumscribed. As Chief Executive, the President faces an often intractable bureaucracy. As Chief Legislator, under the constitutional separation of powers, he faces an independent and often hostile Congress. As military and foreign policy leader, he must consider sentiment in Congress and the bureaucracy. The Twenty-second Amendment limits the President to two terms and thereby weakens his power in the second term (since everyone knows he will not be President again). Federal law may restrict his options. The Supreme Court may strike down his programs. Public opinion may turn against him. The necessities of politics occasionally force him to weigh his actions in terms of their effect on his party. Finally—though such action is most unlikely today—he may be impeached and removed from office, a fate that Andrew Johnson escaped by one vote in 1868.[55]

Whether the Presidency is too powerful, or not powerful enough, depends, then, to some extent, not only on how a President uses his power but also on what he hopes to accomplish. Presidents have different *goals*. Recent Democratic Presidents have tried to press forward with energetic programs of social reform. Other Presidents, such as Eisenhower, have tried to cool things down.

The answer to the question of whether Presidents have "too much" power depends ultimately on what one expects of the office and of the American political system. In the domestic arena, those who regard the Presidency as an essential instrument to meet the social challenges and problems of the nation today, do not tend to regard that office as too powerful. Others, alarmed at the size of the federal bureaucracy and opposed to social welfare programs, may take a different view of the Presidency.

In any event, presidential power fluctuates, depending in part on the situation in which it is being exercised. Franklin Roosevelt was able to wield enormous economic powers during the early years of the New Deal because the nation was in the throes of an acute depression. By 1938, he was encountering substantial domestic opposition. When the Second World War came along, he was able to exercise great powers once more—people expected it.

The power a President exercises not only depends on the times and the circumstances, but also on the policy area involved. A strong argument can be made that there are relatively few effective curbs on the President

---

[55] Johnson was the only President tried in an impeachment proceeding. Only the House can vote to impeach a President. He is tried by the Senate with the Chief Justice presiding, and may be removed only if convicted, by two-thirds of the Senators present, of "Treason, Bribery or other high Crimes and Misdemeanors."

in committing American military power—the undeclared war in Southeast Asia illustrates the point. In the domestic field, however, his powers may not be strong enough. For example, although the President is expected to manage prosperity, he has not been granted discretionary power to change tax rates to respond to threats of inflation or recession.

Given the problems that face the nation today, a President must act. The President (along with the Vice-President) is the only official of the American government elected by all of the people. The Presidency, there-fore, is the branch of government best able to view and act upon national problems in the interest of a national constituency. In a pluralist democracy of conflicting interests and competing groups, he is the only official who represents the people as a whole, and who can symbolize their aspirations. He is the custodian of the right to life of unborn generations. Despite the limitations on his powers, he can be the greatest force for national unity—or disunity. He can recognize the demands of minorities for social justice or he can repress their rights. He can lead the nation into war or preserve the peace. Such is his power that he leaves his indelible mark on the times, with the result that the triumph or tragedy of each Presidency is, in some measure at least, also our own.

SUGGESTED READING

Burns, James MacGregor. *Roosevelt: The Lion and the Fox* * (Harcourt Brace Jovanovich, 1956). A political biography of Franklin D. Roosevelt, one of the foremost practitioners of the art of presidential leadership. Focuses primarily on the Roosevelt Presidency during the New Deal years prior to the Second World War.

Burns, James MacGregor. *Roosevelt: The Soldier of Freedom* (Harcourt Brace Jovanovich, 1970). The concluding volume of Burns' political biography of Franklin D. Roosevelt, focusing on the war years. Burns presents Roosevelt as a statesman and war leader who was at the same time a master politician maneuvering to preserve his political power.

Corwin, Edward S. *The President, Office and Powers* * (New York University Press, 1957). A classic analysis of the American Presidency. Stresses the historical development and the legal powers of the office of President.

Evans, Rowland, and Novak, Robert. *Lyndon B. Johnson: The Exercise of Power* * (New American Library, 1966). A detailed, anecdotal, and il-luminating account by two Washington columnists of Lyndon Johnson's rise to the Presidency and his early years in the White House. Particularly revealing in its analysis of Johnson's leadership techniques in the Senate.

Fenno, Richard F., Jr. *The President's Cabinet: An Analysis in the Period from Wilson to Eisenhower* * (Harvard University Press, 1959). A thoughtful analysis of the development of the Cabinet and its role as a distinct political institution. Examines the dual role of Cabinet members as presidential advisers and department heads and the place of the Cabinet in the larger political system.

Koenig, Louis W. *The Chief Executive,** rev. ed. (Harcourt Brace Jovanovich, 1968). An excellent, readable, and comprehensive study of the many facets of the Presidency. Numerous illustrative examples.

Neustadt, Richard E. *Presidential Power* * (Wiley, 1960). A knowledgeable exploration of the problems faced by a modern President in seeking to exercise his power. The book was influential in the Kennedy administration, in which its author served for a time as a special consultant.

Reedy, George E. *The Twilight of the Presidency* (NAL-World, 1970). A critical analysis of the Presidency by a former press secretary to President Johnson. Reedy argues that the status of the institution isolates the President from the world of political reality and adversely affects the type of judgment required for modern leadership.

Rossiter, Clinton. *The American Presidency,** rev. ed. (Harcourt Brace Jovanovich, 1960). A short, lucid analysis of the American Presidency. Develops the concept of a varied, overlapping set of presidential roles and views the Presidency as the central political force in the American system.

Schlesinger, Arthur M., Jr. *A Thousand Days* * (Houghton Mifflin, 1965). A well-written, detailed account of the Kennedy years by a scholar and former presidential aide. Although Schlesinger was not at the center of power in the Kennedy White House, he had the advantage of viewing events with the eye of a trained historian.

Sidey, Hugh. *A Very Personal Presidency: Lyndon Johnson in the White House* (Atheneum, 1968). A short, readable account of the Presidency of Lyndon Johnson by a skilled journalist who observed him at close range. Suggests how a President's personality may influence his decisions and policies.

Sorensen, Theodore C. *Kennedy* * (Harper and Row, 1965). The Kennedy Presidency seen through the eyes of his closest adviser and speechwriter. Includes behind-the-scenes accounts of presidential decision-making during such events as the Bay of Pigs invasion, the confrontation with the steel industry, and the Cuban missile crisis.

* Available in paperback edition

11

The Bureaucracy

As the decade of the 1970's began, a subcommittee of the United States Senate heard conflicting and highly controversial testimony on a subject of great popular interest: the Pill. At the time, birth control pills had been on the market for ten years; an estimated 8.5 million American women were taking them.

At the hearings in January 1970, medical witnesses warned that the pills might cause breast cancer in women as well as death through blood clotting. Other witnesses disputed these warnings, but the testimony was front-page news around the country. As the debate mounted, the Food and Drug Administration (FDA) sent a letter to 300,000 physicians urging them to discuss frankly with patients the risks of birth control pills. "In most cases," the letter said, "a full disclosure of the potential adverse effects of these products would seem advisable." And the FDA sent telegrams asking drug manufacturers only to issue promotional materials for the pills that reflected the official label warning required since January 1, 1970. The new

FIGURE 11-1

Death and the Pill

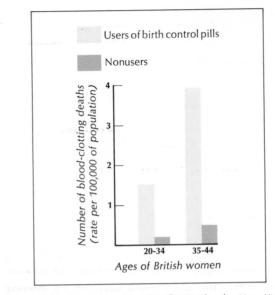

Source: *New York Times*, January 25, 1970. © 1970 by the New York Times Company. Reprinted by permission.

labeling, publicizing the danger of blood clots, was based partly on the results of British studies published in 1968. (See Figure 11-1.)

There had been suggestions of possible risks connected with the Pill for several years.[1] In 1966, an advisory committee studying the problem for the FDA found "no adequate scientific data at this time" to prove the pills "unsafe for human use." However, the panel recommended further studies, and in 1968, after receiving the British data, the FDA put into effect a label warning that was strengthened in 1970 on the basis of a study by the FDA advisory panel that confirmed the British findings.

The controversy over the safety of birth control pills was by no means resolved. But how, it might be asked, could the government have allowed 8.5 million women to take the Pill without publicizing and emphasizing the risks sooner? Why did the FDA wait until a Senate hearing was under way to urge doctors to discuss these risks with their patients?

The answers to such questions may be found, in part, in the general nature of *bureaucracy*. In theory, bureaucrats are public servants who sim-

[1] See, for example, Morton Mintz, "Are Birth Control Pills Safe?" *Washington Post*, December 19, 1965, p. E1. Prior to that date there had been numerous warnings by medical authorities.

ply administer policy decisions made by the accountable officials of the government—the President, his principal appointees, and Congress. In fact, government administrators by their actions—or inaction—often make policy. As Francis E. Rourke has noted, "Bureaucrats themselves have now become a central factor in the policy process: in the initiation of proposals, the weighing of alternatives, and the resolution of conflict." [2]

Bureaucrats have great *discretionary powers;* what they decide to do, or not to do, constitutes a policy output. Certainly the Food and Drug Administration made government policy by its handling of the Pill. The American bureaucracy is deeply involved in politics as well as policy. As in the case of the President and members of Congress, government agencies have *constituencies.* These are interest groups, or clientele, either directly regulated by the bureaucracy or vitally affected by its decisions. The drug industry is a major constituent of the Food and Drug Administration. Since the drug industry's sales of birth control pills at the time of the hearings amounted to more than $100,000,000 a year, the industry had a considerable stake in keeping the Pill on the market.

Sometimes, through close political and personal association between a government agency and its clientele group, the regulating agency becomes a captive of the industry it is supposed to regulate. "In its most developed form," Rourke observes, "the relationship between an interest group and an administrative agency is so close that it is difficult to know where the group leaves off and the agency begins." [3]

The close relationship of government agencies with their constituent groups can work to the disadvantage of consumers. For example, in evaluating drug safety the FDA must rely almost completely on drug studies performed by the industry itself. A secret FDA report made public by United Press International in 1969 disclosed that in the previous four years, several hundred drugs had been recalled as a result of mislabeling or defects discovered *after* the drugs had been placed on sale to the public; and it concluded that in the general area of consumer protection "we are currently not equipped to cope with the challenge." [4]

Although a government bureau may be influenced by its clientele, it may at the same time be sensitive to, and responsive to, pressures elsewhere in the political system. As a unit of the Department of Health, Education, and Welfare, a Cabinet department answerable to the President, the FDA is expected to be aware of the larger public affected by its decisions— the American consumer. Since the safety of the Pill was a potentially ex-

[2] Francis E. Rourke, ed., *Bureaucratic Power in National Politics* (Boston: Little, Brown, 1965), p. vii.

[3] Francis E. Rourke, *Bureaucracy, Politics, and Public Policy* (Boston: Little, Brown, 1969), p. 15.

[4] Congressional Quarterly, *Weekly Report*, August 22, 1969, p. 1552.

plosive political issue affecting the health of millions, the FDA reacted when the Senate investigation focused public attention on its activities.

The bureaucracy, therefore, acts and reacts in a political way. It responds to pluralist pressures because it is at once accountable to several groups—its "clients," the public at large, the press, Congress, and the President.

BUREAUCRACY AND THE DEMOCRATIC PROCESS

"Bureaucrat" is a neutral word—it simply means an administrator—but its connotations are far from complimentary. "Bureaucrat" and "bureaucracy" are words that, to some people, conjure up an image of self-important but inefficient petty officials wallowing in red tape. It has been wryly suggested, and is widely believed, that, once established, bureaucracies tend to mushroom under "Parkinson's Law": "Work expands so as to fill the time available for its completion." [5]

The bureaucracy and bureaucrats are convenient political targets to blame for society's ills. Such criticism is not limited to government bureaucracy. The student in the "multiversity" feels crushed by an impersonal bureaucracy. So may an employee of a huge corporation. The growth of computers and the tendency to assign numbers to individuals (credit cards, bank accounts, social security, selective service) has made many people feel that they are mere cogs in a vast bureaucratic machine.

Some of the sentiment directed against the federal bureaucracy can be traced to the social welfare programs of the New Deal, which vastly expanded the role of government in the lives of individual citizens. For three decades much of the criticism of the bureaucracy came from Republicans and conservatives opposed to the welfare state and the concentration of power in Washington. (Yet, during eight years of Republican rule under President Eisenhower, the Federal Government increased in size.) During the 1964 presidential campaign, Barry Goldwater, the Republican candidate, decried "the steady drift of this country into the swampland of centralized collectivism. . . . government is becoming master instead of servant. Increasingly, power is gravitating to the White House, away from our towns, counties, cities and states—the spread of federal bureaucracy must be arrested—before it cannibalizes us all." [6]

In the late 1960's, similar thoughts began to be voiced by Democratic liberals and the New Left. Ideological disenchantment with the federal bureaucracy had come full circle; conservatives and liberals joined in an antibureaucratic alliance of sorts. While campaigning for the Democratic presidential nomination in 1968, Robert Kennnedy declared: "To

[5] C. Northcote Parkinson, *Parkinson's Law* (Boston: Houghton Mifflin, 1957), p. 2.
[6] In the *New York Herald Tribune*, October 1, 1964, p. 8.

A large part of the time of all employees of the Federal Government is spent in the processes of paperwork. The cost is staggering, $8 billion.

It takes 360,000 different forms, prepared in 15 billion copies to keep the wheels of government turning.

In fiscal year 1966, the Federal Government is believed to have spent over $53 million to print its forms.

The billion letters produced annually in the Federal Government cost approximately $1.5 billion. They vary from an average of 25 cents for a form letter to an average cost of $2.75 for an individually typed letter.

Records holdings now total more than 25 million cubic feet. Throwing away a page a second of these records it would take 2,000 years to discard them all.

It costs $550 million a year to prepare "input" to "feed" the machines.

A computer can make a stack of records 20 feet high each day. Working on full weekly 7-day shifts (less five holidays) this stack could be 1.3 miles high in a year. This is one computer. The Federal Government has 2,600 computers.

Rapid-copying equipment—Once documents are made easily, cheaply, and quickly, they are bound to multiply. Organization after organization has been aghast at the number of copies their copying equipment turns out. One copy in ten is now "rapid copy."

A qualitative analysis of paperwork involves such questions as, "Why are we doing this?"

—Selections from *How to Cut Paperwork*,
Committee on Post Office and Civil Service, U.S. House of Representatives, October 1966.

return to the local community real power to act on the conditions which shape men's lives—the education of their children, the design and renewal of their cities, the recreational facilities of their rural areas—to bring back that kind of control has been a dream of liberals and conservatives alike." He advocated new kinds of programs to place "money directly into com-

Paperwork at the Securities and Exchange Commission.

The bureaucracy: Can anyone control it?

munities, instead of flowing through an inefficient, over-structured, often tyrannical bureaucracy." [7]

Some critics, such as Peter F. Drucker, have gone so far as to conclude that "modern government has become ungovernable." [8] Drucker contends that because of bureaucratic inertia and "administrative incompetence" government is unable to perform the tasks assigned to it. He adds: "There is no government today that can still claim control of its bureaucracy and of its various agencies. Government agencies are all becoming autonomous, ends in themselves, and directed by their own desire for power, their own rationale, their own narrow vision rather than by national policy." [9]

Even if such criticisms are overstated, they raise important, valid questions about the role of bureaucracy in modern society. As long as people demand more and more services from their government—social security, Medicare, aid to education, housing, and the like—some form of bureaucracy is inevitable. As long as there is bureaucracy, the question of how to control it persists.

The classic concept of the bureaucracy was developed by the pioneering German sociologist Max Weber, who saw it as a strict hierarchy, with authority flowing from the top down within a fixed framework of rigid rules and regulations. In Weber's view, the bureaucracy draws its power from its expertise. Political rulers are in no position to argue with the technical knowledge of the trained bureaucrat: "The absolute monarch is powerless opposite the superior knowledge of the bureaucratic expert." [10] Even

[7] Prepared text of remarks by Senator Robert F. Kennedy at Salt Lake City, Utah, and Brigham Young University, Provo, Utah, March 27, 1968.
[8] Peter F. Drucker, *The Age of Discontinuity* (New York: Harper & Row, 1969), p. 220.
[9] *Ibid.*
[10] In H. H. Gerth and C. Wright Mills, *From Max Weber: Essays in Sociology* (New York: Oxford University Press, 1953), p. 234.

the Russian czar of old, Weber noted, could seldom act against the wishes of his bureaucracy.

Today the bureaucracy has sources of strength other than sheer technical superiority over its nominal political masters. (These sources of strength are discussed on pp. 433–43.) Because civil servants are not elected, and are free of direct control by the voters, the bureaucracy is semipermanent in character and, at times, an independent center of power. Can the President, or Congress, control it? In a democracy, this is a serious question, for democratic institutions should be *responsive* to the people.

The bureaucracy must also be *effective* if government is to solve the social problems that face it. A Medicaid program that fattens doctors' bank accounts but fails to meet the medical needs of the poor, a pollution program that creates jobs but fails to eliminate smog—these add to the taxpayers' burden without alleviating social ills. Should the bureaucracy be broken up, decentralized? Is greater community control the answer? Closely tied to these questions is the important question of whether the bureaucracy has been captured by its constituency; whether government regulators are tools of the regulated. In short, is the bureaucracy a responsive democratic institution, or does it make public policy solely by its own decisions?

A PROFILE OF THE AMERICAN BUREAUCRACY

In 1792, the Federal Government had 780 employees. Today, there are approximately 3,000,000 [11] civilian members of the federal bureaucracy. A study of this total reveals some surprising facts. In the first place, "the bureaucracy in Washington" is not in Washington—at least most of it is not. One recent statistical breakdown, for example, showed that only 328,000 government employees—slightly more than 10 percent of the federal total—worked in the metropolitan Washington area. The rest were scattered throughout the fifty states and overseas. California alone had 326,000 federal workers; some 244,000 federal employees worked overseas. [12]

Who Are the Bureaucrats?

In 1970, 43 percent of the full-time civilian employees of the Federal Government worked for the Department of Defense—a startling figure even for a nation still locked in the Vietnam war, as America was in 1970. The 1.1 million Pentagon workers added to the more than 560,000 Postal Service employees comprised two-thirds of the entire full-time federal

[11] Total includes part-time workers. Permanent, full-time employment in the executive branch totaled slightly less than 2,600,000 in fiscal 1971.
[12] Statistics in this section are from "Special Analysis H" in *Special Analyses, Budget of the United States*, Fiscal Year 1971, pp. 99–107.

bureaucracy. In contrast, the State Department employed only 23,000 persons and the Department of Health, Education, and Welfare employed 105,000 persons. These figures, like the federal budget itself, reveal something of America's priorities as it moved into the 1970's; 43 percent of the bureaucracy was involved in military affairs and 4 percent was employed by HEW to meet social challenges at home.

The federal civilian bureaucracy of some 3,000,000 persons is unquestionably large compared to private industry; General Motors, the biggest corporation in America, had 794,000 employees in 1970. Yet, federal workers comprise only 22 percent of total (federal, state, and local) government in the United States. More than twice as many people work for local governments than for the Federal Government. As of 1970, local governments had some 7,200,000 employees (including close to 2,000,000 teachers) and state governments employed 2,700,000 persons. A comparison of federal, state, and local bureaucracies is shown in Figure 11-2.

Figure 11-2

Government Employment—Federal, State, and Local

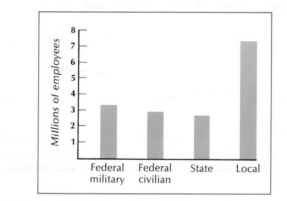

Source: U.S. Bureau of the Census; U.S. Civil Service Commission; U.S. Department of Labor. All data as of February 1970.

A rough portrait can be drawn of the "average" federal bureaucrat in 1969: he was 41.3 years old, had worked for the government for thirteen years, and earned an annual salary of $8,769.[13] The President receives $200,000 a year, the Vice-President $62,500, and members of the Cabinet $60,000. But 85 percent of the bureaucracy are members of the career civil service, with their salaries in many cases fixed on a General Schedule that

[13] *Federal Civilian Manpower Statistics,* December 1969, U.S. Civil Service Commission, p. 5. Salary average from *Survey of Current Business,* Office of Business Economics, Department of Commerce, July 1969, p. 40.

ranges from a starting salary of $4,326 for clerks (GS-1) to $35,600 for a relative handful of top civil servants (GS-18).

What kinds of workers make up the bureaucracy? Although about half a million fit the conventional image of "bureaucrats"—general administrative and clerical employees—the government also employs 147,000 engineers and architects, 114,000 accountants and budget specialists, 94,000 doctors and health specialists, 84,000 scientists, 33,900 social scientists, psychologists, and welfare workers, 8,400 librarians and archivists, and 2,400 veterinarians. Thirty-one percent of the federal employees (slightly over 905,000) are women.[14]

As we noted in Chapter 10, the federal bureaucracy consists of three basic types of agencies: the Cabinet departments, the independent executive agencies, and the independent regulatory commissions. Figure 11-3 shows the *major* executive branch agencies as of 1970, but there were approximately one hundred smaller independent units of government in existence, some even too small to warrant a line in the *United States Government Organization Manual*. In addition, there were 850 interagency committees, 1,400 citizen advisory groups, and sixty presidential committees, commissions, and task forces.[15]

As Richard E. Neustadt has emphasized, the executive branch is not a monolith: "Like our governmental structure as a whole, the executive establishment consists of separated institutions sharing powers. The President heads one of these; Cabinet officers, agency administrators, and military commanders head others. Below the departmental level, virtually independent bureau chiefs head many more."[16]

A President attempts to control the bureaucracy through his White House staff and other units of the Executive Office of the President—particularly the Office of Management and Budget—and through his department heads. Because of the sheer size of the Federal Government, however, no President can really hope to supervise all the activities of the bureaucracy.

The Cabinet Departments. The eleven Cabinet departments are the giants of the federal bureaucracy. Some idea of the structure of the executive branch, and the problem of presidential control, can be grasped by studying the organization chart of a Cabinet department. At first glance,

The Structure of the Bureaucracy

---

[14] *Study of Employment of Women in the Federal Government, 1968,* June 1969, U.S. Civil Service Commission, Bureau of Management Services, p. 161.
[15] Statement of Dwight A. Ink, Bureau of the Budget, before the Special Studies Subcommittee of the Committee on Government Operations, House of Representatives, Ninety-first Congress, Second Session, March 17, 1970.
[16] Richard E. Neustadt, *Presidential Power* (New York: Wiley, 1960), p. 39.

FIGURE 11-3

Executive Branch of the Government

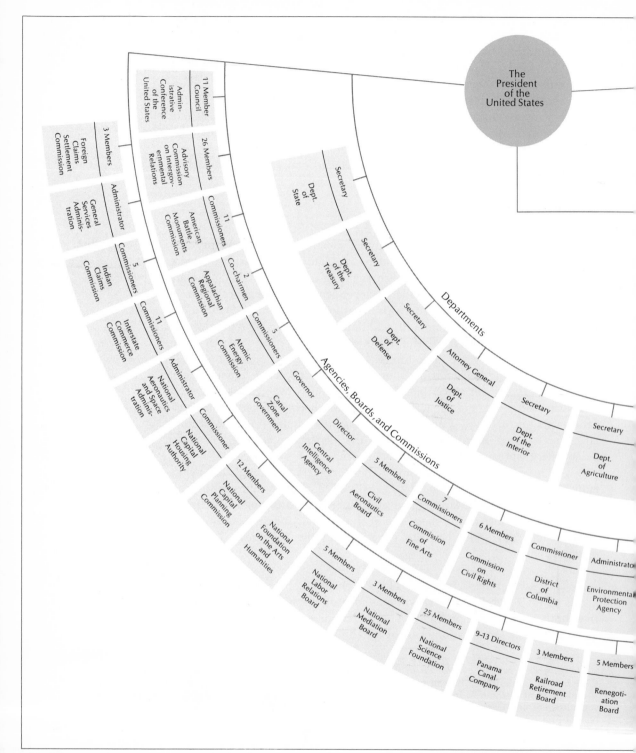

The President of the United States

Departments

Agencies, Boards, and Commissions

Dept. of State — Secretary

Dept. of the Treasury — Secretary

Dept. of Defense — Secretary

Dept. of Justice — Attorney General

Dept. of the Interior — Secretary

Dept. of Agriculture — Secretary

11 Member Council — Administrative Conference of the United States

26 Members — Advisory Commission on Intergovernmental Relations

11 Commissioners — American Battle Monuments Commission

2 Co-Chairmen — Appalachian Regional Commission

5 Commissioners — Atomic Energy Commission

Governor — Canal Zone Government

Director — Central Intelligence Agency

5 Members — Civil Aeronautics Board

7 Commissioners — Commission of Fine Arts

6 Members — Commission on Civil Rights

Commissioner — District of Columbia

Administrator — Environmental Protection Agency

3 Members — Foreign Claims Settlement Commission

Administrator — General Services Administration

5 Commissioners — Indian Claims Commission

11 Commissioners — Interstate Commerce Commission

Administrator — National Aeronautics and Space Administration

Commissioner — National Capital Housing Authority

12 Members — National Capital Planning Commission

National Foundation on the Arts and Humanities

5 Members — National Labor Relations Board

3 Members — National Mediation Board

25 Members — National Science Foundation

9–13 Directors — Panama Canal Company

3 Members — Railroad Retirement Board

5 Members — Renegotiation Board

Source: Adapted from *The Budget in Brief,* Fiscal 1971 (Washington, D.C.: U.S. Government Printing Office, 1970).

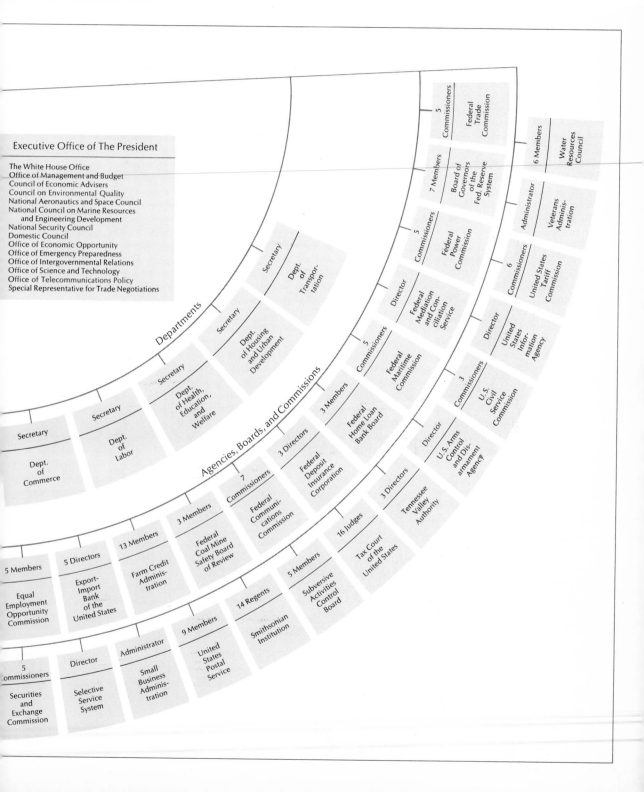

Executive Office of The President

The White House Office
Office of Management and Budget
Council of Economic Advisers
Council on Environmental Quality
National Aeronautics and Space Council
National Council on Marine Resources
   and Engineering Development
National Security Council
Domestic Council
Office of Economic Opportunity
Office of Emergency Preparedness
Office of Intergovernmental Relations
Office of Science and Technology
Office of Telecommunications Policy
Special Representative for Trade Negotiations

Departments

Agencies, Boards, and Commissions

Secretary — Dept. of Transportation

Secretary — Dept. of Housing and Urban Development

Secretary — Dept. of Health, Education, and Welfare

Secretary — Dept. of Labor

Secretary — Dept. of Commerce

5 Commissioners — Federal Trade Commission

7 Members — Board of Governors of the Fed. Reserve System

5 Commissioners — Federal Power Commission

Director — Federal Mediation and Conciliation Service

5 Commissioners — Federal Maritime Commission

3 Members — Federal Home Loan Bank Board

3 Directors — Federal Deposit Insurance Corporation

7 Commissioners — Federal Communications Commission

3 Members — Federal Coal Mine Safety Board of Review

13 Members — Farm Credit Administration

5 Directors — Export-Import Bank of the United States

5 Members — Equal Employment Opportunity Commission

6 Members — Water Resources Council

Administrator — Veterans Administration

6 Commissioners — United States Tariff Commission

Director — United States Information Agency

3 Commissioners — U.S. Civil Service Commission

Director — U.S. Arms Control and Disarmament Agency

3 Directors — Tennessee Valley Authority

16 Judges — Tax Court of the United States

5 Members — Subversive Activities Control Board

14 Regents — Smithsonian Institution

9 Members — United States Postal Service

Administrator — Small Business Administration

Director — Selective Service System

5 Commissioners — Securities and Exchange Commission

FIGURE 11-4

Department of Transportation

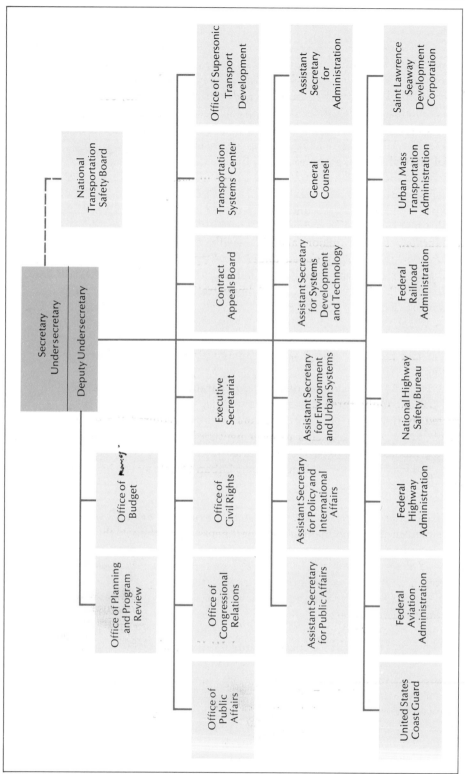

Source: United States Government Organization Manual, 1970–1971.

it might appear to be a tightly organized agency, with lines of authority flowing upward to the secretary, who in turn reports to the President. In fact, the chart masks entrenched bureaus and key civil servants, some of whom enjoy lateral ties with interest groups and congressional committees, relationships that give them power independent of the Cabinet secretary and the President. The sheer size of most departments would seem to defy presidential control. To take one example, the Department of Transportation, formed in 1966, had some 70,000 employees in fiscal 1971. As shown in Figure 11-4, the department was headed by a secretary, an undersecretary, a deputy undersecretary, and five assistant secretaries, each with responsibility for several offices down the line.

In addition, several major agencies—with sometimes competitive client groups—were loosely grouped under the Department of Transportation, including the United States Coast Guard, the Federal Aviation Administration, and the Federal Highway Administration. Although the organization chart does not show it, the Department of Transportation, like the other Cabinet departments, is dispersed geographically. The air traffic controllers of the FAA operate airport towers across the United States; the Coast Guard and the Federal Highway Administration have field offices in several cities.

The creation of the Cabinet departments parallels the growth of the American nation. Only three departments—State, War, and Treasury—were created in 1789. But new areas of concern have required the establishment of executive departments to meet new problems. This fact is reflected in the names of the departments created in recent decades—Health, Education, and Welfare in 1953, Housing and Urban Development in 1965, and Transportation in 1966.

The Executive Agencies. The *independent executive agencies* report to the President in the same manner as departments, even though they are not part of any Cabinet department. Their heads are appointed by the President and may be dismissed by him. The fact that these agencies are independent of the departments does not necessarily mean that they are small. The Veterans Administration (VA) is the third biggest agency of the government, ranking just after Defense and the United States Postal Service in number of employees. In fact, the VA, with more than 150,000 people, is larger than Health, Education, and Welfare, a Cabinet department.

Included among the executive agencies are the American Battle Monuments Commission and the Railroad Retirement Board, but others are better known and more powerful units of the bureaucracy: the National Aeronautics and Space Administration, the Central Intelligence Agency, the Selective Service System, the United States Information Agency, and the United States Arms Control and Disarmament Agency, to name a few.

Grouped with the executive agencies but somewhat different in status are *government corporations*. At one time these were semiautonomous, but through legislation since 1945 they have been placed under presidential control. Some examples of government corporations are the Federal Deposit Insurance Corporation, the Tennessee Valley Authority, and the St. Lawrence Seaway Development Corporation.

The Regulatory Commissions. The *independent regulatory commissions* occupy a special status in the bureaucracy, for they are administratively independent of all three branches of the government. In fact, however, as has been made abundantly clear over the years, the regulatory commissions and agencies are susceptible to pressures from the White House, Congress, and the industries they regulate. The regulatory agencies decide such questions as who shall receive a license to operate a television station, open a new airline route, or build a natural gas pipeline to serve a large city. These licenses are worth millions of dollars, and the competition for them is fierce. As a result, the regulatory agencies are the target of intense pressures, including, at times, approaches by skillful and high-priced Washington lawyers who go in the "back door" to argue their clients' cases in private meetings with agency officials. The agencies were created because of the need for rule-making and regulation in highly complex, technical areas involving the interests of the public. In awarding licenses, they also exercise a quasi-judicial function.

Commission members are appointed by the President with the consent of the Senate, but, unlike Cabinet members, they do not report to the President. Although members of the regulatory commissions must, by law, be drawn from more than one political party, the President designates the chairman. Through his appointive powers a President may in time gain political control of the commissions. For example, within a year of taking office, President Nixon had named Republicans to head five of the "Big Six" regulatory commissions, and Republicans had gained majority control of four.

In endowing the regulatory commissions with significant power, "the Congress intended them to be independent not only of the executive, but also of those subject to regulation." [17] Bernard Schwartz, chief counsel to a House inquiry into regulatory agencies, demonstrated during a dramatic series of hearings in 1958 that the agencies have, in many cases, become servants of industry instead of regulating in the interest of the larger public. The House committee, which had not really wanted to embarrass the commissions and their powerful interest groups by digging too deeply, fired Schwartz for his pains.

[17] Bernard Schwartz, *The Professor and the Commissions* (New York: Knopf, 1959), p. 48.

But the hearings, and subsequent disclosures, revealed a pattern of fraternization by commissioners and regulated industries. Some commission members have accepted free transportation, lecture fees, hotel rooms, and gifts from businesses subject to their authority. Others have left the commissions for big jobs in the regulated industry. Many have seemed more concerned with protecting pipeline companies, airlines, railroads, and television networks than with making sure the industries are serving the public satisfactorily. It would seem that the "independent" regulatory agencies are occasionally independent primarily of the interests of the majority of the public.

The major regulatory agencies, in order of their creation, are:

1. *The Interstate Commerce Commission* (1887): eleven members, seven-year terms; regulates and fixes rates for railroads, trucking companies, bus lines, freight forwarders, oil pipelines, express agencies.
2. *The Federal Trade Commission* (1914): five members, seven-year terms; regulates industry; responsible for preventing unfair competition, price-fixing, deceptive advertising, mislabeling of textile and fur products, false packaging, and similar abuses.
3. *The Federal Power Commission* (1930): five members, five-year terms; fixes rates and has jurisdiction over electric utilities, natural gas companies, hydroelectric projects, and construction of interstate gas pipelines.
4. *The Federal Communications Commission* (1934): seven members, seven-year terms; licenses and regulates all television and radio stations in the United States; regulates frequencies used by police, aviation, taxicabs, "ham" operators, and others; fixes rates for telephone and telegraph companies in interstate commerce.
5. *The Securities and Exchange Commission* (1934): five members, five-year terms; created to protect the public from investing in securities on the basis of false or misleading claims; requires companies offering securities for sale to file an accurate registration statement and prospectus; registers brokers; regulates stock exchanges.
6. *The Civil Aeronautics Board* (1938): five members, six-year terms; grants domestic airline routes and sets air fares; grants overseas routes subject to presidential approval; passes upon airline mergers.

Several other agencies of the government have regulatory functions in whole or in part. For example, the Federal Maritime Commission regulates shipping, the National Labor Relations Board prohibits unfair labor practices, and the Board of Governors of the Federal Reserve System regulates the money supply, interest rates, and the banking industry. Many units of executive departments, such as HEW's Food and Drug Administration, also have regulatory functions.

Shortly before Richard Nixon moved into the White House, the *New York Times* posed an interesting question for its readers: "What's a new Administration anyhow?" The newspaper went on to say that offi-

The Men at the Top

cially, at least, it is "one President, 12 Cabinet appointees, 300 sub-Cabinet officials and agency heads, 124 ambassadors and 1,700 aides, assistants and confidential secretaries." [18] Most of the 3,000,000 federal workers are civil servants, not "the President's men." They are not appointed by him to the key policy jobs in the bureaucracy.

In presidential election years, the House Post Office and Civil Service Committee obligingly publishes something known affectionately in Washington as "the plum book" (as in political plum), a listing of the non-civil-service jobs that the incoming President may fill.[19] For White House aides assigned to screen patronage appointees for the new administration, the plum book is an indispensable reference guide.

When he took office in 1969, President Nixon had to make approximately 2,000 key appointments, for the most part, exempt from civil service requirements. Of this total, perhaps less than 500 were considered important policy-advisory posts.

To recruit the 2,000 appointees, President Nixon assigned two White House aides, Peter M. Flanigan, who had been deputy campaign manager, and Harry S. Flemming, a former assistant to the Republican national chairman. Flemming took the unusual step of mailing a form letter to nearly every person listed in *Who's Who in America*, soliciting names for possible appointees to the administration. He got 60,000 replies, but only about 11,000 that were "worth considering." These were screened with the aid of a computer that belonged to the Office of Emergency Preparedness and was, according to Mr. Flemming, hidden in a cave "somewhere in Virginia, I'm not sure where." [20]

What sort of executive-level administrators emerged from Mr. Flemming's cave? During the campaign, Nixon had declared: "I don't want a government of yes-men. . . . I do want a government drawn from the broadest possible base—an administration made up of Republicans, Democrats and Independents, and drawn from politics, from career government service, from universities, from business, from the professions." [21]

A study by the Center for Political Research, using figures supplied by the Brookings Institution and the White House, indicated that the final composition of the administration was less broadly based than Nixon's campaign address had suggested. The study showed that of the approximately 2,000 appointees, 28 percent came from business (compared to 20 percent under Johnson, 17 percent under Kennedy, and 34 percent under

---

[18] Max Frankel, "Priorities for the Nixon Team," *New York Times*, November 15, 1968, p. 32. As of 1970, there were *eleven* Cabinet appointees.
[19] *United States Policy and Supporting Positions*, House Committee on Post Office and Civil Service (Washington, D.C.: U.S. Government Printing Office, 1968).
[20] John Pierson, "Nixon Talent Hunt: Off to a Good Finish," *Wall Street Journal*, May 9, 1969, p. 18.
[21] Speech by Richard M. Nixon, "The Nature of the Presidency," delivered on the NBC and CBS Radio Networks, September 19, 1968.

Eisenhower). Seven percent came from the field of education. "Most of Mr. Nixon's appointees were white and Protestant, with relatively few Jews, Catholics and Negroes." And 1,017 appointees were Republicans, 239 Democrats, and the rest either independent or of unknown political affiliation.[22]

Today the vast majority of government jobs are filled through the competitive civil service system. Yet, Presidents have always rewarded their political supporters and friends with government jobs. Although George Washington declared that he appointed officials on the basis of "fitness of character," he favored members of his own party, the Federalists. Jefferson dismissed hundred of Federalists from the government when he became President, replacing them with members of his own party.

The
Civil Service

The Spoils System. After Andrew Jackson was elected in 1828, he dismissed more than a third of the 612 presidentially appointed officeholders and 10 to 20 percent of the 10,000 lesser government officials. Although Jackson thereby continued a practice started by Jefferson, he is generally credited with introducing the "spoils system" to the national government. (Jackson preferred to call it "rotation in office.") In 1832, Senator William Learned Marcy of New York, defending a Jackson ambassadorial appointment, declared: "to the victor belong the spoils." The phrase became a classic statement of the right of victorious politicians to reward their followers with jobs. When Lincoln became President, office seekers prowled the White House stairways and hallways.

Up to a point, the spoils system can be defended. Political parties find it difficult to operate without some patronage, and it is natural for any President to want his own supporters in key positions. In the nineteenth century, few technicians and specialists were needed in the government; Jackson was probably correct in contending that bureaucratic duties were then "plain and simple" enough to be performed by almost any intelligent citizen.

ie. if you believe Plunkett it is impossible

The Road to Reform. Inefficiency and corruption in the Federal Government led to the first efforts at reform in the 1850's. After the Civil War, the reform movement gathered momentum. Although President Grant's administration was riddled by corruption, it was Grant who persuaded Congress in 1871 to set up the first Civil Service Commission. But the reform movement had faltered by 1875 partly because Congress declined to appropriate new funds for the commission.

[22] Center for Political Research, *National Journal*, January 24, 1970, pp. 182, 187. A Republican administration, of course, would not normally be expected to appoint very many Democrats to high-level positions.

It took the assassination of a President of the United States to make civil service reform a reality. In 1880, the Republican party was divided into two factions, for and against civil service reform. James A. Garfield, the Republican presidential candidate, ran on a reform platform. To appease the "Stalwarts," or anti-reform faction, Chester A. Arthur was chosen for Vice-President. In New York, Arthur had run the custom house, the patronage base of the state Republican machine.

After Garfield's election, Charles J. Guiteau, an eccentric evangelist and lawyer, decided he deserved the post of ambassador to Austria or at least the job of Paris consul. In 1881 it was easy to get into the White House, and Guiteau actually had an unsuccessful interview with President Garfield. Brooding over his failure to join the diplomatic service, Guiteau purchased a revolver. On July 2, he approached Garfield at the railroad station in Washington and shot him in the back, crying: "I am a Stalwart and now Arthur is President!" Garfield died eighty days later and his assassin was hanged.

To the dismay of his political cronies, Chester Arthur became a champion of civil service reform. In the wake of public indignation over the assassination, Congress passed the Civil Service Reform Act of 1883 (the Pendleton Act). It established a bipartisan Civil Service Commission under which about 10 percent of federal employees were chosen through competitive examinations.

The basic purpose of the Civil Service Act was to transfer the power of appointment from politicians to a bipartisan commission that would select federal employees on merit. In this century, Congress has placed more and more government workers under the protective umbrella of civil service. Today 85 percent of the federal bureaucracy is appointed under the merit system.

To a degree, the removal of civil service appointments from politics has done the President a favor. No matter whom a President selects for a government post, he may antagonize others. William Howard Taft complained that every time he made an appointment he created "nine enemies and one ingrate." [23]

When President Nixon took office, in 1969, 443,000 government jobs were exempt from the civil service system, but many of these were in agencies such as the Foreign Service of the Department of State and the Federal Bureau of Investigation, which have their own merit systems. One study of the federal personnel structure concluded that only 6,500 patronage jobs were open to the President to fill.[24] And, as previously noted, only about 2,000 of these are at the policy-advisory level.

---

[23] In Louis W. Koenig, *The Chief Executive* (New York: Harcourt Brace Jovanovich, 1968), p. 97.
[24] Congressional Quarterly, *Weekly Report*, January 3, 1969, p. 15.

Recruiting the Bureaucrats.   The Civil Service Commission acts as a recruiting agency for the bureaucracy. It does so through Federal Job Information Centers located in every state. Examinations for various kinds of positions are held by civil service boards located in major population areas. Those who pass are put on a "list of eligibles." When a job opens up in a federal agency, the Civil Service Commission provides the names of three people highest on the eligible list; the federal agency must then choose one of the three names. Under a system of "veteran preference," disabled veterans and certain members of their families receive up to ten extra points on their examination score; most other honorably discharged veterans receive five points.

Before being accepted for government employment, applicants are told that an investigation will be made of their reputation, character, and loyalty to the United States. The Civil Service Commission conducts most of these investigations, but if the job is in the national security area, in which the applicant has access to classified material, the FBI usually conducts the background check. An applicant must also swear that he will not join in a strike against the government or any agency of the government. Within that framework, he is free to join one of the numerous unions and employee organizations that represent federal workers. Under the merit system, he will almost certainly be promoted if he remains in the career service. (Despite the fact that strikes by federal employees are prohibited by law, postal workers struck in March 1970 and President Nixon was forced to send in troops to move mail in New York City. As that walkout ended, federal air traffic controllers staged a slowdown by calling in sick, causing air travel to be snarled across the nation.)

Government workers receive annual vacations that increase from two to five weeks with length of service, and liberal sick leave and fringe benefits (although no maternity leave as such). A federal employee may express political opinions, contribute to political parties, vote, badger his congressman, wear a campaign button, display a bumper sticker on his car, and attend political rallies, but under the Hatch Act he may not take an *active* part in party politics or campaigns, or run for political office. He must normally retire at seventy; depending on length of service, he can retire with a pension between the ages of fifty-five and sixty-two, often with more than half pay for the rest of his life, in the case of an employee with many years of service.

For most of the bureaucracy below the level of political appointees, a government career offers a high degree of security. It is true that a federal employee may be fired for cause (such as misconduct or inefficiency), or if he is adjudged a security risk. (In 1967, for example, 14,600 federal workers were dismissed for cause.) Or an employee may be given little to do, or dull work, or transferred to the bureaucratic equivalent of Siberia, if he offends a superior. But, by and large, unlike white-collar employees in

The State Department instructed me to survey Prague staffing needs, following the Communist seizure of the country, at which time the American staff, which I inherited, numbered 80. Six months after my recommendation, approved by the State Department, that personnel be reduced to 40, I had managed to get rid of two persons—two only . . .

Today, a decade and a half later, it exhausts me to remember the struggle with Washington required to obtain that reduction from 80 to 78 persons. If I had started to dig the projected Nicaraguan Canal with a teaspoon, those 6 months might have shown a more impressive achievement . . .

"Go cut the heads off somebody else's dandelions", was the gist of successive representations lodged in Foggy Bottom.

It was at that point that the Communists got into the act. Far as I know, they had no idea of the personnel war I was fighting—and losing—with Washington. They possibly thought they were dealing the American Ambassador the most painful blow imaginable when they suddenly declared five-sixths of my staff persona non grata. They gave the Embassy 2 weeks to get 66 American employees and all their families over the border.

For 30 months thereafter, I ran the American Embassy in Prague with 12 individuals—13, counting the Ambassador. No propaganda establishment. No country team. No Peace Corps. No Minister Counselor of Embassy for Administration.

The staff . . . included a deputy who acted as charge d'affaires in the absence of the Ambassador, an extremely competent man who used to drive the Communists crazy by talking Eskimo over the telephone on a tapped line . . .

It was the most efficient Embassy I ever had.

—Ellis O. Briggs, testimony to Senate Subcommittee on National Security Staffing and Operations, in *Administration of National Security.*

private industry, he is protected from arbitrary dismissal. Firing a career federal worker is difficult because it entails a complex and lengthy series of hearings and appeals. On the other hand, Congress may end a government program or cut the appropriation, resulting in a "reduction in force" in the bureaucracy. A worker who is thus "riffed" may be transferred to another job in his agency or to some other government unit, or he may be fired. About 24 percent of federal employees leave or retire each year, representing a turnover of some 700,000 employees annually.[25]

The Bureaucratic Image. Since the federal bureaucracy reaches into every aspect of our national life, society has a large stake in having first-rate civil servants staff the government. Some Americans think of the federal service in unfavorable terms: gray corridors and gray desks manned by gray people. To the extent that such views are held by the public, the federal bureaucracy is hampered in its efforts to recruit talented employees.

A study by the Brookings Institution disclosed that the public has a mixed image of the bureaucracy. Although 51 percent of workers outside the government had a "favorable" attitude toward federal civil servants,

[25] Based on *Federal Civilian Manpower Statistics*, U.S. Civil Service Commission, January 1970, p. 16.

many executives, scientists, and engineers in the business world reacted negatively to the idea of working for the government; a relatively high percentage said their families would regard such a change as a step "down the ladder." Thus, "The appeal of federal employment is lowest among those kinds of employed adults for whom the government's qualitative needs are the greatest." [26]

In general, almost all population groups interviewed rated federal employees highest on "honesty." Slightly lower ratings were given on their "interest in serving the public" and "ability." Relatively speaking, they were rated lowest on "drive to get ahead." The study also confirmed that many Americans believe a career in the federal service offers excellent security and fringe benefits in exchange for a certain impersonality and red tape. For example, among the general employed public earning $8,500 and over, 37 percent volunteered that they thought job security and benefits were "likely to be better" in the government than outside, and 27 percent said they thought the "bureaucracy and red tape" were "likely to be worse." [27]

Specialized government programs such as the Peace Corps, the poverty program, and the foreign service may continue to attract highly motivated college graduates to join the federal service. But in times of generally full employment, a recruitment problem remains for the bureaucracy as a whole.

Despite its mixed image, there is a high degree of professionalism in the civil service, and a level of honesty that probably matches that of workers in the private sector. (Members of the public interviewed for the Brookings study rated "top-level people in the federal service" higher on honesty than they rated their counterparts in private business.) By its very nature, however, bureaucracy is not a popular concept. In attracting talent the federal bureaucracy is at some disadvantage, compared to many private employers, because of its sheer size and impersonality.

THE POLITICS OF BUREAUCRACY

A new Cabinet secretary in Washington often discovers that a title does not assure actual authority over his department. "I was like a sea captain who finds himself on the deck of a ship that he has never seen before," wrote one. "I did not know the mecha-

[26] Franklin P. Kilpatrick, Milton C. Cummings, Jr., and M. Kent Jennings, *The Image of the Federal Service* (Washington, D.C.: The Brookings Institution, 1964), pp. 99, 116–17, 210.
[27] *Ibid.*, pp. 122, 219.

nism of my ship; I did not know my officers—even by sight—and I had no acquaintance with the crew." [28]

As the Cabinet member had quickly realized, the bureaucracy has its own sources of power that enable it to resist political authority. Cabinet secretaries come and go; the civil service remains. The expert technician in charge of a bureau within a department may have carved out considerable independence over the years; he may resent the effort of a political appointee to take control of his bureau.

In his study of the politics of bureaucracy, Francis Rourke has developed three central themes: the bureaucracy exercises an *impact on policy;* it does so by *mobilizing political support* and *applying its expertise.*[29] As Rourke points out, the growth of the civil service and the removal of much of the appointment power from politics does not mean that politics has been removed from the bureaucracy. Quite the contrary; federal departments and bureaus are extremely sensitive to the winds of politics. A request or inquiry from a congressman usually brings speedy action by a government agency—its officials know where appropriations come from.

Furthermore, in mobilizing support, the bureaucracy practices politics, often in expert fashion. The bureaucracy draws support from four areas— public opinion, the interest groups it deals with, Congress, and the executive branch.[30]

Bureaucracy
and
Public Opinion

A government agency that enjoys wide public support has an advantage over agencies that do not. The President and Congress are both sensitive to public opinion, and a popular, prestigious agency may receive more appropriations and achieve greater independence than others. The FBI under J. Edgar Hoover managed to build such a favorable image with the general public that for more than four decades both the bureau and its chief enjoyed a status of virtual independence. Almost the first official acts of President Kennedy and President Nixon were to announce that Hoover would be retained as FBI director. In 1964, Johnson an old friend and Washington neighbor of Hoover, signed a special executive order permitting him to remain as FBI chief beyond the compulsory retirement age of seventy. In the mid-1960's, the FBI was sharply criticized by the Warren Commission for failure to coordinate with the Secret Service prior to President Kennedy's assassination; its record in the field of civil rights and in fighting organized crime was challenged elsewhere. But such criticism of the

---

[28] In Richard F. Fenno, Jr., *The President's Cabinet* (Cambridge, Mass.: Harvard University Press, 1959), p. 225. The Cabinet secretary who voiced this nautical complaint was William Gibbs McAdoo, Wilson's Secretary of the Treasury.
[29] Rourke, *Bureaucracy, Politics, and Public Policy.*
[30] *Ibid.,* Chapter 2.

FBI and its legendary director surfaced only late in Hoover's government career.[31]

Similarly, the National Aeronautics and Space Administration (NASA) and its Apollo astronauts captured the public imagination. To enable it to place men on the moon in 1969, NASA received massive appropriations, at a time when some Americans were demanding a reordering of national priorities to meet social needs on earth.

To improve their "image" and enlist public support for their programs, many federal agencies employ substantial numbers of public relations men and information officials. These information specialists issue news releases and answer questions from members of the press and the general public. In 1970, it was estimated that the Federal Government employed about 8,000 people and spent more than $100,000,000 a year on public relations activities.[32] In 1969, Senator J. William Fulbright disclosed that the Pentagon *alone* employed 2,800 publicists at a cost of $27.9 million during the previous year.[33]

While most agencies strive for public support, few achieve it. More often, the bureaucracy is able to mobilize political strength by building a constituency. As Rourke notes: "The groups an agency directly serves provide the most natural basis of . . . political support, and it is with these interest groups that agencies ordinarily establish the firmest alliances. Such groups have often been responsible for the establishment of the agency in the first place. Thereafter, the agency and the group are bound together by deeply rooted ties that may be economic, political, or social in character."[34]

Viewed in this light, the behavior of the bureaucracy becomes somewhat predictable. Thus, the Agriculture Department is a natural spokesman for farmers, the Commerce Department is sympathetic to business, the FDA, tied to the drug industry, is slow to warn women of the possible risks of the Pill and the Pentagon is allied with defense contractors.

The close relationship between the FCC and the broadcasting industry illustrates how some government agencies have mobilized the support of client groups. In 1959, at the height of the public scandal over "rigged" TV quiz shows, the chairman of the FCC, John C. Doerfer, expressed "substantial doubts" that he and the commission had authority to end the

Bureaucracy and Client Groups

[31] See Tom Wicker, "What Have They Done Since They Shot Dillinger?" *New York Times Magazine*, December 28, 1969.

[32] Dom Bonafede, "Nixon Orders 500 Jobs, $10 Million Cut from Public Relations Budgets," *National Journal*, Vol. 2, No. 18 (May 2, 1970), p. 912.

[33] *Congressional Record*, December 1, 1969, p. S15144.

[34] Rourke, *Bureaucracy, Politics, and Public Policy*, p. 14.

deceptive practice.[35] He took this position even though the airwaves are public and the FCC, as their guardian, is required by law to license stations in the "public convenience, interest, or necessity." A broadcasting license is issued for three years; upon expiration, the FCC may take a license away from one station and award it to a competitor if the commission thinks the newcomer might provide better service for the public. Yet, in 1970, the FCC voted to renew licenses of radio and television stations as long as they have "substantially" met community needs. Such a practice, if adhered to, would give TV station owners a virtually permanent license.

The Bureau of Mines of the Department of the Interior is responsible for mine safety and health conditions, including the prevention of coal mine disasters and the "black lung" disease that afflicts many miners. Critics of the bureau contended that for many years it appeared more concerned with promoting industry than promoting safety. One bureau official has been quoted as saying: "I had actually gotten to the point where it made me feel good whenever the price of lead or zinc went up a penny a pound. I hate to admit it, but that's the way we thought around here." [36]

Bureaucracy and Congress

Another source of bureaucratic power stems from the political support that an agency may enjoy in Congress, particularly among influential committee chairmen. For many years, the armed services could count on the friendly support of two powerful Democrats who chaired the House and Senate Armed Services committees—Representative Carl Vinson and Senator Richard B. Russell, both of Georgia. Their successors, Representative L. Mendel Rivers of South Carolina and Senator John Stennis of Mississippi, proved equally friendly. Similarly, the CIA has enjoyed the protection of a small group of influential representatives and senators, including Russell. In 1966, the chairman of the Senate Foreign Relations Committee, Senator J. William Fulbright, proposed the creation of a nine-man Senate Committee on Intelligence Operations to oversee the CIA, replacing the existing shadowy House and Senate subcommittees. During the floor debate, Russell heatedly accused Fulbright of "muscling in on my committee." Fulbright's proposal was rejected.

Agencies that do not enjoy cordial relations with important members of the legislative branch may find their power diminished. Representative Otto Passman, the Louisiana Democrat who heads the House subcommittee on foreign aid, has been the bane of Agency for International Development officials for years. Representative John J. Rooney, a Brooklyn Democrat, is

[35] "Investigation of Television Quiz Shows," Hearings, Subcommittee of the Committee on Interstate and Foreign Commerce, House of Representatives, Eighty-sixth Congress, First Session, October 10, 1959, p. 513.
[36] In Laurence Stern and Richard Harwood, "Uncertainties at Bureau of Mines Cast Doubt on Environment Drive," Washington Post, January 31, 1970, p. A15.

The following exchange took place between a hapless State Department official and John J. Rooney, chairman of a House appropriations subcommittee.

Congressman Rooney: I find a gentleman here, an FSO-6. He got an A in Chinese and you assigned him to London.

State Department Official: Yes, sir. That officer will have opportunities in London—not as many as he would have in Hong Kong, for example—

Congressman Rooney: What will he do? Spend his time in Chinatown?

Official: No, sir. There will be opportunities in dealing with officers in the British Foreign Office who are concerned with Far Eastern Affairs. The British have foreign language specialists as well as we do.

Congressman Rooney: So instead of speaking English to one another, they will sit in the London office and talk Chinese?

Official: Yes, sir.

Congressman Rooney: Is that not fantastic?

Official: No, sir. They are anxious to keep up their practice.

Congressman Rooney: Are they playing games or is this serious business?

Official: This is serious business.

Congressman Rooney: Can you describe how this would happen? This officer, who is an FSO-6, probably would not be on too important a mission to the British Foreign Office, would he?

Official: That is correct.

Congressman Rooney: But he has a counterpart in the British Foreign Office who also is studying Chinese and they sit down and they talk Chinese together; is that right?

Official: Yes.

Congressman Rooney: They go out to Chinese restaurants and have chop suey together?

Official: Yes, sir.

Congressman Rooney: And that is all at the expense of the American taxpayer?

—Adapted from Nelson W. Polsby, *Congress and the Presidency.*

the nemesis of the State Department, whose appropriations are handled by his House subcommittee. Rooney's hostility to "striped-pants cookie pushers" in the foreign service is legendary, and State Department officials dread their annual ordeal of testifying before his subcommittee. The congressman has particularly opposed entertainment funds for United States diplomats, which he has termed "booze allowances." In an effort to flatter Rooney, President-elect Kennedy invited him to Palm Beach in 1960. He was wined and dined and treated like visiting royalty by Kennedy and his family for two days. Rooney relented to the extent of promising a bit more money for some United States embassies.[37] But, by and large, the trip accomplished little; Rooney had a nice time and continued to harass the State Department.

The United States Corps of Engineers is a classic example of a federal agency that has won virtually independent status by mobilizing political support in the legislative branch. Its rivers-and-harbors, navigation, and flood-control projects bring important benefits to local communities—and to members of Congress in those districts.[38]

Government agencies exert considerable effort to maintain cordial

[37] Hugh Sidey, *John F. Kennedy, President* (New York: Atheneum, 1963).
[38] See Arthur Maass, *Muddy Waters* (Cambridge, Mass.: Harvard University Press, 1951) and "Congress and Water Resources," in Rourke, *Bureaucratic Power in National Politics.*

diplomatic relations with Capitol Hill. According to a 1970 study, the Cabinet departments employed 531 persons engaged in liaison with Congress, of whom 312, or 59 percent, worked for the Defense Department.[39] The State Department and HEW even have congressional liaison officers assigned at the level of Assistant Secretary. Liaison officers watch over legislation and other matters concerning their agencies; they also field requests made by congressmen on behalf of constituents who have business pending before their agency. The large number of liaison officers, therefore, reflects congressional demands as well as an effort by government agencies to win support on Capitol Hill.

Bureaucracy
and the President

The image of the department head as a sea captain aboard a strange ship with an unknown crew may be applied as well to a President seeking control over the bureaucracy. We have already seen how, from President Kennedy's vantage point, the bureaucracy moved so slowly that "you can wait while the world collapses." Kennedy was particularly exasperated by vacillation and delay in the field of foreign policy. "The State Department is a bowl of jelly," he once declared. "It's got all those people over there who are constantly smiling. I think we need to smile less and be tougher." [40]

Other Presidents have voiced similar complaints. Franklin Roosevelt complained that the Treasury was set in its ways:

> But the Treasury is not to be compared with the State Department. You should go through the experience of trying to get any changes in the thinking, policy, and action of the career diplomats. . . . But the Treasury and the State Department put together are nothing compared with the Na-a-vy. The admirals are really something to cope with—and I should know. To change anything in the Na-a-vy is like punching a feather bed. You punch it with your right and you punch it with your left until you are finally exhausted, and then you find the damn bed just as it was before you started punching.[41]

Often, Presidents attempt to gain tighter control of the bureaucracy by reorganizing its structure. Postwar efforts toward administrative reform led in 1947 to creation of the first of two Hoover Commissions. Formally entitled the Commission on Organization of the Executive Branch of the Government, the study panel was headed by former President Herbert Hoover. It first reported in 1949, and of its nearly 300 recommendations for

---

[39] Dom Bonafede and Andrew J. Glass, "Nixon Deals Cautiously with Hostile Congress," *National Journal*, Vol. 2, No. 26 (June 27, 1970), p. 1362.
[40] Arthur M. Schlesinger, Jr., *A Thousand Days* (Boston: Houghton Mifflin, 1965), p. 406.
[41] In Neustadt, *Presidential Power*, p. 42.

Kennedy . . . was determined to . . . recover presidential control over the sprawling feudalism of government. This became a central theme of his administration and, in some respects, a central frustration. The presidential government, coming to Washington aglow with new ideas and a euphoric sense that it could not go wrong, promptly collided with the feudal barons of the permanent government, entrenched in their domains and fortified by their sense of proprietorship; and the permanent government, confronted by this invasion, began almost to function . . . as a resistance movement, scattering to the *maquis* in order to pick off the intruders. This was especially true in foreign affairs.

—Arthur M. Schlesinger, Jr., *A Thousand Days.*

streamlining the Federal Government, about half were adopted. Most of the commission's proposals emphasized centralization of authority and the need to simplify the organization of government.[42]

The second Hoover Commission was established in 1953 and reported in 1955. Because it urged that the government eliminate many activities that competed with private enterprise, its proposals were more controversial.[43]

Since New Deal days, attempts at administrative reform have sought to restructure the executive branch of government so that power to make decisions is centered in the hands of policy-level executives in the departments, rather than at the lower levels of the bureaucracy. The assumption is that higher-level officials will be more aware of, and responsive to, the needs of broader segments of the public than are low-level officials, who may be captives of one industry or client group. Thus, the reformers have pushed for more "executive-centered" decision-making.

Since 1918, Congress has from time to time given Presidents the right to restructure the executive branch. Presidents have made extensive use of this power under a series of Reorganization Acts passed since 1939; this power was increased by the Reorganization Act of 1949. The current reorganization plans take effect in sixty days unless vetoed by Congress. In 1953, during the Eisenhower administration, Congress permitted a plan to create a new Cabinet department of Health, Education, and Welfare to go into effect. In 1967, President Johnson remodeled the government of the District of Columbia (under the Reorganization Act of 1965); during his administration all but one of his seventeen reorganization plans were accepted. Between 1949 and 1968, sixty-six out of the eighty-five reorganization plans submitted by four Presidents went into effect.

[42] Commission on Organization of the Executive Branch of the Government, *Reports to Congress* and *Task Force Reports* (Washington, D.C.: U.S. Government Printing Office, 1949).

[43] Commission on Organization of the Executive Branch of the Government, *Reports to Congress* and *Task Force Reports* (Washington, D.C.: U.S. Government Printing Office, 1955).

439

The creation in 1970 of the Office of Management and Budget (OMB), as recommended by the President's Advisory Commission on Executive Reorganization, was designed to shift to the President and his budget officials even tighter control over management of the federal bureaucracy. OMB is a unit of the Executive Office of the President (see Chapter 10, pp. 397–98). The budget process, which OMB manages, is a major tool of presidential control over the executive branch. The Federal Government runs on a fiscal year that starts July 1 and ends the following June 30. Each spring, agencies and departments begin drawing up their requests for the fiscal year starting fourteen months later. Matching these requests against economic forecasts and revenue estimates from his advisers, the President establishes budget guidelines; within this framework individual agency requests are studied by OMB and presented to the President for decision. The budget then goes to Congress in January or February. The in-fighting and competition among government agencies for a slice of the budget pie give the President, through OMB, a powerful lever for bureaucratic control. Indeed, as Aaron Wildavsky has observed, "the budget lies at the heart of the political process." [44]

Although the President uses OMB and other tools in the battle to maintain his control over the bureaucracy, the bureaucracy in turn seeks to mobilize support from the President, from OMB, and from elsewhere within the executive branch. Staff agencies of the President depend completely upon the Chief Executive and are powerful only to the extent that the President wishes. A perfect illustration is the National Security Council—powerful under Eisenhower, almost nonexistent under Kennedy.

The bureaucrat "whose requests are continually turned down in Congress finds that he tends to be rejected in the Budget Bureau and in his own department as well. . . . The Bureau finds itself treating agencies it dislikes much better than those it may like better but who cannot help themselves nearly as much in Congress." [45]

Bureaucracy
and
Policy-Making

In theory, Presidents make policy and bureaucrats carry it out. In fact, officials often play a major role in policy formation. In large part, this is because Presidents rely on bureaucratic *expertise* in making their policy decisions. For example, in 1960, President Eisenhower ordered the secret training and arming of Cuban exiles under the direction of the CIA. The original concept of isolated guerrilla landings in Cuba had evolved by the fall of 1960 into a plan to invade Cuba and topple Premier Fidel Castro.

[44] Aaron Wildavsky, *The Politics of the Budgetary Process* (Boston: Little, Brown, 1964), p. 5.
[45] *Ibid.*, pp. 41–42.

The CIA and, somewhat less enthusiastically, the Joint Chiefs of Staff of the armed services assured President Kennedy early in 1961 that the operation would succeed. The invasion at the Bay of Pigs in April 1961, proved a disaster.

Kennedy's critics charged that the invasion failed because he withdrew air cover, but according to Theodore Sorensen, the President later concluded that the invasion never had a chance of success. A major difficulty, Sorensen said, was that the new administration was not yet well organized, "enabling the pre-committed authors and advocates of the project in the CIA and Joint Chiefs to exercise a dominant influence." [46] Although Kennedy publicly took responsibility for the mess, privately he complained to Sorensen: "All my life I've known better than to depend on the experts. How could I have been so stupid, to let them go ahead?" [47] Of

[46] Theodore C. Sorensen, *Kennedy* (New York: Harper & Row, 1965), p. 305.
[47] *Ibid.*, p. 309.

Presidents rely heavily on bureaucratic expertise in making policy. President Nixon is shown here with economic advisers.

Until late 1968, John McGee and A. Ernest Fitzgerald had never heard of each other. But they had much in common. McGee was a Navy fuel inspector in Thailand. He uncovered large-scale corruption. Instead of rewarding him, the Navy tried to fire him. Fitzgerald was a high-level civilian cost-analyst in the office of the Secretary of the Air Force. He revealed the galloping waste of U.S. taxpayers' money on the big weapons system—the C-5A Galaxy cargo plane, the Minuteman missiles, and the Mark II radar and computer brain for the F-111 fighter plane. Like its sister service, instead of promoting the man who blew the whistle, the Air Force first assigned Fitzgerald to a meaningless job and, later, through a "reduction in force," got rid of him altogether.

—Senator William Proxmire,
Report from Wasteland: America's Military-Industrial Complex.

the Joint Chiefs of Staff, Kennedy bitterly told another visitor: "They don't know any more about it than anyone else."[48]

There was a parallel to all this during the Johnson administration—apparently each President must learn for himself that military advisers can be expected to see things from a military viewpoint. Repeatedly assured by the Joint Chiefs—as well as by key civilian advisers—that some form of military victory could be won in Vietnam, Johnson committed the country to a divisive war. In 1968, as he agonized over what became a decision to reverse his policy by limiting the bombing of North Vietnam and seeking negotiations, he called in former Secretary of State Dean Acheson, who told him bluntly: "With all due respect, Mr. President, the Joint Chiefs of Staff don't know what they're talking about."[49]

It should be clear, however, that in both cases, the Bay of Pigs and Vietnam, civilian as well as military advisers urged Kennedy and Johnson on the course that each followed. McGeorge Bundy, national security assistant to Kennedy and Johnson, his successor Walt Rostow, Defense Secretary Robert McNamara, Secretary of State Dean Rusk and others all share responsibility for American involvement in the war in Vietnam, even though the major decisions were made by Presidents Kennedy and Johnson.

Just as federal officials can promote policies that get the nation into trouble, they can also be instrumental in changing those policies. Townsend Hoopes, former Under Secretary of the Air Force, has related that he, Paul H. Nitze, Deputy Secretary of Defense, and several other Pentagon officials privately urged Clark M. Clifford, who succeeded McNamara as Secretary of Defense in 1968, to try to bring about a reversal of Vietnam policy. In March, Hoopes wrote Clifford a strong memorandum warning that

[48] In David Wise and Thomas B. Ross, *The Invisible Government* (New York: Random House, 1964), p. 185.
[49] In Townsend Hoopes, *The Limits of Intervention* (New York: David McKay, 1969), p. 204.

military victory in Vietnam is a dangerous illusion. . . . At the present level, the war is eroding the moral fibre of the nation, demoralizing its politics, and paralyzing its foreign policy. A further manpower commitment . . . would intensify the domestic disaffection, which would be reflected in increased defiance of the draft and widespread unrest in the cities. Welfare programs on which our domestic tranquility might depend would be eliminated or deeply cut. It is possible that well-placed dissenters in Congress could paralyze the legislative process.[50]

As he studied administration policy in Vietnam—and a request by the military for 206,000 more troops—Clifford gradually became convinced of the folly of further escalation. Although his warm friendship with the President "grew suddenly formal and cool," Clifford, and an advisory group of prestigious civilians, were apparently instrumental in persuading the President to reverse his policies.[51]

"NADER'S RAIDERS": A CASE STUDY

In the summer of 1968, consumer advocate Ralph Nader turned loose a team of seven young law students and attorneys to conduct a top-to-bottom study of the Federal Trade Commission, one of the most lethargic of the federal regulatory agencies and one traditionally friendly to business, which it is supposed to regulate.

The report by "Nader's Raiders," as the group of investigators came to be called, confirmed previous criticism of FTC inefficiency and apparent unwillingness to use its full enforcement powers against deceptive advertisers and businessmen.[52]

Starting in Franklin Roosevelt's administration, the FTC had long been a patronage dumping ground for Boss Edward Crump's Memphis political machine, and the "Raiders" found the commission still closely linked to Tennessee and Southern politics. At the time of the Nader group's study, the FTC's Democratic chairman was Paul Rand Dixon of Nashville, who had been appointed in 1961 by President Kennedy at the urging of Senator Estes Kefauver of Tennessee. The report by the Nader investigators found the FTC legal staff packed with Democrats, and charged that Dixon

[50] *Ibid.*, pp. 187, 192.

[51] *Ibid.*, p. 181, Chapters 8–10. No President likes to think that he is manipulated by the bureaucracy. After he left the White House, President Johnson went to great lengths to counter the widely held image of himself as a beleaguered Chief Executive persuaded by his advisers to reverse his Vietnam policy. He insisted that he himself had ordered a major policy review and that the suggestion to stop the bombing had come from Secretary Rusk, not Clifford. See "LBJ: The Decision to Halt the Bombing," CBS Television News Special, Transcript, February 6, 1970, pp. 18–24.

[52] Edward F. Cox, Robert C. Fellmeth, and John E. Schulz, *"The Nader Report" on the Federal Trade Commission* (New York: Richard W. Baron, 1969). Most of the details in our case study are based on this report.

had violated the Hatch Act by soliciting political contributions from the commission staff.

Under the law, the FTC is required to regulate business in "the interest of the public." But Chairman Dixon, the Nader group charged, was biased in favor of business. The report accused the commission of being "fearful of big corporations," preferring to concentrate on trivia, such as violations in the manufacture or labeling of wool and fur products, rather than tackle deceptive advertising on television. The report also accused the FTC of failure to crack down on consumer frauds in the ghetto. The investigation found a sharp decline in the FTC caseload, a reluctance to invoke fines against businessmen who failed to comply with commission "cease and desist" orders, and perhaps most startling of all—an average delay of more than four years in handling deceptive practice complaints.

Chairman Dixon, the report charged, saw himself as a protector of free enterprise against consumer "zealots." But, the report declared, "it is the ghetto dweller whose home has just been lost to a fraudulent aluminum-siding swindle who knows what real tyranny is. And it is the American housewife exploited by games, gimmicks and deception who is in need of protection."

The investigators reported that they walked into the office of one $22,695-a-year FTC official and found him "fast asleep on a couch with the

"You and Mr. Booth just have a lot in common. Mr. Booth's just been ordered to cease and desist, too."

John A. Ruge
Copyright 1970 Saturday Review, Inc.

Consumer advocate Ralph Nader and some of his "raiders."

sports section of the *Washington Post* covering his head." They awakened the official to ask what his job was, but he gave "a very vague reply."

The report concluded: "Alcoholism, spectacular lassitude, and office absenteeism, incompetence by the most modest standards, and a lack of commitment to the regulatory missions are rampant at these staff levels." It added that Mr. Dixon's "chief and perhaps only contribution to the Commission's improvement would be to resign from the agency that he has so degraded and ossified."

Dixon called the Nader report "a hysterical, anti-business diatribe and a scurrilous, untruthful attack." Other officials of the FTC agreed with the investigators. Philip Elman, a commission member, called the criticism "one of the healthiest things" that ever happened to the FTC.

Following publication of the Nader report, President Nixon asked the American Bar Association (ABA) to study the FTC, and in September 1969 the ABA recommended a sweeping reform of the commission. In January 1970, Nixon replaced Dixon with a new chairman, Caspar Weinberger. Dixon remained a member of the commission.

The publicity did seem to influence the FTC. As the Nader report was issued, the commission, after a two-year study, proposed regulations to protect consumers from gas-station and supermarket promotional games. When Weinberger resigned in August 1970 to become deputy director of the new Office of Management and Budget, he was succeeded by a Philadelphia attorney, Miles Kirkpatrick, who had written the ABA's indictment

The overriding concern with institutions should be how we as individuals can tell our institutions that they are not going to have a momentum of their own . . . that they are going to reflect individual inputs . . . that the individual in these large institutions whether they are companies or government agencies or other organizations, must reassert his rights . . . and that every person who is part of a large organization must have that line drawn for himself beyond which he will no longer subserve himself to the dictates of the organization, beyond which he will say . . . my loyalty to mankind, to my society, to my fellow citizen, overrides my loyalty to my organization and that is where I must place my commitment and knowledge. Unless every individual somewhere in his mind draws that line when he will no longer simply take orders . . . unless every individual has that line drawn for himself he will have within him a potential slice of the Nuremberg problem.

—Ralph Nader, commencement address at Franklin Pierce College, 1970.

of the FTC. Kirkpatrick declared that he would try to determine the full scope of the FTC's statutory authority, and he began to move more actively against questionable business practices.[53]

While the Nader report and the ABA's study shocked the public and led to reform efforts at the FTC, this did not mean that conditions in the regulatory agencies were symptomatic of the federal bureaucracy in general. The tendency of the FTC to defer to its client groups illustrated one of the problems of bureaucracy, and of regulatory agencies in particular: as an agency mobilizes political support among its clientele, its regulatory function may be eroded.

BUREAUCRACY AND SOCIETY

Improving
Democracy

Even the President, as we have seen, must struggle constantly to control the federal bureaucracy and to make it responsive to his will. Because the bureaucracy is able to mobilize political support in the various ways we have discussed, to some extent it is able to operate independently of its elected masters.

The reform efforts of recent years, however, have sought to restructure the federal machinery to give the President tighter control over the executive branch, and to place key decision-making power in the hands of officials with broader perspectives at high levels of the government. These developments have been accompanied by a search for ways of making better decisions and improving the performance of government departments. The creation of the Domestic Council and the Office of Management and Budget in 1970 are examples of this trend.

[53] *Newsweek*, December 14, 1970, pp. 87, 89.

One of the criticisms of bureaucracy is that its decision-making tends to be "incremental"—that is, what was decided yesterday limits the scope of choice today. New policies, instead of replacing old ones, tend to be "added on" to existing programs, because government officials are usually wary of sweeping change or policy innovations.

Peter Drucker has suggested: "Certain things are inherently difficult for government. Being by design a protective institution, it is not good at innovation. It cannot really abandon anything. The moment government undertakes anything it becomes entrenched and permanent." [54]

Because of the obstacles to innovation, bureaucracy may overlook problems that do not fit into established forms. In 1967, for example, the Surgeon General of the United States, Dr. William H. Stewart, told a Senate subcommittee on poverty that the Federal Government did not know the extent of hunger and malnutrition in America. "We just don't know," he said. "It hasn't been anybody's job."

Often, when government is confronted with a new task, a new agency is established to handle it. For example, the Peace Corps was made independent of the State Department, and the poverty program was created as a separate agency, not as a division of HEW. The tendency to start new agencies for new programs to some extent reflects resistance to change on the part of old-line, existing agencies.

In an attempt to break through traditional forms of bureaucratic decision-making, the Federal Government in the 1960's began applying new techniques of management technology to policy problems. The goal of the "rationalists," as advocates of the new techniques were sometimes called, was to arrive at decisions on the basis of systematic analysis, rather than on the basis of guesswork or custom.

The new methods often utilized electronic computers to analyze masses of data at high speed. One of the major new management tools, known as "cost-benefit analysis," "cost effectiveness," or "systems analysis," was inaugurated at the Pentagon in 1961 by Defense Secretary Robert S. McNamara. This technique helped officials to measure the benefits of alternative policies against their dollar costs (see Chapter 14, p. 582).

In 1965, President Johnson ordered that these techniques be applied throughout most of the bureaucracy. Specifically, he established a *planning-programing budgeting system* (PPBS) within the executive branch. Under PPBS, since 1965, federal departments and agencies have been required to (1) define their goals precisely, (2) formulate alternative programs to achieve those goals most efficiently, and (3) estimate the future cost of present decisions.

Although PPBS has been hailed as the most far-reaching change in

Rational
Decision-Making

[54] Drucker, *The Age of Discontinuity*, p. 226.

the effort to reform executive branch management, it has also been criticized. For example, the system works best in areas in which goals can be "quantified"—expressed in dollar amounts. Thus, the Pentagon can use this technique to measure the relative merits and cost of weapons systems and military hardware. But in other areas, such as welfare, education, and foreign policy, correct choices cannot so easily be arrived at by measuring benefits against costs. The long range benefits to American society from an improved educational system, for example, cannot be evaluated wholly by a computer. Cost-benefit analysis is an aid to decision-making but not a substitute for decision-making.

There is some danger as well that PPBS, by marshaling scientific analyses in support of policy choices, may overwhelm all objections. In the Defense Department, these techniques have helped to centralize control in the hands of the Secretary of Defense. But as a result, the possibility is increased that any mistakes will be big ones; scientific techniques could lead to "catastrophe measured out with mathematical precision." [55]

Toward a More Creative Bureaucracy

Because federal agencies are often criticized as unimaginative and frozen in their traditional ways of doing things, efforts have been made to develop more creativity in executive agencies. For this reason, in the early days of the "New Frontier," young lawyers, business executives, and college professors flocked to Washington in great numbers to work for the Kennedy administration in key positions. A turnover in top executives takes place at the start of every presidential term.

In the federal civil service, this method of injecting new life into old agencies is known as "lateral entrance." Instead of promoting all officials from within, capable outsiders are recruited to fill policy posts. The purpose is to bring fresh thinking and new ideas to federal decision-making. But this technique has its drawbacks as well—recruitment of outsiders tends to discourage career employees who see the best jobs going to newcomers. And the outsiders generally lack experience.

As we have seen, both conservatives and liberals have become disenchanted with bureaucracy in recent years. This has given rise to experiments in decentralization, as well as a search for new structures to manage social problems. *Community control*, discussed in greater detail in Chapter 16, is one such device. Under this principle, people directly affected by government services are given a voice in running those services on the local level.

Similar in concept are efforts to give citizens an opportunity to participate in policy-making, and in the operation of federal programs. The law establishing the poverty program, for example, required "maximum feasible participation" of the poor. The Model Cities act of 1966 contained

[55] Rourke, *Bureaucracy, Politics, and Public Policy*, p. 127.

similar provisions designed to give local residents a voice in mounting a concentrated attack on urban blight.

Bureaucracy is big. It is big at a time when the individual is disturbed by bigness in general and by loss of personal identity—the vague feeling that everyone is becoming "just another social security number." The sheer size of bureaucracy sometimes helps to make it unresponsive in an age when people are demanding that American institutions be reformed to make them more responsive.

Checks
on Bureaucratic
Power

There are, however, some visible checks on the power of the bureaucracy. First, government agencies must share power with other elites in the political system, not only competing agencies in the executive branch, but also Congress, the courts, and groups and leaders outside the government. When government agencies mobilize political support among private industry or other "client" groups, they give up some of their independence and power in the process. In addition to sharing power with other parts of government and with interest groups, officials are held in check to some degree by the press. Fear of adverse publicity is a powerful factor in decision-making in Washington, as well as in state and local government.

Finally, there are certain "inner checks" on the bureaucracy. To some extent at least, bureaucrats may be inhibited from abusing their power by the social and political system in which they operate. Like other citizens, bureaucrats have been politically socialized, and in many cases they may tend to adhere to standards of fair play and respect for individual rights. But relying on human nature and individual conscience is a rather uncertain means of controlling public servants, and the search continues for institutionalized methods of control. The device of the *ombudsman*, for example, has proved popular in Sweden and other countries. The *ombudsman* is an official complaint-taker; he tries to help citizens who have been wronged by the actions of government agencies.

As long as government has responsibility for allocating things of value, for deciding who gets what in American society, there will be bureaucrats to help make and carry out those decisions. The problem of controlling bureaucracy and making it serve the people is a continuing challenge to the American system.

At the same time, new problems are arising that the bureaucracy is asked to help solve. In the 1970's, for example, demands were being made for such programs as consumer protection, better forms of mass transportation, and the control of pollution of the environment. These public demands were beginning to have a measurable impact on government. How the political system and the bureaucracy responded to these challenges would go a long way toward determining whether the machinery of government can continue to be reshaped and influenced to meet present demands and future needs.

449

SUGGESTED READING

Altshuler, Alan A., ed. *The Politics of the Federal Bureaucracy* (Dodd, Mead, 1968). Paperback. A useful examination of the role of the federal bureaucracy in the political system. Stresses the political dynamics of how the bureaucracy operates.

Blau, Peter M. *The Dynamics of Bureaucracy: A Study of Interpersonal Relationships in Two Government Agencies*, 2nd edition (University of Chicago Press, 1963). (Originally published in 1955.) Realistic analysis of the actual workings of bureaucratic organizations. Emphasizes the importance of interpersonal relationships among public servants.

Cox, Edward F., Fellmeth, Robert C., and Schulz, John E. *"The Nader Report" on the Federal Trade Commission* (Richard W. Baron, 1969). Paperback. A critical study of a major federal regulatory agency by a team of young lawyers working as investigators for Ralph Nader. Publication of the report influenced changes in FTC procedures and personnel.

Hitch, Charles. *Decision-Making for Defense* (University of California Press, 1965). An informative description of the new techniques for making policy decisions that were introduced in the Department of Defense during the early 1960's. Later, many of these techniques were extended to other areas of the government.

Hoopes, Townsend. *The Limits of Intervention* * (David McKay, 1969). A fascinating account of bureaucratic infighting in the Defense Department during attempts in the late 1960's to reverse the extent of American military involvement in Vietnam. Hoopes is a former civilian official in the Pentagon.

Rourke, Francis E. *Bureaucracy, Politics, and Public Policy* (Little, Brown, 1969). Paperback. A concise and valuable general introduction to the role of the bureaucracy in the making of public policy. Among other topics, the book analyzes the sources of power of government bureaucracies, and new approaches to policy-making in bureaucratic agencies.

Rourke, Francis E. *Bureaucratic Power in National Politics* (Little, Brown, 1965). Paperback. An excellent collection of readings on various aspects of the bureaucracy and the role of government officials in the policy-making process.

Simon, Herbert A. *Administrative Behavior*,* 2nd edition (Macmillan, 1957). A classic theoretical and empirical analysis of the behavior and decision-making of government bureaucracies. This book, first published in 1947, has influenced modern scholarly work on bureaucratic organizations.

White, Leonard D. *The Federalists* (Macmillan, 1948); *The Jeffersonians, 1801–1829* * (Macmillan, 1951); *The Jacksonians, 1829–1861* * (Macmillan, 1954); and *The Republican Era, 1869–1901* * (Macmillan, 1958). A notable and detailed study, in four volumes, of the historical development of the American public service from 1789 to the turn of the twentieth century.

Wildavsky, Aaron. *The Politics of the Budgetary Process* (Little, Brown, 1964). Paperback. A revealing analysis of the nature of the federal budgetary process and its relationship to the making of public policy.

* Available in paperback edition

12

The Congress

On July 30, 1965, President Lyndon B. Johnson flew with twelve senators and nineteen members of the House to Independence, Missouri, to sign the Medicare bill in the presence of former President Harry S Truman. Medicare pays health costs for older Americans under the social security program.

It was Truman who had proposed a system of federal medical insurance twenty years earlier. Eric Goldman has recalled the scene at Independence:

> The eighty-one-year-old former President had to be helped to the microphones, but the blue eyes were bright behind the steel-rimmed glasses and the voice took on all the well-remembered crackle as he read his little speech. . . . "Not one of these, our citizens, should ever be abandoned to the indignity of charity. . . . Mr. President, I am glad to have lived this long and to witness today the signing of the Medicare bill which puts the nation right, where it needs to be right." [1]

[1] Eric F. Goldman, *The Tragedy of Lyndon Johnson* (New York: Knopf, 1969), p. 295.

451

Johnson declared: "We marvel not simply at the passage of this bill but that it took so many years to pass it."[2]

Today, the Medicare program helps up to 19,000,000 Americans aged sixty-five and over to pay hospital and doctor bills. The need for such help was clear enough: in March 1965, a few months before passage of Medicare, the median income of Americans aged sixty-five and over was *$1,355 a year*.[3] Obviously, on such incomes, most older Americans were unable to afford adequate health care in the face of rising medical costs. What is more, the public supported such legislation; a Gallup Poll in 1962 showed 69 percent in favor of Medicare.[4] By 1940, every Western European country had some form of government health insurance. Yet, the United States, the richest country in the world, had failed to act. A powerful interest group, the American Medical Association, fought Medicare as "socialized medicine," and for twenty years Congress would not be moved. By the time it acted, even Harry Truman had become an old man.

The Medicare story raises fundamental questions about the performance of Congress in the American political system. Can it meet the social needs of the American people in the twentieth century? Or is it a hopelessly outmoded institution, hobbled by powerful special interests and by internal procedures that are undemocratic? How well does Congress represent the voters, and should it lead or follow them? What is the role of Congress in the American political system as a whole? How well does it perform that role?

Congress is a much-criticized institution. At the outset, therefore, we shall discuss Congress within the framework of the controversy that swirls around it. We shall examine in some detail the case for and against Congress, the beleaguered branch.

The Case
Against
Congress

The unwillingness of Congress to pass comprehensive health care legislation for twenty years is not an isolated example. In 1964, Congress passed the landmark Civil Rights Act. It provided in part that a black American—a man driving from Chicago to Alabama with his wife and children, for example—could check into a motel or hotel en route without being turned away because of the color of his skin. Congress passed this legislation almost one hundred years after the Civil War.

President Kennedy was killed by gunfire in 1963, his brother, Robert, in 1968, and Martin Luther King that same year. Despite the hue and cry for gun control after each tragedy, America in 1970 had no broadly effec-

---

[2] Peter A. Corning, *The Evolution of Medicare*, U.S. Department of Health, Education, and Welfare (Washington, D.C.: U.S. Government Printing Office, 1969), p. 2.
[3] U.S. Bureau of the Census, *Statistical Abstract of the United States, 1969*, p. 279.
[4] Corning, *The Evolution of Medicare*, p. 93.

tive federal gun control legislation. Congress, under pressure by the gun lobby, passed only limited legislation to deal with the problem.

Representative Richard Bolling, a Missouri Democrat and congressional reformer, has put the question bluntly: "Is the Congress to continue as the least responsible organ of Government, acting, if at all, ten and twenty and thirty years late?"[5]

Even when Congress does act to meet social needs, James MacGregor Burns has argued, that help may come too late in the lifetime of many people. And, he notes: "The furious pace of social and economic change at home and abroad makes delay in government action far riskier than before. We do not enjoy a cushion of time in adjusting to such change, just as we no longer enjoy a cushion of time in coping with enemy attack."[6]

From *The Herblock Gallery* (Simon & Schuster, 1968)

In 1963, Senator Joseph S. Clark of Pennsylvania took the floor of the Senate to criticize the way that body was run. He called it "archaic, outmoded, obsolete as a meaningful democratic institution."[7] Clark attacked the "Senate establishment," which he loosely defined as a bipartisan but mostly Democratic group of influential senators from "one party" (that is, mostly Southern) states. Senators from these states are always reelected, Clark argued, and thereby gain power in the Senate through seniority. The "Senate establishment," Clark charged, "is almost the antithesis of democracy." Moreover, "the establishment is dedicated to the preservation of the status quo not only in the Senate, but in the country."[8]

These criticisms focused attention on the paradox of Congress: the legislative branch, usually characterized as the most "democratic" because it is considered closest to the people, has an internal structure that is, in part, undemocratic. The resulting inner tension permeates the institution.

Critics of Congress who have emphasized this paradox concentrate their fire chiefly on the custom of seniority, the committee system, and the internal procedures of the House and Senate. Under the workings of the seniority system, those members of Congress with longest service have become committee chairmen. The system, its critics argue, tends to reward age (and sometimes senility) rather than competence. Legislators with seniority are generally returned by their districts. Some of these districts are in Northern cities, but many are in the South and Midwest and tend to be conservative, rural, and untouched by issues that may stir other parts of the country. The result, in the critics' view, is the selection of committee chairmen who are not representative of majority sentiment in their party or the nation.

[5] Richard Bolling, *Power in the House* (New York: Dutton, 1968), p. 269.
[6] James MacGregor Burns, *The Deadlock of Democracy* (Englewood Cliffs, N.J.: Prentice-Hall, 1963), pp. 3–4.
[7] Joseph S. Clark and other senators, *The Senate Establishment* (New York: Hill and Wang, 1967), p. 15.
[8] *Ibid.*, pp. 16, 22.

"Tell the peasants we find their appeals amusing."

From The Herblock Gallery (Simon & Schuster, 1968)

Although Congress is elected by the people to legislate in their behalf, it has chosen to conduct much of its business in committees behind closed doors. For example, one recent study found that 37 percent of all committee meetings were closed to the public. Some committees, such as House Appropriations, conduct *all* meetings in secret, and others, such as Senate Armed Services, meet in closed sessions most of the time.[9] (Under the Legislative Reorganization Act of 1970, regular meetings of committees of Congress must be public unless a majority of the committee votes to close the doors; so the change still permits closed meetings.)

Congress is frequently assailed for rules and procedures that often seem designed to block rather than facilitate the passage of legislation. In the Senate, the filibuster is the traditional and powerful weapon of obstruction and delay. In the House, the Rules Committee has extensive control over what bills are brought to the floor for debate. For years, the committee was run by Representative Howard W. Smith of Virginia, a rural, conservative Southern Democrat and a foe of civil rights legislation and other liberal measures. In 1961, President Kennedy narrowly won a battle to enlarge and liberalize the Rules Committee and circumvent Smith, but the struggle demonstrated that a classic Southern courthouse politician from Broad Run, Virginia (population 20), possessed power to obstruct a President elected by 34,000,000 Americans.

To these familiar criticisms of Congress must be added another—that many of the norms and customs of the House and Senate reward conform-

---

[9] *1969 Congressional Quarterly Almanac*, p. 1031. The percentage is an average for committee meetings, 1953–69.

ity and penalize initiative. Although it is less true today than in the past, to some extent the newcomer to Congress is expected to be seen and not heard. The paternalistic atmosphere is best summarized by Speaker Sam Rayburn's famous advice to his colleagues in the House: "If you want to *get* along, *go* along." [10]

In the field of foreign affairs, Congress is criticized today for abdicating its power to the President; in the domestic field, critics assert, Congress largely approves or disapproves programs proposed by the Chief Executive but does not initiate or innovate very much. In the twentieth century, there has been a discernible loss of power by legislatures and parliaments to Presidents and Prime Ministers, and the United States has not been exempt from this "shift of initiative toward the executive." [11]

Finally, Congress has been tarnished by scandal, and by the questionable ethics and activities of some of its members. In 1967, Senator Thomas J. Dodd, a Connecticut Democrat, was censured by the Senate because he had retained for his personal use $116,000 of the $450,000 received from political fund-raising dinners. "It never occurred to me that there was anything wrong with what I did," Dodd said.[12] Some congressmen travel abroad on "junkets" for dubious legislative purposes. Some have relatives on their office payroll. Many accept speaking fees from lobbyists. In 1969, it was revealed that Congressman Seymour Halpern, third-ranking Republican on the House Banking and Currency Committee, had borrowed more than $100,000 at favorable interest rates from fourteen banks.

Influential staff members have used their public office for private gain. Bobby Baker, a protégé of Lyndon Johnson (when the former President was Senate Majority Leader), managed to accumulate a fortune (estimated at $2,000,000) while a Senate official. Martin Sweig, assistant to House Speaker John McCormack, was indicted in 1970 on charges that he had used his position to influence federal agencies on behalf of clients of Nathan Voloshen, a highly paid New York lobbyist. Voloshen pleaded guilty to conspiring to use the Speaker's office to exert pressure on federal agencies, and to perjury before the grand jury that investigated the case. He received a suspended sentence and a fine of $10,000. Sweig was acquitted on the influence charges but convicted on one count of perjury. He was sentenced to two and one-half years in prison and fined $2,000.

Many political scientists who have studied the operation of Congress closely have concluded that Congress does a fairly good job on the whole. Those who defend Congress argue that Congress is a generally

The Case for Congress

[10] In Roger H. Davidson, *The Role of the Congressman* (New York: Pegasus, 1969), p. 180. The slogan is often heard in the Senate as well.
[11] David B. Truman, *The Congressional Party* (New York: Wiley, 1959), p. 7.
[12] Stewart Alsop, *The Center* (New York: Harper & Row, 1968), p. 283.

representative assembly that broadly mirrors the desires of the people. If it fails to act "fast enough" to meet social needs, perhaps it is because the people do not want it to act any faster. And one may ask: "How fast is fast enough?"

Ralph K. Huitt, a leading authority on the congressional process, has noted that much criticism of Congress as "obstructive" comes from persons of liberal persuasion. As Presidents have encountered obstacles to liberal programs, he observes, the critics have urged reform of the structure and procedures of Congress to make it more responsive to the President. But Huitt suggests that "elections do count and representation does work." For example, in 1965, "in the first session of the 89th Congress, with a topheavy Democratic majority that included some seventy generally liberal freshmen, President Johnson got approval of a massive domestic legislative program that might normally have taken twenty years." [13]

It may be argued that, to some degree, an oligarchical internal structure is necessary in Congress so that it can function at all. One study of the House of Representatives notes that "a body of 435 men must process a workload that is enormous, enormously complicated and enormously consequential. . . . To meet the more general problems the House has developed a division of labor—a system of standing committees." [14]

The study concluded that the decision-making structure of the House is "essentially a semi-oligarchy," but that the House enjoys stability as a result of "internal processes which have served to keep the institution from tearing itself apart while engaged in the business of decision-making." For example, it is generally assumed that members will not "pursue internal conflicts to the point where the effectiveness of the House is impaired." [15]

In short, the House operates under a set of rules that may be necessary for *system-maintenance*—that is, to keep a diverse, unwieldy institution functioning. From this basic premise flows the defense of such congressional procedures as seniority, the committee system, and the tradition of elaborate courtesy senators normally display in addressing one another on the floor.

A case may also be made for some of the other procedures of Congress that are often condemned. Much criticism of Congress does originate with liberals and activists who are impatient for the national legislature to get on with the business of meeting social needs. And certainly the filibus-

[13] Ralph K. Huitt, "Congress, The Durable Partner," in Ralph K. Huitt and Robert L. Peabody, eds., *Congress: Two Decades of Analysis* (New York: Harper & Row, 1969), p. 219.
[14] Richard F. Fenno, Jr., "The Internal Distribution of Influence: The House," in David B. Truman, ed., *The Congress and America's Future,* prepared for the American Assembly, Columbia University (Englewood Cliffs, N.J.: Prentice-Hall, 1965), p. 53.
[15] *Ibid.,* p. 70.

ter and the seniority system have been used by Southerners to impede major civil rights legislation. Nevertheless, congressional procedures sometimes protect the country against hasty or misguided action in a crisis that could result from bowing to popular emotion; and the same procedures can be used to advantage by liberals. Seniority brought J. William Fulbright of Arkansas to the chairmanship of the Senate Foreign Relations Committee. As a Southerner, Fulbright voted with the South on civil rights legislation. But as a student of foreign policy, Fulbright was deeply troubled by President Johnson's escalation of the war in Vietnam. Fulbright's televised hearings on the war were a powerful and prestigious forum for raising questions about a policy that, as time passed, proved increasingly unpopular.

In reply to the charge that Congress is run by an elite group of leaders, many scholars emphasize the pluralistic nature of Congress. They dispute the importance or even the existence of a ruling elite, such as Senator Clark's "establishment" or William S. White's "Inner Club." [16] No one who has spent any amount of time watching the United States Senate in action can doubt that some senators are a good deal more influential than others. But Nelson Polsby has argued that the concept of an "Inner Club" may be extremely misleading:

> We must pause to ask: Is there an inner club at all? Or is power distributed in the Senate more widely? It is worthwhile to remember that there are only 100 U.S. Senators. Each one enjoys high social status, great visibility, a large staff, and substantial powers in his own right. Each one has the right, by the rules of the Senate, to speak on the floor of the Senate on any subject for as long as he desires to do so.[17]

As Polsby suggests, uncertainty about the outcome of legislative battles makes senatorial bargaining necessary, which "dilutes the power of the most entrenched, and enhances tremendously the powers of all senators, however low on the totem pole." [18] Ralph Huitt contends that each member of Congress is "essentially on his own. This explains a basic fact of life in the Senate: no one finally can make anyone else do anything." [19]

Some of the institutional factors that have distorted Congress as a wholly representative body are changing. The abuses of malapportionment in the House have been declared unconstitutional by the "one-man, one-vote" decisions of the Supreme Court. With the implementation of these reapportionment decisions, the ideal of equal representation in terms of

[16] William S. White, *Citadel* (New York: Harper & Row, 1957), p. 84.
[17] Nelson W. Polsby, *Congress and the Presidency* (Englewood Cliffs, N.J.: Prentice-Hall, 1964), p. 36.
[18] *Ibid.*, p. 39.
[19] Ralph K. Huitt, "The Internal Distribution of Influence: The Senate," in Truman, *The Congress and America's Future*, p. 80.

Cartoon depicting the original gerrymander of Essex, Mass., in 1812.

population is coming closer to being a reality. (Even though congressional districts must now be nearly equal, the problem remains of how the district lines should be drawn. Where these lines are drawn for political advantage, in order to favor one party or group over another, the district is said to be *gerrymandered.* The question of what constitutes fairness in drawing the boundaries of a political district is enormously complex and has been largely unresolved up to now by the courts.)

To the charge that Congress no longer effectively legislates, and has become a "rubber stamp" for the Chief Executive, one can reply that this was certainly not President Kennedy's view as he struggled to pass his legislative program. President Johnson could not have considered Congress a supine institution when it forced him to cut spending by $6 billion as the price of passing a federal income-tax increase. President Nixon discovered the power of Congress early in his administration, when the Senate rejected his Supreme Court nominations of Clement Haynsworth, Jr., and G. Harrold Carswell.

Nor does Congress confine itself to saying "yes" or "no" to presidential programs. To an extent that is perhaps underemphasized, Congress innovates and initiates, sometimes on matters of great importance. The proposal to amend the Constitution to provide for direct election of the President, for example, was largely the work of one senator, Birch Bayh of Indiana. Senator Edmund Muskie, the Maine Democrat, championed antipollution legislation for many years, even though in 1970 President Nixon seized this issue and sought to make it his own.

Finally, those who view Congress in a more favorable light argue

"Did you ever have one of those days when you didn't know whether to advise or consent?"

WASHINGTON, Nov. 20—Since Aug. 18, when President Nixon announced the nomination of Judge Clement F. Haynsworth, Jr., as Supreme Court Justice, this capital has witnessed a classic example of pressure politics. . . .

"There's a book in it," one administrative assistant to a teetering Southern Democratic Senator said today when asked about the various pressures.

"This crowd (the administration) sure knows how to organize pressure," the aide continued. . . . "An important constituent calls up the Senator . . . and says 'I don't give a damn about this guy Haynsworth but one of these days we're going to have a cotton bill up and we'll need Republican support.' " . . .

One Negro lobbyist . . . is known to have remarked to several Senators that he could not be sure whether "we can control our people" if a man of Judge Haynsworth's views was elevated to the Supreme Court. . . .

Senator Robert W. Packwood, an undecided Republican freshman from Oregon . . . was called to the White House and had 40 minutes alone with the President.

"The President," Mr. Packwood related, "said to me, 'Bob, I want your vote, I need your vote. If you can see your way clear to do it, I would appreciate your vote as a personal favor.' But I was never offered anything, nor was I promised anything or threatened with anything. I do not call this exactly arm-twisting." . . .

Richard S. Schweiker, Republican of Pennsylvania . . . said he got calls from the White House, Cabinet officers, Gov. Raymond P. Shafer of Pennsylvania, the Republican state chairman, county chairmen, and heavy contributors.

"I expect pressure," he said. "I know we're not playing beanbag down here. But some of this was rough."

—E. W. Kenworthy, "The Haynsworth Issue: A Study in Pressure Politics," *New York Times*, November 21, 1969.

that scandal and dishonesty among its members are the exception and not the rule, and that the vast majority of senators and representatives are both hard-working and honest. Not every lawmaker junkets to the French Riviera at the taxpayer's expense, and if the Senate produced Warren Harding and Thomas Dodd it also produced Robert Taft and John F. Kennedy. In fact, four out of the five Presidents elected between 1948 and 1968 had served in the United States Senate.

Congress plays a central role in the democratic process by making laws—the general rules that govern American society.

Most of the controversy over how well or how badly Congress performs focuses on its lawmaking function. But Congress plays other important roles. It has several nonlegislative functions: it proposes amendments to the Constitution; it may declare war; it can impeach and try the President or other civil officers of the United States, including judges; it may rule on presidential disability; it regulates the conduct of its members, and can punish, censure, or expel them; and it has power to decide whether a prospective member has been properly elected or should be seated. The House may choose the President in the event of electoral deadlock. The Senate approves or rejects treaties and presidential appointments, and,

The Many Roles of Congress

459

through the custom of *senatorial courtesy*, individual senators who belong to the same political party as the President exercise a veto power over presidential appointments in their states.

In addition, Congress oversees and supervises the operations of the executive branch and the independent regulatory agencies. For example, when bureaucrats are closely questioned at appropriations hearings, Congress is exercising its supervisory powers. The power of the purse, which the Constitution grants to Congress, carries with it the power to monitor how well the money is spent. For this purpose, Congress conducts investigations and holds hearings. These are ostensibly tied to a legislative purpose, but often they serve a broader function of focusing public attention on specific social problems. During the early 1950's, Senator Joseph R. McCarthy achieved formidable personal political power by abusing the Senate's investigatory function and conducting "witch hunts" in search of alleged Communists in government. McCarthy succeeded in creating an atmosphere of fear in which the rights of witnesses were frequently violated. But congressional investigations can also be used to publicize the risks of birth control pills, the problems of American policy in Southeast Asia, or the tragedy of hunger in the midst of plenty.

Perhaps even more important than some of these formal roles is the function of Congress in legitimizing the outputs of the political system. People are more likely to accept the policy decisions of a political system if major decisions are made by representative institutions. Congress, therefore, at times plays a key role in the *resolution of conflict* in American society. As in the case of all political institutions, Congress is subject to external pressures by organized interest groups, unorganized public opinion, the press, individual constituents, and so on. The AMA—the physicians' lobby—opposed Medicare, but enough other groups and individuals wanted it; Congress made a choice and attempted to resolve the conflict by legislating. Not every problem can be solved by passing a law, but in exercising its powers and in responding to social needs with legislation, Congress can at least help to ease the friction points by mediating disputes and making decisions for society as a whole.

In thus managing conflict (or making conflict manageable), Congress helps to *integrate* various groups and interests within the community by acting, to some extent, as a referee. However, as we noted in Chapter 6, not all groups in a pluralistic society have equal power. Disadvantaged groups—the poor and the blacks, for example—may find it more difficult to influence Congress than does the oil industry. Consequently, in resolving conflict, Congress may still leave many groups unsatisfied. Yet Congress does provide one of several points of access to the political system for many individuals and groups. The inputs, in the form of demands and supports by segments of the community, are transformed by Congress through the legislative process into policy outputs and binding decisions for all of society. But Congress is more than a machine for making decisions. It is also a group of 535 men and women, and who they are is worth examining in some detail, for in many cases it may affect what they do.

THE LEGISLATORS

Portrait
of a Lawmaker

When the Ninety-second Congress convened in January 1971 the average age of its members was 52.7 years.[20] In the previous Congress, a total of ninety-six House members, or 22 percent, were between the ages of sixty and eighty-four.[21] Members of Congress were, on the average, almost eight years older than other adult Americans. The average senator was 56.4 years old, and the average House member was 51.9 years.[22] By contrast, the average age of adult Americans was 44.8.[23]

In part, the age level of Congress is high because of constitutional restrictions: a member of the House must be at least twenty-five (and a citizen for seven years) and a senator must be at least thirty (and a citizen for nine years). In part, of course, it is explained by the fact that senators and representatives usually do not achieve their office without considerable prior experience in politics or other fields.

More than half the nation's population are women, but only eleven women (including one senator, Margaret Chase Smith) served in the Ninety-first Congress. Only thirteen blacks were in the Ninety-second Congress although this was the most since Reconstruction days. Among these were one black senator, Edward W. Brooke, a Massachusetts Republican, and Representative Shirley Chisholm, a Brooklyn Democrat, who was the first black woman ever elected to Congress.

In many other respects, the socioeconomic make-up of Congress is not representative of the general population. For example, almost 60 percent of the Ninety-first Congress, or 310 out of 535 members, were lawyers. In the population as a whole, lawyers make up only 0.35 percent of the labor force. Other major occupational groups of members of Congress were: business or banking, 184; educators, 73; agriculture, 50; and journalism, 47.[24] As Roger Davidson has suggested, representatives "are

---

[20] Congressional Quarterly, *Weekly Report*, November 6, 1970, p. 2770.
[21] Adapted from U.S. Bureau of the Census, *Statistical Abstract of the United States, 1969*, p. 364.
[22] Congressional Quarterly, *Weekly Report*, November 6, 1970, p. 2770.
[23] Data provided by U.S. Bureau of the Census; as of December 1969.
[24] Occupational breakdown from Congressional Quarterly, *Weekly Report*, January 3, 1969, p. 46.

A congressman's work is never done, as seen in this series of photographs of Congressman Fred B. Rooney, Democrat, of Pennsylvania.

A congressman must visit with constituents . . .

Listen to their problems . . .

Hurry to . . .

The Life of a Legislator

Committee meetings . . .

recruited almost wholly from the same relatively high-status occupations." [25]

Although today America is a highly urbanized society, Congress historically has been predominantly Main Street and rural. Donald Matthews reported in a 1960 study that a majority of senators were born in towns of 2,500 to 5,000 in population.[26] Congress is also mostly Protestant; for example, in the Ninety-first Congress there were 379 Protestants, 109 Catholics, and 19 Jews. (Protestants comprised 71 percent of Congress and about 60 percent of the adult population.)

If one were to draw a portrait of the average member of Congress, he would be fifty-three, male, white, Protestant, a lawyer, and a native of a small town in a rural area.

How significant is it that in many ways Congress is not a cross-section of America? The question cannot be answered with precision. Obviously, Congress does not have to be an exact model of the population in order to represent its constituents. Nor is it entirely surprising that lawyers are overrepresented in a body that makes laws. Yet it is not hard to see how blacks, other minorities, white blue-collar workers, the poor, and members of underrepresented socioeconomic groups in general may feel "left out" of a system that produces an overwhelmingly white, Protestant, upper-middle-class, and small-town national legislature.

Samuel P. Huntington has stressed "the growing insulation of Congress from other social groups and political institutions" during this century.[27] Because senators and representatives are likely to come from rural, small-town backgrounds the result, he argued, is a "provincialism of Congressmen," who often belong to local political elites and tend to think in small-town, local ways. Businessmen and leaders in the executive branch generally come from cosmopolitan big-city backgrounds. They tend to be international or national in outlook; congressmen are more likely to put Main Street first. "Old ideas, old values, old beliefs die hard in Congress," Huntington concludes.

"It is true that we just don't have much time to legislate around here." [28] The complaint was voiced by a Republican congressman who participated in a series of round-table discussions about life on Capitol Hill. It could easily have come from almost any one of the 435 members

[25] Davidson, *The Role of the Congressman*, p. 69.
[26] Donald R. Matthews, *U.S. Senators and Their World* (Chapel Hill, N.C.: University of North Carolina Press, 1960), p. 16.
[27] Samuel P. Huntington, "Congressional Responses to the Twentieth Century," in Truman, *The Congress and America's Future*, pp. 8, 12–16.
[28] Charles L. Clapp, *The Congressman: His Work as He Sees It* (Washington, D.C.: The Brookings Institution, 1963), p. 61.

of the House or the 100 senators. There are so many demands on the congressman that any lawmaker soon discovers he cannot possibly do all that is expected of him. One House member attempted a few years ago to list all the aspects of his job. Only a sample is quoted here: "A Congresesman has become an expanded messenger boy, an employment agency . . . wardheeler . . . kisser of babies, recoverer of lost baggage . . . contributor to good causes—cornerstone layer . . . bridge dedicator, ship christener."[29]

Answer the mail . . .

Although members of Congress differ in how they choose to allocate their time, constituents *do* elect legislators, and most congressmen spend a considerable portion of their day trying to take care of their constituents' problems. Many congressmen bounce back and forth between Washington and their districts like ping-pong balls and live a sort of legislative double life.

And the phones . . .

As of 1970, members of the House and Senate received salaries of $42,500 a year, plus funds to hire a staff (senators from populous states are permitted to hire more assistants), and certain other allowances for office supplies, telephone calls, and travel, as well as the franking privilege for their official mail. Although the basic salary plus benefits are considerable, members of Congress also have substantial expenses—many maintain residences both in Washington and their hometowns, for example.

The mail pours in from constituents, and it must, somehow, be answered. Because the volume of mail is so great, many lawmakers use robotypers, machines that type personalized form letters. Few senators and representatives dare to reply to abusive letters as Congressman John Steven McGroarty of California did; he wrote to a constituent: "One of the countless drawbacks of being in Congress is that I am compelled to receive impertinent letters from a jackass like you in which you say I promised to have the Sierra Madre mountains reforested and I have been in Congress two months and haven't done it. Will you please take two running jumps and go to hell."[30]

Meet with student antiwar delegation . . .

On a typical day, a member of Congress may spend an hour reading mail, making calls, dictating memos, then rush off to a 10 A.M. committee meeting, dash to the floor for a vote, eat lunch (if he has time), and return to a committee hearing. Perhaps late in the afternoon he manages to get back to his office, where a group of constituents are waiting to see him. A powerful interest group (a labor union or business association, for example) has invited him to one or more cocktail receptions, and he must dutifully put in an appearance, have a drink, and chew on a rubber shrimp before getting home for dinner—that is, on the nights that he is not attend-

[29] Luther Patrick, "What is a Congressman?" *Congressional Record*, May 13, 1963, p. A2978.
[30] In John F. Kennedy, *Profiles in Courage* (New York: Harper & Row, 1955, 1956), p. 30.

Campaign . . .

Demonstrate that he is a patriot . . .

And loves children.

ing a dinner in some hotel banquet hall. He spends many weekends in his home state or district, flying there to march in the Veterans Day parade or listen to constituents' woes.

Although congressmen do spend a great deal of time mending political fences and handling problems of constituents, more than three-quarters of House members questioned in one study listed legislative work as their most time-consuming job. Of eighty-seven congressmen who responded, 77 percent listed "legislator (including committee work)" as their most time-consuming role; only 16 percent listed "Errand Boy; lawyer for constituents." [31]

The congressman must decide how he wishes to spend his time. He must choose among alternative roles open to him—whether, for example, to concentrate on working for the interests of his district, or seeking to become a party leader, or running for higher office, or specializing in a committee, or seizing an issue that may bring him national recognition.

The job of the congressman can be difficult for his wife and children. Often a congressional wife must attend political dinners on short notice, accompany her husband on the campaign trail, and be ready to entertain small or large groups of constituents. "If I had known how much work was involved in being a politician's wife," said one, "I don't think I would have let my husband run that first time." [32]

The Image of the Congressman

Congress and the individual congressman enjoy a rather mixed public image. Voter attitudes toward Congress fluctuate markedly. For example, in December 1963, only 33 percent of respondents to a Louis Harris Survey rated the performance of Congress "Excellent to pretty good," while 60 percent rated it "Fair to poor," and 7 percent were "Not sure." Yet, a year later, these public attitudes were almost precisely reversed; and by 1965, after Congress passed landmark Great Society legislation, 64 percent of the public rated its performance "Excellent to pretty good," only 26 percent found it "Fair to poor," and 10 percent were "Not sure." [33] However, the percentage of those approving of congressional performance dropped to 49 percent in 1966 and dipped even lower in the next few years: [34]

[31] Davidson, The Role of the Congressman, pp. 98–99.
[32] In Clapp, The Congressman: His Work as He Sees It, p. 395.
[33] Louis Harris, "Public Gives Congress Mixed Confidence Rating for Year's Work," Philadelphia Enquirer, January 13, 1969. Respondents were asked: "How would you rate the job Congress did this past year . . .—excellent, pretty good, only fair, or poor?"
[34] Louis Harris, "Congress Gets Lowest Mark in 5 Yrs.," Washington Post, March 23, 1970, p. 2.

	Positive	Negative	Not Sure
1967	38%	55%	7%
1968	46	46	8
1969	34	54	12

One detailed study of public attitudes toward members of Congress indicated that 64 percent of the employed general public had a generally favorable opinion.[35] Public opinion of members of Congress varies among different groups, however. Congressmen did not fare as well as high-level appointed officials in the Federal Government among groups such as graduate students, college instructors, and college seniors; and only 48 percent of business executives held favorable opinions of congressmen.[36]

Should a member of Congress lead or follow the opinion of his constituents? The question poses the classic dilemma of legislators, mixing as it does problems of the proper nature of representation in a democracy with practical considerations of the lawmaker's self-interest and desire for reelection.

Representation: The Congressman and his Constituent

One answer was provided by Edmund Burke, the eighteenth-century British statesman, in his famous speech to the voters of Bristol, who had just sent him to Parliament. As Burke defined the relationship of a representative to his constituents, "Their wishes ought to have great weight with him; their opinion high respect. . . . But his unbiased opinion, his mature judgment, his enlightened conscience, he ought not to sacrifice to you. . . . Your representative owes you, not his industry only, but his judgment." [37] Parliament, Burke contended, was an assembly of one nation, and local interests must bow to the general, national interest.

The Burkean concept of the legislator as trustee for the people clashes with the concept of the representative as proxy for the people—an instructed delegate who automatically mirrors the will of the majority of his constituents. (Burke himself encountered political difficulties in his own constituency; six years after his speech, he withdrew as the member from Bristol.) On the other hand, a congressman who attempted faithfully to follow opinion in his district would soon discover that it was very difficult

[35] M. Kent Jennings, Milton C. Cummings, Jr., and Franklin P. Kilpatrick, "Trusted Leaders: Perceptions of Appointed Federal Officials," *Public Opinion Quarterly*, Vol. 30 (January 1967), p. 379. Respondents were asked: "If you were to describe your general idea of a United States Congressman, what sort of person would that be?"
[36] *Ibid.*, p. 380.
[37] Edmund Burke, *The Works of the Right Honourable Edmund Burke*, Vol. II (London: Oxford University Press, 1930), pp. 164–65.

In an average week I personally read and sign perhaps fifty letters.

How does the rest of the mail get signed? There is still another gadget widely used on the Hill for coping with this problem. I have one right in my own office, and it cost me $1,200 out of clerk-hire—i.e., my office allotment.

My signature is reproduced, or forged if you will, to practically all my letters by a device known as an "autopen"—a wonderful product of automation which saves precious hours each week. There are three forged signatures. Most answers get the formal "Joseph S. Clark." Politicians who are not intimate get "Joe Clark." Friends get "Joe," as do a fair number who are not friends but call me "Joe" when they write.

—Joseph S. Clark, *Congress: The Sapless Branch.*

to measure opinion accurately. He would find that on some issues many voters had no strong opinions. Even when opinions could be discerned and measured, he would also find that a constituency is made up of competing interests and is really several constituencies; often, he could please one group only at the expense of offending another.

The largest number of congressmen, therefore, reject both the role of trustee and the role of instructed delegate and instead try to combine the two by exercising their own judgment *and* representing constituency views. As Roger Davidson has suggested, "Many congressmen observe that their problem is one of balancing the one role against the other." [38] In interviews with eighty-seven members of the House of Representatives, Davidson found that 28 percent expressed conceptions of their role that fit the "trustee" model; only 23 percent fit the "delegate" model; but 46 percent were "politico" types who sought to blend both the trustee and delegate conceptions.[39]

Sometimes a member of Congress faces the dilemma of local versus national interest; constituents may feel foreign aid is a waste of money, but the legislator may decide it is in the best interests of the United States and vote accordingly. Often, however, local interests are put first—that is where the voters are. And some members of Congress feel that their first obligation is to the constituency that elected them.

To an extent, the dilemma may be artificial; one major study of constituent influence discovered that the average voter knows little about his congressman's activities—a finding that contrasted with the view of most congressmen, who regard their voting record as important to their reelection.[40] Approximately half the voters surveyed in one House election year had heard *nothing* about either their incumbent congressman

[38] Davidson, *The Role of the Congressman*, p. 119.
[39] *Ibid.*, pp. 117–19.
[40] Warren E. Miller and Donald E. Stokes, "Constituency Influence in Congress," *American Political Science Review*, Vol. 57 (March 1963), pp. 53–54.

or his opponent. The study, based on interviews with both congressmen and voters, also indicated that, while legislators tend to think that the views of their constituents match their own, there is often a gap between the actual opinions of constituents and the congressman's *perception* of their views.[41]

Polling Constituents. Even if a member of Congress wants to sample opinion among his constituents to help him in making up his mind on an issue, he faces the practical problem of how to go about it. To gauge the thinking back home, congressmen rely on conversations with friends, party leaders, and newsmen in their states or districts, the mail (particularly personal letters), and local newspapers. And in recent years, increasing numbers of congressmen have been using questionnaires mailed to the voters, or have turned to professional polling organizations for help.

Without professional assistance, Congressional polls are likely to be amateurish and the results distorted. In fact, such polls may be taken not so much to gauge constituency thinking as to promote the legislator by flattering his constituent with a questionnaire.[42]

With the growing use of computers and the increased sophistication of polling, congressmen now have the tools available to them to sample constituent opinion, but they may not have the money.

THE HOUSE

Although Congress is one branch of the Federal Government, the House and Senate are distinct institutions, each with its own rules and traditions and each jealous of its own powers and prerogatives.

One basic difference, of course, was established by the Constitution, which provided two-year terms for members of the House and staggered, six-year terms for senators. The result is that all members of the House, but only one-third of the Senate, must face the voters every other year.

The House is big. Because it has 435 members compared to 100 in the Senate, the House is a more formal institution with stricter rules and procedures. For example, the Senate permits unlimited debate most of the time, but representatives may be limited to speaking for five minutes or less during debate on a bill.

And because there are so many representatives, they generally enjoy less prestige than senators. In the television age, some senators, especially

TO HOUSE WING

---

[41] *Ibid.*
[42] V. O. Key, Jr., *Public Opinion and American Democracy* (New York: Knopf, 1961), pp. 492–93.

those who are presidential aspirants, have become celebrities, instantly recognizable to the spectators in the galleries. By contrast, visitors in the House galleries find it difficult to pick out their own congressman, let alone any other. This unfamiliarity is not surprising; only 39 percent of adult Americans are able to name their congressman.[43] At Washington dinner parties where protocol is observed, House members sit below the salt, ranking three places down the table from their Senate colleagues. (House members are outranked not only by senators, but by governors and former Vice-Presidents.)[44]

Despite its size, the House has achieved a stability of tenure and a role never envisioned by the Founding Fathers. The men who framed the Constitution distrusted unchecked popular rule, and provided an indirectly elected Senate to restrain the more egalitarian House of Representatives (the Seventeenth Amendment in 1913 provided for the direct election of the Senate). As Gouverneur Morris put it: "The second branch [the Senate] ought to be a check on the first [the House]. . . . The first branch, originating from the people, will ever be subject to precipitancy, changeability, and excess. . . . The second branch ought to be composed of men of great and established property—an aristocracy. . . . Such an aristocratic body will keep down the turbulency of democracy."[45]

Ironically, the House and Senate have on some issues exchanged places in terms of these expectations of the framers. One reason is that House seats are safer; in recent decades the turnover in the House of Representatives has been relatively small. A commonly cited standard for a "safe" congressional district is one in which the winner receives 55 percent of the vote or more. Less than that is considered "marginal." According to a study by Congressional Quarterly, between 1952 and 1968 only 20.1 percent of House races were won with less than 55 percent of the vote.[46] Senate seats are less "safe." In 1968, for example, sixteen Senate races, or 47 percent, were won with less than 55 percent of the vote.[47]

Because members of the House are more secure than their colleagues in the Senate, the House is often *less* responsive than the Senate to pressures for change in the status quo. Senators have state-wide constituencies frequently dominated by urban areas with powerful labor and minority

[43] Data from the National Assessment of Educational Progress, *Washington Post*, July 8, 1970, p. A6.

[44] Carolyn Hagner Shaw, *The Social List of Washington and Social Precedence in Washington* (Washington, D.C.: Shaw, 1970), pp. 12, 14.

[45] In Robert A. Dahl, *Pluralist Democracy in the United States: Conflict and Consent* (Chicago: Rand McNally, 1967), p. 35.

[46] Congressional Quarterly, *Weekly Report*, February 20, 1970, p. 451.

[47] Based on data in Congressional Quarterly, *Weekly Report*, Part One, June 6, 1969.

TABLE 12-1

Major Differences Between House and Senate

House	Senate
Larger (435 members)	Smaller (100 members)
More formal	Less formal
More hierarchically organized	Less hierarchically organized
Acts more quickly	Acts more slowly
Rules more rigid	Rules more flexible
Power less evenly distributed	Power more evenly distributed
Longer apprentice period	Shorter apprentice period
More impersonal	More personal
Less "important" constituencies	More "important" constituencies
Less prestige	More prestige
More "conservative"	More "liberal"

Source: Lewis A. Froman, Jr., *The Congressional Process* (Boston: Little, Brown, 1967), p. 7.

group vote blocs; as a result, the Senate today is often the *more* "liberal" branch of Congress.[48]

Another result of the greater stability of House seats has been the "institutionalization" of that body. For many representatives, being a member of the House has become a career, with predictable steps up the ladder. Because the House is decentralized, a number of rewards, such as committee and subcommittee chairmanships, await career members; and as an institution, the House can gain the loyalty of its members.[49]

The organization of Congress has sometimes been compared to that of a medieval state. In the House, the Speaker is the most powerful member, but he must contend with the chairmen of the twenty-one standing committees of the House, each a duke in his own right.

Power in the House: The Leadership

The Speaker exercised great power between 1890 and 1910, during the Republican rule of "Czar" Thomas B. Reed of Maine and "Uncle" Joe Cannon of Illinois. In 1910, however, a coalition of Democrats and Bull Moose Republicans led a successful revolt against Cannon. The rules were revised to strip the Speaker of much of his formal power, including the right to appoint members to committees of the House. But a Speaker with

[48] Lewis A. Froman, Jr., "Why the Senate Is More Liberal than the House," Chapter 6 in his *Congressmen and Their Constituencies* (Chicago: Rand McNally, 1963), pp. 69–84.
[49] Nelson W. Polsby, "The Institutionalization of the U.S. House of Representatives," *American Political Science Review*, Vol. 62 (March 1968), pp. 144–68.

a strong personality and great legislative skill can still exert great influence in the House, as Sam Rayburn of Texas demonstrated during his seventeen-year tenure between 1940 and 1961. Over bourbon and branch water in a small room in the Capitol, Rayburn and his intimates would plan strategy for the House and swap political stories in an informal institution known as the "Board of Education." [50] Despite his loss of *formal* powers since 1910, the Speaker remains a key figure.

The position of Speaker is provided for in the Constitution ("The House of Representatives shall chuse their Speaker and other Officers."). He has a number of official powers: he presides over the House, he has power to recognize or ignore members who wish to speak, he appoints members of special or select committees that conduct special investigations (but not standing committees), and he exercises other procedural controls. His real power, however, stems from his position as *political leader* of the majority party in the House, rather than from his formal duties. Technically, the Speaker is elected by the House, with each party offering a candidate. In practice, he is chosen at the start of each Congress by a caucus, or meeting, of the majority party. Since in the past, at least, the formal voting in the House has been strictly along party lines, the majority party's candidate for Speaker has automatically won.

The Speaker has two chief assistants, the Majority Leader, chosen by the party caucus, and the Majority Whip (appointed by the Democrats, elected in the case of the Republicans). The Majority Leader is his party's floor leader and a key strategist; together with the Speaker and the members of the House Rules Committee he schedules debate and negotiates with committee chairmen and party members on procedural matters. The Majority Whip, along with a number of deputy whips, is responsible for rounding up party members for important votes and counting noses. (The term "Whip" comes from "whipper-in," the man assigned in English fox hunts to keep the hounds from straying.) The minority party also elects a Minority Leader and elects or appoints a Minority Whip. Republican members of the House receive committee assignments from a Committee on Committees. Democrats on the Ways and Means Committee perform the same task on the Democratic side.

In recent years, House Democratic liberals, led by such men as Richard Bolling of Missouri and Morris Udall of Arizona, have sought within the party caucus to challenge the Democratic establishment. A number of the liberals banded together in 1959 in an informal organization known as the Democratic Study Group, which had 140 members and a research staff of twelve people a decade later. In 1969, the liberals won approval for monthly meetings of the Democratic caucus, but in 1970 one

---

[50] Neil MacNeil, *Forge of Democracy: The House of Representatives* (New York: David McKay, 1964), pp. 82–83.

faction of the liberals failed in an effort to unseat John McCormack as Speaker. The reformers did, however, win agreement by the Democratic caucus to a "study" of alternatives to the seniority system. In the spring of 1970, McCormack, under increasing pressure to make way for younger leadership, announced he would retire from Congress that year, and he did.

The House Rules Committee has virtually complete control over what bills will be brought to the floor for debate. Most major legislation cannot be debated without a "rule" from the Rules Committee, which sets the terms of the debate, the time to be allowed for floor discussion, and the extent to which it may be amended on the floor.[51] By delaying a bill, or by refusing to permit it to come to the floor at all, the Rules Committee may effectively block the passage of legislation within its jurisdiction (except in the rare instance when a majority of the House signs a discharge petition to by-pass the committee).

In 1961, President Kennedy barely won his fight to enlarge the House Rules Committee and thus curb the power of its conservative chairman. Democrats at that time controlled the House by a margin of 263 to 174, but a coalition of Southern Democrats and Republicans frequently succeeded in blocking passage of liberal legislation; the same coalition almost defeated any change in the composition of the Rules Committee. Although two liberal Democrats were added to the committee, Speaker Sam Rayburn managed to avoid any basic challenge to the jurisdiction and power of the Rules Committee.[52] Since 1961, however, the Rules Committee has not consistently been as powerful a bottleneck to liberal legislation.

The basic power structure of the House, then, consists of the Speaker, the floor leaders and Whips of the two major parties, the Rules Committee, and the chairmen of the twenty other standing committees. How these individuals and committees interact powerfully affects the fate of legislation. But the business of making laws is also governed by a complicated, even byzantine, set of rules and procedures. Although most citizens are not familiar with them, these procedures can affect policy outcomes; whether a bill is successfully steered through the legislative labyrinth, or gets lost along the way, often depends on how the rules and procedures are applied.

The Rules Committee

The Legislative Labyrinth: The House in Action

[51] For a detailed study of the complex rules and procedures of the House and Senate, see Lewis A. Froman, Jr., *The Congressional Process* (Boston: Little, Brown, 1967); and text of the Legislative Reorganization Act of 1970.

[52] Milton C. Cummings, Jr., and Robert L. Peabody, "The Decision to Enlarge the Committee on Rules: An Analysis of the 1961 Vote," in Robert L. Peabody and Nelson W. Polsby, eds., *New Perspectives on the House of Representatives* (Chicago: Rand McNally, 1963), p. 193.

Less than 3 percent of all bills introduced in Congress become public laws. In the first session of the Ninety-first Congress in 1969, 21,553 bills were introduced but only 190 became public laws.[53]

After a bill is introduced by a House member, it is referred to a committee by the Speaker. Often, his choice is limited by the jurisdictions of the standing committees, but when jurisdictions overlap, or when new kinds of legislation are introduced, the Speaker may have considerable discretion in deciding where to assign a bill. In 1963, the Civil Rights Bill was referred to the Judiciary Committee, headed by Emanuel Celler of New York, rather than to the Interstate and Foreign Commerce Committee, headed by Oren Harris of Arkansas. This strategy was designed to put the bill in friendly hands.

Only about 10 percent of bills get out of committee. The committee chairman may assign the measure to one of the roughly 125 subcommittees of the standing committees (all but three House committees have subcommittees). If the bill is reported out of committee, it is placed on one of five *calendars*, or lists of business pending before the House. The various House calendars and the kinds of bills referred to them are shown in Table 12-2.

Certain bills from the Appropriations, Ways and Means, and several other committees may be taken upon the floor without going through the Rules Committee. On specified days, bills on the Consent Calendar and Private Calendar may be called up directly for House action. And if two-

TABLE 12-2

Regulating Legislative Traffic: The House Calendars

Consent	For noncontroversial bills. Bills on the Consent Calendar are normally called on the first and third Mondays of each month, but debate may be blocked by the objection of any member. The second time a bill is called in this manner, three members must object to block consideration.
Discharge	Motions to force a bill out of committee are placed on the Discharge Calendar when they receive the necessary 218 signatures from House members.
House	Bills that do not appropriate money or raise revenue go on the House Calendar.
Private	Bills that affect specific individuals and deal with private matters, such as claims against the government, immigration, or land titles, are placed on the Private Calendar and can be called on the first and third Tuesdays of each month.
Union	Bills that directly or indirectly appropriate money or raise revenue are placed on the Union Calendar.

[53] *1969 Congressional Quarterly Almanac*, p. 22. It should be noted that many of the bills introduced were either for the benefit of *private* individuals or duplicated another bill. A *public* law applies to whole classes of citizens.

thirds of the members voting agree, any bill may be debated under a procedure permitted twice a month called "suspension of the rules." But most major legislation must first be approved by the Rules Committee.

A quorum consisting of a majority of the House, 218 members, is required for general debate. When the House is considering legislation sent to it by the Rules Committee, however, it sits as a Committee of the Whole, a device that allows the House to conduct its business with less formality (and a quorum of only one hundred members).

Voting in the Committee of the Whole is by unrecorded voice vote, in which members shout "Yea" or "Nay," or by a standing vote, or by teller vote, in which members file down the aisle and are counted.

Until 1970 when the House modified the practice, members' names were not recorded in a teller vote. As a result, a congressman's vote was secret unless reported by a watching newsman—no easy feat since the congressmen filed down the aisle *away* from the press gallery, with their backs to the news reporters. Under this practice, as old as the Congress itself, constituents usually had no way of knowing how their representative voted. And teller votes were sometimes used in regular House voting as well as in the Committee of the Whole.

Growing pressures for reform led the House in 1970 to provide for

FOR CONGRESS: ELECTRONIC VOTING

What does the House of Representatives do more than 400 times a year that takes a half-hour each time but needs to take only three minutes?

The answer is call the roll, and after 180 years of virtually unchanged methods, there is mounting evidence that the House may be ready to take the plunge directly from the quill pen to the transistor as the instrument of recording its members' presence and views.

The House Committee on Standards of Official Conduct urged Speaker John W. McCormack . . . to authorize the installation in the chamber of "a modernized voting system at the earliest possible date" to prevent such irregularities as counting absentees. . . .

To understand how revolutionary such a change would be only requires watching a single House roll-call now. Ordinarily, when the time comes for voting, only a dozen or two of the 435 members are likely to be on the floor, so bells are rung to summon the others from their offices and committee rooms.

The tally clerk calls the roll in alphabetical order as the members straggle into the chamber, and many of them arrive too late to answer in order. These cluster in front of the rostrum and get recognized individually to record their stand. Then there is a long counting process and the result is announced.

During 1968, the 428 roll-calls occupied 198 of the 726 hours that the House was in session, or about 27 per cent of the time.

—Warren Weaver, Jr., "Electric Voting by House Studied,"
New York Times, June 23, 1969.

recorded teller votes on the demand of one-fifth of a quorum. During the debate over the change, Congressman Hale Boggs, Louisiana Democrat and Majority Whip, declared: "All we say is that a man should stand up and be counted. If you don't want to be recorded why did you come here in the first place? This is the day that makes the House relevant." [54] When debate is concluded in the Committee of the Whole, the House may send the bill back to its committee of origin (thereby killing it permanently or temporarily), or it may vote final passage. If one-fifth of the members present demand it, a roll call must be taken and each member's vote recorded. But roll-call votes are employed relatively infrequently; there were only 177 in the House in 1969, for example.

Supporters or opponents of a bill sometimes request roll-call votes as a delaying tactic, to give time to round up their forces. Often, however, they are demanded to place members on the spot; congressmen know that in a roll-call vote their position must become a matter of public record. Some interest groups regularly rate the records of members on the basis of their roll-call votes. Constituents may not pay much attention to how a congressman votes, but an opponent in an election campaign may use the legislator's recorded vote on a key issue against him.

This complicated voting procedure gives House members an opportunity to take both sides of an issue; a congressman may vote *against* a bill on voice vote, but then vote *for* it on the roll call for final passage. Much of the maneuvering in Congress takes place under institutional rules that permit legislators this sort of flexibility.

In enacting its 1970 reform legislation, Congress also limited secret voting in committee. The measure required that roll-call votes taken in committee, and votes in committee to report a bill to the floor, be made a matter of public record. It also required that committee hearings be publicly announced one week in advance. In addition, the House for the first time allowed radio and television coverage of its committee meetings. Other provisions of the reform bill, known as the Legislative Reorganization Act of 1970, made it more difficult to cut off floor debate suddenly, and permitted the House minority equal time in floor debate on the final versions of bills.

THE SENATE

After Joseph S. Clark was elected to the United States Senate, he sought advice over lunch with Senator Hubert Humphrey.

"Tell me how to behave when I get to the Senate," I asked him around half-past twelve.

[54] *Washington Post*, July 28, 1970, p. A6.

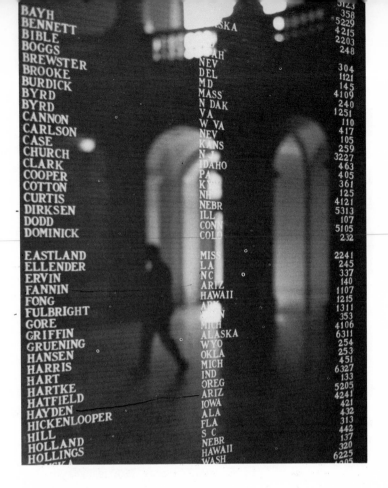

He did—for an hour and a half. I left the luncheon I hope a wiser man, as well briefed as a neophyte seeking admission to a new order can be.

In essence he said, "Keep your mouth shut and your eyes open. It's a friendly, courteous place. You will have no trouble getting along. Paul Douglas and I will help you. Lyndon Johnson runs the Senate and will treat you well." [55]

Although he chose not to follow it, Clark had received knowledgeable advice. The Senate may not be "the most exclusive club in the world" nor a "rich man's club," although it has been called both. It may or may not have an "Inner Club." But it certainly has both the atmosphere and appearance of a club. Its membership is relatively small; its quarters are ornate and gilded; its ways are slow.

William S. White, who meant it as praise, called the Senate "an institution that lives in an unending yesterday." White, then Senate correspondent of the *New York Times*, concluded that the Senate is "both a club and a club within a club. . . . The inner life of the Senate . . . is controlled by the Inner Club. . . . At the core of the Inner Club stand the Southern-

[55] Joseph S. Clark, *Congress: The Sapless Branch* (New York: Harper & Row, 1964), pp. 1–2.

ers, who with rare exceptions automatically assume membership almost with the taking of the oath of office."[56]

Donald Matthews observed in 1960 that the Senate had its "unwritten rules of the game, its norms of conduct." The freshman senator is expected to serve a silent apprenticeship (although this is less true today than when Matthews was writing), to be one of the Senate "work horses" rather than one of the "show horses," to develop a legislative specialty, pay homage to the institution, and observe its folkways.[57] These include the elaborate courtesy with which senators, even bitter enemies, address each other on the floor.

These rules of behavior, Matthews observed, perform important functions: they encourage expertise, soften personal conflict, and promote cooperation. A member may feel great pressure to conform to the rules and to become a "real Senate man" if he wishes to get ahead and be effective.

On the other hand, Nelson Polsby has argued that "the role of the Senate in the political system has changed over the last 20 years," decreasing the importance of Senate norms. He contends that television, with its ability to publicize individual senators, has made the Senate "an incubator of presidential hopefuls" and eroded the significance of its rules of behavior.[58]

Ralph Huitt maintains that the Senate has always had a place for "mavericks" and "independents"—men such as William Borah, Robert La Follette, George Norris, Wayne Morse, and William Proxmire. The senator, he contends, has a choice of what role to play. Although he may pay a price for choosing the role of "outsider," he may also help to resolve social conflicts by championing minority views, and he may bring about new programs by persistently advocating them.[59]

Power in the Senate: The Leadership

Just as the Speaker is elected by the House, the Senate elects a President pro tempore, who presides in the absence of the Vice-President. Although the office is provided for in the Constitution, it has little formal power.

The closest parallel to the Speaker is the Senate Majority Leader. He is the most powerful, elected leader of the Senate, although, as in most political offices, a great deal depends on the man and political circumstances.

Lyndon Johnson, the Democratic Senate leader from 1953 to 1960,

[56] White, *Citadel*, pp. 2, 82–84.
[57] Matthews, *U.S. Senators and Their World*, pp. 92–117.
[58] Nelson W. Polsby, "Goodbye To The Inner Club," *Washington Monthly*, August 1969, pp. 30–34.
[59] Ralph K. Huitt, "The Outsider in the Senate: An Alternative Role," in Huitt and Peabody, *Congress: Two Decades of Analysis*, pp. 159–78.

The extra, indeed the dominant, ingredient was Johnson's overwhelming personality, reflected in what came to be known as "The Treatment."

The Treatment could last ten minutes or four hours. It came, enveloping its target, at the LBJ Ranch swimming pool, in one of LBJ's offices, in the Senate cloakroom, on the floor of the Senate itself—wherever Johnson might find a fellow Senator within his reach. Its tone could be supplication, accusation, cajolery, exuberance, scorn, tears, complaint, the hint of threat. It was all of these together. It ran the gamut of human emotions. Its velocity was breathtaking, and it was all in one direction. Interjections from the target were rare. Johnson anticipated them before they could be spoken. He moved in close, his face a scant millimeter from his target, his eyes widening and narrowing, his eyebrows rising and falling. From his pockets poured clippings, memos, statistics. Mimicry, humor and the genius of analogy made The Treatment an almost hypnotic experience and rendered the target stunned and helpless.

—Rowland Evans and Robert Novak, *Lyndon B. Johnson: The Exercise of Power.*

was widely regarded as an extraordinarily skillful and powerful floor leader. Johnson's power to persuade was formidable. A big man, he towered over most other senators as, on occasion, he subjected them to "The Treatment"—a prolonged exercise in face-to-face persuasion that combined elements of a police "third degree" with Johnson's flair for dramatic acting.

In addition to his powerful personality, Johnson had several tangible tools at his disposal. He could assist a senator in getting legislation passed, he controlled committee assignments, and, above all, he built an intelligence system known as "the Johnson Network." At its heart was Bobby Baker, "a country boy from Pickens, South Carolina, who had come to Washington as a teen-aged Senate page" and whom Johnson made his top assistant.[60] Baker knew how to count noses; because Johnson was well informed of sentiment in the Senate, he was able to anticipate the outcome of close votes. The effect was cumulative: the frequency of Johnson's success allowed him to "fashion a myth of invincibility which was itself mightily persuasive: when he moved, it was taken for granted that 'Lyndon's got the votes.' " [61] Through his network, Johnson came to know the strengths and weaknesses of each senator, and he used that knowledge to further his goals; his was a highly personal leadership.

In contrast, Johnson's successor as Majority Leader, soft-spoken Mike Mansfield of Montana, did not attempt to exercise power in the way that Johnson had. When Mansfield was accused of not providing sufficient leadership for the Senate, he declared: "I am neither a circus ringmaster, the master of ceremonies of a Senate nightclub, a tamer of Senate lions, or a wheeler and dealer." [62]

[60] Rowland Evans and Robert Novak, *Lyndon B. Johnson: The Exercise of Power* (New York: New American Library, 1966), pp. 68, 99.
[61] Ralph K. Huitt, "Democratic Party Leadership in the Senate," in Huitt and Peabody, *Congress: Two Decades of Analysis*, p. 147.
[62] *Congressional Record*, November 27, 1963, p. 22862.

There was a curious parallel on the Republican side to this sea change in Senate leadership style. Senator Everett McKinley Dirksen, the Senate Minority Leader from 1959 to his death in 1969, was a flamboyant, theatrical personality who wielded considerable power; his successor was Senator Hugh Scott of Pennsylvania, a quiet and rather self-effacing leader.

The Senate Majority and Minority leaders represent their party in the Senate. But they may not represent majority sentiment in their party nationally. The wings of each party represented by congressional leaders and by the President are distinct. As a rule, the congressional wings include more conservatives than do the party elements that group around the President (or the titular head of the "out" party). While the Senate Majority or Minority Leader is nominally responsible for steering his party's program through the Senate, he may oppose parts of it. For example, Senator Mansfield, the Democratic Majority Leader, was a critic of the war in Vietnam that was being conducted by President Johnson; as we have seen, Senator Scott, although the Republican Minority Leader, voted against Judge Haynsworth, President Nixon's nominee to the Supreme Court. The role of the Senate leader whose party controls the White House is delicate, because he speaks for both his party and the President. The role varies considerably according to the leader and his personal relationship with the President.

Senate Democrats and Republicans are organized along party lines for both political and legislative purposes:

The *floor whips*. As in the House, the leader of each party is assisted by a whip, and assistant whips, to round up senators for key votes.

The *party conference*. The conference, or caucus, of each party consists of all the senators who are members of that party. The Democratic Conference, although supposedly the highest Democratic party body in Congress, seldom meets more than a few times a year. The Republican Conference is more active. Both party conferences elect leaders, who assume the title of Majority or Minority Leader, depending on which party controls the Senate.

The *Policy Committee*. The policy committee of each party provides a forum for discussion of party positions on legislative issues. In practice, under Lyndon Johnson, the Democratic Policy Committee did little more than ratify his decisions about scheduling major legislation. Under Mansfield, the Policy Committee met often and became a genuine vehicle for discussion of party positions. The Republican Policy Committee also serves as a policy-making body in deciding party positions on legislation.

The *Steering Committee*. The Democratic Steering Committee appoints Democrats to the seventeen standing committees of the Senate. The Republican counterpart is known as the Committee on Committees.

Although the organization of each party appears to be much the same, there are important differences in how the machinery operates. The Democratic party leadership tends to be centralized in the hands of the floor leader. The Republicans tend to spread the party posts around. For example, in the Ninety-first Congress, Senator Mansfield was Majority Leader and chairman of the Democratic Conference, the Policy Committee and the Steering Committee; on the Republican side, the corresponding posts were held by four senators.

Unlike the House, with its complex procedures, five calendars, and tight restrictions on debate, the Senate is relaxed, informal, and less attentive to the rules. Senate bills appear on only one legislative calendar, and they are usually called up by *unanimous consent*. Since a single senator may object to this procedure, the Majority Leader, in conducting floor business, consults with the Minority Leader across the aisle on most major matters to avoid objections.

The Senate in Action

The Filibuster. The Senate allows virtually unlimited debate. Because of this, a single senator, or a group of senators, may stage a *filibuster* to talk a bill to death.[63] Usually, the filibuster is employed to defeat a bill by tying up the Senate so long that the measure will never come to a vote. Historically, Southern senators have used the filibuster to block action on civil rights.

To filibuster, all a senator must do is remain on his feet and keep talking. He may, if he wishes, read the telephone book. The record for such marathon performances by a single senator was set by Senator Strom Thurmond of South Carolina, who spoke against the Civil Rights Act of 1957 for twenty-four hours and eighteen minutes. A group filibuster may go on for many days or even months. When one senator tires, he merely "yields" to a fresher colleague, who takes over. To counter these tactics, the Senate may meet round-the-clock, in the hope of wearing down the filibusterers. But the senators conducting the filibuster may retaliate by suggesting the absence of a quorum (fifty-one senators). Such a demand voiced at, say, 4 A.M. is inconvenient for other senators. So, senators attempting to break the filibuster set up cots in the halls and straggle in to answer the roll; then they try to go back to sleep.

Under Rule XXII of the Senate, a filibuster may be ended if sixteen members petition, and two-thirds of the senators present on the floor vote, for *cloture*. Until 1959, the vote of two-thirds of the *entire* Senate was required to impose cloture. After 1959, when the cloture rule was eased, liberal forces were able to vote cloture to cut off the debate of Southern

---

[63] The word *filibuster* originally meant a privateer or pirate, and its origin in American politics is not certain. (William Safire, *The New Language of Politics* [New York: Random House, 1968], p. 143.)

During a Senate filibuster, members sometimes sleep near the Senate floor to answer roll-calls. This shirtsleeved group of senators napped on cots during the filibuster over the civil rights act of 1960.

SURVIVING A SENATE FILIBUSTER

A filibuster has to be seen to be believed. During its progress the floor is practically empty. One of the eighteen Solid South Senators holds the floor. He will speak for approximately two hours. . . . As one Senator comes to the end of his speech a companion in arms arrives on the scene. The retiring Senator suggests the absence of a quorum. It is always a "live quorum," requiring fifty-one Senators to come to the floor to answer to their names. This often takes as long as an hour. When a quorum is present, the next Southerner takes the floor and a new act of the farce begins.

We went "around the clock" in 1960. . . . the Senate stayed in continuous session for nine days. Those of us who wanted to break the filibuster, somewhat more than a majority but never as many as the two-thirds required for cloture, slept on cots or sofas in our offices or in the rest rooms in the Senate baths. The quorum call bell would ring. We would waken, rub our eyes, pull on our pants and head for the floor. Having answered our names, we would go back to restless sleep—if we could—for another two hours.

Meanwhile, every two hours a well-rested Southerner would turn up on the floor, fresh from a good night's sleep. His schedule had been well planned. He did not have to answer the quorum calls. He would have been pleased had a quorum not shown up. Since there were eighteen participants in the filibuster, it could have gone on indefinitely, making the Senate even more the laughingstock of the country and, indeed, of the civilized world.

In the end, the leadership on both sides of the aisle capitulated to the Southern generalissimo, Richard B. Russell of Georgia. He did not demand unconditional surrender. Indeed, he was a gracious victor. A few crumbs were thrown to the frustrated civil rights advocates. . . .

After the final vote, I spoke briefly, directing my remarks at Senator Russell.

"Dick, here is my sword. I hope you will give it back to me so that I can beat it into a plowshare for the spring planting."

—Joseph S. Clark, *Congress: The Sapless Branch*.

senators on civil rights legislation in 1964, 1965, and 1968. Even with the less restrictive rule, cloture is difficult to impose. Between 1917, when the rule passed, and 1970 cloture was voted only eight times in forty-seven attempts.

Although filibusters are often used by Southerners and conservatives, Northerners and liberals have used them, too. In 1964, the same year that the South filibustered against the Civil Rights Bill, a group of liberals led by Senator Paul H. Douglas of Illinois mounted a filibuster against a rider sponsored by Senator Dirksen, which would have delayed application of the Supreme Court's reapportionment decision to state legislatures. The liberal filibuster was successful.

Voting in the Senate. There are three methods of voting in the Senate: by voice, standing vote, or roll call. As in the House, most voting is by voice; but the Senate has more roll-call votes than the House, since it is a smaller body and calling the roll takes much less time.

THE COMMITTEE SYSTEM

Congressman Mendel Rivers, born in Gumville, South Carolina, was the chairman of the House Armed Services Committee from 1965 to his death in 1970. His power, achieved through seniority, made him one of the most powerful men in Washington, for he sat in judgment on every dollar spent by the Pentagon. White-maned, tall, soft-spoken, and elaborately genteel, Rivers was almost a caricature of the string-tie Southerner. But he ran his fiefdom with an iron hand. One dissident member of the committee complained:

> Here we are dealing with the largest agency of government; it's fantastically complex, and we hear all this testimony for weeks, and then the chairman gets his little group together . . . and they draw up the bill, and we walk in and sit down and here it is already printed up and semiaccomplished—around a billion and a half dollars—and we have 15 minutes to discuss it.[64]

Rivers was only one of the powerful chairmen of the thirty-eight standing committees of Congress. (The House and Senate committees are shown in Table 12-3.)

The complaint voiced by his unhappy committee colleague was not new—both the committee system and the closely related seniority system have often been criticized. Long before he became President, Woodrow

[64] In Marshall Frady, "The Sweetest Finger This Side of Midas," *LIFE*, February 27, 1970, p. 58.

TABLE 12-3

Standing Committees of the Ninety-first Congress

Senate Committees	Chairman	State	Age[1]
Aeronautical and Space Sciences	Clinton P. Anderson	N. Mex.	74
Agriculture and Forestry	Allen J. Ellender	La.	78
Appropriations	Richard B. Russell	Ga.	72
Armed Services	John Stennis	Miss.	68
Banking and Currency[2]	John J. Sparkman	Ala.	70
Commerce	Warren G. Magnuson	Wash.	64
District of Columbia	Joseph D. Tydings	Md.	41
Finance	Russell B. Long	La.	51
Foreign Relations	J. W. Fulbright	Ark.	64
Government Operations	John L. McClellan	Ark.	73
Interior and Insular Affairs	Henry M. Jackson	Wash.	57
Judiciary	James O. Eastland	Miss.	65
Labor and Public Welfare	Ralph W. Yarborough	Tex.	66
Post Office and Civil Service	Gale W. McGee	Wyo.	54
Public Works	Jennings Randolph	W. Va	67
Rules and Administration	B. Everett Jordan	N.C.	73

House Committees	Chairman	State	Age[1]
Agriculture	W. R. Poage	Tex.	70
Appropriations	George H. Mahon	Tex.	69
Armed Services	L. Mendel Rivers	S.C.	64
Banking and Currency	Wright Patman	Tex.	76
District of Columbia	John L. McMillan	S.C.	71
Education and Labor	Carl D. Perkins	Ky.	57
Foreign Affairs	Thomas E. Morgan	Pa.	63
Government Operations	Chet Holifield	Calif.	66
House Administration	Samuel N. Friedel	Md.	71
Interior and Insular Affairs	Wayne N. Aspinall	Colo.	73
Internal Security	Richard H. Ichord	Mo.	43
Interstate and Foreign Commerce	Harley O. Staggers	W. Va.	62
Judiciary	Emanuel Celler	N.Y.	81
Merchant Marine and Fisheries	Edward A. Garmatz	Md.	66
Post Office and Civil Service	Thaddeus J. Dulski	N.Y.	54
Public Works	George H. Fallon	Md.	67
Rules	William M. Colmer	Miss.	79
Science and Astronautics	George P. Miller	Calif.	78
Standards of Official Conduct	Melvin Price	Ill.	65
Veterans' Affairs	Olin E. Teague	Tex.	59
Ways and Means	Wilbur D. Mills	Ark.	60

[1] Ages of chairmen as of January 1, 1970. Because Democrats were in the majority in both houses in the Ninety-first Congress, all committee chairmen were Democrats. Four of the committee chairmen listed in this table were defeated in 1970 and replaced in the Ninety-second Congress. Senator Yarborough was defeated in a primary election, and Senator Tydings in the general election. Representatives Fallon and Friedel were defeated in primary elections. Representative Rivers died in 1970 and Senator Russell in 1971; they were replaced in the Ninety-second Congress.

[2] Name changed to Banking, Housing and Urban Affairs by the Legislative Reorganization Act of 1970, effective January 1971. The same legislation also created a new Senate Committee on Veterans' Affairs beginning in 1971.

Wilson described what he called "government by the chairmen of the Standing Committees of Congress." Wilson saw congressional committees as "little legislatures," and added that the House sat "not for serious dis-

The Senate Commerce Committee meets on Capitol Hill. Congress conducts much of its business in committees, but various aspects of the committee system have been sharply criticized.

cussion, but to sanction the conclusions of its Committees as rapidly as possible." [65]

The growth of the modern Presidency has modified the Wilsonian view of the power of Congress and its committees. The committees are, nevertheless, vital power centers, and it is still true that Congress, for the most part, approves the decisions of its committees. But committees perform the valuable functions of division of labor and specialization in Congress. No member of the House or Senate could hope to know the details of all of the 21,553 bills and resolutions introduced, for example, in 1969. And, as a result of the committee system, congressmen specialize in various fields. Sometimes they become more knowledgeable than the bureaucrats in the executive branch. Finally, many scholars argue that a legislative body should have some forum where members of competing parties can resolve their differences. Committees serve this purpose; they are natural arenas for political bargaining and legislative compromise.

The standing committees are the heart of the committee system. At times, Congress also creates *special* or *select committees* to conduct special investigations. In addition, the Ninety-first Congress had ten *joint committees* of the House and Senate dealing with subjects that ranged from

[65] Woodrow Wilson, *Congressional Government* (New York: World, Meridian Books, 1956), pp. 69, 82–83. Originally published in 1885.

atomic energy to the economy. The Legislative Reorganization Act of 1946 greatly reduced the number of standing committees of Congress and streamlined their operations.

Congressional
Investigations

Although committees basically process legislation, they perform other tasks, such as educating the public on important issues through hearings and investigations. In 1960, Senator Estes Kefauver's hearings on the high price of prescription drugs focused public attention on a major issue, as did Senator Fulbright's later hearings on the Vietnam war.

Some congressional investigations, such as those conducted by Senator Joseph R. McCarthy, have trampled on individual rights. But a series of Supreme Court decisions, starting in 1957, have attempted to give some protection to witnesses before committees. For example, the Supreme Court has ruled that Congress has no power "to expose for the sake of exposure" and that questions asked by a congressional investigating committee must be relevant to its legislative purpose.[66] On the other hand, the Supreme Court in 1959 ruled that a witness could not refuse under the First Amendment to answer questions about his political beliefs if the questions were pertinent to the committee's legislative purpose.[67] Of course, a witness before a congressional investigating committee can invoke the Fifth Amendment on the grounds that his answer might tend to incriminate him. But many people infer that a witness who invokes this constitutional privilege is guilty of something, and the witness may lose his job or suffer other social penalties as a result.

The
Seniority System:
"Let Them Wait"

The House and Senate technically "elect" the chairmen and members of their standing committees. In practice (as of 1970), committee chairmen achieved their power and position by the unwritten rule of seniority. Unless a representative or senator died, resigned, or was defeated, he would eventually move up the seniority ladder and automatically become chairman, if his party controlled the house of Congress in which he served. If he was not a member of the majority party, he became *ranking minority member* of the committee.

In 1970, however, House Republican leaders endorsed a plan to modify the seniority system. Under the new plan, adopted when the Ninety-second Congress convened in January 1971, all House Republicans vote by secret ballot to select the highest ranking Republican on each House committee. The change would not result in elected committee *chairmen* unless the Republicans controlled the House. But the Republican move had placed increasing pressure on the Democrats to modify their seniority system. In January 1971, the Democrats also voted to require approval of committee chairmen by the party caucus, when demanded by ten party members.

[66] *Watkins v. United States,* 354 U.S. 178 (1957).
[67] *Barenblatt v. United States,* 360 U.S. 109 (1959).

No aspect of Congress has been criticized more often than the seniority system (sometimes assailed as "the senility system"). As one popular and highly critical account of Congress put it, "Congress has continued to be a council of elders, dominated by tired old men whose only claim to power is their good fortune in seldom facing serious opposition." [68]

In 1970, the average age of the chairmen of the standing committees of Congress was sixty-six. For chairmen of Senate committees the average age was sixty-five, and for chairmen of House committees it was sixty-six.[69] (See Table 12-3 for the ages of the individual chairmen.)

Discontent with the seniority system has not been limited to critics and reformers outside Congress. Many younger members of the House and Senate have assailed the practice. In 1970, the eighty-one-year-old dean of the New York House delegation, Emanuel Celler, chairman of the House Judiciary Committee, acknowledged in an interview that many of the junior members from his state were frustrated by the seniority system. "They're restless and they complain," he said. "The answer is, let them wait." [70]

The chief argument against seniority has been that it bestows power not necessarily on the most qualified, but on the longest-lived; that the

[68] Drew Pearson and Jack Anderson, *The Case Against Congress* (New York: Simon and Schuster, 1968), p. 263.
[69] Ages as of January 1, 1970.
[70] *New York Times*, February 23, 1970, p. 39.

"Right—we have to watch out for those radical young long-hairs."

Copyright 1970
by Herblock in *The Washington Post*

On April 3, 1964, Everett G. Burkhalter, a Democratic representative in Congress from California, announced that he would not be a candidate for re-election. In an illuminating statement to the press, the California congressman explained why: "I could see I wasn't going to get any place. Nobody listens to what you have to say until you've been here 10 or 12 years. These old men have got everything so tied down you can't do anything. There are only about 40 out of the 435 members who call the shots. They're the committee chairmen and the ranking members and they're all around 70 or 80."

—Nelson W. Polsby, *Congress and the Presidency.*

great individual power of committee chairmen dilutes party responsibility and congressional support for presidential programs; and that committee chairmen returned by "safe" constituencies are not representative of the nation as a whole but tend to be more conservative.

Analysis of the voting records of committee chairmen confirms the common assumption that, *as a group,* they are more conservative than the average member of their party in Congress. For example, in 1969, the average Democratic senator voted in accord with the position of Americans for Democratic Action, a liberal interest group, 61 percent of the time; but Democratic committee chairmen in the Senate voted with ADA only 39 percent of the time. And, in both the House and Senate, committee chairmen received a higher rating from Americans for Constitutional Action, a conservative group, than the average Democrat received.[71] (See Table 12-4.)

TABLE 12-4

Committee Chairmen: Conservative versus Liberal

Every year, various interest groups rate the voting records of members of Congress. By analyzing these data, it is possible to compare "conservative" and "liberal" ratings of committee chairmen and their colleagues. The ADA, Americans for Democratic Action, is a liberal group. The ACA, Americans for Constitutional Action, is a conservative group.

	Average ADA Rating	Average ACA Rating
Senate		
Committee chairmen	39%	46%
Average Democratic senator	61%	31%
House		
Committee chairmen	30%	34%
Average Democratic representative	50%	32%

Source: Based on Congressional Quarterly, *Weekly Report,* February 20, 1970, pp. 569–71. Data for First Session, Ninety-first Congress, 1969.

[71] Based on Congressional Quarterly, *Weekly Report,* February 20, 1970, pp. 569–71.

On the other hand, six chairmen of Senate standing committees and five chairmen of House committees received substantially *higher* ADA ratings than Democrats as a whole in each house. In other words, slightly under 30 percent of all committee chairmen in Congress were rated *more* liberal than the party average in each house; over 70 percent were rated *less* liberal.

The arguments for seniority are that it promotes harmony by providing an automatic road to power, thus preventing conflicts over committee chairmanships; that it guarantees the selection of experienced men to head important committees; and, finally, that it is better than any alternatives.[72]

Among the substitutes for seniority that have been suggested are election of chairmen by members of their committees, or by party caucus; rotation of the chairmen's posts among committee members; and retirement of chairmen at age seventy. Despite the shortcomings of the seniority system, some of the alternatives also pose problems. For example, defenders of the seniority principle contend that election of committee chairmen on "merit" by committee members or party caucus would open the way to backstage political deals, and permit powerful interest groups to try to influence the selection through campaign contributions. Since legislators would very likely disagree on which committee member deserved to be chairman, the procedure could be divisive.

Members of the House and Senate are assigned to committees by the party machinery discussed earlier in this chapter. Since passage of the Legislative Reorganization Act of 1946, most House members are limited to serving on one or two standing committees and senators usually serve on two or three. The Legislative Reorganization Act of 1970 sought to limit senators to one or two committees, but provided a number of complex exceptions to that limitation. By tradition, each party is usually allotted seats on committees roughly in proportion to its strength in each house of Congress.

Members are assigned to committees partly on the basis of seniority, but other factors are taken into account, including the party standing of members, willingness to vote with the leadership, geographical balance, the number of available vacancies, the interests of the legislator's district, and whether the assignment will help his reelection. Certain committees are more important than others. In the House, members compete for places on Appropriations, Rules, and Ways and Means. In the Senate, desirable commitees include Appropriations, Finance, Foreign Relations, and Armed Services.

Committee chairmen generally wield great influence in their commit-

---

[72] For the pros and cons of the seniority system see George Goodwin, Jr., "The Seniority System in Congress," *American Political Science Review*, Vol. 53 (June 1959), pp. 412–36.

tees; they schedule meetings, decide what bills will be taken up, and often control the hiring and firing of the committee staff and the appointment of subcommittee chairmen. In some cases, a committee chairman can pigeonhole a bill simply by refusing to hold hearings on it.

In recent years, however, there has been a trend toward greater democracy within some of the committees. Rules have been adopted by some committees giving rank-and-file members a greater voice in committee operations and providing for regularly scheduled committee meetings. In the House, a majority of members can file a *discharge* petition to dislodge a bill from any committee, including Rules, but the device is little used and seldom successful. Between 1959 and 1969, for example, twenty-six such petitions were filed but only two succeeded.

A BILL IS PASSED

All of these institutions, men, and procedures—the formal organization of Congress, the party leadership, the floor maneuvering, the committee system—bear some relationship to whether a bill will make its way into law. To do so, it must cross hurdles every step of the way.

The formal route that a bill must follow is shown in Figure 12-1. Any member may drop a bill in the "hopper." (Some legislation is introduced as a "Joint Resolution," which becomes law in the same manner as a bill.) Most bills are introduced in both the House and the Senate; they are referred to a committee, which may hold hearings or assign the measure to a subcommittee. Hearings may be open to the public or closed. After receiving the subcommittee's recommendations, the full committee meets in executive session to decide what action to take on the bill. It may do nothing, or it may rewrite the bill completely, or it may report out the original bill to the House or Senate, with or without amendments. A written report, and often a minority report, accompanies the bill from committee. The bill is placed on one of the House calendars or the Senate calendar. If it clears the Rules Committee, it will be debated in the House. In the Senate, it may be called up in order or by unanimous consent or a majority vote.

If a bill is passed by one house, it is sent to the other chamber, which may pass the bill as is, send it to committee, or ignore it and continue to process its own version of the legislation. If there are major differences in the final bill passed by each house, one house may ask for a *conference*. The presiding officer of each house names a conference committee usually composed of senior members of the standing committees that have managed the bill. The conferees attempt to iron out disagreements and reconcile the two versions. Usually, they reach some form of agreement and

FIGURE 12-1

How a Bill Becomes Law

This illustration shows the most typical way in which proposed legislation is enacted into law. There are more complicated, as well as simpler, routes. Most bills fall by the wayside and never become law.

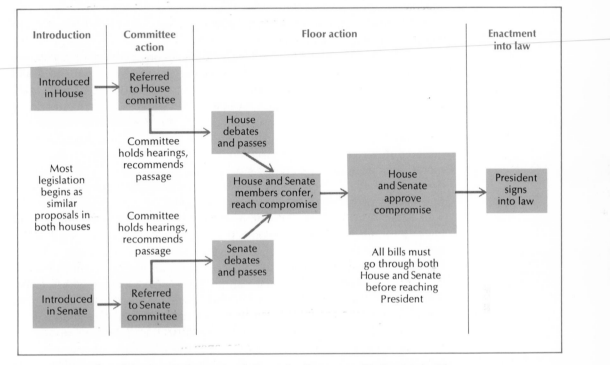

Source: Adapted from *1969 Congressional Quarterly Almanac*, p. 11. Reprinted with permission.

report back to their respective houses. Each house then approves or rejects the conference report. If both houses approve, the final version is signed by the Speaker and the President of the Senate and sent to the President, who may sign the bill into law, let it become law without his signature, or veto or pocket veto the bill, as described in Chapter 10.

Congress functions in a political environment and is subject to all sorts of external pressures: by the voters, who have determined the basic political make-up of Congress, by public opinion, the press, interest groups, the President, by decisions of the Supreme Court, and by specific external events and crises.

These external influences and inputs must often converge if Congress

The
Civil Rights Act
of 1964:
A Case Study

489

is to respond. It was just such a confluence of external pressures that brought about passage of the landmark Civil Rights Act of 1964.[73]

The events that culminated in the most far-reaching civil rights legislation since Reconstruction began in Birmingham, Alabama, in the spring of 1963. Martin Luther King, Jr., led demonstrations designed to desegregate lunch counters and employment in that city. The marchers were met by the high-pressure fire hoses and snarling police dogs of T. Eugene (Bull) Connor, the Police Commissioner.

President Kennedy had moved cautiously on civil rights legislation up to that time. The conflict in Birmingham crystallized national and world opinion and led to widespread demands by many individuals, civil rights groups, and church leaders for legislation to guarantee to black Americans the equality under law that was pledged by the Constitution. "Now the time has come for this Nation to fulfill its promise," President Kennedy declared in a nationwide televised address in June 1963, "We . . . face a moral crisis as a country and as a people. . . . Next week I shall ask the Congress of the United States to act, to make a commitment . . . that race has no place in American life or law."

Later in June, Kennedy submitted his civil rights bill to Congress and began a round of White House meetings to enlist support from civil rights groups. In the House, the Democrats were split, North and South, and the Republicans held the balance of power. Chairman Celler of the Judiciary Committee turned the bill over to an *antitrust* subcommittee whose members were all favorable toward civil rights. Under pressure from civil rights organizations and other sympathetic groups, the subcommittee soon passed a sweeping measure that was even stronger than the President's proposals. It was *backed* by the Southerners—for a reason: "The Southerners on the full committee . . . saw that their chance of defeating any bill lay in putting before the House a bill that appeared extreme, and they rallied to the support of the subcommittee." [74] Attorney General Robert Kennedy negotiated with Republican House leaders and urged that the subcommittee bill be weakened so that it might be passed. The Judiciary Committee backed down and approved a bipartisan, compromise bill, still somewhat stronger than the President's. The measure had just reached the Rules Committee when President Kennedy left for Dallas.

After Kennedy's death, President Johnson moved quickly to mobilize support for the Civil Rights Bill. "We have talked long enough," he said.

---

[73] This case study is based upon James L. Sundquist, *Politics and Policy* (Washington, D.C.: The Brookings Institution, 1968); *Revolution in Civil Rights* (Washington, D.C.: Congressional Quarterly Service, 1965); and John G. Stewart, *Independence and Control: The Challenge of Senatorial Party Leadership*, an unpublished Ph.D. thesis. Mr. Stewart served as legislative assistant to Senator Hubert Humphrey, floor manager of the civil rights bill, during the 1964 debate.
[74] Sundquist, *Politics and Policy*, p. 265.

"We have talked for one hundred years or more. It is time now to write the next chapter, and to write it in the books of law."

But Chairman Howard Smith of the Rules Committee refused to let the bill come to the floor. Celler filed a successful discharge petition and in February 1964, the bill easily passed the House with bipartisan support, 290 to 130. The real test lay ahead in the Senate.

On March 9, 1964, Majority Leader Mike Mansfield moved to take up the House bill, a motion that touched off one of the longest filibusters in the history of the Senate. It was to last for fifty-seven days. The pro-civil-rights senators organized as if for a military siege: one member was put in charge of managing each section of the bill; a special whip system was organized; it was agreed to keep thirty-five Democratic senators in Washington each day to answer quorum calls; and a fifteen-minute strategy meeting was held each morning in the office of Senator Humphrey, the Democratic Whip.[75]

An indication of the importance attached by each side to the civil rights struggle was the fact that it took *six weeks* of maneuvering to make the House bill the pending business of the Senate. As the debate wore on, separate battles took place over amendments to the bill; finally, late in May, a bipartisan, compromise version of the House bill was submitted to the Senate by Mansfield and Dirksen, the Republican Minority Leader. Early in June, the civil rights forces moved for cloture to cut off the debate. On June 10, 1964, the final day of debate, Dirksen, quoting Victor Hugo, intoned: "Stronger than all the armies is an idea whose time has come." [76]

Now the Senate was ready to vote: never in its history had it imposed cloture on a civil rights debate. With all one hundred senators present, the filibuster was broken, 71 to 29. On June 19, the bill passed, 73 to 27. "The Senate had not merely survived its most notable institutional challenge of the postwar era, but its supposed outworn and unworkable procedures never looked better when the Southern Democrats were beaten at their own game." [77] More importantly, the principle of equality for all Americans now had the force of law.

A bill had passed.

CONGRESS AND THE AMERICAN POLITICAL SYSTEM

Congress is the battleground of American democracy. But in attempting to manage the external demands placed upon it, it is caught among the cross-currents of a restless and

[75] Stewart, *Independence and Control: The Challenge of Senatorial Party Leadership*, pp. 185–86.
[76] *Ibid.*, p. 273.
[77] *Ibid.*, pp. 289–90.

rapidly changing society. And, as we have seen, it is subject as well to an "inner tension" between its assigned role as the democratic representative of the people and its own rigid and sometimes undemocratic internal structures.

Its decentralized pattern of organization, with power allocated among various committee dukes and barons, may work against innovative leadership on Capitol Hill. Moreover, programs enacted by Congress may not fit together as a coherent whole. As Ralph Huitt has suggested: "It is not easy for a feudal system to make national policy." [78]

Some scholars have argued that the American political system is not designed to cope with change, that the checks and balances embedded in the Constitution and the conservative bias of Congress make it unable to act. James MacGregor Burns has contended that the system is "designed for deadlock and inaction." [79] He perceives a "four-party system" consisting of congressional Democrats and congressional Republicans, and presidential Democrats and presidential Republicans.[80]

As an alternative to the present system, some have suggested "responsible party government," in which political parties would be held to their campaign promises and the President and his party in Congress would cooperate closely. Representatives and senators would be honor bound to support their party's position on legislation, and at election time, the voters would have a clear choice. Whether this could be made to work in a federal system of shared powers and fragmented political parties, or whether it is even desirable, is a subject of continuing scholarly debate.

Certainly there is ample room for reform in Congress. The behavior of some members who violate ethical standards casts a cloud over all members; the frequent secrecy of congressional committee meetings hardly fits the image of open government.

For many years, however, Congress showed little desire to institute reforms. Its prevailing attitude was reflected by the late Senator Everett Dirksen, who, when questioned about prospects for a particular reform measure, replied: "Ha, ha, ha; and I might add, ho, ho, ho."

A Joint Committee on the Organization of the Congress issued recommendations in 1966 to improve the operation of committees, require more open hearings, and tighten the regulation of lobbying. A bill based on these proposals passed the Senate but died in the House. Nor did individual efforts to change Senate procedures, such as those by Senator Clark, meet with success; and Clark himself was defeated in 1968. (Clark had proposed sweeping reform of the Senate, including election of standing

[78] Huitt, "Congress, The Durable Partner," in Huitt and Peabody, *Congress: Two Decades of Analysis*, p. 229.
[79] Burns, *The Deadlock of Democracy*, p. 6.
[80] *Ibid.*, p. 196.

committee chairmen by a majority of the committee; retirement of chairmen at age seventy; liberalization of the Democratic steering committee to make it more representative of majority sentiment in the party; and enlargement of important committees.)

In the wake of the Bobby Baker and Senator Dodd scandals, both the House and Senate established ethics committees, and, in 1968, both houses adopted weak codes of conduct for their members. The House code required members and principal staff assistants to file annually a limited public report of major financial holdings and sources of income, and a separate report, which was sealed from public view, of how much they were paid by each source. The Senate code restricted outside employment of staff members and the personal use by senators of campaign contributions; in addition, it required senators to file sealed financial statements each year as well as a limited public statement. Congress has also been slow to adopt certain technical improvements in its operations—the use of computers to provide information for members, for example, and electronic voting to end time-wasting roll-call votes. But both proposals were under study by 1970. However in that year, the House rejected a proposal to create a joint congressional committee to develop a computer system for Congress.

The reforms passed by the House in 1970 were the first major changes in its operations since the Legislative Reorganization Act of 1946. But the Democrats, who controlled the House, moved cautiously in January 1971 in altering the seniority system.

Changes in the seniority system—such as the election of committee chairmen by the majority party caucus—might alter power relationships by making chairmen more responsive to the majority sentiment in their party and more representative of the country as a whole. On the other hand, just because seniority has often benefited rural areas, conservatives, and the South in the past, it will not necessarily do so in the future. If large numbers of black or urban voters in the North continue to return the same representatives to Congress, the seniority principle could in time have new political meaning. As the Democratic party loses its grip on the South, that region may not derive the same political advantage in Congress from the seniority system that it has enjoyed in the past. On the other hand, the whole debate over seniority could become moot if Congress, under pressure in the 1970's, continues to modify or abandons the system.

As we have seen, Congress does more than approve legislation. It does innovate and initiate at times, and it serves to give a measure of legitimacy to the process of rule-making for society. Much of the social welfare legislation of the 1960's originated in the United States Senate. Many of the innovative measures that a President finally adopts as his own and that, when passed, seem to be executive measures have, in reality, first been proposed by individual legislators.

493

There are times when Congress seems to be still operating in the nineteenth century. But at other times it is perhaps slow to act because the consensus that it *needs* in a pluralist democracy to act and to innovate is, in itself, slow to develop. To a great extent, Congress reflects the decentralization and pluralism that characterize the American political system as a whole. A powerful argument can be made that Congress does act when the people demand it, their voice is clear, and the need unmistakable. E. E. Schattschneider has described American government as a political system "in which the struggle for democracy is still going on." [81] Viewed in that context, Congress is neither ideal nor obsolete, but rather an enduring arena for political conflict and a crucible for democratic change.

[81] E. E. Schattschneider, *The Semi-Sovereign People* (New York: Holt, Rinehart and Winston, 1960), p. 102.

SUGGESTED READING

Burns, James M. *The Deadlock of Democracy* * (Prentice-Hall, 1963). A forceful statement of the view that Congress is too slow and is inadequate in responding to national needs. Burns argues that in reality the United States has a four-party system—the congressional wings of the Democratic and Republican parties, and the presidential wings of each major party.

Clapp, Charles L. *The Congressman: His Work As He Sees It* * (The Brookings Institution, 1963). An informative insight into the work of United States congressmen. Based on comments made by congressmen in a series of roundtable meetings at which they discussed their job.

Clark, Joseph S. *Congress: The Sapless Branch* * (Harper and Row, 1964). A revealing look at Congress from the inside by a congressional-reform advocate who was then a senator. Clark, a liberal Democrat from Pennsylvania, was critical of the seniority system and other institutional procedures that, in his view, diminished Congress as a representative body.

Fenno, Richard F., Jr. *The Power of the Purse: Appropriations Politics in Congress* (Little, Brown, 1966). A comprehensive analysis of a highly important activity of Congress—the congressional appropriations process.

Galloway, George B. *The Legislative Process in Congress* (Crowell, 1953). A general introductory treatment of the workings of the American Congress.

Huitt, Ralph K., and Peabody, Robert L. *Congress: Two Decades of Analysis* (Harper and Row, 1969). Paperback. Peabody presents an excellent summary and analysis of research on Congress from the mid-1940's to the mid-1960's, and Huitt offers a series of perceptive and influential articles on congressional behavior. Contains a useful bibliography of books and articles on Congress.

Jones, Charles O. *Minority Party Leadership in Congress* (Little, Brown, 1970). A perceptive and thorough exploration of some of the special characteristics of leadership of the minority party in Congress.

Matthews, Donald R. *U.S. Senators and Their World* * (University of North Carolina Press, 1960). A readable and revealing analysis of the United States Senate as of 1960. Examines the senators' geographical and occupational origins, their activities in the Senate, and the nature of the environment in which they work.

Miller, Clem. *Member of the House: Letters of a Congressman* (Scribner's, 1962). A readable and informative examination of life in the House of Representatives, by the late Clem Miller, a former California congressman.

Peabody, Robert L., and Polsby, Nelson W., eds. *New Perspectives on the House of Representatives*,* 2nd edition (Rand McNally, 1969). (Originally published in 1963.) A useful series of articles on various aspects of the House, including specific congressional committees, leadership contests, and legislative-executive relations.

Polsby, Nelson W. *Congress and the Presidency* * (Prentice-Hall, 1965). A concise, readable analysis of the legislative and executive branches of government. Polsby makes useful observations on the Senate and House of Representatives as distinct political institutions, and traces the budgetary process in the executive branch and Congress.

Ripley, Randall B. *Majority Party Leadership in Congress* * (Little, Brown, 1969). An analysis, conducted under the auspices of the American Political Science Association Study of Congress, of the exercise of leadership in the majority party in Congress.

Truman, David B., ed. *The Congress and America's Future* (Prentice-Hall, 1965). Paperback. A valuable series of essays on various aspects of Congress by specialists in the field. Includes essays on congressional elections and the internal distribution of influence in the House and Senate.

Truman, David B. *The Congressional Party* (Wiley, 1959). Paperback. An influential study of congressional leadership and the relationship between the type of constituencies congressmen represent and the congressmen's behavior in the legislature. Based on a detailed analysis of the Eighty-first Congress.

Wilson, Woodrow. *Congressional Government: A Study in American Politics* (Meridian Books, 1956). Paperback. (Originally published in 1885.) A classic study of congressional government in the late nineteenth century. Stresses the separation of powers in the American political system, the importance of congressional committees and committee chairmen, and what Wilson viewed as the predominance of congressional power over that of the President in that era.

* Available in paperback edition

13

Justice

In the high-ceilinged marble chamber of the Supreme Court, on June 23, 1969, the Marshal of the Court rapped his gavel on a wooden block and cried: "The honorable, the Chief Justice and the Associate Justices of the Supreme Court of the United States. Oyez, oyez, oyez. All persons having business before the honorable, the Supreme Court of the United States are admonished to draw near."

As he spoke, Chief Justice Earl Warren and the Associate Justices, wearing their black robes, filed in through the red velvet curtains behind the bench. It was the end of the Court's term, and the end of an era. For this was the final day of the Warren Court, the day that Chief Justice Warren was to retire, and among those who chose to "draw near" were the President of the United States, Richard M. Nixon, and the man he had appointed as the new Chief Justice, Warren E. Burger.

The three final decisions of the Court's term were announced. After that, President Nixon spoke, Earl Warren responded, and Warren Burger was sworn in. With this brief ceremony, power was transferred to a new

Former Chief Justice Earl Warren, President Nixon, and Chief Justice Warren Burger.

Chief Justice of the United States, the official who, more than any other, symbolizes the judicial branch of the Federal Government.

Although the ceremony was conducted with quiet formality, the transfer of judicial power reflected the turbulent political currents that had brought Richard Nixon to the Presidency.

During Earl Warren's sixteen years as Chief Justice, the Supreme Court had a profound impact on politics and government in America. The Warren Court was an extraordinarily activist, innovative tribunal that wrought far-reaching change in the meaning of the Constitution. Among its major decisions, the Warren Court outlawed official racial segregation in public schools, set strict national standards to protect the rights of criminal defendants, required the equal apportionment of state legislatures and the House of Representatives, and ruled that prayers in the public schools were unconstitutional. And it handed down other dramatic decisions that won it both high praise and sharp criticism—and engulfed it in great controversy.

Riding the crest of the tidal wave of social change that swept through America in the 1950's and 1960's, the Court became a natural target of those who felt that it was moving too fast and too far. The political reaction to its bold decisions was symbolized by automobile bumper stickers that read "Impeach Earl Warren" and "Support Your Local Police."

During the 1968 presidential campaign, Nixon promised to appoint to the Supreme Court "strict constructionists who saw their duty as interpreting law and not making law. They would see themselves as caretakers of the Constitution and servants of the people, not super-legislators with a free hand to impose their social and political viewpoints upon the American people." [1] Nixon also declared: "I believe we need a Court which

[1] Campaign speech, November 2, 1968, quoted in Congressional Quarterly, *Weekly Report*, May 23, 1969, p. 798.

looks upon its function as being that of interpretation rather than of breaking through into new areas that are really the prerogative of the Congress of the United States." [2]

Nixon's campaign comments clearly reflected one side of the historical argument over the "proper" role of the Supreme Court. Although the argument was as old as the republic itself, it had, by 1968, taken on new political meaning; for the Warren Court had become linked in the minds of many voters with black militancy, urban riots, rising crime, and the volatile issue of "law and order" and justice in America. By contrast, others viewed the Warren Court as a humanitarian force that had revitalized American democracy.

In Chief Justice Burger, Nixon made it clear, he believed he had found a "strict constructionist" who would fit his political and philosophical requirements. As a judge of the United States Court of Appeals for the District of Columbia, Burger was generally regarded as a moderate on civil rights but a jurist with strong reservations about some of the procedural restraints the courts had placed on police dealing with criminal suspects. He had publicly criticized the Warren Court, charging that it bore "a large measure of responsibility for some of the bitterness in American life today over the administration of criminal justice." [3]

After appointing Chief Justice Burger, Nixon sought to change the political balance on the Court further by nominating a conservative federal

[2] Campaign speech, July 7, 1968, *ibid.*
[3] Congressional Quarterly, *Weekly Report*, May 30, 1969, p. 844.

"My entire portfolio is predicated on the assumption that I won't be elevated to a higher bench."

Drawing by Stevenson; © 1969
The New Yorker Magazine, Inc.

appeals court judge, Clement F. Haynsworth, Jr., of South Carolina, to be an Associate Justice. When the Senate rejected Haynsworth in 1969, after a monumental battle centering on conflict-of-interest charges, Nixon in 1970 nominated another conservative Southerner, G. Harrold Carswell, a federal appeals court judge in Florida. Carswell, too, was rejected after another prolonged and dramatic fight in the Senate. This battle was fought over charges that Carswell had shown racial bias and was a mediocre jurist. Finally, after accusing the Senate of bias against the South, the President nominated Harry Andrew Blackmun, a Minnesota Republican and federal appeals court judge. Blackmun's reputation was that of a moderate; neither his politics nor his ethics were criticized, and he was confirmed.

THE SYSTEM OF JUSTICE

The Supreme Court stands at the pinnacle of the American judiciary, but it is only one part of the fragmented, decentralized system of justice in America, a system that encompasses a network of federal courts, state and local courts and prosecutors, the United States Department of Justice, state and local police, the FBI, prisons and jails, and probation and parole officers and parole boards.

During a time of political activism, as in the 1970's, the police and the courts become the cutting edge and the enforcement arm of the "Establishment" in the eyes of dissident groups—black militants, campus demonstrators, and others with grievances against the status quo. To the mass of Americans, however, the police and courts represent the forces of "law and order."

Some of the young people who came to Washington in November, 1969, to oppose the war in Vietnam were arrested by police during the weekend of protest. One group found that the procedures of American justice and the language of the Bill of Rights do not always match the realities of being jailed. This story of a night behind bars was written by a reporter for the *New York Times* who was arrested while taking notes on the arrest of the demonstrators.

WASHINGTON, Nov. 16—Scummy water an inch deep covered the floor at one end of the long, dimly lit cellblock last night.

One by one, policemen led the young men, arrested during antiwar protests here yesterday, past the dry cells and into those that were flooded until five people crammed each windowless, 4-by-6-foot cubicle.

"Pigs! Pigs!" a youth shouted as the steel door clanged shut behind him.

There was not enough room for everyone to sit down. Two metal bunk frames without mattresses hung by chains in double-decker fashion, but a lip of steel around the edges of the frames dug into the youth's legs, making sitting painful.

At least one man at a time had to stand in a puddle, and water seeped into sneakers and shoes. Most of the dry cells remained empty. About 85 men stayed that way for nine hours

of the night in the basement of police headquarters, and the discomfort produced muttered curses, shouted obscenities, dry humor, some friction, a lot of camaraderie and, for a few, a political shift to the left. . . .

A large proportion of the 85 in the cellblock . . . said that they had been taken into custody while looking for a bus, sitting under a tree or walking along a street from which the radicals had just fled. Two said that they did not favor protests and were not demonstrators at all but had been in Washington sightseeing. . . .

Reed Williams, though, had come to demonstrate. . . .

He looked out through the thick bars of his cell door. "All of a sudden you're put in this cage, and you're not a human being," he said quietly. . . .

Nobody was allowed to make a telephone call during the nine hours behind bars. . . .

The hard fact of jail simply confirmed the radicals' views of the world, but it shocked and outraged the more moderate protesters.

Again and again, a 30-year-old salesman from Boston hammered his fists on the bars, exclaiming, "I'm an American! I'm an American! I came down here as an American for peace! Let me out of here!"

After more than an hour, his hands were cut and swollen, and he collapsed in the water on the floor. His cellmates hauled him into a lower bunk frame.

—David K. Shipler, "A Night in a Jail in Capital: 85 men in Flooded Cells," *New York Times*, November 17, 1969.

In recent years, the whole issue of crime and justice in America has become *politicized*; that is, crime, dissent, the Supreme Court, and the police have in themselves become political issues. Events such as the 1969 battle between police and students at Berkeley, California, over the "People's Park"; the conspiracy trial of Dr. Benjamin Spock on charges of encouraging resistance to the draft; the bloody clash between police and antiwar demonstrators at the 1968 Democratic convention, and the controversial trial of "the Chicago Seven"—the leaders of the Chicago demonstrations—have focused widespread public attention on the American system of justice and raised important questions about its operations, adequacy, and fairness.

What is the "proper" role of the Supreme Court in the American

political system? Should it practice judicial restraint or social activism? What has been the political impact of the Supreme Court's decisions? Since its members are appointed and not accountable to the voters, should the Supreme Court "legislate" and make social policy? What are the dimensions of crime in America? How is the system of criminal justice supposed to operate? How does it really operate? Is it stacked against blacks and other minorities? Does a rich man have a better chance under the system than a poor man?

THE LAW

In a political sense, law is the body of rules made by government for society, interpreted by the courts, and backed by the power of the state. While this is a simple, dictionary-type definition, there are conflicting theories of law and little agreement on how it should be defined.

If law were limited to what can be established and enforced by the state, then Louis XIV would have been correct in saying: "It is legal because I wish it." The men who founded the American nation were influenced by another tradition, rooted in the philosophy of John Locke and in the principle of natural rights. This tradition was the theory that man, living in a state of nature, possessed certain fundamental rights that he brought with him into organized society. The tradition of natural rights was used by the American revolutionaries of 1776 to justify their revolt against England, and more recently, by Martin Luther King, Jr., Dr. Benjamin Spock, and others who have practiced "civil disobedience" against laws they believed to be unjust, unconstitutional, or immoral.

Still another approach to law is sociological. In this view, law is seen as the gradual growth of rules and customs that reconcile conflict among men in societies; it is as much a product of culture, religion, and morality as of politics. There is always a problem of incorporating majority morality into criminal law; if enough people decide to break a law, it becomes difficult to enforce. One example was Prohibition; more recently, there have been pressures to legalize marijuana.

Most American law is based upon English *common law*. In twelfth-century, medieval England, judges began to dispense law, and their cumulative body of decisions, often based upon custom and precedent, came to be called common law, or judge-made law (as opposed to written law made by legislatures). In deciding cases, judges generally relied on the principle of *stare decisis*, the Latin phrase meaning "stand by past decisions." In other words, the judge would attempt to find a *precedent* for his decision in an earlier case involving similar principles. Most law that governs the actions of Americans is *statutory law* enacted by Congress, or by state

503

legislatures or local legislative bodies; but many statutes embody principles of English common law. Most federal law is statutory law and so is most state law.

Laws do not always ensure fairness. If a man discovers that his dogwood trees are gradually being cut down by a neighbor, he can sue him for damages, but the money judgment will not save the trees. Instead, he may, under the legal principle of *equity*, seek an injunction to prevent any further tree-chopping. Equity, or fair dealing, may provide preventive measures and legal remedies unavailable under ancient principles of common law.

Cases considered by federal and state courts are either *civil* or *criminal*. Civil cases concern relations between individuals or organizations, such as a divorce action, or a suit for damages arising from an automobile accident or for violation of a business contract. The government is often party to a civil action—when the Justice Department files a civil antitrust suit against a corporation, for example. Criminal cases concern crimes committed against the public order. Most crimes are defined by local, state, and federal statutes, which set forth a range of penalties as well.

A growing body of cases in federal courts concerns questions of *administrative law*, the rules and regulations made and applied by federal regulatory agencies and commissions.

Supreme Court Justice Robert Jackson once observed that people are governed either by the will of one man, or group of men, or by law. He added: "Law, as the expression of the ultimate will and wisdom of a people, has so far proven the safest guardian of liberty yet devised." [4]

THE SUPREME COURT

The far-reaching decisions of the Warren Court, the appointment of the new Chief Justice, and the bitter battles over the composition of the Burger Court, point up the fact that the Supreme Court is a *political institution* that makes both policy and law. Although insulated by tradition and judicial tenure from the turmoil of everyday politics, the Supreme Court lies at the heart of the ongoing struggle in the American political system. "We are very quiet there," said Justice Oliver Wendell Holmes, Jr., "but it is the quiet of a storm centre."

In giving the Constitution contemporary meaning, the Supreme Court inevitably makes political and policy choices. "To consider the Supreme Court of the United States strictly as a legal institution," Robert A. Dahl has suggested, "is to underestimate its significance in the American politi-

[4] Robert H. Jackson, *The Supreme Court in the American System of Government* (Cambridge, Mass.: Harvard University Press, 1955), p. 27.

cal system. For it is also a political institution, an institution, that is to say, for arriving at decisions on controversial questions of national policy." [5]

A basic reason for the political controversy surrounding the Supreme Court is that its precise role in the American political system was left ambiguous by the framers of the Constitution. The Supreme Court is at the apex of one of the three independent, constitutionally coequal branches of the Federal Government. But does it have the constitutional right to resolve conflicts among the three branches? As Robert G. McCloskey noted: "The fact that the Constitution is supreme does not settle the question of who decides what the Constitution means." [6]

One view of the Supreme Court holds that, because the justices are not popularly elected, the Court should move cautiously and interpret the Constitution "strictly." Popular democracy and the principle of majority rule are more consistent, in this view, with legislative supremacy. An opposite view holds that the Court is the cornerstone of a system of checks and balances and *restraints* on majority rule provided by the Constitution.

The
Supreme Court:
Politics, Policy,
and
Public Opinion

[5] Robert A. Dahl, "Decision-Making in a Democracy: The Role of the Supreme Court as a National Policy-Maker," in Raymond E. Wolfinger, ed., *Readings in American Political Behavior* (Englewood Cliffs, N.J.: Prentice-Hall, 1966), p. 166.
[6] Robert G. McCloskey, *The American Supreme Court* (Chicago: University of Chicago Press, 1960), p. 8.

In this view, the Supreme Court may often be the *only* place in the political system where minorities are protected from the majority.

Since Chief Justice John Marshall's day, the Supreme Court has exercised the right of *judicial review,* the power to declare acts of Congress or actions by the Executive—or laws and actions at any level of local, state, and Federal government—unconstitutional. Lower federal courts and state courts may exercise the same power, but the Supreme Court has the last word in deciding constitutional questions. "We are under a Constitution," Chief Justice Charles Evans Hughes declared, "but the Constitution is what the judges say it is." [7]

Yet why, it is often asked, should "nine old men," who are appointed for life and not elected by the people, have the power in a democratic system to strike down the laws and decisions of popularly elected legislatures and leaders? The question is asked most often by people who disapprove of what the Court is doing at a particular time. Those who approve of the philosophy of a given Court seldom complain that it is overstepping its power.

The debate over the role of the Court in the American system is sharpened by the fact that the Constitution is written in broad and sometimes ambiguous language. As a result, the Supreme Court has interpreted the meaning of the Constitution very differently at different times.

Justice Felix Frankfurter once observed:

> The meaning of "due process" and the content of terms like "liberty" are not revealed by the Constitution. It is the Justices who make the meaning. They read into the neutral language of the Constitution their own economic and social views. . . . Let us face the fact that five Justices of the Supreme Court are the molders of policy rather than the impersonal vehicles of revealed truth. [8]

The Supreme Court must, however, operate within the bounds of public opinion, and, in the long run, within the political mainstream of the times. The Court possesses no armies, and it must finally rely on the executive branch to enforce its rulings. It cannot completely ignore the reaction to its decisions in Congress and in the nation, because, ultimately, as a political institution its power rests on public opinion.

Walter F. Murphy has suggested that the Court's conflicts with Congress ebb and flow in a three-step pattern: First, the Court makes decisions on important aspects of public policy. Second, the Court receives severe

[7] Alpheus T. Mason, *The Supreme Court, Palladium of Freedom* (Ann Arbor, Mich.: University of Michigan Press, 1962), p. 143. Hughes made this comment in 1907 as governor of New York.
[8] Felix Frankfurter, "The Supreme Court and the Public," *Forum,* Vol. 83 (June 1930), pp. 332–34.

CURB THE SUPREME COURT
Help Impeach EARL WARREN
— for Information —
Write to Movement to Impeach Earl Warren, Belmont, 78 Mass.
COURTESY OF MONTGOMERY CHAPTERS OF JOHN BIRCH SOCIETY

criticism coupled with threats of remedial or retaliatory action by Congress. The third step, according to Murphy, has generally been "judicial retreat." [9]

Dahl has concluded that the dominant policy views of the Court "are never for long out of line" with the dominant views of the legislative majority.[10] Or, as humorist Finley Peter Dunne's "Mr. Dooley" put it, "the Supreme Court follows the election returns."

The Constitution gives the Supreme Court power to consider "all Cases . . . arising under this Constitution." The principle of judicial review traces back to English common law, although the Constitution nowhere *explicitly* gives this power to the Court. The question of the framers' intent has never been settled, but Alexander Hamilton argued in *The Federalist* that the judicial branch did in fact have the right to judge whether laws passed by Congress were constitutional.[11]

The power of the Supreme Court to exercise judicial review was established in 1803 in the case of *Marbury v. Madison*.[12] When Jefferson became President in 1801, he was angered to find that his Federalist predecessor, John Adams, had appointed a number of federal judges just before leaving office, among them one William Marbury as a Justice of the Peace in the District of Columbia. When Jefferson discovered that Marbury's commission had not actually been delivered to him, he ordered Secretary of State James Madison to hold it up. Under a provision of the Judiciary Act of 1789, Marbury sued for a Supreme Court writ compelling the delivery of

The Road
to Judicial
Review

[9] Walter F. Murphy, *Congress and the Court* (Chicago: University of Chicago Press, 1962), pp. 246–47.
[10] Dahl, "Decision-Making in a Democracy: The Role of the Supreme Court as a National Policy-Maker," pp. 171, 180.
[11] *The Federalist* No. 78, Edward Mead Earle, ed. (New York: The Modern Library), p. 506.
[12] *Marbury v. Madison*, 1 Cranch 137 (1803).

his commission. The Supreme Court under Chief Justice John Marshall dismissed the case, saying the Court lacked jurisdiction to issue such a writ. The Court held that the section of the Judiciary Act under which Marbury had sued was unconstitutional, a ruling that avoided an open political confrontation with the executive branch over Marbury but at the same time established the power of the Court to void acts of Congress. "The Constitution is superior to any ordinary act of the legislature," Marshall wrote, and "a law repugnant to the Constitution is void." [13]

Although the Court's power of judicial review was thus established, the question of *how* the Court should apply its great power has remained a subject of controversy up to the present day. The debate has centered on whether the Court should practice *judicial activism* or *judicial restraint*.

As Archibald Cox has posed the questions: "Should the Court play an active, creative role in shaping our destiny, equally with the executive and legislative branches? Or should it be characterized by self-restraint, deferring to the legislative branch whenever there is room for policy judgment and leaving new departures to the initiative of others?" [14]

The philosophy of judicial restraint is associated with Justices Felix Frankfurter, Louis D. Brandeis, and Oliver Wendell Holmes, Jr. Briefly stated, that philosophy requires the Court to avoid constitutional questions where possible, and to uphold acts of Congress unless they clearly violate a specific section of the Constitution. Frankfurter held that the Court should avoid deciding "political questions" that could involve it in conflicts with other branches of the Federal Government.

The philosophy of judicial activism was embraced by the Warren Court, which boldly applied the Constitution to social and political questions. In its reapportionment decisions, for example, the Court plunged deliberately into the "political thicket" that earlier Supreme Court justices had avoided. It did so again in ruling that the House had violated the Constitution when it excluded Representative Adam Clayton Powell in 1967. In so ruling, the Warren Court risked a direct power confrontation with the House of Representatives. But such a risk, Warren ruled, "cannot justify the court's avoiding their constitutional responsibility." [15]

The Changing Role of the Supreme Court

Although John Marshall had established the right of judicial review in 1803, the Supreme Court did not declare another act of Congress unconstitutional until the Dred Scott case in 1857. Under Marshall's suc-

[13] *Ibid.*
[14] Archibald Cox, *The Warren Court* (Cambridge, Mass.: Harvard University Press, 1968), p. 2.
[15] *Powell v. McCormack*, 395 U.S. 486 (1969).

cessor, Roger B. Taney (1836–1864), the Court protected states' rights and stressed the power of the states over that of the Federal Government.

After the Civil War, the Court refused to apply the Fourteenth Amendment to protect the rights of black Americans, even though Congress had passed the amendment for this specific purpose (see Chapter 5). Instead, the Court used the amendment's "due process" clause to protect business from state regulation. The Fourteenth Amendment provides that no state shall "deprive any person of life, liberty, or property, without due process of law." The Court accepted the argument that a corporation was a "person" within the meaning of the amendment. In a series of cases, it used the Fourteenth Amendment to protect industry, banking, and public utilities from social regulation. Citing the "commerce clause" of the Constitution and the Fourteenth Amendment, the Supreme Court in the 1890's struck down the federal income tax and emasculated the federal antitrust laws. In general, the Court during this era served as a powerful guardian of the "robber barons"—the businessmen who amassed great fortunes in the late nineteenth century—as well as a champion of *laissez-faire* capitalism.

The Court continued to expound a conservative philosophy under Chief Justice William Howard Taft in the 1920's. The election of Franklin D. Roosevelt in 1932 was followed by vast social change in America; but a majority of the Supreme Court was not in sympathy with the programs of the New Deal. Between 1933 and 1937, the Court struck down one after another of Roosevelt's programs.

In 1936, the average age of members of the Court was seventy-one, and the justices were dubbed the "nine old men." [16] Reelected by a landslide that year, Roosevelt risked his prestige in 1937 when he proposed his famous "court-packing" plan. His objective was to put younger men on the Court who would be more sympathetic to the New Deal. Roosevelt's plan to bring the Supreme Court out of what he termed "the horse and buggy age" provided that whenever a justice refused to retire at age seventy, the President could appoint an additional justice. Under the plan, the Court could have been expanded to a maximum of fifteen members.

The debate raged in and out of Congress all that spring, but in less than six months, the proposal was dead. Although Roosevelt's plan failed, by the time the Court recessed that summer it had already begun to shift to a liberal position and to uphold New Deal programs. As a result, 1937 is regarded as a watershed year in the history of the Supreme Court. From that date on, the Court gradually emerged as the protector, not of big business, but of the individual.

---

[16] A phrase popularized by columnists Drew Pearson and Robert S. Allen. See William Safire, *The New Language of Politics* (New York: Random House, 1968), p. 286.

Before he retired as Chief Justice, Earl Warren was asked to name the most important decisions of the Warren Court.[17] He singled out those dealing with reapportionment, school desegregation, and the right to counsel.[18]

Each of these cases symbolized one of three broad fields in which the Warren Court brought about far-reaching changes in America: the political process itself, civil rights, and the rights of the accused.

In establishing the "one-man, one-vote" principle for legislative districts, the Warren Court required that each citizen's vote count as much as another's. If the quality of a democracy can be gauged, certainly the individual's vote is a basic unit of measurement. Until the reapportionment revolution of the Warren Court, voters were often powerless to correct basic distortions in the system of representation itself.

The *Brown* decision has not eliminated racial segregation in American schools or American society. But by striking down the officially enforced dual school system in the South, the Court implied "that all racial discrimination sponsored, supported, or encouraged by government is unconstitutional." [19] Thus the decision foreshadowed a social upheaval. The civil rights movement and the civil rights legislation of the 1960's followed in the Supreme Court's wake.

In the 1970's, "integration" in itself appeared to be less important to many black Americans than freedom, dignity, and a full share of the economic opportunities of American society. Nevertheless, the *Brown* decision has not become irrelevant; by its action at a time when much of white America was complacent and satisfied with the existing social order, the Supreme Court provided moral as well as political leadership—it reminded the nation that the Constitution applies to *all* Americans.

The third broad area of decision by the Warren Court—the protection of the rights of criminal defendants—was discussed in Chapter 4. In a series of controversial decisions, including *Miranda, Escobedo, Gideon,* and *Mapp,* the Court bit by bit threw the mantle of the Bill of Rights around persons accused of crimes by state authorities. In so doing, the Court collided directly with the electorate's rising fear of crime; it was accused of "coddling criminals" and "handcuffing the police."

The Warren Court moved aggressively in several other areas as well—banning prayers in the public schools, curbing the anti-Communist legislation of the 1950's, and easing the definition of what constitutes "obscenity." All of this activity provided ample ammunition to the Court's con-

[17] *1968 Congressional Quarterly Almanac,* p. 539.
[18] *Baker v. Carr,* 369 U.S. 186 (1962); *Brown v. Board of Education of Topeka, Kansas,* 347 U.S. 483 (1954); *Gideon v. Wainwright,* 372 U.S. 335 (1963).
[19] Robert L. Carter, "The Warren Court and Desegregation," *Michigan Law Review,* Vol. 67, No. 2 (December 1968), p. 246.

"I'm bringing down our dirty books. The Supreme Court says it's all right."

Cartoon by Joseph Farris
The New York Times Book Review

servative critics: the Court, they charged, had tinkered with legislative apportionment, forced school integration, overprotected the rights of criminals, banished prayer from the classroom, tolerated Communists, and encouraged pornography.

Even such scholarly critics as Yale law professor Alexander M. Bickel criticized the Warren Court's "over-confident assault upon large and complex problems of social policy."[20] Moreover, as many of the Court's critics frequently pointed out, it decided many important cases by a narrow 5–4 margin.

Many observers predicted that the Burger Court would move more cautiously in the 1970's. Yet, one leading scholar concluded that

> the doctrines of equality, freedom, and respect for human dignity laid down in the numerous decisions of the Warren Court cannot be warped back to their original dimensions. The attitude of more and more Americans, particularly the members of the young and better-educated generation, is one of intense commitment to human rights. Generations hence it may well appear that what is supposedly the most conservative of American political institutions, the Supreme Court, was the institution that did the most to help the nation adjust to the needs and demands of a free society.[21]

[20] "The Warren Years," NET Journal, June 30, 1969, transcript, p. 40.
[21] William M. Beaney, "The Warren Court and the Political Process," *Michigan Law Review*, Vol. 67, No. 2 (December 1968), p. 352.

The Supreme Court in 1970. Front row: Justices John M. Harlan, Hugo L. Black, Chief Justice Warren E. Burger, Justices William O. Douglas, and William J. Brennan, Jr. Back row: Justices Thurgood Marshall, Potter Stewart, Byron R. White, and Harry A. Blackmun.

TABLE 13-1

The Supreme Court, 1970

Justices	Appointed by	Date
Hugo L. Black	Roosevelt	1937
William O. Douglas	Roosevelt	1939
John Marshall Harlan	Eisenhower	1955
William J. Brennan, Jr.	Eisenhower	1957
Potter Stewart	Eisenhower	1959
Byron R. White	Kennedy	1962
Thurgood Marshall	Johnson	1967
Warren E. Burger[1]	Nixon	1969
Harry A. Blackmun	Nixon	1970

[1] Chief Justice of the United States

The President and the Court

Historically, Presidents have picked Supreme Court justices for their politics more than for their judicial talents. By nominating justices whose political views appear compatible with their own they try to gain political control of the Supreme Court.

When Franklin Roosevelt unsuccessfully attempted to "pack" the Supreme Court, he was aiming not so much at the age of its members as at their political views. As Justice Hugo Black has put it: "Presidents have always appointed people who believed a great deal in the same things that the President who appoints them believes in." [22]

This practice is not necessarily bad if it does not lead to the appointment of mediocre judges. In fact, it is one important way in which the Supreme Court is at least *indirectly* responsive to the electorate. Along with the power of public opinion and the power of the Senate to confirm or reject the President's nominee, the presidential appointment power to some degree links the Court to the voters and the rest of the political system.

Approximately 90 percent of all Supreme Court justices in American history have belonged to the appointing President's political party; some have been selected from the President's inner circle of political advisers. In 1965, for example, President Johnson named Washington attorney Abe Fortas—a Democrat who had been his lawyer and political confidant for many years—to the Supreme Court. (In 1968, the Senate declined to approve Johnson's elevation of Fortas to be Chief Justice. In 1969 Fortas resigned from the Court when it developed that he had accepted a $20,000-a-year lifetime retainer from a foundation controlled by Louis E. Wolfson, a financier who subsequently went to prison for his stock dealings.)

Elected with Southern support in 1968, President Nixon, as we have seen, sought to strengthen the Republican "southern strategy," or political appeal to the South, by successively—but unsuccessfully—nominating two Southern federal judges, Clement F. Haynsworth, Jr., and G. Harrold Carswell to fill the Fortas vacancy.

The requirement that a majority of the Senate approve a Supreme Court nominee restricts the President's ability to shape the Court to his political liking. In 1970, as the Carswell nomination hung in the balance, Nixon charged that the Senate, by withholding its consent, threatened to infringe upon his "constitutional responsibility" to appoint members of the Supreme Court. However, up to 1970, the Senate had failed to approve twenty-eight, or more than 20 percent, of the 130 Supreme Court nominations sent to it. [23]

Supreme Court justices have a way of becoming surprisingly independent once they are on the bench; more than one President has been disappointed to find that he misjudged his man. As governor of California, Earl Warren had helped to elect President Eisenhower. There was nothing in Warren's background as a moderate Republican to make the President think his Chief Justice would preside over a social upheaval. Eisenhower

[22] "Justice Black and the Bill of Rights," interview broadcast over CBS television network, December 3, 1968; transcript in Congressional Quarterly, *Weekly Report*, January 3, 1969, p. 9.
[23] Adapted from the *New York Times*, April 9, 1970, p. 32.

reportedly called the Warren appointment "the biggest damnfool mistake I ever made." [24]

As Supreme Court Justice Jackson once suggested, conflict among the branches of the Federal Government is always latent, "ready to break out again whenever the provocation becomes sufficient." [25]

The Supreme Court, in deciding cases, must worry not only about public opinion, but about how Congress may react. Under the Constitution, Congress can control the appellate *jurisdiction* of the Supreme Court as well as its *size*. In its early history, the Court had five, six, seven, and ten justices. Congress did not fix the number at nine until 1869.

After the Civil War, Congress blocked the Court from reviewing Reconstruction laws by repealing a statute that had given the Court jurisdiction over certain types of cases. During the late 1950's, a coalition in Congress of Southern Democrats and conservative Republicans mounted a legislative assault to curb the power of the Supreme Court and limit its jurisdiction. The effort failed. In 1968, the Senate rejected a provision of the Omnibus Crime bill that would have limited the power of the Supreme Court to review certain kinds of cases in the state courts. So the threat of congressional retaliation is always present.

Congress (in conjunction with the states) also possesses the power to overturn Supreme Court decisions by amending the Constitution.[26] Senator Dirksen's attempts to nullify the reapportionment decisions of the 1960's by this means is one example. The Sixteenth Amendment, establishing the federal income tax, passed by Congress in 1909 and ratified in 1913, was adopted as a direct result of a Supreme Court decision; in 1895, the Court had ruled unconstitutional a legislative attempt by Congress to levy a national income tax.[27]

Finally, Congress may attempt to overturn specific Supreme Court rulings by legislation. For example, Title II of the Omnibus Crime bill of 1968 sought to overturn three major decisions of the Warren Court dealing with the rights of accused persons.[28] That action by Congress reflected the belief of some members of the public that the Warren Court rulings had made it more difficult for police to apprehend criminals. One observer has noted that, in seeking to fix the blame for rising crime rates, "In 1968, the

[24] In Joseph W. Bishop, Jr., "The Warren Court is Not Likely to Be Overruled," *New York Times Magazine*, September 7, 1969, p. 31.
[25] Jackson, *The Supreme Court in the American System of Government*, p. 9.
[26] The Eleventh, Fourteenth, and Sixteenth Amendments to the Constitution reversed specific Supreme Court rulings.
[27] *Pollock v. Farmers' Loan and Trust Co.*, 158 U.S. 601 (1895).
[28] *Miranda v. Arizona*, 384 U.S. 436 (1966); *Mallory v. United States*; 354 U.S. 449 (1957); *United States v. Wade*, 388 U.S. 218 (1967).

members of Congress had only to look across the street, at the Supreme Court." [29]

Most cases never reach the Supreme Court. Under the Constitution the Court has *original jurisdiction* to hear certain kinds of cases directly. These include cases involving foreign diplomats or cases in which one of the fifty states is a party.

The Supreme Court in Action

But the Court rarely exercises original jurisdiction; by far the greatest number of cases reach the Supreme Court under its *appellate jurisdiction.* That is, they are appealed from state or lower federal courts to the Supreme Court. Some cases are appealed on the grounds that they concern violations of constitutional rights, but the Court, which theoretically is obliged to hear such cases, can in practice dismiss them if it decides that no substantial federal question is involved. The majority of cases appealed to the Court come in forms of petitions for a writ of *certiorari* (a Latin term meaning "made more certain"). The Court can choose which of these cases it wants to hear by denying or granting *certiorari.* The Court denies between 85 and 90 percent of all such applications.[30]

Of the more than 10 million cases tried annually in American courts, only some 3,000 are taken to the Supreme Court. Of this total, the Court customarily hears argument on less than 150. In the 1968–69 term, the last year of the Warren Court, the Supreme Court disposed of 3,151 cases. But the Court heard oral arguments in only 140. It handed down written opinions in 130 of these, and set 10 for reargument.[31] The rest of the cases on the Court's docket were dismissed, affirmed, or reversed by written "memorandum orders."

The Court normally sits from October through June. The Court building on Capitol Hill is a majestic structure of white marble, built in 1935 and modeled after the Greek Temple of Diana at Ephesus, one of the seven wonders of the ancient world. The great bronze doors weigh six and a half tons each; the courtroom seats 300 and has a ceiling 44 feet high. Tradition is observed; all Federal Government lawyers appearing for oral argument still wear morning clothes as do a few private attorneys. The rather grandiose setting of the building and the formal atmosphere are designed to preserve the dignity of the nation's highest tribunal, but they also provide some comfort to its critics, particularly political cartoonists, who find it easy to lampoon the Court's elaborate Grecian setting.

A lawyer arguing before the Court usually has one-half hour to make

[29] Fred P. Graham, *The Self-Inflicted Wound* (New York: Macmillan, 1970), p. 12.
[30] Henry J. Abraham, *The Judicial Process* (New York: Oxford University Press, 1968), p. 179.
[31] *1969 Congressional Quarterly Almanac,* p. 128.

his case. Five minutes before his time expires a white light comes on; when a red light flashes on he must stop. But the justices often use up some of this precious time by interrupting to question the attorney, a procedure that can be totally unnerving for a lawyer making his initial appearance before the Supreme Court.

On Fridays when the Court is sitting, the justices meet in *conference* to discuss and vote on pending cases and applications for *certiorari*. The justices, by a tradition established in 1888, shake hands as they file into the oak-paneled conference room. The meetings are secret, and presided over by the Chief Justice. Although theoretically equal to the other eight justices, "the Chief" has four important tools available to him: prestige, the power to influence the Court's selection of cases through his position of leadership, the power to chair the conference, and the power to assign the writing of opinions by the justices. The Chief Justice, therefore, may play a very important role as "Court unifier." [32]

Although the conference proceedings are highly confidential, the veil of secrecy is lifted occasionally, as in this exchange in a televised interview with Justice Black:

> *Q.* What happens in a judicial conference? I know it's so secret that not even the clerks are permitted to come into the room. Could you tell us anything about it?
>
> *Black:* Just discuss the cases. . . . The Chief Justice, if he is with the majority, states that case to the majority and gives his view of what the law should be. . . . He speaks first, and then the next man in rank speaks . . . and so on down to the bottom . . . then . . . we cast a formal vote.[33]

Leadership styles among Chief Justices differ. Charles Evans Hughes, Chief Justice during the 1930's, was popular among the justices on the Court even though he ran the conference with a firm hand. His successor, Harlan Fiske Stone, was much less reserved, and delighted in joining in the debate. " 'Jackson,' he would say, 'that's damned nonsense,' 'Douglas, *you* know better than that.' " [34]

The Chief Justice, if he is in the majority, decides who will write the Court's opinion; otherwise, the ranking justice among the majority assigns the writing of the opinion. Each justice is free to write a dissenting opinion if he disagrees, or a concurring opinion if he reaches the same conclusion as the majority, often for different reasons. Important bargaining takes place backstage among the justices as the opinions are written and circulated informally; and a justice may trade his vote to influence the shape of an

---

[32] David J. Danelski, "The Influence of the Chief Justice in the Decisional Process," in Walter F. Murphy and C. Herman Pritchett, eds., *Courts, Judges and Politics: An Introduction to the Judicial Process* (New York: Random House, 1961), pp. 497–508.

[33] "Justice Black and the Bill of Rights," pp. 7–8.

[34] In Danelski, "The Influence of the Chief Justice in the Decisional Process," p. 501.

opinion. Some legal experts believe that dissents, because they publicly reveal disunity, weaken the prestige of the Court—the large number of 5–4 decisions by the Warren Court, for example, provided fuel for its enemies. But many of the most eloquent arguments of the Supreme Court have been voiced in dissents by justices such as John Marshall Harlan, Sr., Holmes, Brandeis, Cardozo, Stone, Black, and Douglas. Today's dissent may become tomorrow's majority opinion when the Court, as it has frequently done, overrules past decisions to meet new problems.

When it is in session, the Court, by custom, hands down its opinions each week on "Decision Monday," and, occasionally, on other days of the week. The justices read or summarize their opinions in the courtroom, sometimes adding informal comments. The words that echo through the marble chamber, often with enormous consequences for society, become the law of the land, and renew the meaning of constitutional government.

THE AMERICAN COURT SYSTEM

Because the United States encompasses both a federal government and fifty state governments, it has a *dual* court system. "In effect, this means that there exist side by side, two major court systems—one could even say fifty-one—that are wholly distinct." [35]

At the top of the system is the United States Supreme Court. But as we have seen, relatively few cases get there. The average citizen has neither the time nor the money to fight a case all the way to the highest tribunal; in any event the Court only considers cases involving a substantial federal question or constitutional issue, and normally after all remedies in the state courts have been exhausted.

The bulk of the cases that come before the judicial branch of the Federal Government are handled in the "inferior" courts created by Congress under the Constitution. Immediately below the Supreme Court are the United States *courts of appeals*. The nation is divided geographically into eleven judicial circuits, each with a Court of Appeals. Every state and territory falls within the jurisdiction of one of these circuit courts. Each Court of Appeals has from three to fifteen judges, but usually three judges hear a case. The circuit courts hear appeals from lower federal courts and review the decisions of federal regulatory agencies. In 1970, there were a total of ninety-seven circuit court judges. Each year the circuit courts handle about 10,000 cases.

The
Federal Courts

Below the circuit courts are the *federal district courts*. In 1971, there

[35] Abraham, *The Judicial Process*, p. 138.

were eighty-eight district courts in the fifty states, plus one each for the District of Columbia, Puerto Rico, Canal Zone, the Virgin Islands, and Guam. Each district has from one to twenty-four judges, making a total of 402 district judgeships. More than half of the federal judicial districts coincide with state lines, but some populous states, such as New York, are divided into as many as four districts. The federal district courts are trial courts; they handle cases involving disputes between citizens of different states and violations of federal law—for example, of civil rights, patent and copyright, bankruptcy, immigration, counterfeiting, antitrust, and postal laws. In 1969, 110,778 cases were commenced in the federal district courts, of which 33,585 were criminal and the rest civil.[36]

Special
Federal Courts

Congress has created special purpose courts to deal with certain kinds of cases. These include the United States Court of Claims, which has jurisdiction over such cases as claims against government appropriation of property, claims by government workers for back pay, or claims for income tax refunds; the United States Court of Customs and Patent Appeals, which hears tariff, trademark, and patent cases, and the United States Court of Military Appeals, often termed "the G.I. Supreme Court."

The Court of Military Appeals, whose three judges are civilians, is the final appellate tribunal in court-martial convictions. It was established by Congress in 1950, along with a Uniform Code of Military Justice. The code represented the first major overhaul of the system of military justice since the early nineteenth century.

The Vietnam war focused new attention on the process of military justice, and brought much criticism of it. Widespread publicity, some of it unfavorable, arose from the handling of cases involving military defendants in Vietnam and servicemen who participated in antiwar protests. For example, twenty-four soldiers who protested conditions at the Presidio army stockade in San Francisco in 1968 were tried for mutiny, a crime that can be punishable by death. They were initially given long sentences of up to sixteen years; later, most sentences were reduced by the Army to two years.

The cases occurring in Vietnam dramatized the fact that many Americans—more than 3,000,000 in 1970—were subject to military justice and therefore were at least temporarily outside the civilian system of justice as it has evolved under the Constitution. In recent years, however, the Supreme Court has afforded certain protections to military defendants. Although there is no direct appeal from decisions of the Court of Military Appeals, the Supreme Court has asserted a limited right to review certain types of military cases.[37] In a 1967 decision the Court of Military Appeals

---

[36] *Annual Report of the Director, 1969*, Administrative Office of the United States Courts, pp. I-4, 5.
[37] *Burns v. Wilson*, 346 U.S. 137 (1953).

held that the Supreme Court's *Miranda* decision, ruling out involuntary confessions, must also apply in military cases.[38] And in 1969 the Supreme Court ruled that servicemen must be tried in civilian courts for crimes not connected with the service and committed in peacetime while on leave or off duty.[39] Despite such limited protections, there was growing pressure in the 1970's for reform of the whole system of military justice.

State and local courts, not the federal courts, handle most cases in the United States. The quality and structure of the court system in the states vary tremendously with each state, but most states have several layers of courts:

The State Court System

1. *Justices of the Peace,* or magistrates, handle minor offenses (misdemeanors), such as speeding, and perform civil marriages. Most "J.P.'s" do not have law degrees but what they may lack in legal training they make up for in their well-known zeal for convictions, which average 80 percent in criminal cases.[40]
2. *Municipal courts* are known variously as police courts, city courts, traffic courts, and night courts. These courts, generally one step up from the magistrates' courts, usually hear civil cases involving $500 to $1,000, and lesser criminal offenses.
3. *County courts,* also called superior courts, try serious criminal offenses (felonies) and major civil cases. At this level jury trials are held in cases that do go to a jury.
4. *Special jurisdiction courts* are sometimes created at the county level to handle domestic relations, juveniles, probate of wills and estates, and other specialized tasks.
5. *Intermediate Courts of Appeals,* or appellate divisions, exist in some states to hear appeals from the county and municipal courts.
6. *Courts of appeals,* often called state supreme courts, are the final judicial tribunals in the states.

All federal court judges are appointed by the President, subject to Senate approval. But in two-thirds of the *states,* judges are popularly elected. In a few states, judges are appointed, in some cases by a special commission. More than a dozen states employ the merit system for the selection of judges, patterned after the "Missouri plan." The basic elements of that plan, which went into effect in Missouri in 1940, are:

The Judges

1. Nomination of the judges by a nonpartisan commission made up of lawyers, a judge, and citizens.

[38] *United States v. Tempia,* 16 USCMA 629 (1967).
[39] *O'Callahan v. Parker,* 395 U.S. 258 (1969).
[40] Abraham, *The Judicial Process,* p. 140.

2. Appointment by the governor.

3. Approval by the voters after an initial term on the bench.

Despite the efforts to bring about judicial reform, in most cases "it is the politicians who select the judges. The voters only ratify their choices." [41] Political parties sometimes do not run competing candidates for the judiciary; rather, political leaders of both major parties get together and carve up the available judgeships. The nominees then run with the endorsement of *both* parties. In the process, political hacks are sometimes elevated to the bench.

In 1967, a citizens' commission named by President Johnson issued a massive study, with nine supplementary task force reports, on problems of crime and justice in America. The President's Commission on Law Enforcement and Administration of Justice (usually called the President's Crime Commission) emphasized the importance of the judicial selection process, declaring: "The quality of the judiciary in large measure determines the quality of justice." [42] Bad judges do more than administer bad law; in the process they erode public respect for the entire system of criminal justice and the political system of which it is so vital a part.

CRIMINAL JUSTICE IN AMERICA

As the United States moved into the decade of the 1970's, a high-level presidential commission issued the following statement about American justice:

> If welfare assistance is arbitrarily cut off, if a landlord flagrantly ignores housing codes, if a merchant demands payment under an unfair contract, the poor—like the rich—can go to court. Whether they find satisfaction there is another matter. The dockets of many lower courts are overcrowded, and cases are handled in assembly-line fashion, often by inexperienced or incompetent personnel. Too frequently courts having jurisdiction over landlord-tenant and small claims disputes serve the poor less well than their creditors. . . . The poor are discouraged from initiating civil actions against their exploiters. Litigation is expensive; so are experienced lawyers.[43]

[41] Glenn R. Winters and Robert E. Allard, "Judicial Selection and Tenure in the United States," in Harry W. Jones, ed., *The Courts, the Public, and the Law Explosion*, prepared for the American Assembly, Columbia University (Englewood Cliffs, N.J.: Prentice-Hall, 1965), p. 157.

[42] *The Challenge of Crime in a Free Society*, A Report by the President's Commission on Law Enforcement and Administration of Justice (Washington, D.C.: U.S. Government Printing Office, 1967), p. 146.

[43] "Violence and Law Enforcement," in *To Establish Justice, To Insure Domestic Tranquility*, Final Report of the National Commission on the Causes and Prevention of Violence (Washington, D.C.: U.S. Government Printing Office, December 1969), pp. 143–44.

The commission that issued this critical report was headed by Dr. Milton S. Eisenhower and its members included a mixture of liberals, moderates, and conservatives. The report went on to criticize the nation's criminal justice system in words that were often harsh. In fact, the commission said, there is no real *system* of criminal justice:

> There is, instead, a reasonably well-defined criminal *process* . . . through which each accused offender may pass: from the hands of the police, to the jurisdiction of the courts, behind the walls of a prison, then back onto the street. . . . this process is notorious. . . .
>
> Nearly every official and agency participating in the criminal process is frustrated by some aspect of its ineffectiveness, its unfairness or both. . . . criminal courts themselves are often poorly managed and . . . seriously backlogged. . . . prisons . . . are . . . schools in crime. . . . jails . . . are often the most appalling shame in the criminal justice system. . . . the typical prison experience is degrading . . . and the outlook of most ex-convicts is bleak.[44]

Most criticism of the administration of justice in the United States is directed not at the principles of the system—the presumption that a defendant is innocent until proven guilty and the protections of the Bill of Rights—but at the failure of the system to work the way it is supposed to work.

Edward L. Barrett, Jr., Dean of the law school of the University of California at Davis, has focused on precisely this problem: Americans, he notes, tend to think that the procedure of the criminal courts protects the dignity of the individual against the power of the government.

> Such is the general image we have of the administration of criminal justice. But if one enters the courthouse in any sizeable city and walks from courtroom to courtroom, what does he see? One judge, in a single morning, is accepting pleas of guilty from and sentencing a hundred or more persons charged with drunkenness. Another judge is adjudicating traffic cases with an average time of no more than a minute per case. A third is disposing of a hundred or more other misdemeanor offenses in a morning. . . .
>
> Suddenly it becomes clear that for most defendants in the criminal process, there is scant regard for them as individuals. They are numbers on dockets, faceless ones to be processed and sent on their way. The gap between the theory and the reality is enormous.[45]

"Today it is comparatively safe to break the law," Richard Nixon claimed during his 1968 presidential campaign. "Today all across

A Profile
of Crime in America

---

[44] *Ibid.*, pp. 149–52, 155.
[45] Edward L. Barrett, Jr., "Criminal Justice: The Problem of Mass Production," in Jones, *The Courts, the Public, and the Law Explosion*, pp. 86–87.

Half of all major crimes are never reported to police.

Of those which are, less than 25 percent are solved by arrests.

Half of these arrests result in dismissal of charges.

90 per cent of the rest are resolved by a plea of guilty.

The fraction of cases that do go to trial represent less than 1 per cent of all crimes committed.

About 25 per cent of those convicted are sent to prison; the rest are released on probation.

Nearly everyone who goes to prison is eventually released.

Between half and two-thirds of those released are arrested and convicted again; they become repeat criminals known as recidivists.

—Adapted from *To Establish Justice, To Insure Domestic Tranquility*,
Final Report of the National Commission on The Causes and Prevention of Violence.

the land guilty men walk free from hundreds of courtrooms. Something has gone terribly wrong in America." [46]

Nixon's words underscored the fact that in the late 1960's crime had become a major political issue in the United States. As the President's Crime Commission put it, crime and the fear of crime "have eroded the basic quality of life of many Americans." [47]

In 1969, there were almost 5 million serious crimes reported to law enforcement agencies in the United States, of which 655,100, or 13 percent,

TABLE 13-2

Crime in the United States, 1969

Crime Offenses	Estimated Number of Crimes	Rate per 100,000 Inhabitants
Total	4,989,700	2,471.1
Violent	655,100	324.4
Property	4,334,700	2,146.7
Murder	14,590	7.2
Forcible rape	36,470	18.1
Robbery	297,580	147.4
Aggravated assault	306,420	151.8
Burglary	1,949,800	965.6
Larceny $50 and over	1,512,900	749.3
Auto theft	871,900	431.8

Source: Adapted from *Crime in the United States,* Uniform Crime Reports–1969, Federal Bureau of Investigation (Washington, D.C.: U.S. Government Printing Office, 1970), p. 5.

[46] In Richard Harris, *Justice: The Crisis of Law, Order, and Freedom in America* (New York: Dutton, 1970), p. 26; from Nixon's radio address, September 29, 1968.
[47] *The Challenge of Crime in a Free Society*, p. v.

fell into the category of violent crimes that people fear the most—murder, rape, robbery, and assault. (See Table 13-2.) In the United States in 1969, 14,590 persons were murdered. There were nearly 2 million burglaries reported, 56 percent of these in homes. Almost 900,000 cars were stolen. Put another way, on the average a violent crime was committed every forty-eight seconds, a murder every thirty-six minutes, a rape every fourteen minutes, a robbery every two minutes, and a car stolen every thirty-six seconds.[48] (See Figure 13-1.)

But these figures, compiled annually by the FBI from reports received by law enforcement agencies, do not reflect the full magnitude of crime in the United States. Based upon population sampling, the President's Crime Commission estimated that the actual amount of crime committed is "several times" greater than the amount of crime reported to the authorities.[49] People fail to report crimes for a variety of reasons, including a reluctance to "get involved," or doubt that police can do anything about it, or fear of reprisal by the criminal.[50]

There are some popular misconceptions about crime. As the President's Crime Commission has noted, "the risks of personal harm are spread very unevenly. The actual risk for slum dwellers is considerably more; for most Americans it is considerably less."[51] Richard Harris has observed: "By far the greatest number of all crimes reported were committed by slum-dwellers upon slum-dwellers. For a resident of the black slums of Chicago, for instance, the chance of being physically assaulted, on the basis of reported crimes, was one in seventy-seven, whereas for the white resident of a nearby suburb the chance was one in ten thousand."[52]

Crime by youths and juvenile delinquency account for a substantial share of all crime. In 1969, for example, 64 percent of the arrests for violent and serious crimes were of persons under twenty-one. More crimes of this type are committed by thirteen- to fifteen-year-olds than by any other age group. Statistics can be misleading, however—adult crimes account for about 61 percent of *all* crime in the United States. For example, arrests for drunkenness clog the nation's court calendars; of the 1.4 million such arrests in 1969, about 91 percent were of adults.[53]

Narcotics addiction is another source of crime. Estimates vary greatly as to how much crime is committed by heroin addicts in order to get money to support their habit. Some estimates attribute as much as three-quarters

[48] *Crime in the United States*, Uniform Crime Reports-1969, Federal Bureau of Investigation (Washington, D.C.: U.S. Government Printing Office, 1970), pp. 1–46.
[49] *The Challenge of Crime in a Free Society*, pp. 21–22.
[50] *Task Force Report: Crime and Its Impact—An Assessment*, The President's Commission on Law Enforcement and Administration of Justice (Washington, D.C.: U.S. Government Printing Office, 1967), pp. 93–94.
[51] *The Challenge of Crime in a Free Society*, p. 19.
[52] Harris, *Justice: The Crisis of Law, Order, and Freedom in America*, pp. 27–28.
[53] *Crime in the United States*, Uniform Crime Reports-1969, p. 115.

FIGURE 13-1

Crime Clocks—1969

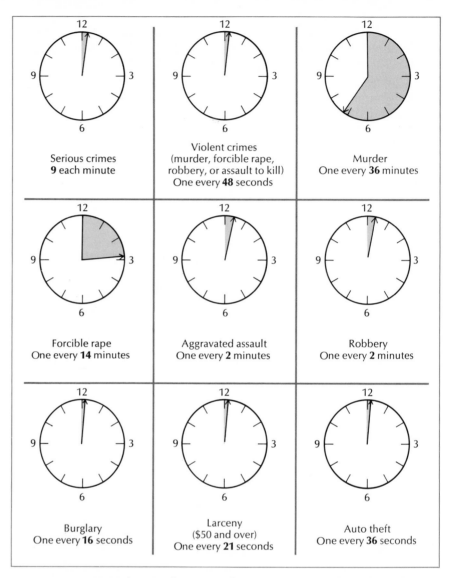

Serious crimes
9 each minute

Violent crimes
(murder, forcible rape,
robbery, or assault to kill)
One every **48** seconds

Murder
One every **36** minutes

Forcible rape
One every **14** minutes

Aggravated assault
One every **2** minutes

Robbery
One every **2** minutes

Burglary
One every **16** seconds

Larceny
($50 and over)
One every **21** seconds

Auto theft
One every **36** seconds

Source: *Crime in the United States,* Uniform Crime Reports-1969, Federal Bureau of Investigation (Washington, D.C.: U.S. Government Printing Office, 1970), p. 29.

of all serious crime in New York City and Washington, D.C., to drug addicts.[54]

There is considerable dispute among criminologists and law enforcement authorities over the *rate* at which crime has increased in America in recent years; in part this controversy is due to inadequate systems of crime

[54] Harris, *Justice: The Crisis of Law, Order, and Freedom in America,* p. 44.

Among all age groups, close to ninety per cent of those arrested for violating the laws on addictive drugs had criminal records, and seventeen per cent of them were armed, presumably to enable them to commit other crimes to support their habit.

It is an exceedingly expensive one. A heroin addict—the principal user involved—needs between fifty and sixty dollars a day to keep himself supplied. Since an addict is rarely able to hold down an ordinary job, let alone a job paying that kind of money, he must steal money or else merchandise that can easily be converted into money. As a rule, stolen goods bring about ten per cent of their value in cash, so, theoretically, the country's sixty-three thousand known addicts must steal three and a half million dollars a day in cash or thirty-five million dollars a day in merchandise, or a combination of the two, in order to survive. In trying to raise funds, the addict most often relies on muggings, holdups, or burglaries, and in the course of committing them he not infrequently assaults or murders his victims.

—Richard Harris, *Justice: The Crisis of Law, Order, and Freedom in America.*

reporting prior to 1958. But that the crime rate has gone up is generally acknowledged; between 1960 and 1969, it is estimated, the rate of violent crime increased 30 percent. (See Figure 13-2.) Even if the crime rate had remained level, there would be more crime, because the population has increased.

FIGURE 13-2

Increase in Violent Crime [1] in the United States, 1933–1969

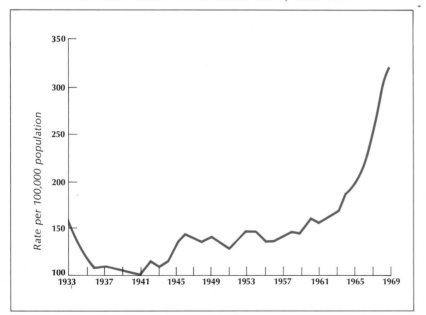

[1] Homicide, forcible rape, robbery, aggravated assault.

Source: *To Establish Justice, To Insure Domestic Tranquility*, Final Report of the National Commission on the Causes and Prevention of Violence (Washington, D.C.: U.S. Government Printing Office, December, 1969), p. xiv; and *Crime in the United States*, Uniform Crime Reports-1969, Federal Bureau of Investigation (Washington, D.C.: U.S. Government Printing Office, 1970) p. 5.

The nation's prisons, instead of rehabilitating offenders, may contribute to the crime rate by serving in many instances as "human warehouses" for the custody of convicts. Half the felons released from prison commit new crimes. There are more than 2,500,000 admissions to America's correctional institutions and jails each year; and in many cases, little is done to prepare them for their return to the outside world. As recently as 1966, thirty state prisons for adults had no vocational training programs. The President's Crime Commission concluded: "For a great many offenders . . . corrections does not correct." [55]

The social and human cost of crime in America can scarcely be measured. In economic terms, the President's Crime Commission estimated the overall cost of crime and related expenditures at $20.9 billion a year (of which $4.2 billion is spent on police, courts, and prisons).

The Police

"He is the most important American. . . . He works in a highly flammable environment. A spark can cause an explosion. . . . If he overacts, he can cause a riot. If he underacts, he can permit a riot. He is a man on a tightrope." [56] When he was Attorney General of the United States, Ramsey Clark used these words to describe the typical police officer. Police today are indeed on a tightrope; vastly underpaid, with inadequate training, manpower, and resources, they are expected to fight rising crime, enforce the law, keep the peace, and provide a wide variety of social and community services. Police must spend much of their time performing such community services—directing traffic, dealing with auto accidents, giving directions to motorists and travelers, responding to medical emergencies, licensing taxicabs, and rescuing stray cats. These duties greatly reduce the amount of time police can spend fighting crime. As the armed embodiment of the law, police are caught between the established order and dissident groups seeking rapid change. Mutual hostility between police and black militants, police and student demonstrators, and police and political protesters is reflected daily in the headlines. Frequently, these tensions have erupted in tragic violence and bloodshed. During 1969, eighty-six police officers in the United States were killed in the line of duty.[57] During the summer of 1970, police in several cities, including Omaha, Chicago, and Philadelphia, were murdered by sniper fire, booby traps, or handguns.

"The policeman," in the words of a task force report to the National Commission on the Causes and Prevention of Violence, "lives on the grinding edge of social conflict, without a well-defined, well-understood notion

[55] *The Challenge of Crime in a Free Society*, p. 159.
[56] In Harris, *Justice: The Crisis of Law, Order, and Freedom in America*, pp. 76–77.
[57] *Crime in the United States*, Uniform Crime Reports—1969, p. 43.

of what he is supposed to be doing there." [58] Called on to play conflicting roles, the policeman is subject to political attack from various directions: "The same policeman in the morning may be called 'soft and ineffective' by our 'forgotten man' and 'fascist pig' by a young revolutionary in the afternoon." [59] Differences in social and cultural background of police and minorities or dissidents may contribute to tension between them. The Violence Commission's task force report argued that "police in the United States are for the most part white, upwardly mobile lower middle-class, conservative in ideology and resistant to change. . . . They tend to share the attitudes, biases and prejudices of the larger community." [60]

One result of the social turbulence of the 1960's and 1970's is that the police have become *politicized*; they are emerging as a powerful interest group in the political system. One controversial Violence Commission staff study concluded that "the police have become increasingly frustrated, alienated, and angry. These feelings are being expressed in a growing militancy and political activism. In short, the police are protesting." [61]

Many Americans—perhaps a majority—strongly support and defend the police. As we noted in Chapter 1, even when police employed violence against demonstrators at Chicago in 1968, 56 percent of the public approved of the way the police had acted. In a time of turmoil and fear of violence, many Americans appear to regard "law and order" as a requirement that takes precedence over all other considerations, including the constitutional right of peaceful dissent.[62]

The controversy over the role of the police in responding to social protest has to some extent tended to obscure the conventional role of the policeman in the system of criminal justice. The police officer is, after all, a highly visible and important public official. As "the cop on the beat" dealing with everyday social conflict and crime, he exercises great discretionary powers.[63] Should a fight be broken up, a speeding car stopped, a

---

[58] James S. Campbell, Joseph R. Sahid, and David P. Stang, *Law and Order Reconsidered*, Report of the Task Force on Law and Law Enforcement to the National Commission on the Causes and Prevention of Violence (Washington, D.C.: U.S. Government Printing Office, 1969), p. 290.

[59] *Ibid.*, pp. 285–86.

[60] *Ibid.*, p. 291.

[61] Jerome H. Skolnick, *The Politics of Protest*, Staff Report to the National Commission on the Causes and Prevention of Violence (Washington, D.C.: U.S. Government Printing Office, 1969), pp. 214–15.

[62] For example, 76 percent of the people questioned in a telephone survey by the Columbia Broadcasting System said extremist groups should not be allowed to "organize protests" against the government; 55 percent said news media should not report stories that the government considers harmful to the national interest; and 58 percent thought that a suspect in a serious crime should be held in jail by police until they can get enough evidence to charge him with the crime. (*The CBS News Poll*, Survey Operations Department, CBS News Election Unit, March 20, 1970, pp. 1–6.)

[63] See, for example, James Q. Wilson, *Varieties of Police Behavior* (Cambridge, Mass.: Harvard University Press, 1968), pp. 7, 278.

street-corner crowd dispersed? The policeman must decide. To a great extent, law enforcement policy is made by the policemen.

Police do not, as a rule, get their man. There is a huge gap between the number of crimes reported and the number of criminals arrested. In 1969, for example, only 20.6 percent of known offenses were "cleared" from police record books by arrests.[64] Crime can be viewed as a series of concentric circles, in which the smallest, innermost circle represents persons actually convicted and sent to prison. (See Figure 13-3.)

FIGURE 13-3

Crime and Law Enforcement

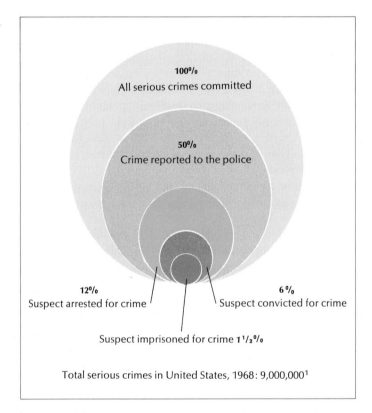

100%
All serious crimes committed

50%
Crime reported to the police

12%
Suspect arrested for crime

6%
Suspect convicted for crime

Suspect imprisoned for crime 1 1/2%

Total serious crimes in United States, 1968: 9,000,000[1]

[1] Aggregate of homicide, forcible rape, robbery, aggravated assault, burglary, larceny over $50, auto theft. Based on estimates.

Source: *To Establish Justice, To Insure Domestic Tranquility*, Final Report of the National Commission on the Causes and Prevention of Violence (Washington, D.C.: U.S. Government Printing Office, December, 1969), p. xviii.

[64] *Crime in the United States*, Uniform Crime Reports—1969, p. 100.

Although criminal justice and law enforcement are primarily the responsibility of state and local authorities, the Federal Government wields increasing power in this field. The Department of Justice in recent years has emerged as a major policy-making agency in relation to a broad range of political, legal, and social issues. The department is headed by the Attorney General, who is both a Cabinet officer and the President's chief legal adviser.

One of the Justice Department's basic responsibilities is to conduct criminal prosecutions in the federal courts. This means that the Attorney General has tremendous power to make political decisions about who will be prosecuted, and who will not. For example, under Attorney General Robert F. Kennedy, the Justice Department implemented the Kennedy administration's pro-civil rights strategy. In 1969, under President Nixon, Attorney General John N. Mitchell asked federal courts to delay enforcement of school desegregation in Mississippi. In both cases, the Justice Department was pursuing political policies.

An Attorney General might publicly throw up his hands in horror at the suggestion that his decisions were political. But it should be remembered that he is a Cabinet officer responsible to the President, and the Attorney General's political viewpoint is normally an important factor in his selection. In exercising discretion about whom to prosecute, he may also reflect his own ideology and outlook. Should an antitrust suit be brought against a big corporation? Should the Black Panthers be tried? Should the department concentrate on prosecuting student radicals? Or should it crack down on organized crime? As a case in point, President Johnson's Attorney General, Ramsey Clark, did not seek to prosecute the "Chicago Seven," the leaders of the protest demonstrations at the 1968 Democratic National Convention. His successor, John Mitchell, asked a federal grand jury in Chicago to act; the "Chicago Seven" were indicted and tried for conspiracy under a 1968 law making it a federal crime to cross state lines with "intent" to "incite a riot."

The Justice Department prosecutes persons accused of federal crimes through its United States attorneys in each of the federal judicial districts. Although United States attorneys are appointed by the President, subject to Senate approval, they serve under the Attorney General. There were 93 United States attorneys and 760 assistant United States attorneys in 1970. Under the supervision of the department's criminal division, the United States attorney in each district initiates investigations and decides whether to prosecute or to seek a grand jury indictment in criminal cases.

Separate divisions of the Justice Department deal with criminal, civil, antitrust, tax, civil rights, natural resources, and internal security cases. A special unit in the criminal division handles cases involving organized crime. The Justice Department also includes the Immigration and Naturalization Service, the Bureau of Narcotics and Dangerous Drugs, the Law Enforcement Assistance Administration—created in 1968 to distribute federal funds through the states to local police—and the Bureau of Prisons, which is in charge of the 25,000 persons in federal prisons and youth centers.

Best known of all the arms of the Justice Department is the Federal Bureau of Investigation. In 1970, the FBI employed 16,700 people (approximately half of all the Justice Department's employees) and had a budget of $232.9 million. About 7,000 of the total were FBI agents; most of the rest were laboratory experts, clerks, and secretaries. The FBI is the investigative arm of the Justice Department and its jurisdiction is limited to suspected violations of *federal* law. It has fifty-nine field offices and a dozen offices abroad for liaison with foreign police and intelligence services. In its files are the fingerprints of 83,670,226 people.[65]

Through movies, a television serial, and guided tours of its headquarters for the millions of tourists who visit Washington each year, the FBI has become more publicized than virtually any other agency of the government. It almost always gets what it wants from Congress—including a $102,000,000 new headquarters building scheduled for completion in 1973. Although technically an arm of the Justice Department, the FBI under J. Edgar Hoover became largely independent of the Attorney General.

The FBI is controversial. The majority of Americans think of it in favorable terms; to them it is an agency adept at catching bank robbers and spies.[66] But many others worry about the concentration of power in the hands of the FBI, and they fear that its wiretaps and the extensive information contained in its dossiers may be used for political ends, or to enhance the power of its director.

The
Criminal Courts

Americans who have never had a brush with the law may tend to think of the system of criminal justice in terms of "due process of law," trial by jury, and the right of counsel—in short, the *adversary system* of justice, in which the power of the state is balanced by the defendant's constitutional rights and by the presumption, not written in the Constitution, but deeply rooted in Anglo-Saxon law, that a man is innocent until proved guilty beyond a reasonable doubt.[67]

[65] *1969 FBI Annual Report*, p. 31.
[66] The Gallup Poll in 1965 asked a cross-section of the American public: "If you had a son who decided to become an FBI agent, would you be pleased or displeased?" Of those questioned, 77 percent said they would be pleased. (Congressional Quarterly, *Weekly Report*, December 26, 1969, p. 2697.)
[67] The Supreme Court has held that the "due process clause" of the Constitution requires the presumption that a criminal defendant is innocent until proven guilty beyond a reasonable doubt. *Davis v. United States*, 160 U.S. 469 (1895); *Coffin v. United States*, 156 U.S. 432 (1895); *In the Matter of Samuel Winship*, 396 U.S. 885 (1970).

Plea Bargaining. These protections may prevail *when* a case goes to trial. But the popular, "Perry Mason" image of American justice overlooks a vital fact: the great majority of cases never *go* to trial. According to one report, "Most defendants who are convicted—as many as 90 percent in some jurisdictions—are not tried. They plead guilty, often as the result of negotiations about the charge or the sentence." [68]

In other words, the machinery of the adversary system of justice exists—but it may not be used. Most guilty pleas are the result of backstage discussions between the prosecutor and defense counsel. The practice is commonly known as "plea bargaining," or, less elegantly, as "copping a plea."

The practice often serves everyone's needs but the defendant's. The government is saved the time and expense of a public prosecution; the defense attorney can collect his fee and move on to the next client; the judge can keep the business of his court moving along. But the guilt or innocence of the accused person is not proven.

Usually, the plea bargaining process works this way: a defendant agrees to plead guilty to a less serious charge than might be proven at a trial; in return the prosecutor agrees to reduce the charges or recommend leniency. In theory, the accused person will get a lighter sentence this way than he might if the case went to trial and he were convicted. There is no guarantee, however, that the judge will act as the prosecutor has promised.

A task force report for a presidential commission notes that

> Few practices in the system of criminal justice create a greater sense of unease and suspicion than the negotiated plea of guilty. . . . The system usually operates in an informal, invisible manner. . . . Although the participants and frequently the judge know that negotiation has taken place, the prosecutor and defendant must ordinarily go through a courtroom ritual in which they deny that the guilty plea is the result of any threat or promise. . . . The judge, the public, and sometimes the defendant himself cannot know for certain who got what from whom in exchange for what.[69]

In 1970, the Supreme Court upheld the practice of plea bargaining. It did so in the case of a man sentenced to fifty years for kidnapping who claimed he had been coerced into pleading guilty to avoid the death penalty. The Court held that a guilty plea, entered voluntarily and intelligently with the advice of counsel, was constitutional.[70]

Court Delay. American courts do not have enough judges to handle

---

[68] *The Challenge of Crime in a Free Society,* p. 134.
[69] *Task Force Report: The Courts,* The President's Commission on Law Enforcement and Administration of Justice (Washington, D.C.: U.S. Government Printing Office, 1967), p. 9.
[70] *Brady v. U.S.,* 396 U.S. 809 (1970).

The courts in the [New York] metropolitan area, as nearly everyone connected with them readily admits, are overcrowded, understaffed and months behind in their work.

"If everyone who came here wanted a trial, there'd be no way to give them one," Assistant Administrative Judge Vincent A. Massi of the Criminal Court said a few days ago. . . .

In Brooklyn's dilapidated Criminal Court, some sessions are held in judges' robing rooms, where, before the sessions begin, guards look in the closets for defendants who may have escaped.

In the Bronx, because there is no air-conditioning in the Criminal Court, windows are left open in the summer—even though the elevated trains next door are so noisy that, as one judge said, "you can't hear yourself, much less the defendant; it's impossible to try a case." . . .

A number of judges and lawyers have also pointed out problems common to most, if not all, the courts: judges so harried they often spend whole days doing no more than adjourning the cases on the day's calendars; correction facilities so overcrowded that some judges say they hesitate to sentence the people they convict; serious charges are dismissed because witnesses, after going to court a few times only to hear the case adjourned, have stopped appearing.

The pressures are so great on all concerned that one day recently Criminal Court Judge Milton Shalleck, after arraigning scores of people at an average speed of 2 minutes 2½ seconds per defendant, finally blurted out: "There is no justice here. I'm not dispensing justice."

—Lesley Oelsner, "The Creaky Courts: Overhaul Needed to End Delays," *New York Times*, April 7, 1970.

the volume of cases that come before them. In a single year, the courts may dispose of 4,000,000 misdemeanor cases.[71]

The high caseload, the lack of judges, and poor administration of the courts all result in major delays in the criminal process. The courts are badly backlogged; in many large cities the average delay between arrest and trial is close to a year. In Great Britain, the period from arrest to final appeal frequently takes four months, but the same process in many states in America averages ten to eighteen months.

Bail Reform and "Preventive Detention." During the long wait for his trial, an accused person may be free on bail or detained. Bail is a system designed to ensure that a defendant will appear in court when his case is called; typically, the arrested person goes before a judge or magistrate who fixes an amount of money to be "posted" with the court as security in exchange for the defendant's freedom. If the defendant does not have the money, a bondsman may post bail for him, but the defendant must pay the bondsman a premium of 5 to 20 percent. If the accused person cannot raise bail either way, he may have to remain in jail until his case comes up. If he goes free on bail but fails to appear for his trial, the bail is forfeited.

The rights of the individual and the community conflict during the pretrial period. The accused person may have a job, and a family to sup-

[71] *Task Force Report: The Courts*, p. 31; data for 1962.

port; and he needs his freedom to prepare his defense. The community demands that he appear for trial and not endanger society by committing a crime in the meantime; that is the rationale of the bail system.

Such a system obviously discriminates against the poor man, who may not be able to buy his way out of jail. "Millions of men and women are, through the American bail system, held each year in 'ransom' in American jails, committed to prison cells often for prolonged periods before trial," Ronald Goldfarb has written. "Because they are poor or friendless, they may spend days, weeks, or months in confinement, often to be acquitted of wrongdoing in the end." [72]

Until the Bail Reform Act of 1966, federal judges had often deliberately set a high bail for defendants they considered dangerous, in the hope that the bail could not be paid; the practice was an illegal but widespread system of pretrial detention. Under the 1966 act, this subterfuge was no longer possible. Federal (but not state or local) judges were required to release defendants before trial except in capital cases—in which death was the possible punishment—and unless there were good reasons to believe that the defendant would flee if released. A federal judge might still set bail, but a defendant could no longer be held because he did not have the money.

But bail reform created problems. In the District of Columbia, where *all* cases go before federal courts, a high percentage of arrested persons released on bail committed crimes while awaiting trial on the first charge. One study of persons indicted for robbery in the District of Columbia in 1966–67 showed that 35 percent were rearrested for at least one additional

THE BAIL SYSTEM: PUNISHMENT FOR THE CRIME OF POVERTY

The American bail system discriminates against and punishes the poor. The rich can afford to buy their freedom, and do; the poor go to jail because they cannot afford the premium for a bail bond. The average amount of bail is about $500, and the average premium for a bail bond—$25 to $50 is 5 percent or 10 percent of the amount of the bond, but many of the poor do not have a ready $25 or $50, and for lack of it go to jail while the rich or the comfortable go home.

The economic facts of the bail system go even further. When the defendant who cannot afford bail goes to jail before trial, he loses his present earning capacity, and often his job. His family suffers. Some people have been forced onto relief rolls as a result of lost earning capacity caused by pretrial detention. All of this happens before trial, without regard to their guilt or innocence. It is, in effect, punishment for the crime of poverty.

—Ronald Goldfarb, *Ransom.*

[72] Ronald Goldfarb, *Ransom* (New York: Harper & Row, 1965), p. 1.

felony while free on bond.[73] Many people considered this situation intolerable, and in 1969, President Nixon submitted a controversial proposal for pretrial "preventive detention," for up to sixty days, of defendants in federal cases found by the judge to be "dangerous." Senator Sam J. Ervin, Jr., of North Carolina, argued that the bill was "unconstitutional and smacks of a police-state rather than a democracy under law." It would, he warned, "result in the imprisonment of many innocent persons."[74] In 1970, after lengthy debate, Congress enacted a crime bill for the District of Columbia that included a provision for pretrial detention, as well as the controversial "no-knock" entry by police, discussed in Chapter 4. Under the bill, a defendant in the nation's capital charged with a dangerous or violent crime can be jailed for up to sixty days after a hearing, if the judge finds convincing evidence that his release might endanger "the safety of the community." The controversy over preventive detention was a classic example of the continuing conflict in the American political system between the demands of order and individual liberty.

Capital Punishment. In 1970, 504 men and women sat in death row cells in the United States awaiting execution. Since the Federal Government began keeping statistics on executions in 1930, 3,859 men have been executed by civil authority in the United States. Increasingly, however, the death penalty has come under attack for moral and legal reasons. By 1970, nine states had abolished capital punishment and four had restricted its use.

In 1968, the Supreme Court ruled that no person may be sentenced to death by a jury from which persons opposed to capital punishment have been excluded.[75] Justice Potter Stewart wrote for the Court: "A hanging jury cannot be squared with the Constitution. The State of Illinois has stacked the deck against the petitioner. To execute this death sentence would deprive him of his life without due process of law." In 1970, the Supreme Court returned to a lower court the case of William L. Maxwell, an Arkansas man sentenced to death in a rape case. The Court ordered that the penalty be set aside under its 1968 decision if it were determined that persons opposed to capital punishment had been excluded from the jury.[76] Other cases pending before the Supreme Court raised the constitutional issue of whether the Eighth Amendment's ban on "cruel and unusual punishments" prohibits the death penalty. Up to 1970, the Supreme Court had declined to face that constitutional question directly, but it was under increasing pressure to do so.

[73] Ronald Goldfarb, "A Brief For Preventive Detention," *New York Times Magazine,* March 1, 1970, p. 73.
[74] *New York Times,* July 12, 1969, pp. 1, 40.
[75] *Witherspoon v. Illinois,* 391 U.S. 510 (1968).
[76] *Maxwell v. Bishop,* 385 U.S. 650 (1970).

Capital punishment has been a controversial political issue, with some state governors favoring it as a means of "tough" law enforcement, but many others dreading the responsibility of taking a human life. During 1968 and 1969 there were no executions in the United States because the states delayed action while awaiting Supreme Court decisions on capital punishment.

The Trial. In Chapter 4, we discussed the broad range of rights to which accused persons are entitled under the Constitution as interpreted by the Supreme Court. Almost all of these rights now apply in the states as a result of Supreme Court interpretations of the Fourteenth Amendment.

Although procedures vary in different jurisdictions, in general, an arrested person is brought before a magistrate for a preliminary hearing at which he is either held, or released on bail. He may be assigned counsel if he cannot afford a private attorney. The district attorney or prosecutor may seek a grand jury indictment, or he presents the case to a judge who may issue an information, an official criminal charge made without action by a grand jury. Now formally accused, the defendant is arraigned— which means that the formal charges in the indictment or information are read to him—and he pleads guilty or not guilty. (In some cases he may plead "no contest" and put himself at the mercy of the court.) At every critical stage, a criminal suspect is entitled to have the advice of a lawyer, and defendants too poor to hire one must be offered or assigned counsel in serious criminal cases.

Jury trials are required in *federal* courts in all criminal cases and in all common law civil suits where the sum involved is larger than $20. Under a 1968 Supreme Court decision, *states* must also provide jury trials in "serious" criminal cases,[77] which the Supreme Court defined in 1970 as all cases in which the penalty for conviction could exceed six months.[78] Federal juries must render a unanimous verdict, but many states permit a less-than-unanimous verdict (usually by three-fourths of the jurors) in civil cases, and five states—Oregon, Louisiana, Texas, Montana, and Oklahoma—permit conviction by a split verdict in certain types of noncapital criminal cases. In 1970, the Supreme Court agreed to consider two cases testing whether a less-than-unanimous verdict in criminal cases in state courts was constitutional. At the federal level it is usually possible to waive the right to a jury trial, but many states do not permit this practice.

In 1970, for the first time, millions of Americans were able to watch a criminal trial on television.[79] The states of Colorado and Texas permit television cameras in the courtroom with the consent of all the parties.

[77] *Duncan v. Louisiana*, 391 U.S. 145 (1968).
[78] *Baldwin v. New York*, 399 U.S. 66 (1970).
[79] "Trial—The City and County of Denver vs. Lauren R. Watson," NET Journal, March 23–26, 1970.

Under this procedure, a film of the trial in Denver of a Black Panther leader charged with "resisting and interfering with a police officer" was broadcast over National Educational Television.

The televised trial provided an excellent illustration of courtroom procedure. First the jury was impaneled (in Denver, six men and women are chosen, rather than twelve), with the prosecution and the defense each having the right to challenge and replace prospective jurors.[80] The defense attorney complained bitterly that the jury was all white and included no young people—that for his black client it was not really a "jury of our peers." The prosecutor presented his case; the defense cross-examined the prosecution witnesses. Then the defense presented its own witnesses, who were cross-examined, in turn. Judge Zita Weinshienk was called on to make important procedural decisions at several points. Gradually, as the strategies of the defense and the prosecution emerged, the tension built up. Finally, the judge delivered her charge to the jury, explaining the law and emphasizing that the defendant's guilt must be proven beyond a reasonable doubt.

The white jury found the defendant, Lauren R. Watson, not guilty. But Watson argued to the television audience that this was not really "justice." He had this exchange with his attorney, Leonard Davies:

> *Watson:* See, that's exactly the point. The very fact that I am a black man . . . I could care less whether six white people that live on the other side of town think I'm guilty or not. . . . What the hell do I care what they think? . . . and yet they're sitting up here, you know, making decisions about my life. That's not justice. . . .
>
> *Davies:* But Lauren, how many trials have we had now? Five? Six? . . . You've been acquitted on each one, with the exception of one minor charge, right? Don't you think that after a while, aren't you going to start to decide maybe the system does work? We've been successful?
>
> *Watson:* The system does not work, because I'm still the victim. What has happened to the officers who brutalized me, surrounded my home . . . dragged me off to jail? They haven't been penalized for this trial. They get paid while they're sitting there, trying to get their lie together. It's a just system for white people. . . . Because the people who created the injustice in the first place were not on trial here today. The officers should have been on trial.[81]

The tumultuous trial of the "Chicago Seven" raised a host of new questions about the judicial process. The defendants sought to dramatize their political views by turning the Chicago courtroom of federal judge Julius J. Hoffman into a sort of theater of the absurd. Their hostility to-

---

[80] The constitutionality of six-man juries was upheld by the Supreme Court in *Williams v. Florida*, 399 U.S. 78 (1970).

[81] "Trial—The City and County of Denver vs. Lauren R. Watson," *The Final Day*, NET Journal, March 26, 1970, pp. 24–25.

ward the judge was matched only by his apparent distaste for the defendants and their views. The tense atmosphere in the courtroom grew worse when the attorney for Bobby Seale, chairman of the Black Panther party, became ill, and Judge Hoffman refused to grant Seale's request for a delay in his trial. When Hoffman also refused to permit Seale to act as his own attorney, Seale called the judge a "pig" and a "fascist." Hoffman had him bound and gagged, then declared his case a mistrial and sentenced him to four years for contempt. The remaining defendants did their best to disrupt the trial; they wore black robes to mock Hoffman, shouted "Heil Hitler" at the judge, and called him "Julie" and "Mr. Magoo."

In February 1970, after five months of hearing testimony, the jury found five of the defendants guilty of violating the federal antiriot law but acquitted all seven on conspiracy charges. Even before the jury had delivered its verdict, Judge Hoffman had sentenced the defendants and their lawyers to prison sentences, ranging from two months to four years, for contempt of court.

The statute under which the Chicago defendants were tried made it a crime to cross state lines with "intent" to "incite a riot." Some legal scholars regarded the law a clear violation of the First Amendment's guarantees of free speech and assembly. Regardless of how the Supreme Court might eventually rule on the constitutionality of the law, the trial posed the difficult additional question of how the courts should cope with disorder in the courtroom. Shortly after the jury's verdict, the Supreme Court, in a separate case, ruled that trial judges could deal with a disorderly defendant in three ways: punish him for contempt, remove him from the courtroom while the trial continued, at least until he agreed to "conduct himself properly," or as a last resort, "bind and gag him." [82]

ORGANIZED CRIME

In 1970, a flurry of federal indictments, along with tape recordings of "bugged" conversations made public by the FBI, suggested the extent of the power of organized crime in Newark, New Jersey. Much of the power in Newark, at least according to these documents, was wielded not by the elected mayor, Hugh Addonizio, but by the local crime chieftain, Anthony ("Tony Boy") Boiardo, heir to a crime empire built by his father, Ruggiero ("Richie the Boot") Boiardo.[83]

The FBI transcripts included these conversations between Angelo ("Gyp") De Carlo and an associate named "Joe":

[82] *Illinois v. Allen*, 397 U.S. 337 (1970).
[83] Fred J. Cook, "The People v. the Mob; Or, Who Rules New Jersey?" *New York Times Magazine*, February 1, 1970.

Joe: You know . . . it's going to take three weeks but we'll own this Hughie [Addonizio]. This guy here. I'll guarantee we'll own him. I'll use that term—in three or four weeks. . . .

Ray: Hughie [Addonizio] helped us along. He give us the city.[84]

According to another tape-recorded conversation, "Tony Boy" and De Carlo discussed an important question—who should be appointed police director of Newark. "Tony Boy" said the decision was up to De Carlo.[85] Summoned before a federal grand jury, the mayor of Newark invoked his constitutional immunity and declined to answer any questions about his alleged ties with the mob. In July 1970, after losing the mayoralty race to Kenneth Gibson (who became the first black mayor of Newark), Addonizio, along with four codefendants, was convicted of extorting money from a contractor doing work for the city. The contractor testified that racketeer Anthony Boiardo had ordered him to pay the kickbacks. He said Boiardo had been described to him by a city official as "the real boss of Newark." [86] Addonizio was sentenced to ten years in prison and fined $25,000.

The power of organized crime in Newark was not a complete surprise; after the 1967 riots in that city's black ward, a state investigating commission listed as an underlying cause "a pervasive feeling of corruption" in Newark.[87] And Henry S. Ruth, Jr., who had served as deputy staff director of the President's Crime Commission, told a state legislative committee: "Official corruption in New Jersey is so bad that organized crime can get almost anything it desires." [88]

There is still argument over whether organized crime in America should be called the Mafia, the Cosa Nostra, the mob, or the syndicate, but there is no longer any doubt that it exists on a major scale. (In 1970, Attorney General Mitchell, in a memo to the Justice Department and the FBI, asked that the terms Mafia and Cosa Nostra be dropped because they gave "gratuitous offense" to law-abiding Italian Americans.) Organized crime controls gambling, loan sharking, narcotics, and other illegal activities. It also owns legitimate businesses and infiltrates labor unions. In some instances, it corrupts public officials by paying them to permit the mob to operate.

And organized crime is big business—illegal betting on numbers and on horse races and other sports events may total $20 billion a year. From such gambling activities, its biggest source of income, the crime syndicate reaps a profit officially put as high as $7 billion annually.[89]

The President's Crime Commission has estimated that the mob op-

[84] *New York Times*, January 7, 1970, p. 28.
[85] Cook, "The People v. the Mob; Or, Who Rules New Jersey?" p. 36.
[86] *Washington Post*, July 23, 1970, p. 1 and June 24, 1970, p. A3.
[87] Cook, "The People v. the Mob; Or, Who Rules New Jersey?" p. 33.
[88] *Ibid.*, p. 34.
[89] *The Challenge of Crime in a Free Society*, p. 189.

THE COST OF CORRUPTION

Narcotics dealers, gamblers and businessmen make illicit payments of millions of dollars a year to the policemen of New York, according to policemen, law-enforcement experts and New Yorkers who make such payments themselves. . . .

A detective with many years of experience in the narcotics division said one of his colleagues had arranged payoffs to the police from major heroin dealers of up to $50,000, in return for such favors as the destruction of evidence gathered on secret wiretaps. . . .

Some aspects of police corruption in New York and the related costs were discussed recently in a report by the Joint Legislative Committee on Crime. The committee charged that gambling in the slums of New York "could not function without official tolerance induced by corruption. . . . ghetto residents are perfectly aware of the corrupt relationship between racketeers and certain elements in the Police Department, and, for this reason, have a

deep cynicism concerning the integrity of the police in maintaining law and order in the community."

Another aspect emerged in the anger of a Brooklyn bookmaker who complained that the plainclothes men he regularly bribed continued to demand payments even after they had been transferred out of gambling enforcement to the narcotics division. He said his payment was $1,200 a month, divided by four levels of the department including one unit at headquarters. . . .

Putting an exact price tag on corruption is impossible. The Joint Legislative Committee on Crime recently reported, however, that the city's 10,000 small Puerto Rican grocery stores were estimated to give the police $6.2-million a year in small weekly payments and free food to avoid summonses on minor charges.

Numbers operators, according to Federal and state agencies and private researchers' estimates, make payoffs between $7-million and $15-million a year.

—David Burnham, "Graft Paid to Police Here Said to Run Into Millions,"
New York Times, April 25, 1970.

erates in 80 percent of all cities of more than one million residents.[90] In 1969, President Nixon declared: "Investigations of the national crime syndicate, La Cosa Nostra, show its membership at some 5,000 divided into 24 'families' around the nation."[91] According to the Crime Commission, each "family" is organized to resemble the structure of the Mafia that has operated for more than a century in Sicily: a "boss" at the top; an underboss; a counselor; several lieutenants; beneath them, the "soldiers" or "button men"; an "enforcer" whose job is "the maiming and killing of recalcitrant members," and a "corrupter" who buys off public officials. (See Figure 13-4.) "The highest ruling body of the twenty-four families is the 'commission,'" a combination supreme court and board of directors composed of nine to twelve of the most powerful bosses.[92]

"All available data indicate that organized crime flourishes only where it has corrupted local officials," the President's Crime Commission has emphasized.[93] Donald R. Cressey, a sociologist and an expert on organized

[90] *The Challenge of Crime in a Free Society*, p. 191.
[91] President Nixon's message to Congress on organized crime, *New York Times*, April 24, 1969, p. 30.
[92] *The Challenge of Crime in a Free Society*, pp. 193–94.
[93] *Ibid.*, p. 191.

FIGURE 13-4

An Organized Crime Family

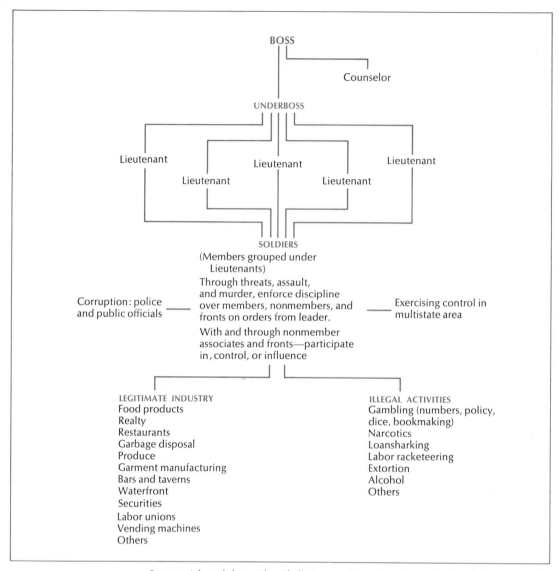

BOSS

Counselor

UNDERBOSS

Lieutenant   Lieutenant   Lieutenant

Lieutenant   Lieutenant

SOLDIERS
(Members grouped under
Lieutenants)

Corruption: police
and public officials

Through threats, assault,
and murder, enforce discipline
over members, nonmembers, and
fronts on orders from leader.

Exercising control in
multistate area

With and through nonmember
associates and fronts—participate
in, control, or influence

LEGITIMATE INDUSTRY
Food products
Realty
Restaurants
Garbage disposal
Produce
Garment manufacturing
Bars and taverns
Waterfront
Securities
Labor unions
Vending machines
Others

ILLEGAL ACTIVITIES
Gambling (numbers, policy,
dice, bookmaking)
Narcotics
Loansharking
Labor racketeering
Extortion
Alcohol
Others

Source: Adapted from *The Challenge of Crime in a Free Society*, A Report by the President's Commission on Law Enforcement and Administration of Justice (Washington, D.C.: U.S. Government Printing Office, 1967), p. 194.

crime, reports that in one instance a United States congressman resigned when ordered to do so by a crime boss: "In this district, Cosa Nostra also 'owns' both judges and the officials who assign criminal cases to judges. About 90 percent of the organized-crime defendants appear before the same few judges." [94]

[94] Donald R. Cressey, *Theft of the Nation* (New York: Harper & Row, 1969), pp. 252–53.

Despite efforts by the Federal Government in recent decades to combat organized crime, President Nixon reported in 1969: "Not a single one of the 24 Cosa Nostra families has been destroyed. They are more firmly entrenched and more secure than ever before." [95]

Organized crime could not thrive if the public did not demand the services it provides, and if law enforcement and elected officials refused to be bought. Corruption of the political system is the most disturbing threat posed by the mob. And the President's Crime Commission maintains, "The extraordinary thing about organized crime is that America has tolerated it for so long." [96]

JUSTICE AND THE AMERICAN POLITICAL SYSTEM

Although the Supreme Court and the Constitution may seem remote from the lives of most citizens, the decisions of the Court—the ultimate outputs of the system of justice—have direct, immediate relevance for the individuals involved and much broader meaning for the political system as a whole. In 1969, for example, the power of the Supreme Court meant that Dick Gregory could not be convicted of disorderly conduct in Chicago while taking part in a peaceful protest. For Mrs. Susan Epperson, a high school teacher from Little Rock, it meant she could teach Darwinian theory in Arkansas. For Robert Eli Stanley, of Atlanta, it meant he could watch all the orgies he wished on eight-millimeter stag films in the privacy of his home. For Ted Steven Chimel of Santa Ana, California, it meant that he could not be convicted of burglary on the basis of evidence seized when police ransacked his house without a warrant.

The list is much longer. Although each case affected only one person directly, the implications for society as a whole are obvious: in *Chimel* the Supreme Court was saying, for example, that the Bill of Rights means that *no* American can be convicted if police burst into his house without a warrant and search it from top to bottom for evidence. That is a rather important distinction between a democracy and a police state.

The decisions of the Supreme Court have great *political* significance for society. In the field of civil rights, the Warren Court was well ahead of the executive branch or Congress. The other branches of government had not acted to remedy inequality of representation; with its reapportionment decisions the Court stepped in to provide the remedy. Of the three branches of the Federal Government, the Supreme Court has, in recent decades, often proved to be the most dynamic and responsive to change.

[95] President Nixon's message to Congress on organized crime, p. 30.
[96] *The Challenge of Crime in a Free Society*, p. 209.

Because its power rests on public opinion, the Court cannot get too far ahead of the country, but it can, in the words of Archibald Cox, attempt to respond to the "dominant needs of the time."[97] And it can also serve as the conscience of the nation and a guardian of minorities, the poor, and the forgotten.[98]

There are serious inequalities and flaws in the American system of justice, as we have seen—backlogged criminal courts and a bail system that penalizes the poor and minorities; plea bargaining in the place of trial by jury; some judges and officials who are puppets for organized crime; prisons that do not rehabilitate. Some of these problems can, of course, be solved by specific reforms—bringing defendants to trial more rapidly by appointing more judges, strengthening law enforcement, improving facilities for handling juvenile offenders, and so forth. But the President's Crime Commission also concluded that "the most significant action that can be taken against crime is action designed to eliminate slums and ghettos, to improve education, to provide jobs. . . . We will not have dealt effectively with crime until we have alleviated the conditions that stimulate it."[99]

Ultimately, as Justice Jackson perceived, the third branch of government, the judiciary, maintains "the great system of balances upon which our free government is based"—the balances between the various parts of the federal system, between authority and liberty, and between the rule of the majority and the rights of the individual.[100] Chief Justice Earl Warren confessed on the day he retired that performing this task is extremely difficult, "because we have no constituency. . . . We serve only the public interest as we see it, guided only by the Constitution and our own conscience."[101]

The resolution of conflict in American society through law, rather than through force, depends upon public confidence in the courts and the process of justice. But confidence in the system of justice requires that the words "Equal Justice Under Law" carved in marble over the entrance to the Supreme Court be translated into reality at every level of the system.

[97] Cox, *The Warren Court*, p. 5.
[98] See, for example, Justice Black's opinion in *Chambers v. Florida*, 309 U.S. 227 (1940).
[99] *The Challenge of Crime in a Free Society*, p. 15.
[100] Jackson, *The Supreme Court in the American System of Government*, p. 61.
[101] *New York Times*, June 24, 1969, p. C24.

SUGGESTED READING

Abraham, Henry J. *The Judicial Process*,* 2nd edition (Oxford University Press, 1968). A very useful general introduction to the American judicial process. Explains the operations of local, state, and federal courts and the legal system, and compares the United States judicial system with that of other countries.

Bickel, Alexander. *The Supreme Court and the Idea of Progress* * (Harper and Row, 1970). A critical and detailed assessment of some of the major areas of judicial decision-making by the Warren Court. Argues that the Court went further than was prudent in a number of decisions with controversial public-policy consequences.

Campbell, James S., Sahid, Joseph R., and Stang, David P. *Law and Order Reconsidered*, Staff Report to the National Commission on the Causes and Prevention of Violence (U.S. Government Printing Office, 1969; Bantam, 1970). Paperback. A task force report to a presidential commission, analyzing crime, social protest, law enforcement, and flaws in the American system of criminal justice. Includes a valuable chapter on role conflicts and social attitudes of police.

The Challenge of Crime in a Free Society, A Report by the President's Commission on Law Enforcement and Administration of Justice (U.S. Government Printing Office, 1967; Avon, 1968). Paperback. A wide-ranging and informative analysis of the extent and consequences of crime in the United States. Supplemented by nine task force reports on specific aspects of crime in America.

Clark, Ramsey. *Crime in America: Observations on Its Nature, Causes, Prevention, and Control* (Simon and Schuster, 1970). A broad indictment of the system of criminal justice in the United States, especially the police departments, the courts, and the prisons. The author, a former Attorney General in the Johnson administration, stresses the social roots of crime.

Cressey, Donald R. *Theft of a Nation* * (Harper and Row, 1969). A comprehensive study of organized crime in the United States by a sociologist who served as consultant to the President's Crime Commission. Describes the corruption of law enforcement and government by organized crime.

Graham, Fred P. *The Self-Inflicted Wound* (Macmillan, 1970). A perceptive analysis of the Supreme Court's controversial decisions protecting the rights of criminal suspects. Concludes that the Supreme Court cannot, by itself, police the police.

McCloskey, Robert G. *The American Supreme Court* (University of Chicago Press, 1960). A lucid and penetrating analysis of the role of the Supreme Court in the American system of government.

Murphy, Walter F. *Elements of Judicial Strategy* (University of Chicago Press, 1964). An informative study of the nature of judicial decision-making and its consequences for public policy. Analyzes the Supreme Court's role as a major decision-maker in the political system.

Shubert, Glendon. *Judicial Policy-Making* * (Scott Foresman, 1965). An introduction to the role the judiciary plays in the making of public policy. Applies systems theory to the activities of the courts.

To Establish Justice, To Insure Domestic Tranquility, Final Report of the National Commission on the Causes and Prevention of Violence (U.S. Government Printing Office, 1969; Bantam, 1970). Paperback. Final report of a presidential commission appointed to explore violence in American society. Deals with the history of violence in the nation, crime, civil disobedience, political violence, and assassinations.

* Available in paperback edition

PART FOUR

Government in Operation

14

Foreign Policy

and National Security

On May 1, 1970, angry student anti-war demonstrations took place on several college campuses across the nation. At the same time, Washington was enveloped in an atmosphere of crisis. The morning headlines told why: in a televised address to the nation the previous night, President Nixon had unexpectedly announced that American troops in Vietnam had crossed the border and were attacking Communist forces inside Cambodia. "This is not an invasion of Cambodia," the President said, but many of his critics in and out of Congress disagreed; they charged that the President had widened the war in Southeast Asia and had done so without consulting Congress.

Four days after Mr. Nixon's decision, Ohio national guardsmen who had been sent to Kent State University to curb campus unrest, shot and killed four students and wounded eleven others. The tragedy solidified campus opposition to the President, bringing together radicals and mod-

547

A girl cries out in grief as she kneels beside one of four students killed when national guardsmen opened fire at Kent State University in May 1970.

erates, students and faculty. The students' anger was aggravated by Mr. Nixon's reference to students who used violence as "these bums." [1]

After Interior Secretary Walter J. Hickel sent an extraordinarily blunt letter to the President, warning that the administration had lost touch with American students, the President hastily met with student groups and university presidents and held a press conference to try to cool the anti-administration feeling on the campuses. On May 9, some 75,000 to 100,000 persons took part in an orderly protest demonstration on the ellipse, just south of the White House. Tragedy struck anew less than a week later when two black students were killed, and twelve wounded, as Mississippi highway patrolmen and police opened fire on a group of students outside a dormitory at Jackson State College, in Jackson, Mississippi. Protests were

[1] *Washington Post*, May 2, 1970, p. 1.

held on more than 400 college campuses in the wake of the two shootings, and some colleges shut down for a time. The country was sharply divided over Cambodia, and it was apparent that the President had not anticipated the intensity of the reaction to his decision to deploy American troops there. (Later in 1970, Nixon fired Hickel, in part because of his outspoken letter.)

On the night that President Nixon announced his critical move into Cambodia, the war in Vietnam had already claimed more than 40,000 American lives. Polls indicated that a majority of Americans considered the United States' involvement in Vietnam to have been a mistake.[2] The war had directly influenced President Johnson's decision to leave the White House; now it had created political risks for President Nixon.

Yet the President's foreign policy problems on that day were not limited to the war in Southeast Asia. The front pages that told of the move into Cambodia also reported new danger in the Middle East: Israel, claiming that Soviet pilots were flying Russian planes for Egypt, was renewing its demands for United States jet fighters. The House of Representatives was debating Nixon's request to widen the Safeguard Anti-Ballistic Missile system.[3] And in Vienna, United States and Russian representatives were holding another round of Strategic Arms Limitation Talks (SALT), in a new effort to curb the onrushing nuclear arms race.

This mix of developments on a single day in the 1970's illustrates some of the complex, paradoxical elements faced by a President in conducting the nation's foreign policy: attempting to extricate the United States from a protracted war in Indo-China, the President felt it necessary to enlarge its geographic boundaries; at the same time, he had to devote attention to the danger of war in the Middle East. While negotiating at Vienna to reduce the nuclear "balance of terror," he was also pushing deployment of the ABM—and all this while measuring domestic political consequences and juggling congressional and student opposition.

Not long before, President Nixon had sent to Congress an unprecedented "State of the World" message, setting forth his view of America's foreign policy and military goals.[4] The 40,000-word document indicated that America in the 1970's would assist friendly nations but would no

---

[2] For example, a Gallup Poll of June 1970 indicated that 56 percent of the public considered that the United States had made "a mistake" in sending troops to Vietnam. The percentage of people who answered "yes" when asked "Do you think the United States made a mistake sending troops to fight in Vietnam?" rose above 50 percent for the first time in August 1968, and remained above 50 percent thereafter. A Louis Harris poll made public in May 1970, reported that 50 percent of the public thought that "President Nixon was right in ordering the military operation into Cambodia"; 43 percent had "serious doubts" and 7 percent were "not sure."

[3] *New York Times*, May 1, 1970, p. 1.

[4] "President's message on foreign policy for the 1970's," *Congressional Quarterly, Weekly Report*, February 20, 1970, pp. 516–45.

longer do so alone. "Others now have the ability and responsibility to deal with local disputes which once might have required our intervention," the message declared.

But the President's controversial decision to attack Communist forces in Cambodia came only two months later. That decision, which the President asserted was necessary to protect American troops in Vietnam, illustrated not only how deeply America had become involved in affairs far from its shores; it also demonstrated how easily American power can be committed by presidential action alone. Congress took no part in the decision announced by the President.

These factors disturbed many Americans because of the new and terrifying dimension added to the conduct of international relations since the Second World War. For the first time in the history of man, nations possess the technological power to destroy each other. The threat of nuclear annihilation overshadows all other foreign policy considerations; for small wars now carry the potential of growing out of control into nuclear war. All men, everywhere, share the peril. There is, as Senator Fulbright has suggested, "a kind of madness in the dialogue of the nuclear age," for how can nations and people really achieve security in the atomic era? [5]

Against this background, we may ask: What is foreign policy? Who makes it? What should America's objectives be in its relations with the rest of the world? How much of the nation's resources should go into defense spending? How, in a democratic society, can people make their views felt and influence foreign policy? What are the dangers posed to American institutions by a multibillion dollar defense budget?

THE UNITED STATES AND WORLD AFFAIRS

American
Foreign Policy

Foreign policy is the sum of the goals, decisions, and actions that govern a nation's relations with the rest of the world. But the world changes, and so does foreign policy. A President may adopt one policy only to discard it later; a new President may reverse the policies of his predecessor. Alliances shift; the Soviet Union, America's ally against Nazi Germany in the Second World War, became its principal adversary in the "Cold War" that began soon afterward. Japan, America's wartime enemy, became its peacetime ally, as did West Germany.

Moreover, foreign policy goals may conflict. For example, containment of communism is a goal that has characterized American foreign policy in the postwar world; yet, at the same time, the United States has also supported the principle of "self-determination," the right of nations to choose

[5] J. W. Fulbright, *Old Myths and New Realities* (New York: Random House, 1964), p. 54.

their own form of government free of outside interference. What should American foreign policy be when, in exercising the right of self-determination, a nation chooses a Communist leader? Other goals may also appear contradictory; United States support of the principles of freedom and democratic government, for example, collides with the economic and military aid it has given to dictatorships in Latin America and Greece.

So "foreign policy" is an elusive and changing concept. Roger Hilsman, a former Assistant Secretary of State, has suggested that the problem of foreign policy is not so much one of relating decisions to a single set of goals as it is "precisely one of choosing goals" in the midst of onrushing events and crises, and of reconciling the advocates of competing goals and policies. "The making of foreign policy," he concluded, "is a political process." [6]

The preservation of national security is a basic consideration in the formulation of foreign policy. But "national security" is so broad a term that it can be used to justify almost any action that a nation or a President takes. Paul H. Nitze, a former high official of the State and Defense departments, has suggested that there are two approaches to the question of national security and American foreign policy. One view emphasizes United States security and "the direct threat to that security" posed by the power of Communist or unfriendly nations. Another regards the interests and security of the United States as dependent on some form of world order "compatible with our values and interests." [7] This second view of American foreign policy holds that there can be no real security for the United States without world peace and security for all people.

Yet security is a relative term in the thermonuclear age. During the Cuban missile crisis of 1962, President Kennedy's advisers knew that their decisions, if wrong, "could mean the destruction of the human race." [8] So any description of national security and foreign policy must take into account the changed nature of the world since the beginning of the atomic age.

Since the Second World War, the United States and the Soviet Union have dominated the world stage. The two superpowers have confronted each other and sometimes clashed in Europe, the Middle East, Cuba, and other parts of the world. And twice since 1945, the United States has fought a protracted war against Communist power in Asia. Confronted with often hostile, armed Communist nations, the United States has maintained a high level of military strength. American policy-makers have argued that this

[6] Roger Hilsman, *To Move a Nation* (Garden City, N.Y.: Doubleday, 1967), pp. 12–13, 541.
[7] Paul H. Nitze, "The Secretary and the Execution of Foreign Policy," in Don K. Price, ed., *The Secretary of State*, prepared for the American Assembly, Columbia University (Englewood Cliffs, N.J.: Prentice-Hall, 1960), pp. 6–7.
[8] Robert F. Kennedy, *Thirteen Days* (New York: Norton, 1969), p. 44.

costly arms burden must be borne to protect the national security, American liberties at home, and the freedom of other nations. Only the shield of American power, they have contended, has prevented Communist expansion to a degree that would threaten American security.

At the same time, military preparedness has created several paradoxes. The spiraling arms race threatens the future of all mankind. And America faces the problem of how to balance its military needs against social needs at home. Billions of dollars that might, in part at least, have been used for education, housing, transportation, and similar programs, have been siphoned off into arms. A "military-industrial complex" spawned to protect American security has created numerous problems for American society.

Some critics of American foreign policy have focused on what Senator Fulbright has called an "excessive moralism." [9] Especially in the 1950's when John Foster Dulles served as Secretary of State under President Eisenhower, the rhetoric and sometimes the reality of American foreign policy took on the aspect of a missionary crusade against communism. The Vietnam war illustrated the limits of American world power, and by the 1970's much of the crusading zeal that had marked the nation's foreign policy had given way to a more cautious, less moralistic approach. President Nixon said in 1970: "We will view new commitments in the light of a careful assessment of our own national interests . . . and of our capacity to counter . . . threats at an acceptable risk and cost." [10]

The Historical Setting

It would be impossible to review the entire history of United States foreign policy in these pages, but some recurring strands and major themes that are relevant to today's world may be sketched.

One deeply rooted historical characteristic of American foreign policy was that of *isolationism*. President George Washington declared that it was the nation's policy "to steer clear of permanent alliance," and Jefferson said that America wanted peace with all nations, "entangling alliances with none."

During the nineteenth century, the diplomats of Europe maneuvered to preserve the "balance of power" in the Old World; America, protected by the broad Atlantic, could afford to remain relatively aloof from the problems of Europe. In 1823, the Monroe Doctrine warned European powers to keep out of the Western Hemisphere and pledged that the United States would not intervene in the internal affairs of Europe. American isolation, of course, was only relative. The United States fought a war with Great Britain in 1812; it annexed Texas in a war with Mexico in 1846; and it acquired Puerto Rico and Guam in the Spanish-American War in 1898 (as

---

[9] Fulbright, *Old Myths and New Realities*, p. 45.
[10] "President's message on foreign policy for the 1970's," p. 517.

well as the Philippines, which gained independence in 1946). However, the United States did not become a major colonial power, with vast overseas territories, on a scale comparable to Great Britain or some of the nations of Europe.

By the end of the nineteenth century, an opposite strand of American foreign policy, that of *interventionism*, was visible. In the early twentieth century, the United States practiced "gunboat diplomacy," intervening militarily in Mexico, the Caribbean, and Latin America. The First World War brought major United States military involvement in Europe for the first time. After the war, however, the United States declined to join with other countries in the League of Nations. Woodrow Wilson's dream of world order was shattered, and America retreated "back to normalcy" and isolationism.

But during the Second World War, the United States emerged in the position of a great world power. America traded its former position of isolationism for one of *internationalism*.

A world weary of war and destruction centered its hopes for peace on the United Nations, created in 1945. It quickly became clear, however, that the future of the postwar world would be shaped not in the UN but in the relations between the two major powers, the United States and the Soviet Union. At a speech at Fulton, Missouri, in March 1946, Winston Churchill declared that from the Baltic to the Adriatic seas, "an iron curtain has descended across the continent." In retrospect, it became clear that a "Cold War" had begun.

During this period, the United States adopted a policy of *containment* of the Soviet Union, first elaborated in an article in the quarterly, *Foreign Affairs,* by George F. Kennan, a senior American diplomat who later became ambassador to Russia. Kennan, who was a State Department official in 1947 when the article was published, signed his name "X" to preserve his anonymity. The article set forth a doctrine that became "the Bible of Western foreign policy in the mid-twentieth century." [11] Kennan argued that the Soviet Union would expand its power wherever it could to challenge Western institutions. He advocated that United States policy toward the Soviet Union be one of "firm and vigilant containment of Russian expansive tendencies." [12]

In the immediate aftermath of the Second World War, the United States moved to counterbalance Soviet power. Under the "Truman Doctrine," Washington began a program of military aid to Greece, which was fighting Communist guerrillas, and Turkey, which was under pressure to cede military bases to the Soviet Union. As enunciated by President

[11] H. Bradford Westerfield, *The Instruments of America's Foreign Policy* (New York: Crowell, 1963), p. 165.
[12] Mr. X, "The Sources of Soviet Conduct," *Foreign Affairs,* July 1947, pp. 566–82.

Robert Censoni
Copyright 1970 Saturday Review, Inc.

"The First World War's connected to the Second World War. The Second World War's connected to the Korean War. The Korean War's connected to the Vietnam War. The Vietnam War . . ."

Truman, the doctrine declared that American security and world peace depended on United States protection for the "free peoples of the world." [13]

In the summer of 1947, the United States launched the Marshall Plan (named for its creator, Secretary of State George C. Marshall) and poured more than $13 billion in four years into Western Europe to speed its postwar economic and social recovery. The Soviet Union and other Eastern European nations declined to join the Marshall Plan.

In 1949, the United States and many of the nations of Western Europe joined the North Atlantic Treaty Organization (NATO), whose members were pledged to defend each other against attack. NATO was the first and most important of a series of postwar collective security pacts signed by the United States. These arrangements were greatly expanded during the Eisenhower administration. By 1970, the United States was pledged under security pacts to defend forty-three nations. (See Figure 14-1.)

Although America was preoccupied with European recovery and collective security, and with containing Soviet expansion, it was in the Pacific that a new war broke out only five years after the end of the Second World

[13] Harry S. Truman, *Memoirs by Harry S. Truman*, Vol. II, *Years of Trial and Hope* (Garden City, N.Y.: Doubleday, 1958), p. 106.

FIGURE 14-1

United States Collective Security Pacts

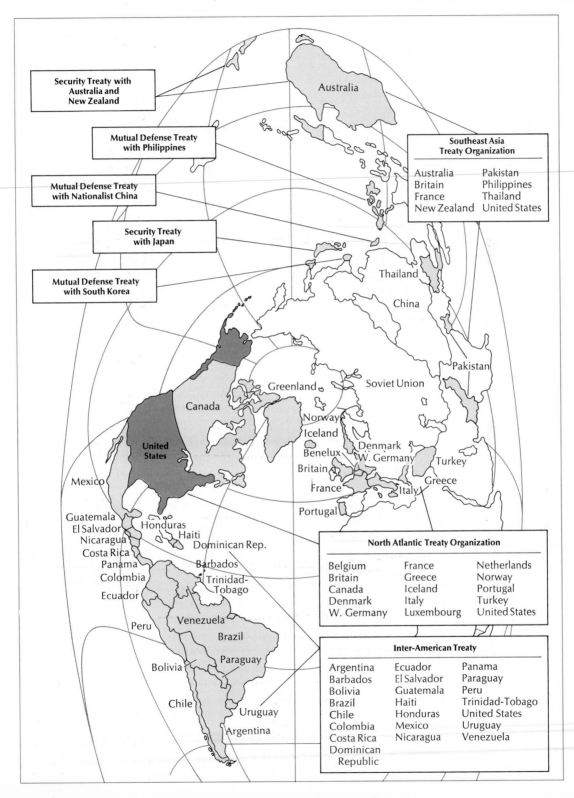

Security Treaty with Australia and New Zealand

Mutual Defense Treaty with Philippines

Mutual Defense Treaty with Nationalist China

Security Treaty with Japan

Mutual Defense Treaty with South Korea

Australia

Southeast Asia Treaty Organization

Australia	Pakistan
Britain	Philippines
France	Thailand
New Zealand	United States

Thailand

China

Greenland

Canada

Norway
Iceland
Denmark
Benelux
W. Germany
Britain
France
Italy
Portugal
Turkey
Greece

Soviet Union

Pakistan

United States

Mexico

Guatemala
El Salvador
Nicaragua
Costa Rica
Panama
Colombia
Ecuador

Honduras
Haiti
Dominican Rep.
Barbados
Trinidad-Tobago

Venezuela

Brazil

Peru

Bolivia

Paraguay

Chile

Uruguay

Argentina

North Atlantic Treaty Organization

Belgium	France	Netherlands
Britain	Greece	Norway
Canada	Iceland	Portugal
Denmark	Italy	Turkey
W. Germany	Luxembourg	United States

Inter-American Treaty

Argentina	Ecuador	Panama
Barbados	El Salvador	Paraguay
Bolivia	Guatemala	Peru
Brazil	Haiti	Trinidad-Tobago
Chile	Honduras	United States
Colombia	Mexico	Uruguay
Costa Rica	Nicaragua	Venezuela
Dominican Republic		

War. During the Korean War (1950–53), the United States became involved for the first time in a land war in Asia.

New forces, sometimes obscured by the rhetoric of the Cold War, were loose in the world. The United States, the sole nuclear power at the end of the Second World War, lost that advantage when the Soviet Union acquired atomic weapons in 1949. At the same time, however, world Communist unity began to come apart. As early as 1948, Yugoslavia's President Tito had broken with the Soviet Union, and in the next two decades the Soviet Union encountered increasing difficulties in maintaining its power in Eastern Europe. By 1962, Russia and its former ally, Communist China, were open and bitter adversaries.

During the same postwar period, a rising tide of *nationalism* brought independence to various nations in Africa, Asia, and the Middle East and stirred political currents in Latin America. In 1947, India and Pakistan gained their independence from Britain, and in 1949, Indonesia became free of Dutch control. The 1960's saw a second wave of nationalism in Africa. As European powers withdrew from what remained of their nineteenth-century colonial empires, the "Third World" became a new battleground in which the United States, the Soviet Union, and Communist China competed for influence and power. By the 1970's, Africa had declined as an arena of Cold War conflict, but the United States and the Soviet Union competed for power in the Middle East. In many of these areas of the globe, poverty, hunger, disease, illiteracy, and political instability were combined in a volatile mixture.

In Vietnam, the United States gradually moved into the power vacuum created when the French withdrew from Indo-China following their defeat in 1954 by Ho Chi Minh's forces at Dienbienphu. Presidents Eisenhower and Kennedy supported the government of South Vietnam, and Kennedy sent 16,000 troops there as "advisers," but it was President Johnson who, in 1965, committed the United States to full-scale war against Communist North Vietnam and the National Liberation Front, or Vietcong.

The policy of containment still conditioned American thinking. Townsend Hoopes, a former Defense Department official, describing President Johnson's plunge into Vietnam, has observed: "Like everyone else in the United States over forty, the President's advisers were children of the Cold War." [14]

Johnson proclaimed that "the grasping ambition of Asian commu-

[14] Townsend Hoopes, *The Limits of Intervention* (New York: David McKay, 1969), p. 9.

nism" would "certainly imperil the security of the United States itself" unless the United States stood firm in Vietnam.[15] Assured by his military and civilian advisers that superior United States airpower, firepower, and ground forces would quickly defeat a small nation such as North Vietnam, Johnson ordered the bombing of North Vietnam and committed half a million American troops to South Vietnam. The cost was high, in lives as well as in other ways.

More than $125 billion was poured into the longest war in American history. The Vietnam issue divided the nation and cast a shadow over the quality of American life. President Nixon, having pledged to end the war, began what he promised would be a complete withdrawal of American combat ground forces from Vietnam. Regardless of the outcome, the costly United States involvement in Southeast Asia would surely have a lasting impact on American politics and foreign policy. For the nation was engaged in a major military undertaking that no longer enjoyed a wide base of popular support. At the same time, the lengthy war caused many Americans to become disillusioned with the workings of the political system itself. For that reason alone, the cost of the Vietnam war may be felt for many years to come.

HOW FOREIGN POLICY IS MADE

The President
and
Foreign Policy

In the field of foreign affairs, as President Kennedy once remarked, "the President bears the burden of the responsibility. . . . The advisers may move on to new advice."[16]

In Chapter 10 we noted that the President is both Chief Diplomat and Commander in Chief. Particularly in the twentieth century, the two roles overlap. National security, foreign policy, and domestic programs are closely related because the President must decide how much money to allocate for each area within the overall framework of his annual budget. A large defense budget means less money for meeting priorities at home; and the level of defense expenditures affects the economy. As a Senate subcommittee headed by Senator Henry M. Jackson put it: "The boundary between foreign and domestic policy has almost been erased."[17]

[15] Press Conference, July 28, 1965, in *Public Papers of the Presidents of the United States, Lyndon B. Johnson, 1965* (Washington, D.C.: U.S. Government Printing Office, 1966), p. 794.

[16] Television and Radio Interview: "After Two Years—a Conversation With the President," December 17, 1962, in *Public Papers of the Presidents of the United States, John F. Kennedy, 1962* (Washington, D.C.: U.S. Government Printing Office, 1963), p. 889.

[17] "Basic Issues," Subcommittee on National Security Staffing and Operations, Committee on Government Operations, United States Senate, in *Administration of National Security* (Washington, D.C.: U.S. Government Printing Office, 1965), p. 7.

The President has the responsibility of deciding whether to use nuclear weapons. In Richard Neustadt's words, the President "lives daily with the knowledge that at any time he, personally, may have to make a human judgment . . . which puts half the world in jeopardy." [18]

The vast power of the President in the realm of foreign policy carries with it great risks—risks that a President will exercise his judgment unwisely, or that he will act without public or congressional support. By 1970, after five years of combat by American troops in Vietnam, substantial segments of both the public and Congress were deeply concerned over the extent of presidential power to commit the American people to war.

In conducting the nation's foreign and military policies, the President must often choose among conflicting advice as he makes his decisions. "The State Department wants to solve everything with words, and the generals, with guns," President Johnson was quoted as saying.[19] A President's background, experience, and beliefs may strongly influence his attitude toward foreign affairs. President Johnson, for example, had not been identified with international affairs as a senator, and as President he might have preferred to concentrate on building a "Great Society" at home. In time, however, the Vietnam war overshadowed and restricted his domestic programs and his Presidency.

> Together we shall save our planet, or together we shall perish in its flames.
>
> —John F. Kennedy, address to the General Assembly of the United Nations, September 25, 1961.

LBJ AND FOREIGN POLICY: WRONG COLLEGE?

The Eastern intellectuals still bothered him. . . . He was serious one afternoon when he said very early in his Presidency, "I'm not sure whether I can lead this country and keep it together, with my background." He paused during one of those soul-cleansings after the day's work was done and looked far off and in a very subdued voice said, "I do not think that I will ever get credit for anything I do in foreign policy, no matter how successful, because I did not go to Harvard."

—Hugh Sidey, *A Very Personal Presidency: Lyndon Johnson in the White House.*

[18] Richard E. Neustadt, testimony to Subcommittee on National Security Staffing and Operations, Committee on Government Operations, United States Senate, March 25, 1963, in *Administration of National Security*, p. 76.
[19] Eric F. Goldman, *The Tragedy of Lyndon Johnson* (New York: Knopf, 1969), p. 383.

Congress
and
Foreign Policy

Under the Constitution, power to conduct foreign and military affairs is divided between Congress and the President. While the Constitution gave the President power to appoint ambassadors and command the armed forces, Congress was given power to declare war, raise and support armies, and appropriate money for defense; and the Senate was granted power to approve or disapprove treaties made by the President.

But the Constitution does not spell out the boundaries of the power that each branch shall exercise. The result has been intermittent conflict between the President and Congress over foreign policy. At various times in history, one branch has dominated. Since the Second World War, Congress has lost to the President much of its war power and control over foreign policy. In the late 1960's and early 1970's, as a result of the increasing unpopularity of the war in Vietnam, a movement began in Congress to try to restore some war power to the legislative branch. But it was not likely that any President would easily yield the control over foreign policy acquired in recent decades.

Between 1950 and 1970, five American Presidents committed United States troops to foreign soil (in Korea, Lebanon, the Dominican Republic, Vietnam, and Cambodia) without any declaration of war by Congress. In no case did the President do so with clear, specific, prior congressional approval, although in four instances Congress had passed resolutions broadly supporting presidential action in various geographic areas: the Formosa resolution of 1954; the Middle East resolution of 1957; the Cuba resolution of 1962; and the Tonkin Gulf resolution of 1964, in which Congress said the President might "take all necessary steps, including the use of armed force" in Southeast Asia.

Congress passed the Tonkin Gulf resolution after President Johnson announced on nationwide television on August 4, 1964, that two United States destroyers, the *Maddox* and the *Turner Joy*, had been attacked in the Gulf of Tonkin off Vietnam. Secretary of Defense Robert S. McNamara declared that the two ships had been under "continuous torpedo attack." Up to this point 163 Americans had died in Vietnam and there were 16,000 troops there as "advisers." After passage of the Tonkin Gulf resolution, President Johnson—beginning early in 1965—vastly expanded the war.

It developed, however, that reports of the attack in the Tonkin Gulf had been considerably exaggerated. For example, the captain of the *Maddox*, Commander Herbert L. Ogier, later said he thought that two torpedos were fired but that subsequent reports of torpedos were actually sonar readings from the destroyer's own propellers. He added: "I felt like I'd more or less been tricked or something by myself." [20] Indeed, the task

[20] In David Wise, "Remember the Maddox!" *Esquire*, April 1968, p. 126. See also, Joseph C. Goulden, *Truth is the First Casualty* (New York: Rand McNally, 1969).

force commander warned Washington that, "Freak weather effects and over-eager sonarman may have accounted for many reports." [21] At a Senate hearing four years later, Senator Albert Gore, Democrat, of Tennessee, told Secretary McNamara to his face: "I feel that I have been misled, and that the American people have been misled." [22]

Angered by how easily it had been persuaded to write a virtual blank check for the Vietnam war, Congress in 1969 attempted to reaffirm its power in foreign affairs. The Senate passed the National Commitments Resolution, which sought to reassert the power of Congress in decisions committing the United States to defend other nations. The resolution did not have the force of law, require approval by the House, or bind the President. But it put the Senate on record against any future use of United States armed forces or funds to assist another country unless such action was taken by both Congress and the President through a treaty, statute, or specific resolution of both Houses of Congress. Less than a year later, however, President Nixon's decision to send troops into Cambodia was taken without consulting Congress.

Reacting to the Cambodian intervention, in the summer of 1970 the Senate engaged in a prolonged debate over foreign policy. It voted to repeal the Tonkin Gulf resolution and then, after seven weeks of discussion, adopted an amendment sponsored by Senators Frank Church of Idaho and John Sherman Cooper of Kentucky barring the deployment of American combat troops or advisers in Cambodia after July 1. But the Senate defeated a so-called "amendment to end the war" sponsored by Senators Mark Hatfield of Oregon and George McGovern of South Dakota. That measure would have required the President to withdraw all American troops from Vietnam after the end of 1971. Thus the Senate to a limited extent reasserted its power, but stopped far short of tying the President's hands and forcing a complete troop withdrawal from Vietnam. Just before adjourning, the House completed the repeal of the Tonkin Gulf resolution and approved restrictions on sending troops to Cambodia.

One major reason Congress has lost so much of its power over foreign affairs to the President is that diplomatic, military, and intelligence information flows directly to the President. As a result, Congress and the public have tended to assume that the President "has the facts" and is acting on the basis of expert advice. Second, foreign policy decisions are often made in crisis situations, in what has been called "an atmosphere of real or contrived urgency." [23] This, too, puts pressure on Congress to

[21] *The Gulf of Tonkin, The 1964 Incidents,* Hearing before the Committee on Foreign Relations, United States Senate, February 20, 1968, p. 54.
[22] *Ibid.,* p. 91.
[23] *National Commitments,* Report of the Committee on Foreign Relations, United States Senate, November 20, 1967, p. 14.

defer to presumed presidential wisdom. More recently, however, there has been an increasing realization that the extensive flow of information to the President does not guarantee that his foreign policy decisions will necessarily prove correct or wise.

The Machinery

Although the President is the principal figure in the conduct of national security policy, until 1947 no formal centralized machinery existed to aid him in his task. In that year, Congress attempted to give the President the tools to match his responsibilities.

The National Security Council. The National Security Act of 1947 created the National Security Council to advise the President on the integration of "domestic, foreign, and military policies relating to the national security." In one sense the act, amended and expanded in 1949, represented an effort to institutionalize the power that had been wielded over military-diplomatic affairs by President Roosevelt in the Second World War. It also represented an effort to provide continuity from one administration to the next in the conduct of national security affairs. As a presidential instrument, however, the NSC has been used very differently by a succession of Chief Executives. Eisenhower made frequent use of the NSC, as noted in Chapter 10. At times it has been used for public relations purposes, to give the appearance during a crisis of somber decisions being made by the President with his highest national security advisers. During the Kennedy and Johnson administrations, for example, the NSC was sometimes used for "window-dressing" of this kind; real decisions were reached in less formal meetings. But even those Presidents who made less formal use of the NSC have promulgated major national security decisions *within* the administration in the form of NSC directives. This was true under both President Kennedy and President Johnson.

By the time President Kennedy was inaugurated in 1961, the NSC had spawned a formidable growth of subcommittees and coordinating groups; paperwork was beginning to overwhelm policy formation. Secretary of State Christian Herter testified: "Sometimes you get yourself so bogged down in the editing of a word or a sentence that you say, 'My God, why am I spending so much time on this?' "[24] President Kennedy's national security adviser, McGeorge Bundy, "promptly slaughtered committees right and left."[25] Kennedy used the NSC infrequently and infor-

---

[24] *Organizing for National Security*, Subcommittee on National Policy Machinery, Committee on Government Operations, United States Senate, Vol. III, Staff Reports and Recommendations (Washington, D.C.: U.S. Government Printing Office, 1961), p. 37.
[25] Arthur M. Schlesinger, Jr., *A Thousand Days* (Boston: Houghton Mifflin, 1965), p. 210.

mally, and some critics contended that the result was a lack of foreign policy coordination. President Nixon directed that the NSC "be reestablished as the principal forum for Presidential consideration of foreign policy issues."[26] Various interagency groups, special panels, and review committees began to flourish once again under Nixon and his adviser for national security, Henry A. Kissinger.

The State Department. George F. Kennan has described the American State Department in a less turbulent era: "The Department of State . . . in the 1920's when I entered it, was a quaint old place, with its law-office atmosphere, its cool dark corridors, its swinging doors, its brass cuspidors, its black leather rocking chairs, and the grandfather's clock in the Secretary of State's office."[27]

Today, the State Department is huge; it occupies a large antiseptically modern building that houses more than half of its 23,000 employees. Department couriers hand-carry diplomatic documents 12,500,000 miles a year in travels between Washington and its 113 embassies abroad.[28] High speed coded communications link the Secretary of State to American embassies overseas, handling more than 300,000 words daily. In an Operations Center on the seventh floor, behind a locked door that is opened by a buzzer, the Secretary can monitor a developing crisis. A device called a Telecon flashes incoming cables on a screen, and the center can communicate with any United States post abroad in two minutes. There are green phones for "scrambling" conversations, white phones linked to the White House, a yellow phone to the Pentagon, a blue phone to the Central Intelligence Agency (CIA).

Despite all this, the State Department's level of efficiency has been the target of periodic criticism. As the United States became a world power, the size of the department increased vastly; bureaus and assistant secretaries proliferated. One reason that the State Department is slow to form policy is the "clearance factor"—the tendency of each branch of the department to check and clear matters with other branches and bureaus and other agencies of government. Clearance assures that all officials concerned with a particular policy will have seen relevant staff studies and documents, but it also means that reaching decisions in the foreign policy field can be a slow process. President Kennedy's impatience with the department's snaillike replies to his requests was a constant source of frustration in the White House. According to Arthur M. Schlesinger, Jr., Kennedy "would

[26] Congressional Quarterly, *Weekly Report*, February 20, 1970, p. 518.
[27] George F. Kennan, *American Diplomacy* (Chicago: University of Chicago Press, 1951), pp. 91–92.
[28] *Your Department of State* (Washington, D.C.: U.S. Government Printing Office, 1969).

The intellectual exhaustion of the Foreign Service expressed itself in the poverty of the official rhetoric. In meetings the men from State would talk in a bureaucratic patois borrowed in large part from the Department of Defense. We would be exhorted to 'zero in' on 'the purpose of the drill' (or of the 'exercise' or 'operation'), to 'crank in' this and 'phase out' that and 'gin up' something else, to 'pinpoint' a 'viable' policy and, behind it, a 'fall-back position,' to ignore the 'flak' from competing government bureaus or from the communists, to refrain from 'nit-picking' and never to be 'counterproductive.' Once we were 'seized of the problem,' preferably in as 'hard-nosed' a manner as possible, we would review 'options,' discuss 'over-all' objectives, seek 'breakthroughs,' consider 'crash programs,' 'staff out' policies— doing all these things preferably 'meaningfully' and 'in depth' until we were ready to 'finalize' our deliberations, 'sign on to' or 'sign off on' a conclusion (I never could discover the distinction, if any, between these two locutions) and 'implement' a decision. This was not just shorthand; part of the conference-table vocabulary involved a studied multiplication of words. Thus one never talked about a 'paper' but always a 'piece of paper,' never said 'at this point' but always 'at this point in time.'

—Arthur M. Schlesinger, Jr., *A Thousand Days.*

say, 'Damn it, Bundy and I get more done in one day in the White House than they do in six months at the State Department. . . . They never have any ideas over there,' he complained, 'never come up with anything new.' " [29]

The role of the Secretary of State varies greatly according to his personal relationship with the President. John Foster Dulles was a powerful

[29] Schlesinger, *A Thousand Days*, p. 406.

Secretary of State William Rogers fields question from a newsman.

architect of foreign policy who enjoyed the full confidence of President Eisenhower; but Kennedy found his Secretary of State, Dean Rusk, somewhat baffling. Rusk, a self-effacing bureaucrat, seldom took a position in the behind-the-scenes debates leading to policy decisions. As a result, Kennedy is said to have complained: "You never know what he is thinking." [30] The role of the modern Secretary of State is further complicated by the fact that while he is in theory principal foreign policy adviser and the ranking officer of the Cabinet, he may be overshadowed by the President's national security assistant and the Secretary of Defense, or even by prestigious subordinates. To some extent, this was Rusk's fate during the Kennedy administration.

To help administer the department and its annual budget of almost $500,000,000, the Secretary of State has an Executive Secretariat, which controls the flow of paperwork and tries to keep the Secretary from being drowned in a sea of words. Beneath the Secretary are the Under Secretary of State, a second Under Secretary for Political Affairs; two Deputy Under Secretaries, thirteen Assistant Secretaries, and a Policy Planning Staff to consider long-range problems. There are five geographic bureaus: African Affairs, European Affairs, East Asian and Pacific Affairs, Inter-American Affairs, and Near Eastern and South Asian Affairs. Within the geographic bureaus are forty-one country desks. In addition, there are functional bureaus for security and consular affairs, congressional relations, public affairs, education and cultural affairs, economic affairs, intelligence, politico-military affairs, and international organization (the bureau that manages United States policy at the United Nations).

The United States Foreign Service is the corps of professional diplomats who represent the United States overseas and staff key policy posts in the State Department in Washington. Most foreign service personnel are stationed abroad as ambassadors, ministers, and political and consular officers. Posts are normally rotated, and members of the foreign service periodically return to Washington for about four years before their next tour of duty overseas.

After the Second World War, the foreign service was a small, elite corps of diplomats who enjoyed status beyond that of the civil service employees who provided the department with many specialized skills and talents. Acting on the basis of a 1954 report by Dr. Henry M. Wriston, the President of Brown University, the department merged the two groups. Thus, beginning in the mid-1950's the foreign service changed in character and size; from a small, sometimes clubby group of generalists, it was expanded to include people with a wide range of skills and social and economic backgrounds. In 1970, the foreign service numbered more than

9,000 men and women, of whom 3,121 were foreign service "officers"—the professional diplomats. That year, under the Nixon administration, an effort was launched to reduce the size of the foreign service and increase the specialization of its members even further. Many foreign service officers today are young, dedicated, and tough-minded professional career officials. Yet despite the changed nature of the foreign service, it has had some difficulty living down its past. In the public mind, an aura of elitism still clings to it—a suspicion that some of its members are preoccupied with social niceties, excessively cautious, and overly concerned with their position on the bureaucratic ladder.

Arthur M. Schlesinger, Jr., not an admirer of the foreign service, has written: "One almost concluded that the definition of a Foreign Service officer was a man for whom the risks always outweighed the opportunities. Career officers had always tended to believe that the foreign policy of the United States was their personal property, to be solicitously protected against interference from the White House and other misguided amateurs." [31] It is true that many foreign service officers do pride themselves on their professionalism, but they may sometimes with good reason resent an ambassador whose chief qualification for an important overseas post is the size of his financial contribution to the President's election campaign.

Overseas, the ambassador is the President's personal representative to the Chief of State and government to which he is accredited. Appointed by the President and subject to Senate confirmation, the ambassador is formally in charge of the entire United States mission in a foreign capital. The mission may include representatives of the Agency for International Development (AID), the United States Information Agency (USIA), the military service attachés, military assistance advisory groups, and agents of the CIA. This comprises the so-called "country team," but often it is a team in name only, with each element reporting back to its own headquarters in Washington, and some officials working at cross-purposes to the ambassador. "To a degree," a Senate subcommittee concluded, "the primacy of the ambassador is a polite fiction." [32]

In addition to problems of coordination with other agencies of government, the State Department also faces competition from those agencies. It competes for the President's attention not only with the White House national security adviser, but with other agencies involved in foreign policy—the Office of International Security Affairs in the Defense Department, for example, and the CIA. To some extent, the State Department must even compete with outside sources of advice in foreign policy—defense research firms, the universities, presidential task forces, private

[31] *Ibid.*, p. 414.
[32] "Basic Issues," in *Administration of National Security*, p. 16.

organizations interested in foreign policy, and former government officials who may be called in and consulted by the President.

Intelligence and Foreign Policy: The CIA. More than a decade after he left the White House, President Truman wrote: "For some time I have been disturbed by the way the CIA has been diverted from its original assignment. It has become an operational and at times a policy-making arm of the government. . . . I never had any thought that when I set up the CIA that it would be injected into peacetime cloak-and-dagger operations." [33]

The CIA was created by Congress in 1947 to advise the National Security Council and to acquire political, military, and economic knowledge about other countries on which the President could base his foreign policy decisions. In addition to collecting intelligence, the CIA has engaged in secret political action within other countries.

Prior to the Japanese attack on Pearl Harbor in 1941, the United States had no centralized intelligence-gathering agency. After Pearl Harbor, President Roosevelt created the Office of Strategic Services (OSS) to gather intelligence and conduct secret political warfare and sabotage operations behind enemy lines during the Second World War. The CIA was the direct descendant of the wartime OSS. The director of the CIA wears one hat as head of that agency, but he is simultaneously chairman of the board of all government intelligence agencies, including the National Security Agency (NSA), the code-making and code-breaking arm of the Pentagon; the Defense Intelligence Agency (DIA), the military rival to the CIA; the FBI; and the State Department's Bureau of Intelligence and Research (INR). All of these agencies are represented on the United States Intelligence Board, of which the CIA director is chairman. The board submits to the President periodic National Intelligence Estimates predicting developments in foreign countries.

The CIA has two principal divisions. An *Intelligence Division* engages in overt collection, research, and analysis of foreign intelligence. Most of the criticism of the CIA has been directed at its *Plans Division*, which engages in the secret collection of intelligence (espionage), and in secret political warfare. On occasion, it has helped to overthrow governments—in Iran in 1953 and Guatemala in 1954, for example. Although the CIA has no police power within the United States (as does the FBI) and was created to collect foreign intelligence, in 1967 it was disclosed that the agency was subsidizing the National Student Association and dozens of foundations and private groups *within* the United States. President Johnson ordered that most of the secret funding be ended. The CIA's size and budget are

[33] Harry S Truman, syndicated article for North American Newspaper Alliance, in the *Washington Post*, December 22, 1963.

The Central Intelligence Agency (CIA) is the most highly secret agency of the federal government. In recent years, it has become increasingly important in the formulation and execution of American foreign policy.

The dangers in an operation like that of the Central Intelligence Agency and in the extension of its powers are: first, that it can become a kind of law unto itself, operating independently even of the President of the United States; second, that operating under the direction of the President, it may perform acts which would otherwise not be authorized or approved. . . .

Defenders of the CIA assert that the President, with the help of his Cabinet and the National Security Council, controls and directs the CIA. Theoretically this is right. But the President is the nominal head of hundreds of agencies and cannot be kept fully informed at all times of the activities of an agency as large and as powerful as the CIA. . . .

The Inner Ring of a secret agency is privileged. It becomes a kind of secular order of the elect. Full individual choice and responsibility are limited by oath of obligation to the agency. Individual conscience is eased in the general certainty of the over-all good of the object being pursued.

The anonymity of the service becomes a kind of habit, a rejection of the world of name and credit and recognition. In the end, the process may become the end, and doing the wrong things for the right reasons becomes increasingly easy.

—Eugene J. McCarthy, *The Limits of Power.*

secret, but it has been unofficially estimated that the agency spends $1.5 billion a year and employs well over 15,000 people.[34] The CIA has its headquarters in a secluded, wooded area of Langley, Virginia, just across the Potomac River from Washington.

During the 1950's, under its director, Allen W. Dulles, the CIA toiled largely out of the limelight. The loss of the U-2, a CIA spy plane, on a flight over the Soviet Union in 1960 and the disaster at the Bay of Pigs in 1961 thrust the CIA into the headlines and focused attention upon its activities. By 1964, critics charged that the CIA stood at the center of what had become "an invisible government." [35]

Former Assistant Secretary of State Roger Hilsman wrote: "The root fear was that the CIA represented . . . a state within a state, and certainly the basis for fear was there." [36] Robert Kennedy noted: "In some countries that I visited, the dominant U.S. figure was the representative of the CIA." [37] Arthur M. Schlesinger, Jr., wrote that by 1961, "The CIA's budget . . . exceeded State's by more than 50 percent. . . . in a number of embassies CIA officers outnumbered those from State. . . . The CIA had its own political desks and military staffs; it had in effect its own foreign service, its own air force, even, on occasion, its own combat forces." [38]

[34] David Wise and Thomas B. Ross, *The Espionage Establishment* (New York: Random House, 1967), pp. 146n, 172.
[35] David Wise and Thomas B. Ross, *The Invisible Government* (New York: Random House, 1964), p. 3.
[36] Hilsman, *To Move a Nation,* pp. 64–65.
[37] Kennedy, *Thirteen Days,* p. 115.
[38] Schlesinger, *A Thousand Days,* p. 427.

Critics of the CIA have charged that it operates at times without sufficient control by the President and Congress, that it sometimes makes policy instead of confining itself to gathering and interpreting facts, and that its covert political operations occasionally interfere with the internal affairs of other countries and embarrass the United States.

Defenders of the CIA argue that it already operates under sufficient control. For example, Allen Dulles wrote that "the CIA has never carried out any action of a political nature, given any support of any nature to any persons, potentates or movements, political or otherwise, without appropriate approval at a high political level in our government *outside the CIA.*"[39]

Dulles argued that the United States "is being challenged by a hostile group of nations," and that only the CIA could learn the defense secrets of the Soviet Union and Communist China. "The special techniques which are unique to secret intelligence operations are needed to penetrate the security barriers of the Communist Bloc," he wrote, adding: "Today it is impossible to predict where the next danger spot may develop. It is the duty of intelligence to forewarn of such dangers, so that the government can take action. No longer can the search for information be limited to a few countries. The whole world is the arena of our conflict." An intelligence service, he said, "is the best insurance we can take out against surprise." As for covert CIA operations inside other countries, Dulles contended that the United States could not limit its activities "to those cases where we are invited in."[40]

Because the CIA is a secret agency, and usually does not make any public comment, it is sometimes blamed for things it does *not* do. Despite the controversy over the CIA, Congress has not strengthened its control over the intelligence agency. In 1966, the Senate rejected a proposal for the creation of a formal nine-man committee to oversee the CIA.

However necessary it may be to protect American security, the existence of a clandestine intelligence and espionage establishment creates special problems in a free society. The operations of the CIA and the other United States intelligence agencies pose the continuing dilemma of how secret-intelligence machinery can be made compatible with democratic government.[41]

Other Instruments: AID, USIA, and the Peace Corps. Today the State Department must compete in the foreign policy field not only with the President's NSC staff, the CIA, and the Pentagon, but with many other

---

[39] Allen Dulles, *The Craft of Intelligence* (New York: Harper & Row, 1963), p. 189.
[40] *Ibid.*, pp. 48–51, 235–36.
[41] See Harry Howe Ransom, *Can American Democracy Survive Cold War?* (New York: Doubleday, 1963).

agencies and units of the Federal Government. A State Department official surprised a Senate committee in 1969 by disclosing that *less than 20 percent* of the personnel of major United States embassies abroad are State Department employees. In many embassies, he told the Senate Foreign Relations Committee, the department was overwhelmed by AID, USIA, and military personnel. In India, he said, State Department people accounted for only 8 percent of the embassy staff. "The State Department role today," he concluded sadly, "isn't anything like it was." [42]

One of the agencies with foreign policy responsibilities both in Washington and in the field is the *Agency for International Development* (AID), a semi-independent arm of the State Department. AID, as its initials imply, is responsible for carrying out programs of financial and technical assistance to less economically developed nations. Since the initiation of the Marshall Plan, the United States has spent more than $162 billion on foreign aid. For fiscal 1971, for example, the President's budget request for economic aid totaled $1.8 billion, and included economic assistance for sixty-nine countries in Latin America, Asia, and Africa, as well as United States contributions made through such international financial institutions as the Inter-American Development Bank and the Asian Development Bank. Although foreign aid appropriations have declined in recent years, the United States has placed greater emphasis on channeling aid through such multilateral institutions, and it has increased its participation in the International Bank for Reconstruction and Development (World Bank), which makes loans to, and promotes foreign investments in, underdeveloped nations.

AID is politically unpopular because many Americans regard it as a "giveaway" program with little visible benefit to the taxpayers. The agency's image has not been helped by occasional scandals, such as the disclosure that it paid $24,000 for shipment to Vietnam of a drug that proved to be pure sea water, or its dispatch of $2,800 in bubble gum to the Dominican Republic. Public disenchantment with the foreign aid program has been reflected in declining aid budgets in recent years—Congress has repeatedly slashed presidential aid requests and, on occasion, has cut off aid to nations considered unfriendly or pro-Communist.

But the aid program can be defended both on humanitarian grounds and, more narrowly, on political grounds. As the richest nation in the world, the United States has felt a moral obligation to try to alleviate poverty, disease, and malnutrition in other nations. At the same time, supporters of the aid program contend, peace and stability are unlikely to be achieved for the United States or the world as a whole as long as such conditions exist in these poorer nations.

[42] Idar Rimestad, Deputy Undersecretary of State for Administration, quoted in the *Washington Post*, September 24, 1969, p. A26.

"We don't consider ours to be an underdeveloped country so much as we think of yours as an overdeveloped country."

John A. Ruge
Copyright 1970 Saturday Review, Inc.

Despite some popular misconceptions, most foreign aid is not given to other countries in the form of cash. Most AID dollars are spent in the United States to buy commodities and to hire technical experts for projects overseas. AID provides technical assistance by sending abroad specialists in such fields as health, education, and agriculture. Through development loans, repayable in dollars, AID offers other countries long-term, low-interest financing for such projects as highways, dams, schools, and hospitals. AID also attempts to increase the flow of private investment capital to these nations. In addition, the United States donates and sells agricultural commodities at low cost under the Food for Peace program.

In September 1970, President Nixon urged Congress to overhaul the foreign aid system so that the great bulk of American assistance would be channeled through multilateral institutions. He proposed that AID be abolished and that the remaining United States bilateral aid program be administered by a new United States International Development Corporation, a quasi-independent government agency.

The *United States Information Agency* (USIA), according to an official description, helps to achieve the objectives of United States foreign policy "by influencing public attitudes in other nations." [43] The USIA is, in short, the official foreign propaganda agency of the United States government. The USIA was created in 1953 under a presidential reorganization plan as a successor to the government information programs that operated during the Second World War.

Wary that such an agency might be used by a President to influence domestic opinion, Congress has generally restricted the USIA to operations overseas. The agency has 10,000 employees and has branches in 102 countries. Its libraries and information centers in foreign countries are sometimes visible and popular targets of anti-American mob violence. Each USIA mission is headed by a Public Affairs Officer (PAO) who is a member of the "country team" and may act as official spokesman for the ambassador.

Through the Voice of America, the USIA each week beams abroad 848 hours of news broadcasts, music, and feature programs in thirty-six languages. Since the early 1960's, the "Voice" has attempted to maintain its credibility among foreign audiences by balanced reporting of race riots and other unfavorable aspects of American life. Nevertheless, its basic task is to explain United States policies to its listeners and to enhance America's "image"; as a government radio station, it operates under policy restrictions and guidelines set by the State Department.

The *Peace Corps* was created by President Kennedy in 1961 to provide a trained corps of highly motivated young American volunteers to help people in developing nations. A decade later, almost 9,000 Peace Corps volunteers were in training or were serving overseas in sixty-two countries as teachers, agricultural aides, doctors, and in many other capacities. Peace Corps volunteers serve abroad for two years and receive $75 per

[43] *United States Government Organization Manual, 1969–70*, p. 515.

A Peace Corps volunteer teaches arithmetic in La Paz, Bolivia.

month, plus allowances for food, clothing, housing, and other living expenses.

The *Arms Control and Disarmament Agency* was established by President Kennedy in 1961. Although technically not a division of the State Department, the director is an adviser to the Secretary of State and the President. The agency prepares and manages United States participation in international arms control and disarmament negotiations, but it also has important responsibilities in conducting long-range research on techniques of arms control. The development of imaginative techniques for inspection and control could increase confidence among nations and form a practical basis for disarmament pacts. With the creation of the post of the President's science adviser in 1957, and of the disarmament agency, the President no longer has to rely exclusively for scientific advice on the Pentagon and the Atomic Energy Commission, which have their own viewpoints.

AID, the USIA, the Peace Corps and the disarmament agency all receive policy guidance from the State Department. The State Department itself must share the foreign policy field with dozens of other agencies of the Federal Government involved in various aspects of foreign affairs. These include the departments of Defense, Agriculture, Labor, Commerce, Justice, and Transportation.

When the twenty-fifth anniversary of the United Nations was commemorated in 1970, the occasion was a reminder of how far the world —and the UN—had fallen short of man's hopes for peace.

The UN was founded at San Francisco in 1945 to fulfill the dream of a community of nations, a world body that could take collective action to keep the peace and work for the dignity of man. The opening words of the UN charter declare its principal goal: "We the peoples of the United Nations determined to save succeeding generations from the scourge of war, which twice in our lifetime has brought untold sorrow to mankind. . . ."

The United Nations, however, has generally been unable to keep the peace on issues that divide the major world powers. Decisions affecting world peace are made in Washington, Moscow, Peking, and other capitals, but seldom at UN headquarters in New York City. In part, this was predictable from the structure of the UN and the nature of international relations. The Security Council, with fifteen members, cannot act over the veto of any of the five permanent members—as of 1970, the United States, the Soviet Union, Britain, France, and Nationalist China. Because the Soviet Union has frequently cast a veto in the Security Council, UN members sought a way to circumvent the Council. In November 1950, the General Assembly decided that it could act to meet threats to peace when the Security Council failed to do so because the permanent members lacked una-

The
United Nations

nimity. There is no veto power in the General Assembly, to which all member nations belong. Although the General Assembly has thus increased somewhat in importance, it, too, has proved unable to cope with major conflicts.

The UN has acted with varying success in several world crises; in Korea in 1950, in Suez in 1956, the Congo in 1961, and Cyprus in 1964. But the UN was not able to end the tragic civil war in Nigeria, or the fighting in Vietnam; and it had scant success in the Middle East during the Arab-Israeli Six Day War in 1967.

The United States, which provides about one-third of the UN's budget, lost much of its influence in that organization in the 1960's as the UN shifted from a pro-Western to a neutralist stand. As many of the former colonial territories of Africa and Asia gained independence, they joined the UN, and the United States could no longer count on winning its political battles in that body. The new face of the UN was symbolized by the selection in 1961 of U Thant of Burma, a neutralist and an opponent of colonialism, as Secretary General.

By 1970, the UN had expanded from its original 50 to more than 125 members. The United States is represented by an ambassador who heads a United States mission in New York. To some extent the decline in the influence of the UN was reflected in the fact that when President Nixon took office he did not follow past custom of appointing a well-known figure as United States ambassador to the UN. Instead he assigned a career State Department diplomat, in effect treating the United States mission to the UN as another American embassy. Two years later, Nixon named George Bush, a Republican congressman from Texas, to the UN post.

Although the UN has had limited success as a peace-keeping agency, it has served some other useful and constructive purposes. It provides a forum for discussion, a place where new and small nations can be heard. It sometimes helps to defuse world crises by allowing nations to talk instead of fight. And its economic, social, and health agencies have made significant contributions in improving the lives of millions of people all over the world. In the late 1960's and 1970's, the UN was also having some success in dealing with such international environmental problems as the peaceful use of outer space and seabeds, and pollution of the oceans. Finally, the UN, for all of its inadequacies, still remains a symbol of hope, the tangible embodiment of man's fragile dream of peace.

The Politics of Foreign-Policy-Making

Over a period of time, widespread or intense domestic reaction to foreign policy may have an impact on government. Domestic protest against the war by students, professors, and many other members of the public in the 1960's eventually won majority support and helped to create a climate in which President Johnson felt it prudent to leave the White

House. And growing opposition to the war provided the political backdrop for President Nixon's decision in 1969 to begin the withdrawal of American troops from Vietnam. Nevertheless, the process seemed to take a long time, and many Americans, particularly those in colleges, still felt a sense of alienation and powerlessness.

The Role of the Public. Despite public awareness of such highly publicized issues as Vietnam, some political scientists have argued that on most foreign policy issues, the public is both uninterested and uninformed. Gabriel Almond has observed that "Americans tend to exhaust their emotional and intellectual energies in private pursuits." While members of the public may develop well defined views on domestic questions that affect them directly, he has argued, on questions of foreign policy they tend to react in changeable, "formless and plastic moods."[44] Almond has suggested that relatively small leadership groups play the major role in the making of most specific foreign policy decisions, and that the public's role is largely confined to the expression of mass attitudes that provide a framework within which officials may work.[45]

James N. Rosenau has also differentiated between public response to domestic issues and foreign policy issues, but he emphasizes that when a foreign policy question becomes so big that it involves "a society's resources and relationships" it quickly turns into a domestic political issue—and he cites Vietnam as an example.[46]

Nevertheless, a President has wide latitude in conducting foreign policy. Kenneth N. Waltz has suggested that as a rule, "The first effect of an international crisis is to increase the President's popular standing." Furthermore, Waltz points out, a President sometimes risks political unpopularity no matter what he does. A President who increases American involvement in Vietnam, for example, will be blamed, but so will a President who permits North Vietnam to conquer South Vietnam.[47]

Failure of the government to respond to persistent and broadly based protest on foreign policy issues raises serious questions about the workings of democratic institutions. But there is another side to the problem. Foreign policy also requires leadership. A President who responds too readily to public opinion may be pushed into dangerous choices if public sentiment is running high for quick or simple solutions. Just as the public may demand peace, at other times it may demand retaliation that risks war. Hawkish voices are sometimes heard in Congress; for example, in

[44] Gabriel A. Almond, *The American People and Foreign Policy* (New York: Praeger, 1960), p. 53.
[45] *Ibid.*, pp. 4–6.
[46] James N. Rosenau, "Foreign Policy as an Issue-Area," in James N. Rosenau, ed., *Domestic Sources of Foreign Policy* (New York: Free Press, 1967), p. 49.
[47] Kenneth N. Waltz, "Electoral Punishment and Foreign Policy Crises," in Rosenau, *Domestic Sources of Foreign Policy*, pp. 273, 283.

January 1968, when North Korea captured the USS *Pueblo*, a spy ship, Senator Richard B. Russell, Democrat, of Georgia, then chairman of the Senate Armed Services Committee, called the seizure "almost an act of war." [48] Senator Wallace F. Bennett, Republican, of Utah, declared that, if diplomacy failed, "our armada should steam into Wonsan, throw a tow line about the *Pueblo* and tow it out." [49] President Johnson chose to ignore the suggestion. Eventually the ship and crew were returned through diplomatic channels.

Domestic influence on foreign policy is not limited to mass public opinion, as reflected in polls, letters, and protest demonstrations. Congress, individual legislators or committee chairmen, interest groups, private organizations concerned with foreign policy, opinion leaders, the press, TV commentators, and proximity to an election may all have some effect on policy outcomes. Some foreign policy questions are of special importance to particular groups. Appeals to ethnic groups by political leaders have declined somewhat in importance since the decades of mass European immigration to the United States, and today most foreign policy issues are national in scope. But not entirely. A President who is interested in carrying New York, California, and Illinois, for example, may frame United States policy toward Israel with at least some thought to the likely reaction among the many Jewish voters in those states. (For the same reason, the mayor of New York has been known to snub visiting Arab potentates.) On Polish patriotic days, members of Congress from heavily Polish areas such as Buffalo or Chicago rise in the House and Senate and carefully pay homage to the contribution of Polish heroes to the nation's heritage.

The Credibility Gap. A President's conduct of foreign policy depends in large measure on whether he is able to carry the public along with him on big decisions. Without public trust in his leadership, he may fail. President Johnson suffered from a "credibility gap" that seriously hampered his Presidency. The Tonkin Gulf episode, already discussed, was one example of an event that took on a far different coloration after the fact. Again in 1965, after Johnson sent troops to the Dominican Republic, he told a news conference: "Some fifteen hundred innocent people were murdered and shot, and their heads cut off. . . . Our ambassador . . . was talking to us from under a desk while bullets were going through his windows." [50] None of this happened. Addressing troops in South Korea in 1966, Johnson got carried away and announced that "my great-great grandfather died at the Alamo," which, reporters discovered, was not the case. [51]

[48] *Washington Post*, January 24, 1968, p. 1.
[49] *Washington Star*, January 24, 1968, p. A15.
[50] Goldman, *The Tragedy of Lyndon Johnson*, p. 396.
[51] James Deakin, *Lyndon Johnson's Credibility Gap* (Washington, D.C.: Public Affairs Press, 1968), p. 55.

Other Presidents have encountered credibility problems. Since the Second World War, the government has on more than one occasion told official lies designed to protect secret intelligence operations. Under Eisenhower, for example, the administration claimed at first that the U-2 spy plane shot down 1,200 miles inside the Soviet Union was a "weather research" aircraft that had strayed off course. Under Kennedy, the government initially denied, but later admitted, that it was responsible for the CIA-backed invasion of Cuba at the Bay of Pigs. Public statements about certain foreign policy decisions, in short, have contributed to an erosion of public confidence in government honesty.

Political Parties, Campaigns, and Foreign Policy. The two-party system tends to push both major parties toward the center on foreign policy issues. Kenneth N. Waltz explains that "failure to do so will give a third party the chance to wedge itself in between its two larger competitors. . . . The policy positions of two competing parties begin to approach one another, and the candidates even begin to look and talk very much alike." [52]

Advocates of *bipartisanship* in foreign policy contend that both major political parties should broadly support the President, and that foreign policy issues should not be sharply debated in political campaigns. They argue that it is in the nation's interest to appear united to the rest of the world. In this context, for example, President Johnson asserted that peace demonstrations in the United States encouraged North Vietnam to prolong the war.

Bipartisanship flourished particularly in the period shortly after the Second World War. It was symbolized by the phrase, "Politics stops at the water's edge," a concept popularized in 1950 by Senator Arthur H. Vandenberg, a Michigan Republican who had served as chairman of the Senate Foreign Relations Committee under a Democratic President, Harry Truman.

The argument against bipartisanship is that it denies democratic choice and blurs responsibility. The essence of democracy is the right of the people to choose among alternatives, to dissent from existing policies, and, when they are dissatisfied with past performance, to elect new leaders. Foreign policy issues, seen in this light, must be discussed in political campaigns precisely *because* those issues are so important today.

There is, nevertheless, still a strong strain of bipartisanship on Capitol Hill. As Burton M. Sapin points out, "The party not in control of the executive is under considerable pressure, patriotic as well as political, to go along with the President and his foreign policy." [53] On the other hand, opposition to the Vietnam war by the Senate Foreign Relations Committee,

[52] Kenneth N. Waltz, *Foreign Policy and Democratic Politics* (Boston: Little, Brown, 1967), p. 86.
[53] Burton M. Sapin, *The Making of United States Foreign Policy* (New York: Praeger, 1966), p. 57. Published for the Brookings Institution.

the passage of the National Commitments resolution in 1969, and congressional discontent over President Nixon's venture in Cambodia in 1970 all indicate that bipartisanship is often more a slogan than a reality. Both parties, in fact, were split internally by a foreign policy issue as important as Vietnam. Moreover, for more than two decades, foreign policy issues have figured prominently in presidential election campaigns, either in general terms or as specific issues in the campaign, and that, too, is not likely to change.

THE DEFENSE ESTABLISHMENT

Near Great Falls, Montana, Aberdeen Angus cattle graze placidly on a grassy hillside. Some fifty feet below, two officers of the Strategic Air Command control ten Minuteman missiles, each tipped with a hydrogen bomb. Within thirty seconds after receiving an order, the two officers could fire the missiles. World War III would have begun.

This was the setting described to readers of the *New York Times* a few years ago when the Department of Defense permitted a reporter to visit the Minuteman launch control center at Malmstrom Air Force Base. The story explained:

> No one here knows the targets. Each missile's destination is determined by the . . . Strategic Air Command. The target is put on magnetic tape, which is fed into the guidance system of each rocket. . . . "The purpose of the ball game is to throw a warhead," said Col. Rex Dowtin, the missile wing commander. . . . A statement made by Captain Johnson . . . illustrated the [missilemen's] language. "When a launch is voted anywhere in the system of 50 missiles, a bell rings," he said ringing it manually to show how the trump of doom would sound in that small room. "We can go to inhibit launch. We have 205 seconds to signal inhibit." . . . The young officers wear pistols—to use on each other to prevent a take-over of control of a missile firing center. Further, the two [launching] keys must be turned simultaneously, and in locks about 10 feet apart. "Murder to get control would be useless," said Captain Crislip.[54]

Although the dialogue might have come from the satiric motion picture, *Dr. Strangelove*, it was real. Across the Arctic Circle, the Soviet equivalent of the SAC officers sat in *their* missile silos ready to launch huge SS-9 ICBMs at the United States. Secretary of Defense Robert McNamara estimated in 1967 that in a nuclear exchange 120 million Americans and an

[54] Wallace Turner, "Minuteman Missile Squads are Poised on Montana Hillsides Ready to Launch Hydrogen Bombs," *New York Times*, February 28, 1965, p. 90.

equal number of Soviet citizens would be killed.[55] And by 1970, both sides were increasing the size and sophistication of their nuclear arsenals.

Since the Second World War, the United States has spent $1.1 trillion on national defense; in fiscal 1971, the Defense Department budget stood at $72 billion. Because of expanding technology, however, weapons systems become obsolete even as they are deployed. And because of the nuclear threat, a strong argument can be made that as spending for armaments has increased, national security has actually diminished. Aside from this paradox, the existence of a multibillion dollar military machine has created numerous problems for American society. Within the "military-industrial complex," whole industries depend on government defense contracts; aerospace industry lobbyists attempt to guard their clients' interests in Washington; and some universities compete for classified military research contracts. A society that devotes 40 percent of its total national budget to war and defense-related spending cannot allocate as much as it otherwise might to eliminate slums and poverty or improve health, schools, and the natural environment. The "cost" of a defense economy cannot be measured simply in terms of the size of the annual Pentagon budget.

The nuclear weapons have remained in their underground silos and beneath the sea in submarines. But since the Second World War the United States has fought a series of costly, so-called limited or conventional wars in Korea and in Southeast Asia. Despite its vast weaponry, manpower, and technology, the United States learned in Vietnam that superior size and resources were of little advantage against an elusive enemy skilled in guerrilla warfare.

The United States could not employ nuclear weapons against a smaller nation without being morally condemned by most of the rest of the world as well as by millions of citizens at home. And the use of tactical or strategic nuclear weapons in a conventional "limited war" carries with it the threat of escalation into a big war, some argue, for it might bring the Soviet Union or Communist China into the conflict. To a great extent, therefore, the United States is a chained giant. Recent experience has taught that its vast military power cannot be applied very effectively in view of the risks of an ultimate holocaust. Its "usable power" has been limited. Furthermore, domestic opposition to United States involvement in Southeast Asia has created additional *political* risks and limitations for American leaders pursuing military solutions to foreign policy problems.

Foreign policy and defense policy are intimately linked. Ideally, as Sapin notes, "Foreign policy establishes the broad outlines within which the defense establishment must do its work." [56] A modern President, however, must contend with the problems of controlling a huge, powerful mili-

---

[55] *1967 Congressional Quarterly Almanac*, p. 214.
[56] Sapin, *The Making of United States Foreign Policy*, p. 136.

tary establishment with its friends and protectors in Congress and its clients in private industry. He must see that the generals serve his foreign policy goals, rather than the other way around.

<table>
<tr><td>The Department
of Defense</td><td>The principle of civilian control over the American military establishment is deeply rooted in the Constitution and the nation's tradition. The President is constitutional Commander-in-Chief of all the armed forces, and the Secretary of Defense, by law, must be a civilian. Yet the effectiveness of civilian control of the military is a major problem that concerns many Americans today.</td></tr>
</table>

Across the Potomac River from Washington, in Arlington, Virginia, lies the Pentagon. Completed in 1943 at a cost of $83,000,000, the Pentagon houses some 27,000 civilian and military employees. In its concourse is a shopping center large enough for most suburban cities. The Pentagon has its own bank, post office, barber shop, department stores, florist—even an optometrist and medical and dental clinics. The Secretary of Defense is the world's biggest employer, boss of 1,100,000 civilians and 3,000,000 members of the armed forces as of 1970. (Indirectly, he is the biggest private employer in America as well, since the Pentagon grants defense contracts amounting to some $45 billion a year.)

The National Security Act of 1947, as amended in 1949, unified the armed forces under the control of a single Secretary of Defense. Additional legislation and a series of internal reorganizations strengthened and centralized his control over such functions as intelligence, procurement, and research. Below the secretary is a deputy secretary and seven assistant secretaries. The Army, Navy, and Air Force continue to exist as separate entities within the Defense Department, each with its own secretary. The

The Pentagon

Pentagon has its own "little State Department," the Office of International Security Affairs (ISA), which serves both as the Defense Department's link with the State Department and as a competing source of foreign policy formulation. The Pentagon also has its own intelligence organization, the Defense Intelligence Agency (DIA), created in 1961, as well as the super-secret National Security Agency (NSA), which intercepts the codes of other nations and conducts electronic espionage.

The members of the Joint Chiefs of Staff are the chairman, the chiefs of staff of the three armed services and, when Marine Corps matters are under consideration, the Commandant of the Marines. The Joint Chiefs wear three brass hats. By law, they are (1) the principal military advisers to the President and the National Security Council, (2) the principal military advisers to the Secretary of Defense, and (3) the chiefs of their respective military services. Although they serve within the Defense Department under the Secretary of Defense, the Joint Chiefs also have direct access to the President.

The
Joint Chiefs
of Staff

The chairman and other members of the Joint Chiefs are appointed by the President for four-year terms. The chairman serves at the discretion of the President for a two-year term, and may be reappointed by him to one additional term. In selecting a member, the President may skip over senior officers to appoint a more dynamic, younger service chief. The chairman of the Joint Chiefs outranks his colleagues. Together, the Joint Chiefs are responsible for day-to-day conduct of military operations as well as long-range strategic planning. They are assisted by a Joint Staff of not more than 400 officers selected about equally from the three services.

Although the President relies on the Joint Chiefs for military advice, he may choose to disregard their views. The President has the responsibility to weigh military risks against the nation's total foreign policy objectives.

Robert Kennedy has related that during the Cuban missile crisis, one member of the Joint Chiefs advocated the use of nuclear weapons. "I thought, as I listened, of the many times that I had heard the military take positions which, if wrong, had the advantage that no one would be around at the end to know." [57] President Kennedy, he wrote, was distressed that his military advisers "seemed to give so little consideration to the implications of steps they suggested. They seemed always to assume that . . . a war was in our national interest. One of the Joint Chiefs of Staff once said to me he believed in a preventive attack against the Soviet Union." [58]

[57] Kennedy, *Thirteen Days*, p. 48.
[58] *Ibid.*, p. 119.

Yet, a whole series of leading military figures in recent decades, generals such as George Marshall, Omar Bradley, Matthew Ridgeway, James Gavin, and Maxwell Taylor proved themselves capable of viewing foreign policy in its broadest context—not merely in narrow, military terms. Another military career man, General Eisenhower, successfully resisted the advice of some of his military advisers and refused, for example, to intervene in Southeast Asia in 1954. More recently, some military officers and ex-officers have criticized the war in Vietnam. For example, General David M. Shoup, Commandant of the Marine Corps for four years, became a leading opponent of the war after his retirement in 1963.

Decision-Making in the Pentagon

The sheer size of the Pentagon and the military establishment almost defies effective management and control. In 1961, President Kennedy appointed Robert S. McNamara, then President of the Ford Motor Company, as Secretary of Defense. McNamara brought with him to Washington a team of civilian analysts ("the Whiz Kids") and quickly established himself as an extraordinarily powerful and strong-willed administrator. Somewhat ascetic in appearance, with steel-rimmed glasses and slick hair combed straight back, McNamara had a mind often compared in its precision to a computer or a slide rule.

McNamara installed a new technique for making decisions within the Pentagon. The new method, alternatively termed "cost effectiveness" or "systems analysis," sought to measure the military value of weapons against their cost in money. (See Chapter 11, pp. 447–48.) As McNamara explained it, the new method attempted to determine "the cost effectiveness of each system, i.e., the combat effectiveness per dollar of outlay." [59] This approach, applying complex computer analysis and scientific method to strategic decision-making, was as appealing to defense intellectuals and to the press as it was annoying to the generals. The system had its limits, however—the computer did not seem able to win the war in Vietnam, which some critics dubbed "McNamara's War." Even Charles J. Hitch, the Defense Department Comptroller under McNamara, noted that there will always be considerations that relate to "the very fundamentals of national defense which are simply not subject to any sort of rigorous, quantitative analysis." [60]

After McNamara's departure from Defense to assume the presidency of the World Bank, a Senate investigating committee chaired by Senator William Proxmire of Wisconsin uncovered multibillion dollar "cost overruns" on the Lockheed C-5A transport plane and other weapons systems

[59] In William W. Kaufmann, *The McNamara Strategy* (New York: Harper & Row, 1964), p. 181.
[60] In Schlesinger, *A Thousand Days*, p. 314.

that turned out to be much more expensive than original estimates.[61] Transcripts made public in 1970 of secret Pentagon meetings on the controversial F-111 fighter-bomber (formerly called TFX) provide, in the words of one Washington observer, "an unsurpassed picture of McNamara, the gifted administrator, frantically trying to control a runaway machine."[62]

The McNamara approach aroused hostility among the armed services, which felt that the systems analysts had taken control of decisions that should be made by the military. Powerful congressional leaders sided with the armed services. Partly in response to these pressures, President Nixon's Secretary of Defense, Melvin Laird, modified the role of systems analysis in the Pentagon. Under his rule, the Defense Department's Office of Systems Analysis prepared spending limits for the armed services, but the services were permitted to study and make recommendations on weapons systems.

Early in the spring of 1969, two prominent scientists, both former high government officials, testified before a Senate subcommittee. At the time, Congress was considering President Nixon's request to deploy the Safeguard Anti-Ballistic Missile system (ABM). The scientists argued that deployment of the ABM could mean that the President would lose control over the use of atomic weapons. Dr. Herbert F. York, professor of physics at the University of California, at San Diego, formerly director of research and development for the Pentagon, observed that the ABM must be maintained on a "hair trigger status" because of the short warning time in a nuclear attack. Therefore, he said, "the power to make certain life-and-death decisions is inexorably passing from statesman and politicians to more narrowly focused technicians, and from human beings to machines. The direction we are going in . . . is not toward the ultimate weapon but toward ultimate absurdity. We are getting to the point . . . where there is no time for humans, and decisions are made by machines."[63]

Strategic Arms: The Balance of Terror

Dr. George B. Kistiakowsky of Harvard, former science adviser to President Eisenhower, testified that because of the time factor, it would be "impossible" for the President to make a decision on use of the ABM. "The decision has to be made automatically by a computer or by a comparatively junior military officer."[64]

These possibilities did not dissuade Congress, which voted funds to begin deployment of the multibillion dollar ABM at two Minuteman missile sites in North Dakota and Montana. (The Senate approved the project by

[61] William Proxmire, *Report from Wasteland* (New York: Praeger, 1970).
[62] Bernard D. Nossiter, "McNamara and the F-111: A Chronicle of Futility," *Washington Post*, April 26, 1970, p. 133.
[63] *New York Times*, March 12, 1969, p. B3.
[64] *Ibid.*

one vote.) President Nixon argued that the ABM was necessary to protect United States missile sites against a possible Soviet or Chinese attack, or against "any irrational or accidental attack." [65]

Since the 1950's, the world has lived with the knowledge that it is only fifteen minutes away from nuclear disaster. The American nuclear monopoly was broken when the Soviet Union exploded an atomic bomb in 1949. In 1957, the Soviet Union launched the first Sputnik, or earth satellite. The military implications were clear; if Russia possessed the technology to boost a satellite into outer space, it had long-range missiles that could be targeted on American cities.

While campaigning for the Presidency in 1960, John F. Kennedy charged that the United States had fallen behind the Soviet Union in building ICBMs. The result, he claimed, was a "missile gap." Three weeks after Kennedy's inauguration, Defense Secretary McNamara called reporters to his office for a "backgrounder"—a Washington custom in which a government official meets with the press but asks to remain anonymous. He disclosed that there was, in fact, no "missile gap." [66] In October 1964, Communist China exploded its first nuclear bomb, and the "nuclear club" now had five members—the United States, the Soviet Union, Britain, France, and China.

Since the Second World War, the United States has adopted a policy of *strategic deterrence*. The theory of deterrence, developed in the Pentagon, with the assistance of defense "think tanks" such as RAND and the Institute of Defense Analyses (IDA), involved deploying enough nuclear weapons so that an enemy would not, in theory, attack the United States, for fear of being attacked in retaliation.

But how, if it relied on nuclear arms alone, could the United States respond to nonnuclear military challenges? President Kennedy believed it was necessary for the United States to supplement its nuclear power by expanding its capacity to fight "conventional" wars. During the 1960's, the policy of massive nuclear retaliation changed to one of "limited" or "flexible" response; and the Pentagon trained its Special Forces in guerrilla warfare and "counterinsurgency."

Henry A. Kissinger, who became President Nixon's national security adviser in 1969, argued in 1957 that the United States must be able to fight a "limited nuclear war," [67] a position from which he later retreated. [68]

---

[65] President's news conference, March 14, 1969, Congressional Quarterly, *Weekly Report*, March 21, 1969, p. 414.
[66] *New York Times*, February 9, 1961, p. 4.
[67] Henry A. Kissinger, *Nuclear Weapons and Foreign Policy* (New York: Harper & Row, 1957), pp. 174–202. Published for the Council on Foreign Relations.
[68] Henry A. Kissinger, *The Necessity for Choice* (New York: Harper & Row, 1961), p. 81.

FIGURE 14-2

Potential Destruction from Nuclear Weapons

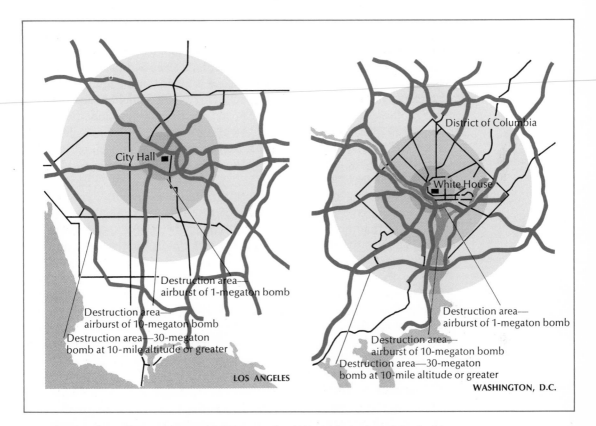

Source: Abram Chayes and Jerome B. Wiesner, eds., *ABM: An Evaluation of the Decision to Deploy an Antiballistic Missile System* (New York: Signet Books, 1969), pp. 274–75. Originally published by Harper & Row.

Some defense intellectuals shocked many people by their attempts at rational analysis of an essentially irrational process—thermonuclear war. For example, Herman Kahn wrote in 1960 that "objective studies" indicated that a nuclear war "would not preclude normal and happy lives for the majority of survivors and their descendants." [69] The picture of nuclear survivors living happy lives amid the debris did not convince everyone. Others, such as Ralph E. Lapp, argued that the nation's arsenal of weapons had

[69] Herman Kahn, *On Thermonuclear War* (Princeton, N.J.: Princeton University Press, 1961), p. 21.

grown into "a monstrous stockpile which could not only kill, but overkill, any possible enemy."[70]

The strategy of deterrence has a language all its own. Military theorists speak of "first strike capability" and "second strike capability," "stable deterrent," "finite deterrent," or "counterforce." By the late 1960's the jargon included ominous new acronyms: MIRV (Multiple Independently Targetable Reentry Vehicle), FOBS (Fractional Orbital Bombardment System), and ABM. Whatever parity had been achieved in the mutual "balance of terror" was threatened by new technology—the simultaneous development of the ABM as a defense against ballistic missiles, and the MIRV, designed to overwhelm the ABM system by firing from one missile a cluster of real and dummy warheads to confuse radar defenses. Both the United States and the Soviet Union were deploying these weapons in various forms in 1970.

The spiraling arms race, in short, threatened to go out of control. The history of United States development of the ABM illustrates the problem: in public testimony in January 1967, Secretary McNamara said the United States had "positive evidence" that the Soviet Union had deployed an ABM system around Moscow. However, he strongly opposed deployment of the ABM by the United States, warning that Soviet countermeasures would leave both countries with no net increase in security. But the Chairman of the Joint Chiefs of Staff, General Earle G. Wheeler, testified in favor of the ABM. Powerful groups in Congress also favored the program. In June, Communist China exploded its first hydrogen bomb. By late summer, the Johnson administration had reversed its course. In a speech at San Francisco in September, McNamara proposed that the United States build a "thin" ABM defense against Communist China. President Johnson's critics suggested that the decision was essentially political, designed to show a firm Democratic defense posture in advance of the 1968 election. Columnist James Reston characterized it as "an anti-Republican missile defense."[71] Although President Nixon modified Johnson's ABM plan and changed the system's name from Sentinel to Safeguard, the United States by 1970 had embarked on a new round of strategic spending for the ABM that would cost the taxpayers many billions of dollars.

Arms Control and Disarmament

The arms race and the strategy of deterrence, however "logical," could lead to disaster. One obvious but elusive alternative is arms control and disarmament, the subject of intermittent negotiations between Moscow and Washington since the Second World War.

In recent years, the spread of nuclear weapons to more countries has

---

[70] Ralph E. Lapp, *Kill and Overkill* (New York: Basic Books, 1962), p. 10.
[71] James Reston in the *New York Times*, September 22, 1967, p. 46.

complicated the picture. In 1963, in a speech at American University in Washington, D.C., President Kennedy announced that the United States had reached agreement with the Soviet Union to begin talks on a nuclear test ban treaty. The treaty, banning tests in the air, underwater, and in outer space—but not underground—was signed in Moscow in July 1963, and ratified by the United States Senate. More than one hundred nations signed the treaty, but two atomic powers—France and Communist China —refused to do so.

In 1968, the United Nations General Assembly voted approval of a draft treaty banning the spread of nuclear weapons to states not already possessing them. The United States, the Soviet Union, and sixty other nations signed, and the Senate ratified the Nonproliferation Treaty in March 1969. But Israel, India, and Japan, all potential nuclear powers, did not sign, nor did France or Communist China.

The major problem, reduction and control of nuclear weapons by the two superpowers, remained. Late in 1969, the United States and the Soviet Union opened SALT (Strategic Arms Limitation Talks) discussions. MIRV

ARMS CONTROL: NOT ONE CENT FOR COLOR TV

Congress is willing to spend billions for defense but some of its members are skeptical of spending for disarmament, as the following colloquy on the floor of the House of Representatives suggests:

Mr. Rooney of New York: As to the Arms Control and Disarmament Agency . . . The Committee is at a distinct loss to understand how color television sets and new electric refrigerators purchased with the American taxpayers' dollars, and installed in the private offices of those in the upper echelons of this agency, will materially contribute to arms control and disarmament activities. . . . When we . . . inquired as to why they would want $400 apiece brand new color television sets, we were informed that they wanted to hear President Nixon at his press conferences. . . .

We did not inquire as to what they were going to put in the brand new refrigerators. I thought they were pretty highhanded in doing what they did and using the taxpayers' money for such purposes. . . .

Mr. Gross: Would they come back down to their offices at night to see those night press conferences on television?

Mr. Rooney of New York: Now the gentleman is asking me a question I cannot answer.

Mr. Gross: It is incongruous to think they would have to have a color television set in their offices downtown in order to see a night Presidential press conference.

Mr. Rooney of New York: They could have gotten a $12 radio and heard it over the radio. . . .

Mr. Kyl: The gentleman would admit there are some things to be seen on color television sets, and some things which could be taken from the refrigerator which could be disarming.

Mr. Rooney of New York: The horse racing, I am told, is very good on Saturday afternoon in color.

Mr. Gross: In living color.

—*Congressional Record,* May 14, 1970.

and the ABM cast a long shadow over the negotiations. In 1969, President Nixon announced that the United States was renouncing germ warfare and would no longer stockpile *biological* weapons. However, he said the United States would continue to engage in "defensive research" in biological weapons. At that time the United States did not renounce *chemical* warfare, including the production of deadly nerve gases such as GB, or Sarin, a tiny drop of which kills instantly. President Nixon did reaffirm that the United States would not be first to use "lethal chemical weapons." [72] In 1970, President Nixon submitted to the Senate the Geneva Protocol outlawing chemical and biological warfare among nations. The United States had signed the treaty in 1925, but the Senate had never ratified it.

THE MILITARY-INDUSTRIAL COMPLEX

In his final speech to the nation, President Eisenhower warned against what he called "unwarranted influence" by the "military-industrial complex." [73] Eisenhower thus focused attention on the consequences for America of a vast military establishment linked to a huge arms industry. In the years after Eisenhower's 1961 warning, the concept of the "military-industrial complex" was expanded to encompass universities conducting defense research, scientists, laboratories, aerospace industry contractors, and research firms such as the Institute for Defense Analyses and the Rand Corporation.

Government defense contracts totaled $44 billion in 1968, and 3.6 percent of the labor force, or almost three million workers, were employed in defense-generated jobs.[74] Entire communities in some areas were dependent on defense industries or military installations. In fiscal 1969, Lockheed Aircraft Corporation received $2 billion in defense contracts from the government, topping the list of the hundred largest defense contractors in

[72] Congressional Record, *Weekly Report*, November 28, 1969, p. 2427.
[73] Dwight D. Eisenhower, *The White House Years, Waging Peace 1956–1961* (New York: Doubleday, 1965), p. 616.
[74] *Statistical Abstract of the United States, 1969*, pp. 247–49.

EISENHOWER'S WARNING: THE MILITARY-INDUSTRIAL COMPLEX

This conjunction of an immense military establishment and a large arms industry is new in the American experience. The total influence —economic, political, even spiritual—is felt in every city, every State house, every office of the Federal government. We recognize the imperative need for this development. Yet we must not fail to comprehend its grave implications. Our toil, resources and livelihood are all involved; so is the very structure of our society.

In the councils of government, we must guard against the acquisition of unwarranted influence, whether sought or unsought, by the military-industrial complex. The potential for the disastrous rise of misplaced power exists and will persist.

We must never let the weight of this combination endanger our liberties or democratic processes. We should take nothing for granted. Only an alert and knowledgeable citizenry can compel the proper meshing of the huge industrial and military machinery of defense with our peaceful methods and goals, so that security and liberty may prosper together.

—Dwight David Eisenhower,
Farewell Address to the American People, January 17, 1961.

the United States.[75] Companies such as Lockheed and General Dynamics are private only in a legal sense; in 1968, for example, defense contracts accounted for more than 80 percent of their sales. A list of the top ten defense contractors in America is shown in Table 14-1.

Defense spending fattens the congressional "pork barrel." Powerful individual legislators can, and do, obtain multimillion dollar contracts for their states and districts. Another example of the interrelationships within the military-industrial complex is the fact that retired military officers are

TABLE 14-1

Top Ten Defense Contractors in Fiscal 1969

Rank	Company[1]	Amount of Defense Contracts (in billions of dollars)
1	Lockheed Aircraft Corp.	2.04
2	General Electric Co.	1.62
3	General Dynamics Corp.	1.24
4	McDonnell Douglas Corp.	1.07
5	United Aircraft Corp.	.99
6	American Telephone and Telegraph Co.	.91
7	Ling Temco Vought Inc.	.91
8	North American Rockwell Corp.	.67
9	Boeing Co.	.65
10	General Motors Corp.	.58

[1] Includes subsidiaries

Source: Adapted from Congressional Quarterly, *Weekly Report,* November 28, 1969, pp. 2388–89.

[75] Congressional Quarterly, *Weekly Report,* November 28, 1969, p. 2388.

frequently hired by aerospace industry contractors; Senator Proxmire disclosed that the nine firms that stood to gain the most from production of the ABM employed a total of 465 retired officers.

The effect of the military-industrial complex is pervasive, and difficult to measure. But with many billions of dollars at stake, the scramble for contracts, the pressure on Congress and the Pentagon, and the political and economic rewards involved have, it may be argued, given some Americans a substantial interest in an economy geared to defense production.

One result of the military-industrial complex is that the United States has become arms salesman to the world. In 1970, the Pentagon estimated that United States arms sales abroad totaled almost $2 billion, or 40 percent of total world arms sales. About half the United States total represented direct sales by the Pentagon to other countries. In addition, the United States ships war materiel, ranging from rifles to jet planes, to other nations under a military assistance program that totaled $350 million in 1971.

The military-industrial complex has also had social and political effects. Demographically, it has been partly responsible for increased population in states such as California, Texas, and Florida with large defense or aerospace industries. This, in turn, has increased the political power of those states. Committee chairmen in Congress, such as the late Representative Mendel Rivers of South Carolina and Senator Richard Russell of Georgia, have been able to channel huge defense expenditures to their states, bringing economic benefits to those states and political benefits to the legislators.

THE MILITARY-INDUSTRIAL COMPLEX: SHE-CRAB SOUP AND CAMELLIAS

Until his death in 1970, Chairman L. Mendel Rivers of the House Armed Services Committee was one of the most powerful members of Congress in the area of military affairs, as the following account suggests.

For a number of years now Rivers has staged in Washington an annual luncheon featuring quail and a Charleston delicacy called she-crab soup, an event that employs three government kitchens. These affairs . . . are attended by the Joint Chiefs, the Secretaries of the services, assorted admirals and generals and Congressional Medal of Honor winners, along with dignitaries from such government contractors as Signal Oil, Avco, Lockheed, Sperry Gyroscope and the Chrysler Corporation, all of whom dine among camellias whisked up by the Charleston postmaster in his private plane. One guest came away from the occasion not long ago and remarked, "I used to wonder exactly what they meant by the military-industrial complex, exactly what it was. Now I know. I have beheld the military-industrial complex and it sits on the right hand of L. Mendel Rivers."

—Marshall Frady, "The Sweetest Finger This Side of Midas," *LIFE*, February 27, 1970.

On the other hand, in the 1970's, there were some counterpressures to military spending and military influence that did not exist a decade earlier. Some members of Congress were resisting a continued high level of defense expenditures. Public support for the war in Vietnam had eroded. And for the first time in recent history, the United States was a nation without a military hero.

AMERICA'S WORLD ROLE IN THE 1970'S

By the start of the 1970's, American losses in Vietnam and dissension at home had begun to bring about a reexamination of the nation's basic foreign policy and national security goals.

To some Americans, it appeared that a quarter of a century as a dominant world power had brought about a reversal of national priorities in American society. The United States had been engaged in a war in Southeast Asia for more than five years. American society had become increasingly polarized, with deep divisions between young and old, between doves and hawks, between social classes, between black and white. The nation had paid a price in more than 40,000 killed and 300,000 wounded. It paid a price in high taxes and inflation. It paid a price in neglect of its cities, its slums, its public schools, and its environment.

Perhaps there were other, less easily measurable, costs to the American character in prolonged exposure to violence and war. In 1970, for example, the Army brought charges against a number of American soldiers for the alleged murder of civilians in My Lai 4, a small hamlet in South Vietnam.[76] No one could really estimate the long-range effect on the American consciousness of a war that went on so long, took so many lives, and that was brought home nightly into millions of American living rooms on television.

And the United States—and the world—still lived under the shadow of nuclear disaster. Two new trends were discernible at the beginning of the 1970's: (1) increasing pressure at home for the United States to reduce its military involvement abroad and (2) some attempts to restrict the power of the President to commit the nation to war without approval of Congress.

Even if these pressures succeeded in forging new policies, the nuclear threat remained. As long as both sides possess atomic weapons there is a danger that they will be used. Presidents and others have warned of the possibility of accidental nuclear war. For these reasons, disarmament and arms control are urgent problems for America and the rest of the world.

The United States emerged from the Second World War as a major power, and it cannot wish away its power and global responsibility. But

[76] See Seymour M. Hersh, *My Lai 4* (New York: Random House, 1970).

What kind of peace do I mean? What kind of peace do we seek? Not a Pax Americana enforced on the world by American weapons of war. . . . I am talking about genuine peace, the kind of peace that makes life on earth worth living, the kind that enables men and nations to grow and to hope and to build a better life for their children—not merely peace for Americans but peace for all men and women —not merely peace in our time but peace for all time. . . . Total war makes no sense . . . in an age when the deadly poisons produced by a nuclear exchange would be carried by wind and water and soil and seed to the far corners of the globe and to generations yet unborn. . . .

First: Let us examine our attitude toward peace itself. Too many of us think it is impossible. . . .

We need not accept that view. Our problems are manmade—therefore, they can be solved by man. . . . No problem of human destiny is beyond human beings. . . . And if we cannot end now our differences, at least we can help make the world safe for diversity. For, in the final analysis, our most basic common link is that we all inhabit this small planet. We all breathe the same air. We all cherish our children's future. And we are all mortal.

—John F. Kennedy, Commencement Address at American University in Washington, June 10, 1963.

former Undersecretary of State George W. Ball has suggested that America can honestly redefine its foreign policy goals. Ball argues that while proclaiming itself in exaggerated rhetoric as the champion of freedom the United States has in reality been pursuing the more modest goal of maintaining a balance of power with the Soviet Union and mainland China. "But while practicing balance-of-power politics, we felt compelled to disavow it. . . . Thus we have gone steadily forward talking one game while playing another. . . . So now we are in a mess, and we have misled our children because we have not been honest either with them or with ourselves." [77]

One outcome of United States involvement in Southeast Asia was the growing conviction that America should exercise great caution in intervening in armed conflicts beyond its borders. Urgent domestic problems increased the pressures on the national leadership to weigh the legitimate concerns of American national security against the need to focus greater attention on the challenges at home, to take up the unfinished task of translating American ideals into reality.

[77] George W. Ball, "Foreign Policy is Camouflaged," *Washington Post*, May 10, 1970, p. B2.

SUGGESTED READING

Almond, Gabriel A. *The American People and Foreign Policy* * (Praeger, 1960). (Originally published in 1950.) An influential and valuable study of public opinion on foreign policy questions and how it relates to the formulation and conduct of American policy overseas.

Barnet, Richard J. *The Economy of Death* * (Atheneum, 1969). A critical examination of the military-industrial complex and the basic assumptions behind the defense budget. Offers concrete proposals for reducing military influence on government policy-making and argues for a reordering of national priorities.

Bauer, Raymond A., Pool, Ithiel de Sola, and Dexter, Lewis Anthony. *American Business and Public Policy: The Politics of Foreign Trade* (Atherton, 1963). A detailed analytical study of the varied factors affecting the development of American trade policy. Provides a useful assessment of the activities and influence of interest groups in this policy area.

Fulbright, J. W. *The Arrogance of Power* * (Random House, 1966). An examination of America's world role by one of its foremost congressional critics, the chairman of the Senate Foreign Relations Committee.

Hersh, Seymour M. *Chemical and Biological Warfare, America's Hidden Arsenal* * (Bobbs-Merrill, 1968). A detailed study of America's development of chemical and bacteriological weapons and of the secrecy surrounding them. Hersh, a Washington journalist, has helped to create an increased awareness of these controversial weapons among the public and in Congress.

Hilsman, Roger. *To Move a Nation: The Politics of Foreign Policy in the Administration of John F. Kennedy* * (Doubleday, 1967). An informative analysis of the foreign policy objectives and activities of the Kennedy administration. Hilsman served as a high official in the State Department during that administration.

Kennedy, Robert F. *Thirteen Days* * (Norton, 1969). A short, fascinating account of the Cuban missile crisis of 1962, as it appeared to a key participant in the crucial decisions made by the Kennedy administration. Reflects the great tension during the world's first nuclear confrontation.

Robinson, James A. *Congress and Foreign Policy Making,** rev. ed. (Dorsey Press, 1967). A careful and comprehensive analysis of congressional institutions and procedures for the consideration of foreign policy matters. Provides insights into the domestic roots and constraints of American foreign policy making.

Rosenau, James N., ed. *Domestic Sources of Foreign Policy* (Free Press, 1967). A useful series of essays on the interrelations between domestic politics and American foreign policy, written by a number of specialists in the field.

Sapin, Burton M. *The Making of United States Foreign Policy* * (The Brookings Institution, 1966). A comprehensive description and assessment of the institutions and political factors involved in the making of American foreign policy. Sapin, a foreign policy scholar, has also served in the Department of State.

Schlesinger, Arthur M., Jr. *A Thousand Days* * (Houghton Mifflin, 1965).

This account of the Kennedy Presidency, by a historian and former White House aide, contains useful insights into Kennedy's relations with the State Department and the administration's response to specific foreign policy crises.

Waltz, Kenneth N. *Foreign Policy and Democratic Politics: The American and British Experience* * (Little, Brown, 1967). A thoughtful analysis of the problems faced by democratic states in making foreign policy. Contains useful comparative data on Great Britain and the United States.

* Available in paperback edition

15

Promoting

the General Welfare

Pollution. The environment. The words are familiar today; only a few years ago they were not. As the decade of the 1970's began, however, significant numbers of Americans were becoming more aware of their environment. The fact that man, in the technological age, was slowly destroying nature and the earth itself—and endangering his own survival—had become a subject of major concern. It began to dawn on Americans that the air they breathed did not *have* to be polluted with chemicals. Their cities did not *have* to be enveloped in smog. Rivers did not *have* to be clogged with human and industrial waste. Seabirds and shorelines did not *have* to be destroyed by oil spills.

As these new attitudes emerged, greater public interest focused on the science of ecology, which deals with the relationship of living organisms and their environment. On April 22, 1970, millions of Americans observed "Earth Day" to demonstrate their concern.

The upsurge of interest in the quality of the natural environment was soon reflected in the political environment. Sensing an issue of explosive

595

importance, political leaders across the nation scrambled to stake out a position. By early 1970, President Nixon was attempting to seize the environmental high ground from the Democratic Congress. Leaders of both major parties vied with one another to claim credit for antipollution programs.

President Nixon sent a message to Congress in 1970 proposing that the Federal Government be given authority to regulate and levy fines against major polluters of the environment. In the past, congressional legislation had given the *states* primary responsibility for setting standards and enforcing antipollution laws. The President's program proposed $10 billion over a five-year period for construction of sewage treatment plants and penalties of $10,000 a day for cities and industries that violated federal air and water pollution standards. In addition, the President asked for legislation giving the Federal Government the power to force oil companies to remove lead from gasoline. And, he announced a federal research program to produce "an unconventionally powered, virtually pollution-free automobile" by 1975.[1]

Congress adopted many of these proposals in enacting the Clean Air Act Amendments of 1970. The measure, steered through the Senate by Edmund Muskie, Maine Democrat and chairman of a Senate subcommittee on pollution, provided for federal air quality standards governing major forms of pollution by industry. To enforce the new standards, the bill included tough criminal penalties: fines of up to $50,000 a day and two years in prison for violators. The bill also required that 1975- and 1976-model automobiles achieve a 90 percent reduction over 1970 levels in the emission of various pollutants.

In moving against pollution the Federal Government was taking a belated step toward requiring automobile manufacturers and other private corporations to comply with standards for the benefit of society as a whole. If the federal program proved effective, it would regulate one segment of society for the greater good of the majority of the people.

This responsibility of the national government to make *social policy* was recognized at the beginning of the American nation, for the Constitution was established, among other purposes, to "promote the general welfare."

It would be very difficult, if not impossible, for people, or even for for groups, to force American industry to eliminate pollution of the environment. But government, supported by public opinion and public demands, possesses the power to accomplish that task.

E. E. Schattschneider has suggested that "the struggle for power is largely a confrontation of two major power systems, government and busi-

[1] *New York Times*, February 11, 1970, pp. 1, 33; Congressional Quarterly, *Weekly Report*, February 13, 1970, p. 437.

Those of us who were born after 1900, or even after 1920, inherited a land that was generally pleasant, livable, and lovely to look at. To be sure, there were slums and tenements and soft coal soot, and quite a lot of mud mixed with the horse manure, but the quality of life, as measured in clean air, clean water, and verdant hills, was something to remember with wonder—and with dismay.

For the generations of this century have squandered that inheritance. Never was so great a trust so grossly violated. We turned our valleys into dust bowls and our rivers into sewers, killed the lakes, fouled the air, choked the cities. With the brute efficiency of systematic vandals, we combined stupidity and greed. Now we measure the quality of our life by the tons of litter we leave behind. The hallmark of our society is stamped on 10 million roadside bottles: No deposit, no return.

—James J. Kilpatrick, *Washington Evening Star,* January 8, 1970.

ness." The function of democracy, he argues, has been "to provide the public with a second power system, an alternative power system, which can be used to counterbalance the economic power." [2]

To "promote the general welfare," the Federal Government fills several major roles. It is regulator, promoter, manager, and protector. It performs these roles in a wide variety of ways. It regulates business and labor. But it also promotes business and labor. It assists farmers. It directly manages the armed forces, and such civilian agencies as the Atomic Energy Commission and the Tennessee Valley Authority. It tries to manage the economy through fiscal and monetary policies. It acts as protector in consumer affairs, health, education, welfare, science, poverty, hunger, and the environment.

The government does not necessarily perform all of these roles well. As we have seen throughout this book, there are many areas in which American government and society have failed to live up to American expectations. So in discussing government-in-operation, a distinction must be made between the various roles of the government and its actual performance.

A government like that of the United States, which takes responsibility for the welfare of its citizens in such areas as social security, housing, and education, is sometimes described as a "welfare state." The term is often used in criticism; in 1964, for example, the Republican candidate, Barry Goldwater, based his presidential campaign on such criticism of the welfare state. But the broad responsibility of the Federal Government to make social policy has been well established in this century, particularly since the days of the New Deal. The terms of the argument today usually concern the proper *extent* of government intervention in domestic problems, as well as *how* government should respond to national needs.

Where people stand on social welfare may be related to their eco-

[2] E. E. Schattschneider, *The Semisovereign People* (New York: Holt, Rinehart and Winston, 1960), pp. 118, 121.

Taxes pay for government social welfare programs. But there is wide disagreement on how tax money should be spent.

nomic, social, and political background. Government services require government spending, and the size of government programs is directly related to the level of taxes. The homeowner in a comfortable suburb may have less interest in federal welfare-assistance programs than the mother of four children living in a rat-infested Harlem tenement.

How and to what extent should government "promote the general welfare"? How well does it do so? How efficiently does government regulate corporate power on behalf of the consumer? How well has it performed in the field of social welfare, in eliminating poverty and hunger, in coping with rising medical costs and educational needs, in protecting the environment?

GOVERNMENT AS REGULATOR AND PROMOTER

The Constitution, as Justice Oliver Wendell Holmes, Jr., once wrote, "is not intended to embody a particular economic theory." [3] But the Supreme Court, which interprets the meaning of the Constitution, has often embodied the particular economic theory of its time. For half a century, from the late 1880's until 1937, during Franklin Roosevelt's New Deal, the Court generally intrepreted the Constitution in such a way as to prevent government from regulating industry. It adopted the prevailing *laissez faire* philosophy, which held that government should intervene as little as possible in economic affairs.

During the late nineteenth century economic power was concen-

Government and Business

[3] *Lochner v. New York*, 198 U.S. 45 (1905).

trated in the "trusts" and in the hands of the "robber barons." But a rising tide of populism created public demands that led to the passage of state and federal laws regulating industry. Nevertheless, the Supreme Court, as we noted in Chapter 13, interpreted the Fourteenth Amendment to protect business from social regulation by the states and by Congress.

Justice Holmes made the comment quoted at the beginning of this section in his famous dissent in the *Lochner* case. In that 1905 decision, the majority of the Supreme Court struck down a New York State law that had limited bakery employment to "sixty hours in any one week," and "ten hours in any one day." Today, it might seem incredible that the Supreme Court would permit a bakery owner to work his employees more than sixty hours a week. But in 1905, the Supreme Court refused to approve the use of the power of the state to regulate private property—in this case a bakery.

The Great Depression and the New Deal brought about a reversal of Supreme Court thinking. Since 1937, the Court has upheld laws policing business; and the right of government to regulate wages, hours, and working conditions of employees is now firmly established.

Regulating Business: Antitrust Policy. In 1890, Congress passed the Sherman Antitrust Act, which was designed to encourage competition in business and prevent the growth of monopolies. The Supreme Court severely limited the scope of the act, however, by ruling that it was up to the states to control industrial monopolies. Then in 1914, Congress passed the Clayton Act, which sought to put teeth into the federal antitrust law by defining illegal business practices and by providing the remedy of court injunctions and giving the FTC power to issue cease and desist orders. The same measure exempted labor unions from antitrust actions.

Subsequent legislation has strengthened the antitrust laws, and both the antitrust division of the Justice Department and the Federal Trade Commission have blocked many large corporate mergers. In a famous case in 1957, the Supreme Court, under the Clayton Act, forced du Pont to divest itself of 23 percent of the stock of General Motors.[4] The degree of enforcement of the antitrust laws varies, however, with the attitudes of the administration in power in Washington.

Although government regulation has had some success at blocking *monopoly*, control of a market by a single company, it has not been able to prevent *oligopoly*, the concentration of economic power in the hands of a relatively few large companies. Economist John Kenneth Galbraith has noted that "in the characteristic market of the industrial system, there are only a handful of sellers." [5]

---

[4] *United States v. E. I. du Pont de Nemours and Co.*, 353 U.S. 586 (1957).
[5] John Kenneth Galbraith, *The New Industrial State* (Boston: Houghton Mifflin, 1967), p. 179.

The 500 largest corporations in the United States control more than two-thirds of all manufacturing assets. In 1967, the revenues of General Motors were more than four times those of the state of Ohio. The ten largest corporations in the United States are shown in Table 15-1.

TABLE 15-1

The Ten Largest Industrial Corporations in the United States, 1969

Rank (by sales volume)	Company	Employees	Sales (in billions)	Assets (in billions)
1	General Motors	793,924	$24.3	$14.8
2	Standard Oil (N.J.)	145,000	14.9	17.5
3	Ford Motor	436,414	14.8	9.1
4	General Electric	400,000	8.4	6.0
5	International Business Machines	258,662	7.2	7.4
6	Chrysler	234,941	7.1	4.7
7	Mobil Oil	76,000	6.6	7.1
8	Texaco	72,572	5.9	9.2
9	International Tel. & Tel.	353,000	5.5	5.1
10	Gulf Oil	60,000	5.0	8.1

Source: Adapted from *Fortune*, May 1970, pp. 184–85. Reprinted from the Fortune Directory by special permission. © 1970 Time Inc.

Despite government regulation, American corporations are increasing in both size and diversity. Nothing illustrates the trend better than the rise in recent years of giant *conglomerates*, multi-interest corporations that may, under one corporate roof, manufacture products ranging from missiles to baby bottles. In 1970, the International Telephone & Telegraph Corporation was one of the largest conglomerates in America. It controlled such diverse companies as Avis-Rent-A-Car, Levitt & Sons (the builders), and the Sheraton hotels.

Because conglomerates are formed by mergers of companies in unrelated fields, they have long been considered exempt from antitrust prosecution. In recent years, however, the Justice Department, other branches of the Federal Government, and Congress have placed increasing pressure on conglomerates; the Tax Reform Act of 1969 eliminated some of the tax advantages of these giant companies.

The ordinary consumer cannot keep up with the complexities of corporate ownership in what Galbraith has called "the new industrial state." Ownership of industry has become more and more impersonal and remote. It is increasingly difficult for the private citizen to fix responsibility for corporate actions. But the issue of corporate responsibility extends beyond individual problems to the larger question of the responsibility of corporations toward society as a whole. The consumer movement, public concern over pollution by industry, and similar pressures have led a number of corporations to take steps to improve their public image in the area of corporate responsibility. Several large companies, for example, have participated in efforts to solve urban ills through such organizations as the Urban Coalition and the Committee for Economic Development. In the wake of well-publicized pressure by minority stockholders for the appointment of three directors to serve "in the public interest," the General Motors Corporation in 1970 named five directors to serve on a Public Policy Committee to investigate "all phases" of GM operations that affected the community at large. Such steps reflected corporate response to increasing public demands for pollution-free, safer automobiles. Increasing awareness of this issue of broader responsibility has led recently to the emergence of *public interest law firms* composed of young law school graduates. Instead of joining traditional, old-line law firms representing large corporations, they have offered their skills for the protection of consumers, minorities, and the poor.

The Regulatory Agencies. Although the Federal Government has responsibility for fostering competition through the antitrust laws, much of the day-to-day relations between government and industry are carried on through the giant federal regulatory commissions discussed in Chapter 11. Thus, the Securities and Exchange Commission (SEC) has responsibility for regulating the stock market; the Federal Communications Commission (FCC), the broadcast industry; the Interstate Commerce Commission (ICC), the transportation industry; the Federal Power Commission (FPC), power companies and utilities; the Civil Aeronautics Board (CAB), airlines; and the Federal Trade Commission (FTC), industry as a whole.

As Chapter 11 pointed out, many of these commissions have to varying degrees become captives of their client industries. A case in point is the railroad industry, which has long claimed that its passenger operations lose money while its freight operations make money. Although responsible for regulating the railroads in the public interest, the ICC permitted passenger service to decline to a point approaching extinction. An American visiting Japan or Italy will find better rail service in cleaner, more modern trains than he will find in his own country. In June 1970, Penn Central, the largest railroad in America, filed a bankruptcy petition. Because government did *not* effectively regulate the railroads in the past, it may find it necessary to take a more direct and costly role in the future.

In 1970, Congress passed legislation to establish a federally subsidized national rail network of passenger trains. The law created a government-sponsored corporation to run many of the nation's intercity passenger trains (but not commuter lines). Under the law, railroads are permitted to transfer operations between cities to the National Railroad Passenger Corporation, popularly known as Railpax. In return, the railroads receive stock in the government-subsidized corporation, or a tax deduction. The measure was enacted and signed into law by President Nixon amid considerable skepticism that it would reverse the decline in railroad passenger service. Not only in the area of passenger rail service, but in some other fields, government regulation of industry had proved inadequate.

Aiding Business. Related to the concept of government as regulator is that of government as promoter. Government promotes commerce by providing services and direct and indirect subsidies to producers and farmers. Many businessmen, farmers, veterans, and students, among others, benefit from government aid.

Appropriations for highways are indirect subsidies to truckers, bus lines, and automobile manufacturers. The Federal Government subsidizes airlines and railroads to carry the mail; it helps support the merchant marine through subsidies to shipbuilders. It finances airport construction and has spent millions on development of the highly controversial Supersonic Transport (SST) for commercial aviation.

In the "alphabet soup" of government agencies in Washington are several service agencies for industry—the Commerce Department and the Small Business Administration (SBA), for example, as well as the Agriculture Department, to serve farmers.

In addition to subsidies and services, the Federal Government assists industry through its *trade and tariff* policies. In the United States, a tariff is a federal tax on imports. A high tariff discourages other nations from sending goods to United States markets, and is therefore "protective" of American manufacturers. But a tariff wall can work two ways; other countries have retaliated by raising their tariffs on imports from the United States. Pressure from American industry seeking foreign markets for its products has resulted in a gradual reduction of United States tariff barriers since the 1930's. In 1947, the United States and twenty-two other nations signed the General Agreement on Tariffs and Trade (GATT), which provided a formal framework for international tariff reductions. The Trade Expansion Act of 1962 gave President Kennedy broad tariff-cutting authority, and more trade barriers fell during the 1960's.

During the 1960's, however, foreign industry in Japan and Western Europe threatened the competitive advantage previously enjoyed at home by American business. Protectionist sentiment succeeded in placing many restrictions on tariff reductions—for example, by imposing quotas on certain categories of imports. By 1970, in addition to the existing import quotas on oil, cotton textiles, tuna fish, potatoes, whiskbrooms, peanuts, cheddar cheese, and several other agricultural products, Congress was considering bills to restrict imports of textiles, shoes, and steel. Textile-producing states such as North Carolina were feeling the pressure from competing with textile imports from Japan; and New England shoe factories were suffering from competition with imports from Italy and Spain. In a post-election congressional session, the House passed a controversial bill setting quotas on importation of textiles and shoes. The measure also sought to restore the President's authority to reduce tariffs, which had lapsed in 1967. The Senate did not pass the trade bill in 1970.

Government and Labor

As in the case of business, labor is both regulated and assisted by the Federal Government. Today, organized labor wields great economic and political power in the United States. This was not always the case; the history of the labor movement in America is one of long struggle, intermittent violence, and only gradual recognition.

The industrialization of the nineteenth century brought the American laborer job opportunities in factories but scant bargaining power with his employers. As a result he worked long hours, at low wages, and under hazardous working conditions. In 1881, Samuel Gompers, a London-born cigarmaker, founded what became the American Federation of Labor (AFL). The Federation fought for "bread-and-butter" improvements—the eighthour day, higher pay, fringe benefits, and restrictions on child labor. The AFL was largely a federation of craft unions—groups of skilled workers organized by trades: construction, printing, railroads, mining, clothing manufacture, and others.

The Great Depression, which threw millions of people out of work, and the liberal policies of the New Deal created a favorable climate for labor expansion. In the mid-1930's, a group of labor leaders within the AFL began to organize industrial unions in the mass production industries, thus bringing unskilled workers into a labor movement dominated until then by craft unions. Led by John L. Lewis, head of the United Mine Workers, the dissidents formed a new labor organization that became known in 1938 as the Congress of Industrial Organizations (CIO). The CIO rapidly won recognition from the automotive, steel, rubber, and other industries. In 1955, the AFL merged with the CIO. By 1970, there were about 20 million union members in the United States, of which 14 million belonged to unions in the AFL-CIO.

In its early years the labor movement was unable to gain protection in the courts, so in the 1920's it turned to Congress for help. As early as 1926, the Railway Labor Act stated labor's right to organize and established a National Mediation Board to assist in settling rail strikes. The Norris-LaGuardia Act of 1932 sharply restricted the power of the courts to issue injunctions in labor disputes. Up to that time, employers were frequently able to break strikes by obtaining court injunctions against the unions. The National Labor Relations Act of 1935 was labor's great milestone. Sponsored by Senator Robert F. Wagner, Democrat, of New York, it established labor's right to collective bargaining and barred employers from setting up "company unions" (unions controlled by the employer) or discriminating against any worker for union activity or membership. The act also established the National Labor Relations Board (NLRB), an independent regulatory agency that supervises union elections and determines unfair labor practices. The Fair Labor Standards Act of 1938 established a minimum wage for American workers, a maximum forty hour work week, and time-and-a-half for overtime. It also outlawed child labor. Over the years, the minimum wage law has been amended by Congress and its coverage expanded. By 1970, the minimum wage was $1.60 per hour, and the law covered 44.5 million workers.

The power gained by labor during the New Deal inevitably brought a political reaction. The National Labor Relations Act had placed restrictions on employers but none on unions. In 1947, Congress passed the Taft-Hartley Act, which sought to shift some of labor's newly won power back to management. The act prohibited the "closed shop," under which only union members may be hired, but it did permit the "union shop," under which any person may be hired provided he joins the union within a specified time. Under Section 14B of the Taft-Hartley Act, nineteen states (nine in the South) passed state "right to work" legislation to outlaw the union shop. The act also defined and prohibited unfair labor practices by unions; expanded the membership of the NLRB, an agency that employers had considered too favorable to labor; barred labor unions from making political contributions; and outlawed strikes by government employees. Finally, the law provided that in strikes creating a national emergency, the President can seek a court injunction against a union during an eighty-day "cooling off period."

In the late 1950's a Senate committee held a series of hearings to investigate labor racketeering. The committee, under Senator John L. McClellan, an Arkansas Democrat, probed a number of unions, including the Teamsters' Union and the Textile Workers. Disclosures of union corruption, infiltration of labor unions by organized crime, and extortion received widespread publicity. Two successive Teamsters' Union presidents, Dave Beck and James R. Hoffa, eventually went to jail, and the AFL-CIO expelled the Teamsters. The televised hearings brought national recognition to the Senate committee's chief counsel, Robert F. Kennedy. It also led to demands for reform legislation.

The Labor Reform Act of 1959 (Landrum-Griffin Act) grew out of the hearings. The act (1) required unions to file elaborate financial reports, constitutions, and by-laws with the Secretary of Labor, (2) granted union members the right to elect officers by secret ballot, (3) barred ex-convicts from holding union office, and (4) tightened Taft-Hartley provisions against secondary boycotts, organizational picketing and certain other labor practices which employers felt gave unions an unfair advantage.

605

Despite the extensive labor legislation passed during this century, in an era of big business and big labor no effective mechanism exists to protect the *public* against strikes that may inconvenience millions of people—airline, rail, and garbage strikes, for example. Compulsory arbitration to settle major labor disputes has not won wide acceptance, and the problem of dislocating strikes in an industrial society remains.

Because unions have concentrated on bread-and-butter gains through collective bargaining, labor has made great economic progress in the United States. (The average bricklayer earns more than the average schoolteacher in America.) The extent of labor's *political* power is less clear. Unlike many industrial nations, the United States has never had a major, enduring "labor party." Rather than run its own candidates for political office, labor has usually worked through the two-party system. Since the New Deal era labor has usually supported the national Democratic party, but it carefully watches the records of members of Congress in both parties and supports those whom it considers friendly to labor. Although labor support is vital to many political candidates, the concept of a deliverable "labor vote" is dubious since union members are also Republicans and Democrats, as well as members of other groups. By 1970, President Nixon was actively wooing labor leaders and inviting them to dinner at the White House. And leaders of the Democratic party were worried that many blue-collar union members were slipping out of the Democratic fold in a backlash against student radicals, antiwar protesters, and other issues on which, in the view of some workers, Democrats were too "permissive." In 1968, for example, many blue-collar workers supported George Wallace even though their union leaders urged them to vote for Hubert Humphrey.

The Department of Labor, which achieved Cabinet status in 1913, administers and enforces laws relating to the welfare of wage earners in the United States. Its responsibilities include manpower and job training programs, administering the wages and hours law, and enforcing the safety and health standards for workers set by various federal laws.

MANAGING THE ECONOMY

In the spring of 1970, the United States was in the grip of serious inflation. Steadily rising consumer prices and high unemployment threatened the nation's economic health. Housewives, in an attempt to cope with supermarket price increases, watched for meat sales and tried as best they could to stretch the family food dollar. Young couples seeking to buy their first home frequently found they could not obtain a mortgage loan because money was scarce and bank interest rates too high. In May, after President Nixon sent American troops into Cambodia, the stock market plunged downward day after day to its lowest point in eight years. The president of the New York Stock Exchange and a group of the nation's leading businessmen—including the heads of General Motors, General Electric, and AT & T—joined forces and took action: they flew to Washington and saw the President.

No one expressed surprise that the business leaders of a nation that prides itself on a system of "free enterprise" should look to the President in Washington to provide a solution to the country's economic problems. Today, most people expect the Federal Government to exercise a major responsibility for the health, stability, and growth of the national economy.

The United States supposedly has a system of free enterprise, or capitalism. In theory, under such a system people own private property, either directly or as shareholders, and as consumers they participate in a free marketplace that responds to the laws of supply and demand. In practice, however, the United States has a *mixed* free enterprise system in which both private industry and government play important roles.

The individual's economic freedom is sharply limited by federal, state, and local economic policies. To begin with, if a person pays high federal, state, and local taxes, he will obviously have less to spend on consumer goods than he would if taxes were lower. If government fails to prevent a recession, he may be out of work. If government fails to prevent inflation, his dollar buys less; retired people living on pensions and savings may find their fixed incomes inadequate.

In general, Democrats tend to favor a larger role for government in regulating the welfare of society and the individual, and Republicans favor less government intervention. But the basic responsibility of government for the economy is now well established. In his Economic Report for 1970, President Nixon declared: "We have learned that Government itself is often the cause of wide swings in the economy. . . . The quality of life in America depends on how wisely we use the great influence that Government has." [6]

In 1933, at the height of the Great Depression, 13 million people— 25 percent of the labor force—were unemployed. The economy recovered rapidly during the Second World War. National growth with full employment became a major goal in the postwar world.

The Employment Act of 1946 spelled out in law the responsibility of the Federal Government for the economy: "It is the continuing policy and responsibility of the Federal Government to use all practicable means . . . to promote maximum employment, production and purchasing power." Although the act also stressed the responsibility of government to foster "free competitive enterprise," the major focus was on the role of govern-

---

[6] *Economic Report of the President,* transmitted to the Congress February 1970, together with the Annual Report of the Council of Economic Advisers (Washington, D.C.: U.S. Government Printing Office, 1970), pp. 3, 5.

ment in formulating economic policy. The law set up three pieces of machinery. First, it directed the President to submit an annual economic report to Congress. Second, it created a three-man Council of Economic Advisers to assist the President (see Chapter 10, pp. 398–99). Third, it created a Joint Economic Committee, made up of members of the House and Senate, to study the President's report and the economy.

The Federal Government attempts to influence the total shape of the economy through two sets of tools: *fiscal policy* and *monetary policy*. The fiscal tools of the government are spending, taxation, and borrowing. The monetary tools are control of the supply of money and credit through the Federal Reserve System.

Fiscal
Policy

Since the New Deal, many government economists have been influenced by the thinking of the British economist John Maynard Keynes. Keynes argued that when people did not consume and invest enough to maintain national income at full employment levels, government must step in, usually by cutting taxes or increasing spending in the public sector, or both. Keynesian economists and their modern successors place major emphasis on fiscal policy to manage the economy, although they recognize the role of monetary policy. More recently, the "Chicago school" of economists, led by Milton Friedman of the University of Chicago, has suggested that the money supply alone—the quantity of money in circulation —is the key to government regulation of the economy. He argues that interest rates, which are one aspect of monetary policy, and fiscal policy— taxes and spending—have little impact or importance. Friedman's views have by no means been universally accepted, and there is sharp disagreement among economists over what levers should be pulled to maintain price stability, full employment, and economic growth.

The Budget. The federal budget reflects an allocation of resources by the national government. But the budget is also an economic tool, embodying the President's fiscal policies. During a time of inflation, the President may cut spending and ask for higher taxes to cool down the economy. Or in a recession, he may propose a bigger budget, more public works spending, and lower taxes. By planning a budget surplus or deficit, the Federal Government attempts to pump money in or out of the economy to stimulate it or slow it down.

But the President must share with Congress his fiscal control over the economy. Only Congress can vote to spend federal funds. It does so in a two-step process. First, it passes *authorizations* to spend federal money. Second, it passes *appropriations* bills to pay for the spending it has authorized. Since an authorization without an appropriation is meaningless, the system places great power in the hands of the House and Senate appropriations committees and subcommittees. Congress may increase or cut the President's appropriations requests.

Once the money is appropriated, Congress has its own accountant to check up on how it is spent. He is the Comptroller General of the United States, who heads the General Accounting Office (GAO). Expenditures of public funds are audited under a joint accounting system developed by the GAO, the Treasury, and the Office of Management and Budget.

Taxes. "The Congress shall have Power To lay and collect Taxes." And Congress, as every taxpayer knows, exercises this constitutional authority. Under the budget for fiscal 1971, the Federal Government planned to spend $200 billion, all but a small fraction of it to be raised from taxes. Of every dollar the government took in during fiscal 1971, 45 cents came from individual income taxes, 17 cents from corporation income taxes, 24 cents from social insurance taxes, 9 cents from excise taxes (taxes on commodities), and 5 cents from other revenue sources.[7] Estimated tax receipts for 1971 appear in Table 15-2.

TABLE 15-2

The Federal Budget: Where the Money Comes From

Source	1971 Estimate (in billions)	Percent
Individual income taxes	$ 91.0	45%
Corporation income taxes	35.0	17
Social insurance taxes and contributions	49.1	24
Excise taxes	17.5	9
All other receipts	9.5	5
Total budget receipts:	$202.1	100%

Source: Adapted from *The Budget of the United States Government,* Fiscal Year 1971, p. 12.

As these figures show, individual income taxes are the Federal Government's largest single source of revenue. The federal income tax is graduated, on the theory that persons with higher incomes should pay more taxes. But taxpayers at all levels grumble about the tax squeeze; not many people enjoy paying their taxes or consider them low.[8]

[7] Estimates for fiscal 1971, in *The Budget of the United States Government,* Fiscal Year 1971, p. 6.
[8] In 1969, when a sample of the population was asked "Do you consider the amount of Federal income tax which you have to pay as too high, about right, or too low?" 69 percent replied "too high." (The Gallup Poll, April 12, 1969.)

Until this century the Constitution required the Federal Government to collect taxes based on state population. The Sixteenth Amendment, ratified in 1913, permitted the government to levy a general income tax. Since that time, however, various interest groups have lobbied Congress and won special tax advantages. The oil industry has its "depletion allowance." Businessmen enjoy liberal "expense account" deductions. People who sell property or stocks pay a lower "capital gains" tax than most ordinary wage earners pay on income. There are many other "loopholes" in the tax law. A rich person can afford to hire a high-priced tax attorney to find them. People in high income brackets may set up foundations, invest in tax-free municipal bonds, or take business losses that enable them to avoid high taxes. In 1959, five persons with incomes of more than $5 million each and one with an income of $20 million paid no federal income tax at all; in 1961 seventeen persons with incomes of $1 million or more also paid no tax; in 1967, twenty-three millionaires paid no income tax.[9]

By the end of the 1960's, growing public awareness of inequalities in the federal tax laws led to talk of "a taxpayer's revolt." Congress responded by passing the Tax Reform Act of 1969, which, among its many provisions: (1) raised personal exemptions from $600 to $750, as of 1973, (2) raised social security benefits by 15 percent, (3) reduced the oil depletion allowance from 27½ percent to 22 percent, (4) exempted 5.5 million low-income taxpayers from paying any tax at all, (5) established a *minimum* income tax of 10 percent on some kinds of formerly tax-free income over $30,000, and (6) tightened the tax laws applying to foundations.

The politics of taxation results in intense pressures on Congress from interest groups when changes in the structure of the tax laws are under consideration. And Congress and the President often fight political battles over how tax policy should be used as a fiscal tool to slow down or stimulate the economy.

The use of fiscal policy to control the economy depends, in theory, on delicate timing; but Congress tends to move very slowly in passing tax legislation. In 1964, Congress voted an $11.5 billion tax cut to promote economic growth more than a year after the original request by President Kennedy. In 1968, after another delay of almost a year, Congress granted President Johnson's request for a 10-percent tax surcharge to help finance the war in Vietnam. But it first insisted he cut $6 billion in spending. (The surcharge expired in 1970.) In 1962, President Kennedy asked for standby power to raise or lower taxes up to 5 percent, but Congress declined to give up this power to the Chief Executive.

[9] Philip M. Stern, *The Great Treasury Raid* (New York: Random House, 1964), p. 4; 1967 data from *Statistics of Income 1967, Individual Income Tax Returns* (Washington, D.C.: U.S. Government Printing Office, 1969), p. 27.

Borrowing. When the Federal Government spends more than it earns, it has to borrow. The national debt stood at $16.2 billion in 1930; by fiscal 1971 it was estimated at $382.5 billion. The government borrows by selling federal securities to individuals, corporations, and other institutions. In 1917, Congress passed a statutory debt limit, or ceiling, on government borrowing, but the limit has been revised upward many times. Borrowing costs money; in fiscal 1971, the government spent $17.7 billion, almost 9 percent of the federal budget, on interest payments.

Government also attempts to regulate the economy by *monetary policy*—controlling the supply of money and the cost and availability of credit. It does this through the operations of the Federal Reserve System. "The Fed," as the system is often called, was established in 1913. Prior to that time, the United States had no way to expand and contract the money supply according to the needs of the economy. To provide such an *elastic* system Congress created the Federal Reserve.

Monetary Policy

The Fed is headed by the Board of Governors of the Federal Reserve System. Although the board's seven members are appointed by the President with the approval of the Senate, they serve overlapping fourteen-year terms and are largely independent of both Congress and the White House. The chairman, appointed by the President for a term of four years, can, and sometimes does, oppose the policies of the administration. The Fed is the central banking system of the United States; it operates through twelve Federal Reserve Banks and twenty-four branches across the nation. All national banks and about 14 percent of state banks are members of the system.

When an individual or a corporation needs money, it normally borrows from a bank. When banks need money, they may borrow from the Federal Reserve System. The Federal Reserve is, therefore, a banker's bank. When it lends to the banks, it can, in effect, create new money.

Through its control of the flow of money and credit within the United States, the Fed attempts to pump more money into the economy when a recession threatens. In a time of rising prices and excessive spending, the Fed normally tries to tighten the supply of money and credit so that people will have less to spend. As one chairman remarked, the Fed tries "to lean against the prevailing economic winds." It does so chiefly in four ways:

1. Open Market Operations. Banks lend money to people in relation to the amount of reserves the banks have on deposit with the Federal Reserve. When the Fed sells government bonds on the open market, the effect is to reduce bank reserves and tighten credit; banks then have less money to lend to people. Or, the Federal Reserve can buy government securities and expand credit.

2. The Fed can raise or lower the "rediscount rate" that it charges member banks for loans. This affects interest rates in the economy generally.
3. It can raise or lower the size of the reserves that member banks must keep in the Federal Reserve banks against their deposits and thus tighten or expand credit.
4. It can raise or lower the "margin requirements" for persons buying securities. The margin requirement defines how much money people can borrow to purchase stocks.

Most United States economists believe that a stock market crash and depression as severe as that which began in 1929 are unlikely to happen again because there are more built-in economic stabilizers today. But there is wide disagreement among economists and politicians over the best way to promote employment and economic growth. Some measures are politically safer to take than others; for example, it is easier for government to spend money on public works to combat recession than it is to enforce wage-price guidelines to fight inflation. Whatever steps an administration takes carry great political risks if they fail. Prosperity and "bread-and-butter" concerns are often key election issues, and both the President and Congress try to steer a safe course between the twin reefs of recession and inflation.

GOVERNMENT AS PROTECTOR

During the 1964 presidential campaign, Barry Goldwater spent a good deal of time explaining that he did not really favor abolishing social security. What he *had* proposed, Goldwater said, was that it be made "voluntary." Even so, President Johnson used the issue against Goldwater to good effect, for millions of Americans were drawing social security retirement benefits.

In the past four decades, the national government has enacted multibillion dollar social welfare programs—ranging from social security to antipoverty measures. Although a majority of Americans grumble about high taxes, by and large they expect the government to act as protector of the general welfare. Proposing to tamper with or modify these established programs carries a high political risk, as the Goldwater campaign suggested.

By 1970, the strength of the consumer and environmental movements in America indicated that government may be asked to do more, not less, in the future. Clearly, major battles lay ahead in these and other public policy areas. In the rest of this chapter, we shall explore some of the important aspects of government-as-protector.

By the end of the 1960's, many Americans were aware that government had often failed to protect ordinary consumers from the perils of the marketplace. Much of that public awareness was the work of a single crusader for consumer protection, attorney Ralph Nader (see Chapter 11).

In *Unsafe at Any Speed,* published in 1965, Nader charged that the automobile industry bore partial responsibility for many highway accidents and deaths by making cars that emphasized style over safety.[10] Nader was then investigated by private detectives hired by attorneys for the General Motors Corporation. A Senate subcommittee disclosed that the private detectives had put Nader under surveillance and had even checked into his sex life. As a result of the Senate investigation, James M. Roche, the president of GM, found it prudent to apologize publicly to Nader at a committee hearing.[11]

Government and the Consumer

[10] Ralph Nader, *Unsafe at Any Speed* (New York: Grossman, 1965).
[11] In 1970, four years after the Senate hearings, GM paid Nader $425,000 in an out-of-court settlement of his invasion of privacy suit. (*New York Times,* August 14, 1970, p. 1.)

J. B. Handelsman
Copyright 1969 Saturday Review, Inc.

"Typical. You don't look at what you're buying
and then you come back crying to us."

613

In 1965, Ralph Nader, a thirty-one-year-old Connecticut attorney, criticized the safety of American automobiles, particularly, General Motors' Corvair, in his book *Unsafe at Any Speed*. General Motors, through an attorney in Washington, hired a "private eye" to investigate Nader. Senate investigators found that the New York detective agency, Vincent Gillen Associates, Inc., had issued the following instructions to its "gumshoes."

The above apparently is a freelance writer and attorney. Recently he published a book "Unsafe at Any Speed," highly critical of the automotive industry's interest in safety. Since *then our clients' client apparently made some cursory inquiries into Nader to ascertain his expertise, his interest, his background, his backers, etc. They have found out relatively little about him, and that little is detailed below. Our job is to check his life, and current activities to determine "what makes him tick," such as his real interest in safety, his supporters, if any, his politics, his marital status, his friends, his women, boys, etc., drinking, dope, jobs—in fact all facets of his life. This may entail surveillance which will be undertaken only upon the OK of Vince Gillen as transmitted by him to the personnel of Vincent Gillen Associates, Inc.*

—Hearings before the Subcommittee on Executive Reorganization, Committee on Government Operations, United States Senate, *Federal Role in Traffic Safety*, March 22, 1966.

The congressional investigation of GM's shocking action against a private citizen made Nader a national figure overnight. In the years that followed, he played a vital role in the passage of five major federal consumer laws. GM removed the Corvair from production after Nader's charges that the car was hazardous to drive under certain conditions. The response to Ralph Nader's crusades reflected a growing interest in consumer affairs by the public, the press, Congress, and the executive branch.

The basic demand of the consumer movement is that government step in to protect buyers from hazardous products, shoddy merchandise, mislabeling, fraudulent sales techniques, consumer credit abuses, and other deceptive or dangerous practices. "Consumerism" holds that when business will not police itself, government must act.

The housewife who must send her coffeepot to the repair shop three times before it is fixed properly; the child playing with an inflammable toy; the ghetto resident talked into buying an overpriced bedroom suite for "only $399"; the family injured in an auto crash because of defective tires—all are victims of consumer abuses. Many products that Americans buy seem to have "built-in" obsolescence—that is, they are designed to wear out after a certain amount of time.

Consumer frauds victimize the most those who can afford it the least. Various studies have shown that "the poor pay more." Residents of urban ghettos often buy low quality merchandise at high prices. Why? One reason is that neighborhood merchants extend "easy" credit terms to poor people who may not be able to buy on credit in major department stores. And, as David Caplovitz has noted in his study of poverty areas in Manhattan, "neighborhood merchants . . . compensate for extending credit to poor risks by high markups." [12] The result is that poor families often end up paying higher prices for appliances such as television sets, phonographs, and washing machines than do more affluent families.[13] To deal with customers who cannot keep up the payments, the merchant can use the weapons of repossession and salary garnishment, backed by the power of the law.

In Philadelphia in 1963, an elderly black couple, Mr. and Mrs. John Gallman, signed up with a salesman to have some painting and home repairs done and a new storm door installed, all for $650. In reality, the job was worth $250. Soon they received a notice from the Mid-Penn Discount Corporation that they owed $1,632, a figure that apparently included $982 in finance charges. When the couple dropped behind on their payments after many months, the finance company demanded that their property be put up for auction; two sheriff's deputies and eight policemen smashed the glass in the front door and broke into the couple's home to take their furniture. Mrs. Gallman "became hysterical and attempted to ward off the men with a barbecue fork." Injured in the fight, she was taken to the hospital. Her husband was overpowered by the police, who removed their furniture, valued at more than $2,000 and acquired over thirty-five years of marriage.[14]

During the 1960's, legislation was passed to deal with consumer problems, and limited machinery to deal with consumer problems was established within the executive branch. Presidents Kennedy, Johnson, and Nixon all appointed staff assistants for consumer affairs. Several federal agencies are involved in consumer matters, but the principal responsibility is in the hands of the much-criticized Federal Trade Commission. (See Chapter 11, pp. 443–46.) In 1970, Congress considered legislation to create a single Consumer Protection Agency in the executive branch to act as an advocate and protector of consumers. The measure passed the Senate that year but was blocked in the House Rules Committee.

The principal consumer laws passed during the 1960's dealt with:

1. *Auto safety* (1966). One law required manufacturers to meet federal standards for automobile and tire safety, and another required each state to establish federally approved highway safety programs or lose 10 percent of federal highway construction funds.
2. *Truth-in-packaging* (1966). To help shoppers make price comparisons, a law was passed requiring manufacturers to label their products more clearly. But it did not require standard package sizes, which would have aided housewives in threading their way through the supermarket jungle of "jumbo," "family," and "large economy" sizes.

[12] David Caplovitz, *The Poor Pay More* (New York: Free Press of Glencoe, 1963), p. 85.
[13] *Ibid.*, p. 84.
[14] Senator Warren G. Magnuson and Jean Carper, *The Dark Side of the Marketplace* (Englewood Cliffs, N.J.: Prentice-Hall, 1968), pp. 46–48.

3. *Meat and poultry inspection* (1967 and 1968). Two laws were designed to tighten consumer protection against poor quality meat and poultry. Prior to this legislation these products were subject to federal inspection when shipped between states, but products consumed within a state were subject only to state inspection. And, seven states had *no* meat inspection at all.
4. *Truth-in-lending* (1968). This legislation requires merchants and lenders to provide full, honest, and understandable information about credit terms. For example, a customer who agrees to pay "only 3 percent per month" must now be told that the *annual* interest rate is actually 36 percent.

Other important consumer measures enacted into law were designed to protect children and householders from inflammable and dangerous products, to limit the emission of radiation by color TV sets, and to tighten pipeline safety standards. In almost every case, industry lobbied against these bills and often succeeded in weakening the final versions.

There is, in fact, some danger that the passage of consumer legislation will create the appearance of government regulation without the reality. In 1970, a report to a panel established by Congress charged that three major consumer laws had merely created "a facade of consumer protection." [15] The study group of the National Commission on Product Safety singled out for criticism the laws dealing with auto safety, inflammable fabrics, and

ACCELERATING PROBLEMS OF THE CONSUMER

The gas gauge was nearing "empty" so the University of Arizona co-ed pulled off the freeway into the nearest service station. All went routinely enough until suddenly she noticed white smoke billowing out from under the open hood. The attendant, standing over it with a properly concerned expression, informed her that the car needed "a new accelerator in its generator" and that if she tried to drive out of the station without having it fixed, the car would be ruined.

One tank of gas and $119 later the student was back on the freeway, heading for the university campus. To confirm her growing suspicion, she took the car to her regular mechanic for a recheck. His verdict: Potassium powder had been used to simulate smoke, and she had been "conned" (a generator does not have an accelerator).

The case is not as exceptional as one might think. Despite stepped-up efforts by law-enforcement agencies and more widespread and vehement complaining on the part of car owners, deceptive auto-repair practices persist as a major consumer problem.

—*Christian Science Monitor*, January 29, 1970.

[15] *New York Times*, June 3, 1970, p. 1.

hazardous substances. The report said that the government agencies responsible for enforcing these laws were weak and understaffed, and added: "One consequence of these conditions has been a widespread public deception. Contrary to broad public expectations, urgent problems of product safety are not being handled." [16]

In 1970, about 26 million Americans—retired or disabled workers and their dependents—received about $33 billion in social security payments. Another 12 million people received public assistance (welfare) payments of $9 billion, of which the Federal Government paid about 60 percent (with state and local governments paying the rest). In addition, a weekly average of 1.3 million jobless workers collected about $3 billion in unemployment insurance.

The
General Welfare

Yet, prior to 1935, these programs did not exist. The hardships of old age, ill health, poverty, unemployment, blindness, or disability were problems for individuals, their families, private charity, and states and local communities.

The depression of the 1930's changed all that. Millions lost their jobs, and a blight of hunger and poverty descended on the land. "Brother, can you spare a dime?" was a popular song of 1932. America realized that individuals needed help from the national government to maintain their income in hard times. In the midst of the Great Depression, Franklin D. Roosevelt proposed, and Congress passed, the landmark Social Security Act of 1935. Although to some Americans it seemed a revolutionary step at the time, the United States was the last major industrial nation in the world to adopt a general system of social security.

There are two kinds of social welfare programs in operation, both designed to guarantee personal economic security to individuals. One is called *social insurance*. The social security program is, in effect, a compulsory national insurance program, self-financed by taxes on employers and employees. The other kind of program, *public assistance*, has no pay-as-you-go features; it simply distributes public funds to people who are poor. (Recipients are usually said to be on "relief" or on "welfare.") The distinction is important, because each approach has significant political consequences.

Social insurance is widely accepted because it is "earned." People assume they have a "right" to retirement income after a lifetime of work. But "welfare" programs do not enjoy the same easy acceptance by the public. Many Americans who receive welfare payments, and many others who do not, believe society has a responsibility to care for those who are less fortunate. However, as Gilbert Steiner points out, some Americans

[16] *Ibid.*

resent supporting those who can't make their own way. . . . The idea of "toughening up" is forever popular. Toughening up, it is argued, will drive the cheaters out, the slackers to work, the unwed mothers into chastity; and it will save money. It is this clash between the ideas of public aid as a right and public aid as a matter of sufferance, to be granted with suspicion, with strings, and with restraints, that is reflected in public policy debates and political action.[17]

Social Security.   The Social Security Act of 1935 and its later amendments provide for *both* social insurance and public assistance programs. The insurance aspects fall into four categories: old-age insurance, survivors and disability insurance, Medicare, and unemployment insurance.

When people talk about receiving "social security," they generally mean the monthly cash payments received by retired, older people. When a man reaches the age of sixty-five (age sixty-two for a woman), he may draw social security payments if he has worked enough years to qualify—five years in 1971, increasing gradually to ten years by 1991. The payments depend on his average earnings over a period of years. In 1970, *average* monthly benefits were $116 for a single person and $196 for a couple. (Examples of social security payments are shown in Table 15-3.)

TABLE 15-3

Examples of Monthly Cash Payments Under Social Security

	Average Yearly Earnings after 1950	
	$3000 (average yearly earnings)	$7800 (average yearly earnings)
Retired worker—65 or older / Disabled worker—under 65	$132.30	$250.70
Wife 65 or older	66.20	125.40
Widow under 62 with two children	202.40	434.40
One child of retired or disabled worker	66.20	125.40
Maximum family payment	202.40	434.40

Source: "Your Social Security," U.S. Department of Health, Education, and Welfare, Social Security Administration (Washington: U.S. Government Printing Office, 1970), p. 12. Data as of 1970.

As originally passed, Social Security provided only retirement benefits. In 1939, the program was expanded to provide payments to dependents and survivors of workers covered by the system. And in 1956, it was expanded to include disabled workers.

[17] Gilbert Y. Steiner, *Social Insecurity, The Politics of Welfare* (Chicago: Rand McNally, 1966), pp. 7–8.

Over the years, Congress has extended social security coverage to virtually all types of workers. The system is financed by a social security tax levied equally on employers and employees. Self-employed persons also pay a social security tax. In 1970, employers and employees each paid 4.8 percent of an employee's income up to a ceiling of $7,800 (earnings beyond this amount were not taxed for social security purposes); self-employed persons paid 6.9 percent. But that year the House approved President Nixon's request to tie social security benefits to the cost of living; it granted a 5 percent increase in benefits, starting in January 1972, and raised the tax base from $7,800 to $9,000. The Senate approved a 10 percent increase in Social Security benefits late in 1970, but the Ninety-first Congress adjourned without reconciling the differences in the two bills.

Medicare. In 1965, Congress added health insurance for persons sixty-five and over to the social security program.[18] Medicare helps to pay hospital bills, and for those who choose to pay an extra amount ($5.30 a month in 1970) it also pays part of doctor bills. In 1970, of the 19.9 million people on Medicare all but 1 million had also enrolled in the voluntary insurance program for doctor bills.

The program will undoubtedly cost more in the future. Medical costs have already greatly exceeded estimates made when the program began. Inflation has affected doctors' fees and hospital costs, but so has Medicare itself: some physicians increased their fees just before the program went into effect.

Unemployment Insurance. The social security benefits discussed above are paid directly by the Federal Government. But the Social Security Act of 1935 also virtually forced the *states* to set up unemployment insurance programs to pay benefits to people out of work. The program is financed by federal and state taxes on employers of four or more persons (and on employees in three states). Every state has an unemployment insurance program, but the size of benefits and the amount of time they are granted vary greatly. In 1970, about 58 million workers were covered but 17 million were not; most states paid unemployment benefits for twenty-six weeks, but a typical maximum weekly payment of $45 was scarcely enough to support a jobless worker with a wife and children.

Welfare: Politics and Programs. "America's welfare system is a failure that grows worse every day," President Nixon told Congress in 1969.[19] He used those words in a message to Congress proposing a complete reform of the nation's welfare programs.

---

[18] Part of the total social security tax, 1.6 percent, went to pay for Medicare benefits.
[19] Congressional Quarterly, *Weekly Report*, August 15, 1969, p. 1521.

WELFARE: A PRESIDENT'S PLEA FOR REFORM

Our states and cities find themselves sinking in a welfare quagmire as caseloads increase, as costs escalate and as the welfare system stagnates enterprise and perpetuates dependency. What began on a small scale in the depression '30s has become a monster in the prosperous '60s. The tragedy is not only that it is bringing states and cities to the brink of financial disaster, but also that it is failing to meet the elementary human social and financial needs of the poor.

It breaks up homes. It often penalizes work. It robs recipients of dignity. And it grows.

—President Nixon, televised address to the nation, August 8, 1969.

The Social Security Act of 1935 created three public assistance, or "welfare" programs: old-age assistance, aid to the blind, and the largest program, known later as Aid to Families with Dependent Children (AFDC). In 1950, a fourth program was added, aid to the permanently and totally disabled.

The cost of these programs and the number of people receiving welfare payments have steadily increased. For example, during the decade of the 1960's, federal, state, and local welfare spending doubled, from $3 billion to $6 billion, and the number of recipients increased from about 7 million to more than 10 million.

The Federal Government provides most of the money for the welfare system in the form of grants to the states. In some states, local governments also assume part of the cost. State and local welfare agencies run the programs.

When President Nixon proposed his reforms the welfare system was under attack on several grounds. First, it did not cover all the poor. The Census Bureau estimated that in 1969 24.3 million Americans were living in poverty, defined in that year as an income of $3,743 a year or less for a nonfarm family of four.[20] But only 8.9 million people, or slightly more than one-third of the total number of poor people, were receiving welfare assistance in 1969.

Because the states controlled the programs, benefits varied sharply. Southern states paid lower welfare benefits than the big industrial states of the North. For example, in 1969, monthly payments to a family of four with dependent children averaged $171 nationally, but payments ranged all the way from $263 a month in New Jersey down to $38.75 a month in Mississippi.

One of the worst features of the welfare system was that for many years welfare assistance was available only to mothers with children and no male breadwinner. The welfare program therefore encouraged a father to desert his family so that his wife and children could obtain welfare payments. Amendments to federal law in 1967 permitted states to make payments to families with unemployed fathers, but only half the states did so.

[20] U.S. Bureau of the Census, *Current Population Reports*, Population Characteristics, Series P-20, No. 204, July 13, 1970, p. 6.

Another problem was posed by the fact that more than one-third of the states had some kind of rule barring welfare payments to families in which there was a "man in the house" who was not married to the mother. Welfare recipients objected strongly to this attempt by the states to regulate moral behavior. The United States Supreme Court has ruled in recent years that states may no longer restrict welfare payments to dependent children just because there is a "man in the house," unless it can be shown

THE INDIGNITIES OF WELFARE

In San Diego County . . . applicants for AFDC are referred to the Family Support Division of the District Attorney's office regarding maternity. Among the 30 to 40 questions which the mother is required to answer are the following:

When did you first have sex relations with the father? _____

Give number of times you had sex relations with the father before you became pregnant.

_____

After you became pregnant? _____

With whom? _____

How many times did you have sex relations two weeks before _____ *and two weeks after* _____ *you became pregnant? With whom?* _____

If the AFDC applicant refuses to follow through on the referral to the Family Support Division or refuses to "cooperate," her application for assistance is automatically denied.

Of course, we have no way of knowing how many nonwhites, dependent on public assistance, have "cooperated" out of fear that this tenuous lifeline might otherwise be severed.

—Robert H. Cohen, "Welfare: Race and Reform," *Civil Rights Digest,* Fall 1969.

Ain't no lazy people on Welfare. . . . But every time you want something extra from them, it's a whole nuisance. Like carfare. Sometimes I got to spend ninety cents for carfare for me and the kids to go off to Bellevue, because, as I told you, you can't leave them alone if you got to go there for some reason. And when I come back from Bellevue clinic, I got to rush over here to 28th Street for that carfare money or else I'm going to run short on food. Well, even so, they don't just give you your money like that. Sometimes they want proof. Sometimes they say they will owe it to you. You got to be careful about the ones who say that. I learned you got to insist right then and there you want that carfare or else you don't get it. So you just got to sit there and wait for the man until he gives it to you. You think they care? Sometimes I spend half my life waiting somewhere for ninety cents.

—Barbara Dugan, quoted in Richard M. Elman, *The Poorhouse State.*

that he is actually contributing some of his income to the support of the children.[21]

The welfare system has frequently been criticized on the grounds that it degraded those whom it was attempting to help. Welfare agencies regularly investigated those on relief, and poor people often regarded welfare workers as unwelcome detectives. Sometimes, welfare agencies staged midnight raids to try to catch a "man in the house." Behind all this is the public suspicion that many welfare recipients are "loafers" and "chiselers."

The welfare program that emerged from the New Deal was criticized on the basis that it "creates a class of dependent persons and then sustains them in their dependency." [22] During the 1960's an alternative approach evolved, sometimes called a "guaranteed annual income" or a "negative income tax." Its basic premise is that people are poor because they lack money; and that therefore the way to cure poverty is to give poor people money.

In modified form, this approach was adopted by President Nixon when he submitted his welfare reforms to Congress in 1969. Nixon's program, called the Family Assistance Plan, worked as follows: All families with children and a yearly income below certain levels—$3,920 for a family of four, for example—would receive a federal cash payment of $1,600 a year. A father or mother who worked could, in addition, keep $60 a month, but on all earnings above that amount, the welfare payment would be reduced 50 cents for each dollar earned, up to the cutoff point of $3,920. Thus the program, President Nixon predicted, "would create a much stronger incentive to work."

The Family Assistance Plan would cover about 28 million people. For the first time, it would provide welfare benefits to poor people who work,

[21] *Lewis v. Martin,* 397 U.S. 552 (1970); *King v. Smith,* 392 U.S. 309 (1968).
[22] Daniel P. Moynihan, "One Step We Must Take," *Saturday Review of Literature,* May 23, 1970, p. 22.

but whose incomes are still very low. In twenty states, the $1,600 annual payment exceeded average family benefits under the Aid to Families with Dependent Children program. But the thirty states in which benefits exceeded $1,600 would be required to maintain the previously existing levels.

Critics of the Nixon program attacked the $1,600 figure as much too low, noting that it was less than half of the income level below which the Census Bureau officially considers a family of four to be "poor." The militant National Welfare Rights Organization, for example, demanded an annual cash benefit of $5,500 for a family of four.

In April 1970, the House passed President Nixon's welfare reform program, including the new $1,600 annual federal payment. But over the summer the bill appeared to be in serious trouble in the Senate Finance Committee. In August, in an attempt to rescue the legislation from oblivion, the President agreed to an amendment offered by Senator Abraham Ribicoff, Democrat of Connecticut, to test the program for one year in selected areas of the country before it went fully into effect in January 1972. Before the 1970 elections, the Senate Finance Committee voted down the President's original welfare reform proposals. In October, in an effort to save

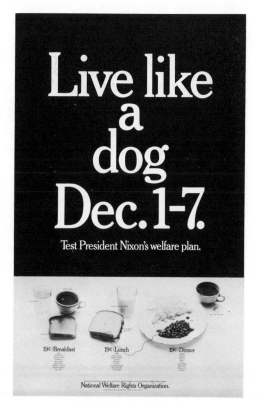

The National Welfare Rights Organization used this dramatic poster to criticize President Nixon's plan to reform the welfare system.

the plan, the administration offered an amendment to increase the minimum payment to $2,200 by eliminating the federal food-stamp program and substituting an all-cash payment to welfare recipients. In addition, the amendment provided that poor persons who worked could earn up to $4,380 a year (instead of $3,920) before benefits would be cut off completely. But the welfare reform plan remained embroiled in controversy in the Senate when Congress reconvened in the 1970 post-election session and the Senate adjourned without approving welfare reform.

The Politics of Poverty — "This administration," President Lyndon B. Johnson declared in his first State of the Union Message, "today here and now declares unconditional war on poverty in America." [23]

When President Johnson spoke these words in January 1964, many Americans might have wondered what he was talking about. Through the picture window of split-level suburbia, the poor could not be seen. Yet they were there, millions of people living in poverty in the mountains of Appalachia and the slums of the great cities. When the black urban ghettos exploded in flames during the second half of the decade, the poor became more visible.

The federal antipoverty program was sparked by the publication in 1963 of Michael Harrington's *The Other America*, a book that described in forceful language the extent of poverty in the United States and had a substantial impact among segments of the public and within the Federal Government. The poor, he noted, were "across the tracks," out of view of more comfortable Americans.[24] The poor lived, in Ben Bagdikian's words, "in the midst of plenty," occupying "a world inside our society in which the American dream is dying." Yet, poor people "are not made so differently from their fellow Americans." [25]

Who are the poor?

The Federal Government answers the question in terms of how many people have incomes below a certain "poverty" level. But to some extent poverty is a relative term; a person may feel poor if he has a good deal less than most other people have. And, with affluence no farther away than the commercials shown on television, the poor person in American society is constantly reminded of his poverty.

In statistical terms, the Census Bureau, as we have noted, estimated that in 1969 there were 24.3 million poor people in the United States. The profile of the poor included these facts:

[23] *1964 Congressional Quarterly Almanac*, p. 862.
[24] Michael Harrington, *The Other America* (New York: Macmillan, 1962), p. 4.
[25] Ben H. Bagdikian, *In the Midst of Plenty* (Boston: Beacon Press, 1964), pp. 6–7.

1. There were more than twice as many poor white people as poor blacks—16.7 million as compared to 7.6 million. But a higher percentage of black Americans were poor—almost one out of every three blacks as opposed to one out of every ten whites.
2. About 12 percent of the nation's population was poor.
3. The number of poor people has decreased by more than 14 million in the last decade, and the proportion of poor people in American society has been declining.

In response to President Johnson's "war on poverty," Congress in 1964 passed legislation creating the Office of Economic Opportunity (OEO). Among its major programs were these:

The Job Corps. This program was designed to provide education and vocational training for young school "drop-outs," ages sixteen through twenty-one, by establishing training camps in rural areas and in the cities.

Volunteers in Service to America (VISTA). Sometimes called a "domestic peace corps," VISTA trained young Americans to work in poverty-stricken areas, among Indians, in hospitals and schools, and with the mentally ill or retarded.

Community Action Programs. This aspect of the antipoverty program, which became highly controversial, was designed to give federal grants to a wide range of programs organized and administered by local public or private groups "with maximum feasible participation" of the poor. While successful in some areas, the community action programs led in some other cases to what one critic, Daniel P. Moynihan, has termed a "maximum feasible misunderstanding." [26]

The political struggle that erupted over the poverty program in the mid-1960's had its roots in the early 1960's, when a group of young government officials and academics joined to propose the idea of community action. They called themselves "guerrillas," for they lived "as one of them later put it, 'off the countryside of the government and foundations.'" [27] Traditionally, social planners have advocated services to individuals—better education and jobs, for example—as the best way to eliminate "the culture of poverty." The "guerrillas" argued that through community action, the poor could be organized *politically* to voice their grievances in direct confrontations with the "power structure."

Soon big city mayors and other critics of OEO charged that the Federal Government was financing rebellion, funding community action groups to march on City Hall and challenge the entrenched power of local political organizations.

[26] Daniel P. Moynihan, *Maximum Feasible Misunderstanding: Community Action in the War on Poverty* (New York: Free Press, 1969).
[27] Richard Blumenthal, "The Bureaucracy: Antipoverty and the Community Action Program," in Allan P. Sindler, ed., *American Political Institutions and Public Policy* (Boston: Little, Brown, 1969), p. 133.

Conflict was inevitable. For, as James L. Sundquist has suggested, "can a national government maintain, for long, a program that sets minorities against majorities in communities throughout the land? Clearly it cannot, even if it should. The affluent majority will not be persuaded that tranquility is not also an objective of society—and one superior, if a choice must be made, to the eradication of poverty itself." [28]

In Chicago, Mayor Richard J. Daley, the most powerful urban boss in the Democratic party, demanded and won control of the local poverty agency. Community action programs in many other cities were also placed directly or indirectly under the control of City Hall.

Under increasing attack from Southern politicians, OEO in 1969 narrowly missed being disbanded and its functions turned over to the states. As it was, President Nixon closed fifty-nine Job Corps centers, and moved the corps to the Labor Department; he also moved Project Head Start—a widely publicized program for preschool children—to the Department of Health, Education, and Welfare. The antipoverty program faced an uncertain future.

The Politics of Hunger

"The moment is at hand to put an end to hunger in America itself for all time," President Nixon declared in a message to Congress in 1969. "There can be no doubt that hunger and malnutrition exist in America, and that some millions may be affected." [29]

How many millions? Figures on the extent of hunger in America vary, but it has been estimated that as many as 15,000,000 people have incomes so low that they cannot afford proper nutrition.[30] America was largely unaware of the hunger problem until a Senate subcommittee toured the Mississippi delta in April 1967. Citizens groups, the CBS television documentary *Hunger in America*, and hearings conducted by Senator George McGovern, Democrat, of South Dakota, spurred congressional and public response to the problem over the next few years.

Although pressures to alleviate hunger in America gained momentum in the late 1960's, influential Southern chairmen of key congressional committees succeeded in blocking or restricting proposals for increased federal spending on food programs.

In 1961, President Kennedy initiated a food stamp program to increase the buying power of low-income families. Under it, a poor family could purchase stamps worth much more than their actual cost in dollars when presented in a store for food; the Federal Government reimbursed the grocer for the full cost of the food. But critics charged that the stamps were

[28] James L. Sundquist, *Politics and Policy* (Washington, D.C.: The Brookings Institution, 1968), p. 152.
[29] *1969 Congressional Quarterly Almanac*, p. 51-A.
[30] Nick Kotz, *Let Them Eat Promises* (Englewood Cliffs, N.J.: Prentice-Hall, 1969), p. 23.

This is the story of hunger in the America of the $900 billion gross national product, of the $200 billion federal budget, of the 1.2 cars and 1.3 television sets per family, of eight million pleasure boats, of block-long supermarkets with entire meals frozen to be prepared instantly in automated kitchens. This is the America that pays farmers $3 billion annually not to plant food because it has developed an ingenious ability to produce far more than paying customers can eat, the America that spends millions on dieting because the affluent consumer can afford to eat too well. For the first time, this is the America fully equipped with the ability, the technology, and the wealth to fulfill its most sacred promises—life, liberty, and the pursuit of happiness.

Yet this nation in the late 1960s looked hunger in the eyes but could not see it, glimpsed the truth about hunger but called only for more study of the problem, discounted hunger as a result of either laziness or ignorance, and finally—even after it reluctantly accepted the problem—could not arrange its national priorities to feed more than a fraction of the malnourished and hungry poor in 1970.

—Nick Kotz, *Let Them Eat Promises.*

still too expensive for many poor people to buy, and that, in any event, they provided less than even a minimal diet. In addition to food stamps, the Federal Government distributed surplus food crops to the poor through local welfare agencies, and it financed a school lunch program and a special milk program for children.

By fiscal 1971, the Federal government had budgeted a total of $1.5 billion for food assistance, and Congress had more than doubled the food stamp program. A federal study estimated, however, that it would take $7 billion a year to close the hunger gap.[31]

Health

In 1971, the Federal Government spent about $20 billion, or 10 percent of the national budget, for health services.[32] The funds were spent for research, training and education, hospital construction, Medicare and Medicaid, and prevention of disease.

The *Medicare* program, discussed earlier in this chapter, provides hospital and medical services to persons aged sixty-five and over through the social security program. *Medicaid*, also established in 1965, is a public assistance program to help pay hospital, doctor, and medical bills for persons with low incomes. It is financed through general federal, state, and local taxes. Under a formula, Washington pays from 50 to 83 percent of the cost of state programs established under Medicaid. In 1971, it was estimated that Medicaid would pay out $5.7 billion to aid 11.3 million people; the federal share of the cost would be about $2.9 billion. In 1970,

[31] Robert Sherrill, "Why Can't We Just Give Them Food?" *New York Times Magazine,* March 22, 1970, p. 101.
[32] "Special Analysis K," in *Special Analyses,* Budget of the United States, Fiscal Year 1971, p. 148.

President Nixon proposed a compulsory health insurance program to replace Medicaid for all persons receiving income payments under the proposed Family Assistance Plan. Medicaid would still be available for other persons with low income.

The Medicaid program is a prime example of the difficulties the government sometimes encounters in attempting to translate good intentions into practice. Soon after the program was enacted, it became clear that it was costing much more than Congress had intended. Between 1968 and 1970, Medicaid costs increased by 57 percent while the number of people helped increased by only 19 percent.[33]

Legitimate increases in medical costs were only one aspect of the problem; lax administration was another. Some physicians were profiting greatly from the federal programs. For example, the Senate Finance Committee staff reported in 1969 that up to 5,000 physicians had received payments of $25,000 or more from Medicare, and thousands of others had received similar amounts from Medicaid. In 1970, the Treasury Department reported that one out of every three of these doctors had underreported his income from the federal payments.[34]

The federal programs described above have assisted the aged and the needy, but they have not helped the majority of Americans to obtain adequate health care at a reasonable cost. The cost of hospital rooms, physicians' care, and other health services has increased at an alarming rate. Pressure for a general federal program of health insurance was growing in 1970.

Education

At the start of the 1969–70 school year, almost 60,000,000 students were enrolled in the nation's schools and colleges. Of the total, 7.4 million were enrolled in colleges, 14.5 million in high schools, 33.8 million in elementary schools, and 4 million in kindergarten and nursery schools.[35]

In 1970, the Federal Government spent about $10 billion on various kinds of aid to education—five times the total spent in 1960. (See Table 15-4.) This aid was channeled in two ways: to *educational institutions* and to *individuals*.

As far back as 1862, Congress had passed the Morrill Act to establish "land-grant" colleges. And millions of veterans of the Second World War went to college under the federally financed GI Bill of Rights. In 1958, after the Soviet Union launched its Sputnik earth satellite, Congress enacted the National Defense Education Act to provide loans for college students in the fields of science, engineering, mathematics, and foreign languages. In

[33] Congressional Quarterly, *Weekly Report*, April 23, 1970, p. 924.
[34] *New York Times*, September 22, 1970, p. 1.
[35] U.S. Bureau of the Census, *Current Population Reports*, Population Characteristics, Series P-20, No. 199, April 22, 1970.

TABLE 15-4

Federal Outlays For Education, 1960–1970
(in billions of dollars)

	1960	1962	1964	1966	1968	1970 (est.)
Elementary and secondary education	$0.4	$0.5	$0.6	$2.2	$3.2	$ 3.3
Higher education	1.1	1.3	1.7	2.7	4.4	5.0
Adult and other education	.5	.6	.8	.9	1.2	1.8
Total	$2.0	$2.4	$3.1	$5.8	$8.8	$10.1

Source: Adapted from "Special Analysis I," in *Special Analyses, Budget of the United States,* Fiscal Year 1971, p. 112.

1963, Congress began appropriating funds for the construction of college classrooms.

Not until 1965, however, did Congress pass a law providing for general federal aid to education. In that year, the high-water mark of President Johnson's "Great Society," it enacted the Elementary and Secondary Education Act and the Higher Education Act. Until 1965, the church-state controversy had blocked passage of a general aid to education bill (see Chapter 4, p. 126). The Elementary and Secondary Education Act by-passed that dispute by providing aid to children on the basis of economic need in both public and private schools. Although most counties in the nation were eligible, the bulk of the money was concentrated in urban and rural areas with a high percentage of children from poor families. Under the law, the Federal Government also provides general purpose grants plus money for textbooks, library books, special programs for handicapped children, and teacher training.

The Higher Education Act of 1965 for the first time provided federal scholarships ("educational opportunity grants") for college undergraduates. The law also provided federally insured loans for college students, federal subsidies to pay the interest on loans to students from private lenders, and a work-study program to help the colleges pay the wages of students with part-time jobs obtained through the schools. It channeled money to colleges to buy library books, and created a program of fellowships for graduate students. It also established a Teacher Corps to aid schools in city slums and poor rural areas. In 1971, the Federal Government estimated it would spend $2.3 billion to support 3.5 million college undergraduate and graduate students.

But federal spending had failed to avert a growing crisis in the nation's public schools. Political battles continue over school desegregation. The quality of education in many big-city public school systems has deteriorated. As large numbers of the white middle class have moved to the suburbs, big cities have found their tax dollars dwindling; one result is

629

that schools are often poorest where their services are needed the most—in low-income inner-city communities.

Science

In an age of science and technology some people have come to feel that, more and more, decisions affecting their lives are being made not by elected political leaders, but by "faceless technocrats in long, white coats." [36]

That concern reflects the growing importance of scientists in government decision-making, and the close relationship today, both financial and political, between government and what Don K. Price has called "the scientific estate." [37] Should American astronauts try to land on Mars? Should a new weapons system be developed? Can the United States depend on its spy satellites to police an international agreement to reduce nuclear arms? For the answers to such questions, the President must turn to his science advisers; government today has become far too complicated for political leaders to know all the scientific data they need to make policy decisions.

The Federal Government spends billions of dollars every year on scientific research and development. This kind of spending has raised questions about the relationship of science and government. For instance, what is the proper role of science within the political system? Today, some critics regard science as "something very close to an *establishment* . . . a set of institutions supported by tax funds, but largely on faith, and without direct responsibility to political control." [38] Another question is whether universities can accept government funds for research without restricting or losing their academic independence.

Campus protests during the 1960's forced many universities to discontinue or curb scientific research under government contracts in such fields as chemical-biological warfare and weapons development. In 1970, the Massachusetts Institute of Technology, under student pressure, announced it was severing its ties with the huge Draper Laboratory, which developed specific weapons systems for the Pentagon. (M.I.T. would, however, retain its Lincoln Laboratories, which were engaged in broader defense research, some of it classified.) The effect of the protest was felt in the social sciences as well. In 1966, M.I.T. announced that its Center for International Studies would no longer accept money from the CIA, which had been providing up to 20 percent of the center's annual budget.

In fiscal 1971, the Federal Government spent an estimated $15.8 bil-

[36] Senator E. L. Bartlett, D., Alaska, in Don K. Price, *The Scientific Estate* (Cambridge, Mass.: Belknap Press of Harvard University Press, 1965), p. 57.
[37] *Ibid.*
[38] *Ibid.*, p. 12.

lion on research and development. Almost half the total, $7.7 billion, was spent by the Pentagon. The National Aeronautics and Space Administration accounted for $3.3 billion. Close to $1.5 billion was spent on research in colleges and universities. About $350 million was spent by the National Science Foundation, established by Congress in 1950 to foster basic research through grants to scientists, universities, and laboratories. In 1968, Congress enlarged the scope of the NSF to support applied science and the social sciences. The National Institutes of Health (NIH) carries out a similar program in the field of medical research and health.

As his first public act of the decade of the seventies, President Nixon signed into law a bill declaring the quality of the environment to be a matter of national policy. The 1970's, the President said, must be the years "when America pays its debt to the past by reclaiming the purity of its air, its waters and our living environment. It is literally now or never." [39]

Protecting the Environment

As with most major national problems, progress toward restoring the environment would require cooperation by individuals, corporations, and institutions—but it would also require coercion in the form of government legislation and enforcement.

During the 1960's, traditional efforts toward "conservation" of the nation's wildlife areas and natural resources evolved into a much broader concern over the quality of life on earth and the future of man and his environment. Pollution is a result of industrialization and increased consumption, combined with population growth. The close relationship between pollution and "the population bomb" has been emphasized by Barry Commoner, a leading ecologist. He has predicted that the present population of the earth, about 3.5 billion people, will grow by the year 2000 to between 6 and 8 billion. Somewhere near that population level is what Commoner called "the crash point," at which, he argues, the air, water, and earth can no longer support human life.

Every person in the United States generates an average of seven pounds of trash each day, and the nation as a whole generates 3.5 billion tons of waste annually. Every year, we throw away 7 million cars, 28 billion bottles, and 48 billion cans. Every second, 2 million gallons of sewage pour into the nation's waterways. Each year, automobiles, factories, power plants, and incinerators pour 142 million tons of pollutants into the atmosphere, making the air in many American communities unpleasant to breathe and potentially dangerous to health.

Since 1957, the Federal Government has made grants to local communities for construction of municipal sewage treatment facilities; $1.3

[39] Congressional Quarterly, *Weekly Report*, January 30, 1970, p. 279.

631

"Now maybe they'll be moved to do something about water pollution!"

Drawing by Chas. Addams
© 1969 The New Yorker Magazine, Inc.

billion had been appropriated for this purpose by 1970. In addition, the government sets water quality standards on interstate waterways. But the enforcement procedure has not worked very well because it is so cumbersome. A General Accounting Office report concluded that, "in recent years growing industrial pollution has overwhelmed the reduction in pollutants made possible by the construction of municipal waste treatment plants, usually with federal grants." [40] In short, federal spending on control of pollution has not kept pace with the spread of pollution.

In 1967, Congress established the National Air Pollution Control Administration, chiefly to make grants to state and local clean air agencies. As noted earlier, President Nixon's 1970 pollution control proposals were designed to give the Federal Government direct control over major polluters, instead of relying, as in the past, on state enforcement. The National Environmental Policy Act of 1969—the bill that President Nixon signed on New Year's Day, 1970—established a three-man Council on Environmental Quality to advise the President. The law also required the President to submit an annual "state of the environment" report to Congress. The Water Quality Improvement Act of 1970 required owners of oil tankers and oil companies to pay up to $14 million of the cost of cleaning up oil spills.

Because federal antipollution programs were fragmented among more than a dozen federal agencies and departments, President Nixon in 1970 submitted a reorganization plan to Congress to create a new agency, the Environmental Protection Agency, to take over responsibility for all federal

[40] Charles L. Schultze, with Edward K. Hamilton and Allen Schick, *Setting National Priorities, The 1971 Budget* (Washington, D.C.: The Brookings Institution, 1970), p. 123.

Some ecologists warn that man is approaching a point where the earth will not sustain life. "Earth Day" marchers in 1970 symbolically urged more tender care for the planet.

programs dealing with the environment. The new agency began operating late in 1970.

CAN GOVERNMENT MEET THE CHALLENGE?

In our discussion of government-in-operation we have examined a number of crucial areas in which government—and therefore American society—has failed to solve urgent social problems.

Complex fiscal and monetary policies have not consistently avoided the evils of recession or inflation. In all too many cases, regulatory agencies have served corporate power and have failed to protect the public. The tax structure remains a target of widespread criticism.

In the field of social welfare, the Federal Government has promised much but delivered far less. As one of President Johnson's former assistants has suggested: "The rhetoric of commitment of the Establishment is

633

magnificent, but it is not the language of American reality." [41] President Johnson declared his "war on poverty" in 1964, but six years later, almost 25 million Americans were still poor. The public assistance program, by common agreement of liberals and conservatives, was a failure. Too much had been promised over the years, and too little had changed.

Achieving desirable social ends costs money, however, and not all Americans want to pay the price. For example, if America really wants a better environment, it will have to pay for it, both in terms of expanded government programs and in higher prices as the cost of pollution control is passed on to the consumer. According to one study:

> Electric power output . . . is expected to double by 1980. Cheap electric power is a keystone of high industrial productivity and convenient living. If it is produced with thermal plants, however, it pollutes the air. If it is produced with atomic power, it heats the water of our streams. Reducing the pollution consequences of producing electric power will inevitably add to the price of electricity, and the less the pollution content, the greater the increase in price. [42]

By 1971, the annual gross national product (GNP) in the United States had exceeded 1 trillion dollars; yet the federal budget of $200 billion represents only 20 per cent of the GNP. State and local governments spend about another $116 billion a year, so the total commitment of America for public needs is about 30 percent of the gross national product. By contrast, England spends 38 percent of its GNP in the public sector; Sweden, France, and West Germany spend more.

How to solve the complex social problems confronting America is by no means clear. But massive programs to try to deal with those problems mean hard choices, high taxes, and other sacrifices. The real question facing Americans in the 1970's is whether they are willing to pay the costs of "promoting the general welfare" and building a better society.

[41] Joseph A. Califano Jr., "The Rhetoric and the Reality," *Washington Post*, June 4, 1970, p. A16.
[42] Schultze, Hamilton, and Schick, *Setting National Priorities, The 1971 Budget*, p. 120.

SUGGESTED READING

Davies, J. Clarence, III. *The Politics of Pollution* (Pegasus, 1970). Paperback. A useful analysis of pollution as a political issue, covering federal anti-pollution legislation, the role of Congress, public opinion, and interest groups. The author, a political scientist and former federal official, emphasizes that improvement of the environment depends upon public pressure on the executive branch and on Congress.

Dubos, René. *Reason Awake: Science for Man* * (Columbia University Press, 1970). A collection of essays by a distinguished microbiologist focusing on the threat to man and his environment posed by the technological and population explosions. Analyzes a whole range of man-made problems, from nuclear weapons to urban sprawl, that have resulted from a constantly expanding technology.

Ehrlich, Paul R., and Ehrlich, Anne H. *Population Resources Environment* (W. H. Freeman, 1970). A comprehensive analysis of the global threat facing mankind as a result of the interlocking problems of environmental deterioration, overpopulation, hunger, and war. The Ehrlichs argue that population growth increases the probability of worldwide plague and thermonuclear war.

Harrington, Michael. *The Other America* * (Penguin, 1962; Macmillan, 1970). One of the most widely read introductory surveys of the nature and extent of poverty in the United States in the early 1960's.

Kotz, Nick. *Let Them Eat Promises* (Prentice-Hall, 1969). A critical study of hunger in the United States by a Washington newsman. Explores the dimensions of the problem and relates how the issue finally began to receive government and public attention in the late 1960's.

Moynihan, Daniel Patrick. *Maximum Feasible Misunderstanding* * (Free Press, 1969). Readable account of the origins of the Johnson administration's "War on Poverty," and some of the political problems encountered in attempting to stimulate "maximum feasible participation" of the poor in the development and administration of community action programs.

Nader, Ralph. *Unsafe at Any Speed* * (Grossman, 1965). A provocative critique of the safety standards of American automobiles manufactured in the mid-1960's. This book launched Nader's career as the nation's leading consumer advocate.

Price, Don K. *The Scientific Estate* * (Harvard University Press, 1965). A thoughtful and perceptive analysis of science and scientists, and their relation to public policy making in the United States.

Schlesinger, Arthur M., Jr. *The Coming of the New Deal* (Houghton Mifflin, 1959). A revealing and highly readable historical account of the inauguration of Franklin Roosevelt's New Deal, which established the basis for much of the nation's current economic welfare legislation. Part of a multivolume historical study by Schlesinger of Roosevelt and New Deal politics.

Steiner, Gilbert Y. *Social Insecurity: The Politics of Welfare* (Rand McNally, 1966). A comprehensive examination of the conflicting assumptions, governmental agency viewpoints, and interest groups concerned with welfare policies in the United States.

Sundquist, James L. *Politics and Policy: The Eisenhower, Kennedy, and Johnson Years* * (The Brookings Institution, 1968). An informative and valuable study of the battles in Congress and in the country to pass what became the new domestic social welfare programs of the Johnson administration.

Udall, Stewart. *1976, Agenda for Tomorrow* (Harcourt Brace Jovanovich, 1968). A former congressman and Secretary of the Interior analyzes problems of population, ecology, and the quality of life. Contains recommendations for action by Americans.

* Available in paperback edition

PART FIVE

The American Community

16

State and Local

Government

PROBLEMS AND PATTERNS IN A CHANGING SOCIETY

In the Washington suburb of Suitland, Maryland, five miles southeast of the Capitol dome and far from the familiar paths trod by the tourists, a complex of federal buildings houses a group of men and women whose business, in part, is to peer into the future. And what they see gives some cause for concern.

The building is the headquarters of the United States Bureau of the Census, a division of the Commerce Department. By using electronic computers, and calculating birth and death rates and other factors, the Census Bureau is able to make population projections for the future. It cannot do so with precision, because there is a wide margin for error in such tabulations. Nevertheless, the Census Bureau is able to guess that the population of the United States, which was 204.8 million after the 1970 census, will, by the year 2000, stand somewhere between 266 million and 321 million.[1]

[1] Final population figure of 1970 census from *New York Times*, December 1, 1970, p. 1; projections from U.S. Bureau of the Census, *Current Population Reports*, Population Estimates and Projections, Series P-25, No. 448, August 6, 1970, p. 1; figures rounded.

Even taking the lower figure, an increase of about 60 million people in thirty years would be like adding the present population of England to the United States. And, by the year 2015, the population of the United States will range between 292 million and 407 million, according to Census Bureau estimates.[2] In other words, there seems a reasonably good chance that the 1970 population of just over 200 million will more than double in less than fifty years.

Today American society is burdened with multifold, interlocking problems—racial tensions, pollution, poverty, crime, political polarization, and more. If, as seems possible, the population doubles in less than half a century, will the American political system and American society be able to cope with these problems? To take a random example, would anyone care to visualize what it might be like driving along the San Bernardino Freeway during the morning rush hour in the year 2000? It is bad enough now, as Los Angeles commuters can attest.

"We don't have too many people," the Secretary of the Interior remarked in 1970. "The trouble is that they're concentrated in the wrong places."[3] Walter Hickel was lamenting the fact that about 80 percent of the nation's population is crowded into less than 10 percent of the land area.

Not only the size of the population but its geographic distribution affect the nature of a society. Since 1920, the population of the United

[2] *Ibid.*
[3] Walter J. Hickel, quoted in the *New York Times*, June 20, 1970, p. 14.

L. Herman

States has been more urban than rural. In 1969, when the population stood at a bit more than 200 million, 129 million Americans, or 65 percent, lived in metropolitan areas. Of this total, 58.5 million lived in central cities and 70.6 million in the rapidly growing suburbs.[4]

By 1975, the Census Bureau estimates, almost 80 million Americans will live in metropolitan areas of more than one million.[5] As America has become urbanized, many of the nation's difficult problems have developed in their most acute form in urban areas—in the central "core" cities and

[4] U.S. Bureau of the Census, *Current Population Reports*, Population Characteristics, Population of the United States by Metropolitan-Nonmetropolitan Residence: 1969 and 1960, Series P-20, No. 197, March 6, 1970, p. 1.

[5] U.S. Bureau of the Census, *Current Population Reports*, Population Estimates, Projections of the Population of Metropolitan Areas: 1975, Series P-25, No. 415, January 31, 1969, p. 6. The terms urban, rural, metropolitan, and suburban are subject to varying definitions. The Federal Government has divided the nation into Standard Metropolitan Statistical Areas (SMSA) each of which contains at least one central city of 50,000 persons or twin cities with a total population of 50,000. All areas inside SMSAs are classified by the government as "metropolitan" and all areas outside are classified as "nonmetropolitan." A "metropolitan area" includes both the central city and the surrounding suburbs.

the surrounding suburbs. Obviously, the decisions and actions of state, city, and other local governments have a direct impact on the quality of American life.

Much of this book has focused on the national government and national politics, but in 1970 there were, in addition to the government in Washington, some 81,000 units of state and local government in the United States. The performance of these governments is often criticized. John W. Gardner, former Secretary of Health, Education, and Welfare, has declared: "State government in most places is a 19th century relic; in most cities, municipal government is a waxworks of stiffly preserved anachronisms." [6]

Not everyone would agree with Gardner's critical view of state and local government, but few would contend that those governments have kept pace with the complex problems they face—transportation, housing, slum clearance, pollution, welfare services, schools, crime, narcotics—to name some of the major ones.

This failure to keep pace is not always the fault of the state or community; many of the problems that exist have been compounded by urbanization and patterns of population migration in recent decades. These factors have interacted to place a serious strain on the federal system.

Since the Second World War, for a variety of reasons, increasing numbers of low-income blacks and whites have migrated from rural areas to the big cities. At the same time, many middle-class whites have moved out to the suburbs, taking the city tax base with them. The newcomers to the inner-city have required costly government services—schools, welfare, police and fire protection, for example—but have not had sufficient taxable incomes and property to finance these services. In the late 1960's, there were signs that blacks had begun migrating to the suburbs in significant numbers.[7] The black suburban population increased by almost a million persons between 1960 and 1969, and was increasing at a faster percentage rate than the black population of the central cities. Nevertheless, most black Americans lived in cities; the percentage of blacks living in the central cities was more than twice that of whites.[8]

For the most part, cities rely on the property tax to finance the bulk of municipal services. Suburban governments now collect the taxes on the property of families and industries that have left the cities—and suburban residents have little desire to "bail out" City Hall.

A *New York Times* survey of the nation's cities has reported: "The middle class, once the strength of the city, has largely fled to the suburbs

[6] The Godkin Lectures, Harvard University, quoted in *Time*, April 11, 1969, p. 40.
[7] David L. Birch, *The Economic Future of City and Suburb* (New York: Committee for Economic Development, 1970), p. 30.
[8] U.S. Bureau of the Census, *Current Population Reports*, Special Studies, Trends in Social and Economic Conditions in Metropolitan and Nonmetropolitan Areas, Series P-23, No. 33, September 3, 1970, pp. 2–4.

and become an enemy. Officials of both cities and suburbs acknowledge that suburban residents are apathetic or hostile to the problems of the working class, the old, the black, and the poor left behind." [9]

Big city mayors look to Washington and the state houses for relief. But, the mayors complain, what limited federal funds are available have been siphoned off in part by the states for use in the suburbs and in rural areas. The mayor of St. Louis, A. J. Cervantes, complained in 1970: "Reapportionment was meant to correct the rural overbalance in state legislatures. So what happened? The legislatures are now dominated by suburbia —and that's just as bad for us." [10]

A "mismatch" exists not only between urgent problems and state and local financial resources, but between the magnitude of the problems and the performance of state and local governments. Two overriding conclusions may be drawn from many of the studies of state and local problems:

1. *The problems are larger than the boundaries of the governmental units that are attempting to deal with them.* Smog, for example, respects no city lines, and the issue of commuter transportation in a metropolitan area may involve two dozen local communities.
2. *The solutions cost more than the governmental units have available to spend.* A suburban area cannot possibly afford, for example, to build a

[9] Jack Rosenthal, "Urbanists Find Suburbs Hostile to Cities, Pinched for Money," *New York Times*, May 22, 1970, p. 21.
[10] *Ibid.*

mass transit line to carry its residents to downtown offices, nor can the central cities raise the tax revenues to provide adequate social services for those inner-city residents who need it most.

Against this somewhat discouraging background, we may ask: How well are state and local governments meeting their responsibilities? How are state and local governments organized? What is the relationship among federal, state, and local governments? What are the major problems of the cities and the suburbs? Given the politics and existing structure of state and local governments, can they hope to solve problems that are larger than their geographic boundaries and financial resources? What are the implications of these problems for America's future?

THE STATES

America is a nation of states. The political institutions of the thirteen colonies foreshadowed the shape of the federal system created under the Constitution. The states, in short, were here *before* the American nation. They grew in number as the frontier was pushed westward to the Pacific. They are not mere administrative or geographic units established for the convenience of the central government. Rather, they are key political institutions rooted in the nation's historical development, sharing power under the federal system with the national government in Washington.

But the federal system was constructed when the United States was a small, rural nation. In today's predominantly urban America, a nation of congested cities, black ghettos, and exploding suburban growth, are the

THE STATES: IN LIMBO?

I am suggesting the states do not stand out as important institutions of democratic self-government. They are too big to allow for much in the way of civic participation—think of California and New York, each about as large in population as Canada or Yugoslavia and each larger than 80 percent of the countries of the world. Yet an American state is infinitely less important to citizens of that state than any democratic nation-state to its citizens. Consequently the average American is bound to be much less concerned about the affairs of his state than of his city or country. Too remote to stimulate much participation by their citizens, and too big to make extensive participation possible anyway, these units intermediate between city and nation are probably destined for a kind of limbo of quasi-democracy.

—Robert A. Dahl, *American Political Science Review*, December, 1967.

THE STATES: A DEFENSE

The argument that the states are anachronisms and need to be replaced by more relevant governmental bodies is a facile conclusion for those who are dismayed by the disorder of American government. This is a classroom solution. But the stubborn facts are that the states do exist, have a fairly strong political base, and will be here for the foreseeable future. There are also promises of good in the states which should bring the eager critic to a more cheerful acceptance of the facts.

The states are the focal points in our system of political parties, with presidential campaigns as more or less quadrennial coalitions of state political structures. . . .

In addition, U.S. congressmen and senators are products of the state political systems, usually are responsive to the state political party leadership, and are frequently influenced by governors and state legislatures.

The states have always occupied and still do occupy a strong constitutional position in the nation. The states created the Constitution, if not the Union, and retain constitutional rights and obligations which make them far more than subdivisions or creatures of the national government.

—Terry Sanford, *Storm Over the States.*

states any longer relevant? Can they meet the new demands placed on them by urbanization?

Many critics of state government feel that the states are not doing as much as they should, particularly in the crucial area of urban problems. As Alan K. Campbell and Donna E. Shalala have suggested, "Students of these matters [urban problems] generally agree that of the various parts of the governmental system, states have performed least well." [11]

There are signs, however, that the states have been making an effort to meet their responsibilities. For example, since the Second World War, state and local expenditures have increased at a much faster rate than federal spending. (See Chapter 3, p. 99.) And state taxes have increased at a faster rate than federal taxes. [12]

The states and localities do not, of course, spend as much as the Federal Government, but their level of spending today comes close to matching that of federal spending on domestic needs. In 1970, for example, the Federal Government was spending at the rate of $200 billion a year. But if the $80.5 billion contained in the fiscal 1971 budget for defense, international affairs, and space is subtracted from this total, federal domestic expenditures were running at about $120 billion annually, or not much more than the $116 billion a year being spent by state and local governments. [13]

[11] Alan K. Campbell and Donna E. Shalala, "Problems Unsolved, Solutions Untried: The Urban Crisis," in Alan K. Campbell, ed., *The States and the Urban Crisis*, prepared for the American Assembly, Columbia University (Englewood Cliffs, N.J.: Prentice-Hall, 1970), p. 24.

[12] *Ibid.*, p. 25.

[13] State and local expenditures as of fiscal 1968. U.S. Bureau of the Census, *Governmental Finances in 1967–68*, p. 18.

But a serious imbalance, or income gap, exists between the demands on state and local governments and the revenues they raise through taxes. One reason for this is that state and local governments rely heavily on property and consumer taxes, which do not reflect the general growth of the economy as rapidly as the income tax does. At present, the Federal Government collects about two-thirds of all taxes; the states and communities divide the remainder about equally.

The states have been searching for new sources of revenue. In 1969, thirty-six state legislatures imposed new taxes or increased existing ones, raising state tax receipts by a record $4 billion.[14] Yet, thirteen states had no personal income tax, and many that did taxed incomes at relatively low rates. States are cautious in taxing in part because they must compete with one another. They "must be wary of increasing taxes or redistributing income in a way that will enable neighboring states to attract away industry."[15]

Part of the financial difficulty of the states is caused by the growing demands for services they provide to the public. What do the states do? They have major responsibilities in the fields of education, welfare, transportation, the administration of justice, the prisons, agriculture, public health, and the environment. (See Figure 16-1.) States share with local governments responsibility for the delivery of these and many other vital public services. And this responsibility is the source of many of the difficulties faced by the states, as well as by local governments. To provide these services, state and local governments employ more people than does the Federal Government—with all of the accompanying problems of unionization, strikes, and of controlling the bureaucracy. Even though states are spending more money on public services, they have not proved very innovative in attacking the urban problems they now face. There is a wide variation in the performance and effectiveness of the fifty states, just as there are substantial differences in state politics and state political institutions.

The State
Constitutions

State constitutions spell out the basic structure of each state government. Every state constitution provides for an executive, legislative, and judicial branch. Although each includes a bill of rights, some state constitutions are more progressive than others. For example, the constitutions of the newest states, Alaska and Hawaii, have strong civil rights provisions.

State constitutions tend to be lists of what the state cannot do; they

[14] "Special Analysis O," *Special Analyses, Budget of the United States Fiscal 1971*, p. 221.

[15] James Q. Wilson, "Urban Problems in Perspective," in James Q. Wilson, ed., *The Metropolitan Enigma* (Washington, D.C.: U.S. Chamber of Commerce, 1967), p. 327.

FIGURE 16-1

Expenditures of State and Local Governments, 1967–1968

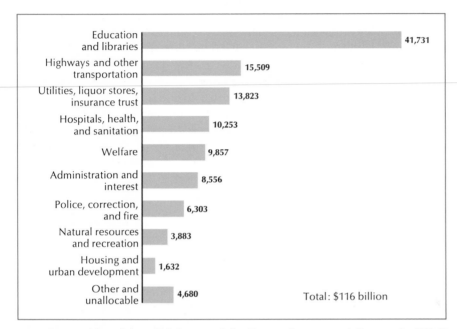

Education and libraries	41,731
Highways and other transportation	15,509
Utilities, liquor stores, insurance trust	13,823
Hospitals, health, and sanitation	10,253
Welfare	9,857
Administration and interest	8,556
Police, correction, and fire	6,303
Natural resources and recreation	3,883
Housing and urban development	1,632
Other and unallocable	4,680

Total: $116 billion

Source: Adapted from U.S. Bureau of the Census, *Governmental Finances in 1967–68,* pp. 18–19.

limit the power of the governor and of the legislatures—to levy taxes and borrow money, for example. As a result, state constitutions are often condemned as restrictive, negative documents that impede the ability of states to meet modern problems.

Yet the importance of state constitutions can be overstressed. Modernizing state constitutions would not in itself improve governmental performance unless there were also changes in the political climate in which those governments operate. For example, in many areas, there is political resistance to massive, costly undertakings by governments to solve urban problems. Although structural obstacles exist in the form of state constitutions, change depends not only on governmental reform but on the political environment as well. For example, New Jersey has one of the most modern state constitutions, but it has not surpassed other states in responding to urban problems.

The state constitutions, as Duane Lockard points out, "have been amended more than 3,000 times and in some instances it is necessary to read the constitution backwards like a Chinese newspaper, in order to see what the last word is on an original provision."[16] The Louisiana constitution, which has been amended 460 times, is 350,000 words long; one of its provisions proclaims Huey Long's birthday a permanent state holiday. The California constitution limits the power of the legislature to regulate the length of wrestling matches. The Georgia constitution provides a $250,-000 reward for the first person to strike oil within the borders of the Peach State.[17]

The most common means of amending state constitutions is by a two-thirds vote of the legislature and approval of a majority of the voters at the next election. But more than a dozen states (mostly in the West) permit the *initiative*. Under this method, proposed constitutional amendments can be placed on the ballot if enough signatures are obtained on a petition. All but a few states also permit the rewriting of constitutions at conventions convened with the approval of the voters.

The Governors

At first glance, it might appear as though the fifty states are federal governments in miniature. Each has the familiar three branches with checks and balances. The governor is usually a reasonably prestigious figure, at least within his state; like the President, he heads an executive branch. And like the President, he has military forces under his command in the form of the state police and the National Guard. Appearances are deceptive, however, for the position of governor in some states is much less powerful than is popularly imagined.

In the first place, the states have come to occupy a less prominent position within the federal system than they enjoyed in years past. The actions of a governor, and of other state officials, and the laws passed by state legislatures, are subject to judicial review by the United States Supreme Court. At Little Rock and elsewhere in the South, federal power has prevailed over that of state governors in confrontations over public school desegregation.

Beyond this, the position of governor has been weakened by historical and political factors. During the colonial period, the royal governors clashed with the elected legislatures. The state constitutions written at the time of the American Revolution reflected the prevailing distrust of executive power; in most states, the legislature chose the governor. During the nineteenth century, popular election of governors spread through the states, but the power of the governors remained relatively weak. Not until the twentieth century were state governments reorganized and executive power

[16] Duane Lockard, *The Politics of State and Local Government* (New York: Macmillan, 1969), p. 85.
[17] *Ibid.*

increased in some states. But even today, the office of governor is weak in many states.

Variations in the power of state governors were dramatically illustrated in a study published in 1967 by a federal panel, the Advisory Commission on Intergovernmental Relations. The commission used five indices to gauge the formal strength of each state governor: (1) the number of other elected executive officials sharing power in the state, (2) the governor's appointive power, (3) his veto power, (4) his term of office, and (5) his power over the state's budget.

The results are shown in Figure 16-2. In only ten states was the governor found to be "very strong." In seventeen states, he was found to be "strong," but in twelve states his power was rated only "medium" and

FIGURE 16-2

Index of the Governor's Authority

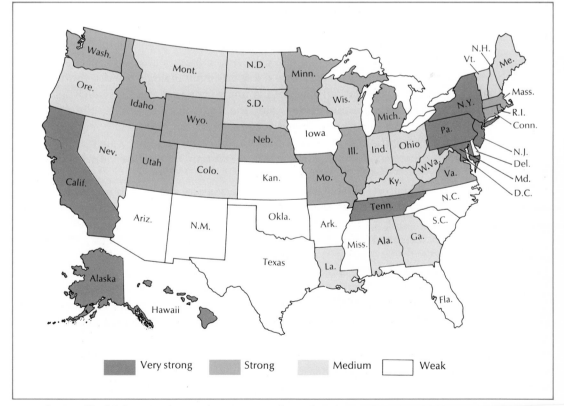

Source: *Fiscal Balance in the American System*, Vol. I, Advisory Commission on Intergovernmental Relations (Washington, D.C.: U.S. Government Printing Office, October 1967), p. 234.

in eleven states "weak."[18] The commission was measuring the *formal powers* of the governor in each case, and not the *influence* he wielded; but the federal panel argued that "Governors with strong formal powers are more likely to be able to exercise effective direction and control."[19]

In all states, the governor shares executive power with at least one other popularly elected official. The 1967 study found that the number of popularly elected state executive officials other than governor ranged as high as thirty-six in Michigan and the median for all states was eight. But in six states the *legislature* also elected state executive officials, ranging from seven in Maine to one hundred in North Carolina.[20] Typically, the officials elected by the voters with the governor may include the lieutenant governor, attorney general, secretary of state, treasurer, auditor, and superintendent of education. The governor's difficulties are increased if one or more of these elected executive branch officials belong to the opposing political party.

The power of governors to appoint important officials (in states where they are not elected independently) varies from state to state; in some cases their choices are subject to approval of the state senate. The 1967 federal study listed the gubernatorial appointment power as "strong" or "very strong" in two-thirds of the states and as "medium" or "weak" in the rest.[21]

All states except North Carolina grant their governors the power to veto state legislation. The veto is one of the few areas in which governors actually have more power than the equivalent power of the President. Governors in forty-three states can exercise an *item veto* over single parts of appropriations bills, and in three states the governor's item veto extends to other bills as well. The President can only veto entire bills (see Chapter 10, pp. 386–88).

Half the states limit the term of office of the governor, restricting him to either two four-year or two two-year terms, or one four-year term. But more than a third of the states now have four-year terms with unlimited succession, and the trend is toward increasing the governor's term and his powers. In general, a governor's power, and his ability to develop long-range policies, is greater if his term in office is four years and he is permitted to succeed himself. Otherwise, to some extent, he becomes a "lame duck" as soon as he is inaugurated. The governor's control over the state budget is another index of his power. In all but a few states, the governor prepares an executive budget and submits it to the legislature. In general, this serves

[18] *Fiscal Balance in the American System*, Vol. I, Advisory Commission on Intergovernmental Relations (Washington, D.C.: U.S. Government Printing Office, October 1967), pp. 233–34.
[19] *Ibid.*, p. 235.
[20] *Ibid.*, pp. 216–18.
[21] *Ibid.*, p. 220.

to increase the governor's strength, but not automatically; much depends on his skill in managing the state bureaucracy and on other fiscal and political practices within the state. Since federal grants-in-aid provided 18 percent of the state revenues in 1970, the governor's power also varies with the degree of his control over state participation in federal programs. Yet, in eighteen states the governor's approval is *not* required when state agencies apply for federal grants.

When the American nation began, state legislatures were powerful and prestigious political institutions. Today, they are sometimes described in unflattering terms. During the nineteenth century, in the era of Jacksonian democracy and again after the Civil War, voters in many states wrote various restrictions on legislative power into the state constitutions, limiting state expenditures and borrowing power, for example. Many of these curbs are still in effect.

The Legislatures

Public respect for state legislators and legislatures has also been eroded by occasional disclosures of corruption among the lawmakers. Probably few state legislators can be "bought" by direct bribes, but there is some feeling among the public that state legislators, one way or another, manage to use their position for private gain. Closely tied to this assumption is the belief that lobbyists and special interest groups can work their will at the statehouse more easily than in Washington. Certainly, an industry, utility, or labor union that exercises great power within a state capital often achieves its legislative aims more easily at the state level than in Congress, where its power may be diffused and it must compete with many other interest groups.

Finally, until the reapportionment decisions of the 1960's, overrepresentation of rural areas in the state legislatures diminished legislative prestige in urban areas. City dwellers grumbled about state legislatures controlled by "appleknockers" and "farmers" who primarily served rural interests.

Every state has a two-house legislature except Nebraska, which has a unicameral legislature. The 7,600 lawmakers serve in legislatures that range in size from 58 in Delaware to 424 in New Hampshire.[22] Typically, the upper house has thirty to sixty members and the lower house about one hundred. Most state senators serve four-year terms; most state representatives of the lower house serve for two years.

In only twenty-six states does the legislature meet annually on a regular basis.[23] In the remainder, the legislatures meet regularly only every

[22] *Book of the States, 1970–71* (Lexington, Ky.: Council of State Governments, 1970), pp. 66–67.
[23] *Ibid.*, pp. 82–83.

two years, normally in January of odd-numbered years. This fact alone tells something of the status and power of state legislatures.

For the majority of state legislators, public service is only a part-time job. About one-half of the states constitutionally limit regular legislative sessions to less than seventy-five days. Even then, the legislators might spend only a few days in the capital each week, often ending the session with a great flurry of last-minute legislation. Sometimes the clock is literally stopped to permit the passage of bills within the time limit.

In 1971, California state legislators were paid $19,200 a year—the highest state legislative salaries in the nation. Although big states such as Michigan and New York paid legislators $15,000 annually, other states paid only a per-diem rate. The median salary of state legislators is about $5,000.

Who are the legislators? State lawmakers tend to come from a higher-than-average social and economic background. As Thomas R. Dye has noted:

> More than three-quarters of the nation's state legislators have been exposed to a college education, a striking contrast to the educational level of the total population. Legislators are also concentrated in the occupations with more prestige. A great majority of legislators are either engaged in the professions, or are proprietors, managers, or officials of business concerns. Farmers constitute a sizeable minority of legislators in all but the most urban states. Lawyers are the largest single occupational group.[24]

Perhaps the most important aspect of state legislatures today is their changing nature as a result of the "reapportionment revolution" discussed in Chapter 9 (pp. 358–61). In *Baker v. Carr* in 1962 the Supreme Court held that the voters of Tennessee did have the right to challenge unequal representation in the state's legislature.[25] And in *Reynolds v. Sims* in 1964 it ruled that apportionment of the upper house must also be based closely on population and the principle of "equal representation for equal numbers of people."[26]

The Court's decisions did not, despite popular expectations, shift the base of state political power from rural areas to the central cities. Instead, as we have noted, the main beneficiary has proved to be the suburbs. "Reapportionment has suburbanized the legislatures," Mayor Wes Uhlman of Seattle complained in 1970, "and the suburbanites are as hostile to the city as the farmers ever were."[27] In Ohio, for example, the "crabgrass

[24] Thomas R. Dye, "State Legislative Politics," in Herbert Jacob and Kenneth N. Vines, eds., *Politics in the American States* (Boston: Little, Brown, 1965), p. 167.
[25] *Baker v. Carr*, 369 U.S. 186 (1962).
[26] *Reynolds v. Sims*, 377 U.S. 533 (1964).
[27] In Jack Rosenthal, "The Year of the Suburbs: More People, More Power," *New York Times*, June 21, 1970, p. 54.

TABLE 16-1

The State Legislatures

	Senate	Length of Term	House	Length of Term	Years Sessions Are Held	Salary[1]
Alabama	35	4	106	4	odd	$ 10 (d)
Alaska	20	4	40	2	annual	6,000
Arizona	30	2	60	2	annual	6,000
Arkansas	35	4	100	2	odd	
California	40	4	80	2	annual	19,200
Colorado	35	4	65	2	annual	10,200 (b)
Connecticut	36	2	177	2	odd	3,250 (b)
Delaware	19	4	39	2	annual	6,000
Florida	48	4	119	2	annual	12,000
Georgia	56	2	195	2	annual	4,200
Hawaii	25	4	51	2	annual	12,000
Idaho	35	2	70	2	annual	10 (d)
Illinois	58	4	177	2	odd	12,000
Indiana	50	4	100	2	odd	4,000
Iowa	61	4	124	2	annual	5,500
Kansas	40	4	125	2	annual	10 (d)
Kentucky	38	4	100	2	even	25 (d)
Louisiana	39	4	105	4	annual	50 (d)
Maine	32	2	151	2	odd	2,500 (b)
Maryland	43	4	142	4	annual	2,400
Massachusetts	40	2	240	2	annual	11,400
Michigan	38	4	110	2	annual	15,000
Minnesota	67	4	135	2	odd	9,600 (b)
Mississippi	52	4	122	4	annual	5,000
Missouri	34	4	163	2	odd	16,800 (b)
Montana	55	4	104	2	odd	20 (d)
Nebraska[2]	49	4	—	—	odd	4,800
Nevada	20	4	40	2	odd	40 (d)
New Hampshire	24	2	400	2	odd	200 (b)
New Jersey	40	4	80	2	annual	10,000
New Mexico	42	4	70	2	annual	20 (d)
New York	57	2	150	2	annual	15,000
North Carolina	50	2	120	2	odd	2,400
North Dakota	49	4	98	2	odd	5 (d)
Ohio	33	4	99	2	odd	25,500 (b)
Oklahoma	48	4	99	2	annual	8,400
Oregon	30	4	60	2	odd	6,000 (b)
Pennsylvania	50	4	203	2	annual	7,200
Rhode Island	50	2	100	2	annual	5 (d)
South Carolina	46	4	124	2	annual	4,000
South Dakota	35	2	75	2	annual	3,000
Tennessee	33	4	99	2	odd	3,600
Texas	31	4	150	2	odd	4,800 (b)
Utah	28	4	69	2	annual	25 (d)
Vermont	30	2	150	2	odd	30 (d)
Virginia	40	4	100	2	even	35 (d)
Washington	49	4	99	2	odd	7,200 (b)
West Virginia	34	4	100	2	annual	1,500
Wisconsin	33	4	100	2	annual	17,800 (b)
Wyoming	30	4	61	2	odd	12 (d)

[1] Salaries annual unless otherwise noted (b) biennial salary, (d) per day.
[2] Unicameral legislature.

Source: Adapted from *The Book of States* (Lexington, Ky.: Council of State Governments, 1970–71), pp. 65–69.

brigade" of suburban legislators is regarded as just as conservative on many social welfare and urban issues as the "cornstalk brigade" from the state's rural areas.[28]

The Judges

Most Americans never see the inside of the United States Supreme Court, or even of a federal district court. But many have been to state and local courts—for example, traffic court to pay a fine, or divorce court—where most criminal and civil cases are handled. The quality of justice in America, therefore, depends to a great extent on the quality of justice in the states and communities. These courts, rather than federal courts, are most visible to the average citizen.

As in the case of the Supreme Court, state courts often strike down state laws as conflicting with their state constitutions. But the decisions of state and local courts must conform to the United States Constitution as interpreted by the Supreme Court. Many of the Warren Court decisions protecting the rights of criminal suspects overruled the opinions of lower state and local courts.

State and local judgeships are important political prizes. A young lawyer who "goes into politics" may serve in the legislature or in a state or municipal administration. But, often, his hope is to be appointed a judge as his safe, prestigious, and ultimate political reward.

The structure of the state and local judiciary and the problems of the nation's criminal justice system are discussed in detail in Chapter 13.

Politics and Parties

In Chapter 7, we examined the structure of state political party organizations, their relation to national parties, the geographic cleavage that exists between "upstate" and "downstate" urban-rural areas in many states, and the decline of big-city political machines. In Chapter 9, we mentioned the various state influences on national politics and the increasing effort of states to isolate themselves from the tides of presidential politics by scheduling elections for governor in the off-years. In Chapter 12, we discussed the effects of one-party state politics on the congressional seniority system. In the American federal system, state politics and state political parties cannot be separated from any discussion of politics and government at the national level.

To the extent that the Nixon administration pursued a so-called Southern strategy, for example, including the unsuccessful nomination of two conservative Southerners to the Supreme Court, the administration was attuned to the politics of Southern and border states. A state governor—

[28] *Ibid.*

George Wallace of Alabama—was as important a political figure as almost any member of the United States Senate.

The states are the building blocks of the national political parties. But among the states, the pattern of party competition differs widely. In the one-party states of the deep South, for example, competition was largely *within* the Democratic party for many years. The real battles were fought for the Democratic nomination; the winner of the nomination was virtually assured victory over his Republican opponent in the general election.

But the emergence of George Wallace's third party in the 1960's, combined with major Republican inroads in the "Solid South," has changed the face of Southern politics. In 1968, President Nixon carried four Southern and two border states, and in 1971, two Southern states had Republican governors.

Some states have vigorous two-party competition. Other states have modified two-party competition—one party is on the average stronger than the other. But in both types of states, control of the statehouse and the legislature can swing back and forth. In a study published in 1965, Austin Ranney characterized eight states as one-party Democratic, nine as modified one-party Democratic, twenty-five as two-party, and eight (including once staunchly Republican Maine and Vermont) as modified one-party Republican.[29] (See Figure 16-3.)

The political parties within the states show considerable ideological variation as well. A Democrat from rural Florida may be much closer to a Republican in ideological hue than he is to a Wisconsin Democrat. The Republican party in Mississippi bears little resemblance to the Republican party in Massachusetts. In 1970, New York's two Republican senators, Jacob Javits and Charles Goodell, were a good deal more liberal in their voting record than a number of Democratic senators. (So much so that the Nixon administration, through Vice-President Agnew, publicly declined to support Goodell, who was defeated in November 1970 by James Buckley, the Conservative party candidate.)

The rise of the direct primary for state political nominations (discussed in Chapter 9) has weakened control of state political machines by party leaders. The primary has at least partially shifted control over nominations to the voters, in those states where they care to exercise that power. In the Democratic primary election in New York in 1970, the voters showed considerable selectivity. They narrowly chose Arthur Goldberg, who had been endorsed by the state convention, to be Democratic candidate for governor, but chose Representative Richard Ottinger as sen-

---

[29] Austin Ranney, "Parties in State Politics," in Jacob and Vines, *Politics in the American States*, p. 65.

FIGURE 16-3

Party Competition in the States

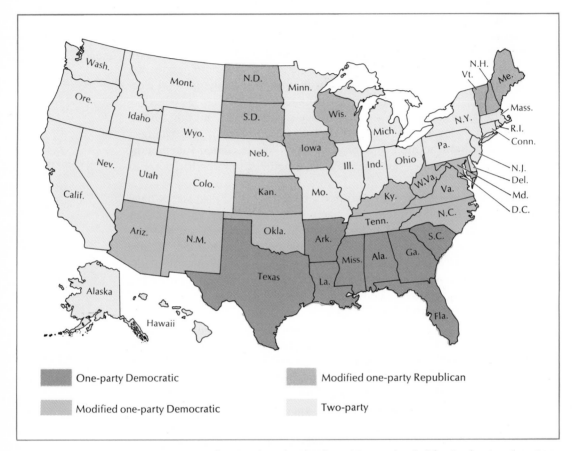

One-party Democratic

Modified one-party Democratic

Modified one-party Republican

Two-party

Source: Herbert Jacob and Kenneth N. Vines, eds., *Politics in the American States* (Boston: Little, Brown, 1965), p. 66. Copyright © 1965 by Little, Brown & Company, Inc.

atorial candidate, rejecting Theodore Sorensen, who had been endorsed by the state Democratic convention.

LOCAL GOVERNMENTS

Recently, a cartoon in the *New Yorker* showed a woman sitting at a table on the terrace of a New York City apartment, calling to her husband, "Hurry, dear, your soup is getting dirty."

For New Yorkers, air pollution is no joke. Whether one lives in a Manhattan skyscraper, a ghetto, or a small town, the quality of local government is likely to have immediate impact on his life. In that sense, local government is "closer" to the citizen, even though the Federal Government may have a greater effect on his life in the long run.

Take New York City. In recent years its residents have lived through strikes by sanitation workers, subway workers, and teachers, and a total power blackout. One way or another, these inconveniences involved the city government. If a New Yorker watches noxious trash piling up on the sidewalks, if he must walk several miles to work, if he cannot send his children to school, or if he is trapped in an elevator in a power failure, he has ample reason to be aware of the impact of local government on his life.

Although the connection is not always well understood, local governments are legal creatures of the states. State constitutions vest power in the state government; localities only exercise the power that the state gives to them.

Cities are municipal corporations chartered by the states. The charters define the municipal powers. About half the states have widely varying provisions for local *home rule*. As the term implies, home rule empowers municipalities to modify their charters and run their affairs without approval by the legislature. Home rule may not help cities solve problems, however. At a time when so many urban problems cut across the boundaries of local governmental units, many urban specialists believe there is a need for greater interdependence and cooperation among local governments, not greater autonomy and independence.

There are three basic forms of city government.

The Mayor-Council Plan. Today, most of the nation's cities of half a million people or more employ a strong mayor-council form of government. Under it, the mayor has substantial formal power over the executive agencies of government and in his dealings with an elected city council. In some cities, however, a weak mayor-council form is still in use. Under it, the mayor is merely a figurehead and must share his administrative power with the council. Some cities employ a mixture of the two systems. Half the cities of more than 5,000 people use the mayor-council plan.

The Commission Plan. When a hurricane and high waves smashed Galveston, Texas in 1900, more than 5,000 people were killed and property damage was estimated to be in the millions. In the emergency, with the city government paralyzed, the Texas legislature appointed a commission of five local businessmen to run Galveston.

The plan caught on and for a time was extremely popular in American

Cities

657

cities. Under it, a board of city commissioners, usually five, is popularly elected (on a nonpartisan ballot in a majority of cities that use the system). The commissioners make policy as a city council, but they also run the city departments as administrators. One commissioner is usually designated mayor, but often has no extra power. In time, the commission plan proved disappointing to reformers. Responsibility was diffused under the system and commissioners frequently lacked the skills needed to administer city departments. Some 250 cities of more than 5,000 people still use this form of local government. In 1960, it was abandoned by Galveston, which turned to the council-manager plan.

The Council-Manager Plan. Staunton, Virginia, and Sumter, South Carolina, adopted the council-manager government before the First World War. Under this system a council elected on a nonpartisan ticket hires a professional city manager, who runs the city government and has power to hire and fire city officials. The council in turn has power to fire the city manager (although the council is not supposed to interfere in the day-to-day administration of city affairs). City managers often receive high salaries and they often bring trained, professional skills to the business of running a city. Although the city manager is nominally "nonpolitical" he may be dismissed as a result of a political battle within the community. About half of all cities under 500,000 have city managers, and the plan is particularly popular in Western states. But it is employed all across the nation, from Portland, Maine, to San José, California.

Counties   In rural areas, the county is the most important geographic unit of local government. There are more than 3,000 counties in the United States. Their size and power vary, but typically, the elected officials include the sheriff, county prosecutor, coroner, clerk, and treasurer. But these officials share governing power with elected county boards, most frequently called a "board of commissioners" or a "board of supervisors." The county court is usually the local center of political power, the gathering place of those local officials, political leaders, and hangers-on often referred to as "the courthouse gang."

Towns and Townships   The New England town meeting has long stood as a symbol of direct, participatory democracy. These meetings are still held in many New England towns: the townspeople come together for an annual meeting in the spring, at which they elect a board of selectmen and settle local policy questions. But urbanization, increased population, and apathy have sapped the town meeting of much of its former strength.

In New England and New York, the "town" includes the village and the surrounding countryside. In the Middle Atlantic States and the Midwest, counties are often subdivided into townships. By order of Congress, many Midwest townships were laid out early in the nation's history in six-by-six-mile checkerboard fashion. For this reason, many townships today are thirty-six square miles in area. Rural townships are declining in importance and number. But in a number of urban areas, townships perform the function of cities.

Special districts are established within states to deal with problems that cut across the boundary lines of local units of government, or to spread the tax burden over a geographic area larger than that of the pre-existing local units. They are created for such purposes as fire protection, sewage, water, and parks. More than half the states also have school districts that are distinct from other governmental units.

Special Districts

The existence of so many different kinds and layers of local government results in fragmentation and overlapping, one of the underlying causes of the inability of local governments to respond effectively to their problems. For example, the existence in so many states of a separate system of governmental control for schools often makes it difficult for local governments to coordinate education with other programs.

CITIES AND SUBURBS: THE METROPOLITAN DILEMMA

One day in 1970—nobody knows exactly when—an event took place of major significance to the American political system. There were no ceremonies to mark the occasion, no presidential ribbon-cutting, no television coverage. But sometime during the year, the number of people who live in the suburbs passed the 71 million mark, and suburbia, by Census Bureau estimates, officially became the largest section of the American population.

What did this demographic milestone mean for the nation's future? One immediate political result can be measured in the increase in suburban representation in Congress and in state legislatures, following apportionment and redistricting based on the 1970 census.

Another result may be to sharpen the conflict between the suburbs and the cities on issues where their interests differ. Even before the suburbs had outgrown the cities in population, the urban-suburban cleavage was clearly visible. In state after state, suburban legislators, sometimes in alliance with rural forces, defeated legislation to aid central cities.

More than half a century ago, George Washington Plunkitt, the Tammany district leader, complained that rural legislators had imposed an unfair tax burden on New York City:

This city is ruled entirely by the hayseed legislators at Albany. . . . In England . . . they make a pretense of givin' the Irish some self-government. In this state, the Republican government makes no pretense at all. It says right out in the open: "New York City is a nice big fat goose. Come along with your carvin' knives and have a slice." They don't pretend to ask the Goose's consent.[30]

Today, the white suburban resident has replaced the "hayseeds" of yesteryear as the adversary of the city dweller. If Boss Plunkitt were around today, he would probably be complaining about the "commuters" in New York City's suburban Nassau and Westchester counties.

The picture of conflict between cities and suburbs might be even bleaker but for two emerging factors. First, the pattern of metropolitan

[30] In William L. Riordon, *Plunkitt of Tammany Hall* (New York: Dutton, 1963), p. 21.

"And then, during the latter part of the twentieth century, as the city choked with ever-increasing taxes, polluted air, and intolerable traffic, one by one the vast corporations moved out across the waste-infested rivers into the more salubrious atmosphere of the countryside."

Drawing by Frascino
© 1970 The New Yorker Magazine, Inc.

growth has created an *interdependence* among all governments in the area, especially in such fields as air pollution, mass transit, and land use, where no single government's boundaries conform to the size of the problem.[31] Suburbs and cities can, and have, cooperated on problems in which their mutual benefit is at stake. Second, some of the problems of the cities—crime, overcrowding, welfare rolls, traffic, housing—have begun to appear in the suburbs as their population has increased. Suburban residents are discovering that, to some extent, they "took the city with them."

As a result, during the 1970's more and more suburbs and cities may come to realize that, on certain issues at least, they are in the same boat. This has happened in Georgia; urban and suburban legislators, formerly political enemies, have joined in an "Urban Caucus"—in part because the area around Atlanta, including Cobb County, began experiencing many of the same problems afflicting the core city.[32]

With the population shift to suburbia, the "urban crisis" in America has become the "urban-suburban crisis," or, more accurately, a "metropolitan crisis."

The Urban Crisis

In Greece, more than 2,000 years ago, planners dreamed of a new city-state called Megalopolis. *Polis* was the Greek word for city-state (from which "politics" is derived), and "mega" comes from the word for "large," so Megalopolis meant a very large city. In 1961, Jean Gottman used the word to describe "the unique cluster of metropolitan areas of the Northeastern seaboard of the United States."[33] Stretching 600 miles, covering all or part of eleven states in a band thirty to one hundred miles wide, Megalopolis in 1960 contained 37 million people and included the cities of Boston, New York, Philadelphia, Baltimore, and Washington.[34] Driving through the area, it seemed almost one continuous community. Some urban experts foresee the time when the United States will have three megalopolises, "Boswash," "Chipitts" (a strip from Chicago to Pittsburgh), and a third one along the West Coast.

But is this how man was meant to live? Since the beginning of civilization, men have clustered together in cities, which have served as magnets of communication, commerce, and culture. But critics of megalopolis have deplored the effect of the modern city on the quality of life. Lewis Mumford has asked: "Will the whole planet turn into a vast urban hive?"[35]

---

[31] See Campbell and Shalala, "Problems Unsolved, Solutions Untried: The Urban Crisis," p. 7.

[32] *New York Times*, June 21, 1970, p. 54.

[33] Jean Gottmann, *Megalopolis: The Urbanized Northeastern Seaboard of the United States* (New York: Twentieth Century Fund, 1961), p. 4.

[34] *Ibid.*, pp. 19, 26.

[35] Lewis Mumford, *The City in History: Its Origins, Its Transformations, and Its Prospects* (New York: Harcourt Brace Jovanovich, 1961), p. 3.

Mumford argued that the modern metropolis has grown in "a continuous shapeless mass," that its residents are subject to constant frustration and harassment in their daily lives; at the same time they have become increasingly removed from nature.[36]

On the other hand, despite all the alarm over the "urban crisis," Edward C. Banfield has argued that "the plain fact is that the overwhelming majority of city dwellers live more comfortably and conveniently than ever before."[37] In Banfield's view, many urban problems—congestion, for example—are overstated: "people come to the city . . . precisely *because* it is congested. If it were not congested, it would not be worth coming to." In defending the city, Banfield adds: "To a large extent, then, our urban problems are just like the mechanical rabbit at the racetrack, which is set to keep just ahead of the dogs no matter how fast they may run. Our performance is better and better, but because we set our standards and expectations to keep ahead of performance, the problems are never any nearer to solution."[38]

Despite Banfield's spirited and controversial defense of the modern American city, a more general view is that the nation's cities *are* in difficulty and that problems such as race, slums, crime, housing, and transportation are not being solved fast enough in the world's richest society.

City Politics: Governing Metropolis

The term "power structure" is often heard today. It was popularized two decades ago by Floyd Hunter, a sociologist who studied community leadership in Atlanta, Georgia.[39] Hunter concluded that a group of about forty people, mostly top businessmen, determined policy in Atlanta and used the machinery of government to attain their own goals.

But in a study of New Haven, Connecticut, Robert Dahl concluded that the city was not run by a power elite of economic or social notables, and that policy decisions were made by changing coalitions of leaders drawn from different segments of the community.[40] As we noted in Chapter 6, scholars have provided diverse answers to the question of "Who governs?" Some scholars argue that power elites make public policy, but other political scientists see American society as pluralistic, with many— although not all—groups sharing in the decision-making.

Edward C. Banfield and James Q. Wilson have contended that, regardless of how decisions are made in various American cities, all cities have one thing in common: "Persons not elected to office play very considerable

[36] *Ibid.*, pp. 543–548.
[37] Edward C. Banfield, *The Unheavenly City* (Boston: Little, Brown, 1970), p. 3.
[38] *Ibid.*, pp. 5, 21.
[39] Floyd Hunter, *Community Power Structure* (Chapel Hill, N.C.: University of North Carolina Press, 1953).
[40] Robert A. Dahl, *Who Governs?* (New Haven, Conn.: Yale University Press, 1961).

parts in the making of many important decisions." [41] Banfield and Wilson have suggested the term "influentials" for these powerful citizens who hold no official position.

When most people think of city government, however, they usually think of decisions being made by officials elected to political office by the voters. As on the national and state levels, parties, politics, and the ballot box play a central role in the decisions made at the city level that affect people's lives.

One result of the migration of many whites to the suburbs has been that more cities with a large black electorate have chosen black officials. In 1970, for example, Cleveland, Ohio, Gary, Indiana, and Newark, New Jersey, all had black mayors; in the latter two cities and in Washington, D.C., black population exceeded the white population. (See Table 16-2.)

TABLE 16-2

Cities Likely to Become More Than
50 Percent Black, 1971–1984[1]

New Orleans	1971	St. Louis	1978
Richmond	1971	Detroit	1979
Baltimore	1972	Philadelphia	1981
Jacksonville	1972	Oakland	1983
Cleveland	1975	Chicago	1984

[1] Estimates based on Census Bureau data.

Source: Adapted from *National Advisory Commission on Civil Disorders* (New York: Bantam Books, 1968), p. 391. © 1970 by The New York Times Company. Reprinted by permission.

Historically, the big-city political machine has characterized urban politics. The political machines traded jobs and social services for votes of immigrants; but, with the changing nature of American society, urban political machines have declined. The power of Tammany Hall was broken in New York City in the early 1960's, and Chicago's powerful political leader, Mayor Richard J. Daley, is often described as the last of the big-city bosses. Often, bossism and urban machines have had close ties with the underworld; in some cases machine politicians have accepted payoffs from organized crime to permit illegal activities to flourish.

Without a tightly structured, old-style political machine, how does a mayor govern a large city? In some cases, the mayor builds a personal machine. Mayor John V. Lindsay of New York, for example, surrounded

[41] Edward C. Banfield and James Q. Wilson, *City Politics* (Harvard University Press and M.I.T. Press, 1963), pp. 244–45.

Nobody thinks of drawin' the distinction between honest graft and dishonest graft. There's all the difference in the world between the two. . . . My party's in power in the city, and it's goin' to undertake a lot of public improvements. Well, I'm tipped off, say, that they're going to lay out a new park at a certain place.

I see my opportunity and I take it. I go to that place and I buy up all the land I can in the neighborhood. Then the board of this or that makes its plan public, and there is a rush to get my land, which nobody cared particular for before.

Ain't it perfectly honest to charge a good price and make a profit on my investment and foresight? Of course, it is. Well, that's honest graft.

—Boss Plunkitt quoted in William L. Riordon, *Plunkitt of Tammany Hall.*

himself with bright, young aides somewhat in the tradition of President Kennedy's "New Frontier" in Washington.

But as one study of urban politics noted, the mayor of New York must share his power with five other groups of participants—party leaders, appointed and elected public officials, the bureaucracy, nongovernmental associations and the media, and officials and agencies of governments outside New York City. Since no one group dominates, decisions are actually the result of "mutual accommodation." [42] In short, the business of governing metropolis usually means that a mayor is constantly striving to build and maintain workable coalitions of interest groups; his power is limited and he is a handy target when things go wrong.

Yet the big-city mayor is not without some tools to govern. Another analyst of politics and power in New York City perceived four roles in which the mayor can lead: first, as a symbol of the city, embodying New York's view of itself as both a glamorous place and a melting pot; second, as chief lobbyist for the city in Washington, in the state capital at Albany, and in the city council; third, as chief employer in the city; and fourth, as umpire among conflicting groups.[43] Since the mayor's power is restricted in many ways, his most successful role may be that of umpire and peacemaker.

The problems of a city such as New York—ranging from corruption to lack of revenue—are so staggering, however, that, in time, they tend to overwhelm the mayor. Up to 1970, at least, no mayor of New York had moved from City Hall to a national political career.

The Plight of the Cities

In 1969, a presidential study group painted a truly appalling vision of what American cities might become "in a few more years," in the absence of massive action to solve urban problems. In its final report, the National Commission on the Causes and Prevention of Violence declared:

[42] Wallace S. Sayre and Herbert Kaufman, *Governing New York City: Politics in the Metropolis* (New York: Norton, 1965), pp. 710–12.

[43] Roger Starr, "Power and Powerlessness in a Regional City," *The Public Interest*, No. 16 (Summer 1969), pp. 3–24.

Central business districts in the heart of the city, surrounded by mixed areas of accelerating deterioration, will be partially protected by large numbers of people shopping or working in commercial buildings during daytime hours, plus a substantial police presence, and will be largely deserted except for police patrols during night-time hours. . . .

High-speed patrolled expressways will be sanitized corridors connecting safe areas, and private automobiles, taxicabs, and commercial vehicles will be routinely equipped with unbreakable glass, light armor, and other security features. . . . Armed guards will "ride shotgun" on all forms of public transportation. . . . the ghetto slum neighborhoods will be places of terror with widespread crime, perhaps entirely out of police control during night-time hours. . . .

Between the unsafe, deteriorating central city on the one hand and the network of safe, prosperous areas and sanitized corridors on the other, there will be, not unnaturally, intensifying hatred and deepening division. Violence will increase further, and the defensive response of the affluent will become still more elaborate.[44]

It should be emphasized that this chilling vision of a fortress America is not shared by all students of the urban condition. Yet, as a warning

ORGANIZED CRIME: CORRUPTING LOCAL OFFICIALS

The mob operates freely only where it is able to bribe public officials for protection. The following conversation, recorded by the FBI, concerns the alleged efforts of organized crime to buy such protection for its gambling operations in the state of New Jersey:

Ray: Do you know what this Cappy [N.J. State Police Superintendent Dominick Capello] wants?
Lucky: No. How much?
Ray: He wants $1,000 for Long Branch and $1,000 for Asbury.
Si: For each town?
Ray: Yeah. Each town. . . .

Si: Do you want to hear the rest of the story? June, July, August and September, he wants double.
Ray: Here's what I figure. Let's move all the offices into Long Branch and we'll just pay him for Long Branch.
Lucky: That's a good idea. . . .
Ray: . . . Did you say you've got the town of Asbury?
Lucky: I ain't got Asbury.
Ray: Well, what have you got? Have you got Neptune? . . .
Lucky: Yeah. We've got the chief, but we ain't got the judge.

—*New York Times*, January 7, 1970.

---

[44] "To Establish Justice, To Insure Domestic Tranquility," *Final Report of the National Commission on the Causes and Prevention of Violence* (Washington, D.C.: U.S. Government Printing Office, 1969), pp. 44–45.

At 10:30 on a recent Saturday morning, a 39-year-old mother of six children was returning from the beauty parlor to her apartment in the Jackson Houses project in the South Bronx when a powerfully built man jumped into the elevator behind her and brandished a knife. He took $80 from her purse, stripped engagement and wedding rings from her fingers and then dragged her to the roof and raped her.

At 9:30 p.m. on another recent Saturday, an insurance man and his wife returned from a party to find a burglar ransacking their apartment in a luxury building at 320 East 58th Street. The burglar pulled out a pistol and fired, hitting the insurance man in the side, and then fled through a patio window.

These stories, both of them recorded on the increasingly heavy police blotters of the city, can be matched in almost every New York neighborhood—rich, middle-income and poor, black and white. They are the substance behind the fear that is making thousands of New Yorkers live ever-larger portions of their lives behind locked doors. . . . "We are living like rabbits in a hutch, afraid of the hawks who are waiting outside," said a professional man who twice since August has been clubbed to the ground and robbed as he was returning to his home on East 87th Street.

—Michael Stern, in the *New York Times*, December 11, 1968.

issued by an official study group, it cannot be lightly dismissed either.

Part of the problem is that cities are no longer performing the same role they performed in the past. In the nineteenth and early twentieth centuries, America's cities were great socializing engines, taking unskilled immigrants from Europe and, in a generation or two, turning many of them into middle-class or even affluent Americans. But to some extent, that process has stopped. The migrants to the cities now are black Americans. And, historically, blacks have not been integrated into American society in the same way as the Irish, Italians, Jews, Poles, and other groups; blacks have faced greater and more persistent discrimination.

Who will pay for the cost of providing schools, housing, and other social services for residents of the inner-city? That remains the core of the dilemma; the cities say they cannot, and the suburbs do not indicate any desire to do so. City mayors complain that the Federal Government has simply not allocated enough money to bridge the gap.

Population Trends. Census Bureau figures tell much of the story of the "sorting out" of city and suburban population. During the decade of the 1960's, the white population of the central cities *declined* by about 2,000,000 persons but the white population of the suburbs *increased* by 14,000,000. During the same period, the black population of the central cities *increased* by 2.7 million persons. As a result, by 1969, 55.2 percent of all black Americans lived in central cities, and only 14.7 percent lived in suburbs surrounding the cities. By contrast, only 25.8 percent of the white

FIGURE 16-4

Distribution of White and Black Population: 1969

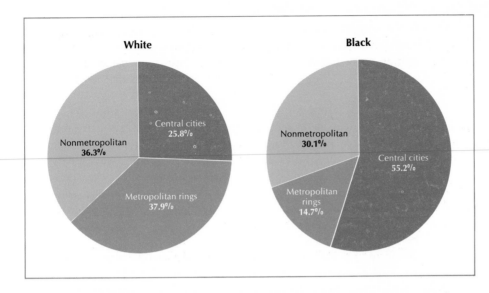

Source: Adapted from U.S. Bureau of the Census, *Current Population Reports*, Population Characteristics, Population of the United States by Metropolitan-Nonmetropolitan Residence: 1969 and 1960, Series P-20, No. 197, March 6, 1970.

population lived in central cities, and almost 38 percent lived in suburbia.[45] (See Figure 16-4.)

As noted earlier in this chapter (and in Chapter 5, p. 183), there were signs by 1970 that black Americans were migrating to the suburbs in increasing numbers. Between 1960 and 1969, according to a Census Bureau survey, the black suburban population jumped from 2.4 to 3.3 million people, an increase of 37 percent. During the same period, white suburbia grew from 51.8 to 66.8 million people, an increase of 29 percent. Thus, even though whites vastly outnumbered blacks in the nation's metropolitan rings, the black suburban population was growing at a faster rate than the white population. The black migration outward was particularly dramatic in the North and West, where the number of black suburban residents increased by 68 percent between 1960 and 1969. [46]

Despite the popular image of poor whites and blacks pouring into the cities to go on relief rolls, one study of urban migration indicates that people come to the cities for jobs, not social services, and that, compared to the nonwhite population already living in the cities, the average nonwhite who

[45] U.S. Bureau of the Census, *Current Population Reports*, Population Characteristics, Population of the United States by Metropolitan-Nonmetropolitan Residence: 1969 and 1960, Series P-20, No. 197, March 6, 1970, pp. 1–2.
[46] U.S. Census Bureau, *Current Population Reports*, Special Studies, Trends in Social and Economic Conditions in Metropolitan and Nonmetropolitan Areas, pp. 2, 8.

comes to the city has a higher occupational and educational background.[47] But the newcomers face job and housing discrimination; they are not in the same position as whites moving to a pleasant suburban neighborhood. As one observer put it, "the Welcome Wagon rarely calls in the ghetto."[48]

Housing, HUD, and Model Cities. Officials of the Federal Government and others who have studied urban problems differ widely on how to break the circle of poverty in the inner-city. In Chapter 15, for example, we noted the two approaches to the welfare problem—providing social services, or providing income for the poor. But that is only one aspect of the debate. Where should government begin in attempting to eliminate poverty and slums? With housing? Schools? Jobs? All of those things at once? Nobody really knows the answer.

The difficulties of making progress in attacking the overall problem can be illustrated by a close look at just one aspect of urban needs: housing. As in the case of many "urban" problems, substandard housing is by no means only a problem of the cities. In fact, in 1960, there was more substandard housing in rural areas than in urban areas.[49] Nevertheless, inner-city slums were, and are, a highly visible, urgent social problem.

How well has the United States coped with that problem? In the Housing Act of 1949, Congress proclaimed the goal of "a decent home and a suitable living environment for every American family." That goal, the law states, shall be met "as soon as feasible."

Yet, in 1960, more than a decade later, 8.5 million families were living in substandard housing in the United States. And, there were still 4.7 million families living in such housing in 1968.

In New York in 1969, a family that asked for an apartment in a public housing project became No. 130,801 on the waiting list. At the existing rate of construction, the family could expect to move into a project *in fifty-one years.*[50]

More than 800 communities and practically every large city in America have participated in the federal urban renewal program since it began in 1949. Under the program, the Federal Government defrays two-thirds to three-fourths of the cost of local slum-clearance projects. Yet the multibillion dollar program has hardly made more than a dent in clearing the nation's slums. Moreover, in many cases urban renewal has *added* to inner-city tensions by forcing poor people from their homes to make way

[47] Charles Tilly, "Race and Migration To the American City," in Wilson, *The Metropolitan Enigma*, pp. 129–31.
[48] *Ibid.*, p. 142.
[49] Bernard J. Frieden, "Housing and National Urban Goals: Old Policies and New Realities," in Wilson, *The Metropolitan Enigma*, p. 153.
[50] David K. Shipler, "The Changing City: Housing Paralysis," in *The Changing City* (New York: New York Times, 1969), p. 25.

for middle- or upper-income housing and commercial centers. Fannie Lou Hamer, an outspoken black civil rights leader in Mississippi, has made this observation on the subject of urban renewal: "We're already living nowhere, and now they're going to move us out of that." [51] In 1969, Congress required for the first time that for each slum home demolished in an urban renewal project, a new low-income dwelling must be constructed.

The responsibility of the Federal Government for housing was given recognition at the Cabinet level in 1965 when Congress established the Department of Housing and Urban Development (HUD). The same year, Congress passed a comprehensive housing bill, including for the first time a program of rent supplements for low-income families.

In 1966, Congress approved a major new Model Cities program under the direction of HUD. The purpose of the program was to demonstrate how the Federal Government could work with city halls in a concentrated and coordinated attack on urban blight. The goal of the Model Cities program was to rebuild entire poverty neighborhoods in selected cities, and to attack social problems as well as the physical problem of decaying buildings. The program was aimed especially at improving conditions in the black urban ghettos. Model Cities was one of the major legislative programs

THE MYTH OF MONEY

There is a wistful myth that if only we had enough money to spend—the figure is usually put at a hundred billion dollars—we could wipe out all our slums in ten years, reverse decay in the great, dull, gray belts that were yesterday's and day-before-yesterday's suburbs, anchor the wandering middle class and its wandering tax money, and perhaps even solve the traffic problem.

But look what we have built with the first several billions: Low-income projects that become worse centers of delinquency, vandalism and general social hopelessness than the slums they were supposed to replace. Middle-income housing projects which are truly marvels of dullness and regimentation, sealed against any buoyancy or vitality of city life. Luxury housing projects that mitigate their inanity, or try to, with a vapid vulgarity. Cultural centers that are unable to support a good bookstore. Civic centers that are avoided by everyone but bums, who have fewer choices of loitering place than others. Commercial centers that are lackluster imitations of standardized suburban chainstore shopping. Promenades that go from no place to nowhere and have no promenaders. Expressways that eviscerate great cities. This is not the rebuilding of cities. This is the sacking of cities.

—Jane Jacobs, *The Death and Life of Great American Cities.*

[51] Speech, Robert F. Kennedy Memorial Journalism Awards dinner, Washington, D.C., June 19, 1969.

passed under President Johnson's "Great Society." The concept was developed by Robert C. Wood of M.I.T., who was appointed the first undersecretary of HUD.

The Federal Government pays up to 80 percent of the cost of the program. By 1970, Congress had provided $1.3 billion for Model Cities in 150 communities, but the program was embroiled in considerable controversy. Critics charged that the program suffered from excessive federal red tape and insufficient federal funding. At the local level there was conflict between city halls and citizen groups over control of the program.

During the first year of the Nixon administration, there was much internal debate over the future of Model Cities. A presidential task force headed by Edward C. Banfield recommended that Model Cities be continued in altered form. By 1970, the Nixon administration had apparently committed itself to this goal. During the Johnson administration, many HUD officials in the field had emphasized citizen control of Model Cities, along the lines of the poverty program's community action projects. Thus, the black ghettos were to be regenerated from within. Under Nixon and HUD secretary George Romney, control of Model Cities was placed in the hands of the mayors. In addition, the Nixon administration stressed greater coordination of all federal programs in participating cities.

Money for Model Cities flows in the form of block grants, giving mayors wide discretion in how they spend the federal funds. Thus, the Nixon White House saw the program as consistent with Nixon's concept of revenue-sharing and the "new federalism." In effect, the administration was remodeling a Great Society program to try to give it a Republican look. Even so, Model Cities remained a controversial program, with its future still somewhat uncertain in 1970.[52]

In the past, at least, some middle-class voters opposed spending tax money for low-income housing for the poor. Yet, middle-income and more affluent homeowners receive what amounts to a huge federal housing subsidy in the form of income tax deductions on mortgage payments. Homeowners can deduct the interest they pay on their mortgage loans in figuring their federal income taxes. Low- and middle-income homeowners benefit as well from the fact that the Federal Housing Administration (FHA) insures the mortgages of many homes. Between 1935 and 1970, 9.5 million families were able to buy homes because of FHA programs. But for three decades the FHA issued insurance only in low-risk areas; as a result it financed the development of the white suburbs but not of the inner-city. During the 1960's, however, FHA's role was expanded to provide federal backing for various kinds of low-income housing.

Despite sharply increased federal spending on housing in the 1960's,

[52] William Lilley III, "Model cities program faces uncertain future despite Romney overhaul," *National Journal*, Vol. 2, No. 28 (July 11, 1970), pp. 1467–80.

city slums had spread and worsened. As recently as 1967, the House initially rejected a $40 million program to exterminate rats in the slums. Some Southern Democrats laughed at the measure, terming it a "civil rats bill," and Representative James A. Haley, Democrat of Florida, suggested that the answer was to "buy a lot of cats and turn them loose." [53] The House refused to vote funds for rat control in spite of the fact that, only a month before, serious rioting had occurred in the black ghettos of Newark. Unfavorable press and public reaction to the House stand brought about a reversal, and Congress passed a modified rat control bill later that summer. Such episodes are not typical but they do raise questions about the degree of national commitment to improving urban conditions.

Taken as a whole, the federal housing program illustrates the lack of meaningful progress on the part of the nation in meeting the urban crisis. The Federal Government has poured billions of dollars into housing. Yet it has not "solved" the housing problem; indeed, some critics argued that other federal programs, such as urban renewal and highways, had dislocated poor neighborhoods and made matters worse. Although housing has finally been recognized as a Cabinet-level problem, the nation's need for decent housing for all Americans remains a goal rather than a reality.

Urban Transportation. Transportation is another urban problem directly affecting the quality of American life. The man in the traffic helicopter seldom broadcasts good news; getting in and out of the nation's cities during morning and evening rush hours, or getting to work within the city limits, is usually an ordeal. Americans spend a substantial part of their lives commuting to and from their jobs; but time spent in a crowded subway, as Lewis Mumford has suggested, takes it toll: "Emerson said that life was a matter of having good days, but it is a matter of having good minutes too. Who shall say what compensations are not necessary to the metropolitan worker to make up for the strain and depression of the twenty, forty, sixty, or more minutes he spends each night and morning passing through these metropolitan man-sewers?" [54]

Metropolitan transportation in the United States has been dominated by the automobile and the highway. Commuter railroads and other forms of mass transit were permitted to decline during the 1950's and 1960's. The Census Bureau reported that as of 1960 64 percent of all work trips in urban areas were by auto and only 20 percent by public transit.[55] Although people tend to complain that commuting takes longer than ever, in fact, travel time in and out of the cities has been slightly reduced over the past

[53] *1967 Congressional Quarterly Almanac*, p. 447.
[54] Mumford, *The City in History: Its Origins, Its Transformations, and Its Prospects*, pp. 549–50.
[55] John R. Meyer, "Urban Transportation," in Wilson, ed., *The Metropolitan Enigma*, p. 35.

"I'm supposed to be in the new U.S. Department of Transportation—if I can get to it."

From *The Herblock Gallery*
(Simon & Schuster, 1968)

decade. But not by much; and many people have chosen to "trade off" improved travel conditions by moving further into the suburbs.[56]

Federal policy has to some extent influenced the dominance of highways over rails. The Federal Government pays 90 percent of the cost of the huge interstate highway program, a massive incentive for states and cities to build roads rather than transit lines. The federal funds come from highway user taxes on trucks and buses, tires, and gasoline; the program, passed by Congress in 1956, is designed to link the nation's cities with 41,000 miles of superhighways, almost all of them four lane. Powerful interest groups have major stakes in highway politics. But the nation has not developed an overall transportation policy, one that would balance highways and rapid transit and ease congestion in metropolitan centers. In 1969, the Nixon administration proposed a mass transit program that would commit the Federal Government to spend 10 billion dollars in twelve years, much of it in the larger cities. The Urban Mass Transportation Act of 1970 embodied these goals and authorized an initial $3.1 billion to enable cities to build or improve rapid rail, subway, and bus commuter lines. The law permits the Federal Government to pay up to two-thirds of the cost of such programs.

Problems interlock. The dominance of the automobile and the highway is directly related to the problem of pollution, since automobiles produce at least 60 percent of total air pollution in the United States (electric power plants and industry account for most of the rest).

[56] *Ibid.*, pp. 39–41.

Poverty.   Poverty remains a pervasive problem in American cities, overshadowing or underlying almost all other problems. By 1968, slightly more poor people were living in metropolitan areas than outside of those areas. Of the 51 percent of poor people living in metropolitan areas, 30.5 percent lived in central cities—but 42 percent of all poor black Americans lived in the central cities.[57]

That does not mean that urban and racial problems are synonymous. But the black, Mexican American, or Puerto Rican child in the inner-city ghetto is caught up in a "culture of poverty" from which there is often no exit. Education may be the key to eliminating poverty, but inner-city schools often occupy the oldest buildings and have the least experienced

[57] U.S. Bureau of the Census, *Current Population Reports,* Consumer Income, Series P-60, No. 68, December 31, 1969, p. 7.

673

teachers, since many white teachers with seniority shun assignments to ghetto classrooms. Blacks and other minorities face discrimination in employment and housing as well. Unlike such physical problems as transportation or air pollution, racial bias involves social attitudes that work against certain minority groups. Many of the problems of the nation's cities, therefore, are bound up with the larger problem of insuring full equality for all Americans.

The Face
of the Suburbs

One of the phenomena of the migration to suburbia after the Second World War was the construction of whole new communities by a single builder. In 1958, Herbert Gans, a young sociologist, moved with his family into one such instant suburb, Levittown, New Jersey. His purpose was to study the community as a participant and observer. In recording the quality of social life in this suburb of Philadelphia, Gans quoted one woman describing her next-door neighbor: "We see eye to eye on things, about raising kids, doing things together with your husband, living the same way; we have practically the same identical background." [58]

The quote summarized both sides of the argument about suburbia. In an impersonal society, where people toil on assembly lines or in beehive offices of large corporations, many Americans long for a sense of identity and belonging. In part, people have moved to the suburbs in "a search for community." To some extent, the migration to the suburbs may be seen as a turning back to the grassroots, a yearning for the small-town America celebrated by Booth Tarkington and Mark Twain. On the other hand, the suburbs have been assailed as centers of conformity and homogeneity, in which community pressures tend to produce narrow social and political attitudes among suburbanites, and massive unconcern for urban and national problems.

Why do people move to the suburbs in the first place? According to Peter Rossi, they are both "pushed" and "pulled." [59] The "push" reasons are often emphasized: crime in the cities, fear of crime, bad schools, deteriorating housing. But the "pull" reasons are also highly important: the desire for more space and to "own our own home" and the attraction of suburban schools, for example. The automobile and FHA mortgage guarantees, allowing lower- and middle-income families to purchase their own homes, have been powerful factors as well.

The move to suburbia has brought change to the center of America's cities. To some extent, "downtown" is disappearing. Not only people, but jobs and industry, have moved to the suburbs. The suburban housewife no longer needs to go to the city to shop; the department stores have moved

[58] Herbert J. Gans, *The Levittowners* (New York: Pantheon Books, 1967), p. 155.
[59] Peter H. Rossi, *Why Families Move* (New York: Free Press of Glencoe, 1955).

to suburban shopping centers to be near *her*. There is still a need for downtown business areas, but less as centers of retail trade than as places for the conduct of businesses that require face-to-face contact—banking, finance, and communications, for example.

Life in the suburbs tends to be centered around home and family. The stereotype of the suburbanite happily barbecuing steaks on his outdoor grill or fussing with his lawn sometimes reflects the reality. But what about his less fortunate fellow citizens back in the city? Gans suggests that the Levittowners "deceive themselves into thinking that the community, or rather the home, is the single most influential unit in their lives. . . . the real problem is that the Levittowners have not yet become aware of how much they are a part of the national society and economy." [60]

Robert C. Wood has also questioned the values held by suburbia, and "its clear indifference to the metropolitan world about it, and on which it clearly depends." [61] Wood argues that grassroots values and democratic values are not one and the same; he sees a confusion between the concept of fraternity, as reflected in the shared values of suburbia, and the idea of democracy, which recognizes diversity and nonconformity.

The suburbanite who takes pride in his shrubs, his home, and his community is also part of a larger American community with many unpleasant problems that cannot be wished away. Sooner or later—and it may be happening sooner—the quality of life in the nation as a whole will be reflected in the suburbs.

Although social problems such as education, housing, crime, and health care have greatest impact in the cities, "they are not unknown to the suburbs and are increasingly being found there. . . . more and more suburban communities have city-like characteristics and all the problems associated with those characteristics." [62]

EXPLODING METROPOLIS AND AMERICA'S FUTURE

If metropolitan problems are larger than the boundary lines of local governments, why not create larger political units to solve these problems? The approach seems logical, but there are many obstacles to metropolitan government. Not the least of these is the reluctance of suburban areas to give up their political independence and to pay for services for residents of the central cities.

Metropolitan Solutions

Yet, efforts are being made in this direction, including the creation of

[60] *Ibid.*, p. 418.
[61] Robert C. Wood, *Suburbia: Its People and Their Politics* (Boston: Houghton Mifflin, 1959), p. 260.
[62] Campbell and Shalala, "Problems Unsolved, Solutions Untried: The Urban Crisis," p. 21.

special districts to handle specific functions, interstate compacts, area-wide planning agencies, consolidated school and library systems, and various informal intergovernmental arrangements. Annexation of outlying areas by the central city and the consolidation of cities and surrounding counties have all been tried; in many cases, they have been found wanting. Another approach has been the plan adopted in Los Angeles, under which the county has assumed responsibility for many area-wide functions, but local communities have retained their political autonomy.

Some urban experts have advocated metropolitan federalism as the best solution. Toronto, Canada, and its suburbs adopted this system in 1953. Mass transit, planning, highways, and many other functions are run by a council made up of elected officials from the central city and surrounding suburbs. London also has a federated system encompassing the thirty-two boroughs of Greater London.

In Florida, Miami and Dade County narrowly opted for "Metro" government in 1957. Under the plan, Miami and twenty-seven suburban cities retain control of local functions, but have ceded to "Metro" area-wide functions such as fire and police protection and transportation. Political control is vested in an elected board of commissioners, which appoints a county manager. Many groups and local communities feared the effects of surrendering power to an area-wide government. To survive, "Metro" had to beat back repeated lawsuits brought by its opponents and a series of referenda aimed at weakening the county-wide government.

In 1962, the city of Nashville, Tennessee, consolidated with Davidson County to form a single metropolitan government. In 1968, Jacksonville, Florida, joined with Duval County. Varying degrees of area-wide consolidation have been established in Baton Rouge, Louisiana; Seattle, Washington; Portland, Oregon; and Indianapolis, Indiana.

As urban growth continues, old concepts of metropolitan areas may change. The cities of the industrial Northeast, for example, may indeed come closer to the concept of "Boswash"—a single, giant city stretching along the Eastern seaboard. One scholar has suggested that tomorrow's metropolis may look less like a fried egg, with a clearly defined center and outer ring, and more like "a thin layer of scrambled eggs over much of the platter."[63]

Inter-
governmental
Relations

Although we have focused on state and local problems in this chapter, any real solution to metropolitan ills depends in large measure on the relationship among federal, state, and local governments.

State and local governments do not have enough revenues to meet

[63] York Willbern, *The Withering Away of the City* (Tuscaloosa, Ala.: University of Alabama Press, 1964), p. 33.

the social demands of both urban and rural areas. The confused, over-lapping program of federal grants-in-aid has been widely criticized. At the same time, state and local revenues have lagged behind national economic growth. The federal system, insofar as intergovernmental fiscal relations are concerned, has become rather creaky at the joints.

One suggested solution is revenue sharing (discussed in Chapter 3). Under such a system, the Federal Government, instead of channeling funds to state and local governments through highly structured federal programs, would simply give states and localities money to spend any way they wished. The plan would supplement rather than replace federal grants-in-aid to state and local governments.

Under the revenue-sharing proposals that President Nixon sent to Congress in 1969, Washington would give the states $500 million the first year, with the amount growing to $5 billion after five years. The money would be distributed under a formula based on population and each state's effort to raise its own revenues. A "pass-through" formula would guarantee that part of each state's share flowed through to cities, counties, and townships. (Nixon greatly expanded his revenue-sharing proposal in 1971.)

Some form of guarantee to local governments is vital to any revenue-sharing plan, since city mayors do not trust state governors to pass on enough money to the cities voluntarily. In 1969, for example, Congress approved a program of "block grants" to the states to strengthen law enforcement. The states were supposed to allocate funds to local agencies, but mayors complained bitterly that most of the money never reached City Hall. For instance, Scranton, Pennsylvania, with an annual police budget of $1 million, received only $5,000 out of the state's $1.4 million federal grant.[64] Solutions to problems of state and local governments depend in large measure on how well the rhetoric of federalism can be translated into the reality of intergovernmental cooperation.

Community Control

When Intermediate School 201 in the heart of New York's East Harlem opened its doors in September 1966, it was—in the opinion of many teachers—a "jungle." Teachers had to brandish sticks to try to maintain order, and large numbers of pupils transferred out because they had been assaulted by other children. Teachers shunned assignments to I.S. 201, and the school had a rapid succession of principals. In 1968, a local governing board was given jurisdiction over the school. One of its first acts was to appoint as principal Ronald Evans, a young black teacher who had grown up in Harlem. By 1970, I.S. 201 had changed for the better. Parents were asking to transfer their children to the school, and discipline problems were greatly reduced. The school had 101 teachers, most of them

[64] Congressional Quarterly, *Weekly Reports*, February 27, 1970, p. 647.

young and intensely committed. The new principal declared that the climate at the school had changed: "We are all working together—the governing board, the parents, the staff—to build a healthy environment for youngsters so they can learn and grow."[65]

On July 1, 1970, an experiment began in the New York City public school system. Its 900 schools, 1.1 million pupils, and 60,000 teachers were placed under a new system of community control. A state law established thirty-one Community School Boards to run the schools. Members of the boards are elected by residents of the neighborhoods in which the schools are located. The local boards have power to employ a district school superintendent and some teachers, to select instructional materials, and to operate recreational centers.

Community control, although still not tested by lengthy and wide experience, may offer a new way for cities to structure social services. According to Alan Altshuler, "*Community control* means the exercise of authority by the democratically organized government of a neighborhood-sized jurisdiction." It means "transfers of authority from the government of large cities to the governments of much smaller subunits within them. Such transfers would constitute political decentralization."[66]

To black residents of the inner-city, community control may prove to be a vehicle for genuine participation in political, social, and economic decision-making. On all levels, as Altshuler has observed, black Americans seek political leaders "genuinely committed to making policy *with* rather than *for* the people."[67] The decade of the 1970's will probably see an increasing number of experiments in community control.

Demands for community control and proposals for area-wide, metropolitan government seem to pull in opposite directions. To bridge the seeming contradictions in these proposed solutions to problems of urban areas, one study has suggested power-sharing by a two-level system of government. Under this plan, some functions would be assigned entirely to an area-wide government, other functions to the local level; but most would be assigned in part to each level.[68]

The American Challenge

The problems discussed in this chapter involve the question of what kind of nation America wants to be. How people live in their local communities reflects the quality of American life.

[65] Leonard Buder, "At I.S. 201 'We've Turned the Corner,'" *New York Times*, July 1, 1970, p. 41.
[66] Alan A. Altshuler, "*Community Control*": *The Black Demand for Participation in Large American Cities* (New York: Pegasus, 1970), pp. 64–65.
[67] *Ibid.*, p. 15.
[68] Committee for Economic Development, *Reshaping Government in Metropolitan Areas* (New York: Committee for Economic Development, 1970), p. 19.

678

Will comfortable or affluent Americans be willing to pay for better schools and for other social needs of the poor and the black? There is no constitutional requirement that an affluent majority take such steps on behalf of a less affluent minority. But the violence and polarization that characterize American society today suggest that the future of the nation's democratic institutions may be affected by the answer. An even larger question, however, is whether political institutions created when America was a rural nation can respond to, and cope with, the demands and problems of a highly urbanized, changing society.

In the spring of 1970, former HEW Secretary John Gardner had been invited to deliver a speech to the Illinois Constitutional Convention in his capacity as chairman of the Urban Coalition, a nonprofit organization concerned with urban problems. Perhaps because the words of his intended speech were strong, his invitation was withdrawn. The text of his address included these thoughts:

"We face two overriding tasks. We must move vigorously to solve our most crucial problems. And we must heal the spirit of the nation. The two tasks are inseparable. If either is neglected, the other becomes impossible." Conflict and violence in America, Gardner suggested, "threaten our survival as a society."

> And while each of us pursues his selfish interest and comforts himself by blaming others, the nation disintegrates. I use the phrase soberly: the nation disintegrates. . . . We must examine every one of our institutions to see where reform or structural redesign will help it adapt to contemporary needs. . . . If Americans continue on their present path their epitaph might well be that they were a potentially great people—a marvelously dynamic people—who forgot their obligations to one another, who forgot how much they owed one another.

American democracy is under pressure; its institutions are being tested. Yet, the problems of American society—racial discrimination, hunger, poverty, crime, pollution, and all the rest—are not necessarily beyond solution if Americans, acting through the political process, insist upon change. To a great extent, the America of tomorrow can be whatever we make it.

More than one hundred years ago, the English philosopher John Stuart Mill voiced much the same thought in his essay *On Liberty:* "The worth of a State, in the long run, is the worth of the individuals composing it."

SUGGESTED READING

Altshuler, Alan A. *"Community Control": The Black Demand for Participation in Large American Cities* (Pegasus, 1970). Paperback. An examination of the case for greater control of governmental programs and services at the local level.

Banfield, Edward C. *The Unheavenly City: The Nature and the Future of Our Urban Crisis* * (Little, Brown, 1970). A provocative assessment of contemporary urban life. Banfield argues that the seriousness of the "urban crisis" is frequently overstated.

Banfield, Edward C., and Wilson, James Q. *City Politics* * (Harvard University Press, 1963). A comprehensive examination of politics in American cities.

Campbell, Alan K., ed. *The States and the Urban Crisis* (Prentice-Hall, 1970). Paperback. A very useful collection of essays on the ability of state governments to cope with today's urban problems.

Gilbert, Charles E. *Governing the Suburbs* (Indiana University Press, 1967). A careful examination of suburban governments and the problems they face. Provides insights into the wide variety of governmental structures and problems encountered in different suburbs.

Gottmann, Jean. *Megalopolis* * (Twentieth Century Fund, 1961). A pioneering examination of the geographical, economic, social, and cultural characteristics of America's largest urbanized corridor, the northeastern seaboard.

Jacob, Herbert, and Vines, Kenneth N., eds. *Politics in the American States* (Little, Brown, 1965). A useful collection of essays on various aspects of the political systems in the states, written by a number of leading authorities in the field.

Key, V. O., Jr. *American State Politics: An Introduction* (Knopf, 1956). A revealing analysis of variations in basic political patterns affecting government in the various states. Focuses on the relationship between state political parties and party systems, and state government.

Lockard, Duane. *The Politics of State and Local Government*, 2nd edition (Macmillan, 1969). A comprehensive analysis of the politics of American state and local governments.

Sayre, Wallace S., and Kaufman, Herbert. *Governing New York City* * (Russell Sage Foundation, 1960). A detailed study of the politics and government of the nation's largest city.

Wilson, James Q., ed. *The Metropolitan Enigma: Inquiries into the Nature and Dimension of America's Urban Crisis* * (Harvard University Press, 1968). A valuable collection of essays on various aspects of urban life, including urban migration patterns, fiscal problems, and mass transit. The contributors are specialists in the field.

Wood, Robert C. *Suburbia: Its People and Their Politics* * (Houghton Mifflin, 1959). A general study of suburban politics and the political ideology and values of the American suburbanite.

* Available in paperback edition

The Constitution

of the United States of America [*]

We the people of the United States, in Order to form a more perfect Union, establish Justice, insure domestic Tranquility, provide for the common defence, promote the general Welfare, and secure the Blessings of Liberty to ourselves and our Posterity, do ordain and establish this Constitution for the United States of America.

ARTICLE I

Section 1. All legislative Powers herein granted shall be vested in a Congress of the United States, which shall consist of a Senate and House of Representatives.

Section 2. The House of Representatives shall be composed of Members chosen every second Year by the People of the several States, and the Electors in each State shall have the Qualifications requisite for Electors of the most numerous Branch of the State Legislature.

No Person shall be a Representative who shall not have attained to the Age of twenty-five Years, and been seven Years a Citizen of the United States, and who shall not, when elected, be an Inhabitant of that state in which he shall be chosen.

[Representatives and direct Taxes shall be apportioned among the several States which may be included within this Union, according to their respective Numbers, which shall be determined by adding to the whole Number of free Persons, including those bound to Service for a Term of Years, and excluding Indians not taxed, three fifths of all other Persons.] [1] The actual Enumeration shall be made within three Years after the first Meeting of the Congress of the United States, and within every subsequent Term of ten Years, in such Manner as they shall by Law direct. The Number of Representatives shall not exceed one for every thirty Thousand, but each State shall have at Least one Representative; and

until such enumeration shall be made, the State of New Hampshire shall be entitled to chuse three, Massachusetts eight, Rhode-Island and Providence Plantations one, Connecticut five, New-York six, New Jersey four, Pennsylvania eight, Delaware one, Maryland six, Virginia ten, North Carolina five, South Carolina five, and Georgia three.

When vacancies happen in the Representation from any State, the Executive Authority thereof shall issue Writs of Election to fill such Vacancies.

The House of Representatives shall chuse their Speaker and other Officers; and shall have the sole Power of Impeachment.

Section 3. The Senate of the United States shall be composed of two Senators from each State, [chosen by the Legislature thereof,] [2] for six Years; and each Senator shall have one Vote.

Immediately after they shall be assembled in Consequence of the first Election, they shall be divided as equally as may be into three Classes. The Seats of the Senators of the first Class shall be vacated at the Expiration of the second Year, of the second Class at the Expiration of the fourth Year, and of the third Class at the Expiration of the sixth Year, so that one-third may be chosen every second Year; [and if Vacancies happen by Resignation, or otherwise, during the Recess of the Legislature of any State, the Executive thereof may make temporary Appointments until the next Meeting of the Legislature, which shall then fill such Vacancies]. [3]

No Person shall be a Senator who shall not have attained to the Age of thirty Years, and been nine

---

[*] The Constitution and all amendments are shown in their original form. Parts that have been amended or superseded are bracketed and explained in the footnotes.
[1] Modified by the Fourteenth and Sixteenth amendments.

[2] Superseded by the Seventeenth Amendment.
[3] Modified by the Seventeenth Amendment.

Years a Citizen of the United States, and who shall not, when elected, be an Inhabitant of that State in which he shall be chosen.

The Vice-President of the United States shall be President of the Senate, but shall have no vote, unless they be equally divided.

The Senate shall chuse their other Officers, and also a President pro tempore, in the absence of the Vice-President, or when he shall exercise the Office of the President of the United States.

The Senate shall have the sole Power to try all Impeachments. When sitting for that purpose, they shall be on Oath or Affirmation. When the President of the United States is tried, the Chief Justice shall preside: And no person shall be convicted without the Concurrence of two thirds of the Members present.

Judgment in Cases of Impeachment shall not extend further than to removal from Office, and disqualification to hold and enjoy any Office of honor, Trust, or Profit under the United States: but the Party convicted shall nevertheless be liable and subject to Indictment, Trial, Judgment, and Punishment, according to Law.

Section 4. The Times, Places and Manner of holding Elections for Senators and Representatives, shall be prescribed in each state by the Legislature thereof; but the Congress may at any time by Law make or alter such Regulations, except as to the Places of Chusing Senators.

The Congress shall assemble at least once in every Year, and such Meeting shall [be on the first Monday in December,] [4] unless they shall by Law appoint a different Day.

Section 5. Each House shall be the Judge of the Elections, Returns and Qualifications of its own Members, and a Majority of each shall constitute a Quorum to do Business; but a smaller number may adjourn from day to day, and may be authorized to compel the Attendance of absent Members, in such Manner, and under such Penalties, as each House may provide.

Each House may determine the Rules of its Proceedings, punish its Members for disorderly Behavior, and, with the Concurrence of two thirds, expel a Member.

Each House shall keep a Journal of its Proceedings, and from time to time publish the same, excepting such Parts as may in their Judgment require Secrecy; and the Yeas and Nays of the Members of either House on any question shall, at the Desire of one fifth of those Present, be entered on the Journal.

Neither House, during the Session of Congress, shall, without the Consent of the other, adjourn for more than three days, nor to any other Place than that in which the two Houses shall be sitting.

Section 6. The Senators and Representatives shall receive a Compensation for their Services, to be ascertained by Law, and paid out of the Treasury of the United States. They shall in all Cases, except Treason, Felony, and Breach of the Peace, be privileged from Arrest during their Attendance at the Session of their respective Houses, and in going to and returning from the same; and for any Speech or Debate in either House, they shall not be questioned in any other Place.

No Senator or Representative shall, during the Time for which he was elected, be appointed to any civil Office under the Authority of the United States, which shall have been created, or the Emoluments whereof shall have been increased, during such time; and no Person holding any Office under the United States shall be a Member of either House during his continuance in Office.

Section 7. All Bills for raising Revenue shall originate in the House of Representatives; but the Senate may propose or concur with Amendments as on other bills.

Every Bill which shall have passed the House of Representatives and the Senate, shall, before it become a Law, be presented to the President of the United States; If he approve he shall sign it, but if not he shall return it, with his Objections, to that House in which it shall have originated, who shall enter the Objections at large on their Journal, and proceed to reconsider it. If after such Reconsideration two thirds of that House shall agree to pass the bill, it shall be sent, together with the objections, to the other House, by which it shall likewise be reconsidered, and if approved by two thirds of that House, it shall become a Law. But in all such Cases the Votes of both Houses shall be determined by Yeas and Nays, and the Names of the Persons voting for and against the Bill shall be entered on the Journal of each House respectively. If any Bill shall not be returned by the President within ten Days (Sundays excepted) after it shall have been presented to him, the Same shall be a Law, in like Manner as if he had signed it, unless the Congress by their Adjournment prevent its Return, in which Case it shall not be a Law.

Every Order, Resolution, or Vote to which the Concurrence of the Senate and House of Representatives may be necessary (except on a question of Adjournment) shall be presented to the President of the United States; and before the Same shall take Effect, shall be approved by him, or being disapproved by him, shall be repassed by two thirds of the Senate and House of Representatives, according to the Rules and Limitations prescribed in the Case of a Bill.

Section 8. The Congress shall have Power To

---

[4] Superseded by the Twentieth Amendment.

lay and collect Taxes, Duties, Imposts and Excises, to pay the Debts and provide for the common Defence and general Welfare of the United States; but all Duties, Imposts and Excises shall be uniform throughout the United States;

To borrow money on the credit of the United States;

To regulate Commerce with foreign Nations, and among the several States, and with the Indian Tribes;

To establish an uniform Rule of Naturalization, and uniform Laws on the subject of Bankruptcies throughout the United States;

To coin Money, regulate the Value thereof, and of foreign Coin, and fix the Standard of Weights and Measures;

To provide for the Punishment of counterfeiting the Securities and current Coin of the United States;

To establish Post Offices and post Roads;

To promote the Progress of Science and useful Arts, by securing for limited Times to Authors and Inventors the exclusive Right to their respective Writings and Discoveries;

To constitute Tribunals inferior to the Supreme Court;

To define and punish Piracies and Felonies committed on the high Seas, and Offenses against the Law of Nations;

To declare War, grant Letters of Marque and Reprisal, and make Rules concerning Captures on Land and Water;

To raise and support Armies, but no Appropriation of Money to that Use shall be for a longer Term than two Years;

To provide and maintain a Navy;

To make Rules for the Government and Regulation of the land and naval forces;

To provide for calling forth the Militia to execute the Laws of the Union, suppress Insurrections and repel Invasions;

To provide for organizing, arming, and disciplining the Militia, and for governing such Part of them as may be employed in the Service of the United States, reserving to the States respectively, the Appointment of the Officers, and the Authority of training the Militia according to the discipline prescribed by Congress;

To exercise exclusive Legislation in all Cases whatsoever, over such District (not exceeding ten Miles square) as may, by Cession of particular States, and the acceptance of Congress, become the Seat of the Government of the United States, and to exercise like Authority over all Places purchased by the Consent of the Legislature of the State in which the Same shall be, for the Erection of Forts, Magazines, Arsenals, dock-Yards, and other needful Buildings; —And

To make all Laws which shall be necessary and proper for carrying into Execution the foregoing Powers, and all other Powers vested by this Constitution in the Government of the United States, or in any Department or Officer thereof.

Section 9. The Migration or Importation of such Persons as any of the States now existing shall think proper to admit shall not be prohibited by the Congress prior to the Year one thousand eight hundred and eight, but a tax or duty may be imposed on such Importation, not exceeding ten dollars for each Person.

The privilege of the Writ of Habeas Corpus shall not be suspended, unless when in Cases of Rebellion or Invasion the public Safety may require it.

No Bill of Attainder or ex post facto Law shall be passed.

[No capitation, or other direct, Tax shall be laid unless in Proportion to the Census or Enumeration herein before directed to be taken.] [5]

No Tax or Duty shall be laid on Articles exported from any State.

No Preference shall be given by any Regulation of Revenue to the Ports of one State over those of another: nor shall Vessels bound to, or from, one State, be obliged to enter, clear, or pay Duties in another.

No Money shall be drawn from the Treasury, but in Consequence of Appropriations made by Law; and a regular Statement and Account of the Receipts and Expenditures of all public Money shall be published from time to time.

No Title of Nobility shall be granted by the United States: And no Person holding any Office of Profit or Trust under them, shall, without the Consent of the Congress, accept of any present, Emolument, Office, or Title, of any kind whatever, from any King, Prince, or foreign State.

Section 10. No State shall enter into any Treaty, Alliance, or Confederation; grant Letters of Marque and Reprisal; coin Money; emit Bills of Credit; make any Thing but gold and silver Coin a Tender in Payment of Debts; pass any Bill of Attainder, ex post facto Law, or Law impairing the Obligation of Contracts; or grant any Title of Nobility.

No State shall, without the Consent of the Congress, lay any Imposts or Duties on Imports or Exports, except what may be absolutely necessary for executing its inspection Laws: and the net Produce of all Duties and Imposts, laid by any State on Imports or Exports, shall be for the Use of the Treasury of the United States; and all such Laws shall be subject to the Revision and Control of the Congress.

No State shall, without the Consent of Congress, lay any duty of Tonnage, keep Troops, or Ships of War in time of Peace, enter into any Agreement or Compact with another State, or with a foreign Power, or engage in War, unless actually invaded, or in such imminent Danger as will not admit of delay.

[5] Modified by the Sixteenth Amendment.

ARTICLE II

Section 1. The executive Power shall be vested in a President of the United States of America. He shall hold his Office during the Term of four years, and, together with the Vice-President, chosen for the same Term, be elected, as follows:

Each State shall appoint, in such Manner as the Legislature thereof may direct, a Number of Electors, equal to the whole Number of Senators and Representatives to which the State may be entitled in the Congress: but no Senator or Representative, or Person holding an Office of Trust or Profit under the United States, shall be appointed an Elector.

[The Electors shall meet in their respective States, and vote by Ballot for two persons, of whom one at least shall not be an Inhabitant of the same State with themselves. And they shall make a List of all the Persons voted for, and of the Number of Votes for each; which List they shall sign and certify, and transmit sealed to the Seat of the Government of the United States, directed to the President of the Senate. The President of the Senate shall, in the Presence of the Senate and House of Representatives, open all the Certificates, and the Votes shall then be counted. The Person having the greatest Number of Votes shall be the President, if such Number be a Majority of the whole Number of Electors appointed; and if there be more than one who have such Majority, and have an equal Number of Votes, then the House of Representatives shall immediately chuse by Ballot one of them for President; and if no Person have a Majority, then from the five highest on the List the said House shall in like Manner chuse the President. But in chusing the President, the Votes shall be taken by States, the Representation from each State having one Vote; a quorum for this Purpose shall consist of a Member or Members from two-thirds of the States, and a Majority of all the States shall be necessary to a Choice. In every Case, after the Choice of the President, the Person having the greatest Number of Votes of the Electors shall be the Vice-President. But if there should remain two or more who have equal votes, the Senate shall chuse from them by Ballot the Vice-President.] [6]

The Congress may determine the Time of chusing the Electors, and the Day on which they shall give their Votes; which Day shall be the same throughout the United States.

No person except a natural-born Citizen, or a Citizen of the United States, at the time of the Adoption of this Constitution, shall be eligible to the Office of President; neither shall any Person be eligible to that Office who shall not have attained to the Age of thirty-five years, and been fourteen Years a Resident within the United States.

[In Case of the Removal of the President from Office, or of his Death, Resignation, or Inability to discharge the Powers and Duties of the said Office, the same shall devolve on the Vice-President, and the Congress may by Law provide for the Case of Removal, Death, Resignation, or Inability, both of the President and Vice-President, declaring what Officer shall then act as President, and such Officer shall act accordingly, until the disability be removed, or a President shall be elected.] [7]

The President shall, at stated Times, receive for his Services a Compensation, which shall neither be increased nor diminished during the Period for which he shall have been elected, and he shall not receive within that Period any other Emolument from the United States, or any of them.

Before he enter on the execution of his Office, he shall take the following Oath or Affirmation:—"I do solemnly swear (or affirm) that I will faithfully execute the Office of President of the United States, and will, to the best of my Ability, preserve, protect, and defend the Constitution of the United States."

Section 2. The President shall be Commander in Chief of the Army and Navy of the United States, and of the Militia of the several States, when called into the actual Service of the United States; he may require the Opinion, in writing, of the principal Officer in each of the executive Departments, upon any subject relating to the Duties of their respective Offices, and he shall have Power to Grant Reprieves and Pardons for Offenses against the United States, except in Cases of Impeachment.

He shall have Power, by and with the Advice and Consent of the Senate, to make Treaties, provided two thirds of the Senators present concur; and he shall nominate, and by and with the Advice and Consent of the Senate, shall appoint Ambassadors, other public Ministers and Consuls, Judges of the supreme Court, and all other Officers of the United States, whose Appointments are not herein otherwise provided for, and which shall be established by Law: but the Congress may by Law vest the Appointment of such inferior Officers, as they think proper, in the President alone, in the Courts of Law, or in the Heads of Departments.

The President shall have Power to fill up all Vacancies that may happen during the Recess of the Senate, by granting Commissions which shall expire at the End of their next Session.

Section 3. He shall from time to time give to the Congress Information of the State of the Union, and recommend to their Consideration such Measures as he shall judge necessary and expedient; he may, on extraordinary occasions, convene both Houses, or either of them, and in Case of Disagreement between them, with respect to the Time of Adjournment, he may adjourn them to such Time as he shall think

---

[6] Superseded by the Twelfth Amendment.

[7] Modified by the Twenty-fifth Amendment.

proper; he shall receive Ambassadors and other public Ministers; he shall take Care that the Laws be faithfully executed, and shall Commission all the Officers of the United States.

Section 4. The President, Vice-President and all civil Officers of the United States, shall be removed from Office on Impeachment for, and Conviction of, Treason, Bribery, or other high Crimes and Misdemeanors.

ARTICLE III

Section 1. The judicial Power of the United States, shall be vested in one supreme Court, and in such inferior Courts as the Congress may from time to time ordain and establish. The Judges, both of the supreme and inferior Courts, shall hold their Offices during good Behaviour, and shall, at stated Times, receive for their Services, a Compensation, which shall not be diminished during their Continuance in Office.

Section 2. The judicial Power shall extend to all Cases, in Law and Equity, arising under this Constitution, the Laws of the United States, and treaties made, or which shall be made, under their Authority;—to all Cases affecting ambassadors, other public ministers and consuls;—to all cases of admiralty and maritime Jurisdiction;—to Controversies to which the United States shall be a Party;—to Controversies between two or more States;—[between a State and Citizens of another State;] [8]—between Citizens of different States,—between Citizens of the same State claiming Lands under Grants of different States, and between a State, or the Citizens thereof, and foreign States, Citizens or Subjects.

In all Cases affecting Ambassadors, other public Ministers and Consuls, and those in which a State shall be Party, the supreme Court shall have original Jurisdiction. In all the other Cases before mentioned, the supreme Court shall have appellate Jurisdiction, both as to Law and Fact, with such Exceptions, and under such Regulations as the Congress shall make.

The trial of all Crimes, except in Cases of Impeachment, shall be by Jury; and such Trial shall be held in the State where the said Crimes shall have been committed; but when not committed within any State, the Trial shall be at such Place or Places as the Congress may by Law have directed.

Section 3. Treason against the United States, shall consist only in levying War against them, or in adhering to their Enemies, giving them Aid and Comfort. No Person shall be convicted of Treason unless on the Testimony of two Witnesses to the same overt Act, or on Confession in open Court.

The Congress shall have power to declare the Punishment of Treason, but no Attainder of Treason

shall work Corruption of Blood, or Forfeiture except during the Life of the Person attainted.

ARTICLE IV

Section 1. Full Faith and Credit shall be given in each State to the public Acts, Records, and judicial Proceedings of every other State. And the Congress may by general Laws prescribe the Manner in which such Acts, Records and Proceedings shall be proved, and the Effect thereof.

Section 2. The Citizens of each State shall be entitled to all Privileges and Immunities of Citizens in the several States.

A Person charged in any State with Treason, Felony, or other Crime, who shall flee from Justice, and be found in another State, shall on demand of the executive Authority of the State from which he fled, be delivered up, to be removed to the State having Jurisdiction of the crime.

[No Person held to Service or Labour in one State, under the Laws thereof, escaping into another, shall, in Consequence of any Law or Regulation therein, be discharged from such Service or Labour, but shall be delivered up on Claim of the Party to whom such Service or Labour may be due.] [9]

Section 3. New States may be admitted by the Congress into this Union; but no new State shall be formed or erected within the Jurisdiction of any other State; nor any State be formed by the Junction of two or more States, or parts of States, without the Consent of the Legislatures of the States concerned as well as of the Congress.

The Congress shall have Power to dispose of and make all needful Rules and Regulations respecting the Territory or other Property belonging to the United States; and nothing in this Constitution shall be so construed as to Prejudice any Claims of the United States, or of any particular State.

Section 4. The United States shall guarantee to every State in this Union a Republican Form of Government, and shall protect each of them against Invasion; and on Application of the Legislature, or of the Executive (when the Legislature cannot be convened) against domestic Violence.

ARTICLE V

The Congress, whenever two-thirds of both Houses shall deem it necessary, shall propose Amendments to this Constitution, or, on the Application of the Legislatures of two-thirds of the several States, shall call a Convention for proposing Amendments, which, in either Case, shall be valid to all Intents and Purposes, as part of this Constitution, when ratified by the Legislatures of three-fourths of the several States, or by Conventions in three-fourths thereof, as the one or the other Mode of Ratification may be proposed by the Congress; Pro-

[8] Modified by the Eleventh Amendment.

[9] Superseded by the Thirteenth Amendment.

685

vided that no Amendment which may be made prior to the Year One thousand eight hundred and eight shall in any Manner affect the first and fourth Clauses in the Ninth Section of the first Article; and that no State, without its Consent, shall be deprived of its equal Suffrage in the Senate.

ARTICLE VI

All Debts contracted and Engagements entered into, before the Adoption of this Constitution, shall be as valid against the United States under this Constitution, as under the Confederation.

This Constitution, and the Laws of the United States which shall be made in Pursuance thereof; and all Treaties made, or which shall be made, under the Authority of the United States, shall be the supreme Law of the Land; and the Judges in every State shall be bound thereby, any Thing in the Constitution or Laws of any State to the Contrary notwithstanding.

The Senators and Representatives before mentioned, and the Members of the several State Legislatures, and all executive and judicial Officers, both of the United States and of the several States, shall be bound by Oath or Affirmation to support this Constitution; but no religious Test shall ever be required as a qualification to any Office or public Trust under the United States.

ARTICLE VII

The Ratification of the Conventions of nine States shall be sufficient for the Establishment of this Constitution between the States so ratifying the same.

Done in Convention by the Unanimous Consent of the States present the Seventeenth Day of September in the Year of our Lord one thousand seven hundred and Eighty seven, and of the Independence of the United States of America the Twelfth. In Witness whereof We have hereunto subscribed our Names.

Articles in Addition to, and Amendment of, the Constitution of the United States of America, Proposed by Congress, and Ratified by the Legislatures of the Several States, Pursuant to the Fifth Article of the Original Constitution.

AMENDMENT I [10]

Congress shall make no law respecting an establishment of religion, or prohibiting the free exercise thereof; or abridging the freedom of speech, or of the press; or the right of the people peaceably to assemble, and to petition the Government for a redress of grievances.

[10] The first ten amendments were passed by Congress September 25, 1789. They were ratified by three-fourths of the states December 15, 1791.

AMENDMENT II

A well regulated Militia, being necessary to the security of a free State, the right of the people to keep and bear Arms shall not be infringed.

AMENDMENT III

No Soldier shall, in time of peace, be quartered in any house, without the consent of the Owner, nor in time of war, but in a manner to be prescribed by law.

AMENDMENT IV

The right of the people to be secure in their persons, houses, papers, and effects, against unreasonable searches and seizures, shall not be violated, and no Warrants shall issue, but upon probable cause, supported by Oath or affirmation, and particularly describing the place to be searched, and the persons or things to be seized.

AMENDMENT V

No person shall be held to answer for a capital or otherwise infamous crime, unless on a presentment or indictment of a Grand Jury, except in cases arising in the land or naval forces, or in the Militia, when in actual service in time of War or public danger; nor shall any person be subject for the same offence to be twice put in jeopardy of life or limb; nor shall be compelled in any criminal case to be a witness against himself, nor be deprived of life, liberty, or property, without due process of law; nor shall private property be taken for public use, without just compensation.

AMENDMENT VI

In all criminal prosecutions, the accused shall enjoy the right to a speedy and public trial, by an impartial jury of the State and district wherein the crime shall have been committed, which district shall have been previously ascertained by law, and to be informed of the nature and cause of the accusation; to be confronted with the witnesses against him; to have compulsory process for obtaining witnesses in his favor, and to have the Assistance of Counsel for his defence.

AMENDMENT VII

In suits at common law, where the value in controversy shall exceed twenty dollars, the right of trial by jury shall be preserved, and no fact tried by a jury, shall be otherwise reexamined in any Court of the United States, than according to the rules of the common law.

AMENDMENT VIII

Excessive bail shall not be required, nor excessive fines imposed, nor cruel and unusual punishments inflicted.

AMENDMENT IX

The enumeration in the Constitution, of certain rights, shall not be construed to deny or disparage others retained by the people.

AMENDMENT X

The powers not delegated to the United States by the Constitution, nor prohibited by it to the States, are reserved to the States respectively, or to the people.

AMENDMENT XI (1798) [11]

The Judicial power of the United States shall not be construed to extend to any suit in law or equity, commenced or prosecuted against one of the United States by Citizens of another State, or by Citizens or Subjects of any Foreign State.

AMENDMENT XII (1804)

The Electors shall meet in their respective States and vote by ballot for President and Vice-President, one of whom, at least, shall not be an inhabitant of the same State with themselves; they shall name in their ballots the person voted for as President, and in distinct ballots the person voted for as Vice-President, and they shall make distinct lists of all persons voted for as President, and of all persons voted for as Vice-President, and of the number of votes for each, which lists they shall sign and certify, and transmit sealed to the seat of the government of the United States, directed to the President of the Senate;—The President of the Senate shall, in the presence of the Senate and House of Representatives, open all the certificates and the votes shall then be counted;—The person having the greatest number of votes for President, shall be the President, if such number be a majority of the whole number of Electors appointed; and if no person have such majority, then from the persons having the highest numbers not exceeding three on the list of those voted for as President, the House of Representatives shall choose immediately, by ballot, the President. But in choosing the President, the votes shall be taken by states, the representation from each state having one vote; a quorum for this purpose shall consist of a member or members from two-thirds of the states, and a majority of all the states shall be necessary to a choice. [And if the House of Representatives shall not choose a President whenever the right of choice shall devolve upon them, before the fourth day of March next following, then the Vice-President shall act as President, as in the case of the death or other constitutional disability of the President.] [12]—The person having the greatest num-

[11] Date of ratification.
[12] Superseded by the Twentieth Amendment.

ber of votes as Vice-President, shall be the Vice-President, if such number be a majority of the whole number of Electors appointed, and if no person have a majority, then from the two highest numbers on the list, the Senate shall choose the Vice-President; a quorum for the purpose shall consist of two-thirds of the whole number of Senators, and a majority of the whole number shall be necessary to a choice. But no person constitutionally ineligible to the office of President shall be eligible to that of Vice-President of the United States.

AMENDMENT XIII (1865)

Section 1. Neither slavery nor involuntary servitude, except as a punishment for crime whereof the party shall have been duly convicted, shall exist within the United States, or any place subject to their jurisdiction.

Section 2. Congress shall have power to enforce this article by appropriate legislation.

AMENDMENT XIV (1868)

Section 1. All persons born or naturalized in the United States, and subject to the jurisdiction thereof, are citizens of the United States and of the State wherein they reside. No State shall make or enforce any law which shall abridge the privileges or immunities of citizens of the United States; nor shall any State deprive any person of life, liberty, or property, without due process of law; nor deny to any person within its jurisdiction the equal protection of the laws.

Section 2. Representatives shall be apportioned among the several States according to their respective numbers, counting the whole number of persons in each State, excluding Indians not taxed. But when the right to vote at any election for the choice of electors for President and Vice-President of the United States, Representatives in Congress, the Executive and Judicial officers of a State, or the members of the Legislature thereof, is denied to any of the male inhabitants of such State, being twenty-one years of age, and citizens of the United States, or in any way abridged, except for participation in rebellion, or other crime, the basis of representation therein shall be reduced in the proportion which the number of such male citizens shall bear to the whole number of male citizens twenty-one years of age in such State.

Section 3. No person shall be a Senator or Representative in Congress, or elector of President and Vice-President, or hold any office, civil or military, under the United States, or under any State, who, having previously taken an oath, as a member of Congress, or as an officer of the United States, or as a member of any State legislature, or as an executive or judicial officer of any State, to support the Constitution of the United States, shall have engaged in insurrection or rebellion against the same, or given aid or comfort to the enemies thereof. But Congress may by a vote of two-thirds of each House, remove such disability.

Section 4. The validity of the public debt of the United States, authorized by law, including debts incurred for payment of pensions and bounties for services in suppressing insurrection or rebellion, shall not be questioned. But neither the United States nor any State shall assume or pay any debt or obligation incurred in aid of insurrection or rebellion against the United States, or any claim for the loss or emancipation of any slave; but all such debts, obligations, and claims shall be held illegal and void.

Section 5. The Congress shall have the power to enforce, by appropriate legislation, the provisions of this article.

AMENDMENT XV (1870)

Section 1. The right of citizens of the United States to vote shall not be denied or abridged by the United States or by any State on account of race, color, or previous condition of servitude—

Section 2. The Congress shall have power to enforce this article by appropriate legislation.

AMENDMENT XVI (1913)

The Congress shall have power to lay and collect taxes on incomes, from whatever source derived, without apportionment among the several States, and without regard to any census or enumeration.

AMENDMENT XVII (1913)

The Senate of the United States shall be composed of two Senators from each State, elected by the people thereof, for six years; and each Senator shall have one vote. The electors in each State shall have the qualifications requisite for electors of the most numerous branch of the State legislatures.

When vacancies happen in the representation of any State in the Senate, the executive authority of such State shall issue writs of election to fill such vacancies: *Provided,* That the legislature of any State may empower the executive thereof to make temporary appointments until the people fill the vacancies by election as the legislature may direct.

This amendment shall not be so construed as to affect the election or term of any Senator chosen before it becomes valid as part of the Constitution.

AMENDMENT XVIII (1919) [13]

Section 1. After one year from the ratification of this article the manufacture, sale, or transportation of intoxicating liquors within, the importation thereof into, or the exportation thereof from the United States and all territory subject to the jurisdiction thereof for beverage purposes is hereby prohibited.

---

[13] Repealed by the Twenty-first Amendment.

Section 2. The Congress and the several States shall have concurrent power to enforce this article by appropriate legislation.

Section 3. This article shall be inoperative unless it shall have been ratified as an amendment to the Constitution by the legislatures of the several States, as provided in the Constitution, within seven years from the date of the submission hereof to the States by the Congress.

AMENDMENT XIX (1920)

The right of citizens of the United States to vote shall not be denied or abridged by the United States or by any State on account of sex.

Congress shall have power to enforce this article by appropriate legislation.

AMENDMENT XX (1933)

Section 1. The terms of the President and Vice-President shall end at noon on the 20th day of January, and the terms of Senators and Representatives at noon on the 3d day of January, of the years in which such terms would have ended if this article had not been ratified; and the terms of their successors shall then begin.

Section 2. The Congress shall assemble at least once in every year, and such meeting shall begin at noon on the 3d day of January, unless they shall by law appoint a different day.

Section 3. If, at the time fixed for the beginning of the term of the President, the President elect shall have died, the Vice-President elect shall become President. If a President shall not have been chosen before the time fixed for the beginning of his term, or if the President elect shall have failed to qualify, then the Vice-President elect shall act as President until a President shall have qualified; and the Congress may by law provide for the case wherein neither a President elect nor a Vice-President elect shall have qualified, declaring who shall then act as President, or the manner in which one who is to act shall be selected, and such person shall act accordingly until a President or Vice-President shall have qualified.

Section 4. The Congress may by law provide for the case of the death of any of the persons from whom the House of Representatives may choose a President whenever the right of choice shall have devolved upon them, and for the case of the death of any of the persons from whom the Senate may choose a Vice-President whenever the right of choice shall have devolved upon them.

Section 5. Sections 1 and 2 shall take effect on the 15th day of October following the ratification of this article.

Section 6. This article shall be inoperative unless it shall have been ratified as an amendment to the

Constitution by the legislatures of three-fourths of the several States within seven years from the date of its submission.

AMENDMENT XXI (1933)

Section 1. The eighteenth article of amendment to the Constitution of the United States is hereby repealed.

Section 2. The transportation or importation into any State, Territory, or possession of the United States for delivery or use therein of intoxicating liquors, in violation of the laws thereof, is hereby prohibited.

Section 3. This article shall be inoperative unless it shall have been ratified as an amendment to the Constitution by conventions in the several States, as provided in the Constitution, within seven years from the date of the submission hereof to the States by the Congress.

AMENDMENT XXII (1951)

No person shall be elected to the office of the President more than twice, and no person who has held the office of President, or acted as President, for more than two years of a term to which some other person was elected President shall be elected to the office of the President more than once.

But this Article shall not apply to any person holding the office of President when this Article was proposed by the Congress, and shall not prevent any person who may be holding the office of President, or acting as President, during the term within which this Article becomes operative from holding the office of President or acting as President during the remainder of such term.

AMENDMENT XXIII (1961)

Section 1. The District constituting the seat of Government of the United States shall appoint in such manner as the Congress may direct:

A number of electors of President and Vice-President equal to the whole number of Senators and Representatives in Congress to which the District would be entitled if it were a State, but in no event more than the least populous State; they shall be in addition to those appointed by the States, but they shall be considered, for the purposes of the election of President and Vice-President, to be electors appointed by the State; and they shall meet in the District and perform such duties as provided by the twelfth article of amendment.

Section 2. The Congress shall have power to enforce this article by appropriate legislation.

AMENDMENT XXIV (1964)

Section 1. The right of citizens of the United States to vote in any primary or other election for President or Vice-President, for electors for President or Vice-President, or for Senator or Representative in Congress, shall not be denied or abridged by the United States or any State by reason of failure to pay any poll tax or other tax.

Section 2. The Congress shall have power to enforce this article by appropriate legislation.

AMENDMENT XXV (1967)

Section 1. In case of the removal of the President from office or of his death or resignation, the Vice-President shall become President.

Section 2. Whenever there is a vacancy in the office of the Vice-President, the President shall nominate a Vice-President who shall take office upon confirmation by a majority vote of both Houses of Congress.

Section 3. Whenever the President transmits to the President pro tempore of the Senate and the Speaker of the House of Representatives his written declaration that he is unable to discharge the powers and duties of his office, and until he transmits to them a written declaration to the contrary, such powers and duties shall be discharged by the Vice-President as Acting President.

Section 4. Whenever the Vice-President and a majority of either the principal officers of the executive department or of such other body as Congress may by law provide, transmit to the President pro tempore of the Senate and the Speaker of the House of Representatives their written declaration that the President is unable to discharge the powers and duties of his office, the Vice-President shall immediately assume the powers and duties of the office as Acting President.

Thereafter, when the President transmits to the President pro tempore of the Senate and the Speaker of the House of Representatives his written declaration that no inability exists, he shall resume the powers and duties of his office unless the Vice-President and a majority of either the principal officers of the executive department or of such other body as Congress may by law provide, transmit within four days to the President pro tempore of the Senate and the Speaker of the House of Representatives their written declaration that the President is unable to discharge the powers and duties of his office. Thereupon Congress shall decide the issue, assembling within forty-eight hours for that purpose if not in session. If the Congress, within twenty-one days after receipt of the latter written declaration, or, if Congress is not in session, within twenty-one days after Congress is required to assemble, determines by two-thirds vote of both Houses that the President is unable to discharge the powers and duties of his office, the Vice-President shall continue to discharge the same as Acting President; otherwise, the President shall resume the powers and duties of his office.

Presidents of the United States

Year	President	Party	Vote	Electoral Vote	Percentage of Popular Vote
1789	George Washington	no designation		69	
1792	George Washington	no designation		132	
1796	John Adams	Federalist		71	
1800	Thomas Jefferson	Democratic-Republican		73	
1804	Thomas Jefferson	Democratic-Republican		162	
1808	James Madison	Democratic-Republican		122	
1812	James Madison	Democratic-Republican		128	
1816	James Monroe	Democratic-Republican		183	
1820	James Monroe	Democratic-Republican		231	
1824	John Quincy Adams	Democratic-Republican	108,740	84	30.5
1828	Andrew Jackson	Democratic	647,286	178	56.0
1832	Andrew Jackson	Democratic	687,502	219	55.0
1836	Martin Van Buren	Democratic	765,483	170	50.9
1840	William H. Harrison	Whig	1,274,624	234	53.1
1841	John Tyler*	Whig			
1844	James K. Polk	Democratic	1,338,464	170	49.6
1848	Zachary Taylor	Whig	1,360,967	163	47.4
1850	Millard Fillmore*	Whig			
1852	Franklin Pierce	Democratic	1,601,117	254	50.9
1856	James Buchanan	Democratic	1,832,955	174	45.3
1860	Abraham Lincoln	Republican	1,865,593	180	39.8
1864	Abraham Lincoln	Republican	2,206,938	212	55.0
1865	Andrew Johnson*	Democratic			
1868	Ulysses S. Grant	Republican	3,013,421	214	52.7
1872	Ulysses S. Grant	Republican	3,596,745	286	55.6
1876	Rutherford B. Hayes	Republican	4,036,572	185	48.0
1880	James A. Garfield	Republican	4,453,295	214	48.5
1881	Chester A. Arthur*	Republican			
1884	Grover Cleveland	Democratic	4,879,507	219	48.5
1888	Benjamin Harrison	Republican	5,447,129	233	47.9
1892	Grover Cleveland	Democratic	5,555,426	277	46.1
1896	William McKinley	Republican	7,102,246	271	51.1
1900	William McKinley	Republican	7,218,491	292	51.7
1901	Theodore Roosevelt*	Republican			
1904	Theodore Roosevelt	Republican	7,628,461	336	57.4
1908	William H. Taft	Republican	7,675,320	321	51.6
1912	Woodrow Wilson	Democratic	6,296,547	435	41.9
1916	Woodrow Wilson	Democratic	9,127,695	277	49.4
1920	Warren G. Harding	Republican	16,143,407	404	60.4
1923	Calvin Coolidge*	Republican			
1924	Calvin Coolidge	Republican	15,718,211	382	54.0
1928	Herbert C. Hoover	Republican	21,391,993	444	58.2
1932	Franklin D. Roosevelt	Democratic	22,809,638	472	57.4
1936	Franklin D. Roosevelt	Democratic	27,752,869	523	60.8
1940	Franklin D. Roosevelt	Democratic	27,307,819	449	54.8
1944	Franklin D. Roosevelt	Democratic	25,606,585	432	53.5
1945	Harry S Truman*	Democratic			
1948	Harry S Truman	Democratic	24,105,812	303	49.5
1952	Dwight D. Eisenhower	Republican	33,936,234	442	55.1
1956	Dwight D. Eisenhower	Republican	35,590,472	457	57.6
1960	John F. Kennedy	Democratic	34,227,096	303	49.9
1963	Lyndon B. Johnson*	Democratic			
1964	Lyndon B. Johnson	Democratic	43,126,506	486	61.1
1968	Richard M. Nixon	Republican	31,785,480	301	43.4

* Succeeded to Presidency upon death of the incumbent.

ACKNOWLEDGMENTS AND COPYRIGHTS

(Continued from page iv)

Marshall Frady. For excerpt from "The Sweetest Finger This Side of Midas," *Life*, February 27, 1970. Reprinted by permission of the author.

Harper & Row, Publishers, Inc. For excerpt from p. 107 in *Kennedy* by Theodore C. Sorensen (Harper & Row, 1965). For excerpt abridged and adapted from pp. 84, 86 in *Why We Can't Wait* by Martin Luther King, Jr. (Harper & Row, 1963). Reprinted by permission of Joan Daves. Copyright © 1963 by Martin Luther King, Jr. For excerpts from p. 60 and pp. 113–14 in *Congress: The Sapless Branch* by Joseph S. Clark (Harper & Row, 1964). For excerpt from p. 32 in *Ransom* by Ronald Goldfarb (Harper & Row, 1965).

Hodder and Stoughton Limited. For excerpt from *Kennedy*, © 1965 by Theodore C. Sorensen, reprinted by permission.

Holt, Rinehart and Winston, Inc. For excerpt from Eugene J. McCarthy, *The Limits of Power* (Holt, Rinehart and Winston, 1967).

Houghton Mifflin Company. For excerpts from Arthur M. Schlesinger, Jr., *A Thousand Days* (Houghton Mifflin, 1965).

Julian Bach Jr. Literary Agency. For excerpts from *The Making of the President 1968* by Theodore H. White.

Alfred A. Knopf, Inc. For excerpt from Carl L. Becker, *The Declaration of Independence* (Alfred A. Knopf, 1942).

Little, Brown and Company. For excerpt from Catherine Drinker Bowen, *Miracle at Philadelphia* (Little, Brown, 1966). For excerpt from William H. Riker, *Federalism: Origin, Operation, Significance*. Copyright © 1964 by Little, Brown and Company (Inc.). For excerpt from Lewis A. Froman, Jr., *The Congressional Process*. Copyright © 1967 by Little, Brown and Company (Inc.).

Look Magazine. For excerpt from the November 4, 1969 issue of Look Magazine. By permission of the editors. Copyright 1969 by Cowles Communications, Inc.

The Macmillan Company. For excerpt from Vine Deloria, Jr., *Custer Died for Your Sins*. Copyright © 1969 by Vine Deloria, Jr. Also for excerpt from Robert D. Novak, *The Agony of the G.O.P. 1964*. Copyright © by Robert D. Novak, 1965.

McGraw-Hill Book Company. For excerpt from *Storm Over the States* by Terry Sanford. Copyright 1967, McGraw-Hill, Inc. Used with permission of McGraw-Hill Book Company. Also for excerpt from *Soul on Ice* by Eldridge Cleaver. Copyright 1968, McGraw-Hill, Inc. Used with permission of McGraw-Hill Book Company.

The New York Times Company. For excerpts from *The New York Times*, © 1969/70/68/58 by The New York Times Company. Reprinted by permission.

W. W. Norton & Company, Inc. For excerpt reprinted from *The City* by John V. Lindsay. By permission of W. W. Norton & Company, Inc. Copyright © 1969, 1970 by W. W. Norton & Company, Inc.

Pantheon Books. For excerpt from Richard M. Elman, *The Poorhouse State* (Pantheon Books, 1966).

Praeger Publishers, Inc. For excerpt from William Proxmire, *Report From Wasteland: America's Military-Industrial Complex* (Praeger, 1970).

Prentice-Hall, Inc. For excerpt from Nelson W. Polsby, *Congress and the Presidency*, © 1964. Reprinted by permission of Prentice-Hall, Inc., Englewood Cliffs, N.J. Also for excerpt from the book *Let Them Eat Promises* by Nick Kotz. © 1969 by Nick Kotz. Published by Prentice-Hall, Inc., Englewood Cliffs, N.J.

Rand McNally & Company. For excerpt from Lester Milbrath, *The Washington Lobbyists*, © 1963 by Rand McNally and Company, Chicago, pp. 220–27.

Random House, Inc. For excerpt from Jane Jacobs, *The Death and Life of Great American Cities* (Random House, 1961).

Reprint House International. For excerpt from William Allen White, *Masks in a Pageant* (1928), quoted in Richard F. Fenno, Jr., *The President's Cabinet* (Harvard University Press, 1959).

Saturday Review. For excerpt from Gladwin Hill, "The Great and Dirty Lakes," *Saturday Review*, October 23, 1965. Copyright 1965 Saturday Review, Inc.

Time. For excerpt from *Time*, May 11, 1970. Reprinted by permission from TIME, The Weekly Newsmagazine; Copyright Time Inc. 1970.

University of North Carolina Press. For excerpt from James Reichley, *States in Crisis* (University of North Carolina Press, 1964).

Washington Star Syndicate, Inc. For excerpt from column by James J. Kilpatrick in *Washington Evening Star*, January 8, 1970.

The World Publishing Company. For excerpt reprinted by permission of The World Publishing Company from *Lyndon B. Johnson: The Exercise of Power* by Rowland Evans and Robert Novak. An NAL book. Copyright © 1966 by Rowland Evans and Robert Novak.

Illustrations

Part I John Messina, Rapho-Guillumette, p. 2.
II Cornell Capa, Magnum, p. 186.
IV NASA, p. 544.
V Elliott Erwitt, Magnum, p. 636.

Chapter 1 Burt Glinn, Magnum, p. 7; Gerald S. Upham, p. 8; (top) John A. Darnell, *Life Magazine* © Time, Inc., (bottom) UPI, p. 15; Burt Glinn, Magnum, p. 16; UPI, p. 27; Donald McCullin, Magnum, p. 37.

Chapter 2 NYPL Picture Collection, p. 42; (top) Eng. by H. B. Hall from a portrait by G. Stuart, NYPL Picture Collection, (center) Eng. from a portrait by Chappel, NYPL Picture Collection, (bottom) Smithsonian Institution, p. 44; National Portrait Gallery, London, p. 46; NYPL Picture Collection, p. 52; The New-York Historical Society, p. 53; Virginia State Library, p. 54; Eng. by Durand from a portrait by Stuart and Trumbull, NYPL Picture Collection, p. 63; George Tames, The New York

Times, p. 68; Smithsonian Institution, p. 69; Brown Brothers, p. 73; Harbrace, p. 74.

Chapter 3 Jeff Kamen, PIX, p. 78; Wide World, p. 82; NYPL Picture Collection, p. 92.

Chapter 4 UPI, p. 108; reprinted by permission of Grove Press, Inc., p. 117; Linda B. Halberstam, p. 121; Wide World, p. 122; cartoon by Ployardt. Reproduced by permission of *The Reporter*, p. 132; UPI, p. 132.

Chapter 5 Bruce Davidson, Magnum, p. 146; UPI, p. 149; Dan Budnick, p. 152; Gene Gordon, p. 156; Wide World, p. 170; *Ebony*, p. 171; Hap Stewart, p. 181.

Chapter 6 (left) UPI, (right) Mary Ellen Mark, Magnum, p. 191; UPI, p. 197; Henry Monroe, DPI, p. 201; UPI, p. 205; Harbrace, p. 208; George Tames, p. 219.

Chapter 7 The Hermitage, p. 233; (top row) Smithsonian Institution, (center) courtesy of The New-York Historical Society, (bottom) Smithsonian Institution Becker Collection, p. 234; (top & center) courtesy of The New-York Historical Society, (bottom left & right) Smithsonian Institution Becker Collection, (center) Smithsonian Institution, p. 235; Charles Harbutt, Magnum, p. 242; Santi Visalli, Photoreporters, pp. 243, 257; UPI, p. 258; Smithsonian Institution, pp. 261, 264.

Chapter 8 Rodney Kamitsuka, p. 272; Cornell Capa, Magnum, p. 273; (center) J. Doyle Dewitt Collection, (bottom) Theodore Roosevelt Birthplace, p. 281; with permission of Doyle Dane Bernbach Inc., photos courtesy of The New York Times, pp. 289–90; CBS, p. 292; Dennis Brack, Black Star, p. 294; Rodney Kamitsuka, p. 295; Wide World, p. 299.

Chapter 9 Paul Seligman, p. 317; UPI, p. 342; (left & center) UPI, (right) Hiroji Kubota, Magnum, p. 343.

Chapter 10 George Tames, p. 371; Cornell Capa, Magnum, p. 373; Wide World, p. 375; UPI, p. 392; Harris & Ewing, p. 404; (left) Wide World, (right) Brown Brothers, p. 407; UPI, p. 408; photo courtesy of Library of Congress, p. 409.

Chapter 11 Wolf von dem Bussche, p. 417; Dennis Brack, Black Star, p. 418; John Zimmerman, *Life Magazine* © Time, Inc., p. 445.

Chapter 12 From *The Herblock Gallery*, Simon & Schuster, 1968, p. 453; (top to bottom) Wolf von dem Bussche, Wolf von dem Bussche, George Tames—The New York Times, Wolf von dem Bussche, Wolf von dem Bussche, p. 456; (top to bottom) Wolf von dem Bussche, Wolf von dem Bussche, Wolf von dem Bussche, Fred Maroon, Wolf von dem Bussche, p. 457; The New York Times, p. 458; Jerome Hirsch, p. 467; Paul Conklin, p. 475; Jerome Hirsch, p. 476; Wide World, p. 480; Paul Conklin, p. 483.

Chapter 13 Wide World, p. 498; The New York Times, p. 500; Declan Haun, Black Star, p. 502; Wolf von dem Bussche, pp. 504–05; Danny Lyon, Magnum, p. 507; UPI, p. 512.

Chapter 14 © The Valley Daily News, Tarentum, Pa., p. 548; (top) Flip Schulke, *Life Magazine* © Time Inc., (bottom) Bernie Boston, p. 557; UPI, p. 564; Paul Conklin, PIX, p. 572; United Nations Photo, p. 573; Black Star, Fred Ward, p. 580; UPI, p. 588.

Chapter 15 Dan McCoy, Black Star, p. 597; Charles Gatewood, p. 599; Hap Stewart, p. 621; Sam Falk, Monkmeyer, p. 633.

Chapter 16 N.Y. Dept. of Commerce, p. 641; Bob Combs, Rapho-Guillumette, p. 643; Jules Zalon, DPI, p. 661; George Gerster, Rapho-Guillumette, p. 671; Burk Uzzle, Magnum, p. 673; D & A Pellegrino, Black Star, p. 678.

Index

Page numbers in *italics* refer to figures and tables.

Americans for Democratic Action (ADA), 486, 487
Americans for Indian Opportunity, 150
Amherst College, 122
Amistad, slave ship, 160
Anderson, Jack, 485*n*
Annapolis conference, 52
Anti-Ballistic Missile (ABM), 583–86, 590; lobby for, 214; and SALT, 587
Antifederalists, 62
Anti-Masons, 246
Antitrust policy, 509, 600
Antiwar protests, 8, 15, 17, 518, 547, 548–49, 574–75
Apollo program, 200, 435
Appropriations bills, 608–09
Arab-Israeli Six Day War, and UN, 574
Arizona, 89, 177, 348
Arkansas, 350; school desegregation in, 81, 89, 165–66
Armed Forces, 69, 436, 580, 581; desertion from, 141; President as supreme commander of, 382–84, 558. *See also* Department of Defense; Draft; Selective Service System; *specific forces under* United States
Arms control and disarmament, 586–88. *See also* Nuclear weapons
Arms Control and Disarmament Agency, 573
Arraignment without delay (in federal case), 135
Arthur, Chester A., 228*n*, 430
Articles of Confederation (1781–89), 50–51, 62, 88–89; expressly delegated powers in, 87; inadequacies of, 51–52, 374; on interstate relations, 90; on relation of Federal Government to states, 89; revision of, 52
Asch, Solomon, 194
Asia, 64, 65, 85, 142, 180, 556, 574; U.S. aid in, 570
Asian Development Bank, 570
Assembly, right of. *See* Freedom of assembly
Associated Press, 202, 354
Atlanta, Ga., 661, 662
Atomic Energy Commission, 596
Atomic weapons. *See* Nuclear weapons
Attainder, bills of, 68
Attorney General, 348, 529; powers of, 172, 173, 175
Attucks, Crispus, 161
Australian ballot (secret), 352
Authorizations, for budget spending, 608
Automobile industry, 309; and air

pollution, 596, 672; and auto safety laws, 602, 615; and highway construction, 603, 671, 672
Aviation industry, 603; regulation of, 427, 602

Bachrach, Peter, 212*n*
Badillo, Herman, 155, 170
Bagdikian, Ben, 624
Bail Reform Act (1966), 533
Bail system, 532–34; and preventive detention, 533
Bailey, Lloyd W., 357
Bain, Richard C., 261*n*, 262*n*, 264*n*, 265*n*, 267*n*
Baker, Bobby, 455, 477, 493
Baker, Charles W., 359
Baker v. Carr, 359, 510*n*, 652
Baldwin, James, 147, 158–59
Baldwin v. New York, 535*n*
Ball, George W., 592
Ballots, 352–54; office-column (Massachusetts), *353*, 354; party-column (Indiana), 352, 354; secret (Australian), 352
Banfield, Edward C., 662, 663, 670
Banking, 509, 611, 612
Baratz, Morton, 212*n*
Barber, James David, 406
Barker v. Hardway, 109*n*
Barnette, Walter, 125
Barrett, Edward L., Jr., 521
Barron v. Baltimore, 137
Bartlett, E. L., 630*n*
Baton Rouge, La., 676
Bates, Daisy, 165
Bay of Pigs, 382, 440–41, 568, 577
Bayh, Birch, 291, 458
Beard, Charles A., 61
Beck, Dave, 605
Becker, Carl L., 45, 255
Becker, John F., 301*n*
Benanti v. United States, 132*n*
Bennett, Wallace, 576
Benton, John Dalmer, 138
Benton v. Maryland, 138
Berelson, Bernard, 324*n*, 325*n*
Berkeley campus, University of California, 36, 121
Berns, Walter, 87*n*
Betts v. Brady, 136*n*
Biafra, 86
Bible reading, in public school, 124
Bickel, Alexander M., 511
Bill of Rights, 41, 71–75, 108, 113–40, 142; "absolutes" in, 114–15; application to states by Supreme Court, 71, 113–40, 510; in colonial constitutions, 50; conflict of basic principles in, 116; and the Constitution, 63, 71, 113, 137; English heritage of, 46–47; provisions of, 71–75, 113–40; re-

strictions of, on states, 89. *See also* Amendments to the Constitution; *specific rights*
Bill of Rights (England, 1689), 47
Bill of Rights, GI, 628
Bills of attainder, 68
Binkley, Wilfred E., 233*n*
Biological weapons, 588
Birch, David L., 183, 642*n*
Birmingham, Ala.: church bombing in, 172; civil rights demonstrations in, 170, 490; Freedom Riders in, 169
Birth control pills, 413–16, 435, 460; and death, *414*
Birth rate, 30, 153
Bishop, Joseph W., Jr., 514*n*
Black, Hugo, 109, 114, 124–25, 128, 136, 512–13, *512*, 516*n*, 617
Black v. United States, 133*n*
Black Americans, 123, 145–48, 150–84, 673, 677–78; African heritage, 160–61; citizenship of, 162; and community control, 677–78; disenfranchisement of, 61, 66, 72, 172, 174, 176, 345; and Dred Scott decision, 162, 508; economic gains of, 145–46, 182–83, 184; employment of, 148, 173, 178, 182; housing of, 147, 174, 178, 182; income of, 149, 182; and Jim Crow laws, 162–63; migration of, 30–31, 159, 177, 183–84, 642, 666, 667; militancy of, 169, 177, 179–80; and Model Cities legislation, 669; political participation of, 31, 182, 259, 334–35, 461, 663, 679; and poll tax, 74, 174, 374; population of, 30, 642, *663*, 667; in Reconstruction era, 162, 174, 514; struggle for equality by, 145–48, 158–84; and urban riots, 5, 6, 177–78, 183, 205; voter registration of, 174–77, *175*, 321; voting of, *176*, 321, 333, 346–47, *347*; and Voting Rights Act (1965; 1970 amendments), *175*, *176*, 347. *See also* Black Panthers; Black Power; Civil rights movement
Black Panthers, 117, 178, 179–80; televised broadcast of Denver trial, 536. *See also* Seale, Bobby
Black Power, 17, 35–36, 178–81, 301; Stokely Carmichael's definition of, 179
Blackmun, Harry Andrew, 500, *512*
Blaine, James G., 286
Blanket (jungle) primaries, 351
Bliss, Ray, 276
Block grants, 101–02, 677
Bluefield State College (W. Va.), 109
Blumenthal, Richard, 625*n*

Central High School (Little Rock, Ark.), 165, 166
Central Intelligence Agency (CIA), 94, 384, 425, 436, 566, 567–69; and Bay of Pigs, 382, 440–41, 577; and Center for International Studies, 630; and FBI, 567; intelligence division of, 567; plans division of, 567; and Senate, 436
Cervantes, A. J., 643
Chambers v. Florida, 542n
Chancellor, John, 254
Character test, as voting requirement, 347–48
Chavez, Cesar, 148–49, 154
Checks and balances, 59
Chemical warfare, 588, 630
Chicago, 608, 663; Democratic National Convention protest demonstrations (1968), 8–9, 111, 120, 255–56; 1966 disorders, 177
"Chicago Seven," 36, 111, 174, 501, 529, 536–37
Chicago Sun-Times, 209
Chicanos, 148, 154
Chief Justice of U.S., 497–98; role of, in Supreme Court, 516
Child labor, 87, 88, 604, 605
Child support, 155
Chimel, Ted Steven, 131, 541
Chimel v. California, 130n
Chinese, barred from immigration (1917–52), 142
"Chipitts," 661
Chisholm, Shirley, 461
Chisholm v. Georgia, 72
Christian Science Monitor, 209, 616
Christopher, George, 299n
Church, Frank, 383, 561
Churches, 49; tax-exempt status of, 125
Churchill, Winston S., 38, 553
Church-state relations, 124–25, 138
CIA. *See* Central Intelligence Agency
CIO (Congress of Industrial Organizations). *See* AFL-CIO
Circuit courts of appeals, 58, 517
Cities, 103, 595; as basic forms of government, 657–58; blacks in, 30–31, 663; central (core), 641; crisis in, 661–62; effect of reapportionment, 643, 651; and federalism, 103, 676–77; licensing by, for "use of public grounds," 120–21; politics in, 662–64; population of, 30–31; 103, 360, 361, 663; problems of, 664–74; and suburbs, 30–31, 659–76. *See also* Urban problems
Citizenship, 140, 162; of American Indians, 150; by birth, 140; and

civil liberties, 107–43; and Fourteenth Amendment, 71, 72, 89, 130, 137, 140, 162, 345, 349, 509, 535, 600; loss of, 141; by naturalization, 140–41; as requirement for representatives and senators, 461; as requirement for voting, 350; rights and responsibilities of, 140–43
City courts, 519
Civil Aeronautics Board (CAB), 427, 602
Civil disobedience, 503
Civil liberties, 107–43; Bill of Rights applied to states, 113–40. *See also* Accused persons, rights of; Bill of Rights; Right(s); *specific freedoms*
Civil Rights Act (1875), 162
Civil Rights Act (1957), 172, 479
Civil Rights Act (1960), 172
Civil Rights Act (1964), 43, 157–58, 172–73, 472; as case study, 489–91, 489; filibuster against, 481; provisions of, 172; and school desegregation, 166–67, 173
Civil Rights Cases (1883), 162
Civil rights movement, 5, 17, 33, 139, 168–84, 240; Birmingham demonstrations, 170; and Black Power, 17, 35–36, 178–81; FBI record in, 434; Freedom Riders, 169–70; legislation brought about by, 145, 172–77; march on Washington, 170–72; and Martin Luther King, Jr. (*see* King, Martin Luther, Jr.); militancy in, 149, 179; and minority groups, 145–50; Montgomery bus boycott, 168–69; and school desegregation decision of Supreme Court, 164, 166, 168, 510; and urban riots, 177–78, 183; and Warren Court, 542
Civil service, 429–33; recruiting for bureaucracy, 431–33, 448
Civil Service Commission, 429, 430; abolishment of loyalty oath of, 129; powers under Voting Rights Act of 1965, 175
Civil Service Reform Act (Pendleton Act) (1883), 430
Civil War, 60, 78, 204; blacks in Union Army, 161; effect on Democrats, 235, 236
Clapp, Charles L., 462n, 464n
Clark, Joseph S., 453, 457, 466, 474–75, 480, 492–93
Clark, Mark, 180
Clark, Ramsey, 526, 529
Clay, Henry, 234
Clayton Act (1914), 600

Clean Air Act Amendments of 1970, 596
"Clear and present danger" test, 114
Cleaver, Eldridge, 179, 180, 248n
Cleveland, Grover, 235, 286, 287
Cleveland, Ohio, 182, 663; disorder (1966), 177
Client groups: and bureaucracy, 415, 435–36; of regulating agencies, 221–22, 244, 415, 435
Clifford, Clark M., 402, 442–43
Closed primaries, 351
Closed shop, 605
Cloture, 173, 175, 479–80, 481, 491
Coalitions, 231, 234, 235, 236, 336, 362
Coattail elections, 251, 337–39
Coffin v. United States, 530n
Cohen, Robert H., 621
Cohen, William, 126n
Cold War, 127, 550, 553, 556
Cole, Donald B., 247n
Coleman, James S., 24n, 190n
Colgrove v. Green, 359
Collective bargaining, 605, 606
Collective defense pacts, 377, 554, 555
Collector v. Day, 87n
College(s): building construction, 629; educational opportunity grants for, 629; federal loans to students, 628, 629; research under government contracts, 631; student enrollment in, 628
Colonialism, 64, 85
Colonies, American, 47–50; governments in, 48
Colorado, 536
Columbia University, student strike (1968), 61, 121
Commission on Campus Unrest, 124
Commission on Civil Rights, 172, 173
Commission on Organization of the Executive Branch of the Government (Hoover Commission), 438–39
Commission on Party Structure and Delegate Selection (Democratic party), 259–60
Commission plan of city government, 657–58
Committee for Economic Development, 602, 678n
Committee system, congressional, 453, 454, 456, 481–87. *See also* House standing committees; Senate standing committees
Committees, congressional. *See* House standing committees; Senate standing committees

Eighteenth Amendment, 72
Eighth Amendment, 71, 138, 141, 534
Eight-hour day, 604
Eighty-ninth Congress, 456
Eisenhower, Dwight D., 74, 265, 374, 380, 381, 382, 394, 403, 406; and ABM, 583; administration of, 172, 377, 552, 554, 577; appointments made by, 429, 513–14; and his Cabinet, 392–93; campaigns of, 281, 290; and CIA, 440; and Congress, 331, 338; and election of 1952, 236, 240, 245, 285, 331, 333; on military-industrial complex, 32, 588, 589; and National Security Council, 396, 440, 562; and Nixon, 283, 287; on politics, 388; on Presidency, 369; sends federal troops to Little Rock, 81, 89, 166; and Taft in convention battle, 245, 263
Eisenhower, Milton S., 521
"Elastic clause," of Constitution, 86
Elazar, Daniel J., 83, 89n
Eldridge, Linda, 10
Election(s): all-white primary, 174, 345; ballots, 352–54, 352, 353; "coattail" effect in, 251, 337–39; and democratic government, 362–64; deviating, 362; direct primary, 351, 655; gubernatorial, 340, 341, 650; landslide, 362; law and order issue in, 38, 132, 134, 184; maintaining, 362, 363; meaning of, 362–63; number of elected officials, 316; off-year, 203, 338; and party identification, 362; presidential (see Presidential elections); primary (see Primaries); as reaffirmation of support, 362; as realigning, 362; relation between national and state, in presidential election years, 340; of representatives to Congress, 67, 203; 318, 337, 345; of senators, 61–62, 67, 72, 337, 345; state, 650; types of, 362; and voting behavior, 315–64; voting patterns in, 333–41; voting rights laws, 177
Electoral college, 13, 14, 68–69, 355–56; abolition of, proposed, 345, 357; deadlock in, 94, 356–57, 459; direct election as substitute for, 357; proportion of electoral and popular votes in 1968 election, 342; vote of, in presidential elections (1928–1968), 334–35
Electoral system, 344–61; counting

the votes, 354–55; direct election proposal, 357–58; electoral college (see Electoral college); fraud in, 355; nominating process of, 350–51; "one man, one vote" (see Reapportionment); and suffrage, 345–50; and two-party political system, 238
Elementary schools, 126–27, 628, 629
Elementary and Secondary Education Act (1965), 629
Eleventh Amendment, 72
Elfbrandt v. Russell, 128n
Ellison, Ralph, 158–59
Elman, Philip, 445
Elman, Richard M., 622
Emancipation Proclamation, 72
Employment, discrimination, in: against Mexican Americans, 153; against women, 149, 155; as cause of black unrest, 173; outlawed by Civil Rights Act of 1964, 157, 158, 173
Employment Act of 1946, 607
Engel v. Vitale, 124n, 125n
Environment: crisis in the, 35, 399, 449, 595–98, 631–33; and federal antipollution legislation, 458, 596, 631–33, 634; international problems in, 574; lobby for, 215; pollution of, by industry, 602, 632; and student protest against pollution, 123
Environmental Protection Agency, 632–33
Epperson, Susan, 541
Equal Employment Opportunity Commission, 173
Equal rights. See Civil rights movement; Minority groups; Right(s)
Equal rights amendment (proposed), 155
Equal time provision, in broadcasting, 290, 294, 312–13
Equality, 21–22; for minority groups, 145–58
Equity, in law, 504
Era of Good Feelings (Monroe), 233
Ehrlichman, John, 397
Eros magazine, 119
Ervin, Sam J., 534
Escobedo, Danny, 134–35
Escobedo v. Illinois, 135, 510
Eskimos, 150
Espionage, 132, 567–69
Esquire magazine, 147, 560n
Estes, Billie Sol, 116
Estes v. Texas, 116n
Ethnic groups: political participation of, 321, 328; political socialization of, 192–94; voter attitudes of, 193, 239–40, 328

Europe: balance of power in, 552; collective defense pacts with, 554, 555; Marshall plan in, 554, 570; and U.S. involvement in First World War, 553
Evans, Ronald, 677–78
Evans, Rowland, 477
Evers, Charles, 182
Evers, Medgar, 182
Everson v. Board of Education, 125n, 126, 138
Executive agencies, 380, 421, 422–23, 425, 448
Executive agreements, 385
Executive branch, 58, 422–23; and bureaucracy, 413–49; and Congress, 460; Constitutional Convention draft recommendations for, 55, 56; departments of, in order of formation, 391; planning-programing budgeting system of (PPBS), 447–48; powers of, under Constitution, 68–69; reorganization of structure of, 438–40. See also Bureaucracy; President
Executive departments, 391. See also specific departments
Executive Office of President, 380, 395–99, 396, 421, 423, 440
Ex post facto laws, 68
Extradition, of fugitives, 90

F-111 fighter-bombers, 583
Fainsod, Merle, 24n
Fair Deal (Truman), 240
Fair Labor Standards Act (1936), 88, 605
Fairness doctrine, in broadcasting, 117
Family, as factor in political socialization, 25–26, 191–92
Family Assistance Plan, 622–23, 628
Fanny Hill, 118–19
Farm workers, 148–49, 154
Farmer, James, 147, 169
Farmer-Labor party, 238n
Farmers, 435, 603
Faubus, Orval, 165, 166
FBI: See Federal Bureau of Investigation
FCC. See Federal Communications Commission
FDA. See Food and Drug Administration
Federal agencies, 422–23, 603; and freedom of information, 117; and liaison with Congress, 437–38; and public relations expenditures, 435; reorganization of, by President, 388. See also Executive agencies
Federal aid: block grants, 101–02,

of party in power (1922–1970), *338*; Minority Leader of, 470; Minority Whip of, 470; passes bill into law, 173, 488–91, *489*; power in, 469–71; powers of, 67; and presidential elections, 345, 356, 357–58; and reapportionment (*see* Reapportionment); reforms in procedure in, 473–74, 493; role conception of members of, 466; salaries in, 463; versus Senate, *469*; seniority system of, 453–55, 481–88; size of, 360; Speaker of, 404, 405, 469–71; state primaries to nominate candidates for, 351; student support of candidates for, 268; voter participation in elections of, *318* (1952–1968), *336* 1928–1968); voting in, 473–74. *See also* Congress; House standing committees; Senate

House standing committees, *482*; Appropriations Committee, 383, 454, 472, 487; Armed Services Committee, 481; Banking and Currency Committee, 455; Campaign Committee, 250; Committee of the Whole, 473; Committee on Committees, 470; Interstate and Foreign Commerce Committee, 472; Judiciary Committee, 472, 490; Post Office and Civil Service Committee, 428; Rules Committee, 454, 470, 471, 473, 487, 490, 491, 615; Ways and Means Committee, 102, 470, 487

Housing, 668–71; public, 215; slum, 147, 148; Housing Act (1949), 668 HUD. *See* Department of Housing and Development

Hughes, Charles Evans, 14, 506
Hughes, Harold E., 259
Hughes, Howard, 288
Hughes Tool Co., 288
Huitt, Ralph K., 456, 457, 476, 477, 492
Humphrey, Hubert, 13, 240; campaign expenditure of (1968), 305, 307; and civil rights (1964), 491; effect of Vietnam war and urban disorders on campaign of, 282–83, 295; and 1960 nominating race, 264, 305–06; 1968 campaign of, 9, 249, 263, 277, 294, 295, 297, 331, 332, 341–44, 606; as senator, 474–75; television expenditure of (1968), *296*
Hunger, 626–27
Hunter, Floyd, 662
Huntington, Samuel P., 462
Hydrogen bomb, 578

I Am Curious (Yellow), 117
ICBMs, 11, 123, 584
Idaho, 177, 351–52, 348
Identity, in nation-building, 65–66
Illinois, 251, 359
Illinois Constitutional Convention, 679
Illinois v. Allen, 537n
Immigration, 141–42; quotas on, 141–42; to U.S. (1820–1967), *29*
Immigration Act (1965), 142
Immigration and Naturalization Service, 140, 529
Impeachment, 459
Income, 182–83; average annual, 149, 156, *157*; Census Bureau survey of, 182–83; effect of discrimination on, 149, 153, 182; poverty, level of, 145, 620, 624; and voter participation, 321; women's versus men's, 149, 156, *157*
Income tax, 72, 101, 509, 514, 518, 609
Independent regulatory commissions. *See* Regulatory agencies
India, 78, 142, 556, 570, 587
Indian Reorganization Act (1934), 152
Indian reservations, 150, 151–52
Indiana, 259, 351
Indiana (party-column) ballot, *352*, 354
Indians, 150–52
Indictment, grand jury, 535
Indo-China, 556
Indonesia, 556
Industry, 435; and antitrust policy, 509, 600; as Commerce Department clientele, 435; conglomerates in, 601; corporate responsibility of, 601–02; defense contracts in, 579, 588–91, *589*; foreign competition with domestic manufacturing, 603–04; and foreign trade and tariff policies, 603; government subsidies to, 603–04; lobbying for, 214, 616; and pollution of environment, 602, 632; regulation of, 88, 426, 427, 443, 444, 599–602; Supreme Court protection of, 509, 600; ten largest corporations in U.S., *601*
Inflation, 33, 606, 607, 611, 612, 633; and consumer prices, 606, 607
Information (criminal charge), 535
Initiative, amendment by, 648
Injunction, 604
Ink, Dwight A., 421
Inner Club, in Senate, 457, 475–76
Inputs, policy, 23, 67, 139, 316, 460

Institute of Defense Analyses (IDA), 584, 588
Insurance: agencies, 312; disability, 618; health, 619; social, 617–19; unemployment, 618, 619
Integration, 66; federal enforcement of, by troops, 81, 82, 89; of schools (*see* School desegregation)
Inter-American Development Bank, 570
Intercontinental ballistic missiles (ICBMs), 11, 123, 584
Interest groups, 94, 189, 211–25; congressional voting rated by, *486*; defined, 212–13; impact of, on government, 17, 211; mediation of, by political parties, 232, 266; operation of, 215–19; regulating, 221–22; and regulatory commissions, 426–27; relationship with government agencies, 415, 435–36; at state level, 651; types of, 214–15; uses and abuses of, 222–24
Interest rates, 427, 612, 616
Intergovernmental relations, 80–81, 101–05, 399, 649, 676–77; interstate, 90–91
Intermediate School 201 (I.S. 201), 677–78
Internal Revenue Service, 133
Internal Security Act (McCarran Act) (1950), 128
International Bank for Reconstruction and Development, 570
International Telephone and Telegraph Corp., 601
Interstate commerce, federal regulation of, 88, 93
Interstate Commerce Commission, 427, 602
Interstate compacts, 91, 676
Interstate Oil Compact, 91
Investment regulation, 427
Iowa, resolution requesting constitutional convention, 359
Irish, Marian D., 65n
Irvin v. Dowd, 116n
Isolationism, 552–53
Israel, 78, 549, 587
Item veto, 388, 650

J. Walter Thompson advertising agency, 295
Jackson, Andrew, 165, 204, 233, 255, 375, 401, 406, 429
Jackson, Henry M., 558
Jackson, Robert H., 138, 142, 164, 165n, 504n, 514n, 542n
Jackson State College (Miss.), 15, 123, 548
Jacksonian democracy, 233, 234, 651

Model Cities act (1966), 83, 104, 448–49

Model Cities program, 668–71; lobby for, 215; purpose of, 669

Moderate, political, 201

Molly Maguires, 180

Monetary policy, 608, 611–12, 633

Money: myth of, 669; supply, 427, 608, 611

Monopoly, 600

Monroe, James, 113, 233

Monroe Doctrine, 552

Montana, 535, 578, 583

Montesquieu, 20, 46

Montgomery, Ala., 168–69, 174; and *New York Times* suit, 120

Morison, Samuel Eliot, 47

Mormons, 126

Morrill Act (1862), 628

Morris, Gouverneur, 5, 53, 57, 374, 468

Morse, Wayne, 476

Mortgages, 670

Moss, John E., 117

Motion pictures, obscenity in, 117, 118, 119

Motorola, Inc., 214

Movement for a New Congress, 268

Moyers, Bill, 394

Moynihan, Daniel P., 622n, 625

Muchmore, Don M., 198

Multiple Independently Targetable Reentry Vehicle (MIRV), 586; and SALT, 587

Multiparty system, 238

Mumford, Lewis, 661–62, 671

Municipal courts, 519

Munn, E. Harold, Sr., 248n

Murphy, Walter F., 506–07, 516n

Murray v. Curlett, 124n

Muskie, Edmund S., 101, 458, 596

Mutiny, 161, *518*

Myers v. United States, 381n

Myrdal, Gunnar, 159

NAACP. *See* National Association for the Advancement of Colored People

Nader, Ralph, 443–46, 613

Nader's Raiders, 443–46

Napolitan, Joseph, 249, 300

Narcotics, 126; and crime, 523–24, 525

Nardone v. United States, 132n

NASA (National Aeronautics and Space Administration), 425, 435

Nashville, Tenn., 676

Nation-building, 64–66; federalism a tool for, 85–86; problems of, 64–65; process of, 65–66

National Advisory Commission on Civil Disorders, 36, 178, 180, 183, 206, 401

National Aeronautics and Space Administration (NASA), 425, 435

National Air Pollution Control Administration, 632

National Association for the Advancement of Colored People (NAACP), 164, 165, 166, 169, 182

National Association of Manufacturers (NAM), 214, 218, 222

National Bank of the United States, 92

National banking system, 86, 312, 611

National Commission on the Causes and Prevention of Violence, 9, 206, 279–80, 522, 526, 527, 644–65

National Commission on Obscenity and Pornography, 401

National Commission on Product Safety, 616–17

National Commitments Resolution (1969), 561, 578

National conventions, 94, 250, 254–65, 311; decision-making at, 262–64; delegates to, 236, 258–62; future of, 264–65; national chairman, 250; national committee, 250, 310; nominating a presidential candidate, 236, 255–58; patterns in presidential nominations, *263*; selection of Vice-President, 256–57, 400; types of nominations, 262. *See also* Preconvention campaigns; Primaries

National Defense Education Act (1958), 628

National Educational Television (NET), 536

National Environmental Policy Act (1969), 632

National Guard, 177; at Kent State University, 15, 123, 548

National Industrial Recovery Act, 88

National Institute of Child Health, 378

National Institutes of Health (NIH), 631

National Labor Relations Act (1935), 88, 154, 604–05

National Labor Relations Board (NLRB), 427, 605

National Liberation Front (Vietcong), 556

National Mediation Board, 604

National Municipal League, 360

National origins, 141–42

National Railroad Passenger Corporation (Railpax), 602

National Science Foundation, 631

National security: arms control and disarmament, 578–88; collective defense pacts, 554, *555*; defense establishment, 578–88; expenditures for, since Second World War, 579; and foreign policy, 547–92; interrelation with foreign and domestic policies, 558–59; machinery for, 562–73; National Security Council (*see* National Security Council); reexamination of goals, 591–92; strategic (nuclear) arms (*see* Nuclear weapons); and world security, 551. *See also* Central Intelligence Agency

National Security Act (1947), 395, 562; amendment (1949), 580

National Security Agency (NSA), 94, 581

National Security Council (NSC), 94, 395–97, 440, 562–63; and CIA, 567–69; Executive Committee of, 396–97

National Student Association, 567

Nationalist China, 285, 573

Native American party, 180, 248

NATO (North Atlantic Treaty Organization), 554, 555

Natural gas industry, 222

Natural rights, 46, 503

Naturalization, 140–41

Navajo Indian, 126, 150

NBC, 254, 271; audience reached by, *210*; Kennedy-Nixon debates televised by, 290; and public opinion, 208; vote projection system of, 354

Near v. Minnesota, 116n, 137n

Negative income tax, 622

Neustadt, Richard E., 381, 386n, 388n, 389, 392n, 401n, 421, 438n, 559

New Deal: effect of, on labor movement, 604, 605; and social policy of government, 598, 617; and social welfare programs, 83, 93; and Supreme Court, 114, 509

New England town meeting, 658

New federalism (Nixon), 84, 102, 670, 677

New Frontier (Kennedy), 236, 240, 448, 664

New Hampshire, 48; 1968 primary, 6–8, 14, 228–29, 344, 651; ratifies Constitution, 63, *64*

New Haven, Conn., 212, 662

New Jersey, 48, 129; constitution, 647; and Port of New York Authority, 91; public assistance payments in, 620; ratifies Constitution, 63, *64*

New Jersey Plan, 55

New Left, 36, 195

contributions of, to campaigns, 310; corruption of public officials by, 538–41, 665; and FBI, 133, 434; and infiltration into labor unions, 605; as political issue, 501; structure of, *540*; and wiretapping, 132–33, 537, 538

Oswald, Lee Harvey, 116, 401
Otis, James, 50
Ottinger, Richard, 655
Outputs, policy, 23, 66, 139, 460–61

Padover, Saul K., *75n*
Paine, Thomas, 44
Palko, Frank, 138
Palko v. Connecticut, 113n, 138
Panetta, Leon, 167
Papert, Fred, 298n
Parker, Edwin B., 379n
Parkinson, C. Northcote, 416n
Parks, Rosa, 168
Parochial schools, 126
Parole, 91
Participation: in nation-building, 66; political (*see* Political participation); voter (*see* Voter participation)
Parties, political. *See* Political parties; *specific parties*
Party-column (Indiana) ballot, *352*, 352–54
Passman, Otto, 436
Paterson, William, 55
Patrick, Luther, 436n
Patronage, 252
Patterson, Haywood, 91
Peabody, Endicott, 301
Peabody, Robert L., 456n, 471n, 477n, 492n
Peace: party best rated for, *285*; strategy of, 592
Peace and Freedom party, 248n
Peace Corps, 142, 236, 240, 432, 447, 569, 572–73
Pearl Harbor, 567
Pearson, Drew, 485n, 509n
Peirce, Neal R., 14n, 247n, 356n
Pendleton Act (Civil Service Reform Act) (1883), 430
Penetration, in nation-building, 66
Penn Central railroad, 602
Pennsylvania, 48; ratifies Constitution, 63, *64*
Pennsylvania Herald, 374
Pentagon, 383, 390, 442, 567, 569, 580, 581; alliance and defense contractors for, 435; and arms sales abroad, 59; budget, 32; decision-making in, 582–83; and defense research, 630, 631; and language of, 586; number of employees in, 419, 579; and

President, 384; and strategic deterrence theory, 584–86; systems analysis in, 447, 582–83

People's Park, 501
People's party (Populists), 235, 248
Perry, James M., 297n, 299n
Peyote, 126
Phelps, Robert H., 120n
Philadelphia, Pa., 661, 674
Philadelphia Convention. *See* Constitutional Convention of 1787
Philadelphia Independent Gazetteer, 63
Phillips, Kevin, 245–46
Physicians, and Medicaid payments, 628
Pierce, Franklin, 228n, 234
Pilgrims, 47
Pill, the: and bureaucrats, 413–16, 435, 460; and death rate, *414*
Pinckney, Charles, 53
Pinckney, Charles Cotesworth, 53, 57
Pincus, Walter, 312n
Planning-programing budgeting system (PPBS), 447–48
Plea bargaining, 531
Pledge of Allegiance to the flag, 112
Plessy, Homer Adolph, 163
Plessy v. Ferguson, 163
Plimpton, Calvin H., 122
Plunkitt, George Washington (Boss), 252, 355, 659–60, 664
Pluralism, 212, 223, 493, 662; defined, 212
Pluralist society, 211–25, 662
Pointer v. Texas, 138n
Police, 133, 177, 427; and black militants, 179–80; and criminal justice, 526–28; at Democratic National Convention riots in Chicago, 8–9, 111, 120, 242, 501, 527; and individual rights, 72, 134; at Jackson State College, 15, 123, 548; murder of, 526; and "no knock" search provision, 130, 534; as political issue, 501, 527; and search warrants, 130–31
Police courts, 519
Policy-makers, 369–410, 413–49, 451–94, 497–542
Policy-making, 447; in bureaucracy, 415, 440–43; and Department of Justice, 529; effect of public opinion and interest groups on, 189–225; and Supreme Court, 504
Political campaigns. *See* Campaign finance; Campaigns; Primary elections; Television and politics
Political issue(s), 282–89; as can-

didate's theme, 282; foreign policy as, 284–85, 289, 577–78; law and order as, 38, 132, 134, 184; and orientation of voters, 202; peace as, *285*; prosperity as, *284*; social progress as, 283–84; Vietnam war as, 38, 229, 344; and voter behavior, 332–33

Political opinion polls, 196–200, 269, 283, 293, 300–01, 467; limits of, 196; operation of, 198–200
Political participation, 14–15, 202–04, 252–54, *253*, 317–21, 678–79
Political parties, 227–69; accounting of, to voters, 266–67; activity in, 14–15, 230, *253*, 431; balanced ticket in, 193, 400; best rated for peace and prosperity, *284*, *285*; campaigns and candidates of, 271–83; caucus, 254–55; coalitions in, 231, 234, 235, 236, 336, 362; coattail voting in, 337–39; conservative, 201–02; control of governorships by, 339, *340*; control of Presidency by, 333–34; development of, 232–37; effect of direct election on, 358; effect of federalism on, 94–96; and foreign policy, 577–78; "four-party system," 492; identification of voters with, 202, 230, 322, *327*, *330*, 331; liberal, 201–02; and midterm loss of power in House of Representatives, *338*; minor parties, 246–48, *247*, 357; moderate, 201; one-party system, 238; organized labor support of, 606; President as chief of, 232, 378, 388–90; and presidential and congressional vote (1932–1970), *337*; state (*see* State political parties); structure of, 249–53; third party, 229, 237, 240; two-party system, 237–48; voting patterns for, *334–35*, 333–41. *See also specific parties*
Political socialization, 24–26, 190–95
Political system, 10, 47–48; adaptability of, 37–38; citizen participation in, 13–17, 142; concept of, 22–26; and Congress, 491–94, 452, 460; constitutional framework of, 75; corruption of, by organized crime, 541; dynamic approach to, 22–23; "four-party," 492; influence of social change on, 33–37; inputs, outputs, and feedback in, 23–24, 139; justice in, 541–42; political parties basic to, 14–15, 232; significance of Supreme Court in,

Pressure groups, 213. *See also* Interest groups
Pretrial publicity, 116
Preventive detention, 534
Price-fixing, 427
Prices, consumer, 33
Primary elections: all white, 174, 345; blanket (jungle), 351; closed, 351; direct, 351; nominations for, 351; open, 351; presidential, 259, 264, 278–79, 305, 351
Primary group, 328–29
Princeton University, 268
Prisons, federal, 530
Pritchett, C. Herman, 516n
Privacy, right to, 132
Private Calendar, 472
Private schools, pupils bused to, 126
Procaccino, Mario, 193
Progressive party: of La Follette (1924), 246, 248; of Theodore Roosevelt (Bull Moose, 1912), 235, 246, 248, 253
Prohibition, 72, 236, 503; repeal of, 70, 74
Prohibition party, 248
Project Head Start, 626
Property ownership, 155; as voting requirement, 61, 62, 345
Proportional representation, 238
Prosperity, 32–33; party best rated for, *284*
Protest movement, 121–24; against defense research in universities, 123, 630; antiwar, 8, 15, 17, 518, 547, 548–49, 574–75; and legal rights of demonstrators, 109–11. *See also* Civil rights movement; Demonstrations, civil rights
Protestant Reformation, 48
Protestants, 29, 462; voter participation of, 321, 328
Proxmire, William, 442, 476, 582, 590
Public: constituency influence in Congress, 465–67; role of, in foreign policy, 575–76. *See also* Public opinion
Public accommodations, 162, 163, 173
Public Affairs Officer (PAO), 572
Public assistance programs, 617, 618, 620–22, 627
Public housing, 215
Public interest law firms, 602
Public opinion, 189–207; and bureaucracy, 434–35; and Congress, 465–67; definition of, 190; in a democracy, 206–07; impact of, on government, 15–16; intensity of, 195; and interest groups, 189–226; mass media

and, 207–11; and President, 206–07, 402–03; stability of, 195–96; and Supreme Court, 506, 514, 542
Public relations, 300, 435
Public schools: and busing of private and parochial school children, 126; community control of, 677–78; consolidated systems of, 676; enrollment in, 628; and federal aid, 629; inner-city, 666; segregation in, 43, 72, 147 (*see also* School desegregation); Supreme Court outlaws prayers and daily Bible reading in, 124–25
Public services, state and local expenditures for, *647*
Public utilities, Supreme Court protection of, 509
"Publius," 63
Pueblo, 576
Puerto Ricans, 148, 154–55, 673
Puerto Rico, 518, 552
Punishment, "cruel and unusual," 71, 138, 534
Puritans, 47–48
Pye, Lucian, 65, 66

Quayle, Oliver A., & Co., Inc., 198n
Quemoy island, 285

Race relations, 173, 177, 183, 184. *See also* Black Americans
Radio pill, 132
Radio stations: fairness doctrine, 117; and freedom of the press, 116–17; licensing of, 116, 427, 436; political broadcasting costs on, 306–07; regulation of, 426–27, 436. *See also* Television and politics
Rafferty, Max, 305n
Railpax, 602
Railroad industry: and "Jim Crow" law, 163; National Railroad Passenger Corporation (Railpax), 602; regulation of, 244, 427, 602
Railroad Retirement Board, 425
Railway Labor Act, 604
Rand Corporation (RAND), 588
Randolph, Edmund, 54, 61n, 63
Ranney, Austin, 251, 655n
Ransom, Harry Howe, 396n, 569n
Rat control bill, 671
Rather, Dan, 254
Rayburn, Sam, 455, 470, 471
Reagan, Ronald, 245, 263, 265, 299
Real estate tax, 101, 642
Reapportionment, 70, 457–58, 481, 510, 643, 651, 652; of congressional districts, 359–61; Dirksen's proposed constitutional

amendment, 70, 359, 514; effect of, on cities, 643, 651; effect of, on suburbs, 643, 652; of state legislatures, 358–59
Recession, 607, 611, 612, 633
Reciprocal Trade Agreements Act (1934), 385
Reconstruction era (1863–1877), 162, 174, 514
Redding, Saunders, 172n
Redress of grievances, 113
Reed, Thomas B., 469
Regulatory agencies, 59, 244, 380, 381, 421, 422–23, 504, 602; and client groups, 415, 426, 435–36; and Congress, 460; and industries subject to regulation, 244, 426–27; licenses issued by, 116, 426; list of, and functions, 427
Reichley, James, 95
Religion, 49; and draft exemption, 42–43; freedom of (*see* Freedom of religion); and political socialization, 192–94; and voter attitudes, *193, 326, 328*; and voter turnout, 321
Reorganization Acts, 388, 439
Representation, congressman and his constituents, 465–67
Republican Congressional Campaign Committee, 220
Republican National Committee, 276, 288
Republican National Convention(s): delegates to, 260; Miami (1968), 197, 241–42; patterns in presidential nominations, *263*; regional strength at (1952–1968), *260*
Republican party, 233n, 242–46, 271–313 *passim*; birth of, 233n, 234; campaign contributions to, *245, 308, 309*; campaign expenditures of, *296, 304, 306*; campaigns and candidates of, 271–313; coalition under Theodore Roosevelt, 235; competition in the states, *655, 656*; conservatives in, 82, 245; and Democrats, 234–37, 238–39, 240–42; effect of Great Depression on, 236; gains of, in 1968, 342; and Goldwater campaign, 236, 237, 327; history of, 234–37; image of, 239–40; liberal-conservative split in, 235, 244–45, *263*; liberals in, 82, 245; major party lineup, President and Congress (1932–1970), *337*; and party identification, *330*; regional strength in, *260*; sectional, representing North and West, 235; split in (1912), 235, 244; split in (1952), 245, *263*; in the South,